About This Book

This book starts where you are likely to start—at the beginning. The design ensures that you learn concepts when you need as you need them, as you start your exploration of NetWare.

By following the book, with its orientation and examples, you will learn simple tasks that build on each other until you have mastered the basics of NetWare. If you faithfully follow the book, you can write and pass Novell's Certified Novell Administrator (CNA) accreditation program.

Anyone with a working knowledge of DOS or Windows can learn how to back up servers, add and delete users, create login scripts, and maintain security.

Who Should Read This Book?

Anyone interested in learning to use NetWare will find something of value in this book. The thrust of the book is, however, toward those who will administer a NetWare network, and must grasp the key tasks.

For both, this book covers NetWare from the basics to tasks and ideas that you will find interesting and useful as you progress beyond the basics.

This book is for you if one or more of the following is true:

☐ You are interested in becoming a Certified Novell Administrator (CNA)

☐ You just found out you will take over administration of an existing NetWare LAN

☐ You were told your company will install NetWare next month

☐ You applied for a new job at a company that uses NetWare LANs exclusively and you want to get the job

☐ You just want to learn about a widely-used network operating system

Conventions

The presentation of NetWare is best accomplished by providing menus and screens as you will see them. You will make choices by working through these menus and screens. As the old Chinese saying goes, "A picture is worth a thousand words."

These visual aids are supplemented with detailed description of everything you need to use or understand the menu or screen. For that reason, as you develop new skills, you'll see figures of NetWare to help in your understanding and to grade your progress.

 Tip: The Tip icon offers advice, teaches an easier way to do something, or explains an undocumented feature.

 Note: The Note icon presents interesting tidbits of information related to the surrounding discussion.

 Warning: The Warning icon warns you about potential problems and helps to steer you clear of disaster, and warns you when you should not skip a task.

Each lesson contains many different tasks. Most tasks are presented in the same format as follows:

Description—Read through a section on a particular task providing you with the basic concepts and terminology for NetWare.

Action—Follow a set of instructions to demonstrate the topic you are working on. Usually, the exercises are strung together to represent realistically the working environment.

Review—Review the tasks you should know after the previous two steps. Each task restates the steps necessary to do the task. This becomes the reference to remind you where you learned the skill. Task lists are logically organized to help you find things.

In addition, each lesson ends with a Workshop that includes a review of key terms, the tasks you should have learned, and questions and answers for the day's tasks.

On some days, you will find an Extra Credit section. This section contains information on other versions of NetWare or other advanced topics. These topics will help you enhance your knowledge of a particular skill or help you avoid a particular pitfall.

Perhaps you might want to come back to the Extra Credit material when you feel secure in your knowledge of the basic NetWare features.

In the text, terms will be treated as follows:

> User-typed entries appear in **bold computer font**.
> Information that appears on-screen appears in `computer font`.
> NetWare/DOS/Windows commands, file names, groups and directories appear in regular UPPERCASE.
> New terms introduced to the reader appear in *regular italics*.

Teach Yourself
NetWare
in 14 Days

Teach Yourself
NetWare
in 14 Days

Peter Davis
Craig McGuffin

SAMS
PUBLISHING

A Division of Macmillan Computer Publishing
201 West 103rd Street, Indianapolis, Indiana 46290

For Finlay, I know you would have enjoyed it.

Peter T. Davis

To all my friends and colleagues—with gratitude for your generous gifts of knowledge, guidance, patience, and understanding.

Craig R. McGuffin

Copyright © 1994 by Sams Publishing

FIRST EDITION

International Standard Book Number: 0-672-30481-3

Library of Congress Catalog Number: 93-87166

97 96 95 94   4 3 2

Interpretation of the printing code: the rightmost double-digit number is the year of the book's printing; the rightmost single-digit, the number of the book's printing. For example, a printing code of 94-1 shows that the first printing of the book occurred in 1994.

Composed in AGaramond and MCPdigital by Macmillan Computer Publishing

Printed in the United States of America

Trademarks

Publisher
Richard K. Swadley

Associate Publisher
Jordan Gold

Acquisitions Manager
Stacy Hiquet

Managing Editor
Cindy Morrow

**Acquisitions and
Development Editor**
Mark Taber

Production Editor
Jill D. Bond

Editors
Cheri Clark
Charles A. Hutchinson

Editorial Coordinator
Bill Whitmer

Editorial Assistants
Carol Ackerman
Sharon Cox
Lynette Quinn

Technical Reviewer
Doug Archell

Marketing Manager
Gregg Bushyeager

Cover Designer
Dan Armstrong

Book Designer
Michele Laseau

**Director of
Production and
Manufacturing**
Jeff Valler

Imprint Manager
Juli Cook

**Manufacturing
Coordinator**
Paul Gilchrist

Production Analysts
Dennis Hager
Mary Beth Wakefield

**Graphics Image
Specialists**
Tim Montgomery
Dennis Sheehan
Susan VandeWalle

Production
Nick Anderson
Katy Bodenmiller
Carol Bowers
Ayrika Bryant
Karen Dodson
Rich Evers
Dennis Clay Hager
Kimberly K. Hannel
Debbie Kincaid
Stephanie J. McComb
Jamie Milazzo
Shelly Palma
Casey Price
Bobbi Satterfield
Michelle Self
Susan Shephard
S A Springer
Marcella Thompson
Scott Tullis
Elaine Webb
Dennis Wesner
Michelle Worthington

Indexers
Charlotte Clapp
Greg Eldred
Rebecca Mayfield

About the Authors

Peter T. Davis

During his 19 years in information systems, Peter Davis worked in data processing in large scale installations in the financial and government sectors, where he was involved in the development and implementation of applications and specification of requirements. Most recently, he worked as director of information systems and audit for the Office of the Provincial Auditor (Ontario). In addition, he was a Principal in an accounting firm's information systems audit practice and has acted as the Canadian representative for a U.S. company specializing in the manufacture and integration of communications products.

He is now Principal of Peter Davis & Associates, a training and consulting firm specializing in the security, audit, and control of information systems.

Peter is the author of *Complete LAN Security and Control*, available from Windcrest/McGraw-Hill. He also is an internationally known speaker on quality, security, audit, and control, speaking frequently at user and professional conferences and meetings. In addition, he has had articles published in *VIP News*, *Access Magazine*, and *Computing Canada*.

He received his Bachelor of Commerce (B. Comm) degree from Carleton University. He also is a Certified Management Accountant (CMA), Certified Information Systems Auditor (CISA), Certified Systems Professional (CSP), Certified Data Processor (CDP), Information Systems Professional (ISP), and Certified Information Systems Security Professional (CISSP).

Peter currently lives in Toronto, Ontario, with his wife and daughter.

Craig R. McGuffin

Craig McGuffin has more than 12 years of experience in the field of computer system implementation, controls, and security. As a senior manager in an international public accounting firm, he assisted clients with all sizes and types of computer environments, ranging from large multi-mainframe installations, to interconnected minicomputers and local area networks distributed across the continent.

He currently is the Principal of C.R. McGuffin Consulting Services, a Toronto-based firm which helps its clients manage and control today's computer technology. The firm provides assistance in the areas of internal controls and security, as well as information resource management, system development and implementation, and special investigations into complex information system problems and issues.

He holds a Chartered Accountant designation, and has a background in computer science obtained through his Bachelor of Mathematics (Honours) from the University of Waterloo. He is a frequent speaker on the use of computer technology, controls, and security, through numerous television appearances, articles published in newspapers and business periodicals, and through public speaking engagements at a variety of conferences sponsored by professional organizations and industry groups.

He has developed and delivered many computer systems-related courses. These include two full-credit university courses required to obtain the professional accounting designation in Canada, as well as a number of customized training programs and presentations on the design and evaluation of computerized security and application controls given for professional staff and client personnel. He has also completed a three-day program for information system professionals on the use of security features in a popular computer operating system.

Overview

Contents

Acknowledgments

Every book requires a great deal of dedication and hard work by many people. Our book is no different. For their part, the authors would like to thank:

Stephen Poland and Gregg Bushyeager for suggesting we talk to Mark.

Mark Taber for going to bat for us in the beginning, and for his patience in the end.

Doug Archell, who kept us honest, for his insight and technical advice.

Jill Bond, Cheri Clark, Chuck Hutchinson, and Scott Parker, whose excellent editing is evident in the final product.

Everyone at Sams who worked on this book that we didn't mention.

Everyone who contributes to NetWire on CompuServe. We found some useful utilities and helpful information about NetWare.

Scott Foerster and Paul Lohnes for their technical help and advice on NetWare.

And, Peter would like to thank Janet and Kelly for their understanding and love during the last few months. Thanks to Janet for doing those chores (all?) I neglected while I was writing this book. My regrets to Kelly for all those times I couldn't watch Power Rangers and the StoogeFest because I was trying to make a deadline.

Craig would like to thank the people who had to put up with me while I was writing this book. *Please* speak with me again. I am indeed fortunate to receive the support of many friends and associates. This project couldn't have happened without each of you, so thanks to you all. Special thanks to Peter for kicking-off, filling-in, and wrapping-up. To Adele Pugliese, many thanks for the great tacos and chocolate. For other raw materials, recognition is due to every pizza joint on Yonge Street, Mr. Sub, and Bill Baker on BBQ (not literally). E-mail sanity and jocularity was provided by Dr. Bruce LaRochelle; thanks Larry. My appreciation to Mom and Bill for your encouragement. To Barry Lewis and Jim Kates, thanks for the suggestions, and to Jim Carroll, thanks, "cuz", for the annoying (but motivating) phone calls. Thanks to Arnold and Axle for the feline company during the 2:00 a.m. writing sessions. To my clients, I appreciate the wealth of experience you have given me. And to the colleagues who have attended my classes and seminars over the years: if even one percent of what you taught me about teaching made it into this book, it will far exceed what I could have done on my own. Thank you.

Introduction

If you are reading this introduction, it's likely that one or more of the following is true:

- [ ] You are interested in becoming a Certified Novell Administrator.

- [ ] You just found out you will take over administration of an existing NetWare LAN.

- [ ] You were told your company will install NetWare next month.

- [ ] You applied for a new job at a company that uses NetWare LANs exclusively and you want to get the job.

- [ ] You just want to learn about a widely-used network operating system.

Whatever your reasons, you certainly will want to learn about NetWare. You recognize that Novell has a very large share of the LAN market, and that knowledge of the product makes you more valuable to your present and future employers.

Regardless of your purpose for wanting to learn NetWare, this book is for you. For the next 14 days, you will find out things you need to operate NetWare efficiently, effectively and economically. Completing the 14 day curriculum will provide you with the confidence and skills to write and pass the Certified NetWare Administrator (CNA) tests. Also, you will have a solid base for embarking on the Certified NetWare Engineer (CNE) and Enterprise Certified NetWare Engineer (ECNE) accreditation programs.

You will build on tasks in each lesson and move progressively to more complex tasks. At the end of the 14 days, you will be certifiable—CNA, that is. Let's look at how the rest of the book is organized.

Organizing the Job of Learning NetWare

As the title of the book suggests, you can learn NetWare concepts in a short period of time—two weeks. Material in this book has been organized to lead you through a logical step-by-step approach to learning NetWare easily and quickly. Obviously, the speed of progression depends on your skills and background knowledge. Even though this is the case, we encourage you to read the book in sequential day and chapter order. Days and chapters tend to build on each other. For example, the concept of networking is introduced early in the book so that you will think about it throughout the book, and build your understanding of NetWare on these key concepts. The following sections give you an idea of what you can expect to cover each day.

Day 1: Starting with the Basics

On Day 1, you explore the role of a NetWare administrator and introductory networking concepts. First, you learn about the major functions of the administrator and where to get help with problems. Also, included in the day's lessons are descriptions of network components and options.

Day 2: NetWare Basics

On this day, you begin learning about NetWare and some of its facilities. Topics covered are NetWare's kernel and memory architecture; NetWare Loadable Modules; how NetWare communicates with its clients, and how it stores files.

Day 3: Getting Your Feet Wet

Day 3 is your introduction to NetWare. In the morning, you learn to log in to the network. Once on the network, you can use the various utilities—command line, menu and console.

You also see basic facilities that show what files you have, who is using the system, and sending electronic notes and mail.

Day 4: Controlling Resources

Day 4 sees you starting on the crux of learning NetWare, that is, system management. You begin to look at the fundamental skills needed to manage effectively a NetWare 3.11 or 3.12 network. Primarily, you learn about the Bindery and its purpose.

During the afternoon, you learn basic account management, such as setting up userids and groups, creating workgroup and account managers, and security equivalence.

Day 5: Controlling User Accounts

By Day 4, you have a basic knowledge of NetWare system administration. You now can log on and add users. Today, you follow on with managing user passwords and learn about account management, restricting users, changing defaults, and detecting and locking out intruders from your system.

Day 6: Customizing Your Users' Environment

Day 6 sees the pace quicken. Today, you learn two useful tools for network management—login scripts and menus. You learn the different types of scripts and how to create them. In the afternoon, you master menus by planning for, setting up and creating menus. Also, you study sample login scripts and menus.

Day 7: Examining NetWare Files

On Day 7, you learn all about how NetWare uses files and directories. You learn about network volumes and drive mappings, and understand how to list and move files around the directory tree.

You also find out about NetWare file attributes and how they are used to control NetWare objects. You will understand how to use the FILER, FLAG, and FLAGDIR utilities.

Day 8: NetWare File and Directory Rights

During Day 8, you learn about how NetWare protects access to files and directories through access rights, and how trustees can be set up. Then you'll explore how to grant and remove these rights using SYSCON, FILER, and other NetWare tools.

Day 9: Talking on the NetWork

Day 9 introduces you to the real-world network standards. In the morning, you learn about cabling systems, network topologies, media access control, network protocols, and interconnectivity devices.

You also learn how other network protocols are supported at the same time and even on the same network cable, using the Open Data Link Interface architecture.

Day 10: Making It Work

With the understanding of NetWare you've developed, lessons on Day 10 will teach you how to configure DOS and Windows workstations and print from your workstation.

Day 11: **Managing NetWare Servers**

Day 11 demonstrates how to perform some of the operational tasks for file servers, such as startup and shutdown. You also see how to set the time on the server, and the time stamp on individual files and directories.

In addition, you learn about ways to protect your NetWare system against loss of data through good backup and recovery planning and procedures. We cover the Transaction Tracking System you can use to log updates to files, and ways to configure your system so that it keeps processing even if there is a hardware failure.

Day 12: **This Must Be Printing**

Day 12 covers the art of printing. In the morning, you cover how to set up and run NetWare print queues and servers so that users can print output at different places on the network using different forms.

You also learn to control print queues and servers, to optimize printing and to troubleshoot printing problems.

Day 13: **Accounting for Users and Usage**

Day 13 shows you how to better secure your NetWare users and data files to minimize the chances of unauthorized access. You also learn about using audit trails to detect whether someone has been trying to bypass your security measures.

NetWare's mechanisms for accounting are explained, which will enable you to set up a system for charging users for the network resources they use.

Day 14: **Tweaking and Tuning**

Day 14 shows you the tools you can use in order to get the best performance, both from your file servers and from the network itself. You learn about the MONITOR utility, and about tuning NetWare with the SET command.

"Summer School"

When you have finished the 14 days and want to learn even more, you can turn to the four useful appendices to supplement the information in the book's lessons.

Appendix A: Installing NetWare on the File Server

Appendix A, "Installing NetWare on the File Server," shows you how you can actually install NetWare on file servers and at client workstations. Of course, if you don't already have a working NetWare LAN, this will have to be the first section you look at. Installing NetWare for the first time isn't the easiest thing for a network novice to try, so we recommend going through Days 1 through 14 on a system that's already up and running.

If you can't get to a working system, however, we'll help you through the installation process. After that, you can go back to Day 1 and work forward from there.

Appendix B: Novell NetWare Certification Programs

Appendix B, "Novell NetWare Certification Programs," provides a useful starting point for the Certified NetWare Administrator Program (CNA), the Certified NetWare Engineer Program (CNE), and the Enterprise CNE Program (ECNE).

Appendix C: NetWare Command Reference

Appendix C, "NetWare Commands Reference," lists the commands used by NetWare in an easy-to-use format.

Appendix D: Glossary

The Glossary contains definitions of the major networking and information processing terms used throughout the book.

Day

1

Morning

1 What Is a NetWare Administrator?

Afternoon

2 Introducing Networking

1

What Is a NetWare Administrator?

People become NetWare administrators through many different avenues. As a child, you may have dreamed of controlling and being responsible for the information resources used by tens or hundreds of people. If so, becoming a NetWare administrator is the realization of that dream. Or, more likely, you were the one person in your office who could spell *LAN*.

In either case, you are assuming a role that is crucial to the effective functioning of a powerful network computing system. Without proper administration, your system can degrade in performance and reliability, your users might abandon the network, and your local area network (LAN) might die a slow and agonizing death. And if this tragedy happens to the LAN, what might happen to its administrator? Not a pretty site.

Understanding Your Role

As the administrator of your NetWare LAN, you are looked to by the user community to keep the network running at a level that meets their expectations. What do most users expect from the LAN? In simple terms, they want no hassles and no surprises. When they need a file on the server, they want to get it easily. When they need to print a document, they want to hit the keystrokes they've learned, walk to the network printer, and find their output. If they want to share a file with another person, they expect that person to be able to get it. If they accidentally delete a file, they want to locate a backup copy. And they want all these capabilities right now. (Users can be a real pain.)

Meeting users' expectations is not an easy task. The amount of time it takes is directly proportional to the size of your LAN—the number of users and workstations, the number and size of the file servers, the number and kinds of printers in use, other types of services provided (such as the ability to dial into or dial out from your LAN). A small network may require only a few minutes of your time every so often, whereas administering large networks may be a full-time job.

Your specific responsibilities and duties as a NetWare administrator vary, depending on what other resources are available to you. You might identify what needs to be done and direct others (such as a third-party support organization) to do it. Or you might do all the work yourself. Regardless of who is executing the steps, a number of areas must be taken care of. You are introduced to these areas in the following sections. The sections also contain cross-references to the chapters where you can find more details on the tasks necessary to run a NetWare LAN.

Backing Up the System

Business data is recognized as a valuable corporate asset. Data can be anything from a customer list or invoice file to corporate accounting records and spreadsheets to strategic plans and budgets to memos and other correspondence and everything in between. Losing data means losing the time, effort, and expense it took to obtain it, manipulate it, and analyze it. Most businesses simply cannot afford to lose their important data.

Back in the information dark ages, when all systems resided on large computers, it was up to the mystical keepers of the mainframe to make backups of key systems and data. But now, with more and more business systems being committed to NetWare LANs, the NetWare administrator must take responsibility for protecting against data loss. As a result, one of the most important functions of the administrator is to make sure that backups of important data stored on a NetWare file server are made. Then, if the original file is lost or unavailable, users can continue processing using backups.

Backing up normally involves copying data from NetWare files onto magnetic tape on a periodic basis. If a file is lost or destroyed, you can reload the file's contents onto the file server. Similarly, if the file server hardware fails, you can load the contents of the tape onto an alternate processor. You learn about using NetWare's SBACKUP utility to copy files to tape in Chapter 22.

More sophisticated and time-demanding environments may use the network itself to perform backups of data to other locations. Here, data is copied from one file server, across the network, to another file server. This approach is more expensive than copying to tape, but it has the advantages of being more convenient and allowing for faster recovery of files.

NetWare provides advanced facilities that also help back up key systems and data. You can use the *System Fault Tolerant* (*SFT*) mechanism and the *Transaction Tracking System* (*TTS*) to minimize the impact of file server failures. As the NetWare administrator, you are involved in the decision on whether to use these facilities. You learn more about advanced backup approaches in Chapter 22.

Administering Users and Groups

No one can make use of NetWare's file server until he or she is *defined* as a user to the system. When a user is defined, NetWare is informed about who the person is, what he or she will use to prove his or her identity (a password), and how and when that user can use the system. As the administrator, you can place a variety of limitations

on users, such as when they can access the file server, what workstations they can use, and how much disk space they have available. NetWare also provides security mechanisms to help protect the server from unauthorized access. Once these measures are defined, NetWare rigorously enforces who can use the server and what each user can or cannot do.

You also can place users together in *groups*. Usage permissions and restrictions are specified at a group level so that NetWare applies them to each user who is a member of the group.

As NetWare administrator, you define standards for using the network (such as the format of *usernames* and whether restrictions are necessary for times users can access the file server). You or your designate then defines each new user to NetWare, adjusts permissions for existing users, and deletes usernames for people who no longer require access. See Chapters 8, 9, and 10 for more details about managing user and group accounts.

Administering Directory and File Security

The main resource on a NetWare server is the files stored there. These files, which contain programs and data needed by LAN users, require protection so that anyone who is not entitled to access them cannot view, use, modify, or delete them.

NetWare provides security mechanisms to help protect directories and their files from access by unauthorized users. *Rights* indicate which users can access files in a directory and in what way they can access them. *Attributes* specify what operations may be performed on a file and serve as indicators of other important file information.

As NetWare administrator, you, in cooperation with your user community, decide how much file system security is necessary. The level of security you choose depends on many factors:

- ☐ The level of sensitivity of programs and data files kept on your NetWare LAN

- ☐ The types of services provided on your LAN (for example, dial-in gateways, mainframe connections, and electronic mail)

- ☐ The size of your LAN and its physical layout

- ☐ The ability and willingness of users to follow security procedures

☐ Any corporate security policy you may have in place

☐ Any contractual, legal, or regulatory requirements under which you must operate

However much security you choose, NetWare's security mechanisms play an important role in protecting your information resources. Chapter 14 explains file attributes, and Chapters 15 and 16 detail how you can use NetWare to protect your files and directories. In addition, Chapter 25 tells you how you can use NetWare to monitor system security to determine whether any unauthorized activities are being attempted.

Supporting Users

Perhaps the most difficult (and potentially the most thankless) job for the NetWare administrator is that of supporting NetWare users. This job involves anything from training users in how to first log in and use the file server to helping them establish advanced network-based applications (such as a client/server database management system), and everything in between. Through your users, you might encounter every conceivable brand of microcomputer, software package, and network hardware, and you are expected to be an expert in them all. Your arrival might bring your users joy, hostility, relief, anger, the sight of a welcome face, or the outline of a convenient target.

One of the main tasks in supporting users is connecting them to the network in the first place. This task might be more difficult than it sounds, due to the many types of network interface cards that can be used to connect a microcomputer to a local area network. Each has its own way of being configured, first to talk with the microcomputer, then to communicate on the network itself, and finally to connect with a NetWare server on the network. Getting this connection to work properly can seem like more of an art than a science. In Chapters 17, 18, and 19, you learn more about how networks exchange data and how to set up DOS-based workstations to communicate with NetWare file servers.

Once your users can access the network, most of your support time is spent in two areas:

☐ Getting the users' existing application programs to function properly in a networked environment. Most programs that reside on a user's workstation continue to function normally, simply accessing network disk drives for data files without any additional steps. Programs that are placed on the file server and that are aware of the network's existence may demand that steps be taken to ensure only one user at a time executes the program. Still you simply may need to reconfigure other programs to use a network correctly. Fortunately, with the popularity of NetWare and the quality of most commercially available software products, setting up programs to function on your NetWare LAN should be a matter of finding and following the appropriate instructions. Some of these issues are addressed in more detail in Chapter 19.

☐ Helping users to print files on network printers. This task may be more difficult, depending on the programs your users have and their knowledge of the existence of the network. Printing also requires a cooperative effort between software running on the workstation and programs and hardware that make up NetWare's print server capabilities. You learn about printing from a workstation in Chapter 20. You can find details on setting up print servers in Chapters 23 and 24.

A key factor in how much time is required to support your users is their level of sophistication—both with microcomputer usage and with network concepts and usage.

Obviously, those people who have less experience with computers need far more hand-holding to become functional on the network. These staff may need help in both microcomputer and network fundamentals. Of course, the advantage often is that these people do not tend to push the network to its limits, in terms of using leading-edge functions.

Other users with greater experience using microcomputers may be virtually self-supporting. After you have them over the hurdle of initially connecting to the network and logging in it for the first time, they may be perfectly able to learn about network functions and operating steps. They also can be counted on to explore the network fully, however, perhaps discovering functions you didn't even know existed (and didn't count on supporting). Or they might issue commands that result in a huge amount of data being transferred across the network—which can flood the network or bring the file server to its knees trying to meet the demand.

In either case, while you're providing support for your users, be prepared for some of the most interesting (and maybe even amusing) activities in your administrative career.

Managing the File Server

At the focal point of most NetWare LANs is the file server. One of the main reasons for installing a LAN in the first place is to enable users to share files, as well as give them access to large amounts of disk storage space. The NetWare administrator is typically responsible for starting up the file server, making sure it keeps going, and occasionally stopping it to perform maintenance activities.

Because the file server provides users with a place to store files and a means to share them, the file server occasionally fills up. As more and more users place more and more files on the server, they may regularly use these files, which possibly increase in size all the time, or they might leave the files there as an archive and forget about them quickly.

Your administrative role requires that you monitor file space usage on the file servers under your control. As available space starts to decrease, you must work with users to determine what files can be deleted, copied to a tape archive, or perhaps compressed. One tool to help you is NetWare's capability to limit how much file space a user can take up. You learn about setting volume/disk restrictions in Chapter 10.

At some point, however, you might want to expand the size or number of disks available on your file server. When to upgrade your server, how much disk space to obtain, and how to configure it are your decisions—along with your user community (and subject, of course, to the financial constraints of your particular situation). Chapter 27 gives you some guidance on adding disks to your server.

As administrator, you also make decisions about the physical security of your file servers. Limiting access to the file server and its command console is important to protect the physical asset itself (often a high-performance computer with a great deal of disk space—a tempting target), as well as the information stored on the server. In Chapter 21, you learn many details about managing a NetWare file server.

Managing Printing

You already read about the need to support users so that they can print files using network print facilities. The good news is that you usually can get users' workstations set up and printing to the network in fairly short order. The bad news is that, in order for printing to work on the network, you must establish a suitable infrastructure, potentially with several different components that must work together. After you set

up this infrastructure, your role as NetWare administrator requires that you monitor both the physical printing components (printers, paper, ribbons, toner cartridges) and the logical components (print queues, print servers) and their users.

Like the file server, printers and the computers they are attached to might need increased physical security. Reports coming off the printer, for example, may be highly confidential. You should help users understand that not all printers on the network are secure and that they should not send confidential information to just any printer on the network.

Managing the print resources on a NetWare LAN can take up quite a bit of time. You learn more about how to set up and manage print servers in Chapters 23 and 24.

Managing Network Applications

A NetWare file server often forms the basis for a *network application*. A network application is a program that resides on the server and is used by many people. It is usually a network version of a commonly used stand-alone program, such as a word processing or spreadsheet package.

The additional functions provided by a LAN, however, also enable the use of new types of applications, such as electronic mail, online messaging, and group scheduling packages. These types of programs often are new to everyone involved in using the LAN and, therefore, require extra time to start up and maintain.

Managing network applications involves installing the software, configuring it for access by users, setting up resources such as shared files and directories, establishing access to network printers, and ensuring that software licensing requirements are respected. Ongoing maintenance usually is required, as is tuning the application so that it performs well. And eventually, you must upgrade to a new version of the software. Upgrades require coordination with the user community, training in new procedures, and perhaps even conversion of old files. Depending on the nature of the application, upgrading may be no small task.

Because network applications tend to be more complex than their stand-alone counterparts, this job can be time consuming. And as more users come to depend on the application, the need for it to be available and reliable increases. Don't underestimate the job of supporting a network application.

How you actually manage a network application is directly related to the nature and size of the application itself; the details can't all be covered here. But rest assured that, throughout this book, you learn more about the tools NetWare provides to help you deal with network applications.

Installing and Changing Hardware

Probably the most prominent piece of hardware in a NetWare LAN is the file server computer. Typically a very powerful PC, the file server is accessed by practically every network user at one time or another. Users store files, they print files, they access network applications, all through the file server. But whereas users tend to be very aware of their own computers, to them the file server is out of sight and so largely out of mind.

The responsibility of taking care of the hardware that is the file server probably falls on you as network administrator. Fortunately, today's computer systems are highly reliable and normally don't require much attention. Still, you must configure and install the file server hardware in the first place and ensure it receives ongoing preventive maintenance (for example, a good vacuuming every so often). You also participate in upgrading the hardware for additional disk capacity or memory, for example. To learn about installing NetWare on a file server, turn to Appendix A. Chapter 21 provides tips about ongoing maintenance of the server.

The ties that bind a NetWare LAN together consist of the cable between computers attached to the network and the Network Interface Cards in each machine. As network administrator, you might play a role in laying out the network configuration in the first place, arrange for cabling (or perhaps even install it yourself), get the file server to talk with the rest of the network, and ensure each user's computer has the right hardware installed so that it can access the network.

Appendix A provides some pointers on tying the file server into the network, and Chapter 19 helps you get DOS-based client computers running. Chapters 17 and 18 offer a general look at the way NetWare LANs handle communication between computers.

Troubleshooting

As they say in all those tough-guy movies, "If you're looking for trouble, you've come to the right place." LANs can be extremely difficult to get running—and sometimes even to keep running. That's not a criticism, just a simple fact of life. LANs are complex, involving cooperating processes on distributed computers communicating over a shared data network. They're not for the faint of heart.

To a great extent, their complexity is a result of the many types of hardware and software that can be used on one NetWare LAN. The price of this flexibility is often some fiddling around trying to get everything working at once. Although most of the hardware and software vendors have done an admirable job of trying to protect you from this complexity, some problem almost always rears its ugly head. And that head is probably facing right at you, the network administrator. Consider it job security.

In your role as network administrator, you can solve many types of problems. Using the suggestions you find throughout this book and with the knowledge you gain from hands-on experience, you quickly will become adept at diagnosing and solving common difficulties. But perhaps the most important troubleshooting skill you can develop is knowing where to turn for additional help. You find some suggestions on key sources of help in the following sections.

Getting Help

By now you've realized that you are going to be the one that everyone else turns to for help. But where can you go for assistance in performing your administrative tasks (besides this book, of course)? Fortunately, NetWare comes with a great deal of support information in electronic and hard-copy form. Plus, the popularity of NetWare as a network operating system has ensured a steady flow of support information from a variety of other places. In the following section, you discover some of the key reference sources you can use to help make your job easier.

NetWare Manuals/ElectroText

If you are like most computer users, you consult the documentation only after every other possible avenue has failed. Not many people actually enjoy reading computer manuals, unless they are insomniacs or gluttons for punishment.

But beware: NetWare is a complex product. You really do need some preparation if you hope to install and use NetWare successfully. This book is a good place to start. In addition, NetWare comes with a full range of documentation describing how to install and use the product.

For version 3.12 of NetWare, the manuals are available in electronic format. Known as *ElectroText*, they come on the same CD-ROM used to distribute the program code. The manuals can be read online using Windows or OS/2 workstation software. Of course, the familiar red manuals that come with version 3.11 are also available through special order.

Online Help

Most NetWare menu utilities (such as SYSCON and FILER) include context-sensitive help screens. Whenever you need information on a menu option or task, you usually can press F1 and receive suggestions and instructions.

In addition, with NetWare command-line utilities, you often can type the name of the command followed by the characters /? to get assistance on how to use the command.

Version 3.11 of NetWare includes an online help facility called *Folio*. Folio provides information on most NetWare commands. Simply type **help <command name>** at the DOS prompt.

> **Note:** Later versions of DOS also come with a help function, and it's started the same way as Folio. Which help facility starts depends on what order directories are searched—and that depends on the setting of your PATH. See Chapter 14 for more details on NetWare's search drives and the DOS PATH variable.

NetWare Support Encyclopedia

The NetWare Support Encyclopedia (NSE) provides two extensive databases in CD-ROM format. A standard version of the database includes update information on available products and services and the NetWare Buyers Guide, technical questions and answers, and a listing of NetWare files. The professional version adds NetWare application notes, help with troubleshooting in the form of decision trees, and supplemental product information. Both versions are updated up to 12 times per year and are available from Novell.

Product Documentation and Support

Most products you use with your NetWare LAN, such as Network Interface Cards and network software, include documentation that specifically addresses how to use the product with NetWare. These vendors realize the widespread use of NetWare and, as a result, are highly motivated to provide customer support to help get you up and running.

The best place to start is with the manual that comes with each product, as well as any README files included on program diskettes. Chances are, you can find a specific section on configuration and use with NetWare. In addition, the manual probably includes a contact telephone and fax number for the vendor. Product support staff at these numbers often can provide invaluable assistance in getting your system running.

Online Services

Online information services available for dial-in by personal computer users are growing in popularity. Besides the other useful information they provide, they also permit fast, direct access to many computer vendors and their support staff, technical bulletins, and program files. Many companies, Novell in particular, have taken advantage of these services to provide support for their customers. Users of products such as NetWare also can exchange questions and answers about common problems they experience. These services aren't free, but they are relatively inexpensive and have the advantage of offering the most up-to-date information to a large user community.

NetWire, Novell's area on the CompuServe Information Service (CIS), provides two software libraries and four forums for discussion of problems.

NetWare Express is available through GE Information Services (GEnie). It also provides access to a database of bulletins and files, plus the NetWare Buyers Guide and the NetWare Support Encyclopedia service.

Whichever service you choose, it will prove to be an invaluable source of information and updates to help keep your NetWare LAN current and fully functional.

Summary

In this chapter, you learned

☐ Some of the key duties and responsibilities of a network administrator, including system backup, administering NetWare user and group IDs, helping to set up proper security, supporting your users, and managing many aspects of the file server and its services. You also saw pointers to places in this book you can gather more details about each task.

☐ About sources of information to help you resolve problems and receive important update details for your NetWare LAN, including help facilities built into NetWare, NetWare manuals in hard copy and electronic form, other types of documentation, and online information services such as CompuServe and GEnie.

Workshop

Terminology Review

administrator—The person responsible for managing a NetWare file server and supporting NetWare users.

backup—The process of copying data files, usually from a hard disk to another media such as magnetic tape. Used to enable restoring data in the event of disk failure or file corruption.

define user/group—The process of creating an entry in NetWare's bindery database so that it knows the identity of each user or group using the file server. Access control mechanisms are based on this identity.

file—A single, named collection of related information stored on magnetic medium.

file server—A computer attached to a LAN which allows other computers to access its data in the form of individual files. In a NetWare LAN, the file server is normally a personal computer running the NetWare Network Operating System.

LAN—See *local area network*.

local area network—A communications system used to allow connected computers shared access to resources on the network.

troubleshooting—Diagnosing and solving problems that invariably occur when using computers.

user—An individual who accesses and makes use of a NetWare file server.

Q&A

Q What are the skills required of an administrator?

A Being a NetWare administrator requires a combination of skills. Certainly, it is important to have an interest in using computers and networks—maybe even a fondness. NetWare can pose some interesting technical challenges, and it's easier to deal with them if you are actually interested in what you are doing and if you derive some feeling of accomplishment from being successful.

Just as important as technical skills, however, are people skills. In your role as administrator, you will deal with all kinds of people—suppliers, technicians, and users. They'll have different levels of understanding about your network, and it's important to try to deal with them at their own particular level. And expect to encounter many different moods, especially from your users. Depending on the problems they've experienced, they may not be the happiest people you've ever met. So your most important people skills may be patience and understanding.

Q Should my NetWare users read this book?

A The book you have in your hands contains a great deal of detail about NetWare. It's definitely more than you need to simply get up and running on NetWare as a basic user.

But if your users want to get the most out of NetWare, then a book such as this one can be a great help. With it, they can gain a better understanding of how NetWare functions. And having a better understanding enables them to utilize NetWare's incredible resources more fully.

Q If my users get too many details about NetWare, won't they be able to mess up the system?

A As the saying goes, "A little knowledge is a dangerous thing." There's a chance that users with a bit more knowledge may wreak havoc on your LAN simply because they try some commands that they don't fully understand and shouldn't use. But look on the bright side—that's one way to help you find and fix future problems (if you don't find and fix the user first).

On the other hand, more knowledgeable users can also be more self-supporting. Having self-sufficient users can relieve you of some of your user-support duties, giving you time to work on other more pressing problems.

So don't let your users gain only a "little knowledge" and be dangerous. Why not encourage them to learn even more about NetWare?

Q How can I view the NetWare ElectroText manuals if I don't have a network up and running?

A The CD-ROM that contains the ElectroText manuals is in a standard format (known as ISO 9660). You can read it on any DOS machine with CD-ROM support. But you need Windows to view the contents of the manual properly.

First, you need to get the file ET.INI from the \DOC\DATA\CONFIG directory on the CD-ROM. Copy this file to your WINDOWS directory and edit the file so that it points to correct directories on your CD-ROM.

Next, you must set a DOS environment variable, using the following command:

```
SET nwlanguage=english
```

Finally, you need to execute the command ET.EXE. You can find it on the CD-ROM or on your NetWare file server in the following \PUBLIC directory.

2

Introducing
Networking

Local area networks are truly amazing creations. With them, you can assemble processing power and storage capacity rivaling that of mainframe computers. Yet LANs give you incredible flexibility. You can add more file servers, increase disk capacity, add more printers, or just reconfigure the whole network far more easily and cheaply than changing a mainframe.

Many aspects of LANs, however, remain shrouded in the mystery of technical jargon and the ever-present Three Letter Acronyms (TLAs). It's easy to be overwhelmed by all the complex-sounding terms and even easier to get lost among the cables, cards, nodes, and all the software that makes the LAN work. Fear not, weary network traveler, for you learn important concepts to help you on your way through the haze of network-ese. You learn to bridge the chasms of misconceptions and portage around the rapids of ever-changing technology.

In this chapter, you learn the key network concepts and their significance to your NetWare LAN. You also look at the major components of the LAN, including servers, clients, and the network interfaces that tie them together.

Later in the book, after you have developed confidence in using NetWare, you explore more technical details about how data is sent between computers on a NetWare LAN. In Chapter 17, you develop an understanding of the cabling systems and the communications protocols used to exchange data across the network.

What Is a Network?

The term *network* can mean many things—from a geometric structure to a collection of consultants sharing office equipment and knowledge. For our purposes, a network refers to a collection of computers linked by some type of cable, to permit sharing of resources such as large disks or fast printers. After the path is opened between these computers and their users, of course, a network permits other useful tasks such as exchanging electronic mail and accessing host computers from the users' desktops. In any event, the key feature of a network is the interconnection of two or more computers.

Note: The most common way to connect computers together is through the use of wire cables. Physical cables commonly are called *bounded media*. These cables contrast with *unbounded media* such as radio frequency links, microwaves, and infrared technologies. But don't worry; all they do is fill in for the physical cable. And that's really all you need to know at this point. If you want to find more information about un-bounded media, look for a book on wireless networking.

For a typical NetWare LAN, the network consists of one or more NetWare file servers, connected through a common cabling system to a number of personal computers acting as clients.

Servers? Clients? What do these terms mean? It's time to find out.

You discover more details on the specific components of a NetWare LAN throughout this book. To set the stage, you first look at important concepts and terminology using the general case of a data network.

Tip: Starting with a good foundation in how networks work makes it easier for you to understand specifics about NetWare later. If you're eager to get right into using NetWare, however, you can jump to Chapter 5, the first chapter in "Navigating through NetWare." But don't forget to come back to this chapter; it's important for your complete understanding of NetWare.

The main components of any data network include the following:

☐ Nodes (also called *endpoints*)

☐ Cabling systems

☐ Communication protocols

☐ Internetworking devices (really just a special type of node)

You examine nodes in more detail in the following sections. You are also introduced to network standards that address cabling systems, communication protocols, and internetworking devices. After you've had a chance to get more comfortable with NetWare, Chapters 17 and 18 give you more specific details on how NetWare LANs are built up from various network standards.

Understanding Network Nodes

A node on a network is simply an endpoint—the point where the cable ends and the computer begins. The exact configuration of how the node is connected depends on the type of network involved.

Computers attached to the network usually fill one of two main purposes; they act as the following:

- ☐ A *server* computer, which provides services to the network, such as storing files, printing data, or connecting to another computer or network

- ☐ A *client* computer, which uses the network to gain access to the available services

On some types of networks, a computer can act as both a client and a server, depending on the particular tasks it is performing.

The terms *server* and *client* have gained great popularity over the past few years. They often are used collectively to give the impression of a leading-edge information system (like calling laundry detergent "new and improved"). The terms, however, really mean something far more straightforward and understandable.

In the following sections, you look at each of the components in more detail.

Understanding Servers

At the simplest level, a server computer offers services to its clients. In a network context, this arrangement normally means accepting requests from other computers on the network, performing some internal processing, and delivering the results back to the requester across the network. Software on the server computer listens for network requests and knows how to deal with them and where to send the results.

Using servers, you can separate some computing tasks (for example, retrieving and storing files) from others (for example, word processing). Rather than use one computer to perform both tasks, you use two or more. You can configure each computer to perform its task most efficiently. You can tune the file server, for example, to store and access files more rapidly than a general-purpose computer.

Server computers can be grouped into two main categories:

- ☐ General-purpose host computers, which provide a variety of computing services to the network

☐ Special-purpose network servers, which are built to provide one particular type of service

Each category of server offers some interesting capabilities, as you learn in the following sections.

General-Purpose Servers

Many types of computers have the ability to be used from a computer network. Everything from mainframe computers to personal computers can be attached to a given network, and allow people or processes from other nodes to use a number of features. Popular and commonly found computer operating systems—with names such as MVS, VM, OS/400, VMS, and UNIX—support communications with end users and their computers across a network.

The most typical service offered by these computers is the ability to *log in*, that is, for the user to supply a username and password and receive a general command prompt. Depending on the user's permissions, he or she then can type commands that are performed by the computer.

These machines also may offer other capabilities to the network. The host computer might do any or all of the following tasks:

☐ *Execute a command or procedure in direct response to a request from the network.* This function, sometimes known as a *remote procedure call,* makes the host behave like a command engine, taking in requests for work and churning out the results. The work requested might be something the host computer does well (for example, computationally intensive tasks) or involve something the host can get to (for example, specific files on a host computer disk).

☐ *Transfer files to or from another computer.* In this mode of operation, the host provides the user with a set of commands that allow sending or receiving a particular file across the network. The transfer mechanisms ensure that the file is transferred completely and accurately.

☐ *Send and receive electronic mail.* The host computer can serve as the central point for all electronic mail entering and leaving the LAN. It can have knowledge not only about people on the LAN and how to communicate with them, but also about how to exchange mail with the outside world.

☐ *Permit other computers to access host files directly.* Here, the host computer allows remote nodes on the network to access its files and appear to the user as if the files are physically on the remote machine. The remote computer translates any references to the files into a request for data that is sent across the network to the host computer. The host responds by supplying the data, as requested. This function often is known as remotely *mounting* a file system. (This role is similar to that of the file server discussed in the next section.)

Special-Purpose Servers

The client/server model of computing really shines with the use of special-purpose network servers. A special-purpose server is designed specifically to perform one or two main tasks and perform them extremely well. If one of those tasks requires more resources (maybe more space for files), then you can upgrade the computer to enhance that particular area (such as more or larger hard disks).

Special-purpose servers come in a number of different flavors—just take your pick of the ones you want to try.

☐ *File servers.* The file server is the most common type of server on a LAN, and it is the heart of most NetWare networks. The file server works in the same manner as described previously for host computers that allow direct access to their files. The remote machine establishes a network connection with the file server disk, allowing it to be treated as if it were physically on the remote computer. It then evaluates any requests for file access and determines which ones it must redirect to the file server. The file server takes requests for data from remote computers and responds by supplying the data as requested.

Note: A common misconception is that file servers actually run the entire network. This nasty and unfounded rumor is spread by a fringe group of radical file servers bent on network domination. Although the file server often is a focal point of the network, it does not control the operation of every node on the network. As you learn in Chapters 17 and 18, each node is responsible for its own behavior. In fact, the network can, and does, continue to operate, exchanging chunks of information between nodes, even in the absence of a file server.

☐ *Print servers.* Another common type of server on a LAN, the print server may be a dedicated computer, or the services may be offered as part of a file server. The print server function can even piggyback on a client computer (clients are described in the next section). The approach taken depends on the volume of printing to be done and how fast it must be performed. To use a print server, a network node simply sends a data file across the network to the server. The print server typically moves the data file onto the back of a queue and eventually prints the output.

☐ *Database servers.* The database server is similar to a file server, representing a special case. Rather than serve up entire files, it receives queries or commands from other computers on the network to retrieve specific database records (which are portions of a file). The database server is optimized so that it can locate and extract quickly the needed records and deliver them to the remote computer.

Database servers are a key feature of many client/server systems because they take the greatest advantage of the separation between different computing tasks (in this case, database lookup as a separate function from other tasks such as dealing with an end user).

☐ *Communication gateway servers.* The purpose of these servers is to receive data from another node on the network and forward it to a host computer that is remotely connected to the gateway. Data received from the host is sent back to the network node. Typically, applications enable someone using a computer on the network to emulate a terminal and allow login to a host computer such as an IBM mainframe. This task often is performed by a gateway computer acting as a System Network Architecture (SNA) node on the mainframe system. Other types of servers can provide terminal sessions to other minicomputer and mainframe computers.

☐ *Other specialty servers.* The flexibility of using a network allows for all manner of other types of servers. Just like Main Street, almost any node on the network can open up shop and offer its services. As a result, servers have been created to provide gateways for electronic mail, perform searches for information, and authenticate users before they are allowed access to other computers on the network.

Of course, some server developers may combine specialty functions onto one machine. NetWare is a good example. Thanks to its flexible design, it not only provides file services, it also can act as a print server and run other applications.

The services offered are limited only by the imagination of those people who design and implement servers. Many more services definitely will come.

Understanding Clients

A *client* computer is simply a computer capable of using the network to take advantage of the services offered by server computers. It typically is a general-purpose computer, and most often a microcomputer (such as a PC or Macintosh) or workstation (such as a UNIX workstation).

The client's software knows when and how to formulate requests for network services, and it maintains information on where to send the requests. Then it just sits back and lets the server do the work of getting the data. After it receives the results, the client carries on with its own processing.

Almost any type of computer can be a client. This list includes the host computers mentioned as being servers because these general-purpose computers can act as both servers and clients at the same time. (They even can run programs that are clients of their own servers). Clients also include the full range of mini- and microcomputers.

Understanding Peer-to-Peer Networks

Some information systems built on data networks enforce clear relationships between nodes. A node is either a server or a client, never both. The general case of a network, however, does not force this distinction. Here, a node on the network may act as a client or as a server or both.

On a peer-to-peer network, each node has equal status and importance. In a typical peer-to-peer network, each computer can offer access to any resources connected to it (for example, disks or printers) as well as access to other computers offering their services. These networks often are used for less formalized sharing arrangements between members of a department or workgroup.

Note: Strictly speaking, almost all data networks are peer-to-peer because each node on the network has an equal opportunity to send or receive data. *As far as the network cable is concerned,* no single station is more important than another. In the real world, however, when someone makes a distinction between peer-to-peer networks and hierarchical

networks, the distinction illustrates that not all nodes offer equal *function-ality* to the network. In a hierarchical network, some nodes are clearly more important than others (as in the case of a file server). In a peer-to-peer network, many nodes offer and use network services (such as members of a workgroup making their files available to others).

Note that NetWare version 3.*x* is *not* considered a peer-to-peer network because its focus is on the file server as the main provider of all services.

Understanding Network Interfaces

Between the computer and the cable sits the *Network Interface Card (NIC)*. The NIC serves as the gateway between the computer's internal components and the network cable. NICs come in many flavors; for example, it can be a hardware device that connects directly to the computer's internal bus, giving it access to the memory and the processor. The other side of the card connects to the network cable.

Or a NIC can be a specialized adapter that connects to the parallel port of your computer. The parallel port then connects to your computer's bus through an input/output card. (Strictly speaking, the specialized adapter is not a card. Because it provides the same functions as a NIC, we lump them together and call it a NIC as well.)

The NIC must obey two sets of rules: those used internally by the computer and those required externally by the network. The rules it must follow are well defined and depend on the type of network the NIC is attached to, as well as the type of computer it is installed on.

Within these constraints, the NIC responds to software running on the computer that directs it to send messages across the network. It receives the data and formats it in a way that is acceptable to the network. This process normally involves attaching the required addresses and related information. When permitted, it places the message on the network for delivery.

The NIC also responds to messages intended for its node that it sees on the network. It captures the message, does its own accuracy checks on the contents, and passes it on to its controlling software.

The Role of the Network Operating System

A discussion of networks usually makes reference to a *network operating system* (NOS). It certainly seems as though this discussion is no exception. What exactly is a NOS?

When it's used in a context such as "Novell NetWare Network Operating System," NOS refers to the programs that run a NetWare file server. Like other computer operating systems, NetWare handles all the basic functions such as deciding what programs run on the file server and when, how memory is allocated to programs, and where files are stored on the disks. NetWare is a network operating system because it includes functionality allowing it to connect to a network and converse across it with other computers.

Note, however, that the NOS does not control the operation of the entire network. Client computers run their own operating systems (for example, MS-DOS). The client's operating system can come with programs to permit network access, or the client can run additional software. Each node has as much right to use the network as any other, and does not need to defer to NetWare or ask its permission to use the network.

Taken in total, the software components required to run the entire network include the following:

- ☐ Programs that control the operation of network servers

- ☐ Programs that control the operation of network clients

- ☐ Communication protocols that govern how data is exchanged across the network cable

You look at each of these components for a NetWare LAN in more detail throughout the rest of this book.

Setting Network Standards

One major reason LANs have gained such prominence among business systems is the development of clear standards regarding how nodes on the network connect together and how they share connections to communicate with each other. Fortunately, instead of network vendors developing proprietary specifications, most vendors have agreed to use certain standards that everyone tries to follow. The result has been improved connectivity between systems and hardware from different vendors.

This standard brings about greater flexibility in what hardware you can purchase and use, increased competition, lower prices, and explosive growth in the size and usefulness of LANs.

In the world of computers, however, and networks in particular, standards are not as standard as they might seem. To paraphrase a well-known quotation on the subject: standards are great, that's why there are so many to choose from.

Attempts have been made to develop a standard model for the entire data communications process. A group known as the International Standards Organization (ISO) developed the *Open Systems Interconnect Model* (*OSI Model*) to illustrate various functions needed for data communication between different kinds of computers.

Although the OSI Model and its standard layers have met with only limited acceptance (and even this level is currently on the decline), it has helped people to understand the data communication process in terms of functions operating at separate *layers*. Each layer plays a role in getting the data between its source and destination.

Several standards are available for individual layers of data networks. Some standards have gained greater popularity than others. But within the more accepted ones, vendors do a fairly good job of creating products that stay true to the specifications and take fewer liberties with the standards. As a result, you can buy hardware and software from many different vendors and be fairly sure that your efforts to get your computers talking together will be rewarded. Your task becomes a matter of stacking the right communication layers on top of each other.

If you are deciding what type of network to use, you have a wealth of standards and products from which to choose. The biggest problem is trying to understand what each standard or product does, how it fits in to what you are trying to do, and whether it interoperates or at least coexists with other products. At the end of the day, the main question is, "Will it all work?"

To answer these questions, you must understand how computers communicate on a network. The process is a complex one, especially if you try to tackle all the bits and bytes at the same time. One approach to improving your understanding is to break down the communication process into *layers*. You learn how to break down the layers in the next section.

Peeling the Layers of a Network

The idea behind viewing a network in layers is part of a divide-and-conquer strategy. Understanding all the functions at one time is virtually impossible. Take them one at

a time, and you stand a much better chance. And the communication process actually lends itself to being viewed in layers. Now look at an example.

When you use a computer to access a a network, many separate activities allow the information you want to come across the network cable.

1. You interact with a program—a word processor, for example—and tell it you want to open a file that is on a remote computer such as a file server. (You actually don't care where it is, you just want it.) You pass the request to the layer below you (the word processing application) and let it worry about how to get the file.

2. The word processor doesn't really know how to use a network either. But it knows it can ask the computer's operating system to open a file, and the operating system works out how to get it. The word processor passes the request to the layer below it (the operating system) and lets it take care of the details from there.

3. Your computer's operating system, or a program working with it, figures out that the file is not local, but on a file server. It has to formulate a request for the file and send it to the remote computer on the network. But it more than likely has no idea how to use the network directly. So it passes the request on to the next layer, a program that knows how to send information across the network.

4. The next lower layer receives the data to be sent (the file request) along with the name of the remote computer. It can then place the data in a *packet* of information and address the packet for the remote computer. But it is unlikely that even this layer knows how to use the network cable. It then passes the request down to the next layer to let it worry about how to transmit the data on the network wire.

5. Finally, you get to a layer that actually can use the cable itself. Software running at this layer knows how and when it can put data on the network, how to use the network to get it to the remote computer, and knows the packets of data it should collect and receive. Even then, it relies on a lower hardware layer to get the message through. So this layer passes the request down one more time.

6. Down at the hardware level, a combination of programs and electronic devices connected to the network cable actually transmits to and receives from the network wire.

On the remote computer, this same process is repeated, only in reverse. Each layer takes from the one below, performs its task, and passes the details up one more layer. All these players are loyal minions working just to bring you your file (and what have you ever done for them?).

The key concept here is that each layer performs one set of functions. Each layer relies on the layers above and below it to exchange data. Although each layer talks only with adjacent layers, the net effect is that each layer exchanges data with its equivalent layer on another computer.

The OSI Model mentioned earlier breaks this process down into seven distinct layers. There's nothing hard and fast about this number of layers—it's just the number the ISO committee believed was appropriate. The layers of the OSI Model are shown in Figure 2.1.

7	Application
6	Presentation
5	Session
4	Transport
3	Network
2	Data link
1	Physical

Figure 2.1. *The Open Systems Interconnect (OSI) Model.*

Each layer has a technical definition of the functions it should perform. The idea of the OSI Model was to define a standard set of functions for which vendors could develop real-world products. Strict compliance with OSI definitions, however, has simply not happened. Instead, vendors have adopted existing real-world standards and developed products complying with them. In some cases, the chosen standards align fairly well with the OSI layers. But many products combine functions that exist at more than one OSI layer or don't implement the full functionality required at even one level.

As a result, the OSI Model serves more as a reference point for comparing various network cabling systems and communications protocols than as a definition of network functions. Later, in Chapters 17 and 18, you see how some of NetWare's mechanisms compare with the OSI Model.

Because few protocols strictly comply with OSI layers, the technical definitions for each aren't that useful. If you really want to know them, you can find the details in many technical books covering the data communication process. But (as we think you'll see) they really don't help out that much in trying to understand what happens where on a network.

A simplification of the seven OSI layers is the three-layer model shown in Figure 2.2. The three layers in this model are more intuitive than the OSI Model because they act in a similar fashion to a telephone network.

- [ ] The *connection level* deals with attaching stations to the network. Attaching stations requires more than just the right physical connector. Various electrical and low-level communication standards also must be met before everything can work properly. Plus, the connection level standards dictate when each station can make use of its connection to the network.

  Not every telephone with a modular connector works with every phone system. A phone designed for use with a Computerized Branch Exchange (CBX), for example, might not work in your home, even though this type of phone uses the same physical connector; the connectors might be electrically incompatible. In the same way, NICs with the same type of connector still may not be able to exchange information. The connection level standards must be the same.

- [ ] The *network level* deals with exchanging data between network nodes. Exchanging data requires standards for identifying each node by a particular address, for placing that address within data packets to indicate their source and destination nodes, and checking that the contents have been received correctly. Network level protocols address this area.

  On a telephone network, each line on the system has a unique telephone number. Reaching local telephones requires telling the network the number you want to reach. Calling long distance requires entering some additional network information (such as area codes or country codes). Data networks also make use of network level standards to exchange data between nodes.

- [ ] The *conversation level* deals with the content of communication between programs residing on each computer. Even though a network session may be established, for any meaningful conversation to take place, both parties must speak the same language. Conversation level protocols deal with this situation.

Using the telephone, you currently can dial households around the globe directly. Unless the parties at each end both speak a common language, however, the fact that they can hear each other is useless. Or you might be able to hear a fax machine screeching in your ear, but that doesn't mean you can receive a fax by yourself.

7	Application		
6	Presentation		Conversation
5	Session		
4	Transport		Network
3	Network		
2	Data link		Connection
1	Physical		

Figure 2.2. *A simplified network model.*

For data networks, connection level and network level protocols might permit two computers to exchange data. But if the data has no meaning to the other party, however, the communication has been for nothing.

Keep these levels in mind as you look at some of the real-world standards you will run across as you gain more familiarity with data networks in general, and NetWare in particular. Although the real-world standards still may not tie in perfectly, they should make more sense.

Summary

In this chapter, you learned the following:

☐ Networks consist of nodes connected by cable. Nodes act as servers, which provide various services to the network, or clients, which make use of servers, or both.

☐ Servers come in many shapes and sizes, and they offer a variety of services. General-purpose computers enable you to log in, transfer files, execute remote commands, and send or receive electronic mail. Special-purpose servers offer these and other dedicated services such as mass file storage and database management facilities.

☐ Client computers perform many or most of their own computing tasks but look to servers for resources such as file storage. Where clients also act as servers and all nodes are of the same importance in terms of what they offer, the network is known as a peer-to-peer network.

☐ The link between the network cable and the node computer is the Network Interface Card (NIC).

☐ Both the OSI Model, and our simplified network model, can be used to help understand the layers operating as part of the data communication process.

Workshop
Terminology Review

cabling system—The type of cable used to network computers together. Also refers to the protocol used to govern use of the cable by each computer.

client—In a client/server system, the computer (usually a workstation) that makes service requests.

client/server—A network system design where a processor or computer designated as a server (file server, database server, and so on) provides services to other client processors or computers.

communication protocol—The agreed set of rules that are followed by every computer on a network to allow exchanging data over the common cable.

login—The process of identifying oneself to a computer and proving that identity, usually by specifying a password. After login, the computer can grant or deny access based on the established identity.

mainframe—A large computer system that supports hundreds or thousands of users with one machine.

network—A collection of computers linked by some type of cable, to permit sharing of resources such as large disks or fast printers

Network Interface Card—A device installed in a computer that serves as the gateway between the computer's internal components and the network cable.

network operating system—Normally refers to an operating system running on a computer that is designed to provide network services such as file sharing. May also refer collectively to all network programs running on both client and server computers.

NIC—See *Network Interface Card.*

node—A point of interconnection to a network.

OSI Model—The Open Systems Interconnect Model, formulated by the International Standards Organization to illustrate functional layers needed for data communication.

peer-to-peer network—A network where each node may act as a server, a client, or both at the same time.

remote procedure call—A request for some type of processing activity, issued by one computer and sent across the network to another computer.

server—A network device that provides services to client stations. Servers include file servers, database servers, and print servers.

workstation—A client computer that performs local processing and accesses network services.

Q&A

Q What type of services will be on my NetWare LAN?

A By far, the most common services available on your NetWare LAN are file and print services. Your NetWare 3.*x* file server is normally the focal point of your LAN and its users. Its main purpose is to provide file storage. Very often, the file server also provides print services. But it is possible to move the actual printing duties off to another computer on the LAN as well.

Other services available on the LAN may be offered by the file server or by other computers on the network. Examples include communication gateways (used to access other computers) and electronic mail gateways (used to exchange e-mail with other computers).

Q Can I mix NetWare with other types of networks on the same cable?

A Because the LAN cable can be used by many protocols at the same time, many other networks can coexist with NetWare. Examples include Windows for Workgroups and LANtastic. Note that getting everyone talking over the same cable at the same time can be a little tricky. See Chapters 17 through 19 for more details.

Q If the NetWare file server fails, is the network "down"?

A On a NetWare LAN, the file server is normally the most important computer. It often contains all the key programs and files that your users want to get to—such as network versions of word processors and spreadsheet programs, as well as their own data files. So for all intents and purposes, when the file server is down, so is the network.

But don't forget, NetWare does not control the entire LAN. Computers other than the file server can still exchange data with each other all by themselves. If you are running a separate service such as a communications gateway, you can still access it, even without the file server (as long as the programs you need to use the gateway aren't kept on the file server). You even can keep playing your favorite network game with your coworkers while you wait for the file server to come back up.

Day

2

3

What Is NetWare?

Novell's NetWare 3.*x* network operating system (NOS) is not simply another program running on a PC. It's not really even a PC DOS application. It is a sophisticated operating system that is purpose-built to deliver high-performance file services to clients connected through a network. Its features and performance have allowed it to play a major role in the downsizing of information systems from traditional mainframe computers to distributed processors connected by local area networks (LANs). That's one of the reasons NetWare has gained such a huge foothold in so many organizations throughout the world.

NetWare has been, and continues to be, very successful in the world of information systems. Teaching yourself about NetWare is definitely a good idea; it allows you to be a part of NetWare's success.

In the preceding chapter, you learned about network concepts and terminology. You now apply what you've learned as we introduce you to NetWare—its structure, how it communicates with others, and how it stores files and makes them available to a variety of systems. By the end of this chapter, you should have a strong foundation in NetWare, preparing you to begin using and understanding its many facilities as you follow through subsequent chapters.

In the following sections, you begin with an overview of NetWare as an operating system.

Getting to Know NetWare

NetWare is not DOS. For some of you, that fact may be a revelation; for others, it is simply cause for relief or even celebration. Because the most popular method of using NetWare, by far, is running on IBM-compatible personal computers (PCs), many people believe that NetWare has some ties to PC DOS. They may think NetWare runs "under" DOS, or somehow ties in to DOS through "exits" or other hooks.

In fact, the main relationship between NetWare and DOS is that they are both operating systems that run on the Intel 80x86 series of microprocessors. Earlier versions of NetWare completely replaced DOS on the PC used as a file server so that DOS no longer even existed on the hard disk. The current versions of NetWare 3.*x* tolerate DOS being around on the file server because having DOS makes installing and starting NetWare easier. DOS also provides NetWare with access to resources such as the file server's floppy disk drives. It keeps out of the way and does something useful occasionally, so NetWare lets DOS hang around in the file server's memory while NetWare runs.

When NetWare starts running, for all intents and purposes, it takes complete control of the PC. NetWare runs the disks, controls memory, schedules which programs run, takes commands from the keyboard, and talks to its clients across the network. It even can remove DOS from memory so that it has more room to work. If DOS is removed, when NetWare finishes (that is, the server is taken down), the computer must be restarted. If not, DOS is allowed to take over the computer again.

NetWare was designed to do one main function and do it well: manage files for clients. By managing, we mean storing and retrieving client files quickly but also safely. NetWare includes many features for high performance, as well as features to protect files against damage due to hardware problems (for example, bad disk areas). It is not a general-purpose operating system like DOS or UNIX or OS/2. NetWare was purpose-built for file serving.

At the core of NetWare is one program that provides its central services. Known as the *kernel*, it consists of a group of routines that perform most of NetWare's basic tasks. The kernel is designed to be fast while maintaining high reliability. NetWare's kernel takes full advantage of the 32-bit architecture offered on the Intel 80386 and 80486 microprocessors. It therefore can move data around the computer in larger portions than operating systems such as DOS. It also can directly address up to four gigabytes of memory.

There's more to NetWare than just the kernel, however. NetWare's design allows a great deal of flexibility to tie supplemental features and functions to the kernel. You can load additional modules into memory and hook them into the kernel, resulting in even more services to help network clients (and network administrators). Figure 3.1 shows the NetWare kernel and its main components.

System Executive	
Scheduler	
IPX/SPX and NCP	
Router	NetWare Kernel
Memory Management	
File System	
Semaphore Management	
Transaction Tracking System	
ODI Multi-protocol Support	

Figure 3.1. *The NetWare kernel.*

NetWare's design also allows it to communicate easily using many different types of networks and to exchange data with a variety of client computers. It establishes core services that are offered through a standard interface. Additional modules that translate between the standard interface and the requirements of other computers and operating systems are then added. These additional modules permit a NetWare server to act as the focal point for computers connected to it throughout the organization.

In the following sections, you examine NetWare's structure and components in more detail.

NetWare's Heart—The Kernel

At the very core of NetWare is something that seems a great deal like a DOS program. After all, to start NetWare, you first have to boot the server computer using DOS. There you are staring at a DOS prompt. You can even use DOS commands such as DIR to look at all the files in the NetWare directory. One file in particular is the heart of it all because it's the program that runs NetWare's kernel. It's known as SERVER.EXE; so to start NetWare, you simply type

SERVER

"Are you *sure* this isn't just a DOS program?" we hear you ponder. Well, after the kernel starts executing, DOS doesn't know what hit it. NetWare loads into extended memory—that portion of the computer's memory above one megabyte. It completely takes over running the computer, while DOS remains in low memory, just waiting to see whether NetWare asks it to do something (such as access a floppy disk drive). Figure 3.2 shows where NetWare and DOS reside in memory.

How the Kernel Controls and Executes Tasks

The approach NetWare takes to executing tasks contributes to its performance; it boils down to how NetWare determines what routines to run and when to run them. Specific details on how NetWare performs this process are described in the following:

☐ *NetWare is a multitasking/multithreaded operating system.* Multitasking means that you can have more than one program active at a time. This capability is key because it allows NetWare to perform many functions at once. A number of tasks are executing simultaneously on a NetWare server, such as taking requests from many different clients, getting their files, and providing results.

	NetWare V3.x OS
1 MB	
	Upper Memory
640 KB	
	DOS Conventional Memory

Figure 3.2. *Memory map of NetWare and DOS.*

Thread refers to the basic unit of execution for NetWare. A thread may be an entire program or a logical group of instructions from within a program. The key point is that each thread may be scheduled for execution by NetWare on the CPU. Multithreaded, therefore, means essentially the same as multitasking. Whereas multitasking refers to the program level, however, multithreaded means that functions within a program can be executed at the same time (assuming that doing so is acceptable to what the program is trying to accomplish). Because control over which functions execute is at a finer level, multithreading can produce improved performance.

Note: If you are familiar with computing models and hardware architectures, you might point out that most traditional computers, and PCs in particular, really perform only one task at a time. It only *appears* that more than one task is running because the computer can quickly switch between programs, allowing each one the capability to accomplish some work. One way to truly perform more than one task at a time is to make use of additional processors that perform operations in parallel.

You see that NetWare can perform many tasks at one time. But how does it decide which task to perform at any instance and how long it gets to run? The answer lies in how NetWare schedules tasks.

☐ *Programs are run on a run-to-completion basis.* Most general-purpose computer operating systems, if they are multitasking, allow a certain amount of time (called a *time slice*) to each program. A scheduling program tracks the amount of CPU time each program receives. After that time has expired, the program is *preempted*, and another program is allowed to run. Time slices are normally equal in size, in an attempt to be fair to all tasks running on the system. (Note, however, that some programs may get a bigger slice of the pie, depending on any higher priorities that can be assigned to them. Shades of the saying "All programs are equal, but some are more equal than others.")

NetWare is not, however, a general-purpose operating system. Its design optimizes the throughput of data. For NetWare, fairness is not the issue; getting the job done is. As a result, NetWare's scheduler allows any thread that is running to complete its task. Run-to-completion means the opposite of preemptive scheduling because all threads are allowed as much time as they need to finish. The benefit of using run-to-completion is that important NetWare tasks are never interrupted. More critical tasks are accomplished because less time is spent monitoring time slices and switching between tasks. This approach also allows the scheduling program to be less complex and, therefore, to run more efficiently.

Run-to-completion, of course, has its drawbacks. Because NetWare does not interrupt execution, a thread can seize control of the CPU and never give it up. Such a miscreant thread can prevent other important threads from executing and generally make a mess of things. NetWare therefore depends on threads being well mannered. Each thread must use the CPU only for as long as it needs to accomplish critical tasks. It then must turn over the CPU so that other threads can run. This process depends on the honor system, and in practice, the approach works effectively.

The Kernel's Relationship with DOS

As we mentioned earlier, you use DOS to boot the computer and then to start the NetWare kernel by typing SERVER at the DOS prompt. DOS then must take a backseat to NetWare but may be asked to help out every so often. The key thing to remember is that NetWare is not running under DOS. NetWare has complete control of the computer and the tasks it is executing.

Whether DOS stays around at all actually is up to you, the system administrator. Leaving DOS available in lower memory allows NetWare to use it to access floppy disk

drives. In addition, after a NetWare server has been stopped and the kernel exited, control is restored to DOS, the C: prompt returns, and the user can continue to use the computer as a regular DOS PC.

Leaving DOS loaded takes up valuable memory, however. You might want to make this memory available to NetWare. Or you might want to ensure that DOS cannot simply be restored after stopping the NetWare server, in order to force the computer to reboot.

In either case, you can completely remove DOS from the NetWare server's memory by using the following console command:

```
REMOVE DOS
```

From that point on, DOS is no longer available unless you reboot the computer.

Note: REMOVE refers to eliminating DOS from the file server's memory, not from its hard disk. A DOS partition still remains on the disk drive.

The NetWare Loadable Module Environment

You've seen that the lowest level of NetWare is the kernel, which performs most of the basic but critical tasks for the file server. NetWare enables you to load and run additional program modules with the kernel, however, to customize its interactions with other hardware and software and to expand the services that NetWare can offer to the network.

To facilitate this process, NetWare includes a *software bus*. Recall that the bus within the PC is a physical configuration of wires and connectors that enables you to add devices. The devices then can talk with the motherboard and CPU. In the same way, the NetWare software bus enables you to add program modules, called *NetWare Loadable Modules* (*NLMs*). The NLMs then can converse with the kernel, drawing on and enhancing its services.

You can load or unload NLMs on the fly; that is, you can start or stop them at any time the kernel is running. No shutdown or regeneration of the kernel is required.

Note: Your ability to load or unload NLMs differs from previous versions of NetWare, where Value Added Processes (VAPs) were first linked to the core NetWare code, and then the server was started. The VAPs remained in effect unless the server was stopped, the code was removed, and NetWare was regenerated.

Five main types of NLMs are available:

☐ Disk drivers

☐ Network Interface Card (NIC) drivers

☐ Name space modules

☐ Management utilities

☐ Server applications

Each of these types of modules is considered more closely in the following sections.

Disk Drivers

NetWare needs to know how to physically read and write data to the disks it accesses. The trouble is that disk controllers come in many types, with each type requiring its own interface. One approach involves building knowledge about all possible disk configurations into the NetWare kernel—a difficult task indeed. And it is inefficient because each computer normally uses only one or two disk types.

The best way to deal with the problem is to build separate disk drivers as NLMs, which contain the instructions necessary to interface with a given type of disk. You need to load only the required disk driver or drivers, after which you can mount the disk for use by NetWare and its users.

A number of standard disk drivers, which you can use with most common disk types, exist. Examples include drivers for use with most IDE and SCSI disk drives. In addition, disk controller manufacturers have the option of creating their own disk drivers for use with NetWare.

Disk driver NLMs are distinguished from other modules by having a DSK filename extension.

Network Interface Card Drivers

NetWare communicates with its clients across the network through one or more Network Interface Cards (NICs). A NIC is simply a card designed to fit in your computer. Network cables are physically attached to the NIC, which acts as a gateway between the computer and the rest of the network. Many different types of networks exist, and each one uses a different type of NIC. And NICs from different vendors typically require their own software to allow communication with other programs running on the computer.

Once again, you have the situation where building all possible NIC interfaces into the NetWare kernel is virtually impossible and inefficient besides. NLMs charge to the rescue. You can create a separate NLM for each type of NIC that is installed on a NetWare server. After you load each NLM and tie it to the appropriate protocol (more on this process later in the chapter), NetWare can receive and send information across the attached networks.

Drivers normally are available from NIC manufacturers. Or, if the NIC behaves like a standard card (such as the NE2000 Ethernet card), you can use one of the drivers available from Novell.

NIC driver NLMs are distinguished from other modules by having the LAN filename extension.

Name Space Modules

A Name Space module is a unique feature that allows NetWare to store files, or more particularly filenames, for non-DOS systems. Whereas DOS filenames are confined to a maximum eight-character name and three-character extension, operating systems such as UNIX, OS/2, and System 7 for the Macintosh allow much larger names. For NetWare to be a useful repository for files for these systems, it must record the full filenames.

NetWare accomplishes this task with Name Space NLMs. Name space information supplements the details recorded in NetWare directories so that full filenames are available to non-DOS clients. Name Space NLMs are loaded for each non-DOS file format to be handled by the server. You can set support for extended filenames using name spaces for each individual NetWare volume. (You examine the details on NetWare directories and volumes later in this chapter.)

Name Space NLMs are distinguished from other modules by having the NAM filename extension.

Management Utilities

NetWare is a sophisticated network operating system that requires proper administration if it is to function efficiently and effectively. Assistance in this task comes from the Management Utility NLMs. These modules help in the administration of the NetWare server and the LAN as a whole. Administration includes installing and maintaining NetWare, as well as monitoring the file server and other portions of the network.

One important example of a Management Utility NLM is the INSTALL module. INSTALL enables you, the administrator, to create NetWare partitions on a hard disk, create volumes within the partition, load NetWare files from the distribution diskettes to their appropriate places on the server, and add and configure other support products.

Another module, MONITOR, provides a wealth of important information about the file server, including key performance measurements, details on memory and other resource utilization, disk and network information, configuration details, and connections with clients.

To see how easy loading an NLM can be, look at how you start the MONITOR utility on the NetWare server in the following task.

Task 3.1: Starting the MONITOR utility.

Step 1: Description

This task describes how you load NetWare's MONITOR utility at the file server console.

Step 2: Action

1. At the file server console prompt, type LOAD MONITOR.

   (You learn about using LOAD and other console commands on the file server in later chapters.)

2. The MONITOR utility menu appears. Figure 3.3 shows what your screen should look like.

3. To leave MONITOR, press Esc until you are asked to confirm your exit.

Step 3: Review

In this task, you started an NLM using the LOAD command at the file server console.

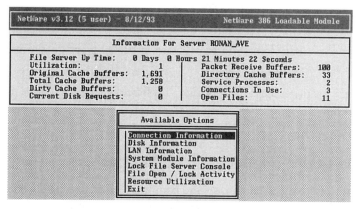

Figure 3.3. *The MONITOR Utility NLM screen.*

An additional set of Management Utility NLMs allows remote access to file server console commands, either from across the network or by dialing in to the server using a modem. Overall, these NLMs provide useful tools to help you as an administrator to perform your server and LAN management tasks.

Management Utility NLMs are distinguished from other modules by having the NLM filename extension.

Applications Running on the Server

NetWare's main purpose is to serve files to clients. It is not intended to be a general-purpose operating system running a variety of programs—that's the role of NetWare's client computers. The NLM environment, however, allows NetWare to perform other tasks that are useful both to NetWare clients and its administrators.

The main example is the print server functions that NetWare can provide. When the print server NLM is loaded, NetWare can access printers attached to the server computer. It maintains queues of print requests on behalf of clients and print files sent to it. Although other computers on the network also can offer print services, the NetWare file server is generally up and available at all times and so provides a handy point for centralized printing needs.

Another example of an application running on the server is the link between the NetWare server and an *uninterruptible power supply* (*UPS*). NetWare can use an NLM to monitor the status of the UPS and determine whether a power failure has occurred. If so, NetWare can advise all users that it will shut down, gracefully close files, and eventually stop processing. This process avoids the potential corruption of files that may occur when power fails and the system simply crashes.

NetWare even provides a simple text editor for use of the file server console, which enables you to modify batch files used during system startup. Although NetWare will likely never run spreadsheets or word processing, it does provide some useful applications in the right place and at the right time.

Like the Management Utility NLMs, Application NLMs also have the NLM filename extension.

Memory Architecture

After NetWare has taken over the computer, it arranges the contents of memory. NetWare's use of a 32-bit architecture means it can deal with up to 4 gigabytes (4G) of memory. That's a hefty responsibility! Because most of today's personal computers accommodate up to only 32 megabytes (32M) of RAM, however, NetWare is not even breaking a sweat managing memory.

The way NetWare arranges and rearranges memory is another contributor to its high level of performance. Now look more closely at how this process works.

How NetWare Categorizes Memory

NetWare uses the server computer's available RAM to maintain three main memory pools:

☐ File-cache buffer pool

☐ Permanent memory pool

☐ Alloc short-term pool

File-Cache Buffer Pool

One of the biggest performance gains for NetWare comes from its use of *file caching*. The motivation behind caching is that moving information to or from a disk drive is relatively slower than moving it to or from RAM. To take advantage of this fact, you can set up a file cache in memory to act like a window into the file. Programs that access the file actually use the cache in memory (and therefore get information quickly). Portions of the file are moved into and out of the file cache as a separate operation.

As an example, suppose that a program requests a specific few bytes of information from a file. Instead of getting only the one piece, a larger portion of the file (a *block*) is brought into the cache. This result is based on the assumption (which is often valid)

that if the program wants one chunk of the file, it will likely want more. If it wants more, at least one portion of the file is already in the cache and can be delivered to the program quickly.

On the write side, caching allows a program to place information rapidly into the cache and then move to the next task. When NetWare gets the chance, it performs the (more time-consuming) physical write to the disk.

> **Note:** Not writing the file to disk immediately can cause problems. If the system stops before the cache is written to disk, the file might be corrupted or at least might not be up to date. That's why NetWare takes steps to make sure that the contents of all file caches have been written to disk before the server is stopped. It's also why a UPS can be a worthwhile investment.

NetWare makes extensive use of caching to enhance performance. It establishes the *file-cache buffer pool* (see Figure 3.4) to hold blocks of files it reads from and writes to. Any new requests for files are assigned a portion of memory called a *buffer* from the pool to hold file blocks. If a file block has not been used for a while, it loses its buffer (but only after the contents have been written to disk). This approach to managing the buffer pool is called the *Least Recently Used algorithm*.

Because file caching is so important to server performance, the file-cache buffer pool is allocated as much memory as possible by NetWare. As you see in the next sections, other pools borrow memory from the file-cache buffer pool (and they may or may not give it back).

Within the file-cache buffer pool are two specific subpools:

☐ *The cache nonmovable pool,* so named because it remains at a fixed location within the file-cache buffer pool. The cache nonmovable pool serves as a constant point of contact for NLMs. During the loading process for an NLM, memory is borrowed from the rest of the file-cache buffer pool. The NLM loads and obtains its own portion of memory. Memory borrowed to perform this process then is returned to the file-cache buffer pool.

☐ *The cache movable pool,* which can be relocated throughout the server's RAM. Moving this cache allows NetWare to use memory more efficiently, avoiding fragmentation. Within this pool reside system tables (like the directory entry tables and file allocation tables), which grow and shrink as the server runs. If a table grows, memory is borrowed from the rest of the file-cache buffer pool. When the table shrinks, memory can be returned. (We look more closely at NetWare's file tables in Chapter 4.)

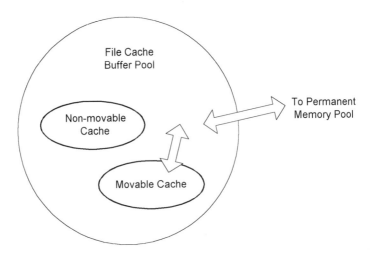

Figure 3.4. *File-cache buffer memory pool.*

Permanent Memory Pool

Permanent memory (shown in Figure 3.5), as its name implies, remains in place after it is established. It is used for processes that require memory for long periods of time, such as directory cache buffers and buffers used to hold incoming packets from the network.

Permanent memory borrows space whenever it needs it from the file-cache buffer pool. As network activity increases, for example, NetWare can increase the number of buffers it has available to hold incoming packets. Unlike the nonmovable and movable cache pools, however, space for permanent memory pools is never returned to the file-cache buffer pool. In this way, permanent memory pool size acts like a high-water mark, never going down even if the peak activity has subsided.

Within the permanent memory pool exists a subpool called *semipermanent memory.* This type of memory is used by NLMs that need small amounts of memory for extended periods. The best examples are the disk and NIC drivers loaded when NetWare started. Each of these NLMs borrows memory from the rest of the permanent memory pool. When use of semipermanent memory stops, the available space is returned for other permanent memory use.

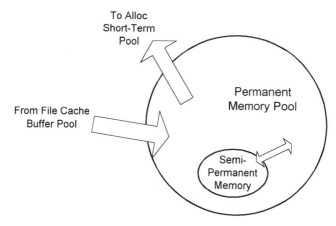

Figure 3.5. *Permanent memory pool.*

Alloc (Short-Term) Memory Pool

Alloc memory (see Figure 3.6) is provided to meet the short-term memory requirements of the kernel and NLMs. When a user logs in, for example, information about his or her connection must be created and stored in memory. After the user logs off, the information is no longer needed. Alloc memory is given while the user remains logged in. Other examples include information on drive mappings, various queues, and tables used by some NLMs.

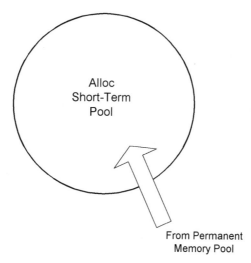

Figure 3.6. *Alloc memory pool.*

To meet these short-term memory requirements, NetWare borrows space from the permanent memory pool, and puts it into the alloc memory pool. As the need for temporary space increases, so does the borrowing from permanent memory (which may have to borrow from the file-cache buffer pool). After the need for temporary memory has ended, the space is made available again to the rest of the alloc memory pool. The free space within alloc memory, however, is not returned to the permanent memory pool.

NetWare's Memory Requirements

Novell offers guidelines on how much RAM a server computer should have to provide acceptable performance. The guidelines are based on criteria such as the size of disk available and the number of name spaces supported.

The rule of thumb can be "the more RAM you have, the better NetWare performs." This rule is due to NetWare's use of file caching to improve performance. The more memory is available, the more file caching can be done. The more caching, the faster NetWare runs. So you probably want to get as much memory as possible for your file server computer. As a check on whether you have enough, you can find the memory guidelines in the NetWare manuals.

How NetWare Protects Memory

NetWare 3.*x* is designed to run on computers using the Intel 80386 or 80486 microprocessor chip. Both chips are based on the 80386 architecture, which includes hardware features to protect programs running in memory. The features allow programs and the memory to be classified into *rings*. Programs running in higher number rings can access memory only within that ring. They cannot get to memory in lower number rings.

The idea behind this approach is to make the system more reliable. You can set certain key programs—an operating system kernel, for example—to run within ring 0. Other programs such as applications run in a higher number ring. If the application program fails, for whatever reason, and starts writing to memory locations that it isn't supposed to, it can only hurt other programs within the same ring. But it can't harm the operating system kernel because the kernel is running within a lower ring. The program may fail, but the operating system continues.

Figure 3.7 shows the ring architecture and how it can be used to protect memory layers (rings). It also shows that NetWare uses only one of these layers.

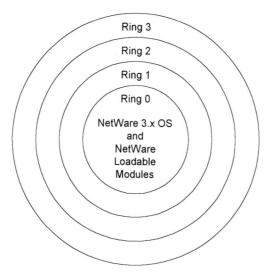

Figure 3.7. *The ring architecture.*

One problem with using multiple rings is that it slows down the system. And NetWare does not want to be slowed down. So NetWare 3.*x* does not use the ring architecture features to protect itself, choosing instead to run all kernel and NLM threads within ring 0. The result is that NetWare executes more quickly than it would if it used the ring architecture. Once again, however, NetWare must trust all its threads to behave properly. In this case, the threads must not inadvertently overwrite the memory used by other threads. Although trust on its own is a wonderful thing, Novell also maintains a certification process for NLMs. The process checks NLMs for reliability to ensure that they are trustworthy.

Summary

In this chapter, you learned the following:

☐ NetWare is a sophisticated network operating system that takes over the operation of a server computer from DOS.

☐ The heart of NetWare is its kernel, which provides basic services such as controlling the execution of threads and allocating memory.

☐ Through the software bus, you can add NetWare Loadable Modules, which supplement the functions of the kernel. Examples include disk drivers, Network Interface Card drivers, Names spaces, management utilities, and other applications.

☐ NetWare maintains three main memory pools, with some subpools. Memory is borrowed from the file-cache buffer pool to serve the needs of permanent memory and alloc memory. More memory on the file server normally gives better performance.

Workshop

Terminology Review

alloc memory pool—The portion of memory used by NetWare for short-term memory needs. Alloc memory space is borrowed from the permanent memory pool but is not returned.

buffer—An area of memory used as a temporary window from which data is moved in and out.

cache movable pool—A subpool within the file-cache buffer pool used for system tables.

cache nonmovable pool—A subpool within the file-cache buffer pool used for loading NLMs.

extended memory—That portion of memory on an Intel 80x86 computer above one megabyte.

file caching—A process that uses memory as a temporary storage area for portions of disk files. Programs that need data from the file or that want to write new data into the file actually access the cache in memory (and therefore move the information more quickly). Portions of the file are moved between the file cache and disk as a separate operation.

file-cache buffer pool—The portion of memory used by NetWare for file caching.

kernel—A group of programs that perform most of NetWare's basic tasks; the core of a NetWare file server. The kernel is started from the DOS command prompt using the command SERVER. Thereafter, it takes over operation of the file server computer.

Least Recently Used algorithm—The methodology used by NetWare to decide which buffers can be reused.

low memory—The first 640 kilobytes of memory on an Intel 80×86 computer.

multitasking—More than one program active (running) on the computer at a time.

multithreaded—More than one thread active (running) on the computer at a time. A thread is a unit of execution that can be an entire program or only a portion of a program.

NetWare Loadable Module—A program module that is loaded on a file server and that interacts with the kernel.

NLM—See *NetWare Loadable Module.*

permanent memory pool—The portion of memory used by NetWare for long-term memory needs. Permanent memory space is borrowed from the file-cache buffer pool but is not returned.

preemptive scheduling—Programs/threads are allowed a certain amount of CPU time. If they are not completed, they are stopped temporarily, and another is allowed its turn.

ring architecture—A hardware feature offered on Intel 80386 and 80486 microprocessors. It prevents programs running in lower number rings from being interfered with by those in higher number rings.

run-to-completion—Programs/threads running on the CPU are not interrupted after a certain time allocation. Instead, they are allowed as much time as they need to finish.

software bus—The facility that allows NLMs to be loaded, interact with the NetWare kernel, and be unloaded.

uninterruptible power supply—A device that provides continuous and regulated electrical power even when the main power lines fail or experience power fluctuations. Normally, it is used with an important computer, such as a NetWare file server, to protect against loss or corruption of data in the event of a problem with normal electrical power.

UPS—See *uninterruptible power supply.*

Task List

In this chapter, you tried your first NetWare file server console command, LOAD MONITOR. You used this command to see an example of a key NetWare Loadable Module (NLM). (You learn much more about the MONITOR NLM in Chapter 27.)

Q&A

Q What workstation operating systems work with NetWare?

A NetWare can support workstation computers running MS-DOS (with or without Windows), OS/2, Macintosh System 7, and UNIX (with NFS). You learn more about how NetWare does this in Chapter 4.

Q Will NetWare run on other types of computers?

A The vast majority of NetWare servers run on computers using an Intel 80386 or 80486 microprocessor. As explained in this chapter, a NetWare file server is started from DOS, but really takes over the computer thereafter.

But a version of NetWare also runs as a set of applications on UNIX computers. NetWare for UNIX runs under UNIX (as opposed to taking over the computer) and provides file services to clients in the same fashion as regular NetWare.

Q Will NLMs run on a DOS-based workstation computer?

A No, because NLMs are not DOS programs, they can't run on a DOS-based workstation. They are designed to tie into NetWare's software bus and so run on the NetWare file server only. They are started from the file server console prompt.

Q Can I run DOS programs on my file server?

A A NetWare file server is started from DOS, so a basic DOS system remains available and can be used on the file server computer. Before you start NetWare, the file can still run DOS programs.

Once you start NetWare, however, DOS programs do not run on the file server. If you try to LOAD a DOS program at the file server console prompt, for example, it does not work.

Q My word processing software is on a NetWare file server. When I run the programs, where does the program execute?

A Any normal DOS program can be stored on a NetWare file server. But that's all NetWare does for the program—store it.

When you log in to the file server from your workstation and then type the name of a program stored on the file server, the program code is sent across the network and loaded into your workstation's memory. The program actually executes on the workstation, *not* on the file server. Many people forget this key point, which results in confusion later on.

4

Understanding NetWare Connectivity

No matter how good NetWare is as a file server, this capability is meaningless unless the file server can communicate with client workstations. Fortunately, NetWare is fluent in several network communication protocols, allowing it to provide file services to many different types of computers on many different kinds of networks.

Learning How NetWare Communicates

If you've ever tried to get different types of computers to communicate, you know that dealing with one sort of network can be frustrating. NetWare permits connections from clients across many different kinds of networks. How does it accomplish such a feat?

NetWare makes use of the same mechanism that allows adding to the kernel's functionality: NetWare Loadable Modules (NLMs). The kernel itself provides support for NetWare's native communication protocols, called IPX/SPX. Through the software bus, you can load NLMs that support other protocols, such as TCP/IP. And because of the design of NetWare's network communication interface, it can support all of these network communication protocols on a single NIC.

Not only can NetWare talk with clients using a number of different communication protocols, it can act as a router for these protocols. You learn in Chapter 17 that a router is a device used to send packets between different networks. Using a NetWare server with both a Token Ring NIC and an Ethernet NIC, for example, routing takes place for packets received on one LAN destined for the other one.

The key to providing all these features is a set of routines within NetWare known as the *Link Support Layer* (*LSL*); see Figure 4.1. The LSL ensures that traffic coming in on each NIC is sent to the appropriate place—IPX packets are sent to the IPX/SPX protocol handlers, IP packets are sent to the TCP/IP protocol handlers, and so on.

In the following sections, you look at some of the highlights, and you see some of the terminology regarding network protocols used in Chapter 2.

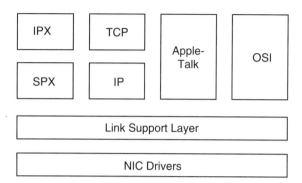

Figure 4.1. *NetWare's LSL with other protocols.*

NetWare's Native Protocol—IPX/SPX

Novell created its own network communication protocol, Internet Packet Exchange/ Sequenced Packet Exchange (IPX/SPX), based on Xerox's XNS protocol. IPX/SPX permits sending information between NetWare servers and their clients across many types of network systems, including Ethernet, Token Ring, and ARCnet. Because support for IPX/SPX is part of NetWare's kernel, the protocol is available whenever the server is running. You only have to direct IPX/SPX to the appropriate NIC driver, and the server is open for business.

IPX operates at the network level of the OSI model. It makes use of a network such as Ethernet to deliver packets between nodes on a NetWare LAN. After IPX is handed information to be delivered by an upper-level protocol, it adds the appropriate addressing for the source and destination node, and then it hands the packet off to the lower-level protocol (for example, Ethernet). IPX also allows packets to be sent to other networks because it includes information on source and destination network numbers, in addition to the node numbers.

IPX does not guarantee the delivery of data because the protocol does not include a provision for sequencing packets or acknowledging their delivery. As a result, a packet sent using IPX may never arrive, or it might arrive in a different order than it was sent in. Although IPX cannot claim to be "reliable" in the pure network sense of the word, it usually does get the packet through; it just can't prove it.

SPX operates at the transport level of the OSI model. It uses IPX as a delivery mechanism but adds information that results in a reliable connection (one that guarantees delivery in the correct order). Some upper-level protocols use SPX so that

they can be sure the packet is delivered. Others take care of ensuring delivery themselves, however, and so use IPX directly rather than incur the extra overhead of SPX.

An important user of IPX directly is the NetWare Core Protocol (NCP), a service providing an interface between programs on client computers and file servers (see Figure 4.2). The client computer determines those requests for resources requiring redirection to the network (for example, when a program tries to open a file residing on a NetWare server). It communicates this information to the file server using NCP as its language of choice. The file server also uses NCP to return the information.

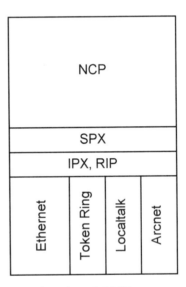

Figure 4.2. *The IPX/SPX protocol stack with NCP.*

Note: Many people using NetWare have never heard of NCP. They usually talk about programs known as either shells or redirectors. These programs act as intermediaries between the client computer operating system and file servers across the network. To do so, the programs speak NCP. You learn more about workstation shell programs in Chapter 18.

Another direct user of IPX is the Routing Information Protocol (RIP). You use RIP packets to advise NetWare routers of the availability of servers, as well as paths to other networks. The routers receive this information and update their internal tables, allowing them to route packets on behalf of the network.

TCP/IP

Transmission Control Protocol/Internet Protocol (TCP/IP) is an open set of network standards and protocols evolving from a U.S. Department of Defense research network known as ARPAnet. It became the basis for the worldwide Internet, a network with millions of connected host computers. But you also can find TCP/IP on stand-alone LANs, connecting small numbers of computers together.

The reason for its popularity in both worldwide and local networks is that the TCP/IP suite of protocols is well defined and available to anyone who wants to implement them. In response, most vendors, including Novell, have included support for TCP/IP in their network software.

On a NetWare server, TCP/IP support is implemented through an NLM. After you load and direct it to the appropriate NIC, NetWare can understand TCP/IP packets that come to it from networks such as Ethernet or Token Ring. NetWare even can deal with TCP/IP on the same Network Interface Card as it uses for IPX/SPX, thanks to the LSL.

IP operates at basically the same level in the OSI model as IPX, that is, the network level. It, too, makes use of a network such as Ethernet to deliver packets between nodes on a NetWare LAN. And, like IPX, it does not guarantee the delivery of packets. It allows higher-level protocols to worry about that. The TCP/IP protocol suite also supports a number of router protocols (including its own version of RIP), which allow routers to learn about the existence of other nodes and paths on the network.

At the transport layer of the OSI model, TCP plays a role similar to that of SPX. TCP is a reliable delivery service because it guarantees that packets arrive and that they are in the correct order. As for SPX, however, a number of higher-level protocols are prepared to take care of ensuring delivery on their own. The TCP/IP protocol suite therefore includes the User Datagram Protocol (UDP), which acts as a transport layer mechanism but does not guarantee delivery.

The main user of TCP/IP is NetWare's implementation of Network File System (NFS); see Figure 4.3. NFS was originally developed by Sun Microsystems but has been licensed to many vendors. It is a popular protocol, particularly among UNIX computers and other users of TCP/IP networks, which allows an NFS client to "mount" a file or a directory of files from a remote NFS server. The remote files appear to be local to the NFS client. (Sounds a great deal like accessing a NetWare file from a PC, yes?)

```
+------------------+------------------+
|   Telnet         |                  |
|   FTP            |    NFS           |
|   SMTP           |    RPC           |
|                  |                  |
+------------------+------------------+
|      TCP         |      UDP         |
+------------------+------------------+
|              IP                     |
+--------+--------+--------+----------+
|        | Token  |        |          |
|Ethernet| Ring   |Localtalk| Arcnet  |
|        |        |        |          |
+--------+--------+--------+----------+
```

Figure 4.3. *The TCP/IP protocol stack with NFS.*

When it's running as an NFS server, the NetWare server provides file and print server access to any client capable of "speaking" NFS across a TCP/IP network. NFS client software is available for many operating systems, including most versions of UNIX and PC DOS.

Other Protocols Available

The flexibility of NetWare's LSL is the key that permits dealing with many different protocols. As you saw for TCP/IP, you only have to load an NLM that supports the required protocol and tie it to the NIC. NetWare's LSL ensures that the appropriate packets are sent to the right place.

Other available protocols include the following:

☐ *AppleTalk Phase 2, including routing.* This protocol supports the AppleTalk Filing Protocol (AFP), which enables Macintosh users to access a NetWare file server as if it were simply an AppleShare Server.

☐ *OSI TP0-TP4, implementing layers zero through four of the OSI model.*
This protocol supports File Transfer Access Management (FTAM), an
application-layer file service protocol.

Understanding NetWare's
File System Support

NetWare 3.*x* is designed in a modular fashion. For example, you saw that the kernel
provides core functions, which can be supplemented by NLMs. In a similar fashion,
the Link Service Level acts as the central coordinator used by a variety of network
protocols.

NetWare's approach to file services maintains this pattern: build strong core functions
and then make them available to many environments using additional software
modules. As a result, NetWare files are accessible by many different types of
computing platforms, including DOS, OS/2, UNIX, and Macintosh. No wonder a
NetWare server can become the focal point for an enterprise-wide network.

In the following sections, you look at how NetWare stores its files.

NetWare Volumes

The highest level of NetWare's storage system is a *volume* (see Figure 4.4). Each
NetWare server can have up to 64 volumes on it. A volume is a logical structure (as
distinct from a physical structure). While a volume can be set up on one physical
device alone, it also can be spread across as many as 32 separate *segments*. A segment
is an area of physical disk that has been prepared for use by NetWare.

Volumes are composed of *blocks*, which are the basic unit in which file storage is
allocated. Each volume can have a block size of from 4 kilobytes to 64 kilobytes (in
integral powers of two). Individual data files are given space an entire block at a time.
Even a 100 byte file, for example, is stored in a block of at least 4 kilobytes in size.

NetWare maintains a mapping for each block, which specifies what segment the block
is on. It translates this information into a physical disk drive and disk sector number
within the drive.

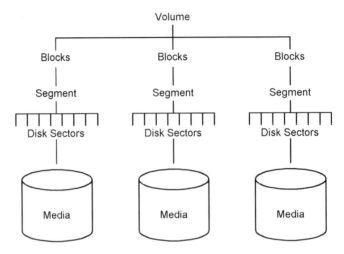

Figure 4.4. *NetWare volumes.*

File Allocation Table

NetWare maintains the *File Allocation Table* (FAT), which contains information about every block on the volume. Each block is either in use by a particular file, or unallocated and available for use.

A NetWare file of any reasonable size spreads across a number of blocks. To keep track of the file, NetWare links together the FAT entries for each block used by the file. To access the file, NetWare simply follows the links to determine each block in use; then it uses the information to find the file at its physical disk locations.

The FAT is cached in memory to permit rapid lookup of file locations and the location of available free space on a disk.

Directory Entry Table

The *Directory Entry Table* (DET) contains details similar to those found in DOS directories. For each file on a NetWare volume, the DET has an entry with the filename, file size, and times and dates for creation and last access. NetWare also tracks security-related information such as the file's owner and who has access to the file. The DET entry also has a pointer to the FAT. NetWare follows this pointer and then uses the FAT information to access the file.

NetWare maintains a cache for DET entries so that frequently used files can be referenced and located quickly. It continues to cache entries until it reaches a set upper limit on the number of directory entries. After that point, the least recently used directory entry is removed and replaced with new entries.

Additional Performance and Safety Features

In addition to FAT and DET caching, NetWare makes use of a number of other features to enhance the performance of its file system. These features include the following:

☐ *File caching*, covered in Chapter 3 as you reviewed the allocation of memory to file-cache buffers. You now understand that it is a volume block that is placed in a file-cache buffer.

☐ *Directory hashing*, which constructs a numeric key based on a file's name. You then can use the key as an index to locate a directory entry more quickly (compared to simply searching for its name in a table).

☐ *Elevator seeking*, which makes disk usage more efficient. Picture an elevator in a building and imagine that the elevator responds to call buttons on each floor in the order that they were pressed. Instead of stopping for passengers as it passes by their floor on the way up or down, the elevator heads all over, first to the first caller and then to the next caller, regardless of their locations. If a disk drive responds to requests to move as they come in, the read/write heads behave in the same way, moving back and forth across the disk. To avoid this situation, NetWare services disk requests to minimize head movement. It deals with them according to where the read/write head is at the time, not according to which request comes first.

NetWare also implements functions that help protect data integrity, including the following:

☐ *Redundant FATs and DETs*. Copies of each are maintained on other areas of the disk available to the server. This capability increases the chance of recovery if the FAT or DET somehow becomes corrupted.

☐ *Disk mirroring and duplexing*. You can duplicate the contents of a disk on another disk attached to the same disk controller. The duplicate is always kept up to date, and so is a mirror image of the first disk. If the main disk fails, the mirror disk can continue processing with exactly the same information. Disk duplexing involves mirroring on a disk that uses a completely separate disk controller.

☐ *Read-after-write verification.* After it writes data to the disk, NetWare rereads and it compares the data to the original source, which is still in memory. If an error exists, the operation is retried up to several times. If the write still fails, the disk area is isolated so that it isn't used again. The original data goes to the hot fix mechanism.

☐ *Hot fix.* Repeated failed attempts to write to a disk cause the data to be moved to the *hot fix redirection area.* As system administrator, you can monitor this area to determine whether disk problems are occurring more frequently than they should.

☐ *UPS monitoring.* As mentioned in Chapter 3, NetWare can monitor an attached UPS to determine whether the power has failed and the system is running on backup sources. If so, NetWare can take action to ensure that all outstanding writes are performed for file-cache buffers, before stopping the system.

☐ *File and record locking.* NetWare permits programs to lock a file, or a record within a file, so that other programs do not attempt to update the information at the same time. This mechanism is crucial in transaction processing systems where multiple client programs might be accessing a common database concurrently. Without locking, data easily can become corrupted.

NetWare also provides mechanisms for System Fault Tolerance (SFT) and the Transaction Tracking System (TTS). They can contribute significantly to NetWare's capability to recover processing in the event of equipment or power failure. Each is discussed in Chapter 22. In Chapters 15 and 16, you also review the security features that NetWare has available to protect directories and files against unauthorized access.

Multiple File System Support

The most common use for a NetWare file server is to provide file storage for DOS-based workstation computers. But you've now been introduced to the NetWare mechanisms that allow it to support other types of computers as well.

To summarize, using the NetWare file system as a basis, network communication protocols as a conduit, and the Name Space NLM for file names, NetWare can allow access by any of the following file system protocols:

- [ ] Network File System (NFS)
- [ ] AppleTalk Filing Protocol (AFP)
- [ ] File Transfer Access Management (FTAM)
- [ ] OS/2 High Performance File System (HPFS)

NetWare's File System Limitations

4

For some areas, NetWare has virtually no limits. It does not have, for example, a fixed limit on the number of files or directories maintained. For other areas, the limits don't seem all that hard to live with. For example,

- [ ] Each file can contain up to 4 gigabytes of data.
- [ ] Each volume can contain up to 32 terabytes of data.
- [ ] A single server can have up to 100,000 file or record locks in place.

> **Note:** NetWare does have one limitation on the number of files and directories you can use because it can keep track of only so many DET entries. Fortunately, the limitation is 2,097,152, so most of the time, this limitation does not pose major problems.

In practice, these limits do not place many real restrictions on the usefulness of NetWare as a file server. The real limitations, which currently come into play, stem far more from server hardware (for example, limitations on the amount of RAM available).

Summary

In this chapter, you learned the following:

- [ ] NetWare supports a variety of network communications protocols. In addition to its native IPX/SPX, NetWare also can deal with TCP/IP, AppleTalk Phase 2, and OSI TP0-TP4.

☐ The NetWare file system consists of blocks within volumes. Blocks are tracked in the File Allocation Table (FAT), which allows NetWare to find each block's physical location. NetWare file directory information is described in the Directory Entry Table (DET), which includes a reference to the FAT.

☐ NetWare includes many features to enhance file system performance as well as protect data integrity.

☐ Support for other file systems allows a NetWare server to offer files to non-DOS clients, such as UNIX (with NFS), OS/2, and Macintosh (with AFP).

Workshop
Terminology Review

block—The basic unit of file storage for NetWare. A block can be any size from 4 kilobytes to 64 kilobytes (in integral powers of two).

Directory Entry Table—A NetWare data structure containing details about NetWare files, such as filename and size.

File Allocation Table—A NetWare data structure containing information about every block on a NetWare volume.

IPX/SPX—The Internet Packet Exchange/Sequenced Packet Exchange network communication protocol; NetWare's native communication protocol.

Link Support Layer—A set of programmed routines that examines packets coming in from the network and routes them to the appropriate handlers, according to the type of protocol found. For example, the LSL sends IPX packets to software responsible for IPX/SPX, whereas IP packets are sent to the TCP/IP protocol handlers. The LSL can be found on NetWare file servers and clients using the ODI architecture (see Chapter 18 for more details on client software).

LSL—See *Link Support Layer.*

segment—An area of a physical disk that has been prepared for use by NetWare.

TCP/IP—The Transmission Control Protocol/Internet Protocol, a widely used network communication protocol that is also supported by NetWare.

volume—A logical data structure analogous to a physical disk. However, a NetWare volume can be spread across many physical disk segments.

Q&A

Q **Can I use more than one type of cabling system on a NetWare server?**

A Yes. NetWare not only supports multiple communication protocols, but also multiple cabling systems (you learn more about cabling systems in Chapter 17). You can add different kinds of NICs to the file server to allow access from a variety of networks, such as Ethernet and Token Ring, so that users on each network can access NetWare.

Q **Can I mix different types of protocols on a NetWare server?**

A Yes. NetWare supports protocols such as IPX/SPX, TCP/IP, and others, all at the same time.

Q **I inherited my NetWare LAN from someone else. How can I tell what kind of network I'm using?**

A From the file server console prompt, you can use two key commands:

```
CONFIG
```

```
MODULES
```

Each provides you with details on which LAN NLMs are loaded. Look for key words such as *Ethernet* or *Token Ring*, which tell you what kind of networks are in use. If you're familiar with the names of different NICs (that is, the ubiquitous NE2000 card), the name of the LAN driver may also tell you something (an NE2000 is an Ethernet card). (You see more about these console commands in Chapter 22.)

Q **Does IPX/SPX get priority on NetWare?**

A No. NetWare is quite fair—it treats all the protocols it supports equally. NetWare's native protocol, IPX/SPX, does not get priority over others such as TCP/IP.

5

Navigating through NetWare

Now that you have a basic understanding of a network, it's time to explore your NetWare network. The easiest way to learn about the network is to jump right in and try some different tasks. In this chapter, you learn how to log in and log out, and how to make your way through NetWare's menu system. The most logical place to start, therefore, is to log in to NetWare.

Connecting to the NetWare File Server

One of the most difficult parts of learning about NetWare is understanding how your workstation gets to the NetWare server in the first place. It also can be a major hurdle—if you can't log in, then you can't do much else in terms of learning about NetWare.

The problem is that the procedures used and programs run to establish your initial connection vary. They depend on the type of network you use, your NIC, the type of computer you use as a client, and even the workstation operating software you are running on the client.

In Chapter 19, you see more specific details about how to get to your NetWare server from a DOS-based client. For now, you just need to log in. Because the steps to log in depend so much on your particular configuration, you must find out how to log in for your particular computer. For help, you walk through a generic login process in the next section. This process might be the one you need to follow to log in. At the least, it should look similar to the procedures you have to use.

A number of programs must run prior to your logging in to the network. These programs can include the following:

☐ LSL, the link support layer running on a client computer. LSL is a layer in the Open Datalink Interface (ODI), an architecture developed jointly by Novell and Apple. ODI is used to allow multiple protocols to run on the network.

☐ A Network Interface Card (NIC) driver, which is a program communicating with LSL and the network card itself.

☐ The network protocol program. For NetWare, the most common protocol is IPX. When it is used with ODI, the program run is called IPXODI.

☐ The workstation *shell* program, that is, NETX. Starting with NetWare version 3.12, the shell program has been replaced by the DOS Requester. If you're using version 3.12, you might have to type **VLM** instead. (You learn details about configuring a DOS workstation in Chapter 18.)

In Task 5.1, you learn the typical sequence to establish a network connection with NetWare.

Task 5.1: Establishing a connection with NetWare.

Step 1: Description

This task provides the means to establish a network connection between a DOS client workstation and a NetWare server.

5

Step 2: Action

1. After you start your workstation, you should see the DOS prompt. You then must change to the directory where the NetWare driver programs are located. These programs might be in your root directory or in another location.

   See the "Extra Credit" section at the end of this chapter for hints on how to find the programs.

2. At the DOS prompt, type **LSL** and press Enter. LSL is the Link Services Layer running on the workstation.

3. Type **NE2000** and press Enter. This step loads the software for the NIC. You should substitute the driver supplied by your NIC vendor, such as 3COM or XIRCOM. We used NE2000 as an example here because it is one of the more popular NICs or is emulated by other cards. NE2000 is a typical network interface card driver, which is a program communicating with the card itself.

4. Type **IPXODI** and press Enter. IPXODI is the IPX network protocol program, which talks with the LSL.

5. Type **NETX** and press Enter. Figure 5.1 shows the screen after you execute these commands. NETX is the workstation shell, which deals with network commands.

```
C>lsl
NetWare Link Support Layer  v2.00 (920904)
(C) Copyright 1990, 1992 Novell, Inc.  All Rights Reserved.
Max Boards 4, Max Stacks 4

C>ne2000
Novell NE2000 Ethernet MLID  v1.10 (901129)
(C) Copyright 1990 Novell, Inc.  All Rights Reserved.
Int 15, Port 300, Node Address 6E22037A
Max Frame 1514 bytes, Line Speed 10 Mbps
Board 1, Frame ETHERNET_802.2

C>ipxodi
NetWare IPX/SPX Protocol  v2.00 (920904)
(C) Copyright 1990-1992 Novell, Inc.  All Rights Reserved.
Bound to logical board 1 (NE2000) : Protocol ID E0

C>netx
NetWare Workstation Shell  v3.32 (930624)  PTF
(C) Copyright 1993 Novell, Inc.  All Rights Reserved.
Patent Pending.
Attached to server RONAN
03-02-94   10:53:27 am

F>
```

Figure 5.1. *Establishing the connection with NetWare.*

Step 3: Review

Loading the right programs in the right order allows your workstation to connect to the NetWare server. After you successfully complete all these steps, your workstation should have access to a new disk drive, which is a network drive, usually shown as your F: drive.

If you change to your F: drive and look at a directory listing, you should see a LOGIN program. You execute LOGIN to inform NetWare about yourself, by logging in to the file server. In the next section, you look at this process more closely.

Behind the scenes, these steps accomplished many important operations, in terms of your ability to use the network. You look at these operations in more detail in Chapter 13. At this point in your exploration of NetWare, the only thing you really need to keep in mind is that your workstation computer now understands that it can access files on the NetWare server. It knows how and when to form requests to be sent to the server, and how to use the network cable to send those requests. It also knows what to do with data it receives from the network. And all these services have been tied in nicely to the regular commands offered by your workstation (such as the DOS DIR command, which you can use on directories sitting on the file server).

What If It Doesn't Work?

If you can't get to your F: drive, your problems have several potential sources. Establishing the network connection between the client and the workstation can seem

to be as much art as science, especially when things don't work correctly. To master the art, you must look at some other sources of information:

☐ If you have access to a working NetWare network, look at how the client computers are configured there. Those configurations may point out where you are going wrong. (Better yet, just use that network until you get further along in learning about NetWare.)

☐ Refer to the documentation that came with your Network Interface Card. Because NetWare is such a popular operating system, most NIC manuals give explicit step-by-step instructions on how to load the appropriate software for NetWare. Normally, NICs come with all the programs that you need on diskette. Just follow the instructions, and you should get to the login prompt.

☐ Ask a Certified NetWare Engineer (CNE) for assistance. CNEs probably can help you get the right configuration and programs up and running quickly.

☐ Review Chapter 19, which gives you more detail on how to access NetWare from a DOS client computer.

Tip: Don't ignore the obvious. The first check you should perform is to ensure the physical connection is complete. So check the wire from the back of the NIC to the wall connection and from the wall to the server.

Logging In to Your NetWare Network

To use a Novell network, you must first log in to a file server. Every user wanting to log in to a server must have a username and optionally a password (see Chapter 9). The login process brings together a username and password for comparison to its internal database entries.

Let's look at how this process works. When you enter the LOGIN command, NetWare prompts you for your username. Usernames provide the first point of access to the network. The username uniquely identifies a user account belonging to you. These names can be anywhere from 2 to 47 characters long—either alphabetic (A–Z) or numeric (0–9). Usernames are objects in the file server bindery and assigned specific properties. In Chapter 7, you learn that the bindery is a database containing information about all objects, their properties, and values, for the server. When you, as network administrator, assign properties to users, you are in effect granting users sufficient rights to do their jobs.

After you type your username, you must verify yourself as the owner of the user account by providing the correct password at the prompt. NetWare checks the password against an entry in its internal database corresponding to the password field of your account. If the passwords match, the login process continues.

Assuming everything so far has worked, you follow the steps in Task 5.2 to log in to the network.

Task 5.2: Logging in to NetWare.

Step 1: Description

This task provides you the means to log in to the network.

Step 2: Action

1. At the DOS F: prompt, type **LOGIN** and press Enter.

2. At the Enter your login name: prompt, type your username and press Enter.

3. At the Enter your password: prompt, type your password and press Enter. Notice that for your protection the password is not displayed on the screen.

Figure 5.2 shows the login sequence.

```
F>login
Enter your login name: supervisor
Enter your password:
Good afternoon, SUPERVISOR.

Drive  A:   maps to a local disk.
Drive  B:   maps to a local disk.
Drive  C:   maps to a local disk.
Drive  D:   maps to a local disk.
Drive  E:   maps to a local disk.
Drive  F: = RONAN\SYS:  \SYSTEM

SEARCH1:  = Z:.  [RONAN\SYS:  \PUBLIC]
SEARCH2:  = Y:.  [RONAN\SYS:  \]
SEARCH3:  = C:\DOS
SEARCH4:  = C:\WINDOWS
SEARCH5:  = C:\
SEARCH6:  = C:\UTILITY

F>
```

Figure 5.2. *Login sequence.*

Step 3: Review

By using the LOGIN command, you executed your first command-line utility on the network. You include your username to identify yourself to the network and your password (if required) to verify your identity.

You may want to log out before the end of the session to change workstations, to go home, to go to lunch, or simply because you are curious. Should you need to log out before finishing this session, go to the section titled "Logging Out from Your NetWare Network."

After you log in, you see a DOS prompt, provided a *menu* or other front-end program is not given to you. Menus might list programs you can run. (In Chapter 12, you have numerous opportunities to learn in detail about creating user menus.) Normally, menus list applications or utilities where you have access. Before you look at NetWare's menu system, however, look at some NetWare utilities described in the following sections.

Understanding Utilities

A number of utilities are available within NetWare. These tools generally are broken down as follows:

- [ ] Command-line utilities (CLU)

- [ ] Menu utilities

- [ ] Supervisor utilities

- [ ] Console commands

Command-line utilities such as NCOPY or NDIR execute from the DOS prompt, or command line. Most command-line utilities include options, variables, or both. Command-line utilities are productive management tools, which provide NetWare functions from a workstation command line. Primarily, system administrators use CLUs, but some utilities have wider appeal. CLUs are plentiful; they are listed and explained in detail in Appendix C, "NetWare Command Reference."

Menu utilities such as SYSCON and FILER provide the same functions as CLUs, but they are more user-friendly due to their menu interface. They execute tasks that you select from options listed in a menu. Also, some menu utilities provide extended functionality beyond that offered with a CLU. These utilities enjoy a great popularity, and as the system administrator, you will use them the majority of the time.

Supervisor utilities are specialized CLUs and menu tools designed for the Supervisor's use. These tools are extremely powerful and must be used wisely. BINDFIX and BINDREST are two Supervisor utilities you learn about in Chapter 7.

Console commands such as LOAD MONITOR or SET are NetWare tools that provide information from and customization at the file server. They are advanced utilities and must be executed from the console. Therefore, you enter them at the NetWare console prompt (:). Console commands work just like command-line utilities. Again, these tools are extremely powerful and must be used wisely.

In the following section, you begin your look at utilities with NetWare menu utilities.

Understanding Menu Utilities

Menu utilities are the most productive and friendly of the NetWare system management tools. An effective menu system is a key ingredient of an easy-to-manage network. NetWare menu utilities provide the same functionality as command-line utilities plus some additional features all wrapped up in a friendly user interface. NetWare provides a variety of menu utilities that perform a variety of tasks. You can break down these tools into two basic categories: user menus and supervisor menus. Some user menus double as supervisor menus. This capability enables Supervisors to perform additional administrative tasks such as user creation, directory maintenance, security, and login configurations.

NetWare menus are a progression of screens that build upon the previous screens in an easy-to-use format. Each menu screen consists of either a single-lined or double-lined border. The single-lined border box is informational, and you cannot edit the contents. On the other hand, you either can view or edit the information in double-lined boxes. All NetWare menu utilities are displayed in the default blue and gold.

Using a menu is straightforward. Novell designed the menus to be easy to use and at the same time provide system management capabilities. Most of the menu functions are self-explanatory, but a few keys, as shown in Figure 5.3, help navigate through NetWare's menu utilities.

You have three basic principles to remember when you're working with menu utilities:

☐ *Choose:* Use the arrow keys to move the highlight (or selection) bar to the menu item of your choice and press Enter.

☐ *Access:* Open the menu screens until you reach the screen required.

☐ *Confirm:* Highlight Yes in the confirmation box and press Enter.

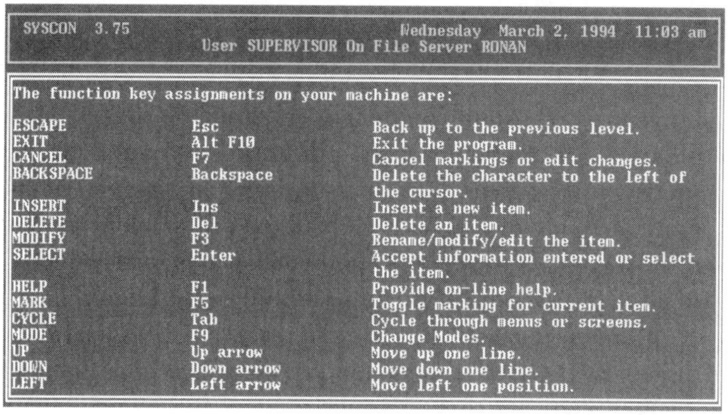

```
 SYSCON  3.75                          Wednesday  March 2, 1994  11:03 am
                   User SUPERVISOR On File Server RONAN

 The function key assignments on your machine are:

 ESCAPE          Esc              Back up to the previous level.
 EXIT            Alt F10          Exit the program.
 CANCEL          F7               Cancel markings or edit changes.
 BACKSPACE       Backspace        Delete the character to the left of
                                  the cursor.
 INSERT          Ins              Insert a new item.
 DELETE          Del              Delete an item.
 MODIFY          F3               Rename/modify/edit the item.
 SELECT          Enter            Accept information entered or select
                                  the item.
 HELP            F1               Provide on-line help.
 MARK            F5               Toggle marking for current item.
 CYCLE           Tab              Cycle through menus or screens.
 MODE            F9               Change Modes.
 UP              Up arrow         Move up one line.
 DOWN            Down arrow       Move down one line.
 LEFT            Left arrow       Move left one position.
```

Figure 5.3. *NetWare keys.*

NetWare menu utility navigation is simple, and you'll soon find yourself working through screens quickly. The following demonstration of a menu utility might also help.

Using a NetWare Utility with a Menu

A number of NetWare utilities, as shown in Table 5.1, have menus.

Table 5.1. NetWare utilities with menus.

Utility	Function
COLORPAL	Enables you to change the colors in NetWare menus
DSPACE	Enables you to restrict the use of disk space
FILER	Enables you to configure files, subdirectories, directories, and volumes
PCONSOLE	Enables you to control printers and print queues
PRINTCON	Enables you to control print job configurations
PRINTDEF	Enables you to define print devices and forms
SESSION	Enables you to control user-specific configurations and features
SYSCON	Enables you to configure users and groups

5

In Task 5.3, you look at a simple example of the SYStem CONfiguration, or SYSCON, utility. You delve into the use of SYSCON in great detail in Chapter 8, when you look at managing accounts.

Task 5.3: Using SYSCON.

Step 1: Description

SYSCON is a powerful utility that you use for many different system management purposes. In this task, however, you use SYSCON as an example of the use of a menu utility.

Step 2: Action

1. At the DOS prompt, type **SYSCON** and press Enter. You should see the Available Topics screen shown in Figure 5.4.

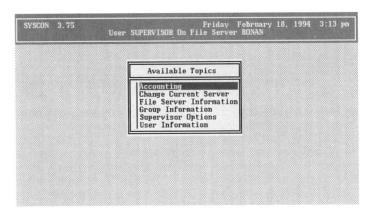

Figure 5.4. *Available Topics menu.*

2. From the Available Topics menu, choose User Information and press Enter. You should see the screen shown in Figure 5.5.

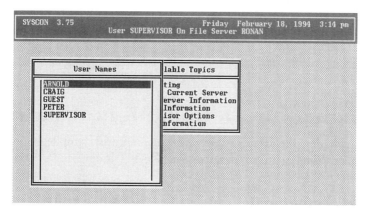

Figure 5.5. *User Names list.*

3. From the User Names list, choose [*your user name*] and press Enter. You should see the screen shown in Figure 5.6.

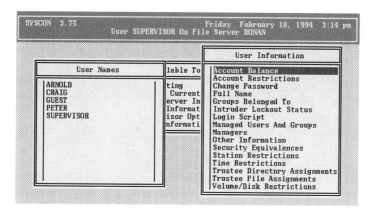

Figure 5.6. *User Information menu.*

4. From the User Information menu, choose Change Password and press Enter. Then change your password.

5. Press Esc until you are asked to confirm your exit.

6. To confirm your intent to exit, select Yes and press Enter.

Step 3: Review

You have just had your first taste of SYSCON. You used SYSCON as an example of a menu utility. By the time you finish the 14 days, you will become thoroughly versed in SYSCON.

Changing the Default Menu Colors

If you don't like the default colors of the menu utilities supplied with NetWare, you can "paint" them with different color schemes.

Task 5.4: Changing the color of a NetWare utility's screen.

Step 1: Description

At some point, you may find that the blue and gold screens provided by Novell get to you. This task introduces you to the COLORPAL utility, which enables you to change the colors of the screens.

Step 2: Action

1. At the DOS prompt, type **COLORPAL** and press Enter. You should see the Defined Palettes menu shown in Figure 5.7.

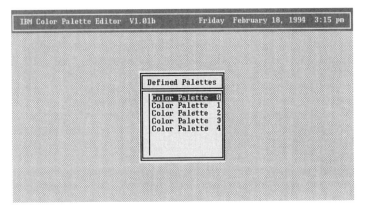

Figure 5.7. *Defined Palettes menu.*

2. From the Defined Palettes menu, choose the palette you want to change. The first five palettes (numbered Color Palette 0, 1, 2, 3, and 4) are NetWare defaults. After you choose your palette, you should see the screen shown in Figure 5.8.

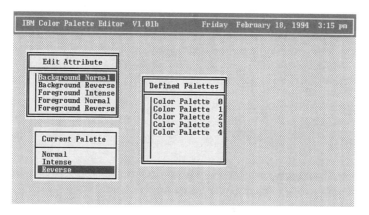

Figure 5.8. *Edit Attribute menu and Current Palette window.*

3. The Current Palette window shows your current settings for Normal, Intense, and Reverse text. From the Edit Attribute menu, choose the attribute you want to change. You then should see the screen shown in Figure 5.9.

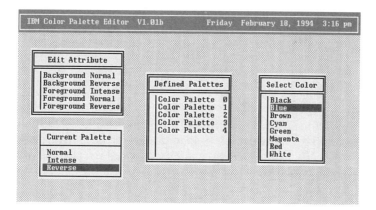

Figure 5.9. *Select Color menu.*

4. From the Select Color menu, choose the color you want. The Current Palette screen will now show the effect of the changes.

5. Repeat steps 3 and 4 for every color style in turn.

6. Repeat steps 3 through 5 for every attribute in turn.

Warning: You should not run COLORPAL in the SYS:PUBLIC directory. Instead, run it from your default directory. Changes made in SYS:PUBLIC also change the IBM$RUN.OVL file for each monitor on the network; therefore, only the Supervisor should run COLORPAL from SYS:PUBLIC. Changing palettes 0 through 4 affects all NetWare menus.

Step 3: Review

If you want to change the colors of the NetWare blue and gold screens, you can use the COLORPAL menu utility.

Note: The color palette for NetWare's menu utilities are configurable using the COLORPAL menu utility. The default menu colors are defined as Palette 0.

If, at any time, you have difficulty with any feature discussed in this book, you can always use a help utility to get more information. For commands, you even can get the syntax and options.

Using Help

NetWare Help is available at all times, from within any menu or from the command line. In version 3.11, you can get Help in three ways. In a menu, press F1 to get help. For the other two ways, you use the online help facility. The first of these ways is to use the Command Line Help utility. Command Line Help provides command syntax, including options.

In version 3.12, NetWare replaced the 3.11 menu utility with ElectroText. Jump to the next section if you have 3.12 installed.

Task 5.5: Using the Command Line Help utility.

Step 1: Description

Everybody requires help in certain circumstances. NetWare, therefore, has an extensive built-in help utility. This task introduces you to the Command Line Help utility.

Step 2: Action

At the DOS prompt, type **HELP [command name]** and press Enter. In place of [*command name*], substitute the name of the command you need help with. In Figure 5.10, you can see the HELP CAPTURE screen. Pressing Esc returns you to the DOS prompt.

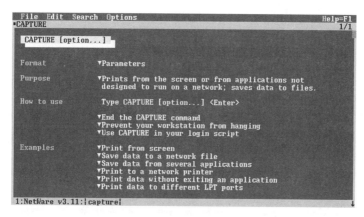

Figure 5.10. *HELP CAPTURE screen.*

Step 3: Review

Now when you have trouble with a specific command, you know to use the HELP command at the DOS prompt.

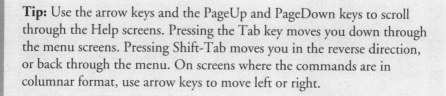

Tip: Use the arrow keys and the PageUp and PageDown keys to scroll through the Help screens. Pressing the Tab key moves you down through the menu screens. Pressing Shift-Tab moves you in the reverse direction, or back through the menu. On screens where the commands are in columnar format, use arrow keys to move left or right.

The other way to get Help is to use the NetWare Help Online Reference utility. This facility actually is the same utility you called when you entered HELP [*command name*]. The difference now, however, is that you use the utility interactively.

Task 5.6: Using the NetWare Help Online Reference utility.

Step 1: Description

As already stated, NetWare has an extensive built-in help utility. But now and then, you might not even know the right command to use. In these instances, you can use the online help utility.

Step 2: Action

1. To change to the \PUBLIC subdirectory, type **F:** and press Enter. The help utility is in the \PUBLIC directory.

> **Note:** Please note that you don't always have to change to the \PUBLIC directory. You do so here to ensure that NetWare finds the command you want to execute. In Chapter 14, you learn to set up NetWare to search the \PUBLIC directory for commands.

2. Type **CD\PUBLIC** and press Enter.

3. Type **HELP** and press Enter. The NetWare Help v3.11 Main Menu appears, as shown in Figure 5.11.

```
 File   Edit   Search   Options                              Help=F1
▪NetWare Help Utility                                         1/2766



                        NetWare Help v3.11 Main Menu

              ▾Commands and Utilities A - J
              ▾Commands and Utilities L - R
              ▾Commands and Utilities S - X
              ▾Index to Printed NetWare Manuals
              ▾Installation, Setup
              ▾Network Concepts
              ▾Administration, Maintenance, Troubleshooting, etc.

              ▾How to use NetWare Help v3.11 (NFOLIO)
              ▾License Agreement, Disclaimer, Other Information




        ┌─────────────────────────────────────────────────────────┐
        │ Tab to a link (▾), then press <Enter>. Press <Escape> to exit │
        └─────────────────────────────────────────────────────────┘
 1:NetWare v3.11:                                                  ↓
```

Figure 5.11. *NetWare Help menu.*

4. Press Tab to move the cursor to Commands and Utilities A-J and press Enter. From the next menu, move the cursor down to a command you want to look at and press Enter.

5. After you are finished and have the information you want, press Esc to return to the previous screen. To exit the utility, press Esc at the Main Menu.

Step 3: Review

You now know two ways to invoke help—through a command-line utility and a menu utility.

Note: At the beginning of each line, and throughout the Help utility, you see a small, inverted triangle. Anywhere you see this symbol, you can tab to this line and press Enter to get more information. At lower levels, if you see the symbol, it means that the particular subject has been exploded into subcategories.

Understanding and Using ElectroText

ElectroText, introduced with 3.12, enables you to view NetWare manuals online. All NetWare v3.12 manuals except the *Quick Access Guide* are available through ElectroText. Hence, you can look at the following manuals:

- ☐ Server Backup
- ☐ Btrieve Installation and Operation
- ☐ Concepts
- ☐ Installation
- ☐ NetWare Management Agent for NetView
- ☐ Print Server
- ☐ System Administration
- ☐ System Messages
- ☐ NetWare TCP/IP Supervisor's Manual
- ☐ Workstation Basics and Installation

☐ Utilities Reference

☐ Workstation for DOS and Windows

☐ Workstation for OS/2

☐ NetWare for Macintosh Installation and Maintenance

☐ NetWare Client for Macintosh

You can install ElectroText on a NetWare server or a local hard disk. ElectroText is available for Windows, OS/2, Macintosh, and UNIX workstation operating systems.

To use ElectroText in Windows, you use the steps outlined in Task 5.7.

Task 5.7: Starting and using Novell's ElectroText.

Step 1: Description

You use ElectroText to get help under NetWare 3.12. ElectroText is available for Windows, OS/2, UNIX, and Macintosh local operating systems. This task demonstrates its use on a Windows workstation.

Step 2: Action

1. At the DOS prompt, type **WIN** and press Enter.

2. Select the Novell ElectroText icon from your Windows desktop and press Enter. You should see an icon like the one shown in Figure 5.12.

Figure 5.12. *ElectroText icon.*

3. Click on the NetWare 3.12 Manuals icon for the bookshelf.

5

Note: After you have the book you want to read, you can do the following:

☐ Move directly to a specific section in the book

☐ Scroll through the book's text

☐ View a graphic or table

☐ Move to another section referenced by the text

☐ Search for a specific word or phrase in the book

4. From the NetWare 3.12 Manuals window, type **IPXODI** in the Search for box and press Enter.

5. Click on OK. The system searches for IPXODI, and those books containing matches to the query have numbers on them as shown in Figure 5.13.

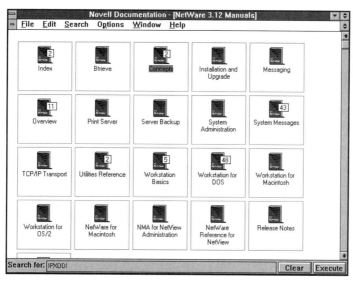

Figure 5.13. *Search results.*

6. Double-click on the Concepts manual. You should see a screen like the one shown in Figure 5.14.

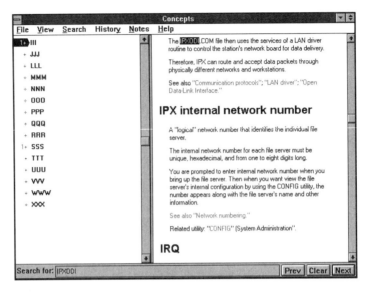

Figure 5.14. *Concepts manual.*

7. The first instance of IPXODI is highlighted; click on Next to see subsequent references.

8. To quit viewing the manual, press Alt-F4.

9. Select C, and the Concepts book is closed.

10. Press Alt-F4 and confirm your intention to leave ElectroText.

Step 3: Review

With NetWare 3.12, Novell replaced the Help menu facility with ElectroText. You can use ElectroText to see any of Novell's 15 online manuals. You can load ElectroText on a PC, which probably is what you will do when first setting up your network. This way, you can read the installation manuals. Most likely, you will move ElectroText to the server later because it uses 30M of hard disk space.

Logging Out from Your NetWare Network

You now have finished your first half-day exploring the network. Now it's time to log out from the network. Logging out disconnects you from the network. You should not disconnect from the network by either turning off or rebooting (pressing

Ctrl-Alt-Del) your workstation. Disconnecting this way can cause problems with open files and programs. Likewise, do not walk away from your workstation without logging out, as doing so exposes your files to other people.

Logging out from NetWare is a simple task. At the DOS prompt, type LOGOUT and press Enter. (See Figure 5.15.)

```
F>logout
SUPERVISOR logged out from server RONAN connection 2.
Login time:    Wednesday  March  2, 1994  11:03 am
Logout time:   Wednesday  March  2, 1994  11:13 am

F>
```

Figure 5.15. *Logging out from NetWare.*

You now know you can log out using the LOGOUT command. In the next chapter, you learn that you can log out from a specific file server and that you can log out from that server and remain logged in to all others.

Summary

You have begun your journey of a thousand miles with a few small steps. In this chapter, you learned how to do the following:

☐ Get on and off the network

☐ Make your way around the network using a few NetWare tools

☐ Use the NetWare help utility for those times when you have questions

Hereinafter, your journey through NetWare rapidly accelerates. Take time to review the terms from this chapter and reconsider the tasks you practiced. These tasks are the basic building blocks of NetWare.

Workshop

Terminology Review

command line—The DOS (>) or NOS (:) prompt.

login—The process of accessing a file server or computer after logical connection has been established.

logout—The process of disconnecting from a file server or computer.

password—Given to or created by the user, privileged information that is entered into a system for authentication purposes. A password is a protected word or secret character string used to authenticate the claimed identity of an individual, a resource, or access type.

shell—A terminate-and-stay resident (TSR) program acting as a redirector on the DOS workstation.

user—Used imprecisely to refer to the individual who is accountable for some identifiable set of activities in a computer system.

username—A name used to identify a user account.

utilities—Useful programs provided with a system. Some examples include tools that enable you to view, rename, copy, format, delete, and otherwise manage accounts, files, and volumes.

workstation—A desktop computer that performs local processing and accesses LAN services.

workstation operating system—Software that controls the internal operations (housekeeping chores) of the workstation. Operating systems are specific to the type of computer used.

Task List

With the information provided in this chapter, you can begin your long journey. Now you can log in and use basic utilities. You also know that when you are stumped, you can get help. You learned how to do the following:

☐ Find key NetWare files

☐ Log in to NetWare

☐ Use a NetWare menu and command-line utilities

☐ Find help

☐ Log out from NetWare

Q&A

Q Is the Help menu utility still available in 3.12?

A As you learned in this chapter, in version 3.11 of NetWare, you can type HELP at the DOS prompt and the Help menu utility appears. In version 3.12, ElectroText replaces the Help utility. You can still type a NetWare command and ask for help, for example, NDIR /? or NDIR /H. This command provides command-line help. Recall from Chapter 1 that with newer versions of DOS, if you type HELP only, then you see the DOS Help.

Q How do I see available servers?

A This answer depends on whether or not you are logged in, or at the console or at a workstation. When you are at the console, type DISPLAY SERVERS and press Enter. If you are logged in, use either SLIST or SYSCON | Change Current Server or SESSION | Change Current Server. If you aren't logged in, use SLIST.

Q Why can I run SLIST when I'm not logged in?

A SLIST is a program in NetWare's LOGIN directory. You can access this one directory before you actually log in. The LOGIN program also resides in the LOGIN directory. SLIST does not tell you the servers where you are logged in or those servers where you have a valid login account. It does, however, provide a list of all the servers that are physically recognized by your internal Network Interface Card.

Q My network drive is not F:. Should I be concerned?

A No, we get used to referring to the first network drive as F: by convention, but this convention is changing. If you want to check the value of your network drives, check either in NET.CFG (VLM) or CONFIG.SYS (NETX). You learn all about checking your drives when you learn to configure DOS workstations in Chapter 19.

Q To use the console, do I have to log in to it?

A No, NetWare does not require you to log in to the console. For this reason, it is wise to allow only authorized physical access to your console. In Chapter 21, you learn that you may need a password to unlock the keyboard, however.

Extra Credit

Automating the Login Process

Typing all the commands used to establish a network connection between your workstation and the NetWare server can be a real nuisance. It's nice to automate this process so that every time you start up your workstation, you are given the opportunity to log in to NetWare. The easiest way to have this opportunity is by inserting on your workstation instructions that are executed automatically for you.

As you remember, DOS runs two files every time you start your workstation—AUTOEXEC.BAT and CONFIG.SYS. These files are stored in the root directory of your C: drive. DOS executes every command in your AUTOEXEC.BAT file every time your workstation boots. Including the necessary commands to get to the doorstep of the network, therefore, is a simple process.

To edit your AUTOEXEC.BAT file, you can use whatever *text editor* is available to you. Simply, a text editor is a program that enables you to create and modify plain text files. You may have Brief, EDIT (DOS 5.0 and later), Editor (DR DOS), QEdit, TED, or The Norton Editor. If you don't have a text editor, you can use a word processing program such as WordPerfect or Microsoft Word, provided you save the file in ASCII format. In WordPerfect, save the file using Ctrl-F5, not F10. Similarly, use the Save as Text Only option with Microsoft Word.

Whatever method you use, open (or create, if required) your AUTOEXEC.BAT file. You should save it on the root directory of the C: drive so that DOS can find it. You also need to complete the following steps.

Before you update the AUTOEXEC.BAT file, you need to know where you can find the protocol driver and workstation shell programs on your workstation disk. Finding these programs can be a trick in itself. Task 5.8 is a suggested approach.

Task 5.8: Finding IPX.COM and NETX.EXE files.

Step 1: Description

This task describes the procedure for finding the network protocol and workstation shell programs.

Step 2: Action

1. Type `CD\`, then `DIR/P NET*` and `DIR/P IPX*`, and press Enter to determine whether IPX and the shell (or requester) are in the root directory.

   Hopefully, you see NETX.EXE and IPXODI.COM. If you have not kept your workstation network software current, you may see a variety of responses to this command. For instance, you might find NET3.COM, NET4.COM, NET5.COM, or NETX with either a COM, VLM, or EXE extension. Also, you might find IPX.COM or IPXODI.COM.

2. If the programs are not in the root directory, check to see whether you have a \NWCLIENT, \NETWARE, or \NOVELL subdirectory. Then type `CD NWCLIENT`, `CD NETWARE`, or `CD NOVELL` and press Enter. Then repeat step 1.

> **Tip:** If you still can't find the programs, check for a directory that may have been created when you loaded your NIC software.

Step 3: Review

This task described the procedure for finding the network protocol and workstation shell (requester) programs. You might need to look through different subdirectories to find these programs. If you installed them using the installation procedure in Appendix A, you will find them in the root directory.

After you find the programs, you can automate the login process as shown in Task 5.9.

Task 5.9: Editing the AUTOEXEC.BAT file.

Step 1: Description

This task describes how to edit your startup file to include commands that start NetWare automatically. You might have to make substitutions because this task shows the use of the generic modules covered earlier.

Step 2: Action

1. Using your favorite text editor, open the AUTOEXEC.BAT file.

2. Type **CD\subdirectory**, at the end of the file. In place of *subdirectory*, substitute the name of the subdirectory where you found the protocol and shell (requester) programs.

3. Type **LSL** on the next line.

4. Type **NE2000** on the next line.

5. Type **IPXODI** on the next line.

6. Type **NETX** on the next line.

7. Type **F:LOGIN** on the next line.

8. Exit and save the file.

When you finish, your AUTOEXEC.BAT FILE should look like the one shown in Figure 5.16.

```
C>type autoexec.bat
cd \nwclient
lsl
ne2000
ipxodi
netx
f:login


C>
```

Figure 5.16. *Sample AUTOEXEC.BAT file.*

Step 3: Review

By editing your AUTOEXEC.BAT file, you can include commands that start NetWare automatically.

Now you are ready to log in to NetWare, as described in "Logging In to Your NetWare Network" earlier in this chapter.

6

Exploring NetWare

In the preceding chapter, you spent your first half-day navigating the NetWare waters. In this chapter, you significantly expand your knowledge of NetWare command-line utilities by delving into more commands. You start with a simple task, one you may ask yourself after studying this material for too long—WHOAMI.

Who Am I?

I assume you know who you are, but occasionally you may be confused or unsure of where you are, what group you belong to, or what rights you have for a volume or file. After logging back in to the network, you can find out more about your user account by typing the following:

WHOAMI [file server] [/option]

You use [*file server*] when you have accounts on more than one server. The options for WHOAMI are listed in Table 6.1. You also can type WHOAMI by itself; you then see information on all servers where you currently are attached or logged in.

Table 6.1. WHOAMI options.

Option	Description	Example
/C[ONTINUOUS]	Continuous display	WHOAMI /C
/G[ROUPS]	Groups belonged to	WHOAMI /G
/O[BJECT SUPERVISOR]	Object Supervisor	WHOAMI /O
/R[IGHTS]	Effective rights	WHOAMI /R
/S[ECURITY]	Security equivalencies	WHOAMI /S
/SY[STEM]	System (network) information	WHOAMI /SY
/W[ORKGROUPS]	Workgroup manager	WHOAMI /G
/A[LL]	All of the above	WHOAMI /A

To see your own account information, follow the steps in Task 6.1.

Task 6.1: Listing your account information.

Step 1: Description

This task describes how to list information about your account. In Chapter 8, you learn how to create and change account information.

Step 2: Action

1. To change to the \PUBLIC subdirectory, type **CD\PUBLIC** and press Enter.

2. Type **WHOAMI** /**A** and press Enter. Your screen should look like the one shown in Figure 6.1.

```
F>whoami /a
You are user SUPERVISOR attached to server RONAN, connection 2.
Server RONAN is running NetWare v3.12 (5 user).
You are a workgroup manager.
Login time: Friday  February  18, 1994  3:59 pm
You are security equivalent to the following:
     EVERYONE (Group)
You are a member of the following groups:
     EVERYONE
[SRWCEMFA]  SYS:
Server RONAN is not in a domain.


F>
```

Figure 6.1. *WHOAMI listing.*

Step 3: Review

You use the WHOAMI command at the DOS prompt to learn information about your account.

Using the SESSION Utility

You can use the SESSION utility to make temporary or "on the fly" changes to your current work session. Using SESSION, you can control file servers and default drive mappings, and you can search drive mappings, send messages, and list users and groups. First, look at using this utility to *attach* to another file server.

Task 6.2: Listing and attaching to other file servers.

Step 1: Description

In this task, you use the SESSION utility to display other file servers or to attach to another file server.

Step 2: Action

1. To change to the \PUBLIC subdirectory, type **CD\PUBLIC** and press Enter.

2. Type **SESSION** and press Enter. The Available Topics menu appears (see Figure 6.2).

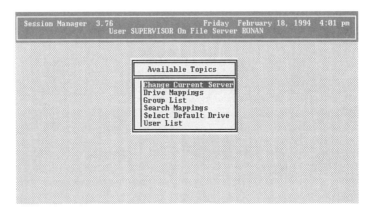

Figure 6.2. *Available Topics menu.*

3. With the cursor on Change Current Server, press Enter. The server(s) you are currently logged in to is displayed, as shown in Figure 6.3.

4. Press Ins to display other file servers.

5. Move the cursor up or down to the name of the file server where you want to ATTACH and press Enter. ATTACH is analogous to login; however, you normally log in to your primary file server and attach to others. Alternatively, you can use the ATTACH command-line utility.

6. At the prompts, enter your username and password, if required.

7. Press Esc repeatedly until you are asked to confirm your intention to leave SESSION.

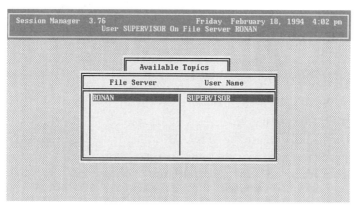

Figure 6.3. *Current servers.*

Step 3: Review

You learned how to use the SESSION utility to display other file servers or to attach to another file server.

You also can use the SESSION utility to log out from a file server, as shown in Task 6.3.

Task 6.3: Logging out from file servers.

Step 1: Description

In the preceding chapter, you learned how to log out from NetWare using the LOGOUT command. Unfortunately, this command logs you out from all servers where you are attached. Occasionally, you might want to log out from only one file server and remain logged in to all others. You can use the SESSION utility to log out from a particular file server.

Step 2: Action

1. To change to the \PUBLIC subdirectory, type **CD\PUBLIC** and press Enter.

2. Type **SESSION** and press Enter. The Available Topics menu appears.

3. With the cursor on Change Current Server, press Enter. Servers you are currently logged in to are displayed on the File Server/User Name window.

4. Move the cursor up or down to the name of the server you want to log out from and press Delete.

> **Tip:** To log out from multiple servers using SESSION, mark each server by moving the cursor to its name and pressing the F5 key. After you mark the servers from which you want to log out, press Delete.

Step 3: Review

You learned how to use the SESSION utility to log out from file servers instead of logging out from the network using the LOGOUT command. You cannot use SESSION to log out from your primary connection.

Continuing Your Exploration of NetWare

Working through NetWare is a lot like a child's development. First, young babies learn about themselves. They slowly discover their own appendages. After this stage of self-discovery, they start to explore their environment. Well after you discover yourself, the next logical step is to learn about the environment you are working in. Start by looking at what files are available to you.

Where Can I Find Files?

On a typical stand-alone microcomputer, you have two, maybe three, disk drives for your use. Drive A: is your first floppy disk drive, and drive B: is your second floppy drive, if you have one. As you probably know, your hard disk is drive C:. When you use the network, you have more drives available for your use.

Remember that a NetWare file server is simply a computer running the NetWare NOS and offering file services to the network. But the NetWare file server does not control the network. You therefore can have many file servers. To find out whether other file servers are available on your network, type SLIST and press Enter. You should see a display like the one shown in Figure 6.4.

SLIST displays the following useful information:

☐ *Known NetWare file servers:* These names are the file servers you can log in to, if you are authorized.

☐ *Status:* This feature shows the file servers where you are connected.

```
F>slist
Known NetWare File Servers              Network   Node Address Status
BALLIOL                                 [    1000][        1]
RONAN                                   [2D222067][        1]Default

Total of 2 file servers found

F>
```

Figure 6.4. *Known NetWare servers.*

At this juncture, do not worry about the other file servers. You should direct your attention toward the default file server. Besides, what you are about to learn also applies to any file server.

To find out what drives are available on the server that you are logged in to, type MAP and press Enter. You should see a display similar to one shown in Figure 6.5. Mapping is when you assign a workstation drive letter to a server directory. In this figure, you see the default mapping set up for your account. You can change the default (you do so later).

```
F>map
Drive  A:    maps to a local disk.
Drive  B:    maps to a local disk.
Drive  C:    maps to a local disk.
Drive  D:    maps to a local disk.
Drive  E:    maps to a local disk.
Drive  F: = RONAN\SYS:   \CRAIG\TYNW14\IMAGES

SEARCH1:   = Z:.  [RONAN\SYS:   \PUBLIC]
SEARCH2:   = Y:.  [RONAN\SYS:   \]
SEARCH3:   = C:\DOS
SEARCH4:   = C:\WINDOWS
SEARCH5:   = C:\
SEARCH6:   = C:\UTILITY

F>
```

Figure 6.5. *Map listing.*

Logging In Automatically to Multiple File Servers

Just as you changed your startup file to start the login process automatically, you can automate logging in to more than one file server. If you make frequent use of file servers other than your default server, you might want to consider including the ATTACH commands for them in your user login script (along with the appropriate mapping commands).

Task 6.4: Attaching and mapping to other file servers automatically.

Step 1: Description
This task shows the procedure for ATTACHing and MAPping to another server. You may default to the HR_SERVER, but frequently you use the ACCT_SERVER. You can automate the login to the second server.

Step 2: Action
1. To change to the \PUBLIC subdirectory, type **CD\PUBLIC** and press Enter.

2. Type **SYSCON** and press Enter. The Available Topics menu appears.

3. Move the cursor down to User Information and press Enter. A list of user names appears. (You performed this task in the preceding chapter if you need a refresher.)

4. Move the cursor to your username in the User Names list and press Enter.

5. From the User Information menu, select Login Script and press Enter.

6. Press Enter to create a blank line. Type **MAP J:=ACCT_SERVER/SYS:** and press Enter. NetWare prompts you for a password, if it is required and not synchronized for your servers. You learn about synchronizing passwords in Chapter 9.

7. Repeatedly press Esc until you confirm your exit out of SYSCON.

Step 3: Review
In this task, you learned that if you need to access another file server often, you can alter your login script to attach to the other file server. The next time you log in, you are prompted to enter the passwords for every file server to which you attach, provided passwords are necessary or different. These passwords can be synchronized; you find out how to synchronize in Chapter 9.

Acquiring Network Drives for Your Use

You can acquire drives by using MAP. First, however, look at what drives are currently mapped to you.

Task 6.5: Displaying drive mappings.

Step 1: Description

In this task, you learn how to display the list of drives currently mapped to you.

Step 2: Action

1. To change to the \PUBLIC subdirectory, type **CD\PUBLIC** and press Enter.

2. Type **MAP** and press Enter. You should see a response like the one shown in Figure 6.6.

```
F>map

Drive  A:   maps to a local disk.
Drive  B:   maps to a local disk.
Drive  C:   maps to a local disk.
Drive  D:   maps to a local disk.
Drive  E:   maps to a local disk.
Drive  F: = RONAN\SYS:  \CRAIG\TYNW14\IMAGES

SEARCH1:  = Z:.  [RONAN\SYS:  \PUBLIC]
SEARCH2:  = Y:.  [RONAN\SYS:  \]
SEARCH3:  = C:\DOS
SEARCH4:  = C:\WINDOWS
SEARCH5:  = C:\
SEARCH6:  = C:\UTILITY

F>
```

Figure 6.6. *Current drive mappings.*

Step 3: Review

In this task, you learned how to display the drive mappings (local and network) for your workstation. You can access any drive according to your access rights, which you also can display using SESSION. In Chapter 15, you master the concept of access rights.

You now have enough information to access directories and files from the network.

Working with Files and Directories from the Command Line

A number of NetWare commands enable you to work with files and directories. Some of these commands are similar in operation to DOS commands. In this portion of your lesson, you practice using the following command-line utilities:

☐ FLAGDIR

☐ LISTDIR

☐ NDIR

☐ NCOPY

Using FLAGDIR

You use FLAGDIR to view or change directory attributes. In Chapter 15, you master access rights, but at this time you need to modify trustee rights to change the attributes for the directory.

Task 6.6: Viewing directory attributes.

Step 1: Description

In this task, you learn how to view directory attributes.

Step 2: Action

1. To change to the \PUBLIC subdirectory, type **CD\PUBLIC** and press Enter.

2. Type **FLAGDIR [path]** and press Enter. For example, FLAGDIR F:\PUBLIC produces a display like the one shown in Figure 6.7. You see the directory \PUBLIC has NORMAL attributes, meaning no other attributes were set.

Step 3: Review

In this task, you learned how to display directory attributes. In Chapter 14, you master the concept of file and directory attributes.

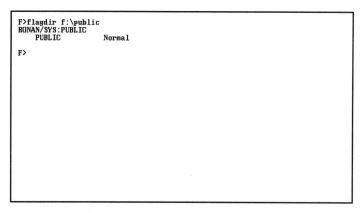

```
F>flagdir f:\public
RONAN/SYS:PUBLIC
     PUBLIC          Normal

F>
```

Figure 6.7. *FLAGDIR listing.*

Using LISTDIR

You use LISTDIR to view directory and subdirectory attributes but not files. Again, in Chapter 15, you learn all about access rights.

Task 6.7: Viewing your access rights in a directory.

Step 1: Description

In this task, you learn how to view your access rights in a directory.

Step 2: Action

1. To change to the \PUBLIC subdirectory, type **CD\PUBLIC** and press Enter.

2. Type **LISTDIR [path] [/option]** and press Enter. Again, *path* is the complete path to a directory. LISTDIR F:\PUBLIC /A, for example, produces a display like the one shown in Figure 6.8.

Table 6.2 lists the LISTDIR options.

Table 6.2. LISTDIR options.

Option	Description	Example
/C[ONTINUOUS]	Continuous display	LISTDIR /C
/D[ATE]	Creation date and time of each directory	LISTDIR /D

continues

111

Table 6.2. continued

Option	Description	Example
/E[FFECTIVE RIGHTS]	Effective rights in each directory	LISTDIR /E
/R[IGHTS]	Rights: Inherited Rights Mask of NetWare version 3.x directories	LISTDIR /R
/S[UBDIRECTORY]	Subdirectory structure	LISTDIR /S
/T[IME]	Creation date and time of each directory	LISTDIR /T
/A[LL]	All of the above	LISTDIR /A

```
F>listdir f:\public /a

The subdirectory structure of RONAN/SYS:PUBLIC
Date      Time    Inherited    Effective    Directory
------------------------------------------------------------
 1-14-94   1:01a  [SRWCEMFA]   [SRWCEMFA]   ->NLS
 1-20-94  10:38a  [SRWCEMFA]   [SRWCEMFA]   ->  ENGLISH
 1-14-94   1:01a  [SRWCEMFA]   [SRWCEMFA]   ->OS2
 1-14-94   1:03a  [SRWCEMFA]   [SRWCEMFA]   ->UNIX
4 subdirectories found

F>
```

Figure 6.8. *LISTDIR of the PUBLIC directory.*

Step 3: Review

In this task, you learned how to view your access rights in a directory. In Chapter 15, you master the concept of access rights.

Using NDIR

You use NDIR to view directory, subdirectory, and file attributes. In Chapter 15, you learn about access rights, but at this time you use NDIR to view directory attributes.

Task 6.8: Viewing directory attributes.

Step 1: Description

In this task, you learn how to view directory attributes.

Step 2: Action

1. To change to the \PUBLIC subdirectory, type CD\PUBLIC and press Enter.

2. Type **NDIR [path] [/option]** and press Enter. For example, NDIR F:\PUBLIC /RO produces a display of files that are read-only in F:\PUBLIC, as shown in Figure 6.9.

```
RONAN\SYS:PUBLIC

Files:                 Size     Last Updated        Flags           Owner
                      -------   ------------     -------------      --------
$RUN        OVL        2,400    7-13-89   9:30a [RoS------------DR] RONAN
ACONSOLE    EXE      118,229    8-06-93   3:13p [RoS------------DR] RONAN
ALLOW       EXE       21,049    5-06-93   5:00p [RoS------------DR] RONAN
APLASER2    PDF        2,986    1-17-92   3:23p [RoS------------DR] RONAN
APPIMAGE    PDF          327   10-25-89  11:49a [RoS------------DR] RONAN
APPLW2FG    PDF        2,696    7-16-92  10:15a [RoS------------DR] RONAN
APPSIT      DLL      812,182    2-14-93   8:25p [RoS------------DR] RONAN
ATTACH      EXE       60,787    5-11-93   1:58p [RoS------------DR] RONAN
BREQUEST    EXE       60,018    6-03-93  12:14p [RoS------------DR] RONAN
BREQUTIL    EXE       28,065    6-04-93  11:07a [RoS------------DR] RONAN
BREQUTIL    MSG          976    6-04-93  11:07a [RoS------------DR] RONAN
BROLLFWD    EXE       82,913    6-04-93  11:19a [RoS------------DR] RONAN
BROLLFWD    MSG        3,719    6-04-93  11:18a [RoS------------DR] RONAN
BTRCALLS    DLL       17,944    6-11-93   9:32a [RoS------------DR] RONAN
CAPTURE     EXE      166,743    5-20-93   2:59p [RoS------------DR] RONAN
CASTOFF     EXE       10,569    4-12-93   5:05p [RoS------------DR] RONAN
CASTON      EXE        6,937    4-12-93   3:48p [RoS------------DR] RONAN
CHKDIR      EXE       19,045    4-14-93   8:24a [RoS------------DR] RONAN
CHKVOL      EXE       33,099    5-06-93   3:45p [RoS------------DR] RONAN

Strike any key for next page or C for continuous display...
```

Figure 6.9. *NDIR of the PUBLIC directory.*

Table 6.3 lists the NDIR options.

Table 6.3. NDIR options.

Option	Description	Example
Sort by directory structure		
/D[IRECTORIES]O[NLY]	Directories only	NDIR /DO
/F[ILES]O[NLY]	Files only	NDIR /FO
/SUB[DIRECTORY]	Subdirectory files in addition to files in the default directory	NDIR /SUB

continues

Table 6.3. continued

Option	Description	Example
Sort by platform		
/MAC[INTOSH]	Macintosh files and subdirectories	NDIR /MAC
/LONG[NAMES]	Long names, for example, Macintosh, OS/2, and NFS (UNIX)	NDIR /LONG
Sort by owner		
/[REV] SORT OW[NER]	Directory and file owners in alphabetical order, or reverse	NDIR /SORT OW, NDIR /REV SORT OW
/OW[NER] [NOT] EQ name	Directories and files owned by one user, or excluding one user	NDIR /OW EQ SUPERVISOR, NDIR /OW NOT EQ SUPERVISOR
Sort files by attribute		
/[NOT] A[RCHIVE]	Archive needed	NDIR /A, NDIR /NOT A
/[NOT] C[OPY]I[NHIBIT]	Copy inhibit (Macintosh only)	NDIR /CI, NDIR /NOT CI
/[NOT] D[ELETE]I[NHIBIT]	Delete inhibit	NDIR /DI, NDIR /NOT DI
/[NOT] E[XECUTE]O[NLY]	Execute only	NDIR /EO, NDIR /NOT EO
/[NOT] H[IDDEN]	Hidden files	NDIR /H, NDIR /NOT H
/[NOT] I[NDEXED]	Indexed files	NDIR /I, NDIR /NOT I
/[NOT] P[URGE]	Purge files	NDIR /P, NDIR /NOT P
/[NOT] R[ENAME]I[NHIBIT]	Rename inhibit	NDIR /RI, NDIR /NOT RI
/[NOT] R[EAD]O[NLY]	Read only	NDIR /RO, NDIR /NOT RO
/[NOT] S[HAREABLE]	Shareable	NDIR /S, NDIR /NOT S

Option	Description	Example
/[NOT] SY[STEM]	System	NDIR /SY, NDIR /NOT SY
/[NOT] T[RANSACTIONAL]	Transactional	NDIR /T NDIR /NOT T

Sort files by date

Option	Description	Example
/AC[CESS] [NOT] BEF[ORE] ¦ EQ[UAL] ¦ AFT[ER] mm-dd-yy	Accessed before, on, or after the date	NDIR /AC BEF 11-11-93, NDIR /AC NOT BEF 11-11-93
/AR[CHIVE] [NOT] BEF[ORE] ¦ EQ[UAL] ¦ AFT[ER] mm-dd-yy	Archived before, on, or after the date	NDIR /AR AFT 11-11-93, NDIR /AR NOT AFT 11-11-93
/CR[EATE] [NOT] BEF[ORE] ¦ EQ[UAL] ¦ AFT[ER] mm-dd-yy	Created before, on, or after the date	NDIR /CR EQ 11-11-93, NDIR /CR NOT EQ 11-11-93
/UP[DATE] [NOT] BEF[ORE] ¦ EQ[UAL] ¦ AFT[ER] mm-dd-yy	Updated before, on, or after the date	NDIR /UP BEF 11-11-93, NDIR /UP NOT BEF 11-11-93
/[REV] SORT AC[CESS]	Accessed in order from earliest to latest, or reverse	NDIR /SORT AC, NDIR /REV SORT AC
/[REV] SORT AR[CHIVE]	Archived in order from earliest to latest, or reverse	NDIR /SORT AR, NDIR /REV SORT AR
/[REV] SORT CR[EATE]	Created in order from earliest to latest, or reverse	NDIR /SORT CR, NDIR /REV SORT CR
/[REV] SORT UP[DATE]	Updated in order from earliest to latest, or reverse	NDIR /SORT UP, NDIR /REV SORT UP

Sort files by size

Option	Description	Example
[REV] SORT SI[ZE]	Smallest to largest, or reverse	NDIR /SORT SI, NDIR /REV SORT SI
/SI[ZE] [NOT] GR[EATER THAN] ¦ EQ[UAL] ¦ LE[SS THAN] n	Bytes greater than, equal to, or less than the number	NDIR /SI GR 10000, NDIR /SI NOT GR 10000

continues

Table 6.3. continued

Option	Description	Example
Other options		
/DATES	Creation, last modified, last accessed, last archived dates	NDIR /DATES
/HELP	Displays these options	NDIR /HELP, NDIR /?
/RIGHTS	All rights and attributes	NDIR /RIGHTS
/UN[SORTED]	No sort	NDIR /UN

Step 3: Review

In this task, you learned how to view your access rights in a directory. In Chapter 14, you master the concept of access rights.

Using NCOPY

The NetWare NCOPY command is similar to the DOS COPY command. The syntax for copying NetWare files is as follows:

```
NCOPY [path 1] [file name] [TO] [path 2] [file name] [/option]
```

Note: Similar to the DOS COPY command, NCOPY also makes use of the wildcard or bingo characters * and ? in the filename. For example, the following is a valid command:

```
NCOPY F:\PUBLIC\*.EXE TO G:\MYDIR\PETER
```

You can copy files from one drive to another over the network using NCOPY. NCOPY also copies from one directory on the file server to another directory. Its use is preferable to the DOS COPY command because it accesses the NetWare File Allocation Table (FAT) and Directory Entry Table (DET) better than COPY. NCOPY works within the memory of the file server and does not need to copy files down to the workstation and back up. Instead, it copies the files in the file server's memory.

Another reason to use NCOPY is that it is safer. NCOPY uses NetWare's read-after-write verification feature, and DOS's COPY does not.

Let's use the NCOPY to copy the NetWare shell to your workstation's hard drive.

Task 6.9: Copying NetWare files.

Step 1: Description

In this task, you learn how to use NCOPY.

Step 2: Action

1. To change to the \PUBLIC subdirectory, type **CD\PUBLIC** and press Enter.

2. Type **NCOPY F:\PUBLIC\NETX.EXE TO C:\ /I** and press Enter. This command copies the workstation shell from F:\PUBLIC to your local C: and warns you if any NetWare attributes will be lost. (See Figure 6.10.)

```
F>ncopy f:\login\netx.exe to c:\ /i
From RONAN/SYS:\LOGIN
To   C:
     NETX.EXE        to NETX.EXE     : DOS copy.

     1 file copied.

F>
```

Figure 6.10. *Example NCOPY command.*

Table 6.4 provides a list of other NCOPY options.

Table 6.4. NCOPY options.

Option	Description
/S[UBDIRECTORIES]	Copies subdirectories
/E[MPTY]	Copies empty subdirectories. Only valid in conjunction with /S

continues

Table 6.4. continued

Option	Description
/F[ORCE]	Copies "sparse" files, usually database files with areas where no data is written
/I[NFORM]	Informs you when non-DOS information will be lost
/C[OPY]	Copies files without preserving NetWare file attributes
/A[RCHIVE]	Copies files with the archive bit set, that is, having the archive attribute
/M	Copies files with the archive attribute and turns it off
/V[ERIFY]	Copies the file and verifies that it is identical to the original
/H[ELP], /?	Provides help for this command

Step 3: Review

In this task, you learned how to copy files using NCOPY. As you just saw, you can copy files from one drive to another over the network using NCOPY.

> **Note:** You can use NCOPY to copy files to local drives, but NetWare file attributes unsupported by DOS are not kept in files on a local drive.

Interacting with Other Users

You might have many reasons to want to know who else is logged in to the network. Before you send messages to another user, for example, you might want to know whether that user is logged in. The NetWare utility USERLIST enables you to list other users.

Task 6.10: Listing other network users.

Step 1: Description

This task describes how to list information about other users on the network.

Step 2: Action

1. To change to the \PUBLIC subdirectory, type **CD\PUBLIC** and press Enter.

2. Type **USERLIST fileserver name/** and press Enter to get a list of users logged in to the file server, as shown in Figure 6.11. Typing only USERLIST provides information about users on your current server.

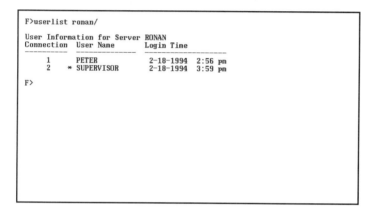

Figure 6.11. *Sample USERLIST.*

3. If you are logged in to multiple servers on the network, repeat step 2 substituting the names of the other file servers.

Step 3: Review

In this task, you learned how to use the USERLIST command at the DOS prompt to get a list of users on any server where you are logged in.

Task 6.11: Listing groups on the network.

Step 1: Description

You can use SYSCON to view *groups* of users on the network. A group is a list of users who have the same access rights to a certain resource on the network.

Step 2: Action

1. To change to the \PUBLIC subdirectory, type `CD\PUBLIC` and press Enter.

2. Type `SYSCON` and press Enter.

3. Use the down-arrow key to move the cursor to Group Information and press Enter. You see a list of group names, as shown in Figure 6.12.

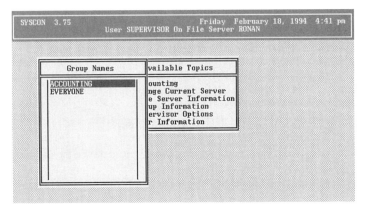

Figure 6.12. *Group Names list.*

4. Use the up- and down-arrow keys to move the cursor to select from Group Names and press Enter. The Group Information menu appears, as shown in Figure 6.13.

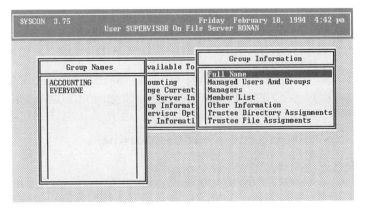

Figure 6.13. *Group Information menu.*

5. Move the cursor down to Member List and press Enter. You then see a list of group members, as shown in Figure 6.14.

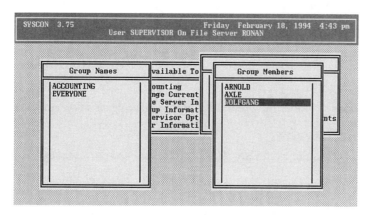

Figure 6.14. *Group Members list.*

Step 3: Review

In this task, you learned that SYSCON provides information about group membership.

Sending a Quick Note

Now that you've identified the users and the groups that you want to send a message to, you can send a message using the SEND command. Understandably, you can send messages only for those servers where you are logged in.

Task 6.12: Sending a message to a user on your network.

Step 1: Description

This task describes how you send a message to another user on your network.

Step 2: Action

1. To change to the \PUBLIC subdirectory, type **CD\PUBLIC** and press Enter.

2. To send the message WELCOME TO TEACH YOURSELF NETWARE to TYN_USER, type **SEND "WELCOME TO TEACH YOURSELF NETWARE" TO TYN_USER** and press Enter. If you don't know the username but know the connection number, you can substitute the connection number.

Step 3: Review

To send a message to another user on your network, you use the SEND command at the DOS prompt. As previously mentioned, you must be logged in to the server to send a message to a user on the server.

Task 6.13: Sending a message to a user on another network.

Step 1: Description

This task describes how to send a simple message to a user on another network.

Step 2: Action

1. To change to the \PUBLIC subdirectory, type `CD\PUBLIC` and press Enter.

2. To send the message WELCOME TO TEACH YOURSELF NETWARE to TYN_USER on ACCT_SERVER, type

   `SEND "WELCOME TO TEACH YOURSELF NETWARE" TO ACCT_SERVER/TYN_USER`

   and press Enter.

Step 3: Review

In this task, you learned that when you want to send a message to another user on another server where you are logged in, you use the same SEND command at the DOS prompt but include the server name.

Task 6.14: Sending a message to a group on your network.

Step 1: Description

This task describes the procedure for sending a message to a group on your network.

Step 2: Action

1. To change to the \PUBLIC subdirectory, type `CD\PUBLIC` and press Enter.

2. To send the message WELCOME TO TEACH YOURSELF NETWARE to the ADMINISTRATION group, type

   `SEND "WELCOME TO TEACH YOURSELF NETWARE" TO ADMINISTRATION`

   and press Enter.

Step 3: Review

In this task, you learned that when you want to send a message to a group on your network, you use the same SEND command at the DOS prompt but include the group's name.

Turning Off Message Reception

Occasionally, you can be inundated by messages. When you receive a message at your workstation, no other instructions or programs can be run until you clear the message by pressing Ctrl-Enter. Sometimes, you may not want your workstation to receive messages sent from the server (for example, warning messages) or from other users (with the SEND command). Usually, you turn message reception off because you are running a program you don't want interrupted.

Task 6.15: Turning off message reception using CASTOFF.

Step 1: Description

This task describes the procedure for blocking messages from other workstations and the file server.

6

Step 2: Action

At the DOS prompt, type CASTOFF [ALL]. Include the ALL option if you want to block file server messages.

> **Note:** The most recent file server message sent to you during message blocking appears on your workstation when you unblock messages. You clear it by pressing Ctrl-Enter.

Step 3: Review

In this task, you learned that CASTOFF enables you to block unwanted messages from interrupting you at your workstation.

You don't always want to block all messages, of course. CASTON enables you to unblock messages.

Task 6.16: Turning on message reception using CASTON.

Step 1: Description

This task describes the procedure for unblocking messages from other workstations and the file server. CASTON enables you to resume getting messages from other workstations and the file server after you have blocked them using CASTOFF.

Step 2: Action

At the DOS prompt, type CASTON.

> **Note:** You must have issued CASTOFF for CASTON to work in a meaningful manner.

Step 3: Review

In this task, you learned that CASTON enables you to resume getting messages from other workstations and the file server.

Sending Electronic Mail

The SEND command is one that can easily get out of hand. You should control its usage to make sure it is being used judiciously. For most electronic mail, you should make use of an e-mail application using NetWare's Message Handling Services (NetWare MHS). Figure 6.15 illustrates NetWare's MHS de facto standard.

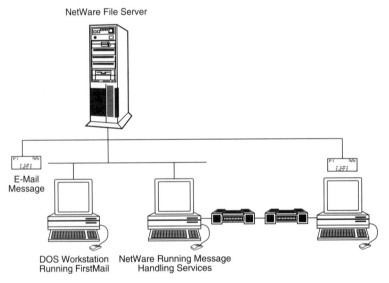

Figure 6.15. *NetWare's Message Handling Services (MHS).*

Most e-mail applications divide into server and workstation parts. The server portion routes mail and stores messages that cannot be delivered in a database. The workstation portion opens messages, deletes messages, creates messages, polls the server, and so forth. A benefit of an e-mail application is that the message is stored, and the recipients can read when they want.

This capability contrasts with what you just learned about the SEND command. If you try to use the SEND command to issue a message to someone not logged on or who has issued a CASTOFF command, you may lose the message. The SEND command does not store the message.

E-mail applications also allow the attachment of files and long messages. For these reasons, you probably should use the SEND command only when warning of some imminent system event—for example, the server is going down.

E-mail is only one service available on most local area networks. In the next chapter, you look at another—print services.

Summary

In this chapter, you learned to do the following:

- [ ] Display account information, users and groups, and directories and files
- [ ] Find and attach to file servers and their network drives
- [ ] Send messages to other users and groups using the SEND utility

You use many of these skills again in other chapters. For instance, you spend a half-day each on print and file servers. You acquired an enormous amount of information in this chapter. Take time to learn by heart the commands you used here. On Day 7, the pace quickens, as you begin gaining system management skills.

Workshop
Terminology Review

attach—To log in a workstation to another file server while the workstation remains logged in to the first.

broadcast—A LAN data transmission scheme in which data packets are heard by all stations on the network.

directory—A pictorial, alphabetical, or chronological list of the contents of a disk. A directory is sometimes called a catalog. The operating system uses it to keep track of the contents of the disk.

file server—A computer that provides network stations with controlled access to shareable resources.

map—To assign a workstation drive letter to a server directory.

network drive—An online storage device available to network users.

Task List

The emphasis of this session has been to explore your way through NetWare by exposing you to different command-line utilities. You will repeatedly use these commands in your daily work—and in this book. The tasks you should grasp from this chapter are as follows:

- ☐ Listing account information
- ☐ Listing and attaching to file servers
- ☐ Logging out from file servers
- ☐ Locating file servers and network drives
- ☐ Displaying directory and file information
- ☐ Displaying users and groups
- ☐ Sending a message

Q&A

Q Is there another way to send messages?

A Yes, you can use SESSION | User List | *current users* | Send Message | Message: or SESSION | Group List | Message:.

Q Can I make my C: drive available to other users?

A You can't make it available through NetWare, but you can provide file service to your local drives through a peer-to-peer network operating system, such as LANtastic or Windows for Workgroups. You therefore would have NetWare client programs and Windows for Workgroups client and service programs, for example. You then make your C: drive available to the other users and provide them with any passwords they need. The users then use Windows for Workgroups client programs to access your drive.

Q Can I use DOS commands on my NetWare files?

A Yes, you can use any DOS command. However, later in this book you learn that NetWare commands preserve NetWare attributes and rights.

Q Can others see what I'm doing on the network?

A Generally, no. Of course, there are exceptions. Anyone using a packet analyzer or grabber program can look at your data. You can protect your password by setting Allow Unencrypted Passwords to OFF at the file server.

7

Understanding the Bindery

Up to now, you have been looking at or using *bindery* objects. Before you learn how to create bindery objects, you need to learn about the bindery. Why a bindery? To support the services on a NetWare network, including accounting and security, the system must have a place to define and maintain objects. The bindery is that place, and it is critical to the operation of NetWare because it is where you define all system objects, such as users, groups, and file servers. When an object is requested, the system can retrieve and use information about the object before carrying out the request. The bindery, therefore, is the heart and soul of the NetWare security system.

Bindery Overview

Every server maintains its own bindery containing the information for that server. The bindery is a simple, flat file database. Each record in the database represents a bindery object. It is an object-oriented database containing definitions for users, groups, and other objects on the network. Each object creates a record. Records in the bindery are divided into fields, which are called *properties*, and each field contains information called *values*.

In a simple database, each record can be identified by its record number. The NetWare bindery identifies each object with a bindery Object Identifier (or Object ID). This identifier is a 32-bit value usually stored as a hexadecimal number.

When you create a new user with a NetWare utility such as SYSCON, you add a new object to the bindery. The object name is the new username you choose. (If you want to add a new user before you learn about the bindery, skip to the next chapter.)

As mentioned previously, servers keep a bindery containing their security information for all users, groups, queues, and so on. Consequently, NetWare access and security is file server-based.

The bindery has three levels, implemented as the following hidden files in the SYS:SYSTEM directory:

- ☐ NET$OBJ.SYS
- ☐ NET$PROP.SYS
- ☐ NET$VAL.SYS

These files store objects, object properties, and property values.

Objects

Every person, process, or device within your network must be represented by an *object* in the bindery. Bindery objects are the actual users, groups, and other named resources. A print server, for example, that stores its print jobs in a NetWare directory must be defined as a bindery object.

Each object has an identification number, name, type, static/dynamic flag, and security byte. The identification number uniquely identifies one object from another. Because remembering a user or group by an identification number isn't easy for most people, objects also get names.

Bindery object names can be up to 48 characters long. Because the name must be zero-terminated, that leaves 47 characters for the actual name. Of course, you need to remember this number when you name users, print servers, and file servers. In the next chapter, you see that usernames are 47 characters long.

Objects in the bindery have type numbers associated with them. There is an entry in the bindery for the object type. The object type makes it possible to lump objects by type and to have different objects with the same name. For example, you can label a server and a group as ACCOUNTING. Because the bindery has assigned each a different object type, the bindery knows they are not the same object.

Novell administers NetWare bindery types and creates new ones as developers ask for them. Table 7.1 lists current object types.

Table 7.1. Current object types.

Object	Type (Hexadecimal)
Unknown	0
User	1
User group	2
Print queue	3
File server	4
Job server	5
Gateway	6
Print server	7

continues

Table 7.1. continued

Object	Type (Hexadecimal)
Archive queue	8
Archive server	9
Job queue	A
Administration	B
Remote bridge server	24
Advertising print server	47

The theoretical limit to the number of bindery objects you can have in NetWare 3.12 is 16,777,216 objects. That's a lot of users, groups, queues, and servers!

Objects and properties in the bindery are either *static* or *dynamic*. A static object exists in the bindery forever or until it is explicitly removed. A Supervisor can delete a static object, but it survives a server restart. Examples of static objects are users, groups, and print queues. You don't want these objects to disappear every time you down the server.

A dynamic object exists in the bindery until explicitly removed or until the server is powered down and brought back up. When the server reinitializes itself, it scans the bindery for dynamic objects and deletes them. An example of a dynamic object is a server (other than the bindery's host). The system tracks file servers by the internal routing mechanism. You don't want a file server to remember the names of other file servers after you've taken down the server. The file server learns the names of other file servers on the network after it reinitializes.

The Security Byte—Object Security

The bindery provides a security mechanism to allow access only to certain objects. It can determine who has access rights to its information. The object security byte controls who can view or write to an object. Separate access rights exist for reading from and writing to the bindery. The byte is broken into parts: the low-order nibble controls reading, and the high-order nibble controls writing.

Following are the five levels of bindery security:

- □ *Anyone.* A program can call a bindery function regardless of who is logged in to the server. The user running the program doesn't even need to be logged in to the server because only a network shell needs to be connected to the server.

- □ *Logged.* A program can call a bindery function when the user running it is logged in to the file server. You only can read a user's full name, for example, when you're logged in to the file server. You can see this capability yourself by logging out from the file server and typing USERLIST.

- □ *Object.* The security level object means that only the object itself (and the Supervisor and the operating system) can run a program to access its bindery information. When you log in, for example, LOGIN.EXE can read your login restrictions from the LOGIN_CONTROL property, but it cannot read anyone else's login restrictions.

- □ *Supervisor.* The security level object means that the user running the program must be the Supervisor or Supervisor-equivalent. The bindery cannot distinguish between the Supervisor and its equivalent. You learn about intruder detection in Chapter 9, for example. Its primary purpose is to lock accounts that appear to be under attack. The ACCOUNT_LOCKOUT property is an example of the Supervisor security level. Only a Supervisor or Supervisor-equivalent can reset accounts that are locked out.

- □ *NetWare.* This security level means that only the operating system can access the bindery information. A good example is the PASSWORD property. Only the operating system can read and write passwords to the bindery. Nobody, including the Supervisor, can read the password directly. Because passwords are one-way encrypted, there is no reason for anyone to read the password. You learn about password encryption in Chapter 9.

Properties and Values

Each object has associated properties. Bindery *properties* are names for information related to a bindery object. The property contains a value. The bindery allows a property to contain one value (an *item*) or many items (a *set*).

Property names are limited to 15 characters and, like passwords, they are case insensitive. Like objects, properties also have flags and the security byte.

Table 7.2 provides samples of property names. This list, like object types, grows as Novell and third-party developers find new types of information to store.

Table 7.2. Bindery properties.

```
ACCOUNT_BALANCE

BLOCKS_READ

CONNECT_TIME

GROUP_MEMBERS

GROUPS_I'M_IN

IDENTIFICATION

LOGIN_CONTROL

MISC_LOGIN_INFO

NET_ADDRESS

NODE_CONTROL

OLD_PASSWORDS

OPERATORS

PASSWORD

PS_OPERATORS

PS_USERS

Q_DIRECTORY

Q_OPERATORS

Q_SERVERS

Q_USERS

SECURITY_EQUALS
```

Different objects have different properties. User objects, for example, have password, account restriction, account balance, security, and login restriction properties. On the other hand, print queues have operators, servers, and users.

Item versus Set

If a property is used, the system assigns one or more values to it. A property can be an item or a set. The PASSWORD item property, for example, contains a single value—the password for the object. It's an item property because at any time an object has only one password.

The OLD_PASSWORDS set property, for example, contains previously used passwords. Because a user can have up to eight old passwords, the OLD_PASSWORDS property must handle more than one value, that is, passwords.

The item property value stores whatever type of data the property requires.

How the Bindery Works

Now that you understand the bindery's components, let's look at how it works. In the next chapter, you get your first taste of creating accounts. But before you do, take a look at how the utility that updates the bindery works.

One task you do a few times is add users. In the following example, you see how the utility uses the bindery when you add a user. To add the user JANET to the ACCOUNTING group, for example, the system does the following:

1. Creates an object named JANET.

2. Adds the property SECURITY_EQUALS to the JANET object.

3. Adds the group EVERYONE to the SECURITY_EQUALS property of the JANET object.

4. Adds the property GROUPS_I'M_IN to the JANET object.

5. Adds the group EVERYONE to the GROUPS_I'M_IN property of the JANET object.

6. Adds the object JANET to the GROUP_MEMBERS property of the group EVERYONE.

7. Adds the property LOGIN_CONTROL to the JANET object.

8. Writes the account restrictions values to the LOGIN_CONTROL property of the JANET object.

9. Adds the property OLD_PASSWORDS to the JANET object.

10. Writes blank values to the OLD_PASSWORDS property of the JANET object.

11. Adds the property ACCOUNT_BALANCE to the JANET object.

12. Adds the property MISC_LOGIN_INFO to the JANET object.

In the next chapter, you work with the SYSCON utility, which provides an easy interface to perform these steps. As you can see, a lot happens when you create a new user. Each step involves at least two packets flowing over the network cable.

Now look at how the same utility creates the ACCOUNTING group. It does the following:

1. Creates an object named ACCOUNTING.

2. Adds the property GROUP_MEMBERS to the ACCOUNTING object.

Very little happens when you add a group. Following is what happens when you add user JANET to the ACCOUNTING group:

1. Adds the object JANET to the GROUP_MEMBERS property of the ACCOUNTING object.

2. Adds the object ACCOUNTING to the GROUPS_I'M_IN property of the object JANET.

3. Adds the object ACCOUNTING to the SECURITY_EQUALS property of the object JANET.

This exercise, too, is simple. Let's look at another example and see how NetWare uses the bindery to create a BALLIOL_PS1 print server. It does the following:

1. Creates an object named BALLIOL_PS1.

2. Adds the property PS_USERS to the BALLIOL_PS1 object.

3. Adds the property PS_OPERATORS to the BALLIOL_PS1 object.

4. Adds the property ACCOUNT_BALANCE to the BALLIOL_PS1 object.

5. Writes unlimited credit limit and zero account balance values to the ACCOUNT_BALANCE property of the BALLIOL_PS1 object.

6. Adds the object SUPERVISOR to the PS_OPERATORS property of the BALLIOL_PS1 object.

7. Adds the object EVERYONE to the PS_USERS property of the BALLIOL_PS1 object.

In addition, you must create a directory for the print server. The directory's name is the bindery identifier for BALLIOL_PS1. Now, look at how NetWare creates a print queue named BALLIOL_Q1; it does the following:

1. Creates an object named BALLIOL_Q1.

2. Adds the object SUPERVISOR to the Q_OPERATORS property of the BALLIOL_Q1 object.

3. Adds the object EVERYONE to the Q_USERS property of the BALLIOL_Q1 object.

That's all there is to this process. However, NetWare also creates the Q_SERVER and Q_DIRECTORY properties. NetWare uses the bindery identifier for BALLIOL_Q1 as the directory's name. Now, turn your attention to the last step, adding a print queue to a print server. You must do the following:

1. Add the object BALLIOL_PS1 to the Q_SERVERS property of the BALLIOL_Q1 object.

2. Create the QUEUE.000 file in the directory of BALLIOL_PS1.

For the last example, look at a user login. When a user attempts to log in to a file server, the system looks up the username to see whether it is a valid user object. If it is a valid user object, the system matches the user-supplied password to the value stored in the PASSWORD property in the bindery. If the passwords match, the user is logged in.

That's it. You have just learned how several NetWare utilities use the bindery. Even though NetWare intended the bindery for system use, applications can access the bindery through NetWare function calls.

7

Applications Using the Bindery

Application programmers can use the bindery to store information. For instance, the bindery can store the user's configuration information for applications. Rather than store the information in a file, the programmer can place it in the bindery. The application then makes bindery calls to get the configuration information.

Alternatively, the bindery can act as a communications agent between two workstations. The messages then survive network outages.

You can think up other applications for the bindery. As you start relying on the bindery even more, backup and maintenance of the bindery become even more important and critical. You already know that the bindery is the primary security mechanism, so backup and maintenance are imperative, as you learn in the following sections.

How to Maintain the Bindery

Regular maintenance of the bindery is necessary. Regularly, you need to use SYSCON to remove old accounts, check TTS$ERR.LOG to make certain it is not getting too big, and keep a backup copy of bindery files.

Because it is important to access the bindery files at times to copy them to a backup device, NetWare function calls to open and close the bindery are available. When the bindery is closed, you can repair and restore it. However, when the bindery is closed, the server cannot provide any services that call for access to the bindery.

Assuming that you have sufficient authority, you know you have a bindery problem when you

☐ Cannot delete a username

☐ Cannot change a password

☐ Cannot modify rights

☐ Get a bindery error message

☐ Get an `unknown server` error during printing

When you discern one of these conditions, you can fix the bindery using BINDFIX.

Task 7.1: Using BINDFIX.

Step 1: Description

This task enables the Supervisor to repair the bindery to fix such problems as the inability to delete or modify user information and rights, error messages regarding the bindery on the file server console, and an `unknown server` message during printing on the default printer.

Step 2: Action

1. At the console prompt, type **SEND "PLEASE LOGOUT IMMEDIATELY. WE HAVE TO REPAIR THE BINDERY"** and press Enter.

2. At the DOS prompt, type **BINDFIX** and press Enter. You see messages as shown in Figure 7.1.

3. Respond **Y** or **N** to `Delete mail directories of users that no longer exist? (y/n):`.

4. Respond **Y** or **N** to Delete trustee rights for users that no longer exist? (y/n):. Your screen now should look something like the one shown in Figure 7.2.

```
F>bindfix
Rebuilding Bindery.  Please Wait.
Checking object's property lists.
Checking properties to see if they are in an object property list.
Checking objects for back-link property.
Checking set consistency and compacting sets.
Checking Properties for proper order.
Checking user objects for standard properties.
Checking group objects for standard properties.
Checking links between users and groups for consistency.
Delete mail directories of users that no longer exist? (y/n):
```

Figure 7.1. *The BINDFIX startup message.*

```
F>bindfix
Rebuilding Bindery.  Please Wait.
Checking object's property lists.
Checking properties to see if they are in an object property list.
Checking objects for back-link property.
Checking set consistency and compacting sets.
Checking Properties for proper order.
Checking user objects for standard properties.
Checking group objects for standard properties.
Checking links between users and groups for consistency.
Delete mail directories of users that no longer exist? (y/n): Y
Checking for mail directories of users that no longer exist.
Checking for users that do not have mail directories.
Delete trustee rights for users that no longer exist? (y/n): Y
Checking volume SYS.  Please wait.

Bindery check successfully completed.
Please delete the files NET$OBJ.OLD, NET$PROP.OLD, and NET$VAL.OLD after you
have verified the reconstructed bindery.

F>
```

Figure 7.2. *The BINDFIX confirmation message.*

5. When BINDFIX finishes, verify the reconstructed bindery and delete the old bindery files afterward.

6. At the console prompt, type **ENABLE LOGIN** and press Enter.

Tip: If the same problems keep recurring, restore the old bindery.

Step 3: Review

In this task, you learned how to fix the bindery when you are experiencing problems. After you start BINDFIX, NetWare backs up the bindery files and closes them so that nobody can access them. The system rebuilds the files, all the time reporting on its progress. In the file-rebuilding process, the utility scans all mounted volumes, removes deleted users from trustee lists, and prompts you to delete mail directories and trustee rights for users who don't exist on the file server. At the end, BINDFIX checks the bindery to make sure that everything worked and that the rebuilt files are usable, and reports its findings. If BINDFIX is unsuccessful, you need to run BINDREST to restore the backup bindery files.

Task 7.2: Using BINDREST.

Step 1: Description

This task enables the Supervisor to restore old bindery files when the current ones are corrupted. You should use BINDREST only when an attempt to fix the bindery using BINDFIX fails to correct the problems.

Step 2: Action

1. At the console prompt or DOS prompt, type **SEND "PLEASE LOGOUT IMMEDIATELY. WE HAVE TO RESTORE THE BINDERY" TO EVERYBODY** and press Enter.

2. At the console prompt, type **DISABLE LOGIN** and press Enter.

3. At the DOS prompt, type **BINDREST** and press Enter.

4. At the console prompt, type **ENABLE LOGIN** and press Enter.

> **Note:** If you restore old bindery files, the passwords in the file may not be current, and users may not remember to what the old ones were set. You therefore need to change the passwords using MAKEUSER or SYSCON. Then users can change their passwords the next time they log in. In Chapter 6, you learn how to change passwords.

Step 3: Review

In this task, you learned how the Supervisor restores old bindery files when the current ones are corrupted, that is, when BINDFIX doesn't work. You should use BINDREST only when an attempt to fix the bindery using BINDFIX fails to correct the problems. Regrettably, you lose everything added to the bindery since the last backup.

Backing Up the Bindery

Backing up bindery files is a key system administration responsibility. In Chapter 22, you learn to use SBACKUP to back up the bindery.

The Last Word on the Bindery

The NetWare Core Protocol (NCP) is the interface for workstations making requests for network services. In reality, NCP's core set of generic services extends the client's workstation operating system by providing services over the network. NCP is a shell that sits on top of the WOS and redirects the network requests to the server and the local requests to the local operating system. This protocol uses the datagram services of the IPX protocol you discovered in Chapter 4. You learn more about this subject when you configure workstations in Chapter 19.

The NCP interacts between the NetWare shell and the NetWare file server. The NCP enables you to name objects and to associate values with one or more properties of the object. The system stores this information in the bindery. Through the bindery, the NOS and NCP implement a comprehensive system of object naming, accounting, and security.

Summary

In this chapter, you learned about the following:

- ☐ The bindery
- ☐ Objects
- ☐ Properties
- ☐ Values
- ☐ Using BINDFIX to fix the bindery
- ☐ Using BINDREST to restore the bindery

You spent a session on the bindery because it is a critical system database. If you take time to understand objects, properties, and values thoroughly, then creating and maintaining users, groups, printers, queues, and servers will be easier to grasp.

Workshop
Terminology Review

bindery—NetWare database for identifying objects, such as users, groups, file servers, and other network objects.

dynamic object—An object removed from the bindery when you reboot the server.

item—A single value in a property.

object—A passive entity that contains or receives data. Access to an object potentially implies access to the information it contains.

property—Field name in the bindery database for information related to a bindery object.

set—Multiple values for a property.

static object—An object that remains in the bindery even when you take down and bring back up the file server.

Task List

With the information provided in this chapter, you now can begin your understanding of NetWare objects. You learned how to do the following:

☐ Fix the bindery

☐ Restore the bindery

Q&A

Q How does the system use the bindery to remove a member of a group?

A To delete the member JANET from the ACCOUNTING group, the system does the following:

☐ Removes the group ACCOUNTING from the SECURITY_EQUALS property of the user JANET.

☐ Removes the group ACCOUNTING from the GROUPS_I'M_IN property of the user JANET.

☐ Removes the user JANET from the GROUP_MEMBERS property of the group ACCOUNTING.

Q Why is the bindery important?

A The bindery is the key accounting and security database on the system. As a system administrator, you constantly create and change bindery objects, such as users and queues.

Q Can you access the bindery directly?

A No. SYSCON, PCONSOLE, and other NetWare utilities provide access to the bindery.

Q Are there other ways to look at the bindery?

A Yes, there are some third-party products that provide information from the bindery, such as Bindview.

Q What happens if the bindery is not available?

A Well, for one thing, users would not be able to log in, because system software consults the bindery to determine whether the username is a valid account, and then matches the password supplied to the one stored in the bindery. You would be unable to create new objects, such as new users or print queues. Also, you would not be able to use any NetWare process or device. So, the short answer is, not very much.

8

Managing Accounts

At this time, you should have a good grounding in NetWare basics. You have studied network components, file systems, some basic NetWare commands, and the bindery. In this chapter, you take your first look at NetWare commands for managing users.

Introducing Accounts

On Day 3, you were introduced to user accounts. User accounts are the foundation of NetWare's security. Usernames are simply a method for referring to those user accounts. You assign usernames and passwords on each NetWare server. In addition, you can specify the times that the user can log in, and you control the location from which the login comes from. You can set the system to detect and report attempts by intruders to gain *access* to your server, and provide a lockout feature after a specified number of unsuccessful attempts. You also can set a minimum character limit for the password length and a limit to the time the password can be kept. These controls reduce the chances that an unauthorized user can guess the password. User accounts and passwords are the basis for login security.

Login security is the first layer of the NetWare security model. The other security layers, which you learn about in this book, are as follows:

☐ Rights security (see Chapters 15 and 16)

☐ Attribute security (see Chapters 13 and 14)

☐ File and print server security (see Chapters 20 and 21)

Login security controls access at the *portal*—the entrance to the network. Login security is effective because it requires an authorized username for identification and a valid password for verification. The username and password must match exactly information kept by the system. Because you enter your account's username first, you look at accounts and usernames first.

Understanding User Accounts

User accounts provide the first point of access. They identify the user of an account. The username is the identification. Usernames are anywhere from 1 to 47 characters in length. You can use any ASCII character, except the space and tab (DOS command-line delimiters), the 32 control characters, and the characters shown in Table 8.1.

Table 8.1. Invalid characters for usernames.

Character	Description
=	Equal sign
>	Greater-than sign
¦	Vertical bar
+	Plus sign
[	Left square bracket
]	Right square bracket
\	Backslash
/	Slash
*	Asterisk
;	Semicolon
:	Colon
.	Period
,	Comma
?	Question mark
"	Double quotation mark

Only Supervisors, Supervisor-equivalents, and Workgroup Managers can create user accounts and usernames.

Within NetWare are a number of special user accounts, including the following:

- ☐ Supervisor
- ☐ Guest
- ☐ Managers
- ☐ Operators

In the following sections, you look at some of these special accounts.

Supervisor Account

When you install NetWare on your file server, the Supervisor account is created automatically. The purpose of the Supervisor account is to manage accounts on the file server. The Supervisor account can do the following:

- ☐ Never be deleted
- ☐ Access any file or directory
- ☐ Create and delete users and groups
- ☐ Create and delete Workgroup Managers
- ☐ Create and delete print queues
- ☐ Assign console operators
- ☐ Create and modify the system login script
- ☐ Set default user account restrictions
- ☐ Set intruder detection parameters
- ☐ Assign a password to a print server
- ☐ Assign a full name to a print server

Note: Users with supervisor-equivalent accounts can do everything on this list, except their accounts can be deleted.

The Supervisor account is omnipotent. You need to control its usage tightly.

Guest Account

Guest is another account that is created automatically on your file server when you install NetWare. Guest has a simple raison d'être. A Guest account allows users to access your server's print queues when they don't have an account on the server. They can use NPRINT and CAPTURE to do so.

A user who doesn't have a connection to your server can specify a print queue on your server when using CAPTURE. The CAPTURE utility attempts to log in to your file server as Guest. If the Guest account on your server doesn't have a password, and Guest is a queue user for the target print queue, then the user attaches to your server

and places a print job in the print queue. If the Guest account on your server does have a password, or Guest isn't a queue user for the target print queue, then CAPTURE prompts the user for a username and password for your server. It attempts to attach to the server in the normal manner with the supplied username and password. If the attachment is successful, the user can use the print queue.

The Guest account also is security-equivalent to the group EVERYONE, which means that any Guest has, at least, access in SYS:PUBLIC and SYS:MAIL. You might want to keep a Guest account, but you may not want it to be security-equivalent to the group EVERYONE.

> **Tip:** You can delete Guest from the EVERYONE group, while still allowing a Guest to print jobs. Just add Guest as a queue user to a print queue using the PCONSOLE utility. In Chapter 23, you learn more about PCONSOLE. If you want to add Guest as a print queue user using the PCONSOLE utility, go to that chapter now.

8

If you don't want users without accounts on your server to print, you can delete the Guest account using SYSCON, which you learn about in this chapter.

Managers

NetWare has two levels of managers:

- ☐ Workgroup
- ☐ Account

Workgroup Managers are assistant Supervisors in a distributed environment. They have been given the right to create, manage, and delete certain users and groups. The Supervisor or Supervisor-equivalent creates Workgroup Manager accounts and assigns them specific users and groups to manage. The Workgroup Manager, in turn, can create and delete users from the workgroup using their Workgroup Manager's account. The Supervisor does, however, limit the Workgroup Manager to managing only those users in the workgroup.

Account Managers, on the other hand, can manage and delete users but cannot create them. An Account Manager's account also can manage bindery objects but cannot create bindery objects. Workgroup Managers (or the Supervisor) create Account Managers for overseeing specific subsets of their groups.

Operators

The Supervisors or Supervisor-equivalents create operators to oversee specific network functions. They can assign functions to control the file server console, print server, or print queues.

File server console operators have full access to the FCONSOLE utility, except for downing the file server or disconnecting other users.

Print server operators are special user accounts that are given rights to manage the print server. They can specify notify lists for printers, issue printer commands, change forms, change the print server for a queue, change queue priority, or down the print server. Print server operators cannot create new print servers or new print server operators. Because the Supervisor account is omnipotent, it is a print server operator on all. Therefore, only the Supervisor or Supervisor-equivalent can assign print server operator status.

Print queue operators are special user accounts with rights to manage, disable, and enable print queues. A print queue operator also can authorize a print server to service a queue. Again, the Supervisor or Supervisor-equivalent is a print queue operator for all print queues. Only the Supervisor or Supervisor-equivalent can assign print queue operator status.

Table 8.2 summarizes the function for the special user accounts.

Table 8.2. Special user accounts.

User Account	Role	Limitations
Supervisor or Supervisor-equivalent	Can create all accounts, including special user accounts, and automatically access any volume, directory, file, and queue	None, omnipotent

User Account	Role	Limitations
Workgroup Manager	Creates, manages, and deletes assigned user accounts and groups and creates Account Managers	No special file rights, cannot create another Workgroup Manager, cannot delete users not assigned or assign rights they don't have
Account Manager	Manages and deletes assigned users and creates other Account Managers	Cannot create user or groups, manage groups, create workgroups, or assign rights they don't have
Print Server Operators	Creates notify lists for printers, changes forms and queue priority, and downs print servers	Cannot create print servers or print server operators, or assign queues to printers
Print Queue Operators	Creates and manages print queues, and assigns queues to printers	Cannot delete print queues or assign print queue operators

Distributing responsibility across a few people is a good control—separation of duties—and gives the Supervisor time to concentrate on system-management functions, as opposed to user-management functions.

Let's look at how to create users using different tools.

Creating User Accounts

You can divide user-account administration into two phases: creating user accounts and maintaining user accounts. You have several ways to create user accounts. The most popular way is using the SYSCON utility because it is an interactive, menu-driven utility that is easy to work with. Most NetWare administrators are familiar with its use. You can use SYSCON when you need to create one or two user accounts. If you need to add more users, you should consider using either the MAKEUSER or USERDEF utilities.

First, you look at SYSCON because you may select it as your tool of choice.

Using SYSCON

Previously, you used the SYSCON menu utility. The Supervisor uses SYSCON to do the following:

- ☐ Create user accounts
- ☐ Delete user accounts
- ☐ Change users' passwords

In the next chapter, you learn about passwords. Here you learn about creating and deleting user accounts.

Task 8.1: Creating user accounts using SYSCON.

Step 1: Description
In this task, you use the SYSCON utility to create new users.

Step 2: Action
1. Type **LOGIN SUPERVISOR** at the DOS prompt and press Enter. Provide a password, if required, and press Enter.

2. Type **SYSCON** and press Enter. The Available Topics menu appears (see Figure 8.1).

3. Move the cursor down to User Information and press Enter. The User Names list appears.

4. Press Ins.

5. Type the new user account name **JANET** in the User Name box and press Enter (see Figure 8.2).

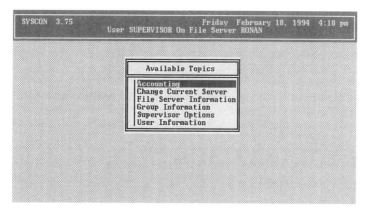

Figure 8.1. *SYSCON menu.*

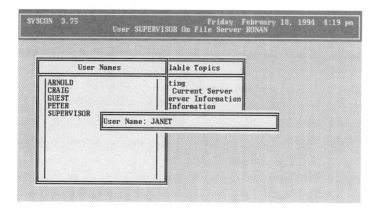

Figure 8.2. *User Name box.*

6. In the Path to Create User's Home Directory box, enter the correct path and press Enter.

7. In the Verify Creation Of New Directory box, select Yes and press Enter to confirm.

8. Press Esc until you are asked to confirm your exit from SYSCON.

Step 3: Review

With this task, you created your first user account. You place some restrictions on this account in Chapter 10.

To delete a user's account, you do basically the same steps as you did for adding a user account. You select the following: SYSCON, User Information, username, and then press Delete.

Using MAKEUSER

In many environments, you must create a large number of users who have similar needs. Creating users one at a time with SYSCON can be a daunting task. Alternatively, you can use the MAKEUSER utility for a batch-creation of users. MAKEUSER enables the Supervisor or Workgroup Manager to create a file to use when creating or deleting users.

The Supervisor can use the MAKEUSER program to create or delete many user accounts. MAKEUSER has its own script language, which you can use to create or delete users and set up individual parameters for them. The Supervisor writes a script controlling how users are created.

Note: Only the Supervisor or Supervisor-equivalent can run the MAKEUSER utility.

Task 8.2: Creating or changing users using MAKEUSER.

Step 1: Description

You use the MAKEUSER utility to create or change a user's password.

Step 2: Action

1. Type **LOGIN SUPERVISOR** at the DOS prompt and press Enter. Provide a password, if required, and press Enter.

2. To change to the \PUBLIC subdirectory, type **CD\PUBLIC**, and press Enter.

3. Type **MAKEUSER** and press Enter. You should see the Available Options menu, as shown in Figure 8.3.

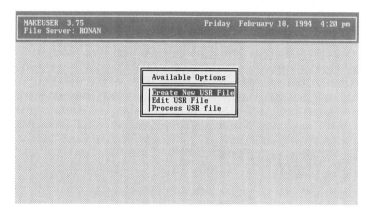

Figure 8.3. *Available Options menu.*

4. Select Create New USR File and press Enter. You then see the Creating a New USR File screen.

5. Type in each command on a separate line and press Enter to move to the next line. A sample USR file is shown in Figure 8.4.

8

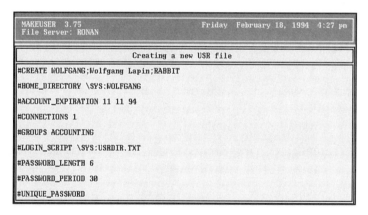

Figure 8.4. *USR file.*

6. To save the file, press Esc and confirm you want to save changes.

7. Type a filename in the Enter the New USR File Name box and press Enter.

8. Press Esc until you are asked to confirm your exit from MAKEUSER.

Table 8.3 provides MAKEUSER commands.

Table 8.3. MAKEUSER commands.

Command	Description	Example
#ACCOUNT EXPIRATION *M D Y*	Assigns an expiration account date for the user	#ACCOUNT EXPIRATION 11 11 93
#ACCOUNTING *balance, low limit*	Assigns balance total and low balance limit	#ACCOUNTING 50,10
#CLEAR or #RESET	Nullifies effect of previous commands on what comes after it in the file	#CLEAR
#CONNECTIONS *n*	Restricts concurrent connections	#CONNECTIONS 1
#CREATE *username* [*;full name*] [*;password*] [*group*] [*;directory path rights*]	Creates a user account and specifies password	#CREATE PETER_DAVIS; PETER T. DAVIS ;PETER ;ACCOUNTING ^
#DELETE *username* [*;username*]	Deletes a user or users	#DELETE PETER_DAVIS ;JANET_DAVIS
#GROUPS *group* [*;group*]	Adds users to the specified group or groups	#GROUPS ACCOUNTING
#HOME_DIRECTORY *path*	Creates or deletes a home directory	#HOME_DIRECTORY \SYS:USRDIR
#NO_HOME_DIRECTORY	Creates no home directory	#NO_HOME_DIRECTORY
#LOGIN_SCRIPT *path*	Copies login script file to user's mail directory	#LOGIN_SCRIPT\SYS:USRDIR
#MAX_DISK_SPACE *vol,n*	Restricts disk space on volume *vol* to number *n* of disk blocks	#MAX_DISK_SPACE F:,100

Command	Description	Example
#PASSWORD_LENGTH *n*	Specifies the minimum password length (1–20 alphanumeric characters)	#PASSWORD_LENGTH 5
#PASSWORD_PERIOD *days*	Assigns number of days a password is valid before forcing a password change	#PASSWORD_PERIOD 30
#PASSWORD_REQUIRED	Requires the user to have a password	#PASSWORD_REQUIRED
#PURGE_USER_ DIRECTORY	Deletes subdirectories below home directories when a user account is deleted	#PURGE_USER_DIRECTORY
#REM or REM	Makes comments in the script file	#REM
#RESTRICTED_TIME *day, start, end*	Specifies the login time that a user cannot be logged on to the server	#RESTRICTED_TIME EVERYDAY
#STATIONS *network, station [;network, station]*	Restricts login locations to network number(s) and station address(es)	#STATIONS 00000001, 0080C77A547A
#UNIQUE_PASSWORD	Specifies that users cannot reuse passwords	#UNIQUE_PASSWORD

Step 3: Review

In this task, you learned the MAKEUSER utility and key words. Remember that once you create a MAKEUSER script, you can use it repeatedly to create new or change existing user accounts. You might find MAKEUSER particularly useful in many instances. You can use MAKEUSER, for example, to restore bindery information by re-creating accounts after a disk failure.

Using USERDEF

The USERDEF utility also creates users in bulk—like the MAKEUSER utility. USERDEF, however, is more powerful and provides more functionality. The difference is that MAKEUSER uses a script format and enables the Supervisor to create and delete users, whereas USERDEF is a template that enables you only to create users.

The additional capabilities provided by USERDEF are as follows:

☐ Assigns disk space limitations to multiple users

☐ Creates print job configurations for new users

These two additional functions make the Supervisor's job easier. Before USERDEF, copying print job configurations to user mailbox directories was tedious. Now USERDEF automates the process.

Note: Only the Supervisor or Supervisor-equivalent can run the USERDEF utility.

Before you can use the USERDEF utility, you must create a template.

Task 8.3: Creating a USERDEF template.

Step 1: Description

In this task, you create or select a template to use the USERDEF utility to create user accounts. The USERDEF template provides a more user-friendly, graphical interface for the Supervisor to customize user parameters.

Step 2: Action

1. Type **LOGIN SUPERVISOR** at the DOS prompt and press Enter. Provide a password, if required, and press Enter.

2. To change to the \PUBLIC subdirectory, type **CD\PUBLIC** and press Enter.

3. Type **USERDEF** and press Enter. You should see the Available Options menu, as shown in Figure 8.5.

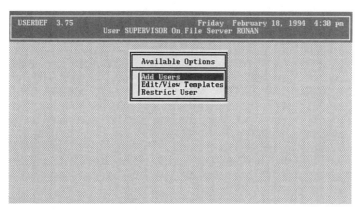

Figure 8.5. *Available Options menu.*

4. Select Edit/View Templates and press Enter. The Templates screen appears.

5. Press Ins and, in the Template box, type in **CLERK** as the template you are creating. Then press Enter.

6. Move the cursor down to Edit Parameters and press Enter. You then see the template parameters on-screen (see Figure 8.6).

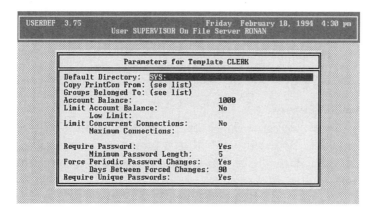

Figure 8.6. *Template parameters.*

7. Change entries from the defaults to your choices and press Esc.

8. Confirm your choices in the Save Changes box.

9. Move the cursor up to Edit Login Script and press Enter. The login script then appears on-screen (see Figure 8.7).

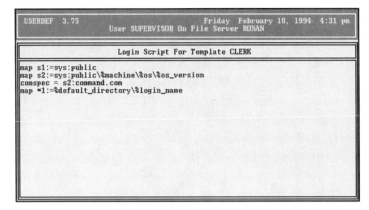

Figure 8.7. *Login script.*

10. Add mappings and other commands for the login script. You learn how to create login scripts in Chapter 11.

> **Warning:** Don't change or delete the default mappings. If you do, NetWare might not be able to find the location of commands entered by the user.

11. Press Esc and confirm changes.

12. Press Esc until you are asked to confirm your exit from USERDEF.

Step 3: Review

With this task, you created or selected a template to use the USERDEF utility to create user accounts. As stated, the USERDEF template provides a more user-friendly, graphical interface for the Supervisor or Supervisor-equivalent to customize user accounts.

Task 8.4: Creating users with USERDEF.

Step 1: Description

In this task, you use the USERDEF utility to create user accounts. The USERDEF template provides a more user-friendly, graphical interface for the Supervisor to customize user parameters.

Step 2: Action

1. As Supervisor or Supervisor-equivalent, log in.

2. To change to the \PUBLIC subdirectory, type **CD\PUBLIC** and press Enter.

3. Type **USERDEF** and press Enter. The Available Options menu appears.

4. Select Add Users and press Enter. The Templates menu appears.

5. Move the cursor to CLERK and press Enter.

6. Press Ins when you see the Users list.

7. Type the full name in the Full Name box and press Enter (see Figure 8.8).

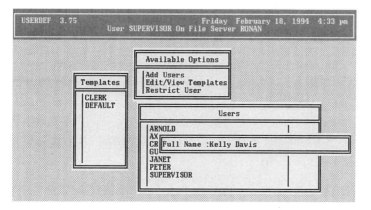

Figure 8.8. *Full Name box.*

8. Type the user's assigned login name in the Login Name: box and press Enter.

9. Repeat steps 5 through 8 for each user you want to add.

10. Press Esc to confirm new users.

11. Select Yes from the Create New Users Using Template CLERK message to exit.

12. Confirm your intent by selecting Yes to create the new user.

13. Press Esc until you are asked to confirm your exit from USERDEF.

Step 3: Review

In this task, you learned that USERDEF provides a means for a Supervisor to create user accounts. Unlike MAKEUSER, you cannot delete users using USERDEF.

Implementing Workgroup Management

To simplify the management of users, you create groups, Workgroup Managers, Account Manager and Supervisor-equivalent accounts. Each has a role in the smooth and safe running of your file server.

Creating Groups

After creating user accounts, you may want to create group accounts and add users to them. Groups simplify administration because you can assign rights at the group level. Let's look at creating group accounts.

Task 8.5: Creating a user group account using SYSCON.

Step 1: Description

In this task, you use the SYSCON utility to create new groups.

Step 2: Action

1. Log in as either the Supervisor or a Supervisor-equivalent.

2. To change to the \PUBLIC subdirectory, type **CD\PUBLIC** and press Enter.

3. Type **SYSCON** and press Enter. The Available Topics menu appears.

4. Highlight Group Information and press Enter. You then see the Group Names list.

5. Press Ins.

6. Type the new user group account name **ACCOUNTING** in the New Group Name: box and press Enter (see Figure 8.9).

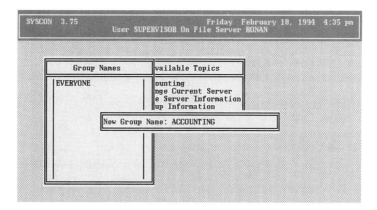

Figure 8.9. *New Group Name box.*

7. Press Esc until you are asked to confirm your exit from SYSCON.

Step 3: Review

With this task, you created your first user group account. You create groups so that users can share files.

8

Assigning Special Accounts

The Supervisor's job can become overwhelming as more and more users are added to the network. User demands and daily management tasks can take over. NetWare therefore provides the capability to distribute network management. NetWare enables the system manager to create a variety of distributed managers and console operators. These managers and operators have unique privileges that allow them to oversee small or large groups of users. SYSCON provides the facility for assigning four of the six distributed network managers—Supervisor-equivalent, Workgroup Manager, user Account Manager, and console operators. Now look at the first: Supervisor-equivalent.

Creating a Supervisor-Equivalent Account

You may find that having just one Supervisor account does not provide you with the timely, efficient service your organization needs. If this is the case, you can create Supervisor-equivalent accounts. Supervisor-equivalents can do anything the Supervisor account can.

Task 8.6: Setting Supervisor-security equivalence using SYSCON.

Step 1: Description

In this task, you use the SYSCON utility to create a user with security equivalence to the Supervisor account. This task shows how the Supervisor can grant Supervisor-equivalence to another user.

Step 2: Action

1. To change to the \PUBLIC subdirectory, type **CD\PUBLIC** and press Enter.

2. Type **SYSCON** and press Enter. The Available Topics menu appears.

3. Move the cursor down to User Information and press Enter.

4. Select the user to get Supervisor-equivalence from the User Names list and press Enter.

5. From the User Information menu, highlight Security Equivalence and press Enter.

6. Press Ins to see the Other Users and Groups list.

7. Move the cursor down to Supervisor and press Enter. Supervisor is added to the Security Equivalences list (see Figure 8.10).

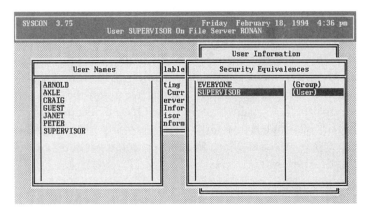

Figure 8.10. *Security Equivalences list.*

8. Press Esc until you are asked to confirm your exit from SYSCON.

Step 3: Review

With this task, you created a Supervisor-equivalent account. You can use the facility to give any user security equivalence to another user.

Task 8.7: Canceling Supervisor-security equivalence using SYSCON.

Step 1: Description

If you determine you don't need a Supervisor-equivalent account or you have too many, you can use the SYSCON utility to delete a Supervisor-equivalent account. This task shows how the Supervisor can cancel Supervisor-equivalence of another user.

Step 2: Action

1. To change to the \PUBLIC subdirectory, type **CD\PUBLIC** and press Enter.

2. Type **SYSCON** and press Enter. The Available Topics menu appears.

3. Highlight User Information and press Enter.

4. Select the user from whom you want to remove Supervisor-equivalence from the User Names list and press Enter.

5. From the User Information menu, select Security Equivalence and press Enter.

6. Highlight SUPERVISOR and press Delete.

7. Press Esc until you are asked to confirm your exit from SYSCON.

Step 3: Review

In this task, you removed Supervisor-equivalent from an account.

You can use the SECURITY command-line utility to determine who has Supervisor-equivalence on your system. SECURITY reports on objects with Supervisor-equivalence. Assigning additional Supervisor-equivalent accounts can open wide a door for a potential unauthorized individual. You should be concerned about the number of these accounts. An easy way for attackers to take over your system is to place what astrophysicist Cliff Stoll called a "cuckoo's egg" on your system. Using SYSCON, you can get a list of users. It then is an easy task to find out Supervisor-equivalents. One way is to look at directories and determine who is updating them. After you determine who's in charge, you just replace one of that person's executables with a made-up name of your own. When the Supervisor-equivalent next runs the program, it executes your changes as well. You have now taken over the system.

Note: Cliff Stoll is the author of the best seller titled *The Cuckoo's Egg*. In this book, Cliff explains how he tries to enlist the aid of those three-letter agencies (for example, the CIA) to track a system cracker. It is fascinating reading.

Task 8.8: Checking for Supervisor equivalence.

Step 1: Description

In this task, you use the SECURITY command-line utility to check for other objects with Supervisor-equivalence. You can view the information online or save it to a file for later analysis. You find the SECURITY CLU in SYS:SYSTEM.

Step 2: Action

At the DOS prompt, type **SECURITY [file name]** ¦ **[/C]** and press Enter. Substitute the name of the file where you want to redirect the output for *file name*. Use /C when you want to have continuous information. Leaving off this variable means that the utility pauses when the screen becomes full and continues when you press any key.

Step 3: Review

In this task, you learned to use SECURITY to check for accounts with Supervisor-equivalence. Chapter 25 provides a more detailed explanation of the SECURITY CLU.

In the following section, you take a longer look at security-equivalence.

Understanding Security Equivalence

At this point, you probably are wondering why you might create an account equivalent to another account. Well, look at some actual examples. How many times have you seen this situation? Someone goes on vacation, and inevitably someone else needs access to the files. To preserve the user's accountability, you don't want to reset the password to provide access. Instead, the Supervisor can make the second user security-equivalent to the first user. When you give a user security-equivalence, he or she not only has his or her own trustee rights, but the rights of the first user.

Warning: Be sure you know what you are doing. Giving Supervisor-equivalence provides access to all files and directories. If all the user needs is access to certain files, you can assign group trustee rights to a directory so that users can share files.

A number-one rule for preserving the accountability of user accounts is that they are not shared. You should never share the Supervisor account! Instead, you can create Supervisor-like accounts. This way, you can remove certain rights from the second account. You also only use the omnipotent account for dire situations.

Following are rules for understanding security equivalence:

☐ Security equivalence is not inherited. If user A and B are security-equivalent, for example, and B and C are security-equivalent, then A and C are not automatically security equivalent. This feature prevents you from granting security equivalence to a group; otherwise, you might make a group Supervisor equivalent.

☐ Security equivalence is unidirectional. If user A is security-equivalent to B, for example, B is not automatically security-equivalent to A.

☐ Security equivalence is nondiscriminatory. If user A is security-equivalent to B, for example, B might be security-equivalent to A, or the rights assigned to one user are available to another user.

Using security-equivalence for managing the use of the Supervisor account is asking for problems. Different users manage the file server differently. This situation can lead to inconsistencies. A better way to manage users and groups is to create Workgroup Managers.

Creating a Workgroup Manager

You can create Workgroup Manager accounts to help with system administration. Earlier in this chapter, you saw that Workgroup Managers can create, manage, and delete assigned user and group accounts. Within their sphere of influence, Workgroup Managers are omnipotent.

Task 8.9: Creating a Workgroup Manager account using SYSCON.

Step 1: Description
In this task, you use the SYSCON utility to create a Workgroup Manager account.

Step 2: Action
1. To change to the \PUBLIC subdirectory, type **CD\PUBLIC** and press Enter.

2. Type **SYSCON** and press Enter. The Available Topics menu appears.

3. Select Supervisor Options and press Enter. The Supervisor Options menu opens.

4. Highlight Workgroup Managers and press Enter.

5. From the Workgroup Managers window, press Ins.

6. From the Other Users and Groups menu, highlight JANET and press Enter. You then see that JANET is added to the Workgroup Managers list, similar to Figure 8.11.

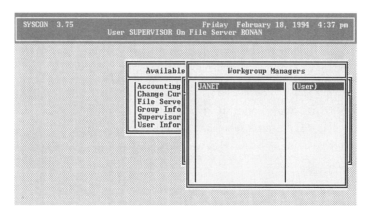

Figure 8.11. *Workgroup Managers.*

7. Press Esc until you are asked to confirm your exit from SYSCON.

Step 3: Review
With this task, you created your first Workgroup Manager account.

Creating an Account Manager

You can create Account Manager accounts to help with system administration. Earlier in this chapter, you saw that Account Managers can manage, and deleted assigned user accounts.

Task 8.10: Creating an Account Manager using SYSCON.

Step 1: Description

In this task, you use the SYSCON utility to create an Account Manager account.

Step 2: Action

1. To change to the \PUBLIC subdirectory, type **CD\PUBLIC** and press Enter.

2. Type **SYSCON** and press Enter. The Available Topics menu appears.

3. Move the cursor down to User Information and press Enter. The User Names list appears.

4. Move the cursor down to JANET and press Enter. The User Information box appears (see Figure 8.12).

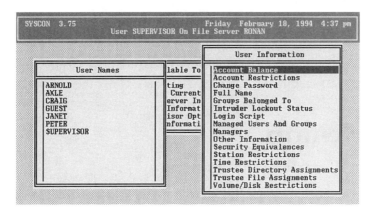

Figure 8.12. *User information.*

5. Move the cursor down to Managed Users and Groups and press Enter.

6. From the Managed Users and Groups window, press Ins.

7. From the Other Users and Groups menu, select ACCOUNTING and press Enter. Making this change means that JANET will manage the group.

8. Press Esc until you are asked to confirm your exit from SYSCON.

Step 3: Review

With this task, you created your first Account Manager account.

For now, you've reached the end of the discussion of special accounts in particular and accounts in general. You most likely would agree that you have covered a great deal of information today. Let's call it a day right now. Don't forget to review the chapter summary and try the workshop.

Summary

In this chapter, you learned about the following:

- ☐ User accounts in general

- ☐ Supervisor and Supervisor-equivalent accounts

- ☐ Workgroup and Account Managers

Now you should be thoroughly familiar with the SYSCON utility. You use it again in subsequent chapters, but you must be comfortable with it now.

Take time to practice using SYSCON to create and delete users. Practice, as they say, makes perfect. On Day 5, you study passwords and their management.

Workshop
Terminology Review

access—The capability and the means necessary to approach, to store, or to retrieve data, to communicate with, and to make use of any resource of a computer system.

access period—A segment of time, generally expressed on a daily or weekly basis, when access rights prevail.

accountability—The quality or state that enables violations or attempted violations of a system security to be traced to individuals who may then be held responsible.

grant—To authorize.

Supervisor—The Network Supervisor is the person responsible for the operation of the network. The Network Supervisor maintains the network, reconfiguring and updating it as the need arises.

Task List

The emphasis of this chapter has been to introduce you to accounts and their management. As a system administrator or Supervisor, you will repeatedly use these commands in your daily work. The tasks you should understand from this chapter are as follows:

- ☐ Using SYSCON
- ☐ Using MAKEUSER
- ☐ Using USERDEF
- ☐ Creating user accounts
- ☐ Creating security-equivalent accounts
- ☐ Finding Supervisor-equivalent accounts
- ☐ Creating Workgroup Managers
- ☐ Creating Account Managers

8

Q&A

Q Should you keep the GUEST account?

A As mentioned, the GUEST account is used to print jobs by users who do not have accounts on your server. So, if your organization's policy is to require users to have unique accounts to provide accountability, you will remove the GUEST account. At the minimum, you may decide to delete GUEST from the EVERYONE group. If you want to allow a GUEST to print jobs, then just add GUEST as a queue user to a print queue using the PCONSOLE utility. You will learn about the PCONSOLE utility in Chapter 23.

Q Should you keep the group EVERYONE?

A You can delete it if you want; however, it has limited security and default login restrictions. The system creates EVERYONE to provide global configuration and security access for all users. The group includes all users on the system, present and future. If you delete the group, you will need another way to send broadcasts and grant security to certain files.

Q Should users share accounts?

A No. The whole reason for having account names is to provide accountability for the actions of the account. If users share an account, how do you tie the actions of the account to one user? You cannot. As soon as you have problems with a shared account, everybody will be doing a lot of finger pointing.

Q When should you use the SUPERVISOR account?

A The SUPERVISOR account should only be used for problem resolution, and for setting up security restrictions and managers and operators. SUPERVISOR and Supervisor-equivalent accounts should not be used for sending electronic mail, accessing network services or composing documents.

Q Who should have Supervisor equivalence?

A Because Supervisor-equivalent accounts are as powerful as the SUPERVISOR account, and they provide a back door to your network, the answer is as few as possible.

Q When would I assign managers and operators?

A The decision to assign managers and operators is really one of decentralization versus centralization. If your organization is centralized, then you will most likely not decentralize the administration of security. On the other hand, if you are decentralized, then create as many operators and managers as you need.

Q What should my usernames look like?

A Your organization should have a standard for the composition of passwords to which all NetWare usernames should adhere. If you are developing a standard for usernames, use something meaningful, for example, the user's last name and first initial. Remember that usernames are not meant to be security mechanisms. You may use them as electronic mail addresses, and they are lot easier to use if they are meaningful.

Day

5

9

Managing Passwords

In the preceding chapter, you looked at creating assorted accounts. In this chapter and Chapter 10, you learn more about controlling accounts. These two chapters deal primarily with account maintenance. Also in Chapter 10, you delve deeply into restricting accounts.

This chapter covers passwords and the parameters associated with them. You probably have direct experience with passwords. Indeed, you might think that passwords are something you know plenty about, but take the time to study this chapter. Because of NetWare's nature, passwords are the major control mechanism on your system. One poorly administered or derived password can put all your valuable data at risk. Many users consider passwords a waste of time. The problem is that once one unauthorized individual has access to one account, that individual can compromise the whole network.

The stories about systems broken into owing to poor passwords are too numerous to name in this book. Maybe you have heard of Robert Morris Jr. and Cliff Stoll's wily hacker. If you haven't, you should pick up a book dealing with local area network security and control. At this time, you should have an appreciation for the need for passwords. Consequently, in this chapter you learn how to manage passwords and ensure that other users understand the need for good passwords.

Understanding User Account Passwords

In NetWare, passwords are optional but highly recommended. They provide an effective strategy for filtering out unwanted users. NetWare provides a number of restrictions for passwords. Password protection can be enhanced by making passwords mandatory, setting minimum lengths, or expiring them after a set period of time.

Note: Supervisors, Supervisor-equivalents, workgroup managers, account managers, and the users themselves can change passwords. You must be aware of this capability as you set up password administration.

It is a good idea to assign a password immediately upon completion of the creation of a user account. Users can then choose and change the passwords you created. In this manner, you are not aware of the users' passwords. This process enhances the users' accountability. The following lesson on how the system uses the password might help your understanding.

Understanding Login Security

The user logs in to the network by specifying the file server name and a username. The system verifies the username by matching it against an object in the NET$OBJ.SYS bindery file. You learned about the bindery and its associated files in Chapter 7.

If the system verifies the username, it searches the NET$PROP.SYS file for a password property. If one exists, the system responds with `Password:`. If a password doesn't exist, the system logs in the individual. The procedure is somewhat different if passwords are required as a system default. In this case, whether or not the username exists, NetWare prompts for a password. This approach fools would-be hackers into thinking they've used a valid username.

Note: Some users may not have passwords. Although logging in users without passwords is not recommended, the system does not prompt these users for a password.

9

Passwords are used to authenticate the user. A generally accepted technique for providing authentication is to exchange privileged information or, in general terms, use a password. To be authenticated, a password must be sent to a file server over the network. Unless the line is physically protected or the password is encrypted, the password is vulnerable to discovery during transmission. Because of this vulnerability, NetWare 3.12 has a password encryption facility.

Note: You must ensure the confidentiality of passwords. In versions up to and including NetWare 2.2, passwords were broadcast across the network in *clear text*. Anyone who could wiretap and read the protocols could capture passwords. NetWare 3.12, however, can protect passwords through *password encryption*, which means that passwords are encoded so that only the file server can decode the password.

At the password prompt, the encryption logic in the login program takes over. You must remember that you still have a connectionless communication. Assuming that the user logs in using the LOGIN.EXE program, LOGIN.EXE sends a message to the server requesting an *encryption key*. The server at this point is still doubtful about the outcome of the relationship, but it returns a 64-bit key to the workstation. The key is unique for every request for a key from a workstation. The LOGIN.EXE program uses the key and encryption algorithm to encrypt the password. The workstation then transmits the encrypted password, as requested by the Password: prompt. Notice that the LOGIN.EXE program prevents the password from being displayed on the screen when you enter it. This capability is another form of protection offered by the LOGIN program.

Note: By default, NetWare 3.12 requires workstations to log in using encrypted passwords. Workstations therefore must use a version of LOGIN that supports encryption.

Warning: You should never place passwords in the AUTOEXEC.BAT file as follows:

```
LOGIN PETER < C:\SECPASS
```

Even though this statement is perfectly legitimate, it represents a serious password exposure. Anyone who can read your AUTOEXEC.BAT file can obtain your username and password, which can affect your accountability.

Because the server knows the key and the algorithm, it can compare the password to the bindery entry. Incidentally, the system stores the password encrypted in the bindery. If the username is valid, NetWare compares the decrypted password to the value in NET$VAL.SYS. If the username is not valid, the system bypasses the search and responds with Access Denied.

Note: Experience will ultimately prove to you that invalid usernames respond more rapidly with Access Denied. NetWare doesn't search the bindery for passwords for invalid usernames. For valid usernames, NetWare takes noticeably longer while it searches the NET$VAL.SYS.

If the user enters a correct username and password combination, the user is granted conditional access[md]conditional, in that NetWare compares your access requests to the bindery for authority. If not, the system responds with `Access Denied`. The user is left at NetWare's portal. If access is not denied, the system matches the username with a variety of additional bindery values—login restrictions. You learn about login restrictions in Chapter 10.

Turning Off Encryption

Throughout the 14 days of learning NetWare administration, you will notice a number of good facilities that you can turn off. Encryption is one of them. Should you decide, you can turn off encryption. Why would you want to turn off this facility? The answer this time is easy. Earlier versions of NetWare (for example, 2.2) don't support encryption. NetWare 386 workstations' LOGIN programs perform encryption, whereas NetWare 286 workstations do not. So, if you need to mix NetWare 2.2 and NetWare 3.12 servers, you must turn off encryption.

Task 9.1: Turning off encryption.

Step 1: Description
In this task, you turn off encryption at the system console.

Step 2: Action
1. At the console prompt, type the following:

   ```
   SET ALLOW UNENCRYPTED PASSWORDS=ON
   ```

   You see the following message on the console:

   ```
   Allow Unencrypted Passwords set to ON
   :
   ```

2. To reverse this command, type the following at the console prompt:

   ```
   SET ALLOW UNENCRYPTED PASSWORDS=OFF
   ```

   You then see the following message on the console:

   ```
   Allow Unencrypted Passwords set to OFF
   :
   ```

9

Step 3: Review

In this task, you toggled password encryption on and off. You should know that NetWare 2.*x* workstations can run NetWare 3.12's NETX and LOGIN. Running these programs is infinitely more desirable than turning off encryption.

Creating Strong Passwords

As you just learned, passwords are an integral part of login security, so it behooves you to create strong passwords. A NetWare password can consist of any ASCII character except the 32 control characters. Passwords are case insensitive—all lowercase passwords are converted to uppercase.

> **Tip:** A space is valid in a password, but you cannot use it to begin or end a password. Because you can use spaces, you can create sentences or phrases. A phrase or sentence may provide extra protection while being easier to remember. EVERY GOOD BOY, for example, is a valid password.

A NetWare password can have from 1 to 127 characters. Thinking of a good password is not easy. A good password is something the user can remember but others won't guess. Some passwords are too obvious or easily guessed. Passwords to avoid are

- ☐ Words in the dictionary
- ☐ First and last names
- ☐ Street and city names
- ☐ Valid license plate numbers
- ☐ Room numbers, Social Security numbers, social insurance numbers, and telephone numbers
- ☐ Beer and liquor brands
- ☐ Athletic teams
- ☐ Days of the week and months of the year
- ☐ Repetitive characters
- ☐ Software default passwords

Other systems prevent users from selecting weak passwords or dictate the format of the password—for example, AAANAA where A is alphabetic and N is numeric. However, NetWare does not prevent weak passwords. Even so, you can educate your users about passwords. Education, in some respects, is one of your best controls anyway. Your users might subvert any password mechanism you put in place should they not understand the need for it, or perceive you as not having the authority to implement and enforce it.

The temptation for users to create weak passwords is overpowering. Paradoxically, you want to allow users to change their passwords, yet you want strong passwords. Fortunately, NetWare provides several password controls from which you can choose. With some password basics under your belt, it's time to make some decisions. For today's tasks, you make decisions about password options and parameters for the system and individual users. Refer to Figure 9.1 for the discussion of these decisions.

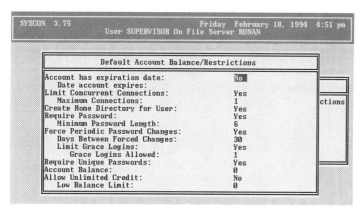

Figure 9.1. *Password parameters.*

Requiring Passwords

Every username created on the system has a bindery password property associated with it. However, NetWare, by default, does not call for a password. You need to change this default quickly because you have valuable information you want to protect.

A review of your network reveals spreadsheet, word processing, and electronic mail applications. These applications sound harmless, don't they? They do until you start investigating what users are really doing out there. A quick review of files might show you sales projections for the new gizmo to be launched next month, lists of credit card numbers including expiration dates, performance appraisals, and memos about a dissatisfied customer. Until you take the time to convince yourself that this example is not the case on your network, you can assume it is. You therefore need to protect users from themselves and others. One good way is to require users to enter a password every time they log in.

Another good reason for using passwords is *accountability*. For example, a payroll clerk phones you in a panic and accuses everybody on the planet of altering a critical and confidential file. So you must investigate these serious allegations. It is a simple task—provided you keep adequate audit trails—to show the clerk that someone in payroll is the culprit. Accountability means that you can trace activities to individuals who may then be held responsible. So due diligence calls for the use of passwords for every user account (yes, including Guest).

Enabling Users to Change Passwords

Another NetWare option enables users to change their own passwords. Normally, you want to relieve yourself of the burden of changing all the passwords. On top of that, users can pick a password that is meaningful to them. Assigned passwords are usually dull, meaningless, and resented. Users are more apt to write down assigned passwords. Furthermore, the accountability principle calls for the user to be the only one who knows the password.

In some instances, you might not allow the users to change their passwords. Can you imagine the potential chaos when someone changes the Guest password used for network printing? You probably can think of other situations where users cannot change their passwords. Hopefully, these situations do not arise because users are sharing accounts. Remember the accountability principle!

Setting Minimum Password Length

If you call for the use of a password, you must set a minimum length. As Supervisor, you can specify a password from 1 to 20 characters for the minimum length. The default minimum is 5 characters. Remember the longer the password, the harder it is to guess. Generally, the shorter the password, the easier it is for someone to guess it. Short passwords are more susceptible to a *brute-force attack*.

Tip: Enterprising individuals have written programs that run against NetWare's bindery to guess passwords. They use computerized trial-and-error attempts to crack passwords by trying dictionary words, or even every possible combination. This approach is known as a brute-force attack because nothing about its approach or methods is subtle.

You discover two lessons here. First, don't allow passwords less than six characters. Second, you should monitor programs running against the bindery. Potentially, you are under a brute-force attack.

Using combinations of seven letters and numbers (exactly 78,364,164,096), there are enough combinations for more than 300 passwords for every person in the United States.

Forcing Periodic Password Changes

Once you require passwords and set a reasonable minimum length, you need to decide whether you want to force users to change their passwords. Again, unless you have a valid business reason for not forcing users to change their passwords periodically, they should.

Setting Days Between Forced Changes

Now comes the hard part. After you decide that users must change their passwords periodically, what should you make that period? The answer is simple: it depends. The system default is 45 days. This number is short for some users and can quickly become bothersome; it is too long for other users, such as you. For users who have limited authority and only use electronic mail, you might want to set the interval to 90 days. That means, these users change their passwords four times a year, which seems a reasonable expectation.

Note: When the periodic password limit expires, NetWare prompts the user for a new password at the next login. If the user isn't allowed grace logins, this is the user's one chance to change the password. Otherwise, the user can log in and use SETPASS or SYSCON to change the password.

On the other hand, any account that is Supervisor-equivalent should change the password more frequently; for example, 30 days.

Once again, you should set the password interval parameters to balance the business need and good security practices.

Setting Grace Logins Allowed and Limited Grace Logins

When the password interval expires, the users must enter new passwords. If the users don't enter new passwords, then the system locks them out, unless they have *grace logins*. Grace logins allow users to log in without selecting new passwords. NetWare defaults to seven grace logins. On the seventh, therefore, they have to change their passwords; otherwise, they cannot log back in with those passwords.

If you can think of any situations where you require a grace login, use it. Otherwise, set grace logins to one and force a change when a change is necessary. When a user reaches the maximum number of logins without changing the password, the system locks out the user, and the Supervisor must unlock the account.

Setting Password Expiration Date

Another option you have to set is a date for the expiration of the password. The password no longer works after that day, regardless of its value. You can use this feature when you believe a password has been compromised.

 Note: Should you call for the use of passwords, the account's password is automatically set to January 1, 1985 when you create a new account.

Requiring Unique Passwords

If you force periodic password changes, you may prevent the user from repeating passwords. If you don't require unique passwords, the user can change the password from alpha to beta and back to alpha. This situation is exactly why this option arose. Normally, you want users to change their passwords because you are worried whether the password is still confidential. You don't require a change to improve typing skills. So allowing users to use the original passwords defeats the purpose of forcing password changes.

If you decide a user needs unique passwords, NetWare maintains a table of the last eight passwords. After the eighth password, the user can repeat the pattern all over again and use the same passwords. Now, you might think that users can just write a routine to change the password nine times back to what it was. Not quite. NetWare makes the users keep each one of their passwords a minimum of one day. So they must spend eight days to get around it. Hopefully, after changing their password for eight days, they'll give up. Changing their passwords in this fashion has to be more work than changing it once a month. However, there is a slight hitch to the password history feature.

> **Note:** NetWare allows you to change your password as many times as you want during a day (as long as it's not on the previously used password list). However, NetWare does a daily save of the current password to the previously used password list.

In Tasks 9.2 and 9.3, you practice what you just learned about passwords.

Task 9.2: Requiring and restricting by default.

Step 1: Description
In this task, you use the SYSCON utility to require users to provide a password.

Step 2: Action
1. To change to the \PUBLIC subdirectory, type **CD\PUBLIC** and press Enter.

2. As the Supervisor, type **SYSCON** and press Enter. The Available Topics menu appears.

3. Highlight Supervisor Options and press Enter. The Supervisor Options menu appears.

4. Highlight Default Account Balance/Restrictions and press Enter. You then see the Default Account Balance/Restrictions box, as shown in Figure 9.2.

5. Move the cursor down to Require Password, type **Yes**, and press Enter.

6. Enter a Minimum Password Length and press Enter. This length ideally should be six or more characters.

7. Type **Yes** for Force Periodic Password Changes and then press Enter.

9

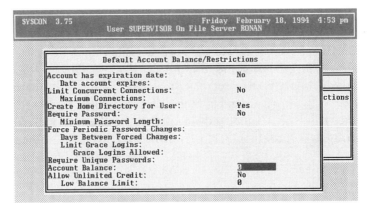

Figure 9.2. *Default Account Balance/Restrictions box.*

8. Enter the number of Days Between Forced Changes and press Enter. This number ideally should be 30 days.

9. Type **Yes** for Limit Grace Logins and then press Enter.

10. Enter the number of Grace Logins Allowed and press Enter. This number ideally should be one day.

11. Type **Yes** for Require Unique Passwords and then press Enter. Your screen now should look similar to Figure 9.3.

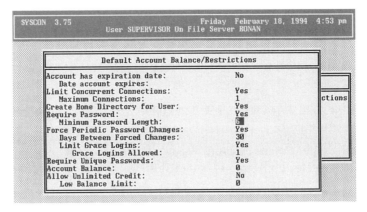

Figure 9.3. *Require unique passwords.*

12. Press Esc until you are asked to confirm your exit from SYSCON.

Step 3: Review

With this task, you set default password restrictions for all users.

Before you go any further and set up restrictions for individual users, you should take a look back at creating strong passwords using NetWare's options.

Task 9.3: Requiring and restricting passwords for individual users.

Step 1: Description

In this task, you use the SYSCON utility to require individual users to provide a password.

Step 2: Action

1. To change to the \PUBLIC subdirectory, type **CD\PUBLIC** and press Enter.

2. Type **SYSCON** and press Enter. The Available Topics menu appears.

3. Move the cursor down to User Information and press Enter. You see the User Names list.

4. Select JANET and press Enter.

5. Move the cursor down to Account Restrictions and press Enter. You then see the Account Restrictions For User JANET box, as shown in Figure 9.4.

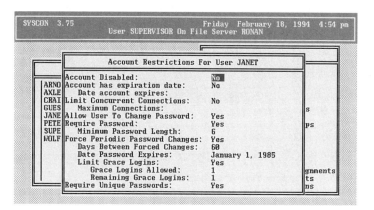

Figure 9.4. *Account Restrictions For User JANET box.*

6. Move the cursor down to Require Password, type **Yes**, and press Enter.

7. Enter a Minimum Password Length and press Enter. This length ideally should be six or more characters.

8. Type **Yes** for Force Periodic Password Changes and press Enter.

9. Enter the number of Days Between Forced Changes and press Enter. This number ideally should be 30 days.

10. Type **Yes** for Limit Grace Logins and press Enter.

11. Enter the number of Grace Logins Allowed and press Enter. This number ideally should be one day.

12. Type **Yes** for Require Unique Passwords and then press Enter. Your screen now should look similar to Figure 9.5.

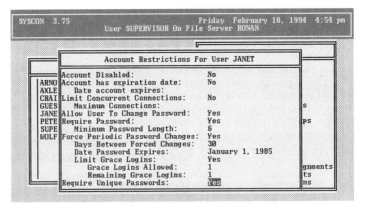

SYSCON 3.75   Friday February 18, 1994 4:54 pm
                    User SUPERVISOR On File Server RONAN

```
          ┌─────────────────────────────────────────────┐
          │       Account Restrictions For User  JANET   │
     ┌────┤Account Disabled:              No             │
     │ARNO│Account has expiration date:   No             │
     │AXLE│   Date account expires:                      │
     │CRAI│Limit Concurrent Connections:  No             │
     │GUES│   Maximum Connections:                       │s
     │JANE│Allow User To Change Password: Yes            │
     │PETE│Require Password:              Yes            │ps
     │SUPE│   Minimum Password Length:    6              │
     │WOLF│Force Periodic Password Changes: Yes          │
     │    │   Days Between Forced Changes:  30           │
     │    │   Date Password Expires:      January 1, 1985│
     │    │   Limit Grace Logins:         Yes            │
     │    │      Grace Logins Allowed:    1              │gnments
     │    │      Remaining Grace Logins:  1              │ts
     └────┤Require Unique Passwords:      Yes            │ns
          └─────────────────────────────────────────────┘
```

Figure 9.5. *Updated Account Restrictions For User JANET box.*

13. Press Esc until you are asked to confirm your exit from SYSCON.

Step 3: Review

In this task, you set password restrictions for an individual user. Setting restrictions is important because you may want to have more stringent controls over some users' network use. A user who accesses the network just to send electronic mail, for instance, calls for a different level of security than the Supervisor.

Creating or Resetting Passwords

Someone in authority needs to create or reset passwords. Resetting passwords is one of the main reasons you set up workgroup and account managers. The Supervisor needs to reset many passwords otherwise. You need to reset passwords because nobody, including the Supervisor, can see unencrypted passwords. If a user forgets a password, the Supervisor or designate can use SETPASS or SYSCON to change the password to something new. This feature preserves the concept of accountability. Otherwise, you cannot hold someone accountable when he or she can show that other people can access his or her password.

Task 9.4: Creating or changing a password using SYSCON.

Step 1: Description

In this task, you use the SYSCON utility to create or change a user's password.

Step 2: Action

1. To change to the \PUBLIC subdirectory, type **CD\PUBLIC** and press Enter.

2. Type **SYSCON** and press Enter. The Available Topics menu appears.

3. Move the cursor down to User Information and press Enter. You then see the User Names list.

4. Move the cursor down to JANET and press Enter. The User Information box appears.

5. Move the cursor down to Change Password and press Enter. The Enter New Password box appears (see Figure 9.6).

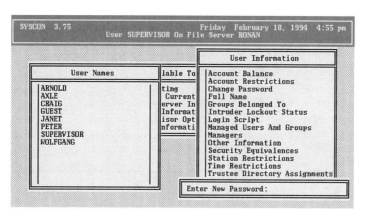

Figure 9.6. *Change Password screen.*

6. Type **ACCMGR** in the Enter New Password dialog box and press Enter.

7. Type **ACCMGR** in the Retype New Password dialog box and press Enter.

8. Press Esc until you are asked to confirm your exit from SYSCON.

Step 3: Review

In this task, you changed a user's password. You should pick passwords that are not easily guessed.

Task 9.5: Changing a password using SETPASS.

Step 1: Description

In this task, you use the SETPASS utility to change your password.

Step 2: Action

1. At the DOS prompt, type **SETPASS** and press Enter.

2. Type your old password at the prompt.

3. Type your new password at the prompt.

4. Retype your new password at the prompt. (See Figure 9.7.)

```
F>setpass
Enter old password for RONAN/SUPERVISOR:
Enter new password for RONAN/SUPERVISOR:
Retype new password for RONAN/SUPERVISOR:
Password for RONAN/SUPERVISOR has been changed.

F>
```

Figure 9.7. *Changing passwords.*

Step 3: Review

Users can use SYSCON or SETPASS to change their passwords. If you are the Supervisor, you can use either SYSCON or SETPASS to change a user's password.

 Typing **SETPASS BALLIOL/JANET**, for example, allows the Supervisor to change the password for account JANET on server BALLIOL.

Remembering many different passwords can be difficult. If you give considerable thought to creating a strong password, you can use it across file servers. You use SETPASS to synchronize your password on all file servers.

When you're deciding on whether you want one password across file servers, you should give some thought to your authorities on each file server. If they are similar on each file server, then using one password is probably okay. We don't recommend that you synchronize your passwords if you are the Supervisor.

Task 9.6: Synchronizing passwords on all servers.

Step 1: Description

In this task, you change your password on one file server and, if you have the same password on multiple servers, change it on them as well.

Step 2: Action

1. Attach to all file servers where you have the same username and password. (Refer to Task 6.4 if you forget how to use the ATTACH command.)

2. At the DOS prompt, type **SETPASS** [*default server name*] and press Enter.

3. Type your old password at the prompt.

4. Type your new password at the prompt.

5. Retype your new password at the prompt.

6. Confirm that you want to synchronize all passwords.

Step 3: Review

In this task, you learned how to use SETPASS to synchronize your passwords on all servers.

Checking Security of Passwords

You should be concerned that users are choosing secure passwords. But how can you monitor their choices when you cannot view user passwords? A number of products, such as BindView, enable you to scan for password problems. Although these products are good, NetWare does come with a command-line utility for looking at security exposures. To inspect your system for potential holes in password security setup, you can run the SECURITY command-line utility found in SYS:SYSTEM, as shown in Task 9.7. This utility checks through the bindery and identifies any password problems it finds.

SECURITY reports on the following password problems:

☐ No password assigned

☐ Insecure passwords

☐ Password too short

"No password assigned" and "password too short" are obvious. You should consider whether this account should really have no password associated with it. One account without a password assigned may be Guest. If you don't require a password for Guest, anyone can log in and use SYSCON, FILER, and other utilities. Using these utilities, this person can obtain a list of users and file servers and scan part of the directory structure (unless the directories are hidden). For more information, see Chapter 14.

Nonsecure passwords are passwords that are the same as the username. SYSCON and SETPASS do not allow nonsecure passwords, but older versions did, and these accounts may be vestigial.

Task 9.7: Checking password security.

Step 1: Description

As Supervisor, you can use the SECURITY command-line utility to monitor users' passwords as shown in this task. You can view the information online or save it to a file for later analysis.

Step 2: Action

At the DOS prompt, type **SECURITY** [> *file name*] ¦ [/**C**] and press Enter. Substitute the name of the file where you want to redirect the output for *file name*. Use /C when you want to have continuous information. Leaving it off means the utility pauses when the screen becomes full and continues when you press any key.

Step 3: Review

With this task, you saw how to use the SECURITY CLU to check for password problems.

Summary

In this chapter, you learned the following:

- ☐ How to create and change passwords

- ☐ Why poor passwords can affect every user on the network.

- ☐ How to master all aspects of password maintenance

- ☐ How to check for the existence of poor passwords

You also should have a healthy appreciation of the need for good password controls—healthy because the health of your network depends upon it. Loose passwords sink ships. Password checking becomes more important if you have a network made up of NetWare 2.*x* and NetWare 3.*x* file servers. NetWare 2.*x* file servers do not have as stringent controls as NetWare 3.*x*. But you should remember that old adage, a chain is only as strong as its weakest link. It must be encouraging to know you now have the tools to search out those weak links and reforge them.

In this chapter—as with other chapters—you acquired an enormous amount of information. If you have kept up and taken the time to review the material, however, you are ready to move on to the next chapter. You revisit accounts and look at ways of creating, maintaining, and protecting accounts.

Workshop

Terminology Review

accountability—The quality or state that enables violations or attempted violations of a system security to be traced to individuals who may then be held responsible.

brute-force attack—A computerized trial-and-error attempt to decode a cipher or password by trying every possible combination. Also known as *exhaustive attack*.

clear text—Information that is in its readable state (before encryption and after decryption).

distributed password system—For security systems, one where passwords are created by the users. The passwords may be accounted for centrally.

encryption—Incorrectly used as a synonym for cryptography; the transformation of plain text into coded form (encryption) or from coded form into plain text (decryption).

grace login—A login to the system after the password interval has expired.

hacker—A computer enthusiast; also, one who seeks to gain unauthorized access to computer systems.

key—In cryptography, a sequence of symbols that controls the operations of encryption and decryption.

wiretapping—Monitoring or recording data as it moves across a communications link; also known as *traffic analysis*.

Task List

The emphasis of this session has been to set up proper password controls. The tasks you should comprehend from this chapter are as follows:

- ☐ Requiring and restricting passwords for the system and individual users
- ☐ Using SYSCON to create or change a password
- ☐ Using SETPASS to change a password
- ☐ Synchronizing passwords across file servers
- ☐ Checking password security

Q&A

Q What do I do if I forget my password?

A You need to contact one of the following:

- ☐ Your Supervisor
- ☐ A Supervisor-equivalent
- ☐ Your workgroup manager
- ☐ Your account manager
- ☐ Your hypnotist to help you remember your password

Q I am the Supervisor. How do I unlock my password after I have used all my grace logins?

A At the console prompt (:), type the following:

```
ENABLE LOGIN
```

Q What three bindery files are involved in the login progress?

A The system uses the NET$OBJ.SYS file for password matching, the NET$PROP.SYS file for password properties, and the NET$VAL.SYS file for encrypted passwords.

Q How do I ensure password encryption is turned on?

A At the console prompt (:), type **SET**. You then see the following:

```
        Setable configuration parameter categories

1.Communications

2.Memory

3.File caching

4.Directory caching

5.File system

6.Locks

7.Transaction tracking

8.Disk

9.Miscellaneous

Which category do you want to view:
```

At the prompt, type **9**. If you have NetWare version 3.11, you answer No to `Do you want to see advanced configuration parameters? (y/n):`. Following are the first two lines that should appear:

```
Allow Unencrypted Passwords: OFF

Description: allow unencrypted password requests to be used
```

Q What is a good password length?

A The length of a passcode determines the potential security of your system. A passcode length of one reduces the potential passcode space to the number of characters in the composition set, for example, 0 to 9 for numeric and A to Z for alphabetic. Increasing the length of a random passcode can make it drastically more difficult to discover. With each additional character, both the number of possible combinations and the average time required to find the password increases exponentially. A length of two characters squares the number and a length of three cubes this number, and so on.

Having said this, the consultant's answer is the length should be such that it cannot be easily guessed during the lifetime of the password. The practical answer is your passwords should be at least six characters long to thwart a brute-force attack.

Q What is the longest password I can have?

A In this chapter, we have stressed the minimum password length, but there is a maximum. The maximum password length is 127 characters. Therefore, a good password is one between 6 and 127 characters in length.

Q Is there any way to help my users create good passwords?

A First, your organization should set password standards. Some issues covered in the standards would be length of the password, how long it can be kept, and the password's makeup. Having a password standard doesn't do much good if you do not tell your users about it. Normally, you would write these standards in conjunction with your users, and get someone with authority to approve them. After your President, Vice-president, or Manager approves the standard, get the word out to your users in the most efficient and effective manner possible. If you have a company newspaper, put a notice in there. You also could send an electronic mail or written memorandum to everybody telling them about the new standard. In addition, when your users request an account, you should tell them at that time about the standards and how to create a good password.

Because your users don't always heed you, you can help users with auto-mated password help. You might, for example, put your SETPASS com-mand in a batch file called SETPASS that calls the SETPASS command. The batch file could echo information on good password selection to the user.

If this still doesn't have any effect, you can buy a program such as Password Coach, which is a C program that helps users create good passwords. When they select a weak password, the Password Coach helps them by telling them the password is in the dictionary, or has repetitive characters, and so on.

Finally, the last way to help them is to check their passwords once a month. From CompuServe's NetWire forum, you can download a program such as

CHKPASS, that compares bindery passwords to a list you create. If a password in the bindery matches the list, the program shows the offending account. When you find a password that is on your list, inform the user, and suggest the user change the password.

9

10

Managing User Access

In the preceding chapter, you learned that login security is the first layer of the NetWare security model. You also learned that usernames and passwords are integral parts of login security. At this point, you learn about another key part of login security. By looking closely at passwords, you gained knowledge about NetWare's verification system. Now you learn about the authentication portion of NetWare's security. What does all this mean? Let's look at the process generically.

Desperately Seeking Data

When you make a request for data, you need to go through the following steps in Figure 10.1.

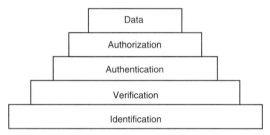

Figure 10.1. *The security process.*

At the first step, you provide a username to the system for identification. The username identifies you as the Supervisor, Fred, or whomever. Associated with a username is a password. You supply the password to prove you are the Supervisor or Fred. The system verifies you are the Supervisor or Fred by matching the password you supplied with the password stored in NET$VAL.SYS (the values bindery file). If the password match is successful, then the system makes assumptions about you.

Next, the system authenticates you by checking restrictions, such as workstation access, time of day, and day of week. If this check is successful, then you can request data. When you request data, the system assures you are authorized to access the data according to the file and directory attributes and your access rights. Should you qualify, the system sends the data back over the network to you.

This chapter introduces you to the authentication step of this process. In Chapters 14, 15, and 16, you look at attributes and rights, and you get your first glimpse of the authorization step.

Restricting User Access

The primary authentication mechanism is login restrictions. Login restrictions include the following:

- ☐ Account restrictions
- ☐ Time restrictions
- ☐ Workstation restrictions
- ☐ Intruder/detection lockout
- ☐ Volume/disk restrictions

You study each one of these restrictions in turn in this chapter.

NetWare account restrictions provide a method for controlling and restricting user access to the NetWare file server. You set account restrictions by using SYSCON in one of the following ways:

- ☐ Accessing Supervisor Options to set default account balances and restrictions
- ☐ Accessing User Information to set individual user account balances and restrictions

Default account restrictions set parameters for new users.

Changing and Setting Account Restrictions

The Supervisor can change account restrictions for individual users or set default values for the entire file server. The following restrictions can be set:

- ☐ Account disabled
- ☐ Account expiration date
- ☐ Limit concurrent connections
- ☐ Account balance

In the following sections, you look at each of these account restrictions in more detail.

Account Disabled

A disabled account means that the account still exists as an object in the bindery, but the user cannot log in to the server. You may want to disable an account for a user on an extended vacation. On the other hand, you can use this feature to create accounts, disable them, and turn them over to workgroup managers to allocate as needed.

Account Expiration Date

Account Expiration Date is a useful tool for temporary employees or students in an academic institution. It enables you to lock an account after a specific date. A locked account cannot be used without being reset. The account therefore expires at midnight the day before the expiry date. By default, the Account Expiration Date is set to No. If you change the value to Yes, today's date appears as the default Date the Account Expires. But you can change the date any time.

Tip: If you enter a date before today's date, all accounts expire on login. You therefore should make all dates in the future.

Limit Concurrent Connections

Limiting concurrent connections is useful against users who like to migrate throughout the LAN or log in from multiple workstations. You can limit a user's concurrent connections by changing the default from No to Yes. An ideal setting is one concurrent connection, which means the user can log in from one workstation at a time. Allowing more than one concurrent connection permits users to log in and leave one or more workstations unattended—a potentially lethal situation if the account is Supervisor or Supervisor-equivalent. This particular account restriction works with station restrictions. You can enhance a user's concurrent connection limitation by combining it with a specific physical workstation.

Tip: If a few users require two or more concurrent connections, then use SYSCON's User Information to change their individual restrictions. Use this method instead of setting the default to two or more concurrent connections.

Account Balance

NetWare has a built-in accounting feature that tracks user logins, logouts, and access to network resources. You can install accounting through the SYSCON menu utility. In addition, you can use SYSCON to define network resources to charge rates for access to those same resources. Account balance is a dynamic measure of each user's accounting usage.

By default, the account balance is 0, and unlimited credit is set to No. These defaults pose a problem because as soon as you turn on accounting, users begin accumulating charges, so accounts force a negative balance. If the low balance limit is set to 0 (a normal number), then users immediately fail on account balance. Once a user's account balance is negative, the system locks the account, and the user cannot log in without intervention. So make sure you set the balance limit to something practical. You don't want to set unlimited credit because that defeats the purpose of an account balance.

Tip: You can use account balance to track how users access resources, rather than for specific resource usage. Within SYSCON | Supervisor Options | Default Account Balance/Restrictions, set Allow Unlimited Credit to Yes, the account balance to 0, and the low balance limit to 0 (see Figure 10.2). Then you charge each user one unit for time usage, blocks written, disk space, blocks read, and processor utilization. By setting Allow Unlimited Credit to Yes, you are allowing the account balance to go negative. The number in the negative account balance provides you with information on how the user accesses network resources.

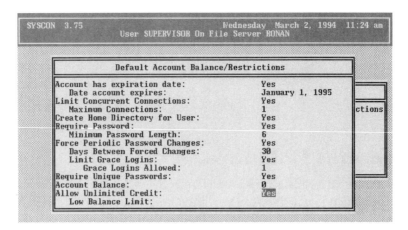

Figure 10.2. *Tracking user access.*

In the following sections and tasks, you practice setting default and individual account restrictions.

Task 10.1: Setting default account restrictions using SYSCON.

Step 1: Description

In this task, you use the SYSCON utility to set default user account restrictions that apply to any new users created.

Step 2: Action

1. Type **LOGIN SUPERVISOR** and press Enter. Provide a password, if required, and press Enter.

2. To change to the \PUBLIC subdirectory, type **CD\PUBLIC** and press Enter.

3. Type **SYSCON** and press Enter. The Available Topics menu appears.

4. Move the cursor down to Supervisor Options and press Enter. You then see the Supervisor Options list.

5. Highlight Default Account Balance/Restrictions and press Enter. The Default Account Balance/Restrictions menu appears. This screen contains 15 fields. You completed the password restrictions in the preceding chapter. Your changes from Chapter 9 are shown in Figure 10.3.

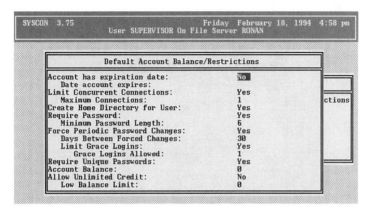

Figure 10.3. *Previous Default Account Balance/Restrictions box.*

6. At Account Has Expiration Date, type **Yes**, and press Enter.

7. Enter an expiry date for Date Account Expires and press Enter. This date ideally should be in the future.

8. Move the cursor down to Limit Concurrent Connections, type **Yes**, and press Enter.

9. Enter the number of concurrent connections you allow for Maximum Connections and press Enter. This number ideally should be one.

10. Move the cursor down to Account Balance, enter the account balance, and press Enter.

11. Move the cursor down to Allow Unlimited Credit, type **Yes**, and press Enter. Your screen should now resemble the one shown in Figure 10.4.

12. Press Esc until you are asked to confirm your exit from SYSCON.

Step 3: Review

In this task, you practiced using the SYSCON utility to set default user account restrictions that apply to any new users created. In the next section, you see how you can override these default settings for individual users.

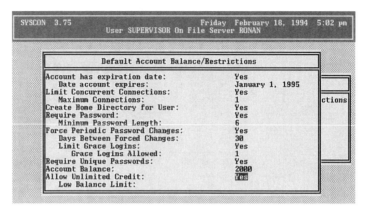

Figure 10.4. *Updated Default Account Balance/Restrictions box.*

Changing Users' Account Restrictions

In Chapter 8, you created your first user account, JANET. At that time, you learned you would place some restrictions on this account. Now is the time.

Task 10.2: Changing a user's account balances using SYSCON.

Step 1: Description

In this task, you use the SYSCON utility to change account restrictions for an individual. SYSCON modifies these parameters to enable you to loosen or tighten specific restrictions based on individual requirements.

Step 2: Action

1. To change to the \PUBLIC subdirectory, type **CD\PUBLIC** and press Enter.

2. Type **SYSCON** and press Enter. The Available Topics menu appears.

3. Move the cursor down to User Information and press Enter. You then see the User Names list.

4. Move the cursor down to the user account name JANET in the User Names box and press Enter.

5. Select Account Balance and press Enter. The Account Balance For User
   JANET box appears. This screen contains three fields, as shown in Figure
   10.5.

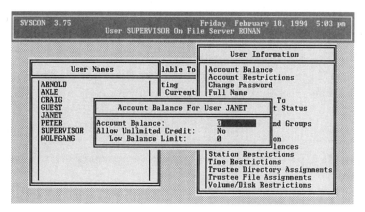

Figure 10.5. *Account Balance For User JANET box.*

6. Highlight Account Balance, enter the account balance, and press Enter.

7. Move the cursor down to Allow Unlimited Credit, type **Yes**, and press
   Enter. Your screen should now resemble the one shown in Figure 10.6.

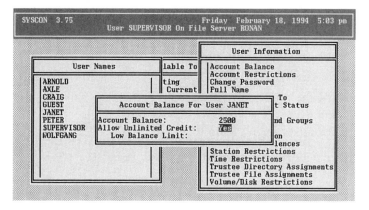

Figure 10.6. *Updated Account Balance For User JANET box.*

8. Press Esc until you are asked to confirm your exit from SYSCON.

Step 3: Review

Occasionally, you may want to override default restrictions. This task showed you how to do that for any individual.

> **Note:** Default account restrictions work for all accounts only after the parameters are set. New default parameters therefore have no effect on existing accounts. Consequently, you should look at setting the default parameters before you start adding all your users.

Task 10.3: Changing a user's account restrictions using SYSCON.

Step 1: Description

In addition to changing account balances, you can use the SYSCON utility to change other account restrictions, as you do in this task.

Step 2: Action

1. To change to the \PUBLIC subdirectory, type **CD\PUBLIC** and press Enter.

2. Type **SYSCON** and press Enter. The Available Topics menu appears.

3. Move the cursor down to User Information and press Enter. You then see the User Names list.

4. Move the cursor down to the user account name JANET in the User Names box and press Enter.

5. Move the cursor down to Account Restrictions and press Enter. The Account Restrictions For User JANET box appears. This screen contains 15 fields, as shown in Figure 10.7.

6. Highlight Account Disabled, type **No**, and press Enter.

7. Move the cursor down to Account Has Expiration Date, type **Yes**, and press Enter.

8. Enter an expiry date for Date Account Expires and press Enter. This date ideally should be in the future. Notice that the system default popped up when you set Account Has Expiration Date to Yes.

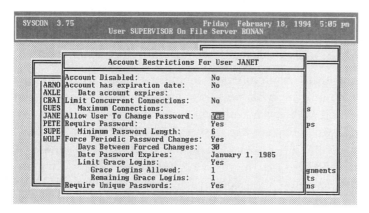

Figure 10.7. *Account Restrictions For User JANET box.*

9. Move the cursor down to Limit Concurrent Connections, type **Yes**, and press Enter.

10. Enter the number of concurrent connections you allow for Maximum Connections and press Enter. This number ideally should be one. Your screen should now resemble the one shown in Figure 10.8.

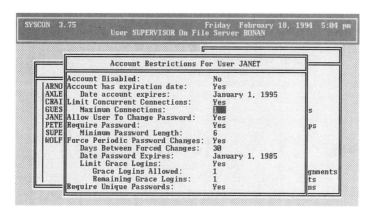

Figure 10.8. *Updated Account Restrictions For User JANET box.*

11. Press Esc until you are asked to confirm your exit from SYSCON.

Step 3: Review

In addition to changing account balances, this task helped you practice using the SYSCON utility to change other account restrictions.

Suppose that you just inherited administration of this system, and you want to lock all accounting users off the system on the weekends—something to do with asset protection. Well, locking off users isn't a problem. In fact, you know part of the answer right now. To change the login restrictions for a large number of users, simply highlight the user by using F5 in the User Information window of SYSCON and press Enter. The Set User Information screen appears with the four choices: Account Balance, Account Restrictions, Station Restrictions, and Time Restrictions (see Figure 10.9). Pick the restriction of your choice and set it.

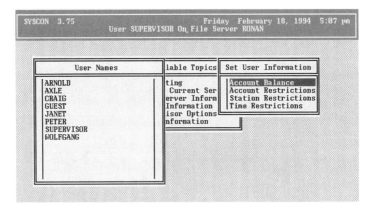

Figure 10.9. *User Information screen.*

Setting Time Restrictions

You can restrict user access to a file server based on the time of day and day of the week. Time restrictions are useful because you can control when users can access the system. You can apply these restrictions as a system default for all users, or you can apply them for individual users. You should remember from account restrictions that default restrictions work only for accounts created after you set the parameters. The default is no time restrictions.

Note: When you apply time restrictions with a plan or according to a company policy, they provide extra protection. On the flip side, improperly conceived parameters hamper the work of your users.

Time restrictions are dynamic; that is, once you come across a blank time period, the system clears your connection. You do, however, have approximately eight minutes to log out. After one minute in a disallowed period, you receive a message telling you to log out. Should you choose to ignore this first message, you receive a second message about six minutes later. If you ignore NetWare's message, NetWare clears your connection in another minute.

Warning: The system tells you twice to log out when a disallowed time period arises. After the system warns you of an impending time restriction violation, you should log out immediately. If you don't log out, the system clears the connection, which means the system does not save the file you were working on.

You can set default time restrictions, similar to account restrictions.

Task 10.4: Setting default time restrictions using SYSCON.

Step 1: Description
In this task, you use SYSCON's Supervisor Options to set default time restrictions for all your users.

Step 2: Action
1. Type **LOGIN SUPERVISOR** and press Enter. Provide a password, if required, and press Enter.

2. To change to the \PUBLIC subdirectory, type **CD\PUBLIC** and press Enter.

3. Type **SYSCON** and press Enter. The Available Topics menu appears.

4. Move the cursor down to Supervisor Options and press Enter. You then see the Supervisor Options list.

5. Move the cursor down to Default Time Restrictions and press Enter. The Default Time Restrictions screen appears (see Figure 10.10). Asterisks

10

appear where you have allowed access for a period. Space over any asterisk for the period where you want to remove access.

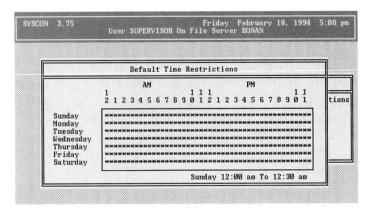

Figure 10.10. *Default Time Restrictions screen.*

6. Press Esc until you are asked to confirm your exit from SYSCON.

Step 3: Review

After carefully studying the requirements of your network, you might decide to set default time restrictions. If you have only one work shift each day, for example, then it is unlikely anyone logs in at three in the morning. You also might want to set time restrictions to prevent workers from logging in at times when they are tired and more apt to make an error. As you saw in this task, you can use SYSCON to set default time restrictions for all your users.

After reading Task 10.4, you might argue that some users need to log in anytime. Agreed. That is why you can change time restrictions on a user-by-user basis, as shown in Task 10.5.

Task 10.5: Using SYSCON to set time restrictions for individual users.

Step 1: Description

In this task, you use SYSCON's Supervisor Options to change the time restrictions for a user. You may want general users to log in only from six to six, for instance, but you need the Supervisor to log in any time, any day.

Step 2: Action

1. To change to the \PUBLIC subdirectory, type **CD\PUBLIC** and press Enter.

2. Type **SYSCON** and press Enter. The Available Topics menu appears.

3. Move the cursor down to User Information and press Enter. You then see the User Names list.

4. Move the cursor down to the user account name KELLY in the User Names box and press Enter.

5. Move the cursor down to Time Restrictions and press Enter. The Allowed Login Times For User KELLY box appears. Present restrictions are shown in Figure 10.11.

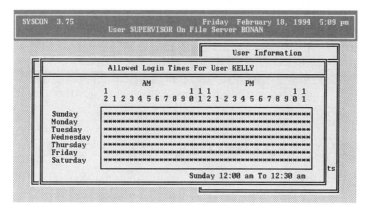

Figure 10.11. *Allowed Time Restrictions For User KELLY box.*

6. Remove asterisks by pressing the spacebar to disallow that time period. Each asterisk represents a half-hour period. Notice that in the bottom right-hand corner the system tells you what time period the cursor is on. The example in Figure 10.12 shows KELLY can log in from 6:00 a.m. to 6:00 p.m., Monday to Friday, and from 12:00 p.m. to 5:00 p.m. on Saturday.

7. Press Esc until you are asked to confirm your exit from SYSCON.

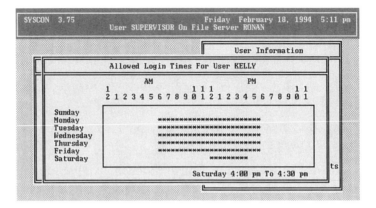

Figure 10.12. *Updated Allowed Login Times For User KELLY box.*

Step 3: Review

In this task, you learned that you can change login times by toggling times on and off. An asterisk denotes that the system allows a login for that time period. To change these half-hour periods, you enter either a space (not allowed) or an asterisk (allowed).

Setting Station Restrictions

Station restrictions are another way to control user access, by restricting the physical workstations where users log in. How do you tie users to workstations? The process relies heavily on the card's internal number. Vendors burn 12-digit hexadecimal addresses into every NIC they manufacture. Every vendor has a unique address because the IEEE controls the allotment of these numbers. The cabling media uses the address to uniquely identify one NIC from another. Because the address number is there, NetWare also can use it to identify workstations when users logically attach to a NIC. In this fashion, you can tie users to workstations.

You configure station restrictions by providing two pieces of information:

☐ A network address

☐ A node address

The *network address* defines the cabling scheme where the workstation attaches. The *node address* is a 12-digit hexadecimal number identifying the Network Interface Card. You probably don't have this information at your fingertips, but you do have a utility to help figure it out. You can use USERLIST to get a list of currently logged-in users along with the addresses of the machines they are using.

Tip: You can capture a USERLIST of each user by typing the following at the DOS prompt:

`USERLIST /A >USERLIST.TXT`

Now that you have a list of node addresses saved in a file, you can use the information to set workstation restrictions.

Station restrictions, like other authentication mechanisms, can enhance access security. When you apply station restrictions with a plan or according to a company policy, they provide extra protection. But similar to time restrictions, improperly conceived restrictions hamper the work of your users. When the user's workstation is broken, the user might not be able to log in to the network. You can handle these contingencies, however, when you create your users' list.

Tip: In Chapter 8, you created Supervisor-equivalent accounts. Now is a good time to make use of equivalency. Because you have users who are Supervisor-equivalent, you can restrict the use of the Supervisor account to a workstation in a physically secure location.

Note: Because station restrictions are linked to the user and the node address, default station restrictions are not practical. It doesn't make sense to restrict all users on the network to the same node address. If you do, all users must log in from the same workstation, which defeats the reason for developing your network.

Task 10.6: Setting station restrictions using SYSCON.

Step 1: Description

In this task, you use the SYSCON utility to restrict users to particular workstations. In this manner, you can improve security.

Step 2: Action

1. To change to the \PUBLIC subdirectory, type **CD\PUBLIC** and press Enter.

2. Type **SYSCON** and press Enter. The Available Topics menu appears.

3. Move the cursor down to User Information and press Enter. You then see the User Names list.

4. Move the cursor down to the user account name KELLY in the User Names box and press Enter.

5. Move the cursor down to Station Restrictions and press Enter. The Allowed Login Addresses box appears.

6. Press Ins to add a station restriction. Your screen now should look something like the one shown in Figure 10.13.

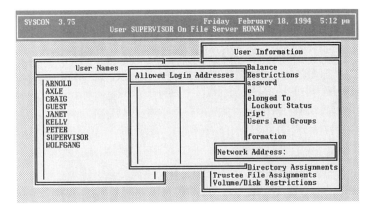

Figure 10.13. *Network Address box.*

7. Enter the eight-digit hexadecimal network portion of the address after Network Address and press Enter. Confirm your intention to allow login from all nodes in the Allow Login From All Nodes box.

   You can find the network address of a workstation by logging in at the workstation and typing **USERLIST /A**. See Figure 10.14 to see a typical listing.

   The entry marked by an asterisk shows the network address. After you press Enter, your screen should look similar to Figure 10.15.

```
F>userlist /a

User Information for Server RONAN
Connection  User Name        Network    Node Address   Login Time
----------  ---------        -------    ------------   ----------
     2    * SUPERVISOR     [        1] [  80C77A547A]   3-02-1994 11:22 am

F>
```

Figure 10.14. *A typical USERLIST.*

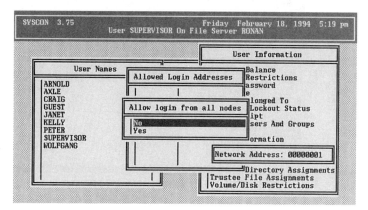

Figure 10.15. *Node address.*

10

8. Enter the 12-digit hexadecimal node portion of the address after Node Address and press Enter.

   You can find the node address of a workstation by logging in at the workstation and typing **USERLIST** /A. The entry marked by an asterisk shows the node address, as well as the network address. Your screen should look something like the one shown in Figure 10.16.

9. Press Esc until you are asked to confirm your exit from SYSCON.

Step 3: Review

Using the SYSCON utility to restrict users to particular workstations is a powerful security tool, as you learned in this task. Make sure that you have implemented your workstation restrictions after careful consideration. Your implementation of this feature should not inhibit the natural work flow within your organization. If you find that you got a little carried away with workstation restrictions, you can backtrack and remove some restrictions.

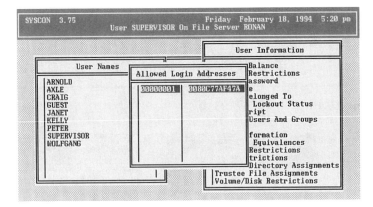

Figure 10.16. *Allowed Login Addresses screen.*

Task 10.7: Deleting station restrictions using SYSCON.

Step 1: Description

In this task, you use the SYSCON utility to delete station restrictions that have been set incorrectly or no longer serve a purpose.

Step 2: Action

1. To change to the \PUBLIC subdirectory, type **CD\PUBLIC** and press Enter.

2. Type **SYSCON** and press Enter. The Available Topics menu appears.

3. Move the cursor down to User Information and press Enter. You then see the User Names list.

4. Move the cursor down to the user account name KELLY in the User Names box and press Enter.

5. Move the cursor down to Station Restrictions and press Enter. The Allowed Login Addresses box appears.

6. Press Delete to delete a station restriction from the Allowed Login Addresses box.

7. Press Esc until you are asked to confirm your exit from SYSCON.

Step 3: Review

As you just learned, you can use the SYSCON utility to delete station restrictions that have been set incorrectly or no longer serve a purpose. Proper initial planning hopefully reduces the number of station restrictions you must remove.

Detecting and Locking Out Intruders

In your travels or reading, you might have heard of intruder detection and lockout. Your first question is probably, "What do you mean by *intruder*?" An intruder is someone who attempts an unauthorized access to someone else's account. Generally, intruders get access by guessing passwords. Intruders may be internal (for example, disgruntled employees) or external (for example, a hacker). If the intruder succeeds in guessing, or otherwise deriving, a password, then the intruder has all the rights and privileges of the account. Unfortunately, Supervisor becomes a target of intruders.

Because the intruder normally doesn't know the password, he or she tries a brute-force attack (see Chapter 9). Hence, the intruder manually or automatically tries random passwords until finding a match. That is where the Intruder Detection/Lockout feature kicks in.

Intruder Detection/Lockout is not so much a restriction but a security feature. The feature tracks invalid login attempts, that is, users who try to log in with incorrect passwords. It keeps track of invalid password attempts and locks a user account when the user reaches the threshold number of password attempts. The name should clue you in to the two components of this feature—intruder detection and account lockout.

Users activate intruder detection as soon as they enter an invalid password. The system increments the Incorrect Login Attempts count for invalid passwords. The Bad Login Count Retention Time is a complementary parameter describing the period during which you track bad logins. After you reach the threshold within that period, you can lock out the user account. Assume, for example, that you set Incorrect Login Attempts to three and Bad Login Count Retention Time to 0 days, 23 hours, and 59 minutes. The system tracks all invalid login attempts every day (a 24-hour period) and locks the user account when the number of invalid login attempts exceeds 3 in a 24-hour period.

You don't have to lock out an account that has passed the threshold; however, you can. You arm account lockout by setting Lock Account After Detection to Yes. Normally, you activate lockout upon detecting an intruder. You therefore need to decide the

10

appropriate time to lock the account. Then you specify the amount of time that must pass before the account automatically unlocks. If you set this number to a day or two, then users must come to you to get reset. By default, this parameter is set to 15 minutes.

> **Note:** The favorite target for intruders is Supervisor. And why not? The Supervisor is omnipotent. You don't have to use finesse when you have this account. Because it is a target, the Supervisor account can become locked. Don't panic; you can remedy this situation. In Chapter 9, you learned how to unlock an account that exceeded the number of grace logins. You use the same procedure when the Supervisor account is locked. At the console prompt (:), type
>
> **ENABLE LOGIN**

Intruder Detection/Lockout is a system-wide parameter, similar to the default account and time restrictions. It applies to all users or none. By default, Intruder Detection/Lockout is set to No. You can set the parameter using SYSCON.

Task 10.8: Setting intruder lockout using SYSCON.

Step 1: Description
In this task, the Supervisor uses the SYSCON utility to turn on the intruder lockout feature and to set the number of invalid logins.

Step 2: Action
1. Type **LOGIN SUPERVISOR** and press Enter. Provide a password, if required, and press Enter.

2. To change to the \PUBLIC subdirectory, type **CD\PUBLIC** and press Enter.

3. Type **SYSCON** and press Enter. The Available Topics menu appears.

4. Move the cursor down to Supervisor Options and press Enter. You then see the Supervisor Options list.

5. Move the cursor down to Intruder Detection/Lockout and press Enter. The Intruder Detection/Lockout menu appears. This screen contains nine fields.

6. For Detect Intruders, type **Yes** and press Enter.

7. Enter a threshold limit for Incorrect Login Attempts and press Enter.

8. Enter days, hours, and minutes for Bad Login Count Retention Time and press Enter.

9. Move the cursor down to Lock Account After Detection, type **Yes**, and press Enter.

10. Enter days, hours, and minutes for Length Of Account Lockout and press Enter. Your screen should now resemble the one shown in Figure 10.17.

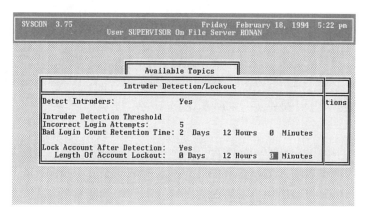

Figure 10.17. *Updated Intruder Detection/Lockout screen.*

11. Press Esc until you are asked to confirm your exit from SYSCON.

Step 3: Review

Intruder detection/lockout is a useful feature, as you learned in this task. Be careful when you set the incorrect login attempts so that you catch intruders and not your own forgetful employees. The Supervisor account is a favorite target of intruders. When you set a lockout number, other employees call upon you to reset their locked accounts. Make sure their reasons for the locked account make sense before resetting the account. You should investigate every lockout thoroughly.

Resetting Locked Accounts

The Supervisor must unlock user accounts locked by the Intruder Detection/Lockout feature. When an account becomes locked, the Supervisor can investigate the incident by calling up the SYSCON/User Information/[user name]/Intruder Lockout Status screen to get information about the locked account and the intruder. Figure 10.18 provides an example of a locked account.

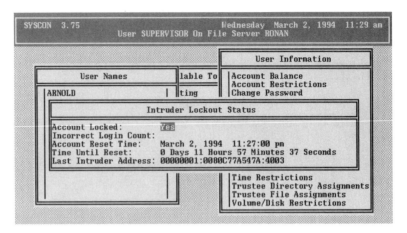

Figure 10.18. *Intruder Lockout Status screen.*

Looking at the screen, you see the address 00000001 :0080C77A547A: 4003, where

☐ 00000001 is the network address of the cabling system that you assigned for the NIC in the file server.

☐ 0080C77A547A is the node address of the NIC in the workstation.

☐ 4003 is the IPX socket number of the workstation where the login program made the request.

You do not need the IPX socket number to determine the physical location of the offending workstation used by the intruder.

After you determine the nature of the incident and satisfy yourself that it was unintentional or you deal with the offender or offending account, you can unlock the account, as shown in Task 10.9.

Task 10.9: Unlocking a user's account using SYSCON.

Step 1: Description

In this task, you use the SYSCON utility to unlock an account.

Step 2: Action

1. To change to the \PUBLIC subdirectory, type **CD\PUBLIC** and press Enter.

2. Type **SYSCON** and press Enter. The Available Topics menu appears.

3. Move the cursor down to User Information and press Enter. You then see the User Names list.

4. Move the cursor down to the user account name JANET in the User Names box and press Enter.

5. Move the cursor down to Intruder Lockout Status and press Enter. The Intruder Lockout Status box for user JANET appears (refer to Figure 10.18).

6. Highlight Account Locked, type **No**, and press Enter.

7. Press Esc until you are asked to confirm your exit from SYSCON.

Step 3: Review

From time to time, you need to use the SYSCON menu utility to unlock user accounts locked by intruder detection, as you learned in this task.

Setting Volume/Disk Restrictions

The final login restriction deals with the use of space on the file server; you can restrict users to specific amounts of disk space on the shared server disk. NetWare tracks disk space by owner. If Limit Volume Space is set to Yes, you must specify the maximum volume space in kilobytes. This parameter deters a user from abusing a volume.

Task 10.10: Setting volume/disk restrictions using SYSCON.

Step 1: Description

In this task, you use the SYSCON utility to limit the amount of space on the shared server disk.

Step 2: Action

1. To change to the \PUBLIC subdirectory, type **CD\PUBLIC** and press Enter.

2. Type **SYSCON** and press Enter. The Available Topics menu appears.

3. Move the cursor down to User Information and press Enter. You then see the User Names list.

4. Move the cursor down to the user account name JANET in the User Names box and press Enter.

5. Move the cursor down to Volume/Disk Restrictions and press Enter. The Select A Volume box for the file server appears (see Figure 10.19).

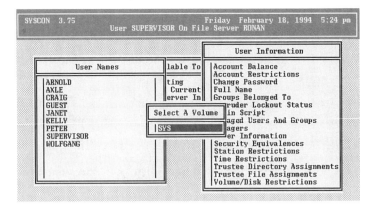

Figure 10.19. *Select A Volume box.*

6. Select a volume and press Enter. The User Volume/Disk Restrictions menu appears.

7. From the User Volume/Disk Restrictions menu, highlight Limit Volume Space?, type **Yes**, and press Enter.

8. Enter the number of kilobytes you want to give the user and press Enter. Your screen should look something like the one shown in Figure 10.20.

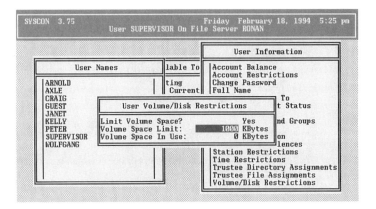

Figure 10.20. *User Volume/Disk Restrictions menu.*

9. Press Esc until you are asked to confirm your exit from SYSCON.

Step 3: Review

This task is the last one you do to set user restrictions. In this task, you learned how to limit the user's space on a volume or disk on the file server.

You must be tired. Now it's time to prepare for tomorrow's sessions by recapping what you learned today.

Summary

In this chapter, you learned about the following:

- ☐ Disabling accounts

- ☐ Expiring accounts on a given date

- ☐ Limiting concurrent connections

- ☐ Setting account balances

- ☐ Restricting accounts based on time, station, and volume/disk

This chapter demonstrated one of NetWare's primary security mechanisms, which is important in understanding how to control users. You should study these account restrictions and use them where they are applicable to improve the security of your network.

Workshop

Terminology Review

authentication—The act of identifying or verifying the eligibility of a station, originator, or individual to access specific categories of information.

authorization—The process that grants the necessary and sufficient permissions for the intended purpose.

identification—The process that enables, generally using unique machine-readable names, recognition of users or resources as identical with those previously described to a system.

intruder—A user or other agent attempting to gain unauthorized access to the file server.

verification—Confirmation that the object is what it purports being. Also, confirmation of the identity of a person (or other agent external to the protection system) making a request.

Task List

The emphasis of this chapter has been to introduce you to accounts and their management. As a system administrator or Supervisor, you will repeatedly use these commands in your daily work. The tasks you should understand from this chapter are as follows:

☐ Setting default account restrictions

☐ Changing a user's account restrictions

☐ Setting default time restrictions

☐ Changing a user's time restrictions

☐ Setting default station restrictions

☐ Changing a user's station restrictions

☐ Setting intruder lockout

☐ Unlocking a user's account

☐ Setting volume/disk restrictions

Q&A

Q If I use intruder detection, what should I set my thresholds to?

A Normally, you would set intruder detection to 3. Anymore than 3 attempts is probably something other than pilot error. Then you should set the Bad Login Count Retention time to 23 hours and 59 minutes. Oh, by the way, you should set the lockout time greater than the bad login account retention time.

Q When and where would I use station restrictions?

A Station restrictions are an excellent control for enforcing program pathing. You might, for example, want to ensure that payroll transactions only come from workstations in the human resources area. Also, you should tie the use of Supervisor to a specific workstation used by the system administrator.

This will obviate the exposure of an unattended workstation in session to the Supervisor. You also may want to tie the Guest account to a specific workstation where print jobs are submitted. Any jobs or processes without passwords should also be associated to a workstation.

Q How many connections should I allow users?

A One, otherwise users are tempted to walk away.

Q If they walk away, with NetWare can I automatically force users off after a predetermined period of inactivity?

A This feature is not standard with NetWare; however, you can buy third-party products that will perform this feature.

10

Day

6

11

Creating and Using Login Scripts

As a network administrator dedicated to serving your users, you want to provide them with a working NetWare environment that is comfortable and easy to use. After users have logged in to the system, they should be able to find and access all their files, use their printers, and execute any of the commands they require. Each user probably has different needs, of course, so each user's working environment must be customized for him or her. Customizing the environment means setting a number of NetWare options each time that user logs in. But the user probably is not crazy about typing in many complex NetWare commands after each and every login. Is there an easier way?

As a network administrator bent on self-preservation and continued sanity, you probably want to place your users in an environment where they can't get into too much trouble. Because they are like your flock, you need to guide them to the right areas of your file server, avoiding dangerous commands and unknown functions. You want to set bounds over where they can go and what they can do, but you can't be there looking over their shoulders and making sure they type only the right commands. Is there a way to keep them safe?

The answer to both questions is to use *login scripts.* Login scripts are files containing commands that are executed when the user logs in to NetWare. Using these commands, you can customize each user's environment so that it is just the way he or she likes it, and at the same time keeps the user safe from some of the perils of network computing.

If you're familiar with DOS batch files, you will find that login scripts are similar. But if you've never created a DOS batch file, don't worry—login scripts are fairly straightforward. In the following sections, you learn all about login scripts and get a chance to try setting up one or two yourself.

Understanding Login Scripts

A login script is just a text file containing commands. The scripts are similar to any other type of computer program because each line contains an instruction to NetWare. Most of these instructions are geared toward setting up the user with a working environment that is right for him or her—such as setting where on the file server NetWare looks for the user's commands and files.

Login script instructions also make use of *identifier variables.* An identifier variable contains information such as the user's name, which NetWare refers to when it performs certain tasks. You see examples of identifier variables later in the chapter.

A login script is essentially a computer program. Like a programming language, login scripts must follow prescribed rules for syntax and semantics. And like other programming languages, login scripts contain logical constructs that can test whether a certain condition is met. Depending on the results of the test, the login script follows one set of instructions or another.

All login scripts work the same way: at the right time, NetWare simply opens the text file containing the login script, reads the instructions, and executes them. Although they all function in the same fashion and use the same commands, NetWare has three different kinds of login scripts:

- The system login script
- A user login script
- The default login script

In the following sections, you look at the purpose of each.

System Login Script

The system login script is executed by every person who logs in to the NetWare server. It's the ideal place to perform instructions and set values that apply to all users. A good example is using the MAP command to set a search mapping to the SYS:PUBLIC directory so that users can get easily to common NetWare commands.

With the decision-making capabilities possible, you can use the system login script to run different commands, depending on an identifier variable such as the user's name, or the group the user belongs to, or even the time of day. You can use any valid script command in the system login script, as long as each command follows the rules for command structure.

As you can imagine, because the system login script affects every user, only the Supervisor (and Supervisor-equivalent users) can edit this text file. The script is stored as a file under the name NET$LOG.DAT in the SYS:PUBLIC directory.

If the system login script exists, it is the first one executed whenever someone logs in. After that, the user can have his or her own login script run, as you see in the next section.

User Login Script

Each user can have a login script that is unique to him or her. The user login script is also a text file, stored under the name LOGIN, and found beneath SYS:MAIL in a subdirectory that is set up for each user. It runs after the system login script, so it can make use of anything set up there—drive mappings, for example. Because it runs after the system login script, commands within a user login script can overwrite or cancel out something done by the system login script.

Using a user login script, you or your user can customize key NetWare settings, such as the drive letters assigned to various directories on the server. With the wide range of software and hardware that can be used on the network, the ability to define an environment for each user is vital. The downside of this flexibility is that creating and maintaining individual login scripts for dozens or hundreds of users can be your worst administrative nightmare. You therefore should try to do as much as possible with the system login script. Although user login scripts are valuable, use them only where necessary.

Default Login Script

What if you don't define a system login script or user login script? NetWare comes to the rescue with a default login script, which is built into the LOGIN.EXE program you used to gain access to the system in the first place. The default login script is built into the login program so that you can't modify it without special tools and special knowledge.

When you first logged in to your newly installed NetWare server, you might have noticed some messages welcoming you to the server and showing you your drive and search mappings. That was the default login script executing.

The default login script executes when no system login script exists. In addition, it runs for any user who does not have his or her own individual login script. It contains some fairly straightforward login script commands, which serve as a good first look at a typical login script. You should review Table 11.1, which shows the default login script commands, along with an explanation of each instruction.

Table 11.1. NetWare's default login script.

Login Script Command Line	Purpose of Instruction
`MAP DISPLAY OFF`	Map commands are not displayed.
`MAP ERRORS OFF`	Errors resulting from map commands are not displayed either.
`Rem: Set first drive to most appropriate directory, depending on who is logging on`	This remark included in the login script helps document the purpose of each instruction.
`.MAP *1:=SYS:`	This line maps the first drive letter to the root directory of the SYS: volume.
`MAP *1:=SYS:%LOGIN_NAME`	This line maps the first drive letter to the user's home directory, taken from the value of the identifier variable `LOGIN_NAME`. If the user has no home directory, the first drive is still mapped to SYS:.
`IF "%1"="SUPERVISOR" THEN MAP*1:=SYS:SYSTEM`	This line tests the value of the identifier variable 1 (which is the first word on the original command line after the word `LOGIN`). If the user's name is SUPERVISOR, the first drive is set to SYS:SYSTEM instead of to the user's home directory.
`Rem: Set search drives.`	This line is another remark for documentation purposes.
`MAP S1:=SYS:PUBLIC`	The first search drive is mapped to SYS:PUBLIC, which contains many useful commands.
`MAP S2:=S1:%MACHINE\%OS\%OS_`	The second search drive is mapped to the `VERSION` directory where files for the user's particular machine variety and operating system type are stored.

continues

Table 11.1. continued

Login Script Command Line	Purpose of Instruction
`Rem: Now display current drive settings.`	This line is another remark for documentation purposes.
`MAP DISPLAY ON`	Map commands can now be displayed.
`MAP`	This command shows the user his or her current drive and search mappings.

Examining Login Script Identifier Variables

In the preceding sections, you learned that login scripts can make use of identifier variables such as `LOGIN_NAME` and `OS_VERSION`. When preceded by a percent sign (for example, `%LOGIN_NAME`), the current value of the identifier variable is substituted.

You can use the results of evaluating an identifier value as part of a command. For example, Table 11.1 includes a `MAP` command that assigns a drive mapping to the user's home directory simply by using the value given by `%LOGIN_NAME`. (Of course, this example assumes that you have set up each person on the network with a home directory that has the same name as his or her username. But this setup is usually the case because it makes administering the network much easier for you, and NetWare defaults point you in the direction of making this change.)

You also can use an identifier variable as part of a test to determine which actions to take. In Table 11.1, the value given by `%1` (which is taken from the `LOGIN` command line) is tested to determine whether it equals `"SUPERVISOR"`. If it does, a specific instruction is followed; otherwise, the line is simply skipped.

NetWare login scripts have many identifier variables available for use. Table 11.2 shows some of the more popular and useful variables that you can use in constructing login scripts.

Table 11.2. Login script identifier variables.

Type of Variable	Identifier Variable	Function
Date	DAY	Day number (01 to 31)
	DAY_OF_WEEK	Name of day (for example, Monday)
	MONTH	Month number (01 to 12)
	MONTH_NAME	Name of month (for example, January)
	NDAY_OF_WEEK	Number of day in week (1 to 7, with 1=Sunday)
	SHORT_YEAR	Last two digits of year (for example, 94)
	YEAR	All four digits of year (for example, 1994)
Time	AM_PM	The a.m. or p.m. indicator
	GREETING_TIME	Phase of day (morning, afternoon, or evening)
	HOUR	Hour (12-hour scale; 1 to 12)
	HOUR24	Hour (24-hour scale; 00 to 23)
	MINUTE	Minute (00 to 59)
	SECOND	Second (00 to 59)
User	FULL_NAME	User's full name
	LOGIN_NAME	User's NetWare login name
	MEMBER OF "group"	True or False indicator depending on whether the user is assigned to the group

continues

11

Table 11.2. continued

Type of Variable	Identifier Variable	Function
	NOT MEMBER OF "group"	True or False indicator depending on whether the user is not assigned to the group
	PASSWORD_EXPIRES	Number of days before password expires
	USER_ID	Unique bindery object number assigned to each NetWare user
Network	FILE_SERVER	Server name
	NETWORK_ADDRESS	Number of the logical network used by the server (eight-digit hexadecimal number)
Workstation	DOS_REQUESTER	Version of the workstation's DOS shell (for example, version 3.31)
	MACHINE	Type of computer (for example, IBM_PC)
	NETWARE_REQUESTER	Version of the NetWare Requester for OS/2 (for example, version 2.00)
	OS	Type of DOS on the workstation (for example, MSDOS, PCDOS)
	OS_VERSION	Version of DOS on the workstation (for example, version 6.2)
	P_STATION	Workstation's node address (12-digit hexadecimal number)

Type of Variable	Identifier Variable	Function
	SMACHINE	Short machine name (for example, IBM)
	STATION	Workstation's connection number
DOS Environment	<variable>	Any DOS environment variable can be used in angle brackets (for example, <PATH>)
Miscellaneous	ERROR_LEVEL	An error number (0=No errors)
	%n	Replaced by parameters the user enters at the command line with the LOGIN utility

To make use of these variables, you need to know some of the more popular login script commands that are available. You see how to use many of these commands in the following section.

Examining Login Script Commands

The login script command language contains a fairly rich set of instructions you can use to set up your users' environments. If you're familiar with any programming languages—even DOS batch files—many of the commands, or at least the types of commands, might seem familiar.

Table 11.3 provides a summary of NetWare's login script commands in alphabetical order. You review the purpose of some of the most popular login script commands in the following sections.

Table 11.3. Login script commands.

#	GOTO
ATTACH	IF ... THEN
BREAK	INCLUDE
COMSPEC	MACHINE
DISPLAY	MAP
DOS BREAK	PAUSE
DOS VERIFY	PCCOMPATIBLE
DRIVE	REMARK
EXIT	SET
FDISPLAY	SHIFT
FIRE PHASERS	WRITE

MAP

Probably the most used command in a login script is the MAP command. You use it to establish pointers to directories on the NetWare file server and to set up search paths for NetWare commands. Proper drive and search mappings are key to problem-free network operation for your users. Because these mappings disappear whenever a user logs off from NetWare, they must be reestablished each time the user logs in. The login script is the perfect place to take care of this task.

You learn all about using the MAP command in Chapter 14. For now, keep in mind that the two most important mappings needed are to the SYS:PUBLIC directory so that users can find common NetWare commands, and to the user's home directory so that they can consistently find their own files.

> **Note:** A key issue for DOS users, which may involve the MAP command, is making sure that their workstations know how to find the all important COMMAND.COM file. One way to find this file is through using a MAP command. See the discussion in the following section on COMSPEC for more details.

To establish the first search map to the SYS:PUBLIC directory, for example, you should add the following line in the login script:

```
MAP S1:=SYS:PUBLIC
```

To establish the first drive map to the user's home directory, you can use the following line:

```
MAP *1:=SYS:%LOGIN_NAME
```

COMSPEC

The COMSPEC command is NetWare's way to tell the DOS workstation where to look for the COMMAND.COM file. This important concept requires some explanation.

COMMAND.COM is critical to the proper running of a DOS workstation. This program, also known as the *DOS command interpreter,* is the interface each user deals with whenever he or she types a DOS command. COMMAND.COM takes the user's keyboard input and performs the appropriate action. This action typically involves starting a program, such as a word processor, at which time COMMAND.COM may be forced to bow out. In this case, after the program is completed, COMMAND.COM must be reloaded so that it can ask the user for the next command. To reload, the workstation has to be able to find COMMAND.COM.

On a stand-alone workstation, COMMAND.COM usually can be found in one of two ways:

☐ It can be found somewhere on the PATH set by the DOS workstation user.

☐ The DOS variable known as COMSPEC can be set to point directly at COMMAND.COM. The workstation user can use the SET command directly or use the SHELL parameter indirectly within the workstation's CONFIG.SYS file.

In either case, finding and reloading COMMAND.COM becomes a simple matter, similar to finding any program.

When you're using NetWare, however, things can become more complicated. If your users rely on keeping COMMAND.COM in their PATH, they should know that search paths can be altered using the MAP command. They may lose track of where COMMAND.COM actually lives, so they end up with a message notifying them that the file cannot be found. Then their workstations stop working. Then they call you.

To solve this problem, you can adopt one of two different strategies:

- ☐ Install various versions of DOS, and COMMAND.COM in particular, in directories on your NetWare server. Include login script commands that make sure the right COMMAND.COM can be found, depending on the version of DOS the users have.

- ☐ Ensure that the workstation's local COMMAND.COM file can be found.

These strategies are discussed in detail in the following two sections.

NetWare-Based Solution

The first approach—installing various versions of DOS—is traditional with NetWare. Whereas it gives you, as administrator, more control over a potential problem area for users, it also can be a nuisance. You might have to install several versions of DOS, depending on how many are in use by your user community. Installing all these operating systems can be quite a bit of work, and the systems take up space on your file server. It also involves ensuring that you adhere to license agreements.

After you install the DOS versions on your server, you must include a configuration file (such as NET.CFG) on each workstation to include variables such as MACHINE and OS_VERSION. Then, within the login script, you include a MAP command, which places the correct directory in the search path. The MAP S2 command in Table 11.1 is an example of what you need. As long as your users don't alter the search drive mapping, the workstation can find the correct COMMAND.COM.

For greater certainty, you can use NetWare's COMSPEC command to tell the workstation where to look for COMMAND.COM. If the second search drive points to the correct directory, for example, use the following command:

```
COMSPEC S2:COMMAND.COM.
```

DOS-Based Solution

A much easier way to deal with the issue of finding the COMMAND.COM is to make sure your users include a simple command line in their CONFIG.SYS file. If DOS resides in the normal way on the workstation's C: drive, for example, include the following command:

```
SHELL=C:\COMMAND.COM
```

This command automatically updates the DOS COMSPEC variable to point to the workstation's COMMAND.COM. It isn't affected by logging in to NetWare, unless you include a COMSPEC command in a login script.

If you use this approach, no additional drive or search mappings are necessary to deal with finding COMMAND.COM. Following this method has a disadvantage, though, because it requires that your users set up their workstations correctly—something that is less in your control. However, this approach saves the administration associated with keeping multiple versions of DOS, as well as file server space, and checking that license conditions are all met.

IF...THEN...ELSE

The IF...THEN...ELSE construct is the key to testing logical conditions and performing actions accordingly. Within a login script, the statement is used in many different ways. The flow of this statement, however, is always the same:

IF (a condition is evaluated to be true)

THEN (perform one or more actions)

ELSE (perform alternative actions)

END (end of statement)

The evaluated condition is anything that can come out to a value of true or false. An evaluated condition is usually the test of an identifier variable against a certain value—for example, to see whether a user is a certain LOGIN_NAME or to take action on specific days of the week. You can combine conditions using the logical operators such as AND and OR. Conditions also can involve tests such as if an identifier variable is greater than or less than a certain value.

The actions performed can be one or more login script commands. If you use more than one command, the keyword BEGIN must follow THEN. All the statements following the BEGIN are executed, up to either an END statement or an ELSE clause.

The ELSE part of the statement indicates what actions should be taken in the event that the condition turns out to be false. Because you often don't want to do anything if the condition is false, the ELSE clause is optional.

IF...THEN...ELSE statements can be nested—that is, placed one within another—up to 10 levels. Nesting is useful when conditions must be tested depending on the results of other conditions.

INCLUDE

The INCLUDE command executes login script commands contained in another file. After the commands in the other file are completed, control returns to the original login script.

This facility is useful to keep the size of one script more manageable and the structure more understandable. If 20 separate commands must be executed when a certain condition is true, for example, you can place the 20 commands between the THEN BEGIN and END statements. Placing one INCLUDE statement that refers to a text file containing the 20 commands is easier and more understandable, however. (For those of you with programming backgrounds, an INCLUDE is similar to a subroutine call.)

An INCLUDE file can itself have INCLUDE statements referencing other files. The number of separate levels you can include is limited only by the amount of memory in the workstation.

(Execute an External DOS Program)

The pound sign is followed by the name of any DOS program to be executed. The program can be any .EXE, .COM, or .BAT file. After the program completes, control returns to the login script.

When you give a program name, it should either be a full path name or make use of previously assigned drive mappings or search mappings. For example, a frequently used method of routing print output to a network printer is using the CAPTURE command. Because it resides in the SYS:PUBLIC directory and because this directory usually is included in the search path, your login script might include the following line:

```
#CAPTURE /L=2 /Q=RONAN_Q
```

This line sends output destined for the workstation's LPT2 to the RONAN_Q on your current file server. (You learn more about printing from a workstation in Chapter 20.)

Or if you want to be more precise, and not rely on the correct setup of search drives, you can use a full path name, as in the following example:

```
#SYS:PUBLIC\CAPTURE /L=LPT2 /Q=RONAN_Q
```

An important thing to remember when you're using the # command is that while the DOS program executes, the contents of the login script remain in the workstation's memory. As a result, the DOS program may not have enough memory available to it for proper execution.

EXIT

The EXIT command ends execution of all login scripts. Once it is encountered in the script file, no more statements are processed. The EXIT command can optionally indicate the name of a DOS program to begin executing. Although this process sounds similar to the # command, it is not the same thing: the login script continues processing after executing the # command, whereas no other script commands are processed after an EXIT.

A typical use of the EXIT command is to start a menu system for a user. You can use it in conjunction with an IF...THEN command to test which menu should be started. If, for example, one menu should be started for your company's managers and another menu used for everyone else, you can use a command like the following:

```
IF MEMBER OF "MANAGERS" THEN
    EXIT "menu managers"
    ELSE
    EXIT "menu others"
END
```

Note: If the EXIT command appears in the system login script, neither an individual user login script (if one exists for the user) nor the default login script (if no user login script exists) is executed. Sometimes this result is desirable—for example, if you don't want users getting themselves into trouble by changing their drive or search mappings. However, users might also need to perform their own customized login script tasks, requiring that the EXIT command must be removed from the system login script. But removing EXIT opens the door to all other users and their own login scripts. One solution is for each user to have a login script that contains only the EXIT command unless he or she needs additional custom settings.

WRITE

The WRITE command displays messages to the user during the login process. The format of the command is as follows:

```
WRITE "text string"
```

The *text string* can contain the results of identifier variables such as %LOGIN_NAME (note the percent sign in front of the variable, causing its results to be included in the string).

DISPLAY

You use the DISPLAY command to have the contents of a file shown on the user's screen. DISPLAY is intended for use with plain ASCII files, that is, files that contain only regular text characters, without special control codes or other extended characters. If a file contains these unusual characters, you can use FDISPLAY, which filters out the unusual characters.

If, for example, you want users to see the results of the latest hockey pool (which you have diligently updated in the POOL.TXT file kept in the SYS:PUBLIC directory), you can use the following command:

```
DISPLAY SYS:PUBLIC\POOL.TXT
```

To be most effective, the text file should not contain more than 24 lines, the size of a typical workstation screen. In addition, you should follow this line with the PAUSE command so that no other commands are executed until the user has a chance to read the screen. After the user has seen everything, he or she hits any key to continue.

DRIVE

Normally, when the login script finishes executing, your user is left at the first available network drive, typically the F: drive. If the first drive has been remapped to somewhere interesting (the user's home directory, for example), that is usually fine. However, the F: drive may still be mapped to the login directory, which doesn't contain anything useful to the newly logged-in user.

As an alternative, the DRIVE command specifies which network drive letter the user sees when the login script is finished executing. If, for example, your login script maps the M: drive to each user's home directory, and you want him or her to be left in his or her home directory after logging in, you can use the following command:

```
DRIVE M:
```

REMARK

A good programming practice is to include several comments throughout your program code. This practice, known as *annotating* a program, helps someone else reading your code to understand exactly what you are doing. Because login scripts are also a form of programming, putting in comments is a good habit to get into.

To insert comments within a login script, simply start a line with any of the following:

REMARK

REM

* (an asterisk)

; (a semicolon)

Any text that follows on the line is ignored.

Entering Login Scripts

Because login scripts are really just text files, you can create and enter them using any standard ASCII text editor such as EDIT, which comes with DOS version 5.0 and later. But NetWare also enables you to modify login scripts using a feature found within the SYSCON utility. You see the steps you use to create and maintain login scripts in the following sections.

Note: The system login script, NET$LOG.DAT, normally carries an attribute of Read Only (see Chapter 14 for more on attributes). If you want to edit this file using a regular text editor, you have to change the attribute to Read/Write. Or just use SYSCON as described in the following section—it takes care of this little adjustment for you.

Creating the System Login Script

If you want to provide your users with a comfortable network environment, but at the same time make your job as administrator as easy as possible, the best place to focus your efforts is on the system login script. Through effective use of the many commands and identifier variables available to you, you should be able to take care of the large majority of user needs for customization. In that way, you can get away with maintaining as few individual user login scripts as possible—maybe none at all. In the long run, having few user login scripts saves you time.

NetWare comes with a default login script, but there's no system login script at all. So you start from scratch when you create the system login script for your file server. To give you some ideas, you walk through a sample system login script in the following task.

Task 11.1: Entering system login script commands.

Step 1: Description

When you are logged in to NetWare as Supervisor or a Supervisor-equivalent, you can use SYSCON to enter or modify the system login script.

Step 2: Action

1. Log in as Supervisor or use a Supervisor-equivalent account.

2. Type **SYSCON** and press Enter. The Available Topic menu appears.

3. Move the cursor down to Supervisor Options and press Enter. The Supervisor Options box appears.

4. In the Supervisor Options box, move the cursor down to System Login Script and press Enter. You then see an empty screen, indicating that no commands exist in the script at this time (see Figure 11.1).

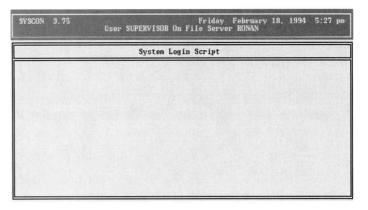

Figure 11.1. *System Login Script entry screen.*

5. In Table 11.4, you see a simple system login script. The table shows the script commands, along with an explanation for each. Enter commands (but not the explanations) in the System Login Script entry screen. After you enter all the commands, double-check your system login script against the one shown in Table 11.4.

6. Press Esc to stop making changes and answer Yes to confirm that you want to save your changes.

7. Exit SYSCON, log off the system, and then log back on as Supervisor, or as any other username you use. Note the effect of the login script commands you entered. You should see results similar to those shown in Figure 11.2.

```
F:\>login supervisor
Enter your password:
Device LPT2: re-routed to queue RONAN_Q on server RONAN.

Drive  A:   maps to a local disk.
Drive  B:   maps to a local disk.
Drive  C:   maps to a local disk.
Drive  D:   maps to a local disk.
Drive  E:   maps to a local disk.
Drive  F: = RONAN\SYS:  \SYSTEM

SEARCH1:  - Z:. [RONAN\SYS:  \PUBLIC]
SEARCH2:  = C:\DOS
SEARCH3:  = C:\WINDOWS
SEARCH4:  = C:\
SEARCH5:  = C:\UTILITY

Good morning, SUPERVISOR.
A reminder - you'll be asked to change your password in 48 days.
Keep your chin up - soon it will be Friday

F:\SYSTEM>
```

Figure 11.2. *Login with new system login script.*

Table 11.4. Sample system login script.

Login Script Command Line	Purpose of Instruction
MAP DISPLAY OFF	Map commands are not displayed.
MAP ERRORS OFF	Errors resulting from map commands are not displayed either.
MAP *1:=SYS:	This line maps the first drive letter to the root directory of the SYS: volume.
MAP *1:=SYS:%LOGIN_NAME	This line maps the first drive letter to the user's home directory, taken from the value of the identifier variable LOGIN_NAME. If the user has no home directory, the first drive is still mapped to SYS:.
IF "%1"="SUPERVISOR" THEN MAP *1:=SYS:SYSTEM	This line tests the value of the identifier variable 1 (which is the first word on the original command line

continues

251

Table 11.4. continued

Login Script Command Line	Purpose of Instruction
	after the word LOGIN). If the user's name is SUPERVISOR, the first drive is set to SYS:SYSTEM instead of to the user's home directory.
`MAP INS S1:=SYS:PUBLIC`	This line includes the SYS:PUBLIC directory (containing commonly used commands) in everyone's search path.
`SET PROMPT = "$P$G"`	This line sets the user's command prompt to display his or her current directory path.
`#CAPTURE /L=2 /Q=RONAN_Q`	This line executes the CAPTURE command to redirect every user's LPT2: to a network print queue.
`MAP DISPLAY ON`	Results of map commands can now be displayed.
`MAP`	This command shows a user his or her current drive and search mappings.
`WRITE`	This command outputs a blank line for aesthetics.
`WRITE "Good %GREETING_TIME, %LOGIN_NAME."`	This line displays friendly greetings to the user.
`WRITE "A reminder—you'll be asked to change your password in %PASSWORD_EXPIRES days."`	This line displays a note indicating when the system will ask for a password change.
`IF DAY_OF_WEEK = "Friday" THEN BEGIN`	This line tests to see whether today is Friday.
`WRITE "Don't forget to attend the weekly Friday Soiree—Social Committee"`	If it is Friday, get people out for some fun.
`FIRE PHASERS 2 TIMES`	This line makes an annoying noise twice in succession (to get attention).

Login Script Command Line	Purpose of Instruction
`ELSE`	Otherwise....
`WRITE "Keep your chin up — soon` `it will be Friday"`	This line provides a message of hope.
`END`	Here is the end of the `IF...THEN...ELSE` statement.
`EXIT`	This command is included to prevent execution of either an individual user login script (if it exists) or the default login script (if no user login script exists).

Step 3: Review

In this task, you learned that most users simply need drive and search mappings established for them when they log in. You easily can accomplish this task by using SYSCON to enter in the appropriate system login script commands. You also can make use of a full set of commands and identifier variables to build sophisticated and complex scripts.

Entering a User Login Script

Each user can have his or her own login script. Just as for the system login script, the user login script can be created with an ASCII text editor or using SYSCON. You learn how to perform the latter method in the following task.

Task 11.2: Entering user login script commands.

Step 1: Description

In this task, you use SYSCON to enter or modify a user login script.

Step 2: Action

1. Log in either as Supervisor, a Supervisor-equivalent account, or the user whose login script is being changed.

2. Type **SYSCON** and press Enter. The Available Topics menu appears.

3. Move the cursor down to User Information and press Enter. The User Names box appears.

4. Select a user to update and press Enter. You then see the User Information screen, as shown in Figure 11.3.

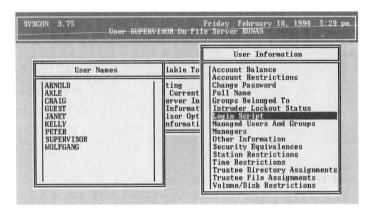

Figure 11.3. *User Information screen.*

5. Move the cursor down to highlight the Login Script selection and press Enter. You are advised that a login script does not exist for the user. The box shown in Figure 11.4 gives you the opportunity to copy an existing script from another user.

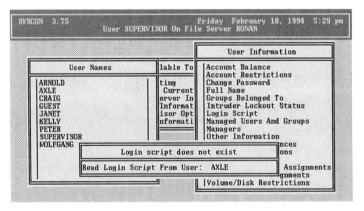

Figure 11.4. *Read from an existing script or start fresh.*

6. To select another user from whom to copy a script, press Ins and select the user's name. Otherwise, press Enter and you are given an empty screen to enter login script commands.

7. Enter the following command into the user's login script, substituting the user's actual name for *<username>*. (Do not use the identifier variable %LOGIN_NAME; you're trying to prove something to yourself here.)

   ```
   WRITE "This is the unique script I created for <username>"
   ```

8. Press Esc to stop making changes and answer Yes to confirm that you want to save changes.

9. For this new user login script to be executed, remove the EXIT command you added to the system login script in Task 11.1. Follow the steps in Task 11.1 to return to the System Login Script entry screen. At the end of the script, place the REMARK command in front of EXIT. Adding REMARK removes the effect of the EXIT command, which is to end execution of all login scripts, without removing the entire command itself. (You might want to restore EXIT later; all you have to do is remove the REMARK.)

10. Exit SYSCON, log off the system, and then log back on as the user. The message you receive is the one you placed in the user's login script. You should see results similar to those shown in Figure 11.5.

```
F:\>login arnold
Enter your password:
Device LPT2: re-routed to queue RONAN_Q on server RONAN.

Drive  A:   maps to a local disk.
Drive  B:   maps to a local disk.
Drive  C:   maps to a local disk.
Drive  D:   maps to a local disk.
Drive  E:   maps to a local disk.
Drive  F: = RONAN\SYS:  \ARNOLD
        ─────
SEARCH1:  = Z:. [RONAN\SYS:  \PUBLIC]
SEARCH2:  = C:\DOS
SEARCH3:  = C:\WINDOWS
SEARCH4:  = C:\
SEARCH5:  = C:\UTILITY

Good morning, ARNOLD.
A reminder - you'll be asked to change your password in 59 days.
Keep your chin up - soon it will be Friday
This is the unique script I created for Arnold

F:\ARNOLD>
```

Figure 11.5. *Log in with new user login script.*

Step 3: Review
In this task, you learned that you can meet unique user requirements by entering individual user login scripts.

> **Note:** Although each user is normally thought to own his or her own script, at times you don't want the user to be able to modify the script. For example, some administrators use the individual user login scripts to place the user into a menu. In this case, you might set permissions on the LOGIN file within the user's SYS:MAIL subdirectory so that the user can't modify the file by himself or herself.

As we pointed out before, you should use the minimum number of individual user login scripts you can because maintaining them can be time consuming. However, it's nice to know the facility is there if you need it.

Summary

In this chapter, you learned how to use login scripts to set up a friendly network environment for your users. Specifically, you learned about the following:

- [ ] NetWare's default login script that it executes in the absence of other login scripts. This script provides users with basic drive and search mappings.

- [ ] The system login script, which is executed for all users whenever they log in.

- [ ] Individual login scripts, executed for each individual user whenever they log in.

In Chapter 12, you see how you can use NetWare's menu facilities to provide an even more friendly user environment on your network.

Workshop
Terminology Review

annotating—The practice of including comment lines within a program such as a login script in order to explain the purpose of instructions.

default login script—The login script built-in to the functioning of the LOGIN.EXE command.

DOS command interpreter—The DOS program that accepts user instructions to DOS and performs the appropriate action. The normal command interpreter is known as COMMAND.COM.

identifier variable—The name of a value tracked by NetWare. An example is the identifier variable DAY, which is set to the number of the current day.

login script—A text file containing commands that are executed when a user logs in to NetWare.

system login script—The login script executed for all users logging in to NetWare.

user login script—The login script executed for an individual user when he or she logs in.

Task List

In this chapter, you entered a sample system login script which is executed for every user logging on to NetWare. You then entered an individual user login script to customize the NetWare environment for one particular user.

Q&A

Q Are login scripts always executed when you access a NetWare server?

A If you ATTACH to a new server after you logged on to another server, any login scripts on the new server will not execute. In addition, if you log in to NetWare from within Windows, login scripts are not executed.

Q Can I create login scripts that apply to Groups?

A There is no facility to create a login script for a particular group. However, you can easily accomplish this with the "IF MEMBER OF" test, and apply the commands you want.

Q Who can modify my login script?

A The capability to modify a login script depends on the rights granted to your LOGIN file—see Chapters 15 and 16 for details on file and directory rights. Certainly the Supervisor, Supervisor-equivalents, and your workgroup manager (if you have one) can make changes.

Q Can a user break out of a login script?

A This is controlled by the BREAK command in a login script. By default, BREAK is OFF. If you set BREAK ON, however, you can abort the normal execution of your login script by pressing Ctrl+C.

12

Customizing and Using Menus

In the preceding chapter, you learned about login scripts. You learned that after NetWare authenticates a user, it runs a series of login scripts. These scripts can contain a variety of setup commands defining the user's environment. After the last login script runs, the user is completely logged in.

Often, the last command executed runs the menu program. This chapter explains the need for menus and the method for creating and implementing them. In the following section, you start with the need for menus.

What's on the Menu?

Why do you need menus? Well, many of your network users probably have limited training and experience when they first use the network. In truth, some users may not even be familiar with microcomputers and their applications. Not surprisingly, the users' primary interest is getting their work done, and not necessarily in becoming techno-wizards. For these reasons and more, your users appreciate a tool that provides a useful and consistent interface.

NetWare provides a menu program that helps you design a customized user interface for programs, utilities, and anything else you might want to put in a menu. The menu program is powerful and DOS-based. You can use it to streamline many tasks that users frequently encounter. Some useful tasks to include in a menu are as follows:

- ☐ Common applications such as word processing and spreadsheets

- ☐ DOS and NetWare commands

- ☐ NetWare utilities

Under NetWare 3.11, you use the MENU utility, but you use NMENU with NetWare 3.12. NMENU has several advantages over the older MENU utility. The main advantage is that NMENU uses less memory on the workstation; in reality, it can use zero memory, when so configured. On the other hand, MENU uses about 50K of RAM.

In this chapter, you learn to

- ☐ Plan for menus

- ☐ Create menus using NMENU and MENU

Regardless of the program you use, you can create different menus for different groups, coordinating the menus they use with the work they perform. For example, you can create a menu for the executives who may just want to use mail, retrieve

reports, and get right off the network. Application developers need database programs and programming languages. Managers need spreadsheets, schedulers, and mail (to respond to executive queries). You can create as many menus as your organization requires. Before you rush off and create a multitude of screens, however, you should sit down and study your organization—in other words, plan.

Planning Menus

In building a menu system, you need to research the needs and experience level of your users. Find out who will use the menu system and what applications or commands they will most frequently use. Determine how much experience they have in using DOS and NetWare.

After you know the users' experience levels and their needs, you must design a user interface that is complete, yet not overwhelming. Also, you must resist the urge to add bells and whistles to your NetWare menus. The goal of every user interface designer is to enable users to use their applications without resorting to manuals. In the case of menu-based systems, menu options should be concise, yet explain clearly what the option does. Menu systems usually are organized in a hierarchy, with menu options that belong together placed under a common heading.

If you have a menu system with DOS and NetWare commands, for example, you should group similar options together. Remember, however, that every new level in a menu system makes the system harder to learn and requires your users to enter more keystrokes to complete their work. Complex menu hierarchies also are difficult to document.

When you're designing your menus, you should try to do the following:

☐ Make the menu structure not too shallow. Try to group related functions under a submenu rather than put them on the main menu. For example, place the word processing or spreadsheet programs in their own submenu when you have more than one, and refer generically to word processing and spreadsheets at the higher level.

☐ Make the menu structure not too deep. In other words, try to reduce the number of steps and menus your users have to traverse to get the option they want.

☐ Visualize the menu the way the users will view the menu. Try to group actions logically as the user does. For example, place Word document printing with the Word application.

12

Tip: You should log in and look at FILER and SYSCON to get an idea of what menus should look like. Try to make your menus look and feel like NetWare's menus. Having a familiar menu structure is comforting to your users. And don't forget to use COLORPAL to change the colors of your menus.

The most appealing thing about NetWare's menu system is that it uses exactly the same function keys and look as other menus, including FILER and SYSCON.

Your next step in the planning process is to chart the menu system. Figure 12.1 provides a sample menu hierarchy.

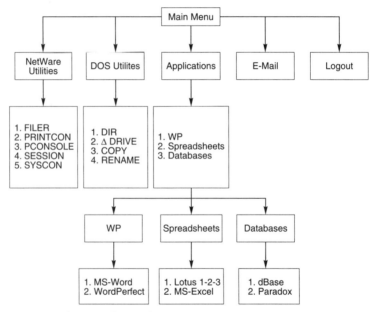

Figure 12.1. *Sample menu hierarchy.*

When the initial design is complete, create a prototype with a few features. Every good program and product starts as a prototype. You will find it very difficult to design and build a finished product in one step. So build a simple menu including the core services and add to it until you have what you want.

Test your menu on sample users. Let these users play with the menu and get back to you with their likes and dislikes. Testing provides valuable feedback from your users, as well as involves them in something affecting them—a process that your users will appreciate immensely.

Refine your design and its implementation to remove any problems. Take all the users' suggestions seriously, try them out, and include useful suggestions.

Don't forget to document your menu system. Complete and accurate documentation will save you time in the future, as well as provide information to other support staff.

NetWare's built-in menu programs provide custom NetWare-looking menus. These programs use a simple script file for building the menus. NetWare's menu program has specific syntax and rules for execution. Before you review the syntax, take a moment to learn about using menus to enhance user productivity.

Note: Novell wrote previous menu programs, but with NetWare 3.12 Novell licensed the NMENU program from Saber Software Corporation. Already, some of you may have Saber's menu system installed because it is the most popular on the market.

After you exploit all of NetWare's menu system features, you might want to look at Saber's product. It offers a login processor, improved security, easier management, and better help.

After you plan your menu system and test the prototype, you can install and implement your menu. Now you're ready to look at how to setup and use your menu system.

Setting Up and Using NMENU

The NMENU utility is new to NetWare 3.12 and adds some features the older MENU program doesn't offer:

☐ NMENU can be set up so that it does not take away any memory from the application the user launches.

☐ NMENU gives you more control over how programs are run.

☐ NMENU enables you to design menu options that ask the user for input and then use the input in the command that is finally executed by the menu.

It's now time to set up NMENU. Setting up NMENU is easy provided you do the following:

1. Install the NMENU programs onto your system.

2. Create a shared directory on the network for the menu files and temporary files that NMENU uses.

3. Use a text editor to create the instructions for the NMENU program.

   Alternatively, you can upgrade the menu files used by the older Novell MENU program. See "Extra Credit" at the end of this chapter.

4. Compile the menu file created in step 3.

5. Set up the users' login scripts to use NMENU so that a menu comes up automatically when the users log in.

Through the course of this chapter, you look at each one of these steps in turn.

Installing the NMENU Program Files

The first step in setting up NMENU is to install the NMENU programs onto the file server. The best place to install these programs is the SYS:PUBLIC directory. You just need to copy the files from your Novell disks or CD-ROM to this directory.

Creating the Shared Directory

NMENU creates two temporary files for each user as it is used. It needs a shared directory to store these files where everyone who uses the menu has full access. The best place to put the shared menu directory is on the SYS: volume. First create the directory and then assign rights to it for everyone.

Task 12.1: Creating the shared directory.

Step 1: Description

This task shows you how to create a shared directory for NMENU.

Step 2: Action

1. At the DOS prompt, type **F:** and press Enter. You should complete this step if your SYS: volume is F:; otherwise, substitute the drive letter of your SYS: volume for F:.

2. Type **CD ** and press Enter. This step ensures that you are in the root directory.

3. Type **MD \MENU** and press Enter. This step creates the MENU directory.

4. Type **CD \MENU** and press Enter.

5. Type **ASSIGN R W F TO EVERYONE** and press Enter. You must assign the EVERYONE group rights to this directory.

Step 3: Review

In this task, you learned how to create a shared directory to store temporary NMENU files for users. Now is the time to create some menus and let users use them.

Creating the Menu

Customizing the menu is the most time-consuming task you have to do for menus, but it also can be rewarding. The process is simple. First, you create a source file of all the commands for the menu. Then you compile that source file into a file that NMENU uses.

At this point, you should have decided on the structure of your menu, so you can start writing the source file using the text editor you are comfortable with. You should create a file called SAMPLE.SRC. You write the source file using the commands shown in Table 12.1.

Table 12.1. NMENU commands.

Command	Description
MENU	Designates the main menu or a submenu
ITEM	Designates an actual menu entry
LOAD	Loads another menu from a different menu file
SHOW	Loads another menu from the same menu file

continues

Table 12.1. continued

Command	Description
EXEC	Instructs NMENU to execute a DOS command
GETO	Allows the menu program to prompt the user for some optional information
GETP	Allows the menu program to store the answer from the user for use later
GETR	Allows the menu program to require the user to respond

Because these commands are not self-explanatory, you look at each one in turn in the following short sections.

MENU

The MENU command delineates a block of commands as belonging to the same menu. The first MENU command in the file defines the top or main menu. Other menus in the file are referenced by their assigned number. The format of the MENU command is as follows:

```
MENU menu_number,menu_name
```

Menu_number is any number from 1 to 255, but each menu must have a unique number. A good idea is to assign your numbers as multiples of 10. Unfortunately, the first menu must be 1. *Menu_name* is any name up to 40 characters in length.

Following are examples of the MENU command:

```
MENU 1,Main Menu...
```

(Main Menu commands follow this line.)

```
MENU 5,Network Utilities
```

(Network Utilities menu commands follow this line.)

ITEM

ITEM marks an individual menu item or entry. The format of the ITEM command is as follows:

```
ITEM item_name {option_1 option_2 ...}
```

Item_name is any name up to 40 characters in length. The *options* are, of course, optional. If you do specify an option, then you must enclose it in braces ({ and }). The options for ITEM are shown in Table 12.2.

Table 12.2. ITEM options.

Option	Description
BATCH	Removes the NMENU program from memory before executing the command
CHDIR	Tells the menu program to return to the previous default directory after ITEM processing is done
PAUSE	Leaves any messages from the DOS command on the screen until the user presses a key to return to the menu
SHOW	Displays the DOS command being executed

Note: If you don't use the BATCH option, then NMENU remains in memory, consuming about 32K of the user's RAM. This might not leave enough memory for some programs to run.

The following examples of the ITEM command use a combination of the options:

```
MENU 5,NetWare Utilities...
ITEM Filer {BATCH CHDIR}...
```

(Filer menu commands follow this line.)

```
ITEM PrintCon {BATCH}...
```

(Printcon menu commands follow this line.)

LOAD

The LOAD command enables you to call a different menu file. You can have a common main menu for all users, for example, and use LOAD to call in customized menus for different functions. LOAD also enables you to link different menus together. The format of the LOAD command is as follows:

```
LOAD menu_filename
```

Menu_filename is any legitimate filename.

Following is an example of the LOAD command:

```
MENU 20,Word Processing
ITEM MS-Word
     LOAD WORD_MNU.DAT
ITEM WordPerfect
     LOAD WP_MNU.DAT
```

SHOW

The SHOW command is similar to the LOAD command. The only difference is that the reference is to another menu within the current menu file. SHOW, like LOAD, enables you to link different menus together. The format of the SHOW command is as follows:

```
SHOW menu_number
```

Menu_number is the assigned reference number for the menu, that is, from 2 to 255.

Following is an example of the SHOW command:

```
MENU 15,Applications
ITEM Word Processing
     SHOW 20
ITEM Spreadsheets
     SHOW 25
ITEM Databases
     SHOW 30
```

EXEC

EXEC causes the command following it to be executed when the menu option is selected. The format of the EXEC command is as follows:

```
EXEC [command] ¦ [option]
```

Command is the name of any executable or command that you want to use. You also can specify options. Again, the *options* are optional. The options for EXEC are shown in Table 12.3.

Table 12.3. EXEC options.

Option	Description
DOS	Enables the users to go into DOS without the menu. When they want to quit DOS, they type EXIT to return to the menu.
EXIT	Exits NMENU. The users must choose an option that explicitly allows exit. Otherwise, the users cannot exit the menu program.
LOGOUT	Exits the menu and logs out the users.

Following is an example of the EXEC command:

```
MENU 5,NetWare Utilities
ITEM Logout
     EXEC LOGOUT
```

GETO

Before you examine GETO specifically, you must understand generally the GETx commands and their purpose. For example, the DISKCOPY command requires you to specify source and target disk drives. Try using the DISKCOPY command without specifying these drives, and you get a message telling you it doesn't work. So you need a method for providing information to DOS commands. The GETx commands are this method. You can have multiple GETx commands before an EXEC command. Each GETx command gets input and places it into the EXEC command.

Now you're ready to look specifically at the GETO command. The GETO command gets input from the user and builds a DOS command with the input just like GETP and GETR do. You execute the DOS command after getting the information. Many DOS commands need information before they can run. This command and its siblings are powerful commands and offer flexibility to customize your menus. The difference between GETO and its siblings is that this command asks for optional information, and the user can choose to enter the information or not. The format of the GETO command is as follows:

```
GETO message {prepend} length,default, {append}
```

The options for GETO are shown in Table 12.4.

Table 12.4. Command options.

Option	Description
message	Prompts the user to enter the required response.
{prepend}	Adds the value in the braces to the front of the user's response, no matter what it is.
length	Specifies the maximum length of the user's response. This option is required.
default	Specifies a value to be displayed as default. The user is given the opportunity to change the default.
{append}	Adds the value in the braces to the back of the user's response, no matter what it is.

Following is an example of the GETO command:

```
MENU 10,DOS Commands
ITEM DOS Directory {SHOW PAUSE}
    GETO Enter the file specification: { } 13,*.*,{/P}
    EXEC DIR
```

In this example, the user can do a directory listing. It prompts the user for a file specification by providing the default *.* (all files). This example also shows the /P parameter appended to the DIR command to pause the command when the screen is full.

GETP

The GETP command, like GETO, gets optional information but stores it in DOS environment variables. The format of the GETP command is as follows:

GETP *message {prepend} length,default, {append}*

The options for GETP are shown in Table 12.4.

Following is an example of the GETP command:

```
MENU 10,DOS Commands
ITEM Copy a Diskette {SHOW PAUSE}
    GETP Enter the source disk drive: {} 01,A, {:}
    GETP Enter the target disk drive: {} 01,A, {:}
    EXEC DISKCOPY %1 %2
```

270

In this example, GETP takes the user's input and creates DOS variables, represented by %1 and %2. You can create variables up to %9. You also can use GETR this way..

GETR

The GETR command asks for required information, which must be provided; otherwise, the menu stops. The format of the GETR command is as follows:

```
GETR message {prepend} length,default, {append}
```

The options for GETR also are shown in Table 12.4.

Following is an example of the GETR command:

```
MENU 10,DOS Commands
ITEM Copy a Diskette {SHOW PAUSE}
    GETR Enter the source disk drive: { } 01,A, {:}
    GETR Enter the target disk drive: { } 01,A, {:}
    GETO Insert source diskette and press {Enter}: {} 00,, {}
    EXEC DISKCOPY
```

In this example, GETR asks for and receives the user's input for the source and target disk drives before doing anything else.

A Sample Menu

Now that you have learned all the menu commands, you can put them all together. Following is a sample menu using the commands you just examined:

```
MENU 1,Main Menu
ITEM NetWare Utilities
    SHOW 5
ITEM DOS Commands
    SHOW 10
ITEM Applications
    SHOW 15
ITEM Electronic Mail
    EXEC EMAIL
ITEM Logout
    EXEC LOGOUT
MENU 5,NetWare Utilities
ITEM Filer {BATCH CHDIR}
    EXEC FILER
ITEM PrintCon {BATCH}
    EXEC PRINTCON
ITEM Pconsole {BATCH}
    EXEC PCONSOLE
ITEM Session {BATCH}
    EXEC SESSION
```

```
ITEM Syscon {BATCH}
     EXEC SYSCON
MENU 10,DOS Commands
ITEM DOS Directory {SHOW PAUSE}
     GETO Enter the file specification: { } 13,*.*,{/P}
     EXEC DIR
ITEM Change Default Disk Drive {}
     GETO Enter new default disk drive: { } 01,, {:}
     EXEC
ITEM Copy a Diskette {SHOW PAUSE}
     GETR Enter the source disk drive: { } 01,A, {:}
     GETR Enter the target disk drive: { } 01,A, {:}
     EXEC DISKCOPY
ITEM Rename a File {SHOW NOECHO PAUSE}
     GETR Enter old file name: { } 30,, {}
     GETR Enter new file name: { } 30,, {}
     EXEC RENAME
MENU 15,Applications
ITEM Word Processing
     SHOW 20
ITEM Spreadsheets
     SHOW 25
ITEM Databases
     SHOW 30
MENU 20,Word Processing
ITEM MS-Word {BATCH CHDIR}
     EXEC WORD.EXE
ITEM WordPerfect {BATCH CHDIR}
     EXEC WP.EXE
MENU 25,Spreadsheets
ITEM Lotus 1-2-3 {BATCH CHDIR}
     EXEC 1-2-3.EXE
ITEM MS-Excel {BATCH CHDIR}
     EXEC EXCEL.EXE
MENU 30,Databases
ITEM dBase {BATCH CHDIR}
     EXEC DBASE.EXE
ITEM Paradox {BATCH CHDIR}
     EXEC PDX.EXE
```

Compiling Menu Files

If you have been following along with the steps in this chapter, then you have a menu in a file such as SAMPLE.SRC. The next step is to take that file and compile it using MENUMAKE.

Task 12.2: Using MENUMAKE.

Step 1: Description

In this task, you compile the menu file you created earlier.

Step 2: Action

1. Type **MENUMAKE SAMPLE.SRC** and press Enter. The output of this command is a new file named SAMPLE.DAT.

2. To run the menu, type **NMENU SAMPLE.DAT** and press Enter. Figure 12.2 shows the main menu using the sample instructions from the preceding section.

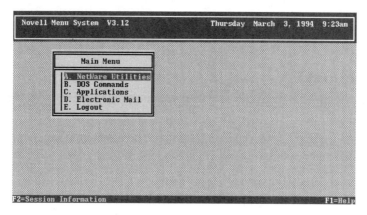

Figure 12.2. *Sample Main Menu.*

Step 3: Review

Compiling menu files you have created is a simple process, as you learned in this task. You use MENUMAKE and add the name of the file to compile. After you have compiled the file, the menu program creates another one. You then can run this menu to see what it looks like. When you are happy with the menu, you can incorporate it into your login scripts (see Chapter 11).

Incorporating NMENU into Login Scripts

The final step in creating menus is to incorporate them into the login scripts for your users. Again, this step involves simply adding the following statements to the login script:

```
SET S_FILEDIR="F:\MENU\"
SET S_STATION="%STATION"
EXIT "NMENU SAMPLE"
```

The first statement here sets the location for the temporary menu files. In this chapter, you set up a MENU directory; however, you should change the path of the MENU directory to match your situation.

The second statement sets each workstation to a unique number. The NMENU program uses the unique number to keep everybody's temporary files in the MENU directory separate.

The last statement exits the login script and passes control to NMENU to execute the SAMPLE.DAT menu.

That's it for menus. Now it's time to recap what you learned today.

Summary

Your network can be scary to some people. The friendlier you can make it for these people, the more likely they are to use your network. You can provide your users with easy-to-use menus, which are simpler to use then remembering some cryptic DOS or NetWare command.

In this chapter, you learned the following:

- ☐ Planning your menus is important

- ☐ NetWare versions 3.11 and 3.12 have different menu systems

- ☐ There are syntax rules for writing menus

- ☐ You can include the menu in a user's login script

That's the menu system. Review the workshop material because it acts as an excellent refresher. If you have not upgraded to NetWare 3.12, then read the "Extra Credit" section to understand about your menu system. In the next chapter, you start your exploration of NetWare files and directories.

Workshop

Terminology Review

menu—A list of options from which users select.

menu options—An option that may perform some action, prompt the user for additional information, or lead to another menu.

submenu—A menu below the main menu.

Task List

The emphasis of this chapter has been to introduce you to menus and their management. As a system administrator or Supervisor, you should understand the role of menus and how to create them. The tasks you should understand from this chapter are as follows:

- ☐ Planning menus
- ☐ Setting up NMENU
- ☐ Installing NMENU program files
- ☐ Creating the shared directory for temporary files
- ☐ Creating a menu
- ☐ Compiling menu files
- ☐ Updating login scripts with menus

Q&A

Q Do I need to have a menu?

A No. Unlike LOGIN scripts, there are no security implications if you do not use menus. However, as mentioned, menus help your users navigate their way easily through the NetWare maze. You will find that your users will appreciate menus.

Q Can users break out of menus?

A With the version 3.11 of NetWare, it was fairly easy to break out of the menu system. The capability to prevent this was improved with the 3.12 version. However, if this is a concern, then you should acquire a third-party menu system.

Q What happens if I make a mistake in building my menu?

A With 3.12, your menu will not compile when your menu syntax is incorrect. If you make a mistake in coding, then the commands may not work. Whatever the mistake, you will get either a NMENU message, a DOS message, or a NetWare message.

Q Can I use my DOS-based menu system?

A Sure, you can use anything that executes DOS commands. If you feel more comfortable with your DOS-based menu system, then use it. Remember, you write menus to make your system easier to navigate, so whatever makes it easy for you should be used.

Extra Credit
Using MENU

Earlier in this chapter, you learned all you need to know about NMENU. Now you can learn everything you need to know about the MENU facility. MENU is the 3.11 version of NMENU. The use of MENU involves two steps. First, you create an ASCII file containing menu headers, options, and commands. Then you execute the MENU utility to compile the ASCII menu file.

To run the application you created, you enter the following at the DOS prompt:

```
MENU {path} <menufile>
```

Note: Normally, you should create a menu file with a filename extension of .MNU. If you use the .MNU extension, then you do not need to supply the full name when running the MENU utility. If you use an extension other than MNU, then you must specify the entire filename.

Creating a MENU File

The creation of the ASCII menu file is relatively simple if you follow the simple steps for creating menus, as shown in Task 12.3.

Task 12.3: Creating a menu.

Step 1: Description

This task walks you through the process of creating a user's menu using the MENU utility.

Step 2: Action

1. Create a text file SAMPLE.MNU in the directory where your users will use the menu.

2. On the first line, type `%Main Menu,0,0,5`. Main Menu is the name of the menu, the first 0 is the horizontal placement of the menu, the second 0 is the vertical placement of the menu, and 5 is the number of the color palette. Use the % symbol (see Table 12.5) to specify a menu's header. Make sure the menu headers are flush with the left margin.

> **Tip:** You can use the following simple formula to calculate the vertical and horizontal placement values for the menus:
>
> `C=A+B/2`
>
> where A is the number of lines above the menu (or to the left of the menu for the horizontal calculation), B is the number of lines in the menu (or the width of the menu for the horizontal calculation), and C is the vertical (or horizontal) center of the menu.

3. On subsequent lines, type main menu options on the left margin, just as you want them to appear.

> **Tip:** The MENU utility automatically sorts the menu options. If the automatic sorting is okay with you, then do nothing. If you want to place the menu options in a specific order, however, then prefix each option with a number.

12

4. Below each option, type the way you want the option executed.

   ☐ *Commands:* Indent three spaces from the left and type the command exactly as you do at the DOS prompt. The command should be on the search path so that the menu utility can execute it. However, you can use the menu to switch drives and mappings to agree with every command.

   ☐ *Submenus:* Indent three spaces from the left and type a percent sign (%) and the menu name.

5. Continue to type options, commands, and subcommands until the menu is complete.

6. Save the text file as SAMPLE.MNU in ASCII format.

Step 3: Review

In this task, you learned the steps for constructing a menu in NetWare 3.11.

Understanding Menu Syntax

You use the characters in Table 12.5 to create menus. The @ sign requires further explanation, however. When a user selects an option to execute a command, NetWare may need to collect more information from the user before executing the command. You can set up the menu to receive input as variables from the user. The @ symbol denotes a variable and indicates where to get the new information. The following command is an example of the use of variables:

```
DIR @1"Enter the file specification " @2"Enter the Options "
```

In the preceding example, you can see the use of two variables (@1 and @2). When you collect additional information this way, you can repeat the use of a variable over multiple commands.

Table 12.5. MENU programming characters.

Character	Description
%	Designates a menu
@	Designates a variable with a user-assigned value
!	Closes all files opened by MENU

Character	Description
\	Indicates the use of a special character (%, @, !, or ") in a literal
"	Encloses strings to display on the screen

Note: The variable assignments are forgotten when a new menu option is encountered. A menu option is not indented from the left margin.

Examining a Sample Menu

Now you can create a menu. Following is a sample menu you might find useful:

```
%MAIN MENU,0,0,5
1.    NetWare Utilities
      %NETWARE UTILITIES
2.    DOS Commands
      %DOS COMMANDS
3.    Applications
      %APPLICATIONS
4.    Electronic Mail
      EMAIL
5.    Logout
      !LOGOUT
%NetWare Utilities,20,10,4
Filer
      FILER
PrintCon
      PRINTCON
Pconsole
      PCONSOLE
Session
      SESSION
Syscon
      SYSCON
%DOS Commands,20,10,4
DOS Directory
      DIR @1"Enter the file specification " @2"Enter the Options "
      PAUSE
Change Default Disk Drive
      @1"Enter new default disk drive:"
      PAUSE
```

12

```
Copy a Diskette
     DISKCOPY @1"Enter the source disk drive:" @2"Enter the target disk
drive:"
     PAUSE
Rename a File
     RENAME @1"Enter old file name " @2"Enter new file name:"
     PAUSE
%APPLICATIONS,20,10,4
1.   Word Processing
     %WORDPROCESSING
2.   Spreadsheets
     %SPREADSHEETS
3.   Databases
     %DATABASES
%WORDPROCESSING,20,10,4
MS-Word
     WORD.EXE
WordPerfect
     WP.EXE
%SPREADSHEETS,20,10,4
Lotus 1-2-3
     123.EXE
MS-Excel
     EXCEL.EXE
%DATABASES,20,10,4
dBase
     DBASE.EXE
Paradox
     PDX.EXE
```

The main menu generated by this sample is shown in Figure 12.3.

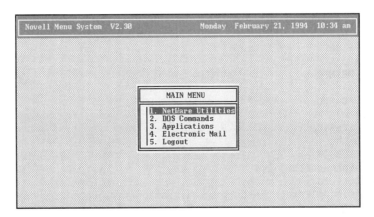

Figure 12.3. *The sample Main Menu.*

Installing a MENU

After you have finished your menu file, save it to a file in the SYS:PUBLIC directory. To bring up the menu, type the following command:

```
MENU SAMPLE.MNU
```

To set up users so that the menu comes up automatically when they log in to the network, add this line to the end of their individual login scripts:

```
EXIT "MENU SAMPLE"
```

You, of course, substitute the name of the menu you want to use for SAMPLE.MNU. You need the quotation marks for the login script command EXIT.

Note: The EXIT command must be the last statement in the login script because nothing following it is executed. Also, you get only one EXIT per login script.

Tip: To save time, you should create a master menu that includes every possible application, utility, and command, and cut selections when creating a customized menu for a user.

If you need to create different menus for various people, then create the different menu files and give each person the appropriate EXIT command to start his or her menu file.

Converting a MENU File

Perhaps you have old MENU files from NetWare 2.*x* or 3.11 that you want to continue to use when you migrate to NetWare 3.12. You can quickly upgrade those menu files with the MENUCNVT utility, included with the new NMENU program. Converting is simple, as you see in the following task.

12

Task 12.4: Converting an old MENU file.

Step 1: Description

In this task, you use the MENUCNVT utility to convert old menu files to the new NMENU format.

Step 2: Action

1. At the DOS prompt, type **F:** and press Enter.

2. Type **CD \PUBLIC** and press Enter.

3. To find the old menu files, type **DIR *.MNU /P**.

4. Type **MENUCNVT SAMPLE.MNU** and press Enter. You repeat this step substituting the name of each menu file for conversion.

5. You can edit SAMPLE.SRC and then compile it to create your new menus.

Step 3: Review

In this task, you learned to convert your old menu files. You can edit these new menu files and compile them to use as menus. Refer to previous tasks in this chapter to see how to edit and compile menus.

13

Exploring
NetWare Files
and Directories

In the last several chapters, you learned how to log on to a NetWare server and navigate around some of the menus and features. You also have acquired knowledge about how to set up users and control how they can access the system. Now it's time to learn more about what it is most users are interested in getting to: directories and files on the file server.

In this chapter, you learn more about how NetWare enables you to organize files into directories, and group directories in other directories. In fact, if you're familiar with DOS and its file structure, you will be pleased to see that NetWare's system is virtually identical.

You learn the commands and utilities that enable you to traverse NetWare's directory structure, move and copy files across the structure, and delete files and directories you no longer need. (And in the next chapter, you learn how to get files back if you didn't mean to delete them.)

This chapter begins with a review of what you learned about NetWare's file structure in Chapter 4.

Reviewing How NetWare Stores Files

In Chapter 4, you learned that NetWare maintains a number of logical structures which it uses to store files. These include the following:

☐ *Volumes*: The highest level of NetWare's storage system. A volume can be spread across as many as 32 separate physical disk areas known as segments. Each NetWare file server may have as many as 64 volumes. Each volume is made up of blocks.

☐ *Blocks*: The basic unit in which file storage is allocated. Each block can be from 4K to 64K (in integral powers of two). Individual data files are given space an entire block at a time.

To get from a block to a physical location on a disk drive, NetWare maintains a mapping for each block that specifies the segment the block is on. NetWare translates the segment into a physical disk drive and disk sector number within the drive.

In order to keep track of all the blocks, NetWare maintains the File Allocation Table (FAT), which contains information about every block on the volume. An actual file simply is a chain of FAT entries for each block used by the file. Each block used by the file contains a link to the next block in use.

To keep track of what files exist, NetWare keeps a Directory Entry Table (DET). The DET contains details very similar to those found in DOS directories. For each file on a NetWare volume, the DET has an entry with key details such as the file's name and size. The DET entry also has a pointer to the FAT. NetWare follows this pointer, and then uses the FAT information to actually access the file.

So once you know the name of a file, NetWare can use the DET to find its FAT entry. The FAT tells NetWare each and every block in use by the file. To access the file, NetWare simply determines each block in use, and then uses the block numbers to actually locate the data at its physical disk locations.

While NetWare's volumes, blocks, FATs, and DETs are all very interesting, your users typically are much more concerned with other data structures—the ones they come into contact with daily. These are files that contain their programs and data, and the directories they use to organize their files into logical groupings. Next, you learn how NetWare provides files and directories to its users.

Understanding the NetWare Directory and File Structure

All the NetWare data structures described previously are created to support the more visible (and usable) creations known as *files* and *directories*. The concept of files and directories is used by many different operating systems including DOS, UNIX, OS/2, and Macintosh System 7. They may be called by different names such as documents and folders, but the purpose for each is the same.

☐ A *file* is used to store data. The data may be anything from a word processing document to an executable program. The easiest way to think of a computer file is as a collection of computer bytes that has a name attached to it. You then can refer to the file by its name, and let the computer worry about where the file is on a disk (or across a network).

☐ A *directory* is like a box that contains files. On the front of the box is a list of all the files inside, as well as information such as the size of the file, and when it was last updated.

Using these concepts, you can imagine that directories containing files can be placed in other directories. When one directory is placed in another one, it normally is referred to as a *subdirectory*. Each directory can contain both files and other directories.

The relationship between directories and files is a hierarchical one. It often is depicted as shown in Figure 13.1, in a structure known as a *tree*. (Because the root is at the top, it really is an upside down tree.) Note that at each level, you can find both subdirectories and files.

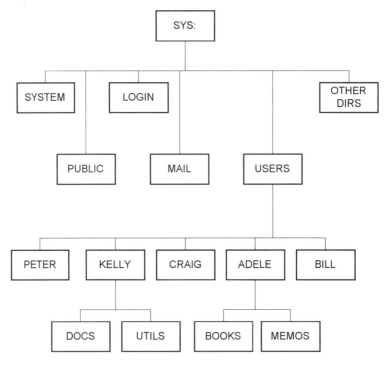

Figure 13.1. *NetWare directories and files.*

Tip: A directory really is just a special type of file. The data it contains gives details on each file in the directory, including its name, size, and other characteristics. If you think of directories simply as special files, the idea of having both directories and files at each level of the tree won't seem quite so strange.

> **Note:** The directory mentioned here is *not* the same as an entry in NetWare's Directory Entry Table. As far as the DET is concerned, the file system directory discussed in this chapter simply is another file containing data. The data it holds just happens to be details about other files.

Uniquely identifying a particular file involves specifying its *pathname*—that is, the name of the file as well as the names of all the directories you follow to get to the file. A *full pathname* is written in the following form:

```
ServerName/VolumeName:Directory1/Directory2/.../Filename
```

For example, the document that contains this chapter is known as CHAP14.DOC. It is stored in a directory called TYNW14, which is a subdirectory of the CRAIG directory, which is kept on the SYS volume on the RONAN server. The full pathname for the file is:

```
RONAN/SYS:CRAIG/TYNW14/CHAP14.DOC
```

ServerName corresponds to the name of your NetWare server as it is known on the network. *VolumeName* is the name of the particular volume on the server. The name of each directory on the path down the tree to the file also is specified. Finally, the name of the file itself appears.

Fortunately, many shortcuts are available so that you don't have to type this full path name every time you want to access a file. These shortcuts are covered later in the chapter.

Recall that, within a particular volume, NetWare can take a file name, consult the DET and FAT, and find the file on a disk. After you specify a particular server and volume, NetWare can begin the lookup process. It takes the full pathname for the file, performs a lookup through its own DET and FAT to see where the file is on disk, and finally retrieves the file's contents.

Listing File and Directory Details

As you probably know, the DOS operating system keeps track of a few details about each of its files—things such as the name of the file, the date it was last modified, and its size. NetWare also keeps track of these details for its files, but it also maintains additional information about each file and directory on the server. Following are examples of these further details:

☐ Key dates and times, including when the file was created, when it was last accessed, when it was last updated, and when it was last archived.

☐ Flags known as attributes, indicating special features or handling for the file (these will be covered in Chapter 14).

☐ Important security information that specifies who can access the directory or file (these are covered in Chapters 15 and 16).

DOS users can utilize all of the same commands they are familiar with to find out about files and directories. The DOS DIR command works just the same way for NetWare files as it does for DOS files.

But NetWare also provides its own commands that enable you to view the additional details it keeps track of (which you learn about in this chapter). You've already seen the main command line utility which serves this purpose: NDIR. In Chapter 6, you used the NDIR command to see what files you have in a directory. In its basic form, NDIR told you the name of the file and its size, plus some other details you learn about later. To review, the syntax of the command is

`NDIR [path] [/option...]`

where [*path*] refers to the pathname for the file, and [*/option...*] refers to the many sorting and selecting options available with NDIR. Now you see some of these options that enable you to find out even more details about your files and directories. This section begins with key dates and times.

Task 13.1: Using NDIR to view dates.

Step 1: Description

Use the NDIR command to view the key dates for files in the current directory.

Step 2: Action

At the DOS prompt on your workstation, type **NDIR \SYSTEM /DATES**. Your output should appear similar to that shown in Figure 13.2.

Note: NDIR does not provide information for local DOS disks attached to your workstation.

```
RONAN\SYS:SYSTEM

Files:              Last Updated   Last Archived  * Accessed   Created/Copied
_____
3C503        LAN    9-01-92 12:51p  0-00-00  0:00  -  1-14-94  1-14-94 12:56a
3C509        LAN    1-07-93  1:09p  0-00-00  0:00  -  1-14-94  1-14-94 12:56a
3C523        LAN    1-13-93  8:58a  0-00-00  0:00  -  1-14-94  1-14-94 12:56a
3CBOOT       NLM    9-30-91  2:32p  0-00-00  0:00  -  1-14-94  1-14-94 12:54a
3CNLAN       LAN   10-14-92  3:59p  0-00-00  0:00  -  1-14-94  1-14-94 12:56a
3NW391R      LAN    9-09-92  4:13p  0-00-00  0:00  -  1-14-94  1-14-94 12:56a
3NW392R      LAN    9-15-92 11:43a  0-00-00  0:00  -  1-14-94  1-14-94 12:56a
3NW89XR      LAN    4-12-93  7:45a  0-00-00  0:00  -  1-14-94  1-14-94 12:56a
ACONSOLE     EXE    8-06-93  3:13p  0-00-00  0:00  -  1-25-94  1-14-94 12:56a
ADAPTEC      NLM    2-13-91  5:07p  0-00-00  0:00  -  1-14-94  1-14-94 12:54a
AFTER311     NLM    5-25-93  4:35p  0-00-00  0:00  -  1-20-94  1-14-94 12:55a
AIO          NLM    6-11-93  2:00p  0-00-00  0:00  -  1-14-94  1-14-94 12:55a
AIOACI       NLM   12-17-92 12:14p  0-00-00  0:00  -  1-14-94  1-14-94 12:55a
AIOCOMX      NLM   12-17-92 12:09p  0-00-00  0:00  -  1-14-94  1-14-94 12:55a
AIOCXCFG     NLM   12-15-92  8:08a  0-00-00  0:00  -  1-14-94  1-14-94 12:55a
AIODGCX      NLM   12-15-92  8:09a  0-00-00  0:00  -  1-14-94  1-14-94 12:55a
AIODGMEM     NLM   12-15-92  8:07a  0-00-00  0:00  -  1-14-94  1-14-94 12:55a
AIODGXI      NLM   12-14-92  2:13p  0-00-00  0:00  -  1-14-94  1-14-94 12:55a
AIOESP       NLM    1-28-93  6:45p  0-00-00  0:00  -  1-14-94  1-14-94 12:55a

Strike any key for next page or C for continuous display...
```

Figure 13.2. *Listing Key Dates/Times for NetWare files.*

Section 3: Review

To determine key dates for NetWare files and directories, use the NDIR /DATES command.

Note the dates provided by the NDIR command. Each one is described in more detail.

☐ Last Updated indicates the date and time the file's contents actually were changed.

☐ Last Archived shows the last date and time the file was copied to tape for backup purposes. The backup process resets the file's archive attribute, while NetWare updates this information. (You learn more about file attributes in Chapter 14.)

☐ Last Accessed shows the date the file was last used in any way (which includes being read or executed).

☐ Created/Copied indicates the date and time when the file was originally placed on this NetWare server.

13

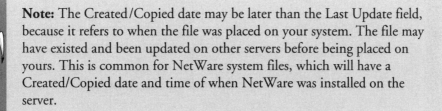

Note: The Created/Copied date may be later than the Last Update field, because it refers to when the file was placed on your system. The file may have existed and been updated on other servers before being placed on yours. This is common for NetWare system files, which will have a Created/Copied date and time of when NetWare was installed on the server.

You can instruct NDIR to display the contents of a directory other than the current one simply by specifying a full path name. For example, the command

```
NDIR SYS:\SYSTEM
```

displays the contents of the SYSTEM directory on your current file server, regardless of the directory you are currently using.

By default, NDIR sorts its output in file name alphabetical order, followed by any subdirectories, also in name alphabetic order. Another useful NDIR option is to sort output according to some other criteria, such as file size. Try listing files from largest to smallest, rather than in alphabetic order.

Task 13.2: Using NDIR sort options.

Step 1: Description
List all the files in the SYSTEM directory in order of decreasing size.

Step 2: Action
Type **NDIR \SYSTEM /REVerse SORT SIze**. This specifies that the output should be sorted by size. By default, this would be in the order of smallest to largest. The /REV parameter indicates the reverse of normal sorting, that is, largest to smallest.

> **Note:** When a portion of a command option appears in capital letters (such as /REVerse) you only have to type the capitalized portion for the option to take effect in the command.

NetWare will produce output similar to that shown in Figure 13.3.

> **Note:** Details on the Flag column are covered in Chapter 14, while the concept of the file's Owner is addressed in Chapter 15.

Step 3: Review
Sorting NDIR output involves specifying SORT options.

```
RONAN\SYS:SYSTEM

Files:                Size      Last Updated       Flags          Owner

CLIB       NLM       305,867   5-19-93   5:27p [RoS------------DR] RONAN
BUTIL      NLM       200,338   1-29-93   2:19p [RoS------------DR] RONAN
TCPIP      NLM       188,871   2-22-93  12:34p [RoS------------DR] RONAN
BTRIEVE    NLM       183,877   5-24-93   6:00p [RoS------------DR] RONAN
SBACKUP    NLM       183,549   5-18-93   8:02a [RoS------------DR] RONAN
BTRIEVE    ORG       180,678   2-19-93   4:49p [RoS------------DR] RONAN
INSTALL    NLM       169,700   8-17-93  10:23a [RoS------------DR] RONAN
NWSNUT     NLM       160,623   6-15-93   3:40p [RoS------------DR] RONAN
IBMFDDIO   LAN       144,095   5-12-93   4:15p [RoS------------DR] RONAN
TSA311     NLM       122,070   6-04-93  10:59a [RoS------------DR] RONAN
TSA312     NLM       122,069   6-04-93  10:54a [RoS------------DR] RONAN
ACONSOLE   EXE       118,229   8-06-93   3:13p [RoS------------DR] RONAN
MONITOR    NLM       117,775  10-26-92   9:21a [RoS------------DR] RONAN
TCPCON     NLM       107,814   1-29-93   1:12p [RoS------------DR] RONAN
RCONSOLE   EXE        94,801   8-06-93   3:13p [RoS------------DR] RONAN
MADGEODI   LAN        78,169   1-05-93   1:40p [RoS------------DR] RONAN
BTRMON     NLM        75,022   1-28-93   2:25p [RoS------------DR] RONAN
BINDFIX    EXE        74,379   4-27-93   9:37a [RoS------------DR] RONAN
BSETUP     NLM        72,329   1-07-93  11:04a [RoS------------DR] RONAN

Strike any key for next page or C for continuous display...
```

Figure 13.3. *NDIR Output sorted by file size.*

NDIR also enables you to limit which items are displayed. You can show only files by using the /FO (files only) option, or only directories by using the /DO option. You can further restrict what is displayed by specifying explicit criteria, similar to querying an information database.

Task 13.3: Using NDIR filtering options.

Step 1: Description
Limit the display of files to only those in the \SYSTEM directory that have been accessed since 1 January 1993.

Step 2: Action
Type the command **NDIR \SYSTEM /ACcess AFTer 12-1-94**. NetWare produces output similar to that shown in Figure 13.4.

Step 3: Review
NDIR allows limiting output by evaluating each item against selection criteria.

> **Tip:** Probably the best thing to remember about the NDIR command, rather than all the possible options, is the way to get help. All you have to do is type **NDIR /help**, (or **NDIR /?**) and NetWare reminds you of the command syntax.

13

```
RONAN\SYS:SYSTEM

Files:                  Size      Last Accessed        Flags            Owner

UBPCETP       LAN     15,148    1-14-94        [RoS-------------DR]  RONAN
TRXNET        LAN      3,075    1-14-94        [RoS-------------DR]  RONAN
TOKENDMA      LAN     10,861    1-14-94        [RoS-------------DR]  RONAN
TOKEN         LAN     10,125    1-14-94        [RoS-------------DR]  RONAN
TCTOKH        LAN     40,039    1-14-94        [RoS-------------DR]  RONAN
TCNSH         LAN      5,861    1-14-94        [RoS-------------DR]  RONAN
TCE32MCH      LAN     17,413    1-14-94        [RoS-------------DR]  RONAN
TCE16MCH      LAN     15,137    1-14-94        [RoS-------------DR]  RONAN
TCE16ATH      LAN     15,043    1-14-94        [RoS-------------DR]  RONAN
TCARCH        LAN      5,877    1-14-94        [RoS-------------DR]  RONAN
T30N4X        LAN     37,463    1-14-94        [RoS-------------DR]  RONAN
T20N4X        LAN     37,440    1-14-94        [RoS-------------DR]  RONAN
SMCARC        LAN      7,076    1-14-94        [RoS-------------DR]  RONAN
SMC8100       LAN     35,946    1-14-94        [RoS-------------DR]  RONAN
SMC8000       LAN     20,944    1-14-94        [RoS-------------DR]  RONAN
PCN2L         LAN      4,726    1-14-94        [RoS-------------DR]  RONAN
NTR2000       LAN     10,133    1-14-94        [RoS-------------DR]  RONAN
NI9210        LAN      5,920    1-14-94        [RoS-------------DR]  RONAN
NI6510        LAN     16,987    1-14-94        [RoS-------------DR]  RONAN

Strike any key for next page or C for continuous display...
```

Figure 13.4. *NDIR output for files accessed since a given date.*

Using LISTDIR

NetWare also provides a command line utility, LISTDIR, that displays directories and their subdirectories in a convenient format. LISTDIR also can provide information on rights, as well as date and time. The syntax of the LISTDIR command is

LISTDIR [*DirectoryPath* [/*Option* ... *Option*]]

with options referring to the types of information that can be included in the listing.

Task 13.4: Using LISTDIR.

Step 1: Description

You can use LISTDIR to provide extensive information about every directory and subdirectory on your file server.

Step 2: Action

Type **LISTDIR /A**. NetWare produces output similar to that shown in Figure 13.5.

Step 3: Review

LISTDIR produces a more visual representation of your directory tree, with additional details available about entries at each level.

```
F>listdir \a

The subdirectory structure of RONAN/SYS:PUBLIC
Date       Time    Inherited    Effective    Directory
──────────────────────────────────────────────────────────
1-14-94    1:01a  [SRWCEMFA]   [SRWCEMFA]   ->NLS
1-20-94   10:38a  [SRWCEMFA]   [SRWCEMFA]   ->  ENGLISH
1-14-94    1:01a  [SRWCEMFA]   [SRWCEMFA]   ->OS2
1-14-94    1:03a  [SRWCEMFA]   [SRWCEMFA]   ->UNIX
4 subdirectories found

F>
```

Figure 13.5. *LISTDIR output using the ALL option.*

Tip: As with some other NetWare commands such as NDIR, the best thing to remember about the LISTDIR command, rather than all the possible options, is the way to get help. All you need to do is type **LISTDIR** /**help**, and you'll be reminded of the command syntax.

Using FILER

NetWare comes with a menu utility that you can use to view file and directory information. FILER provides a very usable interface that enables you to determine quickly a file's key details.

Task 13.5: Using FILER to look at files.

Step 1: Description
The FILER menu utility enables you to view key file and directory details.

Step 2: Action
1. Type **FILER** and then press Enter. The FILER menu now appears, as shown in Figure 13.6.

2. The cursor first appears on Current Directory Information. Press Enter to display details about the current directory. The details should appear similar

to that shown in Figure 13.7. Note the same types of information you saw with the NDIR command, such as Creation Date and Creation Time.

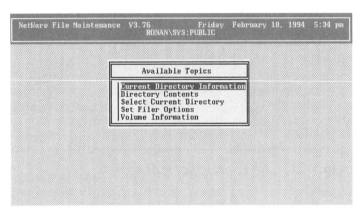

Figure 13.6. *The FILER main menu.*

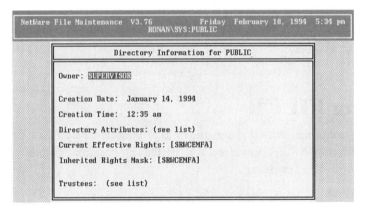

Figure 13.7. *FILER current directory information.*

3. Press Esc to go back to the main FILER menu. Press the down arrow to move down one item so that Directory Contents is highlighted and then press Enter. You see a display similar to that shown in Figure 13.8. This gives details on each item in the directory, including file names, and other directories.

4. Press the down arrow key until the file you want is highlighted, and then press Enter. A new box appears that enables you to select from a number of operations. Highlight View/Set File Information and then press Enter.

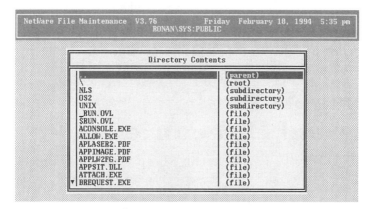

Figure 13.8. *FILER Directory Contents Information window.*

You see a display of file information for the file similar to that shown in
Figure 13.9. Once again, note that the same types of details you were able to
see with the NDIR command such as Creation Date, Last Accessed Date,
Last Archived Date, and Last Modified Date appear.

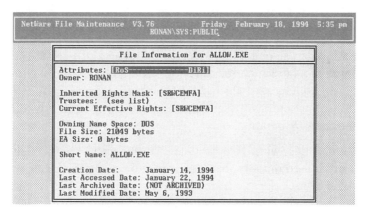

Figure 13.9. *The FILER file information screen.*

Note: The other items of information presented by the FILER utility are
discussed in the following chapters.

5. Press Esc from the FILER utility and return to the DOS command prompt.

13

Step 3: Review

NetWare's FILER utility provides a user friendly menu interface that enables you to obtain details about files and directories on the server.

Moving Around Disks and Directories

As with DOS, you always can specify a full pathname in order to access a NetWare data file or command. Typing the server name, volume name, and every directory on the path to a file, however, can become pretty tedious. Fortunately, NetWare enables you to address this problem in different ways. One mechanism, known as *drive and search mappings* is covered in Chapter 14. Using these maps, you can have NetWare find your files for you.

For this lesson, you can save typing full path names another way. Similar to DOS, NetWare supports the concept of a *current directory*. The current directory is a pointer to a location (a specific directory) in the file hierarchy that can be moved up, down, and around between directories and subdirectories. The importance of the current directory is that DOS and NetWare commands that make use of files generally will refer to the current directory.

For example, if you type a simple command such as DIR or NDIR, by default, they will list all files in your current directory. You then change the current directory by changing the directory to which it points in the file hierarchy. When you type the DIR or NDIR command again, NetWare lists the contents of the new directory to which you currently are pointing.

If you are familiar with DOS, you may remember that the CD (Change Directory) command is used to move the current directory pointer. And, if you type CD on a command by itself, DOS tells you the current directory. You'll be glad to know that things function in exactly the same way in NetWare. You still can use the CD command to move around the directory hierarchy on the file server.

Warning: Using the CD command on NetWare drives known as search drives can cause problems. Search drives provide a mechanism similar to the DOS PATH, so changing the directory to which they point can leave you without the capability to find important files easily. See Chapter 14 for more details on using search drives.

NetWare also enables you to change directories within the menu utilities you use to look at and manipulate files, such as the FILER utility you used earlier in this chapter.

Task 13.6: Using FILER to move around the file hierarchy.

Step 1: Description

The FILER menu utility enables you to move between directories.

Step 2: Action

1. Type **FILER** and then press Enter. The FILER main menu appears.

2. The cursor first appears on Current Directory Information. Press the down arrow key twice to highlight Select Current Directory and then press Enter. You see a display similar to that shown in Figure 13.10. This shows the current directory you are in by giving you the full path name, including the server name and volume.

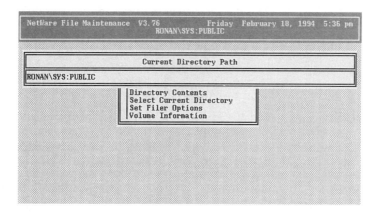

Figure 13.10. *The FILER current directory path.*

3. To change directories, you simply edit this path name. The easiest way to do this is to use the Ins key. This accesses a menu similar to the one shown in Figure 13.11. Press the arrow keys to select the directory to which you want to change and press Enter. You see that the Current Directory Path name is updated. To accept this path, press Esc and then press Enter.

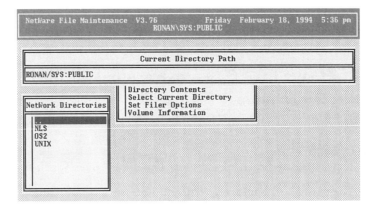

Figure 13.11. *The FILER network directory listing.*

Note: If you keep selecting the parent directory (indicated by ..), you eventually will be offered a choice of volumes on the server. Selecting .. again displays a choice of servers.

4. Another way to alter the current directory is to simply retype the full path name in the Current Directory Path box. To change to a subdirectory of the current directory, for example, type \ followed by the subdirectory name. If you want to change to a completely new directory, press Backspace to delete the path name shown, and then type the new name. After you type the new path name, press Enter. You return to the main FILER menu.

5. FILER also enables you to change directories as you explore the contents of the current directory. To see how this works, highlight Directory Contents and press Enter. You see a display similar to that shown in Figure 13.12.

6. The window that appears lists all entries in the current directory. This includes files (indicated by file in the right-hand column) as well as directories that you can change into directly. The location of the directory is indicated in the right-hand column, as either a subdirectory (contained within the current directory), parent (above the current directory), and root (located at the top of the directory tree). To change directories, highlight the directory you want to change to and press Enter.

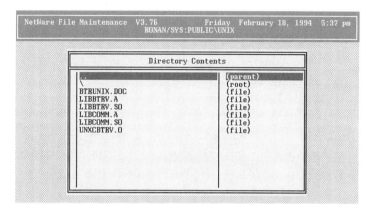

Figure 13.12. *The FILER directory contents listing.*

7. If you chose the parent or root directory, a box will appear prompting you to make the indicated directory the current directory. Press Enter to indicate Yes. If you selected a subdirectory, the Subdirectory Options menu appears. Highlight Make This Your Current Directory, and press Enter. In either case, a new Directory Contents menu appears that lists the contents of the current directory.

8. Press Esc from the FILER utility and return to the DOS command prompt.

Step 3: Review

The FILER menu utility enables you to change the directory in which you are working.

Creating Directories

As you've seen previously, most standard DOS commands work fine on NetWare file hierarchies. Creating directories is no exception. You can continue to use the DOS MKDIR command to create a new directory, and it performs in the same way as you have come to expect on your C: drive.

NetWare's FILER menu utility also enables you to create new directories easily, as you will see in the next task.

Task 13.7: Using FILER to create a new directory.

Step 1: Description

Using the FILER menu utility, you can create a new directory on the file hierarchy.

Step 2: Action

1. Type **FILER** and then press Enter. The FILER main menu now appears.

2. The cursor will first appear on Current Directory Information. Highlight Directory Contents and press Enter. As you saw in Task 13.6, the window displays a list of all entries in the current directory.

3. Press Ins. NetWare prompts you to type the New Subdirectory Name. Your screen should appear as shown in Figure 13.13. Type the name and press Enter. The new subdirectory now appears in the Directory Contents box.

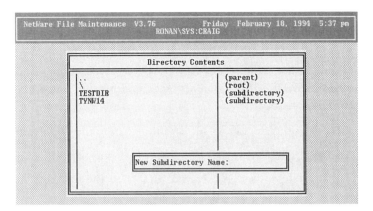

Figure 13.13. *Adding a new subdirectory.*

4. Press Esc from the FILER utility and return to the DOS command prompt.

Step 3: Review

Using the FILER Directory Contents submenu enables you to add a new subdirectory easily.

Deleting Files and Directories

You can delete NetWare files and directories using the normal suite of DOS commands. To erase a file, or example, you can type the command

```
DEL <filename>
```

as you've come to know in DOS. If you prefer, the DOS ERASE command performs the same function.

NetWare's FILER menu utility once again steps in to provide a convenient method of deleting files and directories.

Task 13.8: Using FILER to delete a file or directory.

Step 1: Description

The FILER menu utility enables you to delete a file or directory easily.

Step 2: Action

1. Type FILER and then press Enter. The FILER main menu appears.

2. The cursor first appears on Current Directory Information. Highlight Directory Contents and press Enter. As you saw in Task 13.6, the window displays a list of all entries in the current directory.

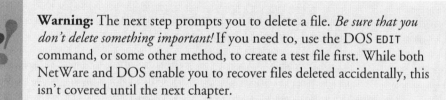

Warning: The next step prompts you to delete a file. *Be sure that you don't delete something important!* If you need to, use the DOS EDIT command, or some other method, to create a test file first. While both NetWare and DOS enable you to recover files deleted accidentally, this isn't covered until the next chapter.

3. Highlight the file you want to delete. Press Delete. NetWare prompts you to confirm that you want to Delete Marked File. Your screen should appear as shown in Figure 13.14. If you press Enter to signify Yes, the file will no longer appear in the Directory Contents box.

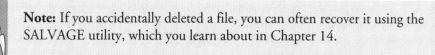

Note: If you accidentally deleted a file, you can often recover it using the SALVAGE utility, which you learn about in Chapter 14.

13

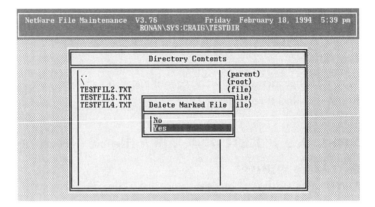

Figure 13.14. *Confirming file deletion.*

Warning: The next step prompts you to delete a subdirectory, and all the files within it. *Be sure that you don't delete something important!* If you need to, use the DOS MKDIR command, or FILER facilities, to create a test directory first.

4. You also can use FILER to delete files within a subdirectory, or the entire subdirectory structure. Highlight a subdirectory you want to delete and press Delete. You will be given two Delete Subdirectory Options, as shown in Figure 13.15.

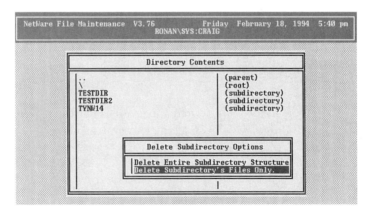

Figure 13.15. *Two Delete Subdirectory Options.*

5. Select Delete Subdirectory's Files Only to erase all files within the subdirectory. To remove the files and the subdirectory itself, highlight Delete Entire Subdirectory Structure and then press Enter.

6. NetWare prompts you to confirm the deletion with a message depending on which option you chose in the preceding action. If you chose Yes to either confirmation, the deletion will take place. If you deleted the entire directory structure, the subdirectory will no longer appear in the Directory Contents box.

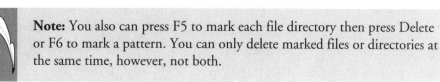

Note: You also can press F5 to mark each file directory then press Delete or F6 to mark a pattern. You can only delete marked files or directories at the same time, however, not both.

7. Press Esc from the FILER utility and return to the DOS command prompt.

Step 3: Review
The FILER Directory Contents submenu enables you to delete files and directories, and prompts you to confirm each deletion as a double check of your intentions.

Moving and Copying Files and Directories

As you probably expect by this point, the familiar DOS commands for copying files work equally well with NetWare. You can use the DOS COPY command to duplicate files, the XCOPY command to copy files and subdirectories, and (in recent DOS versions) the MOVE command to relocate a file from one directory to another.

Note: You also can use the DOS MOVE command to rename a file, by moving from one file name to another in the same directory. And you can rename a file with the DOS RENAME command. You cannot use the RENAME command on directories; however, you can use MOVE. If you want to rename a DOS directory, just use the MOVE command.

13

NetWare comes with its own set of commands for moving and copying files on the server. They have the advantage of knowing about and preserving NetWare-specific file information, such as file attributes. You learn more about file attributes in Chapter 14.

Using NCOPY

NetWare's NCOPY command line utility is very similar to the DOS XCOPY command, and even uses some of the same options. Following is the syntax of the command:

```
NCOPY [path] [[TO] path] [option]
```

Some of the key options available for NCOPY include the following:

/s   Used to copy subdirectories

/e   Used with /s to include empty subdirectories

/a   Copy files with archive bit set

/m   Copy files with archive bit set, clear the bit

/v   Verify copy operation with a read after every write

/i   Inform when non-DOS file information will be lost. (This can occur when copying NetWare files to a workstation running DOS, since it cannot track NetWare-specific information like trustee assignments or NetWare file attributes.)

Note: As with some other NetWare commands such as NDIR, the best thing to remember about the NCOPY command, rather than all the possible options, is the way to get help. All you have to do is type **NCOPY** /h, and you'll be reminded of the command syntax.

Using FILER

NetWare's FILER menu utility provides an easy method of copying and moving files and directories on the file server. You might have noticed these options earlier when you were using FILER to look at the contents of files, and create and delete directories. In the next task, you use FILER to copy and move files and directories.

Warning: During this task, you'll be working on a subdirectory and some of the files it contains. Just so you don't harm anything important, we suggest you create a test directory with some sample files, perhaps in your own home directory. You can create the directory with the DOS MKDIR command, or use the FILER techniques you learned earlier. Then create a simple text file, and make a few copies in the subdirectory under different names.

Task 13.9: Using FILER to copy a file.

Step 1: Description
You can copy files using the FILER menu utility.

Step 2: Action

1. Type **FILER** and then press Enter. The FILER main menu appears.

2. The cursor first appears on Current Directory Information. Highlight Directory Contents and press Enter. As you saw in Task 13.6, the window displays a list of all entries in the current directory. Using the techniques you learned earlier, use FILER features to change into a test directory (the one you set up after reading the preceding Warning).

3. Highlight the file name you want and press Enter. The File Options dialog box appears (see Figure 13.16).

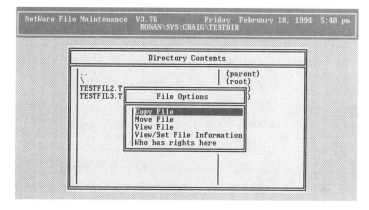

Figure 13.16. *Viewing file options.*

4. To copy a file, highlight the Copy File option and press Enter. The Destination Directory dialog box appears (see Figure 13.17). This box works the same as the Current Directory Path box in Task 13.6. You can use this in the same way to select a new directory path. Alternatively, if you simply want to copy the file within the current directory, just press Enter.

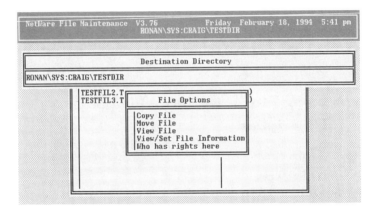

Figure 13.17. *Destination directory in which to copy a file.*

5. After you complete editing the Destination Directory path, press Enter. NetWare then prompts you for the Destination File Name, which is filled in with the name of the file you are copying (see Figure 13.18). If you are copying the file to another directory, you can leave the file name the same and just press Enter. If you are copying within the same directory, however, you must edit the file name so that it is different (otherwise you will be trying to copy a file over itself). When finished, press Enter.

6. NetWare returns you to the File Options dialog box. Press Esc to return to the Directory Contents menu. If you copied the file to a new name in the same directory, the new name now is included in the menu.

Step 3: Review

Using the FILER Directory Contents submenu, you quickly can highlight a file name and copy it to other names or locations.

Moving a file is just as easy with FILER. The only difference between a copy and a move is that, with a copy, a new file is created while the original (source) file stays intact. A move, on the other hand, creates a new file but removes the original.

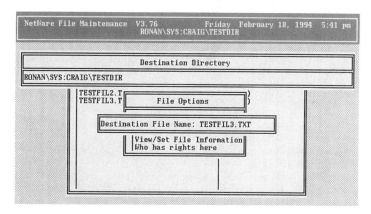

```
NetWare File Maintenance   V3.76        Friday  February 18, 1994   5:41 pm
                    RONAN\SYS:CRAIG\TESTDIR

┌──────────────────────────────────────────────────────────────────────┐
│                      Destination Directory                             │
├──────────────────────────────────────────────────────────────────────┤
│RONAN\SYS:CRAIG\TESTDIR                                                 │
└──────────────────────────────────────────────────────────────────────┘
        ┌TESTFIL2.T┌──────────────────────────────────┐
        │TESTFIL3.T│          File Options             │
        │          └──────────────────────────────────┘
        │
        │    ┌──────────────────────────────────────────┐
        │    │Destination File Name: TESTFIL3.TXT       │
        │    └──────────────────────────────────────────┘
        │         ┌──────────────────────────────────┐
        │         │View/Set File Information         │
        │         │Who has rights here               │
        │         └──────────────────────────────────┘
```

Figure 13.18. *Editing the destination file name.*

FILER also enables you to copy or move entire subdirectories. You have a choice of copying just the files within the subdirectory, or of copying or moving the entire subdirectory structure.

Task 13.10: Using FILER to move a subdirectory.

Step 1: Description

The FILER menu utility enables you to move subdirectories.

Step 2: Action

1. Type **FILER** and then press Enter. The FILER main menu appears.

2. The cursor first appears on Current Directory Information. Highlight Directory Contents and press Enter. As you saw in Task 13.6, the window displays a list of all entries in the current directory. Using the techniques you learned earlier, use FILER features to change to the directory immediately above your test subdirectory. (Did you break down and make one yet?)

3. Move the cursor to highlight the name of your test subdirectory and press Enter. The Subdirectory Options dialog box appears, as shown in Figure 13.19.

4. To move the subdirectory, highlight the Move Subdirectory's Structure option and press Enter. The Destination Directory dialog box appears, as shown in Figure 13.20. This box works just like the Current Directory Path box you saw in Task 13.9. You can use this in the same way to select a new directory path.

13

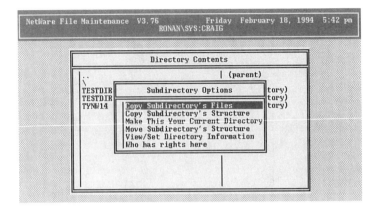

Figure 13.19. *Subdirectory options.*

Note: You also have the option of specifying the same directory you are moving the subdirectory from, but you will be forced to rename the subdirectory for the move to work. This is how you can rename a subdirectory.

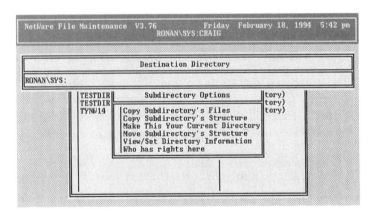

Figure 13.20. *A destination directory for a subdirectory move.*

5. After you complete editing the Destination Directory path, press Enter. NetWare then prompts you for the New Name of the subdirectory which is filled in with the name of the subdirectory you are moving. If you are

copying it to another directory, you can leave the subdirectory name the same and just press Enter. If you are copying within the same directory, however, you must edit the name so that it is different (otherwise you will be trying to copy the subdirectory over itself). When complete, press Enter.

6. You are returned to the File Options dialog box. Press Esc to return to the Directory Contents menu. You no longer see the subdirectory you moved. If you just renamed the subdirectory, to see the effect you must press Esc to return to the main menu and then reselect Directory Contents, or use the Directory Contents menu to move up one directory level, and then back down.

Step 3: Review

The FILER menu utility provides features that enable you to pick up and move entire subdirectories and their files.

Other Useful Commands

NetWare includes other useful commands for dealing with files and directories. The command syntax is given below, along with a brief description for each. The best way for you to learn about them is just to give them a try.

RENDIR *OldDirectoryPath* [TO] *NewDirectoryName*

enables you to rename a NetWare directory.

CHKDIR [*path*]

provides space information for the whole volume and the specified directory.

CHKVOL [*path*] [/Continuous]

provides space information for the entire volume, as well as space available to the user.

One other NetWare menu utility, VOLINFO, can be used to monitor space usage for each of the volumes on the file server. To start the utility, type **VOLINFO** from the DOS prompt on a workstation. A screen similar to that shown in Figure 13.21 appears.

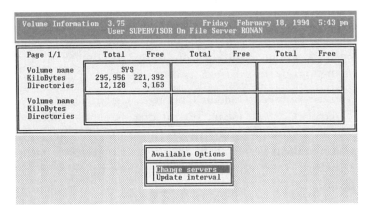

Figure 13.21. *The VOLINFO utility.*

Summary

You've covered a great deal of ground in this chapter about how NetWare enables you to use files and directories. You learned how to do the following:

- ☐ Deal with NetWare files, including how to view them, move them, and delete them.

- ☐ Handle NetWare directories, such as seeing what files are in them, plus how to create, move, and delete them.

- ☐ Use key NetWare command line and menu utilities, such as NDIR, LISTDIR, NCOPY, and especially FILER (one of the most important and useful NetWare utilities).

In Chapter 14, you discover even more important details about NetWare files and directories, including how to recover deleted files, and how to use the all important drive and search maps.

Workshop
Terminology Review

current directory—A pointer to the current location in the file hierarchy. Commands usually operate on files in the current directory, unless a full pathname is provided.

directory—A special file that contains information about files and sub-directories within the directory. The directory provides details such as a file's name and its size.

file—A collection of data bytes, referred to by a name, and stored on magnetic media, usually a disk.

full pathname—The complete list of the path to a file, including file server name, volume name, and all directories on the path to the file.

pathname—The path to a directory or file, usually with respect to the current directory.

subdirectory—A directory within another directory. (Other than the root directory, which resides at the top of a file system, all directories are also subdirectories.)

tree—A representation of NetWare's hierarchical file structure. The hierarchy starts at the root directory, and expands out, through many directories, subdirectories, and files. The structure therefore appears as an upside-down tree.

Task List

In this chapter, your tasks involved files and directories. You learned how to do the following:

- [ ] Use NDIR to sort and selectively view file information.
- [ ] Use LISTDIR to obtain a visual representation of the directory tree.
- [ ] Use FILER to view file and directory details, move around the file hierarchy, create and delete directories, delete files, and copy and move files and directories.

Q&A

Q Can I access NetWare files from Windows?

A After you log on to NetWare, any of the network drives available from DOS also are available from Windows. For example, within the File Manager, notice additional drive icons along the drive bar.

You can make use of additional NetWare functions from within Windows by installing certain programs like NWUSER. See Chapter 19 for more details.

Q Who can use FILER?

A The FILER menu utility is available for use by all NetWare users, unless you restrict users' rights over the FILER program (not normally done).

Q When should I use COPY, XCOPY, and NCOPY?

A COPY and XCOPY are DOS commands used for (amazingly enough) copying files. XCOPY provides the capability to copy entire nodes of a file hierarchy, that is, all the files in a directory, plus files within subdirectories of the directory.

NCOPY provides basically the same features of XCOPY. The advantage of using NCOPY is that it is NetWare-aware. Using it will ensure that NetWare-specific file information (like file attributes which you learn about in Chapter 14) are also copied.

Q What happens if I try to use the DOS CHKDSK or SCANDISK on a NetWare volume?

A DOS will advise you that you cannot perform these functions on a network drive.

14

More on NetWare
Files and
Directories

NetWare is designed to track literally terabytes of data. With it, storage capacities that could only be dreamed of for mainframes a few years ago can now be made available to the network of client computers. Organizing and tracking these massive amounts of information require planning and ongoing administration. In this chapter, you see more NetWare mechanisms that you can use to keep on top of all the data your NetWare file server will be storing. You get details on the following:

☐ Ways to lay out files and directories on your file server

☐ Using drive and search mappings to give you easy access to your files and directories

☐ How NetWare uses file attributes to flag important details about files and directories

But first you see how to recover from one of the easiest-to-make mistakes (and the one most frequently made): accidentally deleting a file.

Recovering Deleted Files

If you're like just about every other computer user, at some point in your life, you will delete a file; then all of a sudden you'll be overcome with a sickening feeling in the pit of your stomach. "(Expletive Deleted)—I didn't mean to do that!" Then you break out in a sweat as you begin to panic. Is there any way to recover that file?

Fortunately, with NetWare, you're in luck. Whenever you delete a NetWare file, the file actually remains available and can be recovered at a later time. All you have to do is use the right tool to peer into the directory where the file used to be—the file actually is still there; you just can't see it with a directory listing. The tool that you use to see the file is the SALVAGE menu utility. Using SALVAGE, you can recover the file and stop perspiring.

And what if you also deleted the directory where the file was? Well, even if you deleted the directory, you can still use SALVAGE to recover the file. Whenever you delete a directory in which deleted files are stored, NetWare saves the deleted files in a hidden directory called DELETED.SAV. Each volume has a DELETED.SAV directory.

After you use SALVAGE to recover a file, it once again appears in the directory you erased it from (or in DELETED.SAV if you also erased the original directory). The file has its original trustee rights and attributes, just as it did before it was erased.

>
> **Warning:** Deleted files don't hang around indefinitely. If the file server starts to run out of disk space, it must get rid of deleted files.

Now you're ready to try an exercise using SALVAGE to recover a deleted file.

Task 14.1: Using SALVAGE to recover a file.

Step 1: Description

Using SALVAGE, you can recover a NetWare file that was deleted previously.

>
> **Warning:** This task asks you to delete a file. Although NetWare can recover the file (that's the object of this exercise), why tempt fate? Make sure you don't delete something important! If you need to, use the DOS EDIT command, or some other method, to create a test file first.

Step 2: Action

1. Choose a file that you want to delete and recover. Change to the appropriate directory and confirm the file's existence by typing **DIR** `<filename>` and then pressing Enter.

2. At the DOS prompt, delete the file by typing **DEL** `<filename>` and then pressing Enter. Confirm that the file no longer exists by typing **DIR** `<filename>` and then pressing Enter. (We hope that you followed our suggestion about creating a test file. If not, have confidence in NetWare's capability to recover the file.)

3. Type **SALVAGE** and then press Enter. The SALVAGE main menu appears, as shown in Figure 14.1.

4. In the Main Menu Options, the selection View/Recover Deleted Files is already highlighted. Press Enter to select this option. SALVAGE responds with a choice of * for the search pattern (meaning all possible filenames).

5. Press Enter to select this default value. The listing you receive next should look similar to the one shown in Figure 14.2. It shows which files have been deleted in the current directory. Among these files should be the name of the file you deleted in step 3.

14

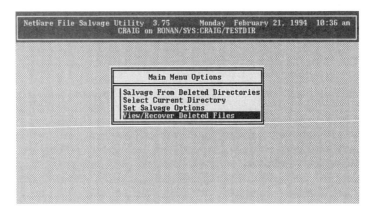

Figure 14.1. *SALVAGE main menu.*

Figure 14.2. *Listing of salvageable files.*

6. Use the cursor keys to highlight the filename and press Enter. SALVAGE responds with a screen similar to the one shown in Figure 14.3.

7. Confirm your desire to recover the file by highlighting Yes and pressing Enter.

8. Exit SALVAGE by using the Esc key. Confirm leaving SALVAGE by selecting Yes to return to the DOS prompt.

9. To demonstrate that the file has, in fact, been restored, at the DOS prompt, type **DIR** *<filename>* and then press Enter. You then see the file as expected. You also can type **TYPE** *<filename>* and press Enter to display the file's contents.

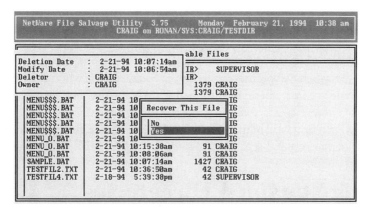

Figure 14.3. *File details and recover prompt.*

Step 3: Review

In this task, you learned that NetWare's SALVAGE menu utility enables you to recover files that were previously deleted.

Standard NetWare Directory Structure

One of the most effective ways of helping you to cope with the massive amounts of data you can store on a NetWare file server is by making good use of directories. Directories enable you to categorize and organize your files, just as they do on your DOS workstation. But with the thousands and thousands of files that can add up on your NetWare server, a well-organized directory structure is even more important.

Using Volumes

At the highest level, you can make use of separate NetWare volumes to segregate different kinds of files or program applications. Recall from Chapter 4 that a volume is a logical grouping of disk blocks that can be spread across up to 32 separate disk segments.

Although a volume doesn't necessarily correspond to a physical disk drive, you can think of it that way. Just as you can store all your programs on one disk drive and all your data on another, you can spread different groups or types of programs and data across NetWare volumes.

Every NetWare file server has at least one volume, known as SYS:. The SYS: volume holds all the directories and files NetWare needs to serve its clients. You learn more about these directories and files later in the chapter.

Whether you have volumes other than SYS: depends on whether you configured more than one volume when you installed your NetWare. For example, some NetWare administrators create a volume called APPS:, which holds all the application programs. You find out about creating NetWare volumes during the installation process described in Appendix A.

Using Standard Directories

As you install NetWare on your file server computer, it creates and populates some standard directories. The result is the file system hierarchy you see in Figure 14.4. A description of each of these key directories follows.

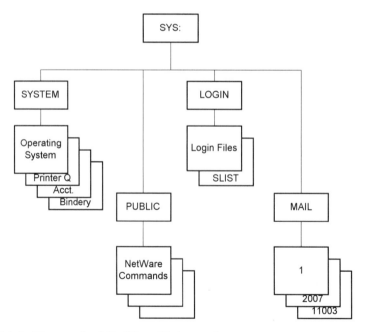

Figure 14.4. *The standard NetWare file hierarchy.*

LOGIN Directory

NetWare's LOGIN directory is the first one you encountered when you accessed the file server. The LOGIN directory contains the LOGIN program, which you use to tell

NetWare your username and password. Before you provide this information, LOGIN is the only directory you have access to. After you log in, you can explore any other directories to which you have access rights.

The two key programs in the LOGIN directory are LOGIN and SLIST. You know what LOGIN is used for, so we won't go over that again. Meanwhile, you can use SLIST to tell you the names of all the file servers you can try to access.

Besides these two programs, the LOGIN directory includes a few other useful files and lets you access them even if you aren't yet logged in to NetWare. If you want more, you must log in so that you can get to the directories listed in the following sections.

PUBLIC Directory

The PUBLIC directory contains programs used by most of the NetWare community. Many of the command-line and menu utilities you've looked at so far, such as FILER, SYSCON, and NDIR, all reside in the PUBLIC directory.

Because the PUBLIC directory contains many useful files, it's important to maintain a search pointer to PUBLIC so that when you type a command, NetWare knows that it should look in this directory to find the command. You see more about how to maintain this pointer later in the chapter.

SYSTEM Directory

As you saw in Chapter 11, when you are logged in as Supervisor, the default login script tries to set up a pointer to the SYSTEM directory because many of the key utilities you use as Supervisor are kept in that directory. Programs such as BINDFIX and SECURITY were never intended for general use. So NetWare collects them all in one spot—the SYSYEM directory—and enforces default protections so that most users can't execute them.

The SYSYEM directory also includes some key configuration files, such as the bindery files you learned about in Chapter 7.

MAIL Directory

If you use SYSCON to add a new user, a subdirectory is created for each person, under the MAIL directory. Creating a subdirectory was originally done in support of NetWare's mail facilities—each user had his or her own MAIL subdirectory as a place to store mail files.

With version 3.12, NetWare now includes an optional mail product called FIRSTMAIL. Even if you don't use this mail system, it's useful to have a standardized place to keep files that apply to each user. The user login scripts you learned about in Chapter 11 are a good example; the login script for each user is stored in his or her own subdirectory of the MAIL directory.

Organizing Directories

When you install NetWare, it gives you a good head start at organizing your directories, as you saw in Figure 14.4. If your file server is typical at all, you probably want to add directories for two main purposes:

☐ To set up a place for users to store their files

☐ To install network applications for use by all your users

Note: Refer to Chapter 11 and what you learned about using the COMSPEC variable so that your users can find their COMMAND.COM files. One approach to this process (although not the one we recommend) is to copy COMMAND.COM files to your NetWare server, one for each version of DOS your users are running. If you take this approach, you also must establish directories for each version of DOS in use.

Keeping all NetWare files in the root directory may be tempting (some people do so with their DOS computers). However, keeping all your files in this directory is about the worst thing you can do if you place a premium on organization—trying to figure out which file is which ends up being just about impossible.

You also might create a subdirectory under the root directory for each user and application you have. This approach is better but still not as easy to maintain as it could be.

Keeping directories and files in order actually is fairly straightforward. All you have to do is create a directory for each type of object you want to keep track of. You then place each object within its own separate subdirectory.

Assume, for example, that you are using only one volume, SYS:. To keep track of user files, you can establish a directory under the root, such as the following:

SYS:\USERS

Then, as you add users, you can give each one his or her own subdirectory within USERS:

```
SYS:\USERS\PETER
SYS:\USERS\CRAIG
SYS:\USERS\ARNOLD
```

What the users do to organize their files within their home directory can be totally up to them. The users can be as structured or as messy as they like. Ideally, each user can set up his or her own subdirectories of the user's home directory and store his or her network files within that structure—but you can leave that decision up to them.

You can deal with applications in a similar fashion. If you are using only the SYS: volume, you can create one directory, under which you set up a separate subdirectory for each application. You end up with a structure like the following:

```
SYS:\APPS\WINWORD
SYS:\APPS\EXCEL
SYS:\APPS\LOTUS
SYS:\APPS\WP
```

Or, if you have the luxury of a separate volume for applications, say an APPS: volume as described earlier, you can simply create separate subdirectories under the root directory:

```
APPS:\WINWORD
APPS:\EXCEL
APPS:\LOTUS
APPS:\WP
```

The application programs probably maintain their own subdirectories for such items as configuration files and data required by the application.

You also might want to establish one other directory that everyone can access. It serves as a place where users can leave files so that others can pick them up—sort of a message board for the file server. You might set up a directory with permissions, for example, so that the group EVERYONE can read and write all files:

```
SYS:\PUBLIC\DATA
```

This directory can let users share files without having to alter NetWare file or directory permissions (which some users are not willing to learn about). They should be careful, however; if a user places a file in this directory, everyone using the file server can read or change it.

If you follow these suggestions, you'll end up with a directory structure similar to the one shown in Figure 14.5.

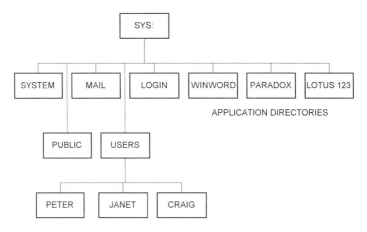

Figure 14.5. *Suggested NetWare directory structure.*

Using NetWare Drive Mappings

As you learned in Chapter 13, you can always specify a NetWare file or directory by referring to its full pathname. Or, using one of the many ways to move around the file hierarchy, you can change to a directory and refer to it by a shorter name. But NetWare also gives you two additional facilities: drive mapping and search mapping. With drive maps, NetWare lets you refer to places in the file hierarchy with a simple letter. And with search maps, NetWare does the looking for you when you type the name of a program. In the following sections, you see how you can use each of these facilities to make life easier for yourself.

Drive Mappings

When you first started using your DOS computer, you quickly learned about an important concept: your current drive. The drive referred to the physical disk you used. The letters A and B usually meant one of the two floppy disk drives, and the letter C referred to your hard disk drive.

NetWare also makes use of drive letters. But it doesn't just assign a single letter to a single physical drive. Instead, NetWare enables you to refer to a number of different directory locations on any of its volumes. Each is assigned its own drive letter. That letter points to a particular directory on the NetWare volume. To refer to any file in that directory or below, all you have to do is use that drive letter. Each of these

references from a drive letter to a particular directory on the NetWare volume is known as a *drive mapping*.

Figure 14.6 shows an illustration of a NetWare volume directory tree and the drive letters assigned to various points.

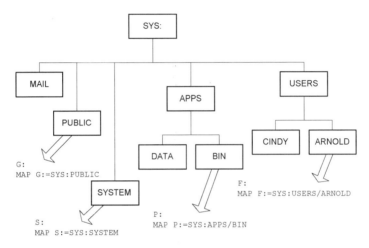

Figure 14.6. *Mapping drive letters to NetWare directories.*

The last letter available for a drive mapping is the letter *Z*. The first letter depends on how you configured your workstation—for example, whether you use NETX or VLM to get to the server, and the related settings in certain configuration files. Chapter 18 gives you details on how to set your first network drive. For now, all you have to remember is that the first NetWare drive (the one you use for logging in) is normally the F: drive.

> **Note:** You may remember that DOS can also assign drive letters to particular directories on a local hard drive, using the SUBSTitute command. You can then refer to a directory using only the drive letter.

To assign drive letters to NetWare drives and directories, you use the MAP command. MAP tells NetWare that when you refer to a particular disk drive by a simple letter, you really mean a specific location on a certain server, a volume within the server, and a directory within the volume.

As you learned in Chapter 11, one of NetWare's login scripts normally establishes a few drive mappings for you. And most of the time, the login script includes a MAP command to show you what drive mappings have been set up. You can use the MAP command at any time to see the drive mappings in place.

Task 14.2: Using the MAP command to set drive maps.

Step 1: Description

In this task, you use the MAP command to determine which drive letters refer to which NetWare volumes and directories, as well as add and delete drive assignments.

Step 2: Action

1. At the DOS prompt, type **MAP** and press Enter. NetWare produces output similar to that shown in Figure 14.7.

```
F>map

Drive   A:    maps to a local disk.
Drive   B:    maps to a local disk.
Drive   C:    maps to a local disk.
Drive   D:    maps to a local disk.
Drive   E:    maps to a local disk.
Drive   F: = RONAN\SYS:  \CRAIG\TESTDIR
Drive   M: = BALLIOL\SYS:  \PUBLIC
         ------
SEARCH1:    = Z:.  [RONAN\SYS:   \PUBLIC]
SEARCH2:    = Y:.  [RONAN\SYS:   \]
SEARCH3:    = C:\DOS
SEARCH4:    = C:\WINDOWS
SEARCH5:    = C:\
SEARCH6:    = C:\UTILITY

F>
```

Figure 14.7. *Sample MAP command output.*

2. To add a new drive mapping, such as pointing to the SYS:\PUBLIC directory with the drive letter P, type **MAP P:=SYS:\PUBLIC** and then press Enter. NetWare responds by telling you that the drive has been mapped.

3. To delete the drive mapping you just assigned, type **MAP DEL P:** and press Enter. You can check that the mapping was deleted by typing **P:** and pressing Enter. DOS then advises you that no such drive exists.

4. If you want to assign a drive mapping and don't care which drive letter is used, you can let NetWare determine the next available letter and assign it. Type the command **MAP NEXT SYS:\PUBLIC** and press Enter. NetWare maps

the next available drive letter to the SYS:\PUBLIC directory, and advises you which drive letter it assigned.

Step 3: Review

In this task, you learned that the MAP command enables you to maintain which drive letters refer to which NetWare directories.

Which drive mappings you establish is totally up to you and your users. Some people like to use many drive letters, pointing to many different NetWare directories. Others prefer just to use one drive letter, more like referring to a single hard drive on a workstation. With NetWare, you have the flexibility to do either.

NetWare also provides the search drive facility to help you locate your files. You learn more about search drives in the next section.

Search Mappings

Back when you were learning about DOS, you also likely found out that DOS maintained a pointer known as the current directory. Your current directory is the one DOS points at, such that if you refer to a simple filename (for example, FILE1.TXT), you knew that DOS looks for it in your current directory. Each drive letter you use has a current directory pointer.

Another important DOS concept you probably learned about was the *search path*. Whenever you type the name of a command, DOS looks at the PATH variable. It then looks for the command in every directory listed in the PATH. If it finds the command, DOS executes it; otherwise, it advises you that it can't find the requested program.

In NetWare, you also can maintain a current directory pointer for each of your drives. In addition, NetWare provides a facility called *search drives*. When you assign a search drive letter to a point in NetWare's directory structure, the drive/directory is included when you search for a command. You can see the effect of assigning a search drive when you type PATH at the DOS prompt. The NetWare search drive letters are included in the PATH, ensuring that the appropriate directories are searched.

The actual letter used for a search drive is less important than the order in which the drives are searched. NetWare numbers search drives in the order S1, S2, and so on. By convention, drive letters are assigned to represent each search drive, starting at the Z: drive and working backward. So the drive letter for S1 is normally Z:, the drive letter for S2 is Y:, and so on. However, the assignments can change with subsequent use of the MAP command to change the search order.

> **Warning:** Because search drives seem just like regular drives, you might be tempted to use them like regular drives. For example, you might have a Z: drive, which is mapped to the directory \PUBLIC. You can change to the Z: drive and, using the DOS CD command, you can change directories so that the Z: drive points elsewhere. Then, all of a sudden, you can't find any of your NetWare commands! You've changed where one of your important search drives is pointing to—the \PUBLIC directory, where many NetWare commands reside. So be careful—and don't lose your search drives.

You see how to set up and modify search maps using the MAP command in Task 14.3.

Task 14.3: Using the *MAP* command to set search maps.

Step 1: Description

In this task, you use NetWare's MAP command to set up search drives.

Step 2: Action

1. To add a new search drive mapping, such as including the SYS:\PUBLIC directory, type **MAP S1:=SYS:\PUBLIC** and press Enter. NetWare responds by telling you that the S1 search drive points to the SYS:\PUBLIC directory, as well as the drive letter assigned.

2. If you want to specify that a directory is searched before other directories, you can tell NetWare to insert the search drive earlier in the path. For example, to have the SYSTEM directory searched before any others, type the command **MAP INSERT S1:=SYS:\SYSYEM** and press Enter. NetWare then maps the next available drive letter to \SYSTEM, although the other search drives maintain their maps. However, the order of the search drives changes.

3. You can confirm the order of the search by typing MAP and pressing Enter. NetWare shows you the current drive mappings, including the updated search drives. Also, type the DOS command **PATH** and press Enter, which shows the updated path variable.

Step 3: Review

The MAP command enables you to maintain search drive assignments, as you learned in this task.

Note: When you're assigning search drive numbers (that is, S1, S2, and so on), you normally must keep track of which numbers have been used so far. If you simply want to add a search drive to the end of the search path, however, you can use the command MAP S16:=*<pathname>* to assign the next available search drive number.

Using SESSION

The MAP command is fine for setting drive maps and search maps in login scripts and at the DOS prompt. However, like it does for many other tasks, NetWare provides a more user-friendly menu-driven utility to accomplish the same tasks. For maps, you use features found within the SESSION menu utility.

Task 14.4: Using SESSION to set drive maps and search maps.

Step 1: Description

NetWare's SESSION menu utility gives you an easy interface to assign, maintain, and delete drive mappings and search mappings.

Step 2: Action

1. To start the SESSION menu utility, type **SESSION** at the DOS prompt and press Enter. The Available Topics menu appears, as shown in Figure 14.8.

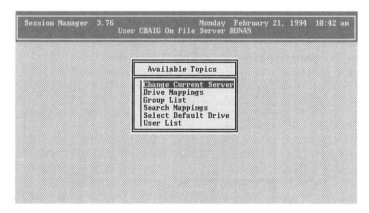

Figure 14.8. *SESSION main menu—Available Topics.*

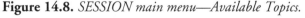

2. To update your drive maps, move the cursor down to Drive Mappings and select the menu option by pressing Enter. You receive a list of your Current Drive Mappings similar to that shown in Figure 14.9.

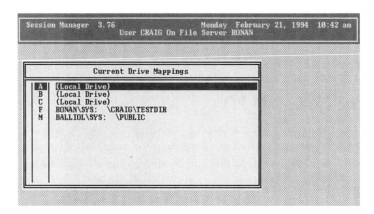

Figure 14.9. *Current drive maps.*

3. Adding a new drive map involves pressing the Ins key. SESSION prompts you with the next available drive letter, as shown in Figure 14.10.

4. You can accept this drive letter by pressing Enter. Or you can backspace over the letter offered and enter the drive letter of your choosing, and press Enter. SESSION then gives you the option to select the directory to which the drive letter is mapped.

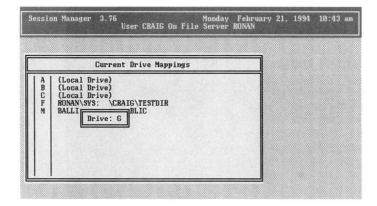

Figure 14.10. *Mapping a new drive letter.*

5. You can type in a full pathname and press Enter. Or you can use the Ins key to have SESSION help you build a pathname. If you take this route, you are presented with a series of menus that enable you to select from servers you are logged into, volumes on the chosen server, and directories on the volume. This process is the same as the one you used in Chapter 13 to build a pathname from within FILER.

6. After you enter or build the path, press Enter to indicate completion. SESSION then asks Do you want to map root this drive? Select No and press Enter. SESSION then displays the updated drive mappings.

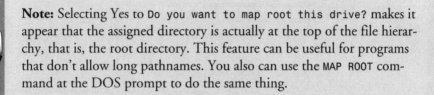

Note: Selecting Yes to Do you want to map root this drive? makes it appear that the assigned directory is actually at the top of the file hierarchy, that is, the root directory. This feature can be useful for programs that don't allow long pathnames. You also can use the MAP ROOT command at the DOS prompt to do the same thing.

7. To delete a drive map, highlight the drive letter and path shown on the Current Drive Mappings screen and press Delete. SESSION then asks you to confirm that you want to delete the drive mapping. If you select Yes, you see that the drive map is missing when SESSION displays the updated maps.

8. Adding a new search map is just as easy as adding a drive map. Press Esc to return to SESSION's main menu. Then select Search Mappings. The Current Search Mappings screen appears, as shown in Figure 14.11.

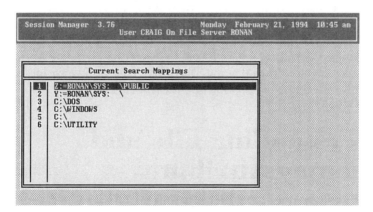

Figure 14.11. *Current Search Mappings screen.*

9. To add a new search map, press Ins. SESSION prompts you with the next available search drive number, as shown in Figure 14.12.

10. You can accept this number by pressing Enter. Or you can backspace over the number offered and enter the number of your choosing, and press Enter.

```
Session Manager   3.76                    Monday  February 21, 1994  10:46 am
                          User CRAIG On File Server RONAN


            ┌─────────────── Current Search Mappings ───────────────┐
            │ 1   Z:=RONAN\SYS:   \PUBLIC                            │
            │ 2   Y:=RONAN\SYS:   \                                  │
            │ 3   C:\DOS                                             │
            │ 4   C:\WINDOWS                                         │
            │ 5                                                      │
            │ 6   ┌─ Search Drive Number: 7 ─┐                       │
            │     └──────────────────────────┘                      │
            │                                                        │
            │                                                        │
            └────────────────────────────────────────────────────────┘
```

Figure 14.12. *Mapping a new drive letter.*

11. You then are asked to select a directory for the search map. As you saw in step 5, you can enter a full pathname or let SESSION help you build a path by pressing Ins. In the latter case, the first choice SESSION offers includes both file servers you are logged into and local disk drives on your work station.

12. After you enter or build the pathname, press Enter. SESSION then displays an updated listing of your current search mappings. To leave SESSION, press Esc until you are asked to confirm that you want to exit.

Step 3: Review

In this task, you learned that the SESSION menu utility provides a convenient and easy-to-use method of updating drive assignments.

Understanding File and Directory Attributes

NetWare keeps track of a great deal of information for each file and directory that it stores. As you saw in Chapters 4 and 13, details about every file and every directory

are recorded in the Directory Entry Table. Key information kept for each entry includes the file name, its size, and the date and time of last update.

These details are similar to the information tracked by DOS for each of its files. But NetWare can maintain other important details on its files and directories. These details, called *attributes*, help NetWare control how a file or directory can be used. They also flag other special handling procedures that NetWare should use with the file, such as tracking transactions or maintaining special index information.

File attributes are taken into consideration by NetWare when performing various operations on files and directories. In addition to checking attributes, NetWare considers the file access permissions that are in place for each user (see Chapter 15). For example, access permissions might enable a user to read and write a file, but if you set a file's attribute to *read-only*, the user cannot write to the file.

> **Note:** A user's ability to update file attributes has a significant impact on the effectiveness of security over the file. For example, if you allow the user to modify file attributes, he or she can easily set read-only to read-write.

The attributes can be broken down into two main categories:

☐ Feature attributes, which flag the status of the file. This status information is referenced by features such as NetWare's Transaction Tracking System.

☐ Security attributes, which indicate restrictions on how the file can be used.

Each attribute is represented by a one- or two-letter code. In the following sections, you examine the various attribute settings and their meanings more closely.

Feature Attributes

The various feature attributes are discussed more fully in the following short sections.

T—Activate Transaction Tracking System

Files marked with the T attribute make use of NetWare's Transaction Tracking System (TTS). TTS ensures that only complete transactions are recorded in a file.

If the file server experiences a power failure during the update of a transaction, the details may not be recorded properly in the file. As a result, the file may be corrupted.

Because TTS monitors to ensure that only complete transactions are recorded, the incomplete transaction is detected. After the file server is recovered, TTS automatically backs out the incomplete transaction, restoring the file to its original state.

I—Indexed

Very large files (those exceeding 64 blocks) can be turbo indexed, meaning that the file's blocks are maintained together in the File Allocation Table (FAT). The I attribute indicates that Turbo FAT Indexing should be maintained.

Sy—System

The Sy attribute indicates that the file or directory is owned by the system. When NetWare sees this flag on a file, it prevents users from deleting, copying, or overwriting the file. It also shows that the file can be used only for system functions. A good example of system files is the three files that make up NetWare's bindery.

A—Not Archived (Archive Needed)

Whenever a file is modified in any way, the archive flag (A) is set on. It tells software used to back up files that this particular file has been modified, and so is a candidate for being copied.

P—Purge

As you learned earlier in this chapter, under normal circumstances, when a file or directory is deleted, the contents still remain on disk. The directory entry is simply updated to indicate that the entry has been deleted. However, you can still recover the file, using the SALVAGE utility.

Sometimes you really do want to completely wipe out the file. If, for example, the file contains sensitive information (your résumé, for instance), when you delete the file, you don't want someone else to be able to recover it. The solution is to have NetWare *purge* the file, by setting the purge attribute (P). The purge attribute indicates that the contents of a file or directory should be wiped clean from the disk if it is deleted. Using P foils attempts to recover the file's contents.

RA—Read Audit

The RA attribute currently performs no function in NetWare 3.12.

WA—Write Audit

The WA attribute currently performs no function in NetWare 3.12.

Security Attributes

The various security attributes are discussed more fully in the following short sections.

S—Shareable

Normally, files are non-shareable. This means that only one user can access the file at a time. Other users are not permitted access until the first user releases the file. Some files, particularly data files, should not be used by more than one person at a time. Limiting access to one user helps prevent file corruption due to more than one person trying to update the file's contents simultaneously.

With the Shareable (S) attribute set, multiple users can access the file at any given point in time. But when sharing a file, caution is required. If use is not coordinated, many people may read the file, change its contents, and attempt to update the file, all at the same time. However, only the changes made by the last user of the file are actually put into place. For this reason, the Shareable attribute is normally used with the Read-Only attribute, described in the next section.

RO—Read-Only

A file with the RO attribute can be opened for reading but not updated. This facility is useful for programs that should be updated only rarely, or not at all. Marking the program as read-only can help prevent any accidental updates of the program by careless users.

RW—Read/Write

A file with the RW attribute can be opened for reading and writing. Anyone with the appropriate security permissions can read or write to the file, as requested.

X—Execute-Only

A file with the X attribute can only be executed. This facility is useful to protect program files so that they cannot be copied or inadvertently updated.

H—Hidden

Files or directories with the H attribute do not appear in DOS DIR listings. However, you can still see the files with NetWare's NDIR command, if you have the File Scan right (covered in Chapter 15). NetWare stops you from copying or deleting Hidden files.

DI—Delete Inhibit

Files with the DI attribute cannot be deleted. This facility can help prevent deleting the file by careless or malicious users.

RI—Rename Inhibit

RI files cannot be renamed. Again, this facility mainly helps protect against inadvertent or malicious acts by users who have permission to access a file.

CI—Copy Inhibit

Files with the CI attribute cannot be copied. However, this only functions with Macintosh files and their users.

Setting and Reviewing File and Directory Attributes

Now that you're familiar with the various file and directory attributes, you're ready to set attributes using the FLAG command and FILER utility.

Using the *FLAG* Command

The most direct way to assign file attributes is to use the NetWare FLAG command. The syntax for the command is as follows:

```
FLAG [<filename>[[+¦-] list of attributes to be added or deleted]
```

Note: To view directory attributes, you use the FLAGDIR command in the same manner as you use FLAG.

To see what attributes are assigned to a file, for example, type the following command:

`FLAG <filename>`

Note that you can use the normal DOS wildcard characters to indicate, for example, all files in the directory. To add an attribute, include the characters you learned earlier in this chapter to introduce each one. To add the attribute Read-Only to a file, for example, type the following command:

`FLAG <filename> RO`

With FLAG, you also can use two additional attributes. Use the attribute ALL if you want to assign all available attributes to a file. Use the attribute NORMAL if you want the file to have the default attributes, that is, Read/Write and no others.

Using FILER

Once again, NetWare provides an easy-to-use menu-driven interface to set file and directory attributes. The FILER menu utility offers the ability to add and delete file attributes.

Task 14.5: Using FILER to set file attributes.
Step 1: Description
In this task, you use the FILER menu utility to set file attributes.

Step 2: Action
1. At the DOS prompt, type **FILER** and press Enter. The FILER menu appears with the cursor on Current Directory Information. Use the techniques you learned in Chapter 13 to select the \PUBLIC directory.

2. After you position yourself in the \PUBLIC directory, from FILER's main menu, select Directory Contents and press Enter. You then see a display similar to that shown in Figure 14.13. This screen gives details on each item in the directory, including filenames and other directories.

3. Move the cursor to a file of your choosing and press Enter. A new box appears, enabling you to select from a number of operations.

4. Move the cursor down to View/Set File Information and press Enter. You then see a display of File Information for the file, as shown in Figure 14.14. The cursor highlights the information you are interested in at this point— the Attributes. Attribute information is presented using the symbols you learned earlier in this chapter.

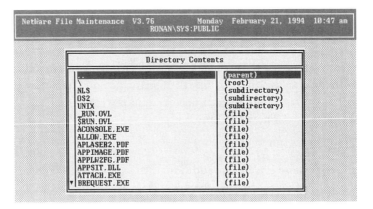

Figure 14.13. *FILER directory contents information for \PUBLIC.*

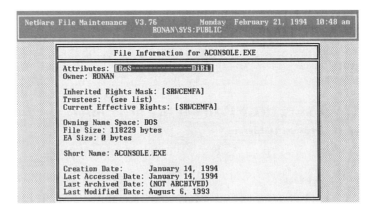

Figure 14.14. *FILER File Information screen.*

5. To change the file's attributes, press Enter. The Current File Attributes menu appears, as shown in Figure 14.15.

6. To add a new attribute, press Ins. FILER responds with a list of other file attributes that have not yet been assigned, as shown in Figure 14.16. Highlight one of the attributes in this list and press Enter.

7. To delete an attribute, highlight the attribute to be deleted and press Delete. FILER asks you to confirm that you want to delete the attribute.

8. After you complete all the changes you want to make, press Esc to return to the File Information screen. The updated attributes then appear.

9. Press Esc to exit the FILER utility and return to the DOS command prompt.

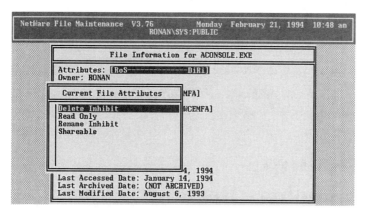

Figure 14.15. *Current File Attributes menu.*

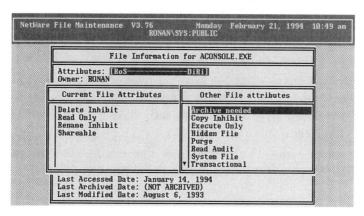

Figure 14.16. *Other file attributes available to be assigned.*

Step 3: Review

NetWare's FILER utility provides a user-friendly menu interface, which enables you to modify file attributes, as you learned in this task.

Summary

In this chapter, you learned the following:

- ☐ How to use the SALVAGE utility to recover files that were accidentally deleted

- ☐ Suggestions on setting up a usable directory structure to best organize the thousands of files on your file server

- ☐ How to set up NetWare drive mappings and search drives

- ☐ The purpose of NetWare file and directory attributes, and how to view and set them

Workshop

Terminology Review

attribute—A flag on a NetWare file or directory that indicates special status, handling requirements, or restrictions.

drive mapping   A drive letter assigned to a particular directory within the NetWare file hierarchy.

purge—To completely eliminate a file so that it cannot be recovered.

search drives—The NetWare facility used to build a search path. Each directory on the search path is assigned a drive letter. When a command is typed without a full pathname, each search drive is checked to find the command.

search path—The list of directories searched when a command is typed without specifying the command's full pathname.

Task List

The tasks in this chapter covered a range of common activities to deal with NetWare files and directories. You practiced how to

- ☐ Use the SALVAGE menu utility to recover a deleted file.

- ☐ Use the MAP command line utility to set up drive maps and search maps.

- ☐ Set drive and search maps using the SESSION menu utility.

- ☐ Set file attributes using the FILER menu utility.

Q&A

Q **Can I use SALVAGE to recover files on my workstation**

A No, SALVAGE only works with files on your NetWare server. If you accidentally delete a file on your DOS-based workstation, you can try the DOS UNDELETE command.

Q **How can I prevent people from salvaging a file I want deleted permanently?**

A Set the Purge attribute on the file, using either the FLAG command line utility, or the FILER menu utility. Whenever the file is deleted, such as by using the DOS DEL command, NetWare will purge it immediately. After that, you cannot use SALVAGE to recover it.

Q **What is the difference between NetWare's search mappings and the DOS PATH variable?**

A The two facilities are similar. Setting a search map also assigns a drive letter to a particular search directory, instead of just building a single list of search directories as is done for DOS. But the concept of specifying which directories to look in for a command is the same. When you maintain search maps within NetWare, you'll even find that your DOS PATH is updated as well.

Q **How do I list hidden files?**

A NetWare's NDIR command shows files that include the Hidden attribute. Also, within FILER, you can set an option that will cause it to show Hidden or System files. From FILER's Available Topics menu, choose Set Filer Options | File Search Attributes. At the Search File Attributes box that appears, you can press Ins to instruct FILER to include either or both of Hidden or System files.

Day

8

15

Introducing NetWare File and Directory Rights

In Chapter 9, you learned login security is the first layer of the NetWare security model. You also learned that usernames and passwords are an integral part of login security. In Chapter 13, you studied security attributes. At this point, you will learn about another key part of security. In this chapter, you will learn about NetWare's *rights* security. NetWare rights security applies to users and groups of users. NetWare rights help you control what directories, subdirectories, and files a user or group can access.

To access files within directories on NetWare volumes, you must have rights to the directories where the files reside. Rights define what a user can do on your network. Rights are a powerful security mechanism in NetWare. You can use them to control who can access programs and data. Take care to assign users rights when they need them to do their jobs. NetWare implements rights security using *Trustee Assignments* and the *Inherited Rights Mask*. You can use these two features together to control access to the file system on the file server. In this chapter, you see that NetWare 3.12 allows users to have rights to individual files within directories, and to the directories themselves. You also learn how to view, create, and delete directory trustees. Chapter 16 shows you how to view and change inherited rights. First, you must understand the different rights types.

Understanding NetWare Rights

Rights are how NetWare indicates the various privileges a user can have on the network. The rights basically break down into the following three high-level categories:

- ☐ **The Canadian Ballet Rights**: that is, look but don't touch. These rights include the capabilities to open and read a file, or to create a directory listing.

- ☐ **The Nintendo Rights**: that is, touch and play. These rights include the capabilities to create, delete, edit, or rename files or directories.

- ☐ **The Alexander Haig Rights**: that is, I'm in control. These rights include the capabilities to alter file attributes, and to completely control the file or directory.

In Table 15.1, you can see the various rights and their effect on files and directories.

Table 15.1. NetWare directory and file rights.

Right	Directory	File
Supervisor	All rights for the directory tree. Removes the effect of any restriction placed on files or directories by the IRM.	All rights for the file
Read	Open files in the directory and read them, execute programs in the directory	Open the files and read contents
Write	Open files in the directory and write to them	Open the file and write to it
Create	Create files and subdirectories in the directory	Salvage deleted file before a purge
Erase	Delete files, subdirectories with files, and directories	Delete a file
Modify	Modify the attributes of files and directories, rename the directory, files, and subdirectories	Modify the attributes of files, rename the file
File Scan	Search for files in the directory	Allows the file name to be seen when the directory contents are listed
Access Control	Control the trustee assignments and the Inherited Rights Mask for the directory or the files in the directory, and can assign every right except Supervisor	Control the trustee assignments and the Inherited Rights Mask for the file, and can assign every right except Supervisor

Notice the bold letters in Table 15.1 displayed whenever you use a utility, such as FILER and RIGHTS. If you grant all rights to a user, then you will see this represented as the following:

```
[S R W C E M F A]
```

If you have not granted a right to a user, then you will see a space where the right should have been. The order [SRWCEMFA] is constant. This constancy shows you at a glance what rights have been given to a user or group. For example, a user with the following can copy files from a directory:

```
[  R        F  ]
```

Now it's time to look at each right in more detail starting with the Supervisor right.

Supervisor

You learned in earlier chapters that SUPERVISOR is a user account. Just to add confusion, NetWare also has a right named Supervisor. This right gives you all rights to the directory, files within the directory, and subdirectories. The person with this right needs no other permissions to grant others access to, remove access from, modify, delete, write, create, or erase a file or directory.

You can only revoke the Supervisor right from the directory in which it was granted, not from a subdirectory or file.

Read

The *Read* right is a directory level right that enables you to open files and read them, or execute programs in a directory. Even though you may have the Read right, you cannot open a file with the Execute Only attribute set. Also, you may not be able to read from a file while another user has the file open and has denied you read access.

Write

Write enables you to open existing files and write to them. A user needs the Create right to make new files.

Even though you may have the Write right, you cannot open (and later write to) a file with the Read Only attribute set. Also, you cannot write to a file if another user has the file open and has denied you write access.

Note: You learned about file and directory attributes in the preceding chapter, should you wish to review the material to help in your understanding of rights and attributes.

Create

The *Create* right enables you to create new files or subdirectories. You need the Read right to read the contents of the file you create.

> **Note:** A user can create a file that the user cannot read or modify. This happens when the user has Create rights, but not Read rights. You can use this feature in all types of applications. Use it wherever you want users to save files in a directory, and not change them later.

When you create a new file, it is automatically opened and you can write to it as well as read from it. It doesn't make sense to read from a file that was just created and has a length of zero; however, you do have the right to position the file pointer so that you can create the file, write to it, reposition the file pointer, and read the data you just wrote.

> **Note:** The Create right changes for a file. You cannot, for example, create a file within a file. Therefore, the Create right only allows you to salvage a deleted file.

Erase

Erase enables you to delete files in the current directory. Even though you may have Erase rights, you cannot erase files whose attributes are set to Delete Inhibit, Read Only, System, or Transactional.

The Erase right also enables you to delete subdirectories and directories as long as the subdirectories and directories are empty and are not in use by other users. Even though you may have Erase rights, you cannot erase directories with the Delete Inhibit attribute set.

Modify

Modify enables you to change the attributes, names, and date/time stamps of files and directories. It does not, however, mean that a user has the right to change a file's contents.

Warning: This is a powerful right! You should not give it to users unless they need it to run their applications.

File Scan

The *File Scan* right makes the files within the directory visible to you when you scan for them and see the directory structure.

Scanning for files means that programs can use the DOS function calls Find First and Find Next. One such program is the DOS resident command DIR. If you do not have File Scan rights, you will get a message saying that there are no files found when you run DIR. Similarly, any programs that search the current directory for file names, such as WordPerfect, will not find any files without this right.

Access Control

The *Access Control* right enables you to modify the rights of others as well as control your rights. You can assign rights to others that you yourself do not have (except the Supervisor right). Because you can control your rights, however, for all intents and purposes, you have all rights.

Now that you understand the rights and their use, you can begin to apply them. The first application is trustee assignment.

Understanding Trustee Assignments

If you have rights to a directory or file, you are a *trustee* for that directory or file. The rights you possess are *trustee rights*. You can assign trustee rights to users and groups. A user gets Trustee Assignments to a directory in one of following three ways:

- ☐ Users have rights to directories and files given by the SUPERVISOR or users with Access Control rights.

- ☐ Users are members of a group that has rights to the directory or file.

- ☐ Users get rights to a directory or file because they are security equivalent to users who have rights to the directory or file.

Note: Groups get rights in the same way users do: the SUPERVISOR or a user with the Access Control right grants rights.

Users gain trustee rights in one of two ways: explicitly or implicitly. *Explicit* trustee assignments are the rights intentionally given to a user in a specific directory. *Implicit* rights are inherited trustee rights flowing down from parent directories.

Generally, the combination of all of these rights is a user's trustee rights. This is the additive feature of trustee rights, which means that a user's trustee assignment in a given directory is the combination of user rights and group rights mentioned previously. Trustee rights also can be nonadditive, which means that when you grant a user explicit rights in a given directory, NetWare takes away all other rights. Hence, explicit rights override implicit or inherited rights.

Note: You can assign a user rights to files within a directory without giving the user rights to all the files in the directory.

You will use the inherited rights feature of NetWare to assign rights. The best approach is to assign group rights for global directories, such as PUBLIC, and user rights for user specific directories, such as USERS\JANET.

Remember that the system created three default accounts: EVERYONE, SUPERVISOR, and GUEST. The group EVERYONE that includes all users has the Read and the File Scan right for SYS:PUBLIC, and the Create right for SYS:MAIL. SUPERVISOR grants all rights to everything. These rights cannot be removed, and neither can the SUPERVISOR account. GUEST has the trustee privileges of the group EVERYONE, and all rights except control to the account's SYS:MAIL directory.

Viewing Your Rights

If you want to see your rights in a directory or file, you can use the following five utilities:

- ☐ NDIR command line utility

- ☐ RIGHTS command line utility

- ☐ TLIST command line utility

☐ SYSCON menu utility

☐ FILER menu utility

You learn about NDIR and RIGHTS in Chapter 16.

Using the TLIST command line utility, you can see directory trustees by typing the following and pressing Enter.

TLIST [path] [USERS ¦ GROUPS]

If you type the following line, you will see a display similar to that in Figure 15.1.

TLIST SYS:PUBLIC GROUPS

```
F>tlist sys:public groups

RONAN\SYS:PUBLIC
Group trustees:
   EVERYONE                                    [ R    F ]

F>
```

Figure 15.1. *The TLIST display.*

Table 15.2 provides examples of the use of the TLIST command line utility.

Table 15.2. TLIST examples.

Command	Meaning
TLIST	Enables you to view all trustees of the current directory.
TLIST . USERS	Enables you to view only the user trustees of the current directory.
TLIST FILESERVER1/SYS:PUBLIC GROUPS	Enables you to view group trustees of the PUBLIC directory on the volume SYS: and the file server FILESERVER1.

The display tells you that the group EVERYONE has Read and File Scan rights to the PUBLIC directory.

SYSCON likewise provides trustee directory and file assignments.

Task 15.1: Viewing trustee assignments for a directory.

Step 1: Description

You can use SYSCON to view all of a user's or a group's directory trustee assignments. You also can use this utility to view your own assignments.

Step 2: Action

1. Type **LOGIN SUPERVISOR** and press Enter. Provide a password if required, and press Enter.

2. To change to the \PUBLIC subdirectory, type **CD\PUBLIC** and press Enter.

3. Type **SYSCON** and press Enter.

4. Highlight one of the following and then press Enter:

   To view user directory trustees, highlight User Information.

   To view group directory trustees, highlight Group Information.

5. In the User Names or Group Names menu, highlight the user or group for which you want to view trustee rights, and press Enter.

6. Highlight Trustee Directory Assignments, and press Enter. You should see a Trustee Directory Assignments screen similar to Figure 15.2.

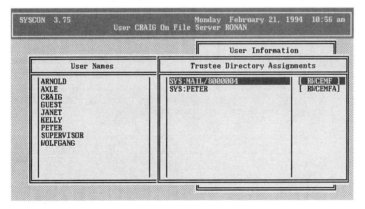

Figure 15.2. *Viewing a Trustee directory assignments screen.*

7. Press Esc until you are asked to confirm your exit from SYSCON.

Step 3: Review

As you just saw, you can use SYSCON to view all of a user's or group's directory trustee assignments and your own assignments. Moreover, you can use SYSCON to view trustee assignments for a file.

Task 15.2: Viewing trustee assignments for a file.

Step 1: Description

This task enables you to view the users and groups who are trustees of a file.

Step 2: Action

1. Type **LOGIN SUPERVISOR**, and press Enter. Provide password if required, and press Enter.

2. To change to the \PUBLIC subdirectory, type **CD\PUBLIC** and press Enter.

3. Type **SYSCON** and press Enter.

4. Highlight one of the following and then press Enter:

   User Information to view user directory trustees.

   Group Information to view group directory trustees.

5. In the User Names or Group Names menu, highlight the user or group where you want to view trustee rights, and then press Enter.

6. Highlight Trustee File Assignments, and press Enter. You should see a Trustee File Assignments screen similar to Figure 15.3.

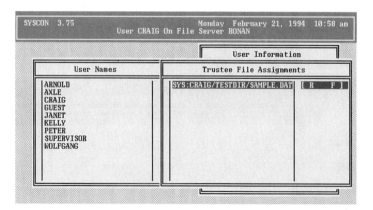

Figure 15.3. *Viewing a Trustee File Assignments screen.*

7. Press Esc until you are asked to confirm your exit from SYSCON.

Step 3: Review
Using what you learned in this task, you can view the users and groups who are trustees of a file. FILER also provides the capability to view directory trustees.

Task 15.3: Viewing directory trustees.

Step 1: Description
You can use the FILER utility to see who has trustee rights in a directory.

Step 2: Action
1. At the DOS prompt, type **FILER** and press Enter.

2. Highlight Current Directory Information, and press Enter. You will see a menu such as that in Figure 15.4.

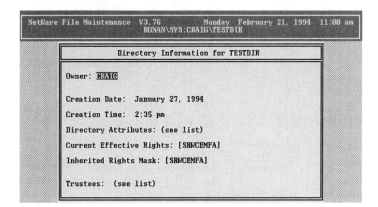

```
NetWare File Maintenance  V3.76         Monday  February 21, 1994  11:00 am
                        RONAN\SYS:CRAIG\TESTDIR

              ┌──────────── Directory Information for TESTDIR ────────────┐
              │                                                            │
              │  Owner: CRAIG                                              │
              │                                                            │
              │  Creation Date:  January 27, 1994                          │
              │  Creation Time:  2:35 pm                                   │
              │  Directory Attributes: (see list)                         │
              │  Current Effective Rights: [SRWCEMFA]                      │
              │  Inherited Rights Mask: [SRWCEMFA]                         │
              │                                                            │
              │  Trustees:  (see list)                                     │
              │                                                            │
              └────────────────────────────────────────────────────────────┘
```

Figure 15.4. *Directory Information for TESTDIR.*

3. Press the down arrow key to highlight Trustees and press Enter. You see a list of trustees such as shown in Figure 15.5.

4. Highlight the user or group you want and press Enter. You will see a list of trustee rights such as shown in Figure 15.6.

5. Press Esc until you are asked to confirm your exit from FILER.

Step 3: Review
The FILER utility enables you to see who has trustee rights in a directory. Once you understand and can view trustee rights, you will want to manage them carefully.

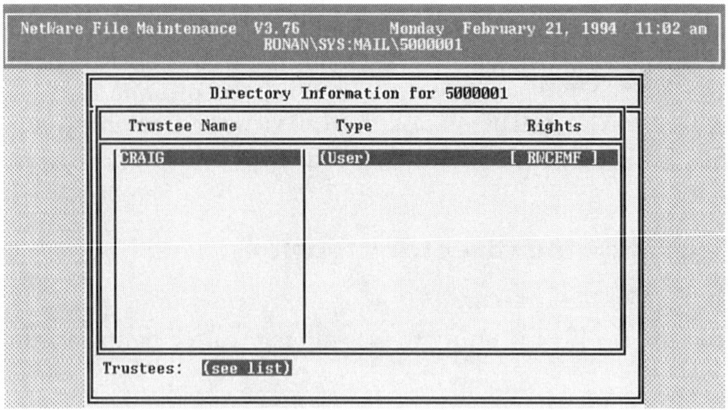

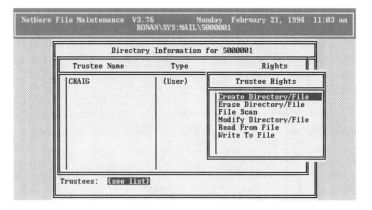

Figure 15.5. *Trustee information.*

Figure 15.6. *Trustee Rights.*

Controlling Rights

You can assign and modify rights in several ways. The following utilities enable you to control rights:

GRANT

REVOKE

REMOVE

SYSCON

FILER

GRANT, REVOKE, and REMOVE are command line utilities for controlling trustee rights. You use the GRANT command line utility to add trustee rights to users and groups without parsing a menu. At the DOS prompt, type

`GRANT R C TO KELLY`

With this command, you have granted (given) Read and Create rights to the user KELLY for the current directory. The complete command syntax is available in Appendix C.

> **Note:** You can specify all the rights for the GRANT command, or you can type **ALL**. Similarly, you can substitute N (no rights), ALL BUT (all rights except one), and ONLY (remove all rights except one listed), for a right.

Table 15.3 provides some other simple examples of the use of the GRANT command line utility.

Table 15.3. GRANT examples.

Command	Meaning
GRANT R W TO CRAIG	Adds the Read and Write rights to a user CRAIG. This does not affect any rights the user had previously.
GRANT ONLY R W TO CRAIG	Grants only the Read and Write rights to a user CRAIG. This affects any rights the user had previously by removing everything except Read and Write.
GRANT ALL BUT R W TO CRAIG	Adds all rights except Read and Write rights to a user CRAIG. This affects any rights the user had previously.
GRANT N TO CRAIG	Gives no rights to a user CRAIG. This affects any rights the user had previously.
GRANT ALL TO CRAIG	Gives all rights to a user CRAIG. This affects any rights the user had previously.

Note: With GRANT, you can substitute a group name for a username you want to add group trustee rights.

GRANT enables you to remove easily all rights from a user or group. The same utility also enables you to remove rights with the ONLY operator. There is an easier way, however. To delete trustee rights from a user or group, you can use the REVOKE command as follows:

```
REVOKE C FROM KELLY /F
```

In this simple example, you remove the Create right from user KELLY for the files in the current directory so that the user only can Read now. The /F is one of two options you may specify. If you do specify, then REVOKE will remove rights from files. The /S option works the same for subdirectories. Table 15.4 provides some other simple examples of the use of the REVOKE command line utility.

Table 15.4. Examples of REVOKE.

Command	Meaning
`REVOKE M A FROM CRAIG /F`	Removes the Modify and Access Control rights from a user CRAIG to all files in the current directory. This affects any rights the user had previously.
`REVOKE M A FROM GROUP ACCOUNTING`	Removes the Modify and Access Control rights from the ACCOUNTING group. This affects any rights the group had previously.
`REVOKE ALL FROM CRAIG`	Removes all rights for a user CRAIG. This affects any rights the user had previously.
`REVOKE ALL FROM GROUP ACCOUNTING`	Removes all rights for the group ACCOUNTING. This affects any rights the group had previously.

Note: With GRANT and REVOKE, you must have either the Access Control or the Supervisor right for the file or directory to grant or revoke rights.

Another command you will use—REMOVE—is similar to REVOKE. But, unlike REVOKE, you will use it when you want to delete users and groups from file and directory trustee lists. You can, for example, use the REMOVE command as follows.

```
REMOVE USER KELLY FROM SYS:APPS
```

At this moment, the user KELLY has been removed from the trustee assignments for the APPS directory in the SYS: volume. Table 15.5 provides further examples of the use of the REMOVE command line utility.

Table 15.5. Examples of REMOVE.

Command	Meaning
REMOVE CRAIG	Removes user CRAIG as a trustee of the current directory. This affects any rights the user had previously.
REMOVE GROUP ACCOUNTING	Removes the ACCOUNTING group as a trustee of the current directory. This affects any rights the group had previously.
REMOVE CRAIG FROM SYS:APPS	Removes user CRAIG as a trustee of the SYS:APPS directory tree. This affects any rights the user had previously.
REMOVE GROUP ACCOUNTING FROM SYS:APPS	Removes the group ACCOUNTING as a trustee of the SYS:APPS directory tree. This affects any rights the group had previously.

As you know, SYSCON and FILER are menu utilities you use to view and assign trustee rights. These utilities control users and groups. Using SYSCON and FILER will be intuitive once you master the use of GRANT, REVOKE, and REMOVE.

Task 15.4: Creating a directory trustee using SYSCON.

Step 1: Description
You can use the SYSCON as the SUPERVISOR to make a user or a group a trustee of any directory.

Step 2: Action
1. Type **LOGIN SUPERVISOR**, and press Enter. Provide a password if required, and press Enter.

2. To change to the \PUBLIC subdirectory, type **CD\PUBLIC** and press Enter.

3. Type **SYSCON** and press Enter.

4. Highlight one of the following options and then press Enter.

   User Information to create user directory trustees

   Group Information to create group directory trustees

5. In the User Names or Group Names menu, highlight the user or group to which you want to give trustee rights, and press Enter.

6. Highlight Trustee Directory Assignments, and press Enter.

7. Press Ins. You should see a Directory In Which Trustee Should Be Added screen similar to the one in Figure 15.7.

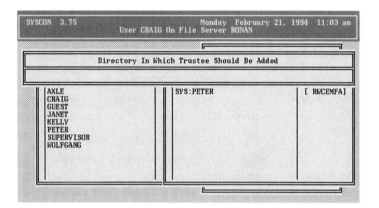

Figure 15.7. *Directory In Which Trustee Should Be Added screen.*

8. Type the path of the directory in which you want to add this user or group as a trustee. You should have a screen similar to Figure 15.8.

9. Press Esc until you are asked to confirm your exit from SYSCON.

Step 3: Review

With this task, you learned to use the SYSCON as the SUPERVISOR to make a user or a group a trustee of any directory. You could use FILER when you have control of the directory.

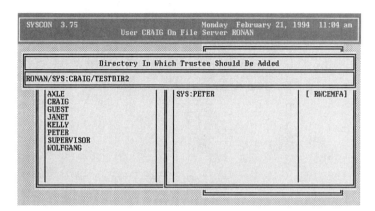

Figure 15.8. *Creating a Trustee Directory Assignments.*

Task 15.5: Creating a directory trustee using FILER.

Step 1: Description

You also can use the FILER menu utility to make a user or group a trustee of a directory you control.

Step 2: Action

1. At the DOS prompt, type **FILER** and press Enter.

2. Select Current Directory Information, and press Enter.

3. Press the down arrow key to select Trustees, and press Enter. You should see the screen similar to the one in Figure 15.9.

4. Press Ins.

5. From the Others menu, select a user or group, or press F5 to choose more than one user or group, and then press Enter. You should see a screen similar to the one in Figure 15.10.

6. Press Esc until you are asked to confirm your exit from FILER.

Step 3: Review

As you just saw, you can use the FILER menu utility to make a user or group a trustee of a directory you control. So the SUPERVISOR could use FILER to change any directory.

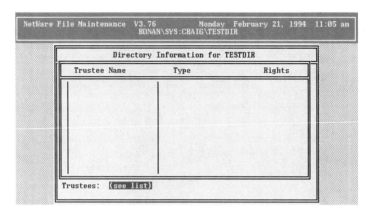

Figure 15.9. *The "before" Trustees screen.*

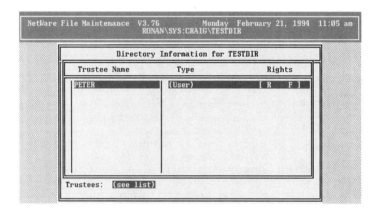

Figure 15.10. *The "after" Trustees screen.*

Task 15.6: Deleting directory trustee rights using SYSCON.

Step 1: Description

You can use the SYSCON utility as the SUPERVISOR to delete a trustee of any directory.

Step 2: Action

1. Type **LOGIN SUPERVISOR**, and press Enter. Provide password if required, and press Enter.

2. To change to the \PUBLIC subdirectory, type **CD\PUBLIC** and press Enter.

3. Type **SYSCON** and press Enter.

4. Highlight one of the following options and then press Enter:

   User Information to delete users as directory trustees

   Group Information to delete groups as directory trustees

5. In the User Names or Group Names menu, highlight the user or group from which you want to remove trustee rights, and press Enter.

6. Highlight Trustee Directory Assignments, and press Enter.

7. Select the directory, and press Delete.

8. Confirm your intent in the Remove Trustee From Directory screen similar to the one in Figure 15.11.

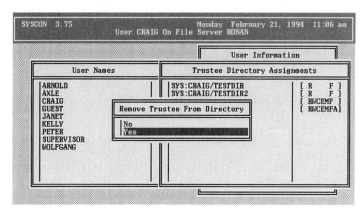

Figure 15.11. *The Remove Trustee From Directory screen.*

9. Press Esc until you are asked to confirm your exit from SYSCON.

Step 3: Review

Using the SYSCON utility, the SUPERVISOR can delete a user or group as a trustee of any directory. A user who controls a directory could use FILER as well as SYSCON.

Task 15.7: Deleting directory trustee rights using FILER.

Step 1: Description

You also can use the FILER menu utility to delete a user or group a trustee of a directory you control.

Step 2: Action

1. At the DOS prompt, type **FILER** and press Enter.

2. Select Current Directory Information, and press Enter.

3. Press the down arrow key to highlight Trustees, and press Enter. Your list should be like the one in Figure 15.12.

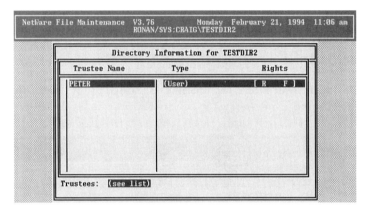

Figure 15.12. *The Trustee Names screen.*

4. Select a user or group to delete, and press Delete.

5. Confirm your intent in the Delete Trustee From Directory menu, and press Enter.

6. Press Esc until you are asked to confirm your exit from FILER.

Step 3: Review

You have seen how to use the FILER and SYSCON menu utilities to delete a user or group as a trustee of a directory.

Now and then, you will need to add directory trustee rights. Again, you can use either SYSCON or FILER.

Task 15.8: Adding directory trustee rights using SYSCON.

Step 1: Description

You can use the SYSCON utility as the SUPERVISOR to add trustee rights to any user or group.

Step 2: Action

1. Type **LOGIN SUPERVISOR**, and press Enter. Provide password if required, and press Enter.

2. To change to the \PUBLIC subdirectory, type **CD\PUBLIC,** and press Enter.

3. Type **SYSCON** and press Enter.

4. Highlight one of the following, and then press Enter.

   User Information to add users as directory trustees

   Group Information to add groups as directory trustees

5. In the User Names or Group Names menu, highlight the user or group to which you want to give trustee rights, and then press Enter.

6. Highlight Trustee Directory Assignments, and press Enter.

7. Highlight the directory that you want to add rights to the user or group, and press Enter. You see the Trustee Rights Granted window.

8. Press Ins. You should see a Trustee Rights Not Granted screen similar to the one in Figure 15.13.

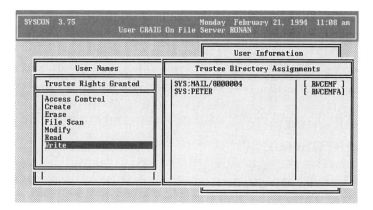

Figure 15.13. *Trustee Rights Granted screen.*

9. Select the right, or press F5 to choose more than one right, and press Enter.

10. Press Esc until you are asked to confirm your exit from SYSCON.

Step 3: Review

This task demonstrated how you could use the SYSCON utility as the SUPERVISOR to add trustee rights to any user or group. You can use FILER to add directory trustee rights.

Task 15.9: Adding Directory Trustee Rights Using FILER

Step 1: Description

You can use the FILER utility to add trustee rights to any user or group you control.

Step 2: Action

1. At the DOS prompt, type **FILER** and press Enter.

2. Highlight Current Directory Information, and press Enter.

3. Press the down arrow key to highlight Trustees, and press Enter.

Tip: With FILER, you can substitute a group name for a username should you want to add group trustee rights.

4. From the Trustee Name list, select a user, or press F5 to select several users, and press Enter. You should see the Trustee Rights window.

5. Press Ins. Now, you should see the Other Rights window.

6. Select the right, or press F5 to select more than one right, and press Enter.

7. Press Esc until you are asked to confirm your exit from FILER.

Step 3: Review

In the previous two tasks, you used SYSCON and FILER to add trustee rights to a directory. In the next chapter, you will discover the steps for completing the same task for files.

Summary

In this chapter, you learned about the following:

☐ The eight different rights

☐ The utilities for viewing rights

You will want to review the different rights and review how they could be used in your particular case. Proper use of rights security can greatly increase the security and effectiveness of your file server and network.

NetWare's rights security provides a flexible, yet powerful system for assigning rights and controlling users. Its power derives from the number of combinations you can create from the basic rights. It is a good idea to spend time discovering how rights security works. For this reason, you will spend the next session creating and deleting trustee rights and inherited rights masks.

Workshop

Terminology Review

access type—An access right to a particular device, program or file, such as read, write, execute, append, allocate, modify, delete, create.

permission—A particular form of allowed access, such as permission to Read as contrasted with permission to Write.

read—A fundamental operation that results only in the flow of information from an object to a subject.

read access—Permission to read data.

rights—User capabilities given for accessing files and directories on a file server.

trustee—A user assigned right to a file or directory.

trustee rights—Right to a directory or file directly or indirectly assigned to a user or group. They are a combination of a user's rights, the group's rights, and the security equivalence rights.

write—A fundamental operation that results only in the flow of data from a subject to an object.

write access—Permission to write an object.

Task List

The emphasis of this chapter has been to introduce you to rights and their management. Frequently, you will be called upon to grant and revoke trustee rights to users and groups. The tasks you should understand from this chapter are:

☐ Viewing trustee assignments for a directory and a file

☐ Viewing directory trustees

☐ Creating and deleting a directory trustee using SYSCON

☐ Creating and deleting a directory trustee using FILER

☐ Controlling rights using GRANT

☐ Controlling rights using REVOKE

☐ Controlling rights using REMOVE

☐ Controlling rights using SYSCON

☐ Controlling rights using FILER

Q&A

Q How do I prevent one user from accessing another user's network files?

A This is precisely the reason for using rights. If the users are in the same group, they may have inheritance from the directory, so you will need to write either an IRM (next chapter) or explicitly REVOKE rights.

Q Should I allow users to maintain trustee rights for their directories and files?

A This is another decentralization versus centralization decision. If you perform most administrative functions centrally, it is unlikely that you will decentralize security. If you decide to decentralize administration, you must remember to provide your users with adequate security training, and acquaint them with security issues.

Q What rights do I need to read a file? Write a file?

A You learn all about the combinations of rights for common tasks in Chapter 16. For now, you need **R**ead to read a closed file and **W**rite+**C**reate+**E**rase+**M**odify to write to a closed file.

Q Should I give Access Control to users?

A You normally should not give Access Control to anybody. Users can do almost everything with Erase, File Scan, Read, Write, and Modify. If you give Access Control, then you have intentionally or unintentionally decentralized security administration.

Q **How do I see who owns a directory or a file? Also, how do I change the ownership for a directory or a file?**

A To see the owner of a directory, use FILER | Current Directory Information. In the Directory Information for DIRECTORY screen, you will see the Owner: field. To change this field, highlight it, press Enter, highlight a new user from the Known Users window, and press Enter.

To see the owner of a file, use FILER | Directory Contents | file name | View/Set File Information. In the File Information for FILE screen, you will see the Owner: field. To change this field, highlight it, press Enter, highlight a new user from the Known Users window, and press Enter.

16

Concluding NetWare File and Directory Rights

In Chapter 15, you were introduced to rights generally and trustee assignments specifically. You saw how you could use the command line utilities GRANT, REVOKE, and REMOVE and the menu utilities FILER and SYSCON to create and delete directory trustees.

By the end of the last session you understood that you must have rights to directories, subdirectories, and files to perform any activity in them. At the moment, you are aware that rights define what a user can do on your network and that they are a primary NetWare security mechanism. In the last session, you looked principally at trustee assignment. You should appreciate by now that explicit assignment is preferable to implicit assignment. The primary reason for this is that network or system administrators rarely predict the flow through of directory rights. With user and group rights, and directory rights cascading, this prediction can be a formidable task. Having said this, you still need to review and understand inheritance, which is the bulk of the material in this chapter.

Before getting to the subject of inheritance, you will need to complete the study of trustee assignments. You learned about directory trustees in Chapter 15. The first section of this session continues on that theme, and shows you how to view, add, and delete a file trustee. Your first task is to view file trustees.

Task 16.1: Viewing file trustees.

Step 1: Description
You can use the FILER utility to see who has trustee rights in a file. As you saw in Chapter 15, trustee rights flow down from the directory rights. These trustee rights, however, can be different than the trustee rights for the directory.

Step 2: Action
1. At the DOS prompt, type **FILER** and press Enter.

2. Highlight Directory Contents, and press Enter. You will see a list of Directory Contents like those in Figure 16.1.

3. Highlight the file you want, and press Enter. You will see the File Options menu shown in Figure 16.2.

—

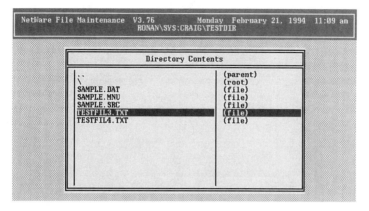

Figure 16.1. *Directory Contents.*

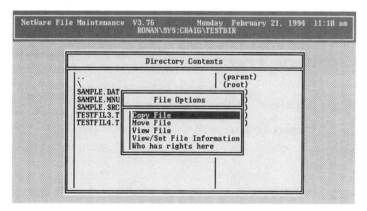

Figure 16.2. *File options.*

4. Highlight Who has rights here, and press Enter. You will see a window similar to Figure 16.3.

5. Press Esc until you are asked to confirm your exit from FILER.

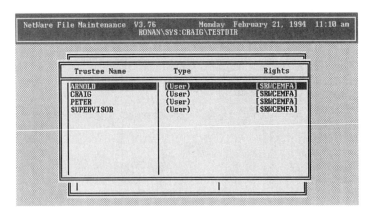

```
NetWare File Maintenance   V3.76        Monday  February 21, 1994  11:10 am
                         RONAN\SYS:CRAIG\TESTDIR

        Trustee Name            Type              Rights

    ARNOLD                   (User)            [SRWCEMFA]
    CRAIG                    (User)            [SRWCEMFA]
    PETER                    (User)            [SRWCEMFA]
    SUPERVISOR               (User)            [SRWCEMFA]
```

Figure 16.3. *Rights screen.*

Step 3: Review

You just practiced how you would view file trustees using FILER. You also will use FILER to add a file trustee.

Task 16.2: Adding a File Trustee.

Step 1: Description

With this task, you use the FILER utility to add a user to the trustee list of a file that you control.

Step 2: Action

1. At the DOS prompt, type **FILER** and press Enter.

2. Highlight Directory Contents, and press Enter. You should see a Directory Contents list comparable to the one in Figure 16.4.

3. Highlight the file you want to add a user to from the Directory Contents list, and press Enter. You will see the File Options Account menu.

4. Highlight View/Set File Information, and press Enter.

5. Press the down arrow key to highlight Trustees, and press Enter. You will see a list of trustees such as those shown in Figure 16.5.

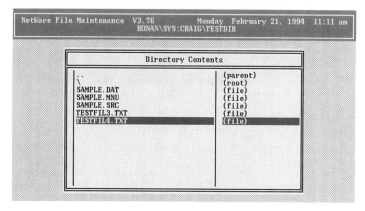

Figure 16.4. *Directory contents.*

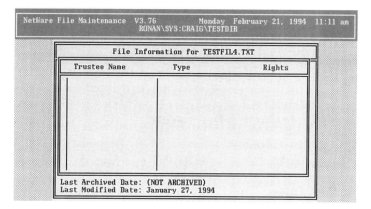

Figure 16.5. *Trustee names.*

6. Press Ins.

7. Highlight a group or user, and press Enter. You will see a list of trustee rights such as those shown those in Figure 16.6.

8. Press Esc until you are asked to confirm your exit from FILER.

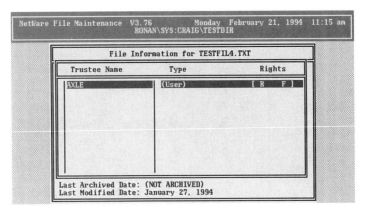

Figure 16.6. *Trustee rights.*

Step 3: Review

At this time, you know how to use the FILER menu utility to look at and create file trustees. Now and then, you will need to delete file trustees. You may need to do this as employees leave or assume new positions.

Task 16.3: Deleting a file trustee.

Step 1: Description

You also use the FILER utility to delete a user from the trustee list of a file.

Step 2: Action

1. At the DOS prompt, type **FILER** and press Enter.

2. Select Directory Contents, and press Enter.

3. From the Directory Contents list, highlight the file from which you want to delete a user, and press Enter. You will see the File Options Account menu.

4. Highlight View/Set File Information, and press Enter.

5. Press the down arrow key to highlight Trustees, and press Enter.

6. Select the user or group you want to delete, and press Delete.

7. Confirm your intent to delete the user in the Delete Trustee From Directory box.

8. Press Esc until you are asked to confirm your exit from FILER.

Step 3: Review

So far in this chapter, you have used the FILER menu utility to view, add, and delete file trustees. Later on in this chapter, you will use the FILER again.

Presently, you are going to expand your knowledge of trustee rights and learn about inheritance and its effect on file security.

Introducing Inheritance

When you have trustee rights in a directory, you have the same rights to the sub-directories and files within those directories. This means that rights flow down, cascade, or are inherited by these lower level files and directories. Hence, when you grant an access right to a trustee for a given directory, the user inherits the privilege for all subdirectories and files.

Suppose that you have Read and File Scan rights to SYS:PUBLIC, and then you have Read and File Scan rights to every subdirectory and file below SYS:PUBLIC. You can relax a little because inheritance doesn't flow up. Now you understand inheritance! Figure 16.7 depicts this flow of rights.

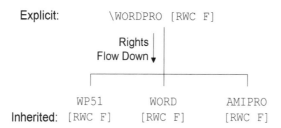

Figure 16.7. *The inheritance of trustee rights.*

> **Note:** If you give rights to anyone in the root of volume SYS, then that individual inherits those rights for all subdirectories of the root—unless you protect the directories in the directories with a mask. The simple solution is don't make anyone a trustee of the root of any volume, particularly SYS.

When you create a file or directory, the inherited rights for the object defaults to all rights. You can change the defaults as you will see in a subsequent section.

Understanding the Inherited Rights Mask

There may be times when you don't want the rights assigned to a parent directory to flow down to subdirectories. If you don't want lower level directories to inherit the rights of the directories above, you can block some or all of these rights from being inherited. You do this with an Inherited Rights Mask (IRM). Basically, the IRM provides the maximum rights you can inherit in a directory. The mask blocks out the rights inherited from the higher level directory, and insists on you having specific rights. There is an inherited rights mask for every directory on your file server. If the SYS:APPS\PAYROLL subdirectory contain sensitive files that shouldn't be read, for example, then you can remove the Read right from the directory. You will need to explicitly grant Read rights in the SYS:APPS\PAYROLL subdirectory.

> **Note:** The IRM only applies to inherited rights, and not explicit rights, which override the IRM.

Also, there is an Inherited Rights Mask for every file on your file server. A file's IRM can block some or all rights from being inherited from the directory where the file resides.

> **Note:** Don't confuse IRM with trustee assignment. An IRM with all rights doesn't mean that users are assigned all rights. It just means all rights are allowed. However, you will explicitly grant rights through trustee assignment.

Even though your users and groups do not have trustee rights to SYS:SYSTEM, they easily could inherit rights if assigned trustee rights to the root volume of SYS. Just for assurance, you should set the IRM for the SYS:SYSTEM directory to Read and File Scan rights. This mask applies to all users except for the SUPERVISOR and supervisor-equivalent. If you really want to ensure that a user does not inherit rights to a directory, then you should make that user a trustee of the directory, and assign the user no rights. Now you have a user with no rights to the directory regardless of the user's trustee rights in the parent directory.

There are two methods for viewing the Inherited Rights Mask. The first way is to type the following at the DOS prompt:

LISTDIR /R

Figure 16.8 provides an example of LISTDIR. From it you can determine whether the user has inherited all rights to the subdirectories.

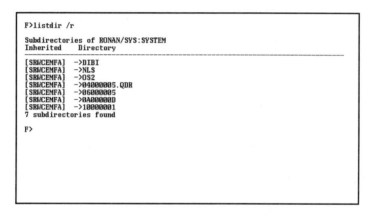

```
F>listdir /r

Subdirectories of RONAN/SYS:SYSTEM
Inherited     Directory
_____
[SRWCEMFA]    ->DIBI
[SRWCEMFA]    ->NLS
[SRWCEMFA]    ->OS2
[SRWCEMFA]    ->04000005.QDR
[SRWCEMFA]    ->06000005
[SRWCEMFA]    ->0A00000D
[SRWCEMFA]    ->10000001
7 subdirectories found

F>
```

Figure 16.8. *Listing Inherited Rights Using LISTDIR.*

In addition to the command line utility, you also can use the FILER menu utility to view the Inherited Rights Mask.

Task 16.4: Viewing a Inherited Rights Mask.

Step 1: Description
You can use the FILER utility to see a directory's inherited rights mask.

Step 2: Action
1. Select Current Directory Information, and press Enter.

2. Press the down arrow key to highlight Inherited Rights Mask. You will see an Inherited Rights window such as Figure 16.9.

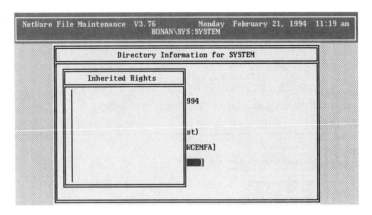

NetWare File Maintenance V3.76   Monday February 21, 1994 11:19 am
                        RONAN\SYS:SYSTEM

Directory Information for SYSTEM

Inherited Rights

994

st)
WCEMFA]

Figure 16.9. *Listing inherited rights using FILER.*

4. Press Esc until you are asked to confirm your exit from FILER.

Step 3: Review

FILER is a handy menu utility. It provides a facility for implementing trustee assignment, inherited rights mask, and attribute level security. In addition, FILER provides a tool for managing NetWare directories, files, and volumes.

FILER incorporates the following associated command line utilities into its menus:

☐ FLAG

☐ LISTDIR

☐ NCOPY

☐ NDIR

☐ RENDIR

☐ DOS XCOPY

You have viewed the IRM, and now you probably are ready to create and change them.

Controlling Inherited Rights Mask

You can create and change inherited rights masks in several ways. The following utilities enable you to control the IRM:

☐ ALLOW

☐ SYSCON

ALLOW is a command line utility for controlling trustee rights. You use the ALLOW command line utility to view or set the Inherited Rights Mask of files or directories. Anyone can use the ALLOW command to view an IRM, but you must have Access Control or Supervisor rights to change an IRM. When IRM is set, the IRM only has the rights specified. NetWare will remove any rights (except the Supervisor right) that you do not specify. For example, at the DOS prompt, you could type the following:

```
ALLOW SYS:PUBLIC TO INHERIT R F
ALLOW SYS:PUBLIC\*.EXE TO INHERIT R F
```

The first command sets the IRM for the SYS:PUBLIC directory to Read and File Scan. In the second command, you have set the IRM of all executable files in the PUBLIC directory to Read and File Scan. Therefore, the executables cannot inherit any other rights but Supervisor from the directory.

After you have played with ALLOW for a spell, you can try doing the same thing using the FILER menu utility.

Task 16.5: Changing an Inherited Rights Mask.

Step 1: Description
This task enables you to grant or revoke a right in the Inherited Rights Mask of a directory where you have the Access Control or Supervisor right.

Step 2: Action
1. At the DOS prompt, type **FILER** and press Enter.

2. Select Current Directory Information, and press Enter.

3. Press the down arrow key to highlight Inherited Rights Mask, and press Enter.

4. Add or revoke a right. To add a right, you can press Ins, select the right, or use F5 to choose more than one right from the Other Rights menu, and press Enter. (See Figure 16.10.)

   To revoke a right, you can press Delete, select the right, or use F5 to choose more than one right from the Other Rights menu, and then press Delete (see Figure 16.10).

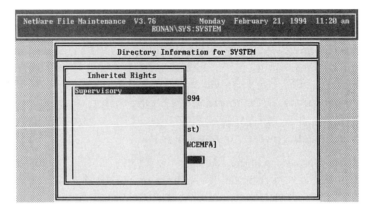

Figure 16.10. *Other Rights.*

5. Press Esc until you are asked to confirm your exit from FILER.

Step 3: Review

The FILER utility provides a means to manage the IRM of a directory, subdirectory, or file.

Using the Types of Rights

As suggested in NetWare's documentation, you will need to review your organization's security policy and develop rights based on the policy before you start assigning rights to users. Because the system restricts users to 32 Trustee Assignments, you will need to work these assignments out carefully and logically. Otherwise, you could rapidly run out of Trustee Assignments.

You also must play around with these rights by testing the ramifications on dummy users. As you have seen in this book, doing something first hand greatly enhances your understanding of the tasks.

Each of the eight access rights corresponds with a particular user function. Five of them correspond to common functions—reading, writing, creating, erasing, and searching. The other three rights—supervisor, modify, access control—are NetWare security related because they assign and modify attributes and rights. With Modify, you can customize file attributes. Access control enables you to change access privileges.

The key to understanding NetWare rights is to understand the rights you need to do common activities. Table 16.1 provides a sample of these.

Table 16.1. NetWare rights combinations.

Activity	Rights
List files in a directory	**F**ile Scan
Read a closed file	**R**ead
Write to a closed file	**W**rite+**C**reate+**E**rase+**M**odify
Execute a program	**R**ead+**F**ile Scan
Execute a program that uses temporary files	**R**ead+**F**ile Scan+**C**reate+**E**rase+**M**odify
Create file/subdirectory	**C**reate
Delete a file	**E**rase
Rename a file or directory	**M**odify(or **C**reate)+**W**rite
Modify file attributes	**F**ile Scan+**M**odify
Copy files into a directory	**C**reate
Copy files from a directory	**R**ead+**F**ile Scan
Set directory attributes	**A**ccess Control
Change trustee rights in subdirectory/directory	**A**ccess Control
Change the Inherited Rights Mask	**A**ccess Control
See the root directory	Any right

As you know, NetWare enables users to control access to directories and to the files and subdirectories within them. The rights users grant at the directory level are effective for all files and subdirectories in the directory. You can, however, override rights of access to files and subdirectories, if you want.

Trustee assignments and inherited rights masks use the same rights shown in Table 15.1 in Chapter 15 to control user access to directories and files on NetWare volumes. The effect of the right depends on whether you are using a trustee assignment or an inherited rights mask. Calculating effective rights is a lost art.

Effective Rights

This chapter and Chapter 15 examine trustee assignment and inherited rights. In this part of your session, you explore how these rights translate into the rights that you actually have for a particular file or directory. These rights are labeled *effective rights*.

As you saw in Chapter 15, your effective rights for a file or directory are an intersection of the following:

- ☐ The trustee assignments of the user
- ☐ The trustee assignments of the user's group (or groups)
- ☐ The inherited rights mask for the file or directory

The method for translating effective rights for a directory differs slightly from that for a file. You determine the effective rights to a directory by doing the following:

1. Determine whether the user has an effective right of Supervisor in the parent directory. You can do this by determining whether the user or a group the user belongs to has Supervisor right to the parent directory, or for a directory on the path leading to the root directory. If you find any of these conditions, then the effective right for the directory is the Supervisor right. Confused? Well, once you assign the Supervisor right to a directory, you can remove it only from that directory, and not from the subdirectory.

2. If you didn't have the Supervisor right, then you will want to determine whether the directory has a trustee assignment. When trustee assignments exist, the effective rights for the directory are equal to the rights in the trustee assignment. If there are no trustee assignments, then you will need to look at the inherited rights mask.

3. Determine whether there is an inherited rights mask for the directory. If all the rights of the parent directory are inherited, then the effective rights of this directory are the same as the effective rights of the parent directory. Otherwise, the effective rights of the directory are equal to the effective rights in the parent directory less the rights that are set in the inherited rights mask.

This is an important concept. So, let's look at another way of saying this. You can determine the effective rights to a directory as follows:

1. When you don't have trustee assignment to the directory, your effective rights to that directory are equal to your effective rights to the parent directory, less any rights blocked by the directory's inherited rights mask.

2. When you do have trustee assignment to the directory, your effective rights to that directory are equal to your trustee assignments, irrespective of the parent directory or the inherited rights mask.

As mentioned, the method for translating effective rights for a file differs slightly from that for a directory. You will use the following method for determining a file's effective rights.

1. Determine whether the user has an effective right of Supervisor for the directory where the file is. If you find this, then the effective right for the file is all rights, because the Supervisor right to a directory gives all rights to the directory, subdirectories, and files.

2. If you didn't have the Supervisor right, then you want to determine whether the file has a trustee assignment. When trustee assignments exist, the effective rights for the file are equal to the rights in the trustee assignment. If there are no trustee assignments, then you will need to look at the inherited rights mask.

3. Determine whether there is an inherited rights mask for the file. If all the rights of the file can be inherited, then the effective rights of the file are the same as the effective rights of the directory where the file resides. Otherwise, the effective rights of the file are equal to the effective rights of the file's directory less the rights that are set in the inherited rights mask.

Note: The trustee assignments always override the inherited rights mask in deriving a user's effective rights for a directory. Strangely, the user's rights for files or subdirectories are determined by the inherited rights mask.

Note: Now is the time to muddy the effective rights waters. The true effective rights to a given directory are determined by the combination of trustee assignments, directory rights, and file attributes. Don't forget to include the use of security attributes when you are trying to figure out effective rights.

You can view your effective rights to a file or directory using either the RIGHTS and NDIR command line utilities or the FILER menu utility. To see your effective RIGHTS for the current directory, type the following and press Enter.

RIGHTS

```
F>rights
RONAN\SYS:
Your Effective Rights for this directory are [SRWCEMFA]
    You have Supervisor Rights to Directory.    (S)
  * May Read from File.                          (R)
  * May Write to File.                           (W)
    May Create Subdirectories and Files.        (C)
    May Erase Directory.                         (E)
    May Modify Directory.                        (M)
    May Scan for Files.                          (F)
    May Change Access Control.                   (A)

* Has no effect on directory.

    Entries in Directory May Inherit [SRWCEMFA] rights.
    You have ALL RIGHTS to Directory Entry.

F>
```

Figure 16.11. *Supervisor's effective rights.*

Figure 16.11 provides a sample display for the RIGHTS command. From the display, notice that the SUPERVISOR account has [S R W C E M F A] rights. This is what you would expect from the SUPERVISOR. Let's, however, try the same directory with a different user. Figure 16.12 shows the RIGHTS display for user KELLY. As you can see, this account has no rights on this directory.

```
F>rights
RONAN\SYS:
Your Effective Rights for this directory are [        ]
    Entries in Directory May Inherit [        ] rights.
    You have NO RIGHTS to this directory area.
F>
```

Figure 16.12. *A User's effective rights.*

The full command is RIGHTS [directory name\file name], which means you can use it for files, too.

Alternatively, you can use NDIR to see your effective rights for a directory by typing the following and pressing Enter.

NDIR [path] /RIGHTS

Figure 16.13 provides a sample display. From the display, notice the inherited rights.

```
RONAN\SYS:

                                    Inherited    Effective
Files:                  Flags       Rights       Rights       Owner
─────────────────────────────────────────────────────────────────────
BACKOUT       TTS  [Rw-A-HSy----------]  [S-------]  [SRWCEMFA]  SUPERVISOR
TTS$LOG       ERR  [Rw-A-------------]  [SRWCEMFA]  [SRWCEMFA]  SUPERVISOR
VOL$LOG       ERR  [Rw-A-------------]  [SRWCEMFA]  [SRWCEMFA]  SUPERVISOR

                       Inherited    Effective
Directories:           Rights       Rights       Owner        Created/Copied
─────────────────────────────────────────────────────────────────────
ARNOLD            [SRWCEMFA]  [SRWCEMFA]  CRAIG        1-24-94  11:39p
AXLE              [SRWCEMFA]  [SRWCEMFA]  SUPERVISOR   2-18-94   4:19p
CRAIG             [SRWCEMFA]  [SRWCEMFA]  SUPERVISOR   1-14-94   1:11a
DELETED      SAV  [--------]  [SRWCEMFA]  SUPERVISOR   1-14-94  12:35a
DOC               [SRWCEMFA]  [SRWCEMFA]  RONAN        1-20-94  10:14a
ETC               [SRWCEMFA]  [SRWCEMFA]  RONAN        1-14-94   1:04a
JANET             [SRWCEMFA]  [SRWCEMFA]  SUPERVISOR   2-18-94   4:19p
KELLY             [SRWCEMFA]  [SRWCEMFA]  SUPERVISOR   2-18-94   5:08p
LOGIN             [SRWCEMFA]  [SRWCEMFA]  SUPERVISOR   1-14-94  12:35a
MAIL              [--------]  [SRWCEMFA]  SUPERVISOR   1-14-94  12:35a
PETER             [SRWCEMFA]  [SRWCEMFA]  CRAIG        1-24-94  10:03a

Strike any key for next page or C for continuous display...
```

Figure 16.13. *The NDIR display.*

If you don't provide any arguments to the command syntax, then the system displays your effective rights for the current directory. RIGHTS and NDIR provides rights for files and directories. The next section deals with using FILER to see effective rights in a directory.

Task 16.6: Viewing your effective rights in a directory.

Step 1: Description
This task shows you the rights you can exercise in the default directory.

Step 2: Action
1. At the DOS prompt, type **FILER** and press Enter.

2. Highlight Current Directory Information, and press Enter. You should see a menu like the one in Figure 16.14.

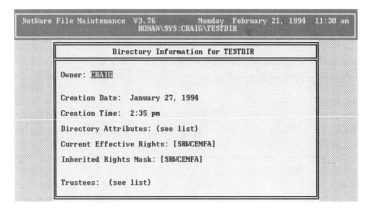

Figure 16.14. *Directory information.*

3. Highlight Current Effective Rights. Again, you should see a listing like the one in Figure 16.5. In the example, you can see the effective rights are [SRWCEMFA], which means this user has *x*, *x*, *x*, and *x* rights for directory *x*.

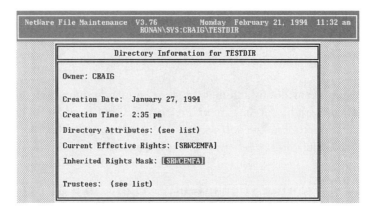

Figure 16.15. *Effective rights.*

4. Press Esc until you are asked to confirm your exit from FILER.

Step 3: Review

With this task, you learned how to view the effective rights for a directory using FILER.

Summary

In this chapter, you did the following:

☐ Finished your review of trustee rights by looking at trustee assignments for files

☐ Studied inheritance and you saw that if you have trustee rights in a directory, you have the same rights to subdirectories and files in the directory

☐ Learned you can block rights (except Supervisor) from being inherited

☐ Learned how to calculate effective rights

Workshop

Terminology Review

effective rights—The actual rights a user has to a file or a directory based on trustee assignments, inheritance, and masks.

Inherited Rights Mask—A mechanism that blocks some rights for a file or subdirectory, which you can inherit from a directory.

rights—User capabilities given for accessing files and directories on a file server.

Task List

The emphasis of this chapter has been to introduce you to inheritance and how to control inherited rights. As a system administrator or SUPERVISOR, you will need to know how to control access as part of your job. Following are the tasks you should understand from this chapter:

☐ Controlling file trustees

☐ Viewing an Inherited Rights Mask

☐ Changing an Inherited Rights Mask

☐ Viewing effective rights in a directory

Q&A

Q Is there a connection between attributes and rights?

A Yes. The last security check performed is to the file attributes. So even if you have Write and Modify rights, you cannot update the file if the file is set to Read Only.

Q Does the IRM add or subtract rights?

A Remember that an Inherited Rights Mask blocks inherited rights for a file or subdirectory from a directory. Therefore, an IRM subtracts rights not specified. The one exception is the Supervisor right, which you cannot block.

Q If I want to ensure that a file is protected, what should I do?

A You should explicitly grant rights. Explicit rights override inheritance. It is a good idea to grant access explicitly to sensitive directories and files.

Q Is there an easy way to detect excessive rights?

A It depends. If you want to see excessive rights to SYS:SYSTEM, SYS:MAIL, and SYS:PUBLIC, you can use NetWare's SECURITY command line utility, otherwise no. Third-party products can help you look at excessive rights of other directories and files.

Q Can I prevent the Supervisor from looking at my files?

A You cannot prevent the Supervisor from looking at your files; you can, however, make them unintelligible. If you are concerned about the Supervisor reading your files, then you should use file encryption. File encryption enables you to write coded information to shared drives. You need the encryption key to retrieve information in clear text.

Day

9

17

Understanding Real-World Network Standards

One of the most difficult parts of learning about local area networks in general, and NetWare in particular, is understanding the data communication process. What goes across the cable between nodes on a network can be mysterious and confusing. You saw some of these issues in Chapters 2 and 4. In this chapter, we unravel more of the mystery for you. While it's not essential to have an *in-depth* understanding of how data communications work, the more you know, the better you will be able to deal with problems which arise on the network.

To help your understanding, we look at some data communication standards in use. Popular standards have evolved at various layers in the data communications model. But regardless of where standards or products fit in any model, the key question remains "What works with what?" You discover some answers to that question later in this chapter.

For now, you learn more about the current standards in use for various parts of the data communication process. If you keep in mind the functions illustrated by the simplified network model covered in Chapter 2, you'll be able to understand better how real-world network hardware and software operate.

The current standards can be broken down into three main areas:

- Cabling systems
- Media access control methods
- Network communications protocols

Together, cabling systems and media access control methods form the connection-level of our simplified network model. (They also represent the first and second levels of the OSI Model.) You see many details about cabling systems and media access control methods in the next section.

Later in the chapter, you learn more about network communication protocols. They form the network-level and converstation-level of our simplified network model (and the top five layers of the OSI Model).

Considering Cabling Systems

Cabling systems refer to the physical means by which data is transmitted between network nodes. This setup normally involves a physical cable to conduct electrical signals, or sometimes light beams, between computers. Physical cable is called *bounded media* because signals are not intended to leave the medium.

Note: The term *cabling systems* also can refer to *unbounded media*, that is, wireless transmission of data over radio frequency waves, microwaves, or infrared. Although these systems are gaining popularity, broadly accepted standards are still evolving. As a result, you do not spend much time examining wireless LANs. In fact, this note is about the full extent of it.

Following are the three most common cabling media:

- ☐ Twisted pair
- ☐ Coaxial cable
- ☐ Fiber optic cable

Next, you look more closely at each of these cable types.

Twisted Pair

Twisted pair wiring consists of two or more conducting wires covered by a plastic sheath. You can find an example in use between an average household telephone and its wall outlet.

It is available in both shielded and unshielded varieties, and with different numbers of electrical conductors within. Shielded twisted pair provides somewhat better protection against stray electrical fields than unshielded. Twisted pair makes use of a variety of connector types, such as the RJ11 connector (also known as a modular phone plug) or the somewhat larger RJ45. Figure 17.1 illustrates a typical twisted pair wire.

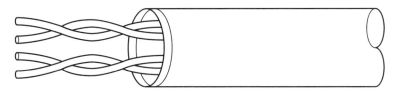

Figure 17.1. *Twisted pair wire.*

Twisted pair, particularly unshielded twisted pair (UTP), has the advantage of being less expensive than other types of cable. It is also commonly available and relatively easy to work with during installation and connection.

Twisted pair also has some limitations, however. Its main drawback is that, because it is more vulnerable to electromagnetic interference than other types of cable, its distance and overall data speed is limited compared to other cables. Of course, engineering improvements continue to reduce these limitations to the point where UTP is used for many LAN connections, with no problems being experienced.

Coaxial Cable

Coaxial cable (also called coax) is made up of two conducting wires running along the same axis (hence the term coaxial). One wire surrounds the other, separated by an insulating layer, and the whole package is covered by a plastic sheath. The types of connectors used vary, but British Naval Connectors (BNC) are often employed. An example of coaxial cable is as close as your cable television hookup.

Coax comes in a variety of sizes and qualities. Each has its own electrical characteristics, which means the various types are not directly interchangeable. Higher-level standards will dictate exactly what type of coax is needed, and what type of connector is used. Figure 17.2 is a depiction of coaxial cable.

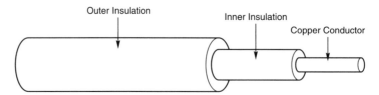

Figure 17.2. *Coaxial cable.*

Although more expensive than twisted pair, coax is still less expensive than other cabling options. It offers improved resistance to interference, and higher data capacities in terms of distance and speed. The thinner varieties remain easier to work with during installation, and connections are fairly straightforward. Coax is also commonly available at computer and electronics shops and suppliers.

Where larger types of coax are used, materials prices can become steep, as do the time and expense of installation.

Fiber Optic Cable

Fiber optic cable is an amazing creation in terms of its data-carrying capacity. Instead of using conventional electrical signals, it conducts light beams along its length.

The cable consists of a thin glass core that conducts light, surrounded by glass cladding that reflects light inward. A plastic sheath protects the entire package.

The availability and ease of use of fiber optic cable is going up, and prices are coming down. It is still reserved for more specialized applications, however. Examples of applications include high bandwidth (capacity) connections over longer distances, which may be needed to connect separate LAN segments. Figure 17.3 shows a fiber optic cable.

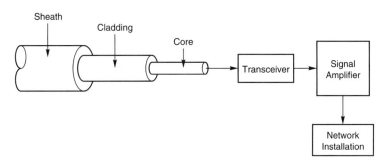

Figure 17.3. *Fiber optic cable.*

As you might expect, with its technology and capacity, fiber optic remains more expensive than wire cables, and much more involved to install and connect. However, benefits such as being able to carry extremely high volumes of data quickly may make the added expense worthwhile.

Considering Topologies

When used for a LAN, cables must be arranged according to a certain *topology*, that is, the physical configuration of how the network nodes are connected. The topology required normally is dictated by the overall standard in use. Ethernet, for example, specifies a bus topology and must be cabled accordingly.

There are many different topologies in use, including the *bus*, the *ring*, the *star*, the *tree*, and the *mesh*. Next, you examine each of these topologies in turn.

Bus Topology

A network bus is similar to the internal arrangement of a personal computer—a number of devices connected in parallel to one set of electrical conductors. For the network, the nodes are connected to a single physical path. The connections involve tapping the line, forming a T-shaped attachment. At each end, the bus must be terminated in order to maintain the correct electrical characteristics. Figure 17.4 shows computers connected in bus arrangement.

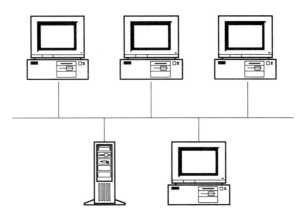

Figure 17.4. *Computers connected using the bus topology.*

The bus topology is relatively simple to use. You simply attach new nodes onto the bus, often by running a cable to their nearest neighbor. This capability makes it ideal for fast, inexpensive connections among small workgroups.

Unfortunately, the bus is vulnerable to disruption. A break anywhere along the line usually disrupts the entire network or at least isolates nodes on one portion of the bus from the other portion.

Ring Topology

The ring topology is formed in exactly the way you think—network nodes are connected to form a circle, with each node inserted into the ring. The electrical path passes through every station on the network and then continues along the ring to the next station. A complete circuit on the ring involves passing through every station. Figure 17.5 is an illustration of computers connected by a ring.

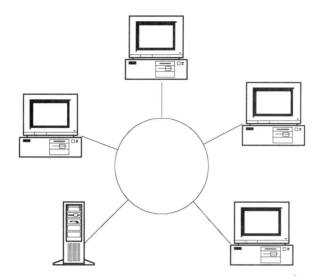

Figure 17.5. *Computers connected using the ring topology.*

A ring is a somewhat more elaborate structure than a bus. To add a new node, you must break the ring, insert the new station into the path, and then resume operation.

The ring also is vulnerable to disruption. A break anywhere in the ring severs the circular path and disrupts the entire network. The use of a ring, together with certain upper-level protocols controlling how it is used, however, offers unique advantages for network performance and reliability.

> **Note:** As you learn in the next section, the physical implementation of a ring makes it appear very different than its theory of operation. For example, in practice a node is inserted into the ring by using a special device, instead of by actually breaking a cable.

Star Topology

You form a star network by connecting computers together through a central point, often called a *hub*. All communications between nodes pass through the hub. The resulting network structure resembles a star, with separate lines merging at a central core. Figure 17.6 illustrates the star topology.

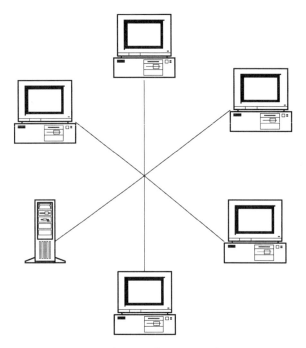

Figure 17.6. *Computers connected using the star topology.*

The star topology depends on its hub for all operations. Connecting a new node involves running a cable from the station to an open port on the hub. This topology can require more actual cabling than the bus or ring because a wire must run from every station to a central point.

Star topologies suffer the disadvantage of a single point of failure because the breakdown of the central hub means the loss of the entire network. However, the star configuration also offers advantages. For example, a break in the wire to one node does not disrupt all the others, thus making it easier for you to identify and isolate problems.

Other Topologies

Networks are also formed using other topologies, although the bus, ring, and star are currently the most popular. The two other main configurations are as follows:

- The tree topology is a special case of bus. A tree allows each tap on the network to be split into other taps, which can be split into other taps, and so on.

An example of a tree topology network is a cable television system. Starting from the head-end (where the antenna facilities are located), the signal is distributed through a series of taps, fanning out over the service area.

☐ The mesh topology involves connecting every computer to every other, permitting a unique data path between each and every machine.

The use of a mesh provides the most robust computer network, with total redundancy for every path. If one link fails, then communications between computers can be rerouted through other nodes. As you can imagine, implementing a mesh is very expensive; however, for computer links that absolutely, positively must be there at all times, the cost is justified. A lower cost alternative is to establish some redundant data paths but not the full mesh with every-to-every connectivity.

Signal versus Wiring Topologies

The issue about topology with the most potential to confuse right-thinking individuals is the apparent wiring topology versus the actual signal topology. In many cases, the two are not the same.

As an example, IBM's Token Ring uses, obviously enough, the ring topology. If you were to view the physical layout of a typical Token Ring LAN, however, you would observe a number of separate cables running from each node to a central hub. Sounds suspiciously like a star topology, yes? Has IBM confused their geometry here? Not at all.

The answer lies in the device that appears to be the hub of the star. The MultiStation Access Units (MAUs) are the central point for connecting each Token Ring node. Each wire from a node is plugged into a spare port on the MAU, just like a star. Within the MAU, however, each of the ports is wired together as a ring. The ring exists within the MAU itself.

So you have a Token Ring LAN with a star wiring topology, but a ring signal topology. This approach provides a number of advantages because you can add and remove stations relatively easily, without having to break the ring physically.

Similarly, an IEEE 802.3 LAN can be wired as a star (using the 10Base-T standard), but it implements a bus as far as its internal signals are concerned. What better illustration of the old adage "You can't judge a book by its cover"?

In the following sections, you learn about standards such as Token Ring, IEEE 802.3, and others.

Understanding Media Access Control

Whenever two or more people converse, generally rules of etiquette are in place (notable exceptions are some government assemblies and most popular talk shows). An explicit or implicit code of conduct is followed by everyone, so everyone gets his or her say, and all others can hear and understand that person. Without such a code, effective communication cannot take place.

Computer networks operate in the same way. Two or more nodes share one physical medium. They therefore must follow the rules of converstation; otherwise, communication is lost or distorted. And although not hearing what the latest guest on *Geraldo* has to reveal may not be a terrible loss, for a computer network, loss of data can be a disaster.

Computer networks control access to the communications medium using two main approaches: *contention* and *deterministic*. You review each of these approaches in more detail in the following sections.

Contention Techniques

Contention methods of media access control are geared towards figuring out whether a collision has occurred on the network, that is, whether more than one station has tried to use the cable at one time. As for most areas of information processing, you need an acronym for such systems: Carrier Sense Multiple Access (CSMA). There are two flavors of CSMA: *collision detection* and *collision avoidance.*

With collision detection (CSMA/CD), when a node has data to send, it waits until no other stations are heard on the network. When silence is detected, the node transmits data but also listens to hear whether any other nodes also are transmitting. If it hears another node, it assumes that a collision has occurred and that its data has been lost. The node then waits (or backs off) a randomly generated amount of time. The random time prevents both nodes from trying to retransmit at the same time. After the time has elapsed, the node attempts the process all over again.

With collision avoidance (CSMA/CA), each node also waits for silence on the network before transmitting. It does not continue to listen on the network for others transmitting, however. Instead, it awaits a formal acknowledgment of its transmission from the intended recipient. If it does not receive an acknowledgment in a set period of time, it assumes that a collision has occurred and that the data is lost. The node then waits for silence, and after a randomly generated period of time, it tries again.

Contention methods are typically used on bus or tree topologies. Examples of contention-based systems are Ethernet and the IEEE 802.3 standard, which both use CSMA/CD. Apple's LocalTalk uses CSMA/CA.

Note: The standards for Ethernet and IEEE 802.3 protocols are similar but not identical by any means. However, they often are used interchangeably.

Contention methods are often called probabilistic techniques because you cannot precisely determine when your node will be allowed to speak on the network. Because randomness is associated with when you get access, you can figure out timing only within a given probability. This method contrasts with the deterministic techniques you learn about in the next section.

Deterministic Techniques

Deterministic methods add a level of certainty to when and how often each node on the network is allowed to send messages. They revolve around the use of a *token* that is passed from node to node. When you have the token, you can speak. Under this approach, it is possible to determine the worst-case time to get access to the cable and send data, hence the name deterministic.

With token passing, each node with data to transmit must await the arrival of the token. After it gets the token, the originating node can send the data, which eventually comes to the intended recipient. The receiving node can only acknowledge receipt, not return any other data. The acknowledgment returns to the sender, who must then give up the token, even if it has more data to send. In this way, every node gets an equal chance to send data.

Token-passing systems tend to be more complex than contention techniques because the system must have facilities to deal with the addition or deletion of nodes, lost tokens, and other problems that come up. They also tend to be quite reliable, however, thanks to the additional mechanisms in place.

The two main examples of the deterministic technique are

☐ The token-passing bus, as described by IEEE 802.4. ARCNet (not the same as IEEE 802.4) makes use of the token-passing bus model.

☐ The token-passing ring, as described by IEEE 802.5. IBM's Token Ring makes use of the token-passing ring model.

Summary of Popular Network Standards

As you may have gathered, a particular network standard dictates the type of cabling, topology, and media access control approach taken. Table 17.1 summarizes the most popular standards and the conventions they follow.

Table 17.1. Summary of network standards.

Name of Standard Control	Type of Cable	Topology	Media Access
Ethernet/IEEE 802.3	Unshielded TP	Star-wired bus	CSMA/CD
	Thin Coax	Bus	
	Thick Coax	Bus	
Token Ring/IEEE 802.5	Shielded TP	Star-wired ring	Token-passing
	Unshielded TP		
ARCNet/IEEE 802.4	Unshielded TP	Star-wired bus	Token-passing
	Coax		

Explaining Network Communication Protocols

So far, you've learned about the connection-level elements of our simplified network model: the cables, how they are laid out, and how each node decides when it can use the cable. They are concerned with the nitty-gritty details of getting bytes of data between Network Interface Cards across a network cable.

But the task of exchanging information over a network involves more than just deciding who can speak on the network and when. What is actually said is just as important. Nodes must know the correct name to use when referring to other nodes. Each node must speak the same language as all the other nodes. And nodes must know what to do with information they receive from the network, that is, who (or what program) to give it to and what to expect in return (if anything).

So we need to consider the upper two layers of our simplified network model:

☐ Network-level protocols, which provide the service of sending data back and forth between network nodes.

☐ Converstation-level protocols, which make sense of the data and supply it to the person or program making the network request.

Together, the network-level protocols and converstation-level protocols make up a complete package, which we refer to here as network communication protocols. Let's take a closer look at what each level does for you.

Network-Level Protocols

Connection-level protocols such as Ethernet and Token Ring maintain their own idea of the identity of each node on the network—each Network Interface Card has an address built into it. But this low-level addressing convention is used only at the connection-level. There also is a network-level address that is used to more conveniently refer to another node on the network. The network-level protocol uses these addresses when it exchanges data with other network nodes, but interacts with a connection-level protocol to get the job done.

The network-level address also enables you to refer to computers on other networks that you can access. You may reach not only the nodes on your local Ethernet, for example, but also servers on a Token Ring with which you have established a connection. (You learn more on ways to interconnect networks in the next section.)

Using this approach, the system assigns each network node its own network-level address. Then the network-level protocol can uniquely identify each node on the network. The protocol requires that the individual network address be used in each message to identify the source of the data, as well as specify the destination node where the data is being sent.

Examples of network-level protocols are IPX (from the IPX/SPX protocol developed for use on Novell networks) and IP (part of the TCP/IP protocol suite used on a wide variety of local and wide area networks). You see more about using IPX in the next chapter when you learn about the ODI architecture. NetWare supports IPX and other network-level protocols.

The network-level protocol usually takes care of getting messages between nodes spread across the network. However, it can also be just a little irresponsible. Normally, it doesn't take the steps necessary to ensure that

☐ Each message actually arrived at its destination

☐ All the messages arrived in the correct order (each one may have taken a longer or shorter route to its destination)

☐ The contents of each message were intact (accurate)

Actually, you don't really want the network-level protocol to worry about such things. You sometimes don't even care whether these things have been achieved. And if you do need these services, you can build them in the converstation-levels of the simplified network model.

However, if you want, these services also can be obtained from within the network-level protocol. An optional protocol mechanism operating within the network level (the transport level for OSI fans) can ensure reliable delivery of data. Reliable means all the data was received, in the right order, and intact. Examples of reliable transport-level protocols are SPX (from IPX/SPX) and TCP (from TCP/IP).

Converstation-Level Protocols

Still higher in the path between the cable and the user are the conversation-level protocols. These protocols are tied more closely to end-user functions on the node computer, such as making a request for a file. The conversation-level protocols interact with the network level. They may require reliable delivery services or may take care of this area themselves.

Many different conversation-level protocols are available, each offering a different range of functions and features. The wide range of services that you can find within this level often makes it difficult to compare one protocol or program with another. The most prevalent conversation-level protocol on a NetWare LAN is NCP, used by the NetWare shell and requester programs (which you learn about in Chapter 18).

An Example of Protocols at Work

By way of example, let's look at how a typical network file request is handled. An application program running on a client computer (for example, a word processor) needs to open a file stored on a NetWare server. The NetWare shell or requester runs on the client computer and interacts with an operating system such as DOS in order to intercept and evaluate any requests for resources such as disk access. Once a request is received, it determines if the file is on an attached NetWare server, in which case it must create a network request.

The shell or requester formulates the request for data from the NetWare server and passes it to a network-level protocol such as IPX to be passed across the network. IPX, in turn, passes the request to the lower-level protocol (for example, Ethernet), and the message makes its way to the server. When the required data is returned, Ethernet brings the data to the node and gives it to IPX, which then hands it up to the shell or requester, which passes it to the word processing program making the request.

Figure 17.7 illustrates the relationship between application programs, the NetWare shell, DOS, IPX, and the lower-level protocols running with the NIC.

17

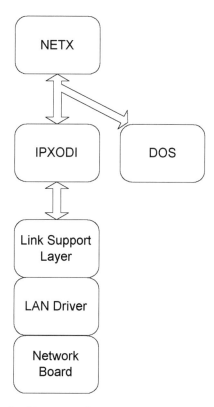

Figure 17.7. *Layers involved in network communications.*

Reviewing Repeaters, Bridges, and Routers

Another key reason for the fantastic growth of LANs has been the increasing ease with which smaller LANs can be interconnected to make much larger ones. This ease of use enables you to join together a collection of departmental workgroups to form an enterprise-wide network. When the network reaches this scale, tools such as electronic mail and corporate databases assume far greater significance and use.

Interconnecting LANs means using a device to allow messages from one LAN to pass through to another, and vice versa. To do so, you can make use of the following:

☐ *Repeaters*, which simply extend the range of one LAN

☐ *Bridges*, which extend the range or partition of a busy LAN into two separate sections

☐ *Routers*, which connect LANs of different hardware types (for example, Ethernet and Token Ring)

Let's examine each of these devices in more detail.

Repeater

A repeater is simply a device you use to overcome some of the physical limitations of a particular network. The Ethernet standard, for example, includes a maximum allowable length for individual cable runs, and for the network as a whole. Each Ethernet segment cannot exceed this length; if it does, it might not work at all.

As an alternative, you can connect two Ethernet segments with a repeater (see Figure 17.8). The repeater amplifies and regenerates signals, passing anything heard on one segment to the other.

As you might have guessed, you can use a repeater only to connect two of the same types of network. You cannot, for example, connect an Ethernet system through a repeater to a Token Ring.

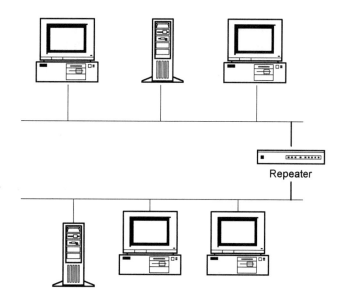

Figure 17.8. *Network segments linked by a repeater.*

Bridges

A bridge is a more sophisticated device than a repeater. It can examine data link level addresses found in packets of information on each of the LAN segments where it is connected (see Figure 17.9). Based on the addresses found, it can forward only those packets that need to be sent on to the other segment (unlike the repeater, which passes everything). When a user from one LAN needs access to a resource on another LAN, the bridge acts as an intermediary.

This capability to distinguish data link addresses is why bridges are used not only to join LANs, but to split them. If the split is performed along departmental lines, for instance, the result is two less busy LANs, with occasional traffic passing between them over the bridge.

Like repeaters, bridges can operate only between the same types of cabling systems.

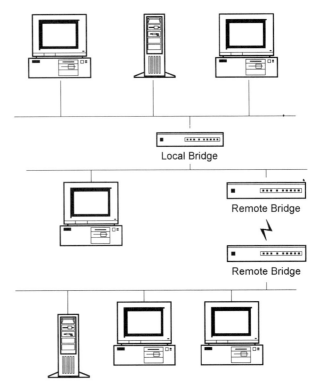

Figure 17.9. *Networks linked by a bridge.*

Routers

Routers are the most intelligent internetworking devices. They operate at the network level, examining, for example, IPX packets received on the LAN segments to which they are attached. Based on routing tables it maintains, a router can forward the IPX packet on to another LAN.

The key benefit of a router is its capability to connect different types of cabling systems (see Figure 17.10). For example, you can place a router between an Ethernet LAN and Token Ring LAN, sending traffic back and forth between the two LANs based on the IPX addresses on each.

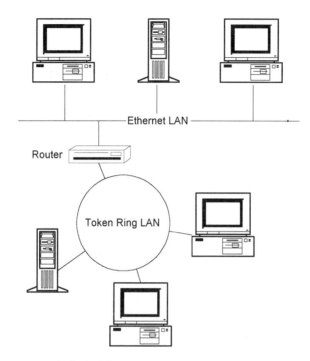

Figure 17.10. *Networks linked by a router.*

You also can use routers to filter packets, preventing certain messages from entering or leaving the network. Often you filter packets to minimize extraneous traffic and provide for increased security. In addition, newer routers handle more than one network protocol at a time (for example, both IPX and IP may be routed by the same device).

Hybrid Devices

The increasing size and sophistication of networks has brought with it an increased need for more sophisticated internetworking devices. As a result, the functions formerly associated with a particular device are now being combined into one hybrid unit. Devices with names such as brouters allow both bridging and routing functions to take place on a selectable basis, depending on the protocol and addresses involved.

All Together Now

You can interconnect LANs across a building, a city, a continent, or the world. You can refer to interconnected LANs forming larger networks by other names, which mainly describe how geographically spread out they are:

☐ Campus Area Networks (CANs) link LANs across a geographical area, such as a university campus or commercial industrial property.

☐ Metropolitan Area Networks (MANs) span a city.

☐ Wide Area Networks (WANs) connect LANs across a country, a continent, or around the world.

Advances in data communication technology allow greater connectivity between computers and the LANs to which they are joined. As capabilities increase, the distinction between LANs, MANs, and WANs becomes more and more obscure, and less and less meaningful. Eventually, we may end up with one huge interconnected network.

For now, the options available to exchange data are driven mainly by the data speed required and the money available to pay for it. As a famous auto racing engineer once said, "Speed costs money—how fast do you want to go?"

A detailed analysis of wide area networking options is beyond the scope of this book. To acquaint you with some of the terms, however, here are some of the available types of connections:

☐ Direct lines established between network nodes:

Leased data lines operating at between 9.6–56 kilobits per second (Kbps)

Leased T-1 data lines operating at 1.544 Megabits per second (Mbps), or sub T-1 lines operating at 64 Kbps

Fiber optic links, terrestrial microwave, or satellite links, each operating at extremely high speeds (and cost)

☐ Packet-switched networks, which link two or more network nodes:

Private networks, constructed with X.25 switches linked by leased lines

Public networks, with switch connections shared among many users

☐ Current and emerging technologies (a collection of other buzzwords designed to wow them at parties):

T-3 (45 Mbps)

Broadband Integrated Services Digital Network (ISDN)

Frame Relay

Asynchronous Transmission Mode (ATM)

Switched Multimegabit Data Service (SMDS)

Synchronous Optical Network (SONET)

Fiber Distributed Data Interface (FDDI)

For the future, the rapid advances in data communication technologies should permit incredible volumes of data to pass at reasonable prices. The resulting level of interconnectivity between LANs across the country and around the world will be truly impressive.

Summary

In this chapter, you discovered the following:

☐ Network standards are established in the areas of cabling, media access control, and communication protocols. Popular low-level standards such as Ethernet and Token Ring have permitted standardized hardware and software to be used to connect many different types of computers. Well-accepted protocols such as IPX/SPX and TCP/IP also have helped establish many network connections.

☐ Internetworking devices permit joining individual LANs into much larger, enterprise-wide networks. Links can be made within a building or over great distances.

Workshop
Terminology Review

bounded media—A medium, such as a wire cable, where electrical signals are not intended to be released as part of the data transmission. Compare to unbounded media.

bridge—A device used to connect to separate segments of a network cable, selectively passing data between them.

bus—A network topology where each node is connected in parallel to a single cable. The ends of the cable are terminated with resistors.

cabling system—The medium used to transmit data between nodes on a network. Normally involves a physical cable used to conduct electrical signals.

coaxial cable—Also known as coax. Two conducting wires running along the same axis, one insulated from, but within, the other. Both wires are covered by a plastic sheath.

collision—Occurs when two nodes on a network send data at the same time. The result is that data is garbled, and is likely not received properly.

collision avoidance—A contention system where nodes wait for a formal acknowledgment of receipt.

collision detection—A contention system where nodes listen while transmitting to see if a collision has occurred.

contention—A media access technique where nodes wait until nothing is heard on the network before trying to send data.

deterministic—A media access technique where each node waits for a token, giving it permission to use the network.

fiber optic cable—A cable constructed of a thin glass core, surrounded by glass cladding and a plastic sheath. Conducts light rather than electrical signals.

hub—The central connection point of a star-wired network.

mesh—A network topology where each node is directly connected to every other node.

repeater—A device used to extend the range of a network cable segment.

ring—A network topology where each node is connected to the next in a series. The first and last nodes are joined together to complete the circle.

router—A device used to connect different types of networks together, and pass data between them as necessary, based on network addresses.

star—A network topology where each node is connected to the others at a central point, often called the hub.

token—A flag or indicator, the possession of which allows a node to use the network.

topology—The physical configuration of how network nodes are connected.

tree—A network topology that is a special case of a bus. Each connection on the bus may be split recursively into other connections.

twisted pair—Two or more insulated conducting wires, twisted together within a plastic sheath. Comes in both shielded and unshielded varieties.

unbounded media—A medium, such as radio frequency waves or micro-waves, involving the wireless transmission of data.

Q&A

Q What is the best topology to use?

A The most common configuration for larger offices is a star-wired configuration. A node in each office or workstation is connected by a wire to a central point, such as a hub in a wiring closet. Both Token Ring and 10Base-T use this configuration (even though one is a ring and one is a bus—see text).

You may find it more simple to run a cable from computer to computer in a bus configuration, as is used for 10Base2. While this normally uses less cable, it is also less flexible when moving nodes around during office reorganizations.

In the end analysis, the topology you use will be driven by the type of network you choose.

Q Can I connect NetWare LANs together?

A You can connect multiple NetWare servers to one LAN. You can also use a NetWare server as a router between two LANs. For example, one server could have both an Ethernet NIC and a Token Ring NIC. It is then capable of talking with workstations from each LAN, as well as routing packets between the two types of networks.

Q What is the difference between a controller, a concentrator, a hub (and other similarly-named network devices)?

A People apply different names to different devices, depending on their computer and network background. That fact, plus the rapidly changing and growing capabilities of many network devices, means the best thing you can do if you're not sure what a device does is: ask. And don't be intimidated by network jargon—let the "network experts" explain exactly what they mean in lay person's terms (which will often serve as an interesting test of their knowledge).

18

Understanding the ODI Architecture

In the last chapter, you learned about communications using a data network, and the concept of a layered architecture. In this chapter, you see the main network architecture that NetWare uses to communicate with its clients—the *Open Data Link Interface*, ODI for short. Using ODI, you not only can talk to NetWare with its native communication protocol, you also can talk to many other types of computers over the same network cable.

The NetWare Open Data Link Interface

The ODI architecture was originally developed jointly by Apple Computers and Novell. It is a set of data communication standards that has enjoyed wide acceptance and is currently supported by most manufacturers of Network Interface Cards (NICs). Using the ODI standard also simplifies life for software vendors (such as Apple and Novell) because ODI makes it easier to develop programs that work with many different types of NICs.

A competing standard to ODI is the *Network Driver Interface Specification* (NDIS), which is used by network operating systems such as LAN Manager and 3+Share. Some network operating systems, such as Windows for Workgroups, can make use of either ODI or NDIS, depending on the NIC installed. In fact, given the increasing availability of support for both protocols, sometimes simultaneously, the question of which one to use can get confusing. Such is the joy of today's multiprotocol and multi-operating system computer networks.

The motivation behind an architecture such as ODI and NDIS is the need to use more than one type of network protocol over the same network cable. If your computer is wired to an Ethernet or Token Ring network, for example, you have access to a high-capacity pipe capable of sending and receiving large volumes of data. But without support for multiple protocols, you can use the pipe for only one purpose at a time. This is because each set of programs that implement a particular protocol wants complete control over the NIC. Without multiprotocol support, if you are using NetWare and want to access a UNIX computer, you have to stop your session and unload your NetWare client programs to release the NIC. You then load the UNIX programs to take over the NIC. What a pain.

Contrast the preceding with the multiprotocol world, where many different network application programs can use your NIC at the same time. A special program works to examine each packet of information it receives from the network and determine to

which application the packet should be given. It also receives packets from applications that are to be given to the NIC, making sure only one program sends data at a time. Using the ODI architecture gives you this kind of capability.

As a side benefit, ODI makes it easier to write network application programs. In the past, a program that implemented the IPX protocol had to be configured specifically to handle each kind of NIC it had to deal with. But under the ODI approach, the NIC manufacturer creates a driver program that offers a standard ODI interface. The program that implements IPX can then be written to deal with the standard interface and be used with any ODI-compliant driver.

Note: The IPX to NIC dialogue is actually done through another layer, called the *Link Support Layer.* You learn more about all the ODI layers in the next section.

The ODI Layers

You may recall the two network models you learned about in Chapter 2. The simplified model presented three main layers:

- [ ] The connection level deals with attaching stations to the network.

- [ ] The network level deals with exchanging data between network nodes.

- [ ] The conversation level deals with the content of communication between programs residing on each computer.

ODI's key layers fit in at the network level. When you think about the ODI architecture in the context of NetWare, however, you usually include reference to the NetWare Shell or DOS Requester. These programs operate at the conversation level. So you can think of ODI as providing both network- and conversation-level functions. As you might expect, ODI sits on top of protocols such as Ethernet or Token Ring, that is, the protocols operating at the connection level.

When ODI is implemented on a DOS workstation, it consists of three main layers:

- [ ] A Multi-Link Interface Driver (MLID)

- [ ] The Link Support Layer (LSL)

- [ ] One or more network protocols. For NetWare use, this layer normally includes IPX/SPX but can also include TCP/IP and AppleTalk.

Figure 18.1 provides an illustration of these ODI layers. You'll see more detail on each layer in the following sections.

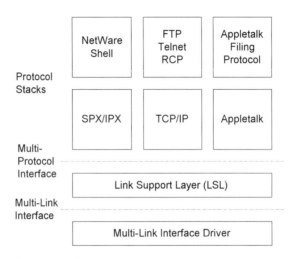

Figure 18.1. *The ODI architecture.*

The Multi-Link Interface Driver

At the very bottom of the ODI model is the NIC itself. Remember that the NIC is a piece of hardware that connects between your computer and the network cable. A NIC is designed to comply with one of the major network cabling systems, such as Ethernet, Token Ring, or ARCnet.

Your client computer needs a piece of software loaded in order to talk with the NIC. This program often is called a *NIC driver* or *LAN driver*. Drivers may come on a diskette with the NIC. In the past, a driver was provided for the popular types of network you might be using—naturally, this included NetWare. In addition, network operating systems provided driver programs for popular types of NICs. But today, most NICs come with an ODI-compliant driver, that is, one intended to be used with any network that supports ODI.

When a NIC driver supports ODI, it is accessed using ODI's Multi Data Link Interface, which is used to talk with the next highest layer. ODI-compliant drivers are called *MLID drivers*, and they support the different kinds of packets that can come across the network destined for multiple applications on the computer.

A popular NIC is the NE2000. Many NICs emulate an NE2000 (making it sort of like the Hayes modem of the NIC world). As a result, one of the most common MLID drivers in use is the NE2000.COM program. Figure 18.2 shows the result when you load this MLID driver on a computer with a correctly configured NE2000 or compatible NIC.

```
C>ne2000
Novell NE2000 Ethernet MLID  v1.10 (901129)
(C) Copyright 1990 Novell, Inc.  All Rights Reserved.

Int 3, Port 300, Node Address 6E22837A
Max Frame 1514 bytes, Line Speed 10 Mbps
Board 1, Frame ETHERNET_802.2
Board 2, Frame ETHERNET_802.3

C>
```

Figure 18.2. *NE2000 MLID driver load message.*

Even if you're not using an NE2000, your NIC driver likely provides a similar type of message.

The Link Support Layer

The next ODI layer is the Link Support Layer (LSL). This layer is key to the multiprotocol nature of ODI because it fills the role of examining packets handed to it via the MLID and passes them along to the appropriate network protocol above.

The LSL can handle several protocols at the same time. When you're using NetWare, of course, the most common protocol you find is IPX/SPX, the native protocol used. But don't forget the reason you're using ODI—so that you can use the network cable for more than just one network operating system. So, in addition to IPX/SPX, LSL supports access to other computers using protocols such as TCP/IP, AppleTalk, and the OSI Protocols.

Figure 18.3 shows the message you receive when you load the LSL program.

```
C>lsl
NetWare Link Support Layer  v2.00 (920904)
(C) Copyright 1990, 1992 Novell, Inc.  All Rights Reserved.

Max Boards 4, Max Stacks 4

C>
```

Figure 18.3. *LSL load message.*

Implementing IPX/SPX with ODI

With the move to ODI-compliance, implementation of the IPX/SPX protocol for a given workstation has gotten much easier. As a result, Novell recommends upgrading workstation software to use ODI-compliant drivers and software.

If you haven't changed to the ODI architecture, you have to do things the old way. This method involves creating a custom version of IPX.COM for use on your workstation. You do so using the diskette labeled WSGEN, which came with NetWare. Insert it in the workstation's disk drive and start the program by typing WSGEN. You then are led through the selection of the NIC you are using. This setup includes selecting which interrupt (IRQ) and Input/Output (I/O) Base Address for the NIC. If your NIC is not listed, you must provide the appropriate file supplied by the vendor. After you complete the setup, the custom IPX.COM is created and stored on the workstation. And you have to follow these steps for each type of NIC you use on your network and each different configuration the card can be used on (for example, different interrupts can be used on different computers).

If you have gone with ODI, life is much simpler. Now you can use one program, IPXODI.COM, on all your workstations. IPXODI implements the IPX/SPX network protocol, interfacing with the LSL through the Multi-Protocol Interface (as does any other protocol using LSL). IPXODI is then used by higher level programs such as the NetWare Shell and DOS Requester programs described in the next section.

Figure 18.4 shows the message you receive when you load the IPXODI program.

```
C>ipxodi

NetWare IPX/SPX Protocol  v2.00 (920904)
(C) Copyright 1990-1992 Novell, Inc.  All Rights Reserved.

Bound to logical board 1 (NE2000) : Protocol ID E0

C>
```

Figure 18.4. *IPXODI load message.*

Shells and Requesters

With NetWare version 3.12, you have a choice of which workstation software you use to access the file server. NetWare's traditional workstation shell program, NETX, is

still available and works well. But for a number of reasons, NetWare has also introduced the DOS Requester to take the place of the shell.

Because you are likely to run into both of these programs on your network, you examine details for each in the following sections.

The NetWare Shell

After you load the required communication programs (such as the ones you've just covered), your workstation knows how to talk to the world, or at least other computers on your network. Any program on your workstation can use the IPX/SPX protocol to exchange packets with other computers. Some computer games take advantage of this setup, letting you do battle with players on other nodes. The games simply exchange IPX/SPX packets over the network. But if you want to access a NetWare file server, you still need to run one more program. The NetWare Shell is the final step in establishing a link to the file server, enabling you to log in. Currently, NETX.EXE is the most used version of the NetWare Shell program (although other versions are available, as you discover later in this chapter).

When the NetWare Shell is run, it provides the most visible link to the file server: the network drive. It's usually the F: drive but can be another letter (depending on the LASTDRIVE parameter set for DOS, which normally is set in the workstation's CONFIG.SYS file). Whichever letter you use, it represents a drive that isn't on your local workstation—it's a network drive. After you change to the drive, you can run NetWare's LOGIN program, type your username and password, and you're on the file server.

The NetWare Shell works by intercepting requests for DOS services such as files and printing. It intercepts by trapping software interrupts generated by programs to request DOS functions. By intercepting these requests, the Shell can determine whether the request needs to be handled by a network file server. If it does, the Shell formulates the appropriate network request and passes it to IPXODI for delivery to the file server. (Of course, IPXODI relies on its lower level associates to send the packet.) If the request is for a local service, however, the Shell simply passes it along to DOS for normal processing. In this way, the Shell acts as a front-end to DOS, sorting out service requests between those handled locally and those needing the network. Figure 18.5 offers an illustration of this process.

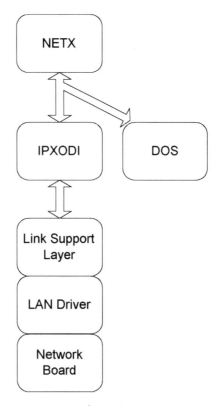

Figure 18.5. *NETX interaction with DOS.*

The NetWare Shell has been, and still is, available in a variety of flavors:

☐ Earlier versions of the NetWare Shell were specific to the version of DOS in use. If you used DOS version 3.*x*, you needed NET3.COM; with DOS 4.*x*, you used NET4.COM; and with DOS 5.*x*, you used NET5.COM.

☐ The most common version is NETX.EXE. As implied by the *X*, it works with all versions of DOS, including the newer versions 6.0 and 6.2.

NETX and its predecessors run in conventional memory, that is, within the first 640 kilobytes of the DOS workstation's RAM. Owing to some limitations of DOS, space in this part of memory can be at a real premium. Loading large network programs into that area might prevent other programs from running. As a result, NetWare includes alternatives to NETX.

Two versions of the NetWare Shell are designed to run in the areas of workstation memory above 640 kilobytes. EMSNETX.EXE works with expanded memory, whereas XMSNETX.EXE uses extended memory. Using either one frees conventional memory, but this use can come at the cost of speed or displacing other applications that use this area of RAM.

> **Note:** If you are confused about the difference between DOS expanded memory and extended memory, join the club. It's best to first give up ever trying to remember; then consult your DOS manual.

18

The NETX.EXE program itself is subject to regular update, so a few different versions are available. You may even have received one with the NIC used for the workstation. Try to stick with one of the more recent versions—but not necessarily the absolute latest. You can always let someone else sort out any bugs or other problems.

The NETX program offers some command options, which are described in Table 18.1.

Table 18.1. NETX command options.

Command Format	Description
NETX /?	Displays a help screen
NETX /PS=<server>	Specifies which server you prefer being attached to
NETX /C=[path\]filename.ext	Specifies a configuration file NETX should read (see NET.CFG later in this chapter)
NETX /U	Unloads a program from workstation memory
NETX /F	Forcibly unloads a program from workstation memory (Forcibly unloading a program may cause the system to crash due to memory problems that relate to terminate-and-stay-resident programs)

Figure 18.6 shows an example of the message you receive after starting one version of NETX.EXE.

```
C>netx

NetWare Workstation Shell   v3.32 (930624)   PTF
(C) Copyright 1993 Novell, Inc.   All Rights Reserved.
Patent Pending.

Running on DOS V5.00

Attached to server RONAN
03-02-94    10:52:01 am

C>
```

Figure 18.6. *NETX load message.*

The DOS Requester

The NetWare Shell has worked well for workstations and continues to work, even with NetWare version 3.12. You therefore might be tempted to follow the quaint but accurate sentiment, "If it ain't broke, don't fix it," and simply keep using NETX.EXE. If so, you can still use your NetWare 3.12 server without problems.

The new DOS Requester, which was designed to replace NETX and offer new functionality, represents a refinement of the approach to providing DOS workstation services, however. The DOS Requester provides the same functions as NETX and maintains full backward compatibility. So if you run software on a workstation that requires NETX, the DOS Requester should be able to fill in. It also adds some new features:

☐ It supports NetWare's Packet Burst protocol used to send multiple packets at one time without waiting for individual acknowledgments. The DOS Requester also supports Large Internet Packets (LIP). You can use both these features to increase the speed of network communications.

☐ It supports NetWare Directory Services, used as part of NetWare version 4.0. NDS is the basis of a move away from individual bindery files on each server to a network-wide database of objects. Because this is likely a trend, support for NDS is an advantage.

The DOS Requester takes a different approach than NETX does in its dealings with DOS. Rather than hijack software interrupts, it makes use of redirection facilities that have been built into DOS. This more cooperative relationship with DOS results in a decrease in the number of conflicts that can arise. The relationship between DOS and the Requester is represented in Figure 18.7.

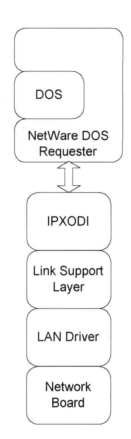

Figure 18.7. *DOS Requester interaction with DOS.*

From the user's point of view, does any of this information matter? In many cases, the answer is no. As mentioned previously, NETX continues to be available and to work. Because the DOS Requester seems to be Novell's future direction for supporting DOS- and Windows-based clients, however, it may be a good idea to jump on board now, rather than wait until the last minute.

The DOS Requester is composed of many program modules, called *Virtual Loadable Modules* (VLMs). Each module performs a separate function and is called in to work whenever needed. At the heart of the DOS Requester is the VLM Manager, known as VLM.EXE. The VLM Manager's job is to load individual VLMs as necessary and provide them with requests for work.

The VLM Manager also takes care of where to load in memory: conventional, extended, or expanded. When it is started, it chooses the best location automatically.

Normally, this location is extended memory outside of the High Memory Area (HMA), allowing DOS itself to make use of the HMA. In the absence of extended memory, the VLM Manager looks for expanded memory and finally conventional memory.

You can think of VLMs in two main categories:

- *Child VLMs.* Each one implements a logical group of functions.

- *Multiplexors.* These VLMs route requests to Child VLMs, according to the needed function. In this way, they also can be thought of as Parent VLMs (sort of like asking your child to cut the grass or shovel the snow).

DOS Requester Layers

You can divide the functions provided by the DOS Requester into three main layers. Following are brief descriptions and the names of VLMs associated with each layer.

- *DOS Redirection Layer.* This layer is responsible for working with DOS to redirect file and print requests to the network, whenever needed. The layer uses the module REDIR.VLM.

- *Service Layer.* This layer provides a number of network services. For example, the NetWare Protocol Multiplexor, NWP.VLM, handles connections to file servers, logins and logouts, and broadcast messages. For file servers running NetWare version 3.12, NWP uses the BIND.VLM module.

    Network file input and output is dealt with at this layer using FIO.VLM, and PRINT.VLM provides the interface to network print services. One additional service, RSA.VLM, implements a popular public-key encryption mechanism used to authenticate network nodes (using NCP Signature packets).

- *Transport Layer.* This layer deals with lower level programs, such as IPXODI, to actually send and receive packets on the network. The IPXNCP.VLM module performs this function with the IPX/SPX protocol. Another module, AUTO.VLM, operates to reconnect workstations if a connection is lost.

Starting the DOS Requester

Loading the DOS Requester is similar to starting the NetWare Shell. At the DOS prompt, you only have to type the command VLM. And like NETX, VLM offers some command options, which are described in Table 18.2.

Table 18.2. VLM command options.

Command Format	Description
`VLM /?`	Displays a help screen
`VLM /MC`	Forces VLM to use conventional memory
`VLM /MX`	Forces VLM to use extended memory
`VLM /ME`	Forces VLM to use expanded memory
`VLM /C=[path\]filename.ext`	Specifies a configuration file VLM should read (see NET.CFG later in this chapter)
`VLM /U`	Unloads a program from workstation memory
`VLM /D`	Displays VLM file diagnostics

NET.CFG Configuration File

Each of the layers you've seen in this chapter has been implemented by a program. As you might imagine, these programs are configurable; that is, they can be provided with information that alters how they operate. Under the ODI model, one text file is referred to by all the layers to obtain important configuration details. Known as NET.CFG, it's really just an ASCII file containing parameters. Some parameters are grouped into sections that apply to a certain program or function. You see some of the more useful NET.CFG parameters in the following sections.

Note that you don't have to include a parameter in NET.CFG unless you need to specify a value different from the parameter's default. As a result, in many cases, your NET.CFG file can remain quite small.

Link Driver Parameters

You use Link Driver Parameters in configuring your NIC and MLID driver. You find them in a section headed with the name of the driver, followed by the parameters

needed. If you use an NE2000 NIC, for example, your Link Driver might look like the following:

```
LINK DRIVER NE2000
INT 3
PORT 300
FRAME ETHERNET_802.3
```

This entry in NET.CFG specifies that the NIC uses hardware interrupt number three and uses an I/O port that starts at address 300. In addition, it uses the frame type Ethernet 802.3 (rather than frame type 802.2, which is the default for version 3.12 servers).

Other parameters include maximum frame size, the RAM memory address used by the MLID, and the Direct Memory Access channel to be used (if needed by the NIC), as well as others.

Link Support Parameters

The Link Support Parameters control how the LSL operates, including the maximum number of packet receive buffers, logical boards, and protocol stacks it can handle, and how much memory it can use. They normally can be left at their default values.

Protocol IPXODI Parameters

You can specify a PROTOCOL section for each network protocol you plan to use. For NetWare, it should be IPXODI, so the NET.CFG entry looks like the following:

```
PROTOCOL IPXODI
BIND NE2000
```

This entry specifies that the IPXODI protocol be tied to the NE2000 NIC. Normally, the protocol binds to the first logical board it finds, so this parameter often is not necessary.

Other IPXODI parameters regulate IPX and SPX packet size and timing, as well as set the software interrupts IPXODI responds to. Other parameters are also available.

NetWare DOS Requester Parameters

The NetWare DOS Requester section customizes how the workstation interacts with file servers. A typical NET.CFG entry might consist of the following:

```
NETWARE DOS REQUESTER
FIRST NETWORK DRIVE N
PREFERRED SERVER = RONAN
SIGNATURE LEVEL 1
```

This entry sets your first network drive to N: (rather than the standard, which is F:). It also tells the Requester that you prefer to be attached to the RONAN_server, rather than the nearest server. Finally, this entry enables your workstation to respond to packet signature requests.

You can enter many other parameters for these software layers as well as for other applications that refer to the NET.CFG file, such as NETX, NetBIOS, and the Task-Switched Buffer Manager. For complete details, you should consult your NetWare manuals.

Loading the ODI Layers

Starting up your DOS workstation involves loading programs for each of the layers you've read about in this chapter—but not exactly in the order you've seen them. The LSL layer is loaded before the MLID driver, despite being higher up in the model, at least conceptually. So, for example, if you are using an NE2000 NIC, you type each of the following commands at the DOS prompt and press Enter after each command:

```
LSL
NE2000
IPXODI
VLM (or NETX)
```

Of course, this example assumes that all programs are in the same directory, along with the NET.CFG file to which they all refer. Because you usually want to log in to the network whenever you start your workstation, you probably put these commands into a file such as AUTOEXEC.BAT, or another batch file, for automatic execution.

Using Multiple Protocols

If you follow the rules for using ODI, you should be able to use multiple protocols and services on your network, in addition to NetWare. That's the theory. However, as a professor of our acquaintance once remarked, "There's no difference between theory and practice in theory—but there is in practice."

Multiprotocol networks are relatively new, and very complex, and getting everything just right can be difficult. Expect to do lots of fiddling and tweaking and trying various software products and versions before everything works the way you think it should. Make sure you collect the telephone numbers of the technical support lines for the vendors of every piece of hardware and software you are using. Better yet, get their fax numbers too, and the numbers of their Bulletin Board Service computer (so you can download technical bulletins and get updated versions of programs such as drivers). Then mark off lots of time in your calendar. You'll probably need it.

Are you worried yet? Well, don't be. Although it may take you a while to get things running, your setup may also go smoothly. That's the element of mystery and excitement about network data communications. If it does work first time, count yourself among the lucky. In any event, enjoy all your new network services.

Summary

In this chapter, you learned about the ODI architecture, including the following:

- ☐ Its capability to support multiple protocols, and its key layers.

- ☐ Which programs are used on a DOS workstation to implement the ODI model.

- ☐ Specific details about both the NetWare Shell and the DOS Requester programs, and the differences in their approach to communicating between DOS-based clients and NetWare servers.

Workshop
Terminology Review

Child VLM—A VLM which implements a logical group of functions.

LAN Driver—See *NIC Driver*.

Link Support Layer—The ODI layer which examines the contents of packets received and passes them to the appropriate upper-level protocol.

MLID Driver—A NIC driver which complies with the ODI Multi Data Link Interface.

Multiplexors—A VLM which routes requests to Child VLMs.

Network Driver Interface Specification—A competing standard to ODI.

NIC Driver—Software which enables communication between a computer and its NIC.

Open Data Link Interface—A data communication architecture, developed jointly by Apple and Novell. Used to enable multiple protocols to communicate over the same NIC. Also specifies a standard interface between data communication layers.

Virtual Loadable Modules—A suite of workstation programs which make up the DOS Requester.

Q&A

Q Can I use NDIS and ODI at the same time?

A You can use NetWare's Open Data Link Interface/Network Driver Interface Specification Support (ODINSUP) program to enable the coexistence of both network driver interfaces. Consult NetWare's Workstation for DOS manual for more details.

However, before you try setting this up, make sure you really need to run both driver interfaces at the same time. You may be able to standardize on ODI, depending on what network software you are using. For example, Windows for Workgroups normally uses NDIS, but supports both NDIS and ODI drivers. So while you could run both types with ODINSUP, it's easier to standardize on ODI so that the workstation can access both NetWare and Windows for Workgroups resources at the same time.

Q Does it matter which order I load the workstation programs in?

A You must load the programs in the order shown in the text (that is, LSL, then your MLID Driver, then IPXODI, then NETX or VLM). Otherwise you'll receive one or more error messages.

Q What do I set the LASTDRIVE parameter in my CONFIG.SYS to?

A When using NETX, you normally set LASTDRIVE=E in the workstation's CONFIG.SYS file. You then change to the F: drive when you want to log in to the network. However, you also can set the First Network Drive = parameter under the NETX section in NET.CFG, in order to set another drive letter as your first network drive.

As you see in the next chapter, VLM requires that you set LASTDRIVE=Z in the workstation's CONFIG.SYS file. You use the First Network Drive parameter in the NETWARE DOS REQUESTER section of NET.CFG to set your login drive letter.

Day

10

19

Configuring DOS-Based Clients

As a NetWare administrator, you will spend most of your time dealing with the file server. The file server is naturally the focus of attention, given the tremendous resources it makes available to the network and the fact that every user will interact with it.

Having such a powerful server isn't much use, however, if clients can't get to it. So you have to spend at least some of your time setting up your users' computers—adding new workstations, changing Network Interface Cards, updating client software versions. And if your NetWare LAN is at all typical, you'll spend most of your time dealing with DOS-based workstations.

In the preceding chapter, you learned about the ODI architecture and how NetWare implements it on DOS-based computers. In this chapter, you'll get details about installing the proper software and configuring it so that your DOS workstations can get to NetWare. You'll also see how NetWare works with Windows to permit access to network files and printers.

Note: Because Novell strongly recommends the ODI approach to workstation software, configuring non-ODI workstations won't be covered in this text.

Compared to the sophistication of NetWare, adding and running a few files on a client computer must be a piece of cake, right? Well, like many other aspects of using NetWare, installing and configuring DOS workstations can go very smoothly. It can also be one of your worst nightmares. With that gentle warning, let's look at the issues involved.

The Workstation Hardware

Other than a standard DOS computer, the only extra piece of hardware you need in order to access the network is a Network Interface Card (NIC). Recall that there are a few popular types of networks, such as Ethernet, Token Ring, and ARCnet. Even within these types, different kinds of connections are made. For example, one Ethernet variety (known as 10Base2) uses coaxial cable, whereas another (known as 10BaseT) uses unshielded twisted pair cable.

The main requirement of your NIC is that it be compatible with the cabling system in use. It also must be compatible with the type of computer bus you have (for

example, a NIC designed for use with an EISA bus won't work on a computer with an ISA bus). Before you buy, consult the documentation that comes with the NIC to make sure that it will work with your network. And while you're at it, review the NIC's manual to ensure that there are detailed and understandable instructions on how to use the card with NetWare.

Physically installing the card is usually straightforward. Just follow the manufacturer's instructions. Getting the card to work, however, might not be so easy, even with good instructions. Depending on the type of NIC and computer you are using, various parameters need to be configured. This might be done by flipping switches or moving jumpers (small connectors) on the NIC, or through commands issued from software.

The most common problem experienced with getting a NIC to work has to do with conflicts caused by incorrect parameter settings. Common settings needed for the NIC include (depending on the kind of card) the following:

☐ The hardware interrupt (IRQ) number

☐ The Input/Output (I/O) address

☐ The Direct Memory Access (DMA) channel used

☐ The address in RAM used by the driver program

These settings can conflict with other cards on the computer, such as serial or parallel port, or the disk controller. The area of RAM used can also collide with that taken by other programs, such as drivers for your video display. Besides your not being able to use the NIC, the most common indicator of a conflict is when the workstation simply locks up.

Fortunately, most NICs come with configuration programs that can help determine the correct settings, or at least diagnose when conflicts occur. In addition, more recent versions of DOS come with the Microsoft Diagnostics program, MSD.EXE (look in your \DOS directory). This program, and others like it, examines the hardware and software on your system and reports details such as what hardware interrupts are being used. These kinds of programs can be very valuable assistants in determining the source of conflicts.

The easiest way to support your users' workstations is to try to use the same type of NIC for every machine. You'll gain experience with the product and its various configurations as you install and configure each NIC. You'll also have only one software driver to worry about. Unfortunately, unless everyone's computer and peripherals are identical, you'll probably still run into the occasional problem, even when using only one type of NIC. But you'll quickly get used to determining and resolving such problems as interrupt conflicts. This approach also makes it easier to test for problems with the NIC itself. If everyone has the same type of card, you can just swap boards between machines to quickly see whether the NIC is at fault.

Using the same NIC won't be possible in all cases—for example, someone's notebook computer probably won't accept a NIC designed to be added to an expansion slot (unless the person has also purchased the expansion chassis for the computer). And after all, variety is the spice of life (although many system administrators might not agree). However, standardizing as much as possible will help reduce the amount of effort required to support your users' workstations.

Sooner or later, you'll get the NIC installed and working. Your next step is to configure it so that it will work with NetWare client software.

Software Installation Overview

There are many ways you can get the software you need onto the workstation. You'll see some of these ways in the following sections. For now, let's review what you're trying to accomplish.

At the end of the installation process, you need to have four programs installed and working correctly:

☐ LSL.COM, handling the Link Services Layer

☐ The correct driver (MLID) for your particular NIC

☐ IPXODI.COM, implementing the IPX protocol

☐ The program (or programs) used to interact with DOS to provide network services. This will be either NETX.EXE, if you decide to stay with the NetWare Shell approach, or VLM.EXE, if you move to the DOS Requester approach.

Note: As you saw in the preceding chapter, instead of using NETX, you can use one of its colleagues, XMSNETX or EMSNETX. Also recall that VLM.EXE relies on a number of VLMs, which must also be present on the workstation.

Tip: As you read in the preceding chapter, using NETX Shell still works with NetWare version 3.12. But moving to the DOS Requester with VLM is a good idea. The installation program used with NetWare version 3.12 installs VLM, so if you do choose NETX, you must install it manually.

If the workstation also uses Windows, you might want some other programs as well. These programs update Windows to make it NetWare-aware so that you can use Windows applications (such as the File Manager) to access network resources more easily.

Note: You don't have to use these special programs. If you log in to NetWare and then start Windows, it will know about your network drives, even if you don't install Windows support. Configuring Windows to know about NetWare simply creates a nicer environment.

Creating Installation Diskettes

You'll see in the next sections that some of the files you require can be gotten from many sources. But NetWare Version 3.12 includes all the required workstation files you need (except, perhaps, a specialized or unusual NIC driver). So NetWare is the best place to start. This is particularly true if you use the DOS Requester, because these newer files are not as widely available from other sources.

The files you need come on the same medium as NetWare's file server programs. Note that earlier versions of NetWare came with a large stack of diskettes, one of which had the files you needed. You just copied the files off the diskette and onto a workstation. However, one way NetWare 3.12 is distributed is on a CD-ROM. You can still purchase the programs on diskette, but after installing NetWare from a CD, you won't want to go back to floppies. Compared with swapping diskette after diskette in and out of a floppy disk drive, sitting back and watching the files being picked up from a CD is a treat. There's one small drawback, however: no more workstation files are easily available on diskette.

To solve this problem, the NetWare CD-ROM includes a batch file called MAKEDISK, located in the directory \CLIENT\DOSWIN. To get to this directory, you must get to the CD-ROM. How you do that depends on what method of CD-ROM drive is made available to you.

For example, to run the MAKEDISK program, you can use any CD-ROM drive attached to a DOS computer to access the required files—it doesn't even have to be on the network. If you have a CD-ROM drive attached to a DOS workstation, it is simply configured as another DOS drive. You can load the NetWare CD-ROM and change to the directory noted previously using the DOS CD command.

It might also be that the CD-ROM drive is attached to your file server. If so, you have two options to access the drive. In the first case, the CD-ROM drive is configured as another DOS drive, just as for the workstation example. You can simply load the NetWare CD-ROM and change to the directory noted previously. Note that you take this action *before starting NetWare*.

In the second case, the CD-ROM drive is mounted as a NetWare volume. This implies that you have a NetWare disk driver which can recognize the CD-ROM drive and that you've mounted the CD-ROM as a NetWare volume. If you have taken this approach, you must start NetWare and log in to a workstation, then map a drive to the right directory on the CD-ROM volume. You'll see more about using CD-ROM drives with NetWare in Appendix A, "Installing NetWare on the File Server."

To create the diskettes, start by formatting three DOS floppies. Next, change to the directory noted earlier, type the command MAKEDISK A: (or whatever drive letter is used by your floppy drive), and press Enter.

The MAKEDISK program prompts you to insert diskettes when necessary and suggests how they should be labeled. At the end, you'll have diskettes that contain DOS and Windows program files, as well as NIC drivers and an installation program.

 Note: Many of the files are packed; that is, they must be uncompressed before you can use them. The installation programs include an unpacking utility for this purpose.

 Tip: You might want to copy the files from the newly created installation diskette into a NetWare directory that everyone can access. Your users can

> then install from the network directory. This might seem strange—after all, if they can get to the directory, they must already be on the network. However, placing the install files on the server enables those using older client software—non-ODI drivers or NETX, for example—to update their own workstations without using diskettes.

Now that you have the installation diskettes (either by creating them with MAKEDISK or by taking them out of the box), you are ready to try an installation.

Installing the Software

NetWare version 3.12 includes a program to install workstation software. You copied this program to the installation diskettes when you ran MAKEDISK. Using this installation program is the easiest way to install the required files on a new workstation. You'll see how this process works in the following section.

Task 19.1: Installing workstation software.

Step 1: Description

Using the INSTALL program placed on the workstation installation diskettes, you can easily load the required workstation software.

Step 2: Action

1. Start the workstation computer in the normal way. However, even if you are a regular Windows user, *do not start Windows.* The installation must be done at a normal DOS prompt, not a DOS session running under Windows.

2. Place the installation diskette labeled WSDOS_1 in the floppy disk drive of the workstation computer. Type **INSTALL** and press Enter. You'll see the program's main menu, as shown in Figure 19.1.

   The screen shows five steps, with the fifth step starting the actual installation process. Before selecting this step, you should at least consider each of the previous ones.

3. For step 1, the cursor highlights the name of the workstation directory that will receive the files. By default, it is \NWCLIENT. Unless this name is unacceptable to you, simply press Enter to confirm. Otherwise, you can change the name to a directory you prefer. In either case, if the directory does not exist, the installation program creates it.

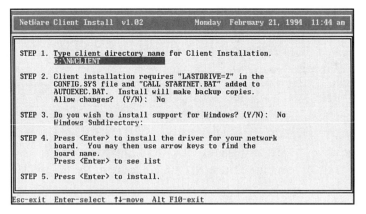

Figure 19.1. *Workstation installation main menu.*

4. For step 2, you are offered the choice of whether the install program will automatically update the workstation's CONFIG.SYS and AUTOEXEC.BAT files. After using the cursor keys to highlight this choice, enter Y or N as desired. If you choose No, the program provides you with samples of what it thinks the updated files should look like, and it places these in the NWCLIENT file. But you must manually update the files.

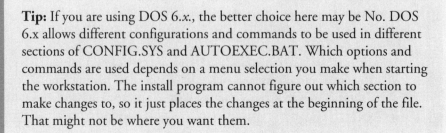

Tip: If you are using DOS 6.*x*., the better choice here may be No. DOS 6.x allows different configurations and commands to be used in different sections of CONFIG.SYS and AUTOEXEC.BAT. Which options and commands are used depends on a menu selection you make when starting the workstation. The install program cannot figure out which section to make changes to, so it just places the changes at the beginning of the file. That might not be where you want them.

5. If you want the Install program to add Windows support files, you can indicate Yes or No in Step 3. Entering Y brings up a field for you to indicate the name of the Windows directory (\WINDOWS by default).

6. Step 4 is used to select which MLID you will install. After you highlight the request for a list and press Enter, you are asked to insert the disk containing DOS drivers, labeled WSDRV_1. The install program reads the diskette,

then offers a choice of many different NICs, as shown in Figure 19.2. If your NIC is listed, you can simply select it. Otherwise, you must press Esc and supply your own driver on diskette (which should have come with the NIC).

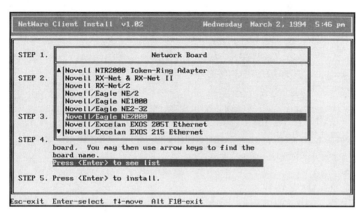

Figure 19.2. *Selecting a NIC.*

7. After selecting a NIC, you are given a menu of options for the NIC, as shown in Figure 19.3. You can change these if you know that your NIC is configured differently—for example, if it uses another hardware interrupt number. Otherwise, accept the default settings.

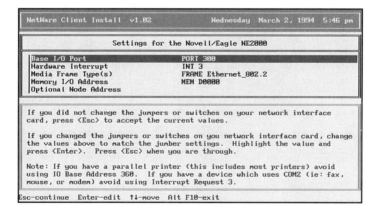

Figure 19.3. *NIC options.*

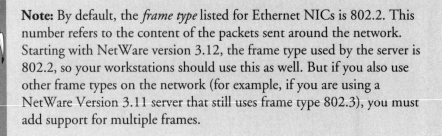

Note: By default, the *frame type* listed for Ethernet NICs is 802.2. This number refers to the content of the packets sent around the network. Starting with NetWare version 3.12, the frame type used by the server is 802.2, so your workstations should use this as well. But if you also use other frame types on the network (for example, if you are using a NetWare Version 3.11 server that still uses frame type 802.3), you must add support for multiple frames.

8. Finally, move the highlight to step 5, and press Enter. The installation program copies the required files to the workstation, as well as making any authorized changes.

Step 3: Review

The installation program leads you through the process of loading client software onto a workstation.

Behind the Scenes

The installation process accomplished several tasks, depending on exactly what you asked it to do. Let's look a bit more closely at the highlights.

1. The CONFIG.SYS file was updated to include LASTDRIVE=Z, and the AUTOEXEC.BAT file was updated to include this line:

```
@CALL C:\NWCLIENT\STARTNET
```

2. Assuming that you didn't change the default, the \NWCLIENT directory was created. Key files copied to the directory include LSL.COM, the MLID for the NIC you selected (such as NE2000.COM for an NE2000 NIC), IPXODI.COM, and VLM.EXE, as well as its related virtual loadable modules. In addition, a NET.CFG file was created that contains the parameters for the MLID, as well as the following section:

```
NETWARE DOS REQUESTER
   FIRST NETWORK DRIVE = F
```

> **Note:** You may note that the issue of what LASTDRIVE parameter to use for the workstation has been simplified, compared to earlier versions of NetWare with NETX. The workstation thinks it has been given all drive letters. VLM then reassigns the drives to achieve the same effect as before: you log in from the F: drive.

3. A file called STARTNET.BAT is created in \NWCLIENT. Its contents will be similar to the following lines:

```
CD \NWCLIENT
LSL
NE2000 (will be replaced by the MLID for your NIC)
IPXODI
VLM
CD \
```

If you chose not to have your CONFIG.SYS and AUTOEXEC.BAT files updated automatically, you must update them now. You can use the DOS EDIT command to make the changes indicated and put them in the right location within each file. In addition, you should comment out any existing references to network programs within AUTOEXEC.BAT.

So when you restart your computer, the STARTNET batch file will be executed to load the network programs, finishing with VLM. If everything works properly, you'll see messages similar to those shown in Figure 19.4.

```
C>lsl
NetWare Link Support Layer  v2.01 (921105)
(C) Copyright 1990, 1992 Novell, Inc.  All Rights Reserved.
Max Boards 4, Max Stacks 4

C>ceodi
Xircom CreditCard Ethernet Adapter MLID V2.02 (931122)
(C) Copyright 1993 Xircom. All Rights Reserved.
Max Frame 1514 bytes, Line Speed 10 Mbps
Board 1, Frame ETHERNET_802.2, LSB Mode

C>ipxodi
NetWare IPX/SPX Protocol  v2.11 (930423)
(C) Copyright 1990-1993 Novell, Inc.  All Rights Reserved.
Bound to logical board 1 (CEODI) : Protocol ID 0

C>vlm
VLM.EXE      - NetWare virtual loadable module manager  v1.02 (930510)
(C) Copyright 1993 Novell, Inc.  All Rights Reserved.
Patent pending.
The VLM.EXE file is pre-initializing the VLMs...........
The VLM.EXE file is using extended memory (XMS).
You are attached to server RONAN

C>
```

Figure 19.4. *Loading workstation programs.*

Updates to Windows Files

As mentioned earlier, you don't have to install support for Windows in order to access NetWare files from within Windows. The act of logging on to NetWare before loading Windows results in NetWare drives being available to your Windows programs.

If you did tell the install program to include Windows support, it also copied files to your \WINDOWS directory. The copied files include two programs, NWPOPUP and NWUSER, as well as related Dynamic Load Library (DLL) files that give you Windows-based NetWare tools. They also include the drivers NETWARE.DRV, VIPX.386, and VNETWARE.386, and the NETWARE.HLP help file.

The install program also makes changes to the Windows initialization files WIN.INI (so that NWPOPUP is loaded), PROGMAN.INI (to add a new program group), and SYSTEM.INI.

After you start Windows, you should see additional menu options on programs such as the File Manager and Print Manager that enable you to access NetWare resources. You'll also have access to the NWUSER program, which should appear in a new program group called NetWare Tools. You'll see more about NWUSER later in the chapter.

If things don't work as planned (for example, if Windows won't start any more), don't worry, you can always fall back to your old configuration. The installation program saves your old .INI files with an extension of .BNW (Before NetWare). Rename the new version of each file to something with a different extension, say .ANW. For example, you could use the following command and then press Enter:

```
RENAME SYSTEM.INI SYSTEM.ANW
```

Then change SYSTEM.BNW back to SYSTEM.INI, and everything should be back to normal.

Any problems that come up probably relate to changes made in SYSTEM.INI. A discussion of Windows SYSYEM.INI parameters is outside of what we want to cover here. But for your information, these are the main parameters changed in this file:

```
[boot]
network.drv=netware.drv
[boot.description]
network.drv=Netware (Vx.x)
[386 Enh]
network=*vnetbios, vipx.386, vnetware.386
TimerCriticalSection=10000
```

These settings advise Windows of the existence of NetWare, and of what files to use while operating in 386 Enhanced mode. The parameters might have been updated by other programs, for example, if you've used other network operating systems in the past. If so, the changes NetWare made might upset the apple cart. Changing them back could fix the problem, but you might not have full NetWare functionality. It's time to call in the Windows experts.

> **Warning:** While we're on the subject of Windows, you should be aware of another problem area. If you use the install program to update a workstation that runs Windows for Workgroups, the updates to SYSTEM.INI will stop Workgroup networking from operating properly. You'll have to focus your attention on updating the secondnet parameters to refer to NetWare files. And if you're using ODI drivers, you'll have to update the \NWCLIENT\STARTNET.BAT file to start ODIHLP.EXE before starting VLM. As you can see, multiprotocol networks offer the most fun!

Installing Files Manually

In some circumstances, you might want to, or have to, install needed workstation files manually. These circumstances are considered in the following sections.

If Using the DOS Requester

If you're going to use the DOS Requester, the install program is the most convenient way to load on the VLM Manager and all the virtual loadable modules. It also performs the required updates to Windows files.

If you've been using NETX and ODI drivers but now want to update to VLM, you might be tempted to manually copy the VLM files to your workstation. This method should work; however, it's probably still easier to use the install program, particularly if you let it update CONFIG.SYS and AUTOEXEC.BAT. If you want to use your existing MLID driver and NET.CFG, you can select any NIC during the installation process and then copy your driver and NET.CFG file into the \NWLCIENT directory. But don't forget to update the STARTNET.BAT file so that it runs your driver. You'll also have to update NET.CFG so that it includes the NETWARE DOS REQUESTER section and parameters.

If Using the NETX Shell

If you've chosen to use the NETX Shell, you'll have to update the workstation software manually. Fortunately, because there are really only four programs to copy, and one text file (NET.CFG) to configure, this process is not too difficult. It involves getting copies of the required files and placing them on the workstation.

Because NETX with ODI drivers is such a widely used approach, many NICs come with all the required software. All you have to do is copy them onto the workstation. The NIC might even come with an installation program to do the copying for you. This method should also create the required NET.CFG file, or at least give you a template to work from.

Drivers are also available from other sources, such as Windows. In the Windows Setup program, you can specify use of a NetWare network. The Setup program prompts you for Windows diskettes that contain LSL, IPXODI, and NETX (you'll have to supply your own MLID).

Failing these sources, you can get some of the required files from the installation diskettes you created earlier. LSL.COM and IPXODI.COM, found on the WSDOS_1 diskette, can be copied directly onto the workstation.

The MLID drivers are kept in a packed format. To unpack them, you must use the NLUNPACK command. You specify the name of the driver file and the name of the target directory to which you want the file unpacked. For example, to unpack the NE2000 MLID to the workstation's \NWCLIENT directory, you would type the following line and then press Enter:

```
NLUNPACK NE2000.CO_ C:\NWCLIENT
```

NETX, or one of the other Shell programs, can be gotten from the network's LOGIN directory. However, if you can get there, you must already have NETX—so this technique would be used to update your version of NETX. If you don't have an older NETX, you can get the most recent version from the LOGIN directory on the NetWare installation diskette labeled SYSTEM_3.

But, you point out, you might not have installation diskettes, because you installed from CD-ROM. Well, in that case, you'll have to get to the CD-ROM in the same way that you saw earlier to use the MAKEDISK command. Change to the following directory (note that there are eight underscore characters in the pathname):

```
\NetWare.312_____\3
```

Copy the file NETX.EXE from this directory to your workstation.

Or just ask around—someone is bound to have a copy of NETX somewhere.

You'll also have to create or edit the NET.CFG file. You saw some of the parameters in the preceding chapter. Those for the LINK DRIVER section are critical so that your MLID can actually talk to the NIC. Make sure that you have entered parameters such as interrupt number (INT) or I/O address (PORT) for which the ones set on the NIC differ from the defaults used by the MLID.

Because you are using NETX rather than the DOS Requester, you won't need the Requester section in NET.CFG. However, you can still add parameters such as PREFERRED SERVER.

As a final consideration, you'll probably want to add these commands to your AUTOEXEC.BAT files so that they are executed every time you start your workstation.

Using NetWare with DOS

Regardless of whether you installed the NetWare Shell or DOS Requester programs, the process you use to log in to NetWare remains the same. All you have to do is change to the first network drive by typing the drive letter. What the drive letter is depends on one of two things:

- ☐ If you are using NETX, your first network drive is the first letter after that specified by the LASTDRIVE parameter on your workstation (usually set in the CONFIG.SYS file).

- ☐ If you are using the DOS Requester, your first network drive is specified by the FIRST NETWORK DRIVE parameter in your NET.CFG file.

Most of the time, your first network drive is the F: drive. When you switch to the F: drive, you are placed in the LOGIN directory. Type the following line and then press Enter:

LOGIN (*your username*)

You're asked to provide a password. Type the password and press Enter, and you're on the system. After that point, all the NetWare commands are at your disposal (subject only to which ones you have permission to execute).

Using NetWare with Windows

The easiest way to access NetWare from Windows is to log in to the file server before you start Windows. You will then have access to NetWare resources from within Windows.

However, you also can start Windows first, then use the NWUSER program to log in to a NetWare server. Let's review how this task is performed.

Task 19.2: Logging on from Windows.

Step 1: Description

In addition to other NetWare administrative functions, the NWUSER program for Windows enables you to log in and off NetWare servers.

Step 2: Action

1. After starting the workstation with all required drivers, but without logging on, start Windows.

2. Locate the NWUSER icon, which is probably located in the NetWare Tools program group. Double-click your mouse on the icon. You should get the NWUSER screen, as shown in Figure 19.5.

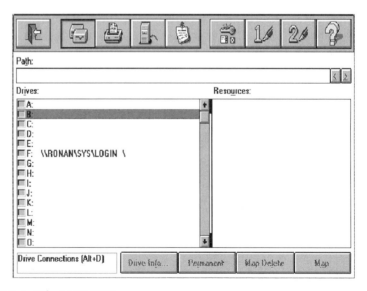

Figure 19.5. *The NWUSER menu.*

3. Using the mouse, click the top button that is the fourth one from the left (a picture of a tower computer, representing NetWare servers). You'll see a list of resources on the right side of the screen, similar to that shown in Figure 19.6. These resources are file servers you can log in to.

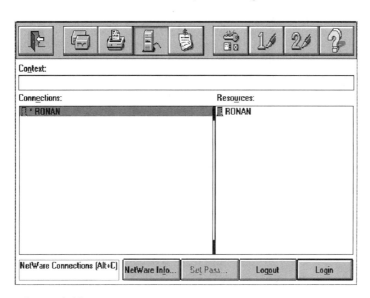

Figure 19.6. *Available servers.*

4. Using the mouse, double-click on the name of the server you want to log in to. You'll receive a Login to NetWare dialog box.

5. Complete the details and press Enter. If you are an authorized user of the file server, the name of the server moves to the left side of the screen, indicating that you are now logged on.

Step 3: Review

You can use the NWUSER program for Windows to log in to NetWare servers.

When logged on, you can use either NWUSER or other Windows programs such as the File Manager and Print Manager to attach to new servers, map drives, and access printers. Although NetWare is easy to use from the DOS prompt, it's even easier to use from the Windows interface. Give it a try!

Summary

In this chapter, you covered the steps for installing the files required by a DOS-based workstation to access NetWare. You saw how to do the following:

☐ Create installation diskettes.

☐ Run the install program to update your workstation with the necessary programs in order to use NetWare's VLMs.

☐ Manually install the files required to use NETX.

☐ Log in to NetWare from DOS and from within Windows.

Workshop

Terminology Review

frame type—Format used for the contents of a network packet. NetWare uses two main frame types for Ethernet packets. Ethernet_802.3 is the default type for version 3.11, and Ethernet_802.2 is the default for version 3.12.

MAKEDISK—A program included with the NetWare CD-ROM. It creates diskettes that are used to install workstation software.

Task List

In this chapter, your tasks involved the following:

☐ Installing workstation files using NetWare's INSTALL utility

☐ Reviewing how to log in to NetWare from DOS and practicing logging in from Windows

Q&A

Q **Sometimes I want to log in to the network automatically when I start my workstation. At other times, I don't want to log in. Is there an easy way to make this setup?**

A You can easily choose whether or not to load your network programs using the correct commands in the AUTOEXEC.BAT file. For example, you can use the CHOICE batch command to prompt you whether you want to run the STARTNET.BAT program installed in the \NWCLIENT directory. To learn about this approach, type **HELP CHOICE** at the DOS prompt to display details from the DOS help facility.

Or you can use the multiple-configuration option available in DOS 6.x. You first define startup configurations within the CONFIG.SYS file. You can then selectively execute commands within the AUTOEXEC.BAT file, based on the startup option chosen. To learn about this approach, type **HELP MULTI-CONFIG** at the DOS prompt.

Q Can I use VLM and NETX at the same time?

A No, use only VLM or NETX, not both. One of the files provided with NetWare version 3.12 is NETX.VLM. This VLM fills in for any workstation program that needs the services offered by NETX. So if you use VLMs, you should not need to try to load NETX.

Q If I don't use the PREFERRED SERVER parameter, can I log in to a server other than the one I was attached to automatically when I started VLM.EXE?

A Yes, you can specify the server name as part of the LOGIN command. For example, if after starting VLM.EXE you were attached to a server called BALLIOL but wanted to log in to a server called RONAN as user CRAIG at the F: prompt, you can type the following:

```
LOGIN RONAN\CRAIG
```

19

20

Printing from
Workstations

In the preceding chapter, you became adept at configuring DOS-based clients. DOS is a primary culprit in printing problems on the network. In this chapter, you will get an overview of DOS and the NetWare printing environment.

First, you'll see how network printing differs from printing on a stand-alone microcomputer. You'll acquire knowledge about the different types of network applications. You'll also learn about the elements involved in printing on the network. You'll start with how printing works.

Printer Operation

On the surface, printing seems like a simple operation. You create something on your screen, you press a few keys, and the results are printed on paper.

All you want is to transform electronic impulses into a glorious combination of ink and paper. Underneath, though, producing printed output is a fairly complex process involving interactions between the computer, the operating system, and the printer hardware. It helps to have a basic understanding of this process, especially when a problem arises with an existing printer or during the installation of a new printer. One way to better understand the network printing process is to compare it with the stand-alone printing process.

Printing on a Stand-alone Microcomputer

On a stand-alone microcomputer with a locally attached printer, several players get involved in printing data from within an application. These players include the application software, the microcomputer's operating system, the BIOS, the I/O bus, the printer port, the printer interface cable, and the printer itself. Figure 20.1 shows the stand-alone printing process. Let's decompose this process.

First, the application sends the operating system a file for printing. The internal process used is fairly standard across all types of applications—the application issues a software interrupt to the operating system, signaling that it needs to use the operating system's print service routine. The operating system's print service routine attempts to establish a connection with the requested DOS print device (for instance, LPT1 or COM1) by issuing a call to the BIOS to open the device. If the print device does not respond, the operating system sends a Printer Timeout or Printer Not Online error back to the application. Then it is up to the application to handle these error messages.

If the device does respond, the operating system establishes a printer connection, and the operating system signals the application to send data. The operating system passes the data to the BIOS, which sends it to the proper printer port over the computer's I/O bus.

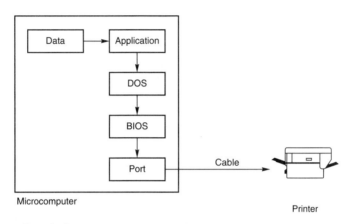

Figure 20.1. *Stand-alone microcomputer printing process.*

At this point, the hardware takes over, and the software no longer has control over the data. The port collects the data in an input buffer and then transfers it one character at a time to another buffer, where the data waits until the printer is ready to accept it. The process of the port and the printer assuring each other that they are ready to transfer data is called a handshake.

After the handshake, the port sends the data one character at a time to the printer over the printer cable. This cable connects the computer and the printer's interface circuitry, literally joining them into one circuit. Each pin on the port corresponds to a specific signal line on the cable. For example, a parallel printer connection involves 15 main signals. Eight of the signal lines carry the actual data, whereas the other lines carry such control signals as Acknowledge, Busy, Ground, On Line, and Paper Out.

The printer holds incoming data in yet another buffer, where the data waits to be sent to the printer head, nozzle, or wires. Data containing control characters (usually in the form of escape characters) causes the printer to perform a particular function, such as switching to compressed mode or to letter-quality output. The data itself is printed in whatever mode the control codes dictate.

Now that you understand printing on a stand-alone microcomputer, you can look at printing on the network.

Printing on the Network

Using a network printer is a little different from using a local printer. With network printing, the paths traveled by data for printing are different from those on a stand-alone microcomputer. The main difference in network printing is that the information to be printed is redirected through the network cabling to a print queue on the file server before being sent to the printer. Understanding this difference is vital for troubleshooting a printing problem on a network.

Figure 20.2 shows how the various printing players interact on the network. Notice that some of these players work the same as in the stand-alone scenario (for example, the application software and the printer interface cable), whereas others are specific to network printing (for example, the redirector or shell and print queue).

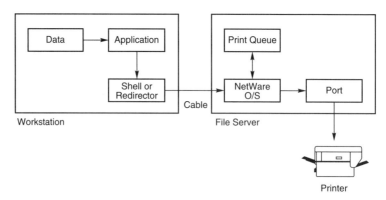

Figure 20.2. *Network printing process.*

The complexity of network printing depends on the design of the application. Some applications are designed to print only to a local printer; to these applications, the network is nonexistent. Many NetWare-specific applications take advantage of the NetWare printing features; these applications establish intricate printer interfaces through the network. What does all this mean? Basically, you can sum it up by saying that NetWare has three ways of printing:

☐ Network-aware or network-intrinsic applications

☐ CAPTURE

☐ PCONSOLE/NPRINT

Network-aware applications communicate directly with file server queues. These applications either are smart enough to be aware of network printing or have network printing as an intrinsic part of their functionality. Network-aware applications, such as Microsoft's Windows and WordPerfect, print directly to NetWare queues and require no intervention from the system manager. Network-intrinsic applications, such as Microsoft's Mail and Lotus Notes, also do not require intervention because they can print directly to queues.

On the other hand, network-ignorant applications, or ones that aren't aware of NetWare's queues, require the CAPTURE printing facility. CAPTURE literally hijacks the local workstation port and redirects print jobs to NetWare queues. The following description of network printing might not apply to network-aware applications that set up printing through NetWare's printing application programming interface (API).

As you can see in Figure 20.2, NetWare (meaning the workstation redirector or shell, the network cabling, and the NetWare operating system in combination) takes over the printing functions that DOS and the BIOS usually handle in a stand-alone scenario. Before running an application, a user issues the NetWare CAPTURE command. CAPTURE tells the redirector or shell to intercept all DOS print commands destined for the local printer port (usually LPT1) and sends them to the file server. When the application issues the interrupt to DOS to request print services, the NetWare workstation redirector or shell (which is memory-resident on the workstation) snatches the interrupt and tells the application that network printing services are available and ready to receive print data. The redirector or shell encapsulates the data into a network packet and sends it out over the network cabling to its destination—the print queue on a file server.

After the packet reaches its destination and the sending workstation receives an acknowledgment, the NetWare operating system takes over. The data is stripped from each packet and stored in a print queue file on the server until all the information for printing is received. The time required for this process is a reason for the delay between the time the application starts sending data and the time the network printer actually begins to print data. Primarily, this delay is because you are actually sending the print job to a print queue rather than directly to a printer. Don't be alarmed if you can see the printer from your workstation and the print job does not begin printing immediately (as it would on a local printer). The print job is not sent to the printer until the print queue has received the entire job. Even so, when printing large jobs (especially if you are used to a local printer), you might be surprised at how quickly you can begin printing the next job.

Several print jobs can arrive at the server at the same time. The jobs are held in the print queue in the order of their arrival until the printer can service them (or their order is changed by a print queue operator).

20

The print server code built into NetWare (or some external print server software) coordinates the transfer of data to the printer. The print server code sends data through the printer port on the file server or print server computer to the printer in much the same manner as in the stand-alone printing process.

In addition, the user has the option of inserting a job directly into a NetWare print queue using either the PCONSOLE menu utility or the NPRINT command-line utility. PCONSOLE and NPRINT enable you to choose print job files and drop them into valid NetWare print queues.

Printing Terms

The previous discussion introduced you to some printing terms that you should be more familiar with at this point: the print queue, the print job, and the print server. You should skip to Chapter 23 if you want a detailed description on how to set up printing.

Print Queue

Conceptually a *print queue* is a holding area where print jobs accumulate prior to printing. Technically, these print queues correspond to subdirectories in the SYS:SYSTEM directory on the file server. When you create a print queue, NetWare assigns it an identification number just as with any other bindery object. As you saw in Chapter 7, a print queue is a bindery object. You will learn more about print queues in Chapter 23.

Print Job

When users send data to a print queue for printing, the data becomes known as a *print job*. Print jobs are stored as files in the print queue's subdirectory in SYS:SYSTEM. Users have control over their print jobs in the queue. As Supervisor, you can reorder, edit, or delete jobs from the queue and modify the status of the queue. As you already saw, you also can assign certain users as queue operators so that they can help you deal with print jobs in a given print queue. Again, you will master these concepts in Chapter 23.

Print Server

A print server is software that takes jobs from the print queue and sends them to the printer. Print servers are very complicated and form the crux of the material in Chapter 23.

Looking at NetWare Printing Services

You have to know the printers available to you on your network before you can start using them. Finding network printers means finding print queues. There is one way to find print queues. You should skip to Chapter 23 if you have a new system without defined print queues.

Task 20.1: Listing print queues.
Step 1: Description

This task lists print queues currently available. In addition, you can see print queue ID numbers.

Step 2: Action

1. To change to the \PUBLIC subdirectory, type **CD\PUBLIC** and press Enter.

2. Type **PCONSOLE** and press Enter. You should have started the printer console utility and seen the screen shown in Figure 20.3.

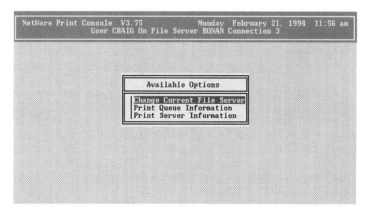

Figure 20.3. *The PCONSOLE screen.*

3. Use the down-arrow key to move the cursor to Print Queue Information, and press Enter. You see a list of available print queues similar to that shown in Figure 20.4.

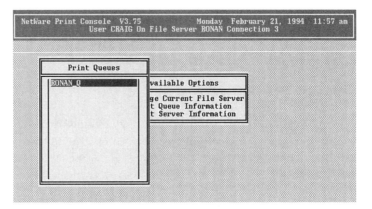

Figure 20.4. *Print Queue Information screen.*

4. To see the print queue ID, select a print queue, and then select Print Queue ID. You should see a screen similar to the one in Figure 20.5.

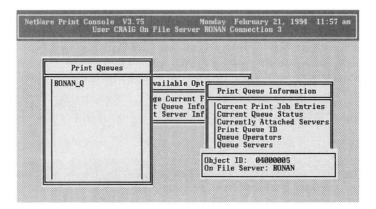

Figure 20.5. *Print Queue ID screen.*

5. Press Esc repeatedly until you are asked to confirm your exit from PCONSOLE.

Step 3: Review

Using PCONSOLE, you can get a list of print queues available to your workstation. You also can use PCONSOLE to view servers currently attached to a queue. To do so, you would make the following menu selections:

```
PCONSOLE ¦ Print Queue Information ¦ queuename ¦ Currently Attached
➥Servers
```

From the Print Queue Information menu, you would select a queue to access the Currently Attached Servers list.

Using CAPTURE

Most of your network printing for applications that are unaware of NetWare's printing features will be done using the CAPTURE command. CAPTURE redirects print jobs from your workstation printer devices to NetWare print queues. This command enables you to print text files, files from applications, screen displays, and any other print output not originally designed for networks—that is, from LAN-ignorant applications. You have to know the printers available to you on your network before you can start using them. Finding network printers means finding print queues.

Task 20.2: Capturing a print queue.
Step 1: Description

After you have found print queues available to your workstation, you can connect to them using the CAPTURE command. Using PCONSOLE, you can locate print queues, and using CAPTURE, you can connect to them.

Step 2: Action

1. Type **PCONSOLE** and press Enter. Locate the print queue where you want to connect.

2. Press Esc and confirm exit from PCONSOLE.

3. To connect to a printer queue located using PCONSOLE, type **CAPTURE Q**=[*queue name*] at the DOS prompt, and press Enter. If you are successful, you will see a message like that shown in Figure 20.6.

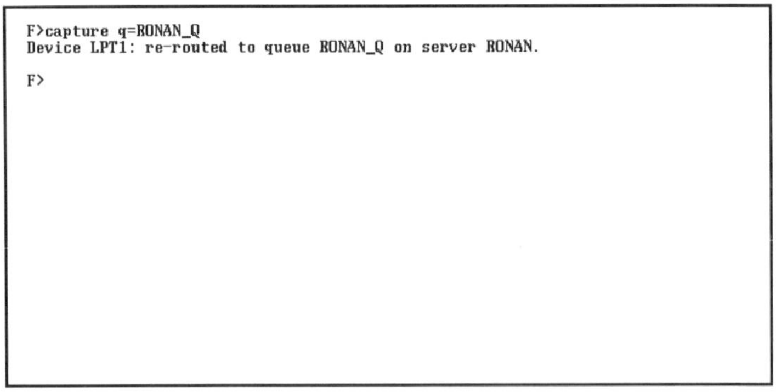

```
F>capture q=RONAN_Q
Device LPT1: re-routed to queue RONAN_Q on server RONAN.

F>
```

Figure 20.6. *The* CAPTURE *message.*

Step 3: Review

Using CAPTURE, you can direct output to print queues. In addition to the Q= option, CAPTURE has other options, listed in Table 20.1.

Table 20.1. The CAPTURE options.

Option	Description
AU[TOENDCAP]	Sends job automatically to a printer or a file upon exiting the application
B[ANNER]=banner	Prints a word on banner page
C[OPIES]=n	Prints specified number of copies from 1–65,000
CR[EATE]=path	Instructs the print job to be sent to a file
DO[MAIN]=domain	Indicates the domain of the printer
F[ORM]=n	Specifies the printer form defined by Supervisor
F[ORM]F[EED]	Enables form feed after your print job is through
J[OB]=job	Tells the printer the print job configuration
K[EEP]	Retains what data is in the queue if your workstation hangs
L[OCAL]=n	Specifies the LPT port number to capture. Valid entries for *n* are 1, 2, and 3
NAM[E]=name	Prints a name on the banner page

Option	Description
N[O]A[UTOENDCAP]	Prevents the job from automatically going to the file or printer upon exiting the application
N[O] B[ANNER]	Prevents a banner page from printing
N[O] F[ORM] F[EED]	Prevents form feed from functioning
NOTI[FY]	Indicates that a message is sent to the user when the job is printed
N[O] NOTI[FY]	Indicates that a message is not sent to the user when the job is printed
N[O] T[ABS]	Keeps tabs exactly as in your application. Do not use if your application has a print formatter
Q[UEUE]=*queue*	Specifies the queue for the print job
S[ERVER]=*server*	Specifies file server, if not the default server
SH[OW]	Shows the LPT ports that are captured
T[ABS]=*n*	Makes all tabs the uniform number of spaces specified (from 1–18; 8 is the default). Do not use if your application has a print formatter
TI[MEOUT]=*n*	Sends job automatically to printer if nothing is added in specified number of seconds

Note: The following CAPTURE command and options are useful in most environments:

```
CAPTURE Q=[queue name] /NB /NT /TI=10 /NFF
```

Note: To print with CAPTURE without exiting the application, include the TI option at the DOS prompt. Your job prints automatically after the specified number of seconds. Use the NA option with CAPTURE only if the default print job configuration has AUTOENDCAP set to YES and enable TIMEOUT set to NO. The TI option overrides the NA option.

Following are a few examples of the use of CAPTURE options.

```
CAPTURE Q=PRNTQ1 /NB /NT /NFF /TI=10
```

This command captures LPT1 (default) and sends the job to print queue PRNTQ1. It specifies no banner, no tabs, no form feed, and a timeout of 10 seconds.

```
CAPTURE Q=PRNTQ2 /L=2 /B=REPORT1 /T=5 /AU
```

This command makes some changes to the preceding command. It captures LPT2 and sends the job to print queue PRNTQ2. It specifies a banner of REPORT1, converts tabs to five spaces, and specifies that the job doesn't print until the application is exited (AU).

```
CAPTURE J=INVOICE
```

This command and option direct CAPTURE to get its configuration from the print job INVOICE created using PRINTCON. You learn about PRINTCON later in this chapter.

Using ENDCAP

When you want to end the printer port redirection in effect at your workstation, type **ENDCAP** at your workstation. You might want to end CAPTURE to print to a locally attached printer for a while.

Task 20.3: Ending a print queue *CAPTURE.*
Step 1: Description
Just as you needed to connect to a printer queue, you also need to disconnect from the queue. To end the capture of a printer port, use the ENDCAP command. This task outlines the procedure for disconnecting from a print queue.

Step 2: Action
1. To end the capture of a print queue located using PCONSOLE, type **ENDCAP** [*option*] at the DOS prompt, and press Enter. If you are successful, you will see a message as in Figure 20.7.

```
F>endcap
Device LPT1: set to local mode.

F>
```

Figure 20.7. ENDCAP *is successful.*

Warning: If you have set up elaborate printing using CAPTURE commands in batch files or log-in scripts, you might want to discourage your users from using ENDCAP haphazardly. Most users will not understand why they suddenly cannot print on the network anymore.

Step 3: Review

With this task, you learned the procedure for ending the capture of a printer port.

Like CAPTURE, ENDCAP has options, which are listed in Table 20.2.

Table 20.2. The ENDCAP options.

Option	Description
ALL	Ends capture of all LPT ports
C[ANCEL]	Ends LPT port capture and discards data without printing
C[ANCEL] L=n	Cancels a particular port and discards data without printing
C[ANCEL] ALL	Cancels all ports and discards data without printing
L[OCAL]=n	Specifies the LPT port number to end capture

Tip: You can use the ENDCAP to force a print job to a printer if you have the TIMEOUT option set too high.

Note: You needn't use ENDCAP unless you first used CAPTURE. Using ENDCAP without first issuing a CAPTURE command accomplishes nothing.

Using PCONSOLE

PCONSOLE is a powerful printing menu utility. It provides a wide range of configuration options for printing, print servers, print queues, and printers. For NetWare printing, you need three things: a print queue, a print server, and defined printers. PCONSOLE can accomplish all three things.

Task 20.4: Using PCONSOLE.

Step 1: Description

Previously, you learned how to use CAPTURE to redirect printer output to a print queue. This task shows you how to place a print job in the print queue using PCONSOLE.

Step 2: Action

1. To change to the \PUBLIC subdirectory, type **CD\PUBLIC** and press Enter.

2. Type **PCONSOLE** and press Enter.

3. Select Print Queue Information, and press Enter. You should see a list of queues similar to that shown in Figure 20.8.

4. Highlight the print queue where you want to connect, and press Enter.

5. Select Current Print Job Entries, and press Ins.

6. Type the directory path, press Enter, and go to step 8. Alternatively, you could press Ins, select the directory from the list shown in Figure 20.9, press Esc to return to the directory box as shown in Figure 20.10, and press Enter.

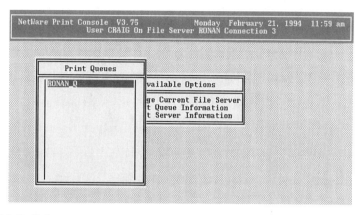

Figure 20.8. *Print queues.*

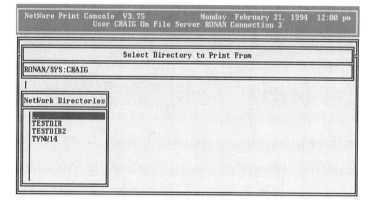

Figure 20.9. *The directory listing.*

7. If you choose the latter method in step 6, then choose the filename, or use F5 to choose more than one.

8. Choose the print job configuration.

9. Make any needed changes to the configuration using the arrow keys, and press Enter.

10. Press Esc and confirm exit from PCONSOLE.

Step 3: Review

This task showed you how to place a print job in the print queue using PCONSOLE. The next section deals with NPRINT, which is another way to direct print output.

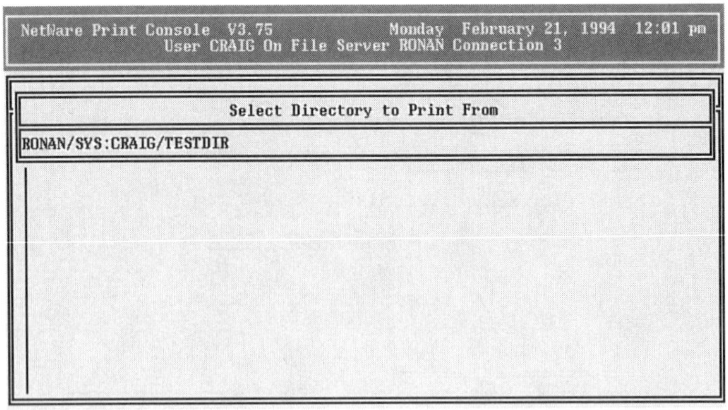

```
NetWare Print Console  V3.75              Monday  February 21, 1994  12:01 pm
                    User CRAIG On File Server RONAN Connection 3


                        Select Directory to Print From
RONAN/SYS:CRAIG/TESTDIR
```

Figure 20.10. *The directory box.*

Using **NPRINT**

NPRINT is a network printing command similar to the DOS PRINT command. NPRINT enables you to send files to a network without being in an application. Most of the time, you'll use NPRINT to print only DOS text files. To use NPRINT, type the following line at the DOS prompt:

```
NPRINT SYS:PUBLIC\NET$LOG.DAT Q=PRNTQ1 NB NFF
```

This command sends the system log-in script to the PRNTQ1 print queue, without a banner and form feed at the end of the job. Available NPRINT options are shown in Table 20.3.

Table 20.3. NPRINT Options.

Option	Description
B[ANNER]=*banner*	Prints a word on banner page
C[OPIES]=*n*	Prints a specified number of copies
D[ELETE]	Automatically erases file after printing
F[ORM]=*n*	Specifies the printer form defined by Supervisor
F[ORM] F[EED]	Enables form feed after print job is through
J[OB]=*job*	Tells the printer the print job configuration

Option	Description
NAM[E]=name	Prints a name on the banner page
N[O]A[UTOENDCAP]	Prevents the job from automatically going to the file or printer on exiting the application
N[O] B[ANNER]	Prevents a banner page from printing
N[O] F[ORM] F[EED]	Prevents form feed from functioning
N[O] NOTI[FY]	Prevents notification that print job is done
N[O] T[ABS]	Keeps tabs exactly as in your application. Do not use if your application has a print formatter
NOTI[FY]	Notifies you when your print job is done
Q[UEUE]=queue	Specifies the queue for the print job
S[ERVER]=server	Specifies file server, if not default server
T[ABS]=n	Makes all tabs the uniform number of spaces specified. Do not use if your application has a print formatter

Following are a few examples of the use of NPRINT options.

```
NPRINT C:\AUTOEXEC.BAT Q=BALLIOL_Q1 /NB /NT /NFF
```

This command prints the AUTOEXEC.BAT file to print queue BALLIOL_Q1, and it specifies no banner, no tabs, and no form feed.

```
NPRINT C:\CONFIG.SYS Q=BALLIOL_Q2 /B=CONFIGURATION
```

This command makes some changes to the preceding command. It sends the file CONFIG.SYS job to print queue BALLIOL_Q2 and specifies a banner of CON-FIGURATION.

```
NPRINT *.DOC
```

This command sends all files with the file extension of DOC to the printer.

```
NPRINT C;\PAYROLL.DAT J=INVOICE
```

This command and option direct NPRINT to get its configuration from the print job INVOICE created using PRINTCON. Let's look at print job configurations.

Print Job Configurations

Print job configurations tell the queue how to handle the print job. PRINTCON is an advanced NetWare system management printing utility used to customize print job configurations. Using PRINTCON, the system administrator can define a specific set of configurations for a user and then attach those configurations to a print job using the CAPTURE or NPRINT commands. PRINTCON provides a facility for permanently storing print job parameters. These configurations are user-specific, and you can find them stored as PRINTCON.DAT in the user's SYS:MAIL subdirectory.

Task 20.5: Choosing the default print job configuration.

Step 1: Description

This task shows you how to choose the print job configuration you want as your default.

Step 2: Action

1. To change to the \PUBLIC subdirectory, type **CD\PUBLIC** and press Enter.

2. Type **PRINTCON** and press Enter.

3. Choose Select Default Print Job Configuration, and press Enter. You should see a list of print job configurations similar to that shown in Figure 20.11.

4. Highlight the print job configuration you want as a default, and press Enter.

> **Warning:** The first print job configuration you create is the default, unless you change it using the procedure described.

5. Press Esc repeatedly and confirm your changes and exit from PRINTCON.

Step 3: Review

This task showed you how to choose the print job configuration you want as your default. Remember, the first print job configuration you create is the default, unless you change it using the procedure described previously. If this default is acceptable, you need not take any action.

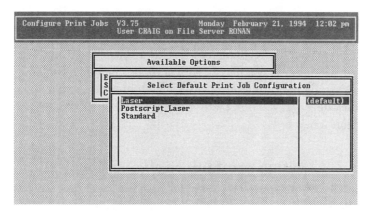

Figure 20.11. *Print job configurations.*

Task 20.6: Copying the print job configuration.

Step 1: Description

You can copy one user's print job configuration file to another user's file using this task.

Step 2: Action

1. To change to the \PUBLIC subdirectory, type **CD\PUBLIC** and press Enter.

2. Type **PRINTCON** and press Enter.

3. Choose Copy Print Job Configurations, and press Enter.

4. In the Source: box, type the username whose file you want to copy, and press Enter.

5. In the Target: box, type the username who needs the file, and press Enter. If the user already had a file of print job configurations, you must confirm the copying by answering Yes to the Delete Existing File prompt.

> **Warning:** You cannot copy a print job configuration. You only can copy a file of configurations, which overlays any existing configuration file in the user's mail directory.

6. Press Esc repeatedly and confirm exit from PRINTCON.

Step 3: Review

Usually, it is easier and safer to copy one user's print job configuration file to another user than to create a new configuration. Unfortunately, you cannot copy one print job configuration, but only a file of configurations. So remember, copying overlays any existing configuration file in the user's mail directory, and it should be done with extreme caution. If you don't want to copy another user's configurations, you always can create a new one.

Task 20.7: Creating print job configurations.

Step 1: Description

You can create three print job configurations as you need for the various printing jobs you have. This task shows you how to create one.

Step 2: Action

1. To change to the \PUBLIC subdirectory, type **CD\PUBLIC** and press Enter.

2. Type **PRINTCON** and press Enter.

3. Choose Edit Print Job Configuration, and press Enter.

4. Press Ins, type the name you have chosen for this configuration, and press Enter. You should have a screen like the one shown in Figure 20.12.

5. Complete the form with the parameters for this type of print job.

6. Press Esc and confirm changes.

7. Press Esc repeatedly to confirm changes and exit from PRINTCON.

Step 3: Review

You can create print job configurations as you need them for the various printing jobs you have. Invariably, you will make a mistake in creating your configuration, so you need to be able to edit it.

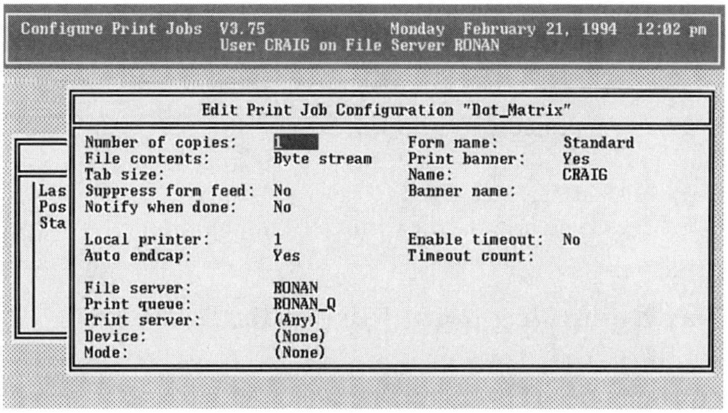

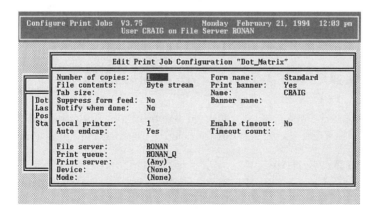

Figure 20.12. *The New Print Job Configuration box.*

20

Task 20.8: Editing print job configurations.
Step 1: Description
This task enables you to change parameters in one of your print job configurations.

Step 2: Action
1. To change to the \PUBLIC subdirectory, type **CD\PUBLIC** and press Enter.

2. Type **PRINTCON** and press Enter.

3. Choose Edit Print Job Configuration, and press Enter.

4. Highlight the print job configuration you want to change, and press Enter. You should have a screen like the one shown in Figure 20.13.

Figure 20.13. *The Edit Print Job Configuration screen.*

5. Edit the parameters on the Edit Print Job Configuration screen.

6. Press Esc and confirm changes.

7. Press Esc repeatedly to confirm changes and exit from PRINTCON.

Step 3: Review

This task showed you how to edit a print job configuration that was previously created.

Task 20.9: Renaming print job configurations.

Step 1: Description

This task teaches you how to rename your print job configuration.

Step 2: Action

1. To change to the \PUBLIC subdirectory, type **CD\PUBLIC** and press Enter.

2. Type **PRINTCON** and press Enter.

3. Choose Edit Print Job Configuration, and press Enter.

4. Highlight the print job configuration you want to rename, and press F3.

5. Type in the new name you want in the Change name to: box.

6. Press Esc and save changes.

7. Press Esc repeatedly to confirm exit from PRINTCON.

Step 3: Review

You might need to rename print job configurations occasionally. For instance, you might want to rename print job configurations tied to a particular print as the print changes its name. You might want to rename print job configurations because of a change in years. For instance, you might have a print job configuration CURRENT_FORM, which changes when the year changes.

Task 20.10: Deleting print job configurations.

Step 1: Description

Now and then you might want to delete print job configurations that are no longer used. This task shows you how to delete a print job configuration.

Step 2: Action

1. To change to the \PUBLIC subdirectory, type **CD\PUBLIC** and press Enter.

2. Type **PRINTCON** and press Enter.

3. Choose Edit Print Job Configuration, and press Enter.

4. Highlight the print job configuration you want to delete, and press Delete.

5. Confirm the deletion.

6. Press Esc repeatedly to confirm exit from PRINTCON.

Step 3: Review

Tasks 20.5 to 20.10 have all dealt with the creation and maintenance of print job configurations. It is easier to create print job configurations than to specify CAPTURE and NPRINT options every time you use the commands. Also, it is easier to change a print job configuration than to change 100 log-in scripts (see Chapter 11).

Managing Print Jobs

As previously mentioned, you will learn about creating print queues, print servers, and print queue operators in Chapter 23. You will learn about some print tasks in this chapter, however. In addition to your maintaining print job configurations, your users will ask you to perform some simple tasks:

☐ Finding out the status of jobs and queues

☐ Managing jobs in a print queue

Let's start with finding print jobs.

Task 20.11: Listing print jobs.

Step 1: Description

This task shows you how to use PCONSOLE to see all the jobs in a queue, including the status of each job, the job number, and the initials of the user who sent it.

Step 2: Action

1. To change to the \PUBLIC subdirectory, type **CD\PUBLIC** and press Enter.

2. Type **PCONSOLE** and press Enter.

3. Choose Print Queue Information, and press Enter.

4. Highlight the print queue where you want to see the jobs, and press Enter.

5. Choose Current Print Job Entries, and press Enter. You should see a screen similar to the one in Figure 20.14.

20

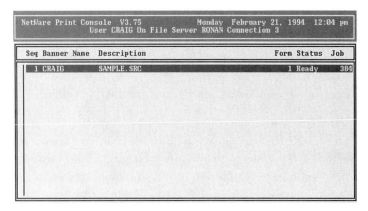

Figure 20.14. *Current Print Job Entries screen.*

6. Press Esc repeatedly to confirm exit from PCONSOLE.

Step 3: Review

This task showed you how to use PCONSOLE to see all the jobs in a queue, including the status of each job, the job number, and the initials of the user who sent it. Armed with this information, you can perform simple job and queue management functions for users. There are three tasks associated with managing print jobs:

☐ Changing the priority of a print job

☐ Holding a job

☐ Deleting a job

To perform these tasks, use PCONSOLE to change print job parameters. Print job parameters are the parameters affecting how a print job is controlled by the print queue, such as its queue order or priority, the number of copies to be printed, whether it is being held in the queue, or whether a banner will be printed before the job. Ordinarily, you will not need to look at the parameters or change them. Occasionally, however, you will find that after sending a print job to the queue, you will change your mind about how the job should be printed. This is when you will want to know how to change your print job parameters.

You can use the PCONSOLE menu utility to change a print job's priority in the queue.

Task 20.12: Changing the priority of a print job.

Step 1: Description

This task enables you to move a print job from its position in the queue to another position in the queue.

Step 2: Action

1. At the DOS prompt, type **PCONSOLE** and press Enter.

2. Highlight Print Queue Information, and press Enter.

3. From the list of print queues, select the desired queue and press Enter.

4. Select Current Print Job Entries, and press Enter to display the current print jobs in the queue.

5. Select the print job you want to change, and press Enter. You should see a screen similar to the one in Figure 20.15.

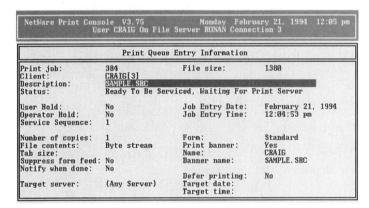

Figure 20.15. *The Print Queue Entry Information screen.*

6. Tab down to Service Sequence, type a new priority number, and press Enter.

Note: Type number 1 to move the job to the top of the queue, or type a number greater than the last job in the queue to move the job to the end.

7. Press Esc repeatedly until you are asked to confirm your exit from PCONSOLE.

Step 3: Review

This task showed you how to move a print job in the queue from its position in the queue to another position in the queue. Moving the job to the end of the queue temporarily puts it on hold, but there is an easier way. But why would you want to hold or delay a job? Sometimes it is necessary to hold a job in the queue to prevent it from printing, usually because at the last moment you notice that something is wrong and needs to be changed, such as the paper type or size. As you already guessed, you use PCONSOLE to change the priority of a print job.

Task 20.13: Holding a print job in the queue.

Step 1: Description

This task enables you to hold a print job in the queue, that is, to stop it from printing until you release the hold on the print job.

Step 2: Action

1. At the DOS prompt, type **PCONSOLE**, and press Enter.

2. Highlight Print Queue Information, and press Enter.

3. From the list of print queues, select the desired queue, and press Enter.

4. Select Current Print Job Entries, and press Enter to display the current print jobs in the queue.

5. Select the print job you want to delete, and press Delete.

6. Tab down to either Operator Hold (if you are a queue operator) or User Hold, press Y, and press Enter.

Note: Remember that the Supervisor has queue operator status for every queue.

7. Press Esc repeatedly until you are asked to confirm your exit from PCONSOLE.

Step 3: Review

You now know how to hold a print job in the queue, that is, how to stop it from printing until you release the hold on the print job. But what if you don't need the

job at all? Sometimes a print job is not needed, the wrong job was sent, or a user requests that a job be deleted. The Supervisor, Supervisor-equivalent, or queue operator can delete a job from the queue. Again, you use PCONSOLE to delete a job from a print queue.

Task 20.14: Deleting a print job from the queue.

Step 1: Description

This task enables users to delete their print job in the queue. As the Supervisor, you can delete any job from any queue.

Step 2: Action

1. At the DOS prompt, type **PCONSOLE** and press Enter.

2. Highlight Print Queue Information, and press Enter.

3. From the list of print queues, select the desired queue, and press Enter.

4. Select Current Print Job Entries, and press Enter to display the current print jobs in the queue.

5. Select the print job you want to delete, and press Delete.

6. Confirm the deletion in the Delete Queue Entry box.

7. Press Esc repeatedly until you are asked to confirm your exit from PCONSOLE.

Step 3: Review

At this time, you can perform some simple queue management tasks. For example, you know how to move a job around in the queue, put a job on hold, or delete it from the queue.

Task 20.15: Viewing queue status.

Step 1: Description

This task shows you how to see the number of entries in the queue, the number of servers attached, and the operators flags that are set.

Step 2: Action

1. At the DOS prompt, type **PCONSOLE** and press Enter.

2. Highlight Print Queue Information, and press Enter.

3. From the list of print queues, select the desired queue, and press Enter.

4. Select Current Queue Status, and press Enter to display the status of the queue.

5. Press Esc repeatedly until you are asked to confirm your exit from PCONSOLE.

Step 3: Review

This final task showed you how to see the number of entries in the queue, the number of servers attached, and the operators flags that are set. All this information will help you better manage the queue.

That's it for workstation printing at this time. In Chapter 23, you will learn about NetWare's print services and the different print servers. You also will learn to define print queues and servers, create print servers, and assign print queues and operators. Let's recap what you learned today.

Summary

In this lesson, you mastered printing from a workstation. Specifically, you learned

☐ The difference between local printing and network printing

☐ The specifics about LAN-intrinsic, LAN-aware, and LAN-ignorant applications

☐ For LAN-ignorant applications, the CAPTURE command

☐ The NPRINT command-line utility and the PCONSOLE menu utility and how to use them for printing

☐ Copying, creating, and deleting print job configurations

☐ How to change a job's priority, place a job on hold, and delete a job from the queue

Workshop
Terminology Review

buffer—The printer's random-access memory (RAM), measured in kilobytes. Because computer chips can transfer data much faster than mechanical printer mechanisms can reproduce it, small buffers are generally inserted between the two, to keep the data flow in check.

control codes—Nonprinting computer instructions such as carriage return and line feed.

handshaking—Used in this context to refer to the controlled movement of bits between a computer and a printer.

off line—Indicates that the printer is not ready to receive data.

Task List

The tasks in this chapter dealt principally with printing from a workstation and helping users print from their workstations. These are the tasks you should understand from this chapter:

- ☐ Listing print queues
- ☐ Capturing a print queue
- ☐ Ending a print queue CAPTURE
- ☐ Using PCONSOLE to place a print job in the queue
- ☐ Using NPRINT to print a DOS text file
- ☐ Creating print job configurations
- ☐ Maintaining print job configurations
- ☐ Listing print jobs
- ☐ Changing the priority of a print job
- ☐ Holding a print job in the queue
- ☐ Deleting a print job from the queue
- ☐ Viewing queue status

Q&A

Q How often will I use CAPTURE?

A You won't use CAPTURE at all if you have Windows and let it handle the redirection of printing to print queues. If you have old DOS software that doesn't, you need to use CAPTURE. Hopefully, this situation is rare.

Q How often will I use PRINTCON?

A PRINTCON defines print job configurations that CAPTURE can use. Because you do not need CAPTURE too often, the need for print job configurations decreases.

Q How do I delete my own jobs?

A Use the steps given for the Supervisor or Queue Operator.

1. At the DOS prompt, type **PCONSOLE** and press Enter.

2. Move the cursor down to Print Queue Information and press Enter.

3. From the list of print queues, select the desired queue and press Enter.

4. Select Current Print Job Entries and press Enter to display the current print jobs in the queue. If you use a restricted account, you see only your print jobs.

5. Select the print job you want to delete and press Delete.

6. Confirm the deletion in the Delete Queue Entry box.

7. Press Esc repeatedly until you are asked to confirm your exit out of PCONSOLE.

21

Managing the File Server

NetWare works fairly well straight out of the box. Needless to say, however, problems can crop up. And system administrators must perform some tasks regularly to keep the file server running smoothly. On Day 14, you will get into tweaking and tuning your file server. This chapter will introduce you to some simple file server management commands.

Let's start at the beginning and see how to start a downed file server.

Starting the File Server

The Supervisor can boot the file server using a DOS executable file on the file server console. To do this, type the following line at the DOS prompt at the file server console:

SERVER [option]

Table 21.1 shows the various options with descriptions for the SERVER command.

Table 21.1. SERVER options.

Option	Description
-S *{path} filename*	Boots with alternate START-UP.NCF file
-C *number*	Boots with different cache buffer size
-NA	Boots without AUTOEXEC.NCF file
-NS	Boots without START-UP.NCF file

Gathering Information About the Network

If you want to see what version of NetWare your file server is running, use the following command-line utility:

NVER

As you can see from the display in Figure 21.1, the versions of NetBIOS, IPX, SPX, LAN driver, redirector or shell, DOS, and the file server are given.

```
F>nver

NETWARE VERSION UTILITY, VERSION 3.75

IPX Version: 3.30
SPX Version: 3.30

LAN Driver:  Xircom CreditCard Ethernet Adapter V1.00
             IRQ 5, Port 0300, Memory D000:0

Shell:       V4.00 Rev. A
DOS:         MSDOS V6.20 on IBM_PC

FileServer: RONAN
Novell NetWare v3.12 (5 user) (8/12/93)

F>
```

Figure 21.1. *View version of NetWare.*

Similarly, if you want to see NetWare configuration, type the following command at the file server console:

CONFIG

As you can see from the display in Figure 21.2, you get the file server's name, its network address, LAN drivers loaded, board settings, node addresses for boards, communication protocol bound to boards, cabling number for boards, frame type assigned for boards, and the board name.

```
RONAN:config
File server name: RONAN
IPX internal network number: 2D222067

Novell NE2000
    Version 3.25    June 17, 1993
        Hardware setting: I/O Port 300h to 31Fh, Interrupt 3h
        Node address: 00006E22037A
        Frame type: ETHERNET_802.3
        No board name defined
        LAN protocol: IPX network 00000001
RONAN:
```

Figure 21.2. *Configuration information.*

Another handy file server command is MODULES, which you can use by typing

MODULES

As you can see from the display in Figure 21.3, you get a list of all the NetWare Loadable Modules (NLMs) currently running on the file server.

```
RONAN:modules
RSPX.NLM
   NetWare 386 Remote Console SPX Driver
   Version 3.12    March 29, 1993
   Copyright 1993 Novell, Inc.  All rights reserved.
REMOTE.NLM
   NetWare 386 Remote Console
   Version 3.12    May 13, 1993
   Copyright 1993 Novell, Inc.  All rights reserved.
NE2000.LAN
   Novell NE2000
   Version 3.25    June 17, 1993
   Copyright 1993 Novell, Inc.  All rights reserved.
ETHERTSM.NLM
   Novell Ethernet Topology Support Module
   Version 2.14    May 17, 1993
   Copyright 1993 Novell, Inc.  All rights reserved.
MSM.NLM
   Novell Generic Media Support Module
   Version 2.14    March 11, 1993
   Copyright 1993 Novell, Inc.  All rights reserved.
ALWAYS.DSK
   Always Technology Disk Driver Version 2.16 (930120)
RONAN:
```

Figure 21.3. *NLMs information.*

Setting Time and Date

If you want to see the date and time set on the file server, type one of the following lines at the file server console:

SET TIME
TIME

You also can see the date and time set on a file server where you are attached by typing the following line at the DOS prompt:

SYSTIME file server

If you find that the date or time are incorrect, you can change either. The Supervisor can set the date and time kept by the file server by typing the following command:

SET TIME [month/day/year] [hour:minute:second]

You type the preceding command at the file server console, substituting the parameters you want. If you don't type a parameter, it remains at its original setting. Following are some sample formats:

```
SET TIME 02/18/94
SET TIME FEBRUARY 18, 1994
SET TIME 18 FEBRUARY 1994
SET TIME 8:30:30
SET TIME 20:30:30
```

Now that you know some background information about your server, let's look at securing it.

File Server Security

The physical security of the network and the file server are of prime importance. Anyone who gains access to either can upset the operation of the network. Physical security of the network refers to controlling what nodes are attached to it. One way some crackers gain unauthorized access to a user's account is to connect a machine to the network physically and capture network packets to local hard-disk storage. If a user logs in to the file server while this machine is active, the cracker can replay the log-in session to discover the user's password.

In the past, system administrators were confident that NetWare volumes were secure because there was no way to access files in a NetWare volume directly by booting the server with DOS. The NetWare file system does not use DOS-formatted volumes— it's more like UNIX. If you booted your NetWare file server with DOS and tried to read the hard disk, DOS would report that the disk was not a DOS disk.

This feature was a major advantage of NetWare when compared to networks in which the server used a DOS file system. Networks based on IBM's PC LAN program are less secure because anyone with physical access to the server has access to the files on the server.

21

Now vendors are selling utility programs for the system administrator that allow access to files on a NetWare volume without the server running the NetWare operating system. One very popular product is NetUtils from OnTrack Computer Systems. You first boot a NetWare server with DOS and then run NetUtils. You then have access to the files on any NetWare volume.

You've seen that storing files on a NetWare server does not necessarily mean they are secure. You need to take other actions to secure your data. This section covers issues in which the universal solution is to physically secure your server.

Physically securing your server can mean putting it in a locked room where nobody can touch it. If you can physically secure your server, NetWare will provide the security you need in order to protect your data. If you do not provide physical security, you run the risk that someone can bypass NetWare's security mechanisms and access your data.

NetWare's servers support console commands that can cause severe disruption of the network if exercised with malicious intent. Someone could, for example, take down the server, clear connections, and disable new logins. You already learned about the last of these three commands, and you will learn about the first two commands in this chapter.

One way to help protect against attacks is to lock the keyboard of the server when the server is out of view of the system administrator. Many machines support this feature with a metal key lock. Most people view keys as a nuisance and prefer to lock the keyboard by entering a password. You can use the MONITOR NLM to lock the keyboard of the server. To lock the keyboard, use the following procedure.

Task 21.1: Using *MONITOR* to lock the keyboard.

Step 1: Description

This task shows you how to lock the file server keyboard so that no unauthorized user can type anything there.

Step 2: Action

1. At the DOS prompt, type **MONITOR** and press Enter. You should see the screen in Figure 21.4.

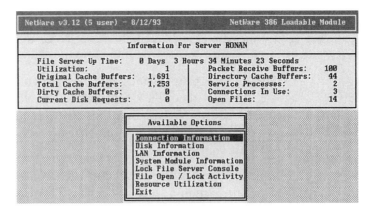

Figure 21.4. *The Available Options screen.*

2. From the Available Options menu, highlight Lock File Server Console and press Enter.

3. At the Password: prompt, enter a password and press Enter. You should see the message shown in Figure 21.5.

4. Type the password to unlock the keyboard.

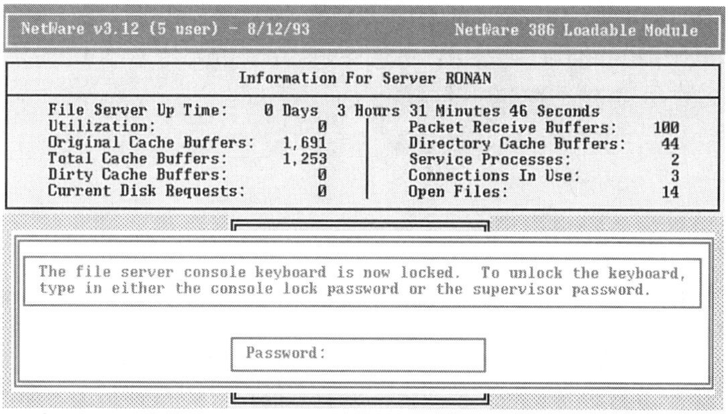

```
NetWare v3.12 (5 user) - 8/12/93              NetWare 386 Loadable Module

                     Information For Server RONAN

     File Server Up Time:    0 Days  3 Hours 31 Minutes 46 Seconds
     Utilization:             0     |  Packet Receive Buffers:   100
     Original Cache Buffers:  1,691 |  Directory Cache Buffers:   44
     Total Cache Buffers:     1,253 |  Service Processes:          2
     Dirty Cache Buffers:     0     |  Connections In Use:         3
     Current Disk Requests:   0     |  Open Files:                14


     The file server console keyboard is now locked.  To unlock the keyboard,
     type in either the console lock password or the supervisor password.


                         Password:
```

Figure 21.5. *A locked console.*

Step 3: Review

Using the MONITOR NLM to lock the keyboard of the server when it is not in use is a good idea. Alternatively, you can keep unauthorized users from loading new NLMs, prevent entry into the OS debugger, and prevent changes to the file server date and time. You can do so by typing the following line at the file server console:

SECURE CONSOLE

Tip: If you forget the password you entered, you can use the Supervisor's password.

Warning: To reverse the SECURE CONSOLE command, you must reboot the file server. Type DOWN and EXIT.

There is another method for preventing the loading of NLMs. Typing the following command at the console returns DOS memory space to file caching and prevents the unauthorized loading of NLMs residing on DOS partitions or local DOS drives:

REMOVE DOS

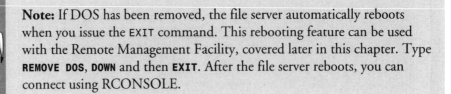

Warning: To reverse the REMOVE DOS command, you must reboot the file server. Type **DOWN** and **EXIT**.

Note: If DOS has been removed, the file server automatically reboots when you issue the EXIT command. This rebooting feature can be used with the Remote Management Facility, covered later in this chapter. Type **REMOVE DOS**, **DOWN** and then **EXIT**. After the file server reboots, you can connect using RCONSOLE.

SECURE CONSOLE also removes DOS from the file server.

Before locking the keyboard, you might want to clear the screen so that the last command is not frozen in time. You can type **CLS** at the file server console to clear the screen.

If you suspect someone has been using the file server console, you could start your investigation by checking the error logs—provided that they weren't erased.

Task 21.2: Checking the error log.

Step 1: Description

Using SYSCON, the Supervisor can see the error log where the system records warning messages displayed for the file server.

Step 2: Action

1. At the DOS prompt, type **SYSCON** and press Enter.

2. Highlight Supervisor Options and press Enter.

3. Highlight View File Server Error Log and press Enter. You should see a log similar to the one shown in Figure 21.6.

4. Press Esc and choose to either delete the error log or not.

5. Press Esc repeatedly until you are asked to confirm your exit from SYSCON.

SAMS
Learning
Center

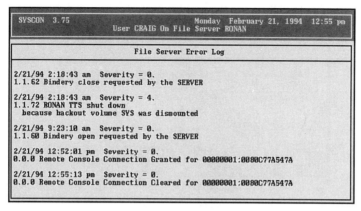

Figure 21.6. *The error log.*

Step 3: Review

The error log warns you if any problems are developing with your file server hardware or software. If you suspect problems with your file server, check the log daily. Novell's documentation provides an explanation of system messages recorded in the error log. On Day 14, you will look at maintaining and fine-tuning your file server.

Task 21.3: Erasing the error log.

Step 1: Description

When the error log gets too large, you will want to erase it. Using SYSCON, the Supervisor can clear the error log where the system records warning messages displayed for the file server.

> **Note:** You should back up your system before erasing any audit trail material.

Step 2: Action

1. At the DOS prompt, type **SYSCON** and press Enter.

2. Highlight Supervisor Options and press Enter.

3. Highlight View File Server Error Log and press Enter. You should see a log similar to the one shown in Figure 21.7.

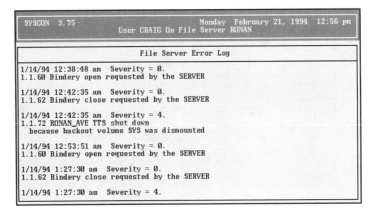

Figure 21.7. *The error log.*

4. Press Esc.

5. Choose Yes to clear the error log.

6. Press Esc repeatedly until you are asked to confirm your exit from SYSCON.

Step 3: Review

This task showed you how to erase the file server error log. When you clear the log, the system immediately restarts the log with new messages after you clear it. You also can delete the error log from the DOS prompt by typing the following:

```
DELETE SYS$ERR.DAT
```

Another important element of any file server security program is an effective virus prevention and control program.

Virus Protection

As with their biological cousin, the AIDS-causing HIV virus, there is a lot of misinformation about viruses. The popular press has whipped up horror stories on computer viruses out of proportion to the number of incidents.

What is a virus? There is confusion over the difference between viruses and worms. A virus is a program that can infect other programs by modifying them to include, say, an evolved copy of itself. A virus normally changes its form or the infected program over time. Furthermore, it is self-replicating, and it attaches itself to either a program or data so that it can hide and travel throughout your network. Virus developers

program them to erase hard disks, delete certain critical files, or prevent log-in by your users. Viruses are either benign—causing disruption but no serious damage—or malignant—destroying data or the integrity of the system. There are other virus strains. For example, a logic bomb is a virus triggered on a specified date and time or after an occurrence of a specific event or events.

Worms are similar to viruses, except their aim is simply to replicate themselves repeatedly. Eventually, worms use all the memory in your network so that nothing can be done.

There are other kinds of computer pestilence—bacteria, tribbles, rabbits, and chain letters—but regardless of their name, they can cause untold damage if not handled correctly.

What Are the Symptoms?

An infected system exhibits noticeable symptoms. The first symptom of a computer virus might be decreased network or workstation performance; one reported virus had so filled the network with copies of itself that it was impossible to get warnings to potential victims.

Another sign is when you experience unexplainable, nonrepeatable problems on the network or workstations.

What Can You Do?

Viruses are for the most part avoidable. Like their biological counterparts, computer viruses mostly come from poor computing habits. You should take a proactive stance to prevent viruses.

First, management must set the right tone by implementing and enforcing good security practices. Second, you should inform your users about viruses, their habits, virus prevention, and recovery procedures. Education, not eradication, is the number one method for controlling the threat of viruses and worms. Forewarn your employees about viruses and worms—an ounce of prevention is worth a pound of cure.

You must be aware that viruses represent a real and potentially catastrophic threat to your network. Users can, however, safeguard their networks to deter viral infection. You must review your user's vulnerability to viruses both in physical terms—who has access—and in administrative terms—what policies are necessary.

Fortunately, industrious entrepreneurs developed flu shot programs to combat computer viruses by scanning programs looking for any potentially harmful instructions. Unfortunately, these corrective programs work only on known viruses. A prophylactic program might take control and raise an alarm, however, when any attempt is made to put data on media. These programs, when loaded into memory, intercept any suspicious activity. You should review these programs and consider implementing one if your network is not already protected.

Recovering from a Virus

What should you do when you suspect you have a virus? If you have a microcomputer or local area network, you should know how to recover from a virus. Many people do not know how to recover from a virus. Following are some steps to take when you discover you are infected and you must recover:

1. Don't panic, because many viruses are malicious, "one false move could wipe out your hard disk" types. Thoughtful analysis now could save you months of work—and possibly your job.

2. Terminate any connections to the outside world. Also, you should isolate parties showing symptoms or positive test results from the network or other workstations. You do not want to risk reinfection while trying to eradicate the virus.

3. Try to recall your activities and previous symptoms. These recollections might help recover your system.

4. Determine the nature and extent of the infection. You should be aware of what happened to your system. For example, was the fixed disk affected, and has the damage stopped?

5. Power down the infected system.

6. Power up using the write-protected, uninfected, original system diskettes.

7. Back up all nonexecutable files and screened files to tape or diskette.

8. Do a low-level reformat of the infected hard disk.

9. Restore the operating system software to the hard disk.

10. Reload all uninfected files that were backed up.

11. Scan all your floppy diskettes for infections, and reformat those that are infected.

Recovering from viruses is serious business. If you do not feel fully comfortable with the foregoing instructions, approach someone who does. Hire a consultant, if need be. It might turn out to be the best money you ever spent on your network.

Helping Users with Crashed Workstations

Users will sporadically call for your help. For example, occasionally users will call with a complaint that their workstations have crashed. As Supervisor, you can help them with this problem.

Task 21.4: Viewing connection information.

Step 1: Description

This task shows you how to see all the file server connections and information about the connection. The information you can view includes connection time, address, file server requests, status, kilobytes read and written, number of semaphores and logical record locks, and a list of open files.

Step 2: Action

1. Type **LOAD MONITOR** on the file server console and press Enter.

2. Choose Connection Information and press Enter.

3. Choose the user connection from the menu and press Enter. You should see information similar to that in Figure 21.8.

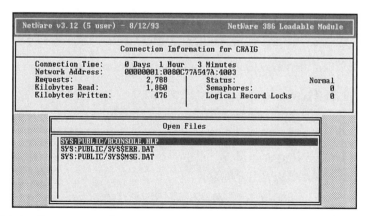

Figure 21.8. *Connection information.*

Step 3: Review

After you have identified the user's connection, you can clear the user's workstation. There are two utilities that enable the SUPERVISOR to clear a workstation's connection abruptly. These utilities, however, remove all file server resources from the workstation and can cause file corruption or data loss when executed while workstations are processing transactions. You should use these utilities only where workstations have crashed or users have turned off their workstations without logging out. In these cases, the workstation's connection would stay open even though the files are not currently used.

The first utility is the console utility CLEAR STATION. To use this command, type the following line at the file server console:

CLEAR STATION n

You substitute the connection number for *n* for the workstation to be cleared. Normally, you would not know the connection number because the workstation gets assigned the number as it attaches, and it changes from session to session. You can view the connection number from MONITOR.

Task 21.5: Closing files on a crashed workstation.

Step 1: Description

This task shows you one way to close files and delete internal tables for a workstation that has crashed.

Step 2: Action

1. Type **LOAD MONITOR** on the file server console and press Enter.

2. Choose Connection Information and press Enter.

3. Choose the user connection from the menu, and press Del.

4. When the Clear Connection prompt appears, answer Yes.

Step 3: Review

Using MONITOR, you can close files and delete internal tables for a workstation that has crashed.

Perhaps when you get an idea of all the work you must do, you will want to create some file server operators to assist you.

Using **FCONSOLE**

You can create console operators through the Supervisor Options in SYSCON. Console operators can access all FCONSOLE facilities except DOWN and CLEAR CONNECTION.

Using FCONSOLE, an operator can take these actions:

- ☐ Change your default server
- ☐ Log in to or log out from an attached file server
- ☐ Change to a different username on an attached file server
- ☐ See the NetWare version your file server is running
- ☐ See connection information
- ☐ Enable/Disable logins
- ☐ Enable/Disable TTS (see Chapter 22)
- ☐ Send a message from the file server to all users or to selected users

Figure 21.9 illustrates the various screens of FCONSOLE.

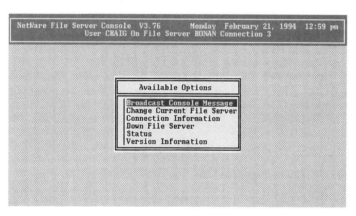

Figure 21.9. *The FCONSOLE menus.*

For those times when FCONSOLE will not suffice or you cannot get to the file server, NetWare provides a remote management facility for you to use.

Remote Management Facility

The Remote Management Facility (RMF) enables you to manage your NetWare servers from a single location. This location can be a workstation attached to the network or any device that can connect asynchronously. The servers regard the device as local, and you can transfer files, install or upgrade NetWare on a remote server, reboot a server, and execute console commands, such as MONITOR, just as if you were sitting at the server's console. RMF greatly expands the system administrator's ability to monitor, administer, and troubleshoot enterprise-wide networks efficiently and economically.

RMF has two main components:

☐ The RMF NLMs

☐ The RMF console program

The RMF NLMs are either REMOTE.NLM or connection NLMs. The REMOTE.NLM manages the information exchange between the server and the remote workstation. Connection NLMs provide communication support for the REMOTE.NLM and the remote workstation.

When using RMF from a workstation on the network, you use the RSPX.NLM as the connection NLM. In like manner, when using RMF from a device via a modem, you use the RS232.NLM as the connection NLM. Regardless of the connection NLM used, you load REMOTE.NLM first.

The RMF console program is either RCONSOLE or ACONSOLE. You use RCONSOLE from a workstation on the network. Before you can use RCONSOLE or ACONSOLE, you must load the RMF NLMs on the file server.

Task 21.6: Setting up the file server.

Step 1: Description
This task shows you how to load the remote management facility NetWare loadable modules required to run either the RCONSOLE or the ACONSOLE program.

Step 2: Action
1. At the file server console prompt, type **LOAD REMOTE** and press Enter. This loads the REMOTE NLM.

2. At the prompt, enter a remote console password.

3. At the file server console prompt, type **LOAD RSPX** and press Enter. You use the RSPX NLM for direct communications links. To use asynchronous links, type **LOAD RS232**.

> **Note:** If you specify RS232, RMF prompts you to specify either 1 for COM1 or 2 for COM2, as well as the modem's baud rate.

Step 3: Review

Using this task, you can now access the console prompt using either PCONSOLE or ACONSOLE. You can run a remote console session from any DOS workstation on the network by using RCONSOLE. Or you can run a remote console session by dial-up using ACONSOLE.

Task 21.7: Using RCONSOLE to access the console prompt.

Step 1: Description

This task enables the Supervisor to use a DOS workstation to access the file server console prompt and thus use the workstation as a file server console.

Step 2: Action

1. At the DOS prompt, type **RCONSOLE** and press Enter. You should see the screen shown in Figure 21.10.

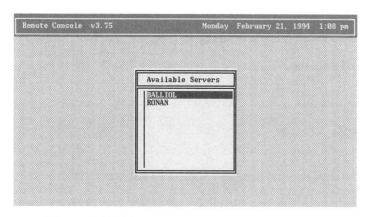

Figure 21.10. *The available file servers.*

2. Choose the file server name from the list and press Enter.

3. At the Password: prompt, type the remote password or the Supervisor password.

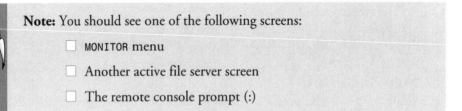

Note: You should see one of the following screens:

☐ MONITOR menu

☐ Another active file server screen

☐ The remote console prompt (:)

Note: A prompt asks for the MONITOR password if MONITOR is loaded in the system with the keyboard lock option available.

Step 3: Review

You just saw how to use RCONSOLE to access the console prompt from a workstation. Using the Transfer Files to Server option, you can upgrade a file server remotely. For instance, you can use RCONSOLE to upgrade a LAN or disk drivers. Sometimes you might not be on the network but still need access to the console. In this instance, you use the ACONSOLE program.

Task 21.8: Using ACONSOLE to access the console prompt.

Step 1: Description

Using ACONSOLE, you can use a DOS workstation to access the file server console prompt and thus use the workstation as a file server console.

Step 2: Action

1. Log in to the network as Supervisor.

2. At the DOS prompt, type **ACONSOLE** and press Enter.

3. When the main menu appears, select Connect to Remote Location, select the phone number of the server where you want to connect, and press Enter.

4. The Modem Result Codes screen appears to show the progress of the connection. When you connect successfully, you will see the Available Servers screen.

5. Choose the file server name from the list and press Enter.

6. At the Password: prompt, type the remote password or the Supervisor password.

Step 3: Review

ACONSOLE is very similar to RCONSOLE, except you use it for asynchronous connections. When you dial up from home or connect via RS232 cables, use ACONSOLE.

When you are finished using RCONSOLE or ACONSOLE, you will want to return your workstation to DOS.

Task 21.9: Reverting to DOS on the workstation.

Step 1: Description

This task enables you to exit the ACONSOLE or RCONSOLE program and resume using your workstation as a workstation.

Step 2: Action

1. At the file server console prompt, press Shift and Esc simultaneously.

2. Confirm your intent to exit.

3. Press Esc.

4. Confirm your intent to exit once more.

Step 3: Review

This task showed you how to exit the ACONSOLE or RCONSOLE program and resume using your workstation as a workstation. You now know how to use RMF. Be sure to establish policies and procedures regarding the use of RMF.

The last task for today is to shut down the system.

Shutting Down the System

Shutting down the file server is potentially one of the most dangerous things you can do. If you don't do it at the right time or in the right way, you could lose files and server statistics and performance information. You occasionally will need to take down the server, however.

Task 21.10: Taking down the file server.

Step 1: Description

This task shows you ways to ensure that all cache buffers are written to disk, that all files are closed, and that the Directory Entry and File Allocation Tables are updated before turning off the power to the file server.

Step 2: Action

1. Send a broadcast message to all users to log out.

2. At the file server console, type **DOWN** and press Enter.

3. At the DOS prompt, type **FCONSOLE** and press Enter.

4. Highlight Down File Server and press Enter. This utility alerts you if any files are open. You can choose to force the server down with open files if you want.

5. Choose Yes and press Enter.

Note: If you issue either of these commands and you don't power off, the file server still receives packets, and you still can issue any command that deals with packets.

Note: You can access DOS after downing the server, assuming that the power is not turned off. Type EXIT at the file server console. The benefit to returning to DOS is that you can do a warm boot of the file server. Remember that you learned you cannot use DOS if you typed either **REMOVE DOS** or **SECURE CONSOLE** at the console.

Step 3: Review

This task showed you how to down your file server using either the DOWN command-line utility or the FCONSOLE menu utility.

Appropriately, that's it for today. After you review today's workshop, you can take your NetWare (and WetWare) down for the day.

Summary

As mentioned, NetWare works fairly well out of the box, but you will see file server maintenance and troubleshooting on Day 14. In this chapter, you learned

☐ About routine commands for the system administrator

☐ How to boot the file server

☐ How to get the version of NetWare your file server is running, see the NetWare configuration, and get a list of all the NetWare Loadable Modules (NLMs) currently running on the file server

☐ To set the date and time for your file server and to see the date and time set on a file server where you are attached

☐ How to secure your console

☐ About virus prevention and recovery

☐ How to view the error log where the system records warning messages displayed for the file server

☐ About and how to look at and clear file server connections

☐ About file server facilities FCONSOLE, RCONSOLE, and ACONSOLE

☐ To use FCONSOLE to down your server

One further comment on this chapter: LAN security and control, auditing, and viruses are the subjects of whole books. You might want to buy another book to pursue these subjects further.

You covered a great deal of material today. Don't forget to review the terminology, the tasks, and the Q&A section.

21

Workshop

Terminology Review

error log—An audit trail of system warning messages displayed for the file server.

virus—A self-replicating program that attaches itself to either a program or data so that it can hide and travel throughout your network. Viruses are either benign or malignant.

worms—Similar to viruses, except their aim is simply to replicate themselves repeatedly until they use all the memory in your network so that nothing can be done.

Task List

The emphasis of this chapter has been to introduce you to simple file server management tasks. As a system administrator or Supervisor, you will repeatedly use these commands in your daily work. These are the tasks you should understand from this chapter:

- ☐ Starting the file server
- ☐ Gathering information about your file server and network
- ☐ Setting time and date
- ☐ Locking the server's keyboard
- ☐ Securing the console
- ☐ Removing DOS
- ☐ Checking and erasing the error log
- ☐ Recovering from a virus
- ☐ Helping users with crashed workstations
- ☐ Using FCONSOLE
- ☐ Using RCONSOLE
- ☐ Using ACONSOLE
- ☐ Downing the file server

Q&A

Q When should I down the file server?

A You shouldn't down the file server when users are logged in. You should use the time restriction feature to provide a period for performing routine maintenance. You have to down the server when you have major changes to make to the software or hardware.

Q Should I delete the error log?

A If you don't delete the error log, it continues to build up so that you have to delete it from time to time. Before you do, make sure that you have a backup copy.

Q How do I remove NLMs that are executing?

A First, if you want to see executing NLMs, type the following at the file server console:

MODULES

When you have identified the NLM you want to remove, type the following at the file server console:

UNLOAD [NLM name]

Then press Enter.

Q How do I get a list of current screens on the console?

A At the file server console, press Ctrl-Esc to see a list like the following:

```
Current Screens

   1. System Console

   2. Monitor Screen

Select screen to view:
```

Q How do I switch between screens?

A To switch between screens at the file server console, press Alt-Esc. When you press Alt by itself, you see the name of the screen reverse-highlighted at the top of the screen.

22

File Backup and Recovery

The data stored on your network is the most valuable part of your network. It might in fact be one of the most important assets in your company or department. Its value is much higher than the cost of the equipment storing it, and its importance is second only to your users who use the information. This information is, however, at risk.

Nobody wants to face facts. It is not a question of whether a disaster will strike but rather of when it will strike. You know what Murphy's Law says. Loosely paraphrased, it is "If anything can go wrong, it will." This definitely applies to networks. So it is important to prepare for a disaster, and that includes developing and testing a plan for recovering with the least amount of disruption.

In this chapter, you will learn about the following topics:

- ☐ Predicting the cost of a disaster to your organization
- ☐ Protecting yourself against a disaster
- ☐ Recovering from a disaster
- ☐ Fault tolerance
- ☐ Backing up your data

Disaster Recovery Planning

A disaster in a network computing environment is any interruption of service significantly affecting user operations. It follows, then, that disaster recovery planning is the process of identifying critical computing resources, determining potential events that could affect these resources, and developing a plan for responding to such events.

While this book is being written, a painful reminder to prepare for disasters flashes across the television screen—the Northridge Quake of '94. Imagine you work in the San Fernando Valley in California. It is Tuesday morning, and your staff comes in to discover that the network is unavailable. If the network is not available immediately, hundreds of productive hours will be lost. Luckily, you developed a disaster recovery plan and everyone knows what to do. If you are like most system administrators, though, you do not have a tested plan.

Why plan? The lack of a plan could have a serious impact on the economic viability of your organization. An important step in any project is the planning process. Successful planning leads to a successful plan.

Disaster recovery planning has two primary goals. A good plan both ensures the safety of your employees and minimizes the impact on the business.

Following are planning steps for disaster recovery:

☐ Identification of critical business functions

☐ Assessment of related exposures

☐ Determination of disaster impact

Identification of Critical Business Functions

Through interviews and discussions, you must identify the data on your network that is critical to your organization. Critical business data contributes to the bottom line and the success of your organization. This process entails a review of the critical business functions served by your network.

Assessment of Related Exposures

You should assess exposures on your network. If you determine that a critical component is the file server's hard disk, you should either provide redundancy for the disk or establish a plan to recover data when a disk crash happens.

Threats affecting the availability of your network could be intentional or unintentional. Obviously, power failures affect availability. Maybe not so obvious are the deliberate attacks against your network. A disgruntled employee could destroy your file server easily and quickly.

Determination of Disaster Impact

You must assess the costs (both tangible and intangible) of a disaster affecting the critical business data if you don't have a plan in place. Normally, the shorter the period specified to recover the critical application, the higher the cost to maintain a plan. Conversely, the longer the recovery period, the lower the cost.

Developing the Plan

After you have determined where your critical data is, what possibly could go wrong, and what the impact is, you can start planning. An effective written plan would address how to take the following actions:

☐ Determine the potential threats

☐ Determine the probability of the threat occurring

☐ Estimate the impact, exposure, or cost of occurrence

☐ Identify solutions for recovery

☐ Estimate the cost of recovery

☐ Establish priorities for recovery

☐ Develop a recovery plan

A documented plan of the actions that must be taken immediately after the disaster happens would include, for example, names and phone numbers of key individuals to be notified, building evacuation procedures, and generally, those activities needed to minimize danger to human life and physical damage to the facility.

After you have completed your plan, you must test it to determine its completeness and practicality. You also must develop procedures to ensure that the plan stays current. There are positive reasons for testing plans. Tests enable organizations to determine the feasibility and compatibility of backup equipment and procedures. In addition, testing identifies and corrects weaknesses in the plan. Many organizations find serious problems during testing. For instance, personnel at one company who had faithfully sent tapes off-site found during testing that they had incorrectly created the tapes, which were of little use. Another good reason for testing is to prove your ability to recover and to increase your confidence in the ability to recover. Finally, tests also provide strong motivation to maintain the plan continually.

Your plans are not static documents; instead, they are dynamic organisms, breathing and growing along with your network. You must analyze changes in your environment and make any necessary modifications or refinements to your original plans. Then you must retest the plan and go through the process again. The process must be cyclical, without an end.

Several good books focused on local area networking disaster recovery are available. Buy one and study it before you start. Most of these books provide useful checklists to use when planning.

The best plan for disaster recovery is to avoid disasters. Fault tolerance is one way to avoid disasters. Novell provides system fault tolerance features with NetWare.

System Fault Tolerance (SFT)

Your organization might use its network for an application in which access to the data and services is extremely important. For instance, your organization might have moved its critical applications off the mainframe and put them on the network. You can see that there is a need for redundancy in today's local area networks. Redundancy provides protection against downtime because of hardware failure.

One application of redundancy is NetWare System Fault Tolerance (SFT) features. SFT builds redundancy into some critical system components and provides software enhancements to ensure data integrity. One software feature is the maintenance of duplicate tables, such as DETs and FATs.

Read-After-Write Verification

Another software feature of NetWare helping to provide data integrity is read-after-write verification. Immediately after the operating system writes a block of data to disk, it reads the same block and compares the blocks written and read. If the blocks match, everything is OK. On a no match, however, the operating system will try again, and if it still does not match, then the system marks the block as bad and writes the data to the hot fix redirection area.

Hot Fix

The hot fix redirection area is part of hot fix. Hot fix locates faulty blocks on volumes and marks them. The data destined for those blocks is then placed in another area.

Disk Mirroring and Duplexing

NetWare supports disk mirroring and disk duplexing. You might decide you require these features after you understand their purpose.

Disk Mirroring

Mirroring is one of the most important features of a successful fault-tolerant system. The overall benefit from mirroring is to provide protection against data loss. It provides fault tolerance to possible hard disk failure by writing the same information to two NetWare-partitioned hard disks. In the event of a hard disk failure, the functioning mirrored disk continues to retrieve and store data. The operating system sends a warning message that disk failure has occurred.

With disk mirroring, the hard disk is duplicated, so you can continue in the event that one hard drive fails. You still can be in trouble if the disk channel goes down, however.

Disk Duplexing

NetWare features disk duplexing, which enables a single server to have redundant hard drives and drive controllers. Disk duplexing enables NetWare to access data stored on a hard disk even if the channel to the disk fails. The channel is the path the data takes to get to the disk, including the disk controller interface card and the cables connecting the components. This means that a drive failure on a NetWare server need not bring the server down. If the server permits hot-swapping, then the server continues operating even while the technician replaces the failed drive.

Disk duplexing, or disk-channel mirroring, provides complete mirroring of the controllers and disks on the disk channel. If any component on the disk channel fails, the operating system still can retrieve and store data on the hard disk. During a failure on the channel, the operating system then sends a warning message of disk channel component failure.

Another benefit of disk duplexing is a NetWare feature called split seeks, which provides concurrent read requests on different disk channels. Disk mirroring cannot do split seeks and multiple seeks.

Disk Arrays

As with NetWare fault tolerance, disk array systems were developed to prevent loss of data and improve disk I/O performance. The most popular concept of disk arrays is known as Redundant Array of Independent Disks (RAID), developed by a team of researchers at the University of California Berkeley. When compared with NetWare's fault tolerance, disk array systems fall short in performance, are costly, and lack flexibility.

UPS

A power outage or interruption can cause considerable damage to your hardware and the data stored on it. Backup power systems provide emergency power in the event of a commercial power outage or interruption. UPS is used generically to refer to these backup power systems. Most people will tell you UPS stands for uninterruptible power supply, but it really stands for uninterruptible power system. Another backup

power system is SPS, or standby power system. The only difference is that a UPS constantly powers your system, whereas an SPS waits to be called into action.

NetWare can work hand in hand with intelligent power systems (IPS) to monitor battery time and recharge times. In coordination with NetWare, an IPS can orchestrate a fail safe and shut down the whole network.

Again, power supply systems are a fairly complicated matter that you should discuss with vendors of power supply systems. This also is another topic to discuss on NetWire. Other system administrators who have gone through the purchase of a UPS or IPS will be happy to share their experiences.

Understanding Transaction Tracking

The Transaction Tracking Services (TTS) is another of NetWare's integrity features. It enables several file or record changes to be grouped together as one logical transaction. NetWare can back out a transaction when the transaction is not completed. This means that a log is made of your transaction so that an incomplete transaction can be backed out to preserve the integrity of your database.

NetWare provides implicit and explicit transactional tracking. An implicit transaction occurs when an application program writes to a file or a record in a file that is locked. This type of transaction tracking is pretty straightforward. An explicit transaction, on the other hand, is controlled by the application that writes data to the server. Your application developers can access functions to employ transaction tracking.

Incidentally, you turn TTS on and off at the file server console using ENABLE TTS and DISABLE TTS. By default, TTS is turned on. You can use the FLAG command to set the TTS file attribute.

> **Note:** Some NetWare files such as the Bindery are transactional by default, and you cannot change the TTS attribute.

TTS is an important part of data integrity. If you decide to implement this feature, research the subject thoroughly. Obviously, heavy overhead is associated with the use of TTS.

A very important part of ensuring availability is regular backup. Backup, however, is performed for two purposes: operational expediency and disaster recovery.

Backups and Archiving

An effective backup plan protects your data against more than just hardware and software failures; it protects you against the most unpredictable part of your network—your users. Accidental deletion of files by users is by far the most common type of data loss in a networked environment. This error usually happens when users delete large groups of files or entire directories. Although deleted files are generally recoverable from a NetWare volume using SALVAGE, sometimes a complete restore from backup media is the only alternative.

Your users will not bother you until their data is gone. You might often overlook NetWare backup because you don't need to use it daily. As soon as the users lose data, however, you will be reminded of the need for disaster recovery planning. A major responsibility of yours is to back up important data on the server. Frequently, NetWare backup can be all that stands between your present career as a NetWare system manager and your next job. Make sure never to neglect your NetWare backup duties.

So how does network backup differ from backing up your microcomputer? NetWare backup is not quite as simple as inserting a diskette and copying files. The complicated process involves the bindery, NetWare compatibility, reliability of backed-up data, maintenance, and efficient restore procedures.

In a stand-alone environment, a backup consists primarily of the data and directories. In a network environment, the backup consists of not only data and directories, but also security rights, file attributes, the NetWare bindery, and users and groups. This is why one of the most important considerations of a NetWare backup system is NetWare compatibility. Many backup systems say they work with NetWare or that they are NetWare comfortable, but that doesn't mean they are NetWare compatible. The key component in NetWare compatibility is whether the system can recognize the bindery. Backing up the bindery is an arduous task because it requires that the bindery be closed and reopened—you cannot easily back up a file that is open.

Few backup systems are capable of accessing the NetWare bindery. They cannot close and open it without bringing down the network—not a desirable feature. Don't despair, however, because many products are indeed NetWare compatible and can satisfactorily back up the bindery.

Other important considerations for backup systems are the user interface, ease of use, and security. For security reasons, it is important that the Supervisor or Supervisor-equivalent be involved in a full backup.

It's a good idea to perform the backup when other users are off the system. Opening and closing of the bindery can cause serious problems for users who might try accessing the bindery in the middle of your backup. Also, it is difficult to back up open files. If users are currently logged in and using data and applications, those files will not be backed up.

Backup Strategies

Because computer hardware and software have become more reliable and robust, users and system administrators have been lulled into a false sense of security concerning the data stored on their network. Although there have indeed been significant improvements in reliability and fault tolerance, the overall level of data safety and integrity is still dependent on a comprehensive backup system spanning all important data on the network.

It is very important to implement an intelligent schedule that provides complete data security without producing 365 tapes per year. The grandfather method, for example, uses 24 tapes and provides at least four or five years' worth of data. This method calls for recycling tapes every day, week, month, and year. Reliability can be ensured in two ways. First, most backup software provides a verify feature to confirm the success of the backup process. And, if you can afford it, reliability is maintained by performing periodic restores to nonactive disks so that you can authenticate that the backup is truly good and that the restore functionality of the backup system works. You spend your days, weeks, months, and years backing up data—and never actually restoring it. More than one company has dutifully rotated tapes off-site that could not be restored because of corrupted data or poor media.

Note: Perhaps you haven't heard of the grandfather method. It involves three versions: son, father, and grandfather. When you create a new backup, the tape is the son, the old son becomes the father, the father becomes the grandfather, and the grandfather returns to the scratch pool.

An effective written backup plan addresses the following information:

☐ The servers needing regular backup

☐ The criticality of your data

☐ The individuals with responsibility for backup and restoration of each server

☐ The time of day and days of the week when it is optimal to do backup

☐ The storage location of backup tapes

☐ The tape rotation schedule

The preceding list needs a little explanation. You will need to determine which file servers need backup and the frequency of that backup. Not all servers need to be backed up the same. Chances are you would back up your production server more frequently than a test server. You might not back up print servers at all. Your organization needs to make a business decision based on the costs and benefits.

You need to analyze your data. Not all data needs to be backed up on the same basis. You might want to segregate executables, such as programs and NLMs, from users' data files, such as word processing documents. Executable programs tend to change rarely, whereas users often make changes to their data. Knowing this, you can perform daily backups of volumes containing user data, and weekly or monthly backups of executable data volumes. These selective backups reduce the amount of time and money needed for backup.

Incremental Backups

You also must decide whether to perform full or incremental backups. Usually, you will want to do a little of both. It is wise to plan to perform incremental backups daily. Incremental backups write only the files and data that have changed since the preceding backup. This method reduces the amount of time and the amount of backup media required. Weekly, you will want to perform a system-wide backup to have a recent reference point from which incremental backups can be performed.

Another twist to a full backup is televaulting. Televaulting allows instantaneous backups to be continually sent to off-site mass-storage devices. The off-site storage devices can be yours or a vendor's. Off-site vendors are now offering televaulting services. The vendor installs a connector at every workstation, terminal, and personal computer at your site. When the system is in place, every keystroke at the device is recorded and transmitted off-site. You can access this information whenever and however you want (for a cost).

Backup Schedules and Storage

When using a mix of backup strategies, carefully plan and coordinate how long each backup tape (or disk) will be safely stored. A common scheme is to keep daily copies of backups for a week, weekly copies for a month, monthly copies for a quarter of a year, and quarterly backups for a year or two. Yearly backups should be kept as long as they are required for business purposes, which might be as long as seven years.

Daily backups should be kept on-site in a safe place such as a vault or a secure, climate-controlled, fire-protected room. Taking this action provides a degree of protection while allowing quick access to backup media. This type of storage is particularly useful for restoring accidentally deleted and purged files, or entire volumes in case of a hard disk or file server failure. Monthly or quarterly backups, or any backups made following a major event (such as the release of a quarterly financial report or the completion of a milestone in the development of a project) should be moved off-site.

Also, you should perform a full backup on any server before it is scheduled to have a hardware or software upgrade, repair, or major system reconfiguration. This is certainly true when new hard disks are added to the server or when disk space on existing servers will be reclaimed by deleting unneeded data from the disk.

Moving the backup media off-site provides an extra degree of protection against possible destruction of data from a fire, flood, or earthquake. If feasible, backups can be rotated around different branches of the same company, or they can be placed in a vault at a third-party supplier of protection facilities and services.

Another important backup issue is media rotation. Magnetic tape has a finite life, and tape rotation helps ensure that the same tape is not used repeatedly. Instead, the use of each tape is rotated, effectively reducing how frequently a particular tape is read or written. By using a pool of tapes rather than using the same tapes over and over, the tape's reliability is increased. Several programs are available to help you manage tapes used for backing up your NetWare server. Some backup software employs the Tower of Hanoi method, which is a compromise between full and incremental backups. This software typically uses seven tapes and rotates them through the backup schedule.

A word on backup hardware and media. The type of backup hardware and media you select depends on your network. You should weigh the costs and benefits of each type. You should consider the following features when making your decision:

- ☐ Cost

- ☐ Flexibility of backup and restore features

☐ Storage capacity

☐ Speed

☐ Reliability

Unattended Backups

What about unattended backup? Baby-sitting a backup program is not the way you want to spend your evenings and nights. Recognizing this fact, vendors of most backup systems include the capability to schedule automatic, unattended backup sessions. The best strategy is to have a system that logs in the user, performs the backup, and logs out the user—automatically. You can schedule the backup to run in the middle of the night when your users are gone. Remember that you can use time restrictions to ensure a window for backup.

Now that you have developed a backup strategy and plan, you can back up your data. You can purchase a third-party backup program, or you can use NetWare's SBACKUP utility to perform the backup.

Using SBACKUP

SBACKUP, or server backup, is backup software available as part of Novell's Storage Management Services (SMS). It is a collection of NLMs loaded at the file server console. Using SBACKUP, the system administrator can back up data from and restore data to NetWare 3.11 and 3.12 servers. With SBACKUP, the backup device attaches directly to the file server. This feature is important because it means that data is not transmitted over the network. The data is simply transmitted between the tape device and the server's hard disk. In addition, security is enhanced because a workstation is not left logged in with the Supervisor account and its privileges. SBACKUP is quickly gaining support because of its improved performance over NBACKUP, internetworking support, and name space capabilities. If you have version 3.12, then you have no choice but to use SBACKUP.

Note: Using RCONSOLE, you can run SBACKUP remotely from your workstation. See Chapter 21 to refresh your memory on using RCONSOLE.

SBACKUP supports non-DOS name spaces, including DOS, Macintosh, OS/2, and UNIX. You also can use it to back up other NetWare servers. SBACKUP relies on the concept of a host file server and target file server. Figure 22.1 illustrates host and target file servers. The host file server runs the SBACKUP NLMs and has the tape backup drive attached. The target NetWare file server loads target service agents (TSA) that provide for a centralized backup of remote file servers. SBACKUP supports eight file server connections at one time. Finally, SBACKUP has enhanced performance because it does not cause additional load on the network. The tape unit connects directly to the file server, and SBACKUP communicates directly with the internal shared hard disk.

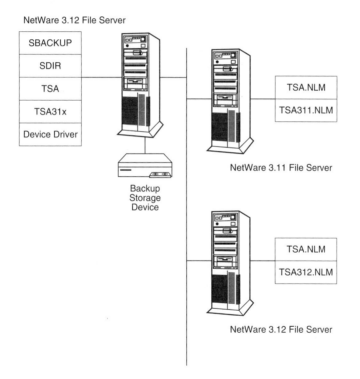

Figure 22.1. *Host and target NetWare servers.*

In addition, SBACKUP supports various backup devices. NetWare keeps an SBACKUP configuration file, DIBI2$DV.DAT, in the SYS:SYSTEM\DIBI subdirectory for configuring independent tape device drivers. The system administrator can add different drivers to the DIBI2$DV.DAT file, and SBACKUP automatically picks them up as possible choices. SBACKUP supports any device compatible with Novell's Device Independent Backup Interface-II (DIBI-II) specification. By default, SBACKUP supports the following tape device controller combinations:

☐ WANGTEK tape device with a PC36 controller

☐ WANGTEK tape device with a Quick 02 controller, including all devices with a DIBI2 certified driver

☐ Drivers supporting Quick 02 and SCSI boards

SBACKUP relies on the host/target methodology. The SBACKUP host runs the SBACKUP NLM and communications software. The target software runs the target service agent NLMs. Host software includes SBACKUP.NLM, SIDR.NLM, and corresponding tape device NLM. The tape device NLM can be one of three NLMs provided with NetWare: WANGTEK.NLM, ASPIDIBI.NLM for SCSI tape drives, and TAPEDC00.NLM for DIBI2 tape drives. There are other NLMs; it is best to read the README file provided on your system disks to get a current list. You also might check NetWire for additional help with device drivers.

SBACKUP has three components. The SBACKUP.NLM contains the backup interface. It reads and translates requests, determines the type of session being started, and decides the modules to activate. SIDR.NLM is Novell's data requester. It passes data requests to and from the host and target agent components. The SIDR.NLM uses Novell's built-in SMSP (Storage Management Services Protocol).

The third component is the tape device NLM. The target service agent NLMs consist of TSA.NLM and TSA-312.NLM (or TSA-311.NLM). TSA.NLM is the link between the data requester, the SIDR, and the target-specific module, such as TSA-312. TSA-312.NLM is the target-specific part of server backup for file servers running NetWare 3.12. It processes data using the target's data structure.

Even though the following NLMs have nothing to do with the backup, you need to load them for server backup:

☐ STREAMS.NLM

☐ SPXS.NLM

☐ TLI.NLM

☐ CLIB.NLM

☐ NUT.NLM

> **Warning:** Never mount or dismount a volume during a backup or restore session. It could cause irreparable damage to the volume and NetWare bindery.

Task 22.1: Backing up data on your file server.

Step 1: Description

Backing up data on your file server is a complicated procedure. This task works you through the major steps in the procedure.

Step 2: Action

1. At the file server console prompt of the target server, type **LOAD WANGTEK** and press Enter. You should substitute the applicable device driver for your backup hardware. This step loads the device driver for your backup device.

2. At the file server console prompt of the target server, type **LOAD TSA** and press Enter. This command loads the TSA modules on the target file server.

> **Note:** The host server also can be the target server, but you still must load TSA on the server.

> **Warning:** You also must load the applicable TSA on the target server, for example, TSA-311.NLM.

3. At the file server console prompt of the host server, type **LOAD SBACKUP** and press Enter. This command loads the SBACKUP NLM modules on the host file server. You should see a window similar to the one in Figure 22.2.

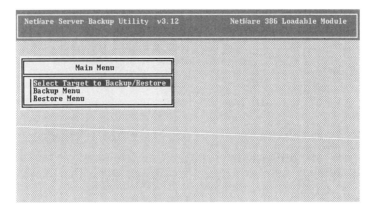

Figure 22.2. *SBACKUP Main Menu contents.*

4. Enter the username and password for the server. Generally, you can use the Supervisor account and its associated password.

5. Select the device driver corresponding to the backup hardware you will use to back up your server.

6. From the Main Menu, highlight Select Target to Backup/Restore, and press Enter.

7. Enter the username and password for the NetWare server you selected.

8. Press Esc.

9. From the Main Menu, highlight Backup Menu and press Enter.

10. From the Backup Menu, highlight Select Working Directory, and press Enter.

11. Enter the full path of the working directory, including the volume name and the directory path. If you don't know the full path, press Ins and build the path one level at a time.

12. Press Esc.

13. From the Backup Menu, highlight Backup Selected Target, and press Enter. You should see a screen similar to the one in Figure 22.3.

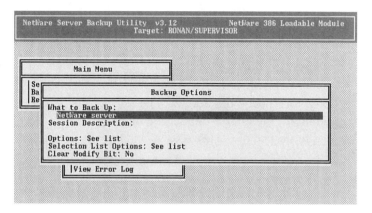

Figure 22.3. *The Backup Options screen.*

14. On the Backup Options screen, enter `File Server` for What to Back Up:, and press Tab. File Server is the default, and SBACKUP archives each volume currently mounted on the file server. You can also select The Bindery, a Volume, and a Directory. The Bindery option backs up all the bindery files. The Volume option backs up all directories, subdirectories, and files for the volume you select. The Directory option backs up every file in the directory.

15. Enter some descriptive information regarding the backup, and press Tab. You might want to include the date of the backup, the kind of backup (incremental, full, and so on), and the name of the person performing the backup. You should include anything that might provide useful information about the backup.

16. With See List for Options highlighted, press Enter. A form is displayed on which you can exclude certain files from the backup based on the attributes of the files or the trustee information. The default for all is No, meaning that all attributes are included.

17. Choose Hidden and press Enter.

18. With See List for Selection List Options highlighted, press Enter. A form is displayed on which you can specify the files and directories you want to include or exclude from the backup. This form is for fine-tuning what you selected in What to Back Up:. The default is None, meaning that no changes are made to what you selected earlier.

19. Press Esc.

20. Enter No for Clear Modify Bit, and press Tab. The Clear Modify Bit enables you to specify whether the backup process should clear the Modified since last archived bit field for the backed-up data.

21. Enter No for Append this Session. The Append this Session enables you to record more than one backup session on a tape. If you select Yes, the tape is wound to the end of the last session, and new data is written starting there.

22. Press Esc twice.

23. Confirm your intent to proceed by answering the Proceed with Backup? prompt.

24. Select the time that you want to start the backup from the Start Backup Menu.

25. To start the backup now, enter the media label information at the prompt, and press Enter. Go to step 27.

26. To start the backup later, enter the date and time in the Start Backup Timer form. Press Esc to save the specified time. Enter the media label information at the prompt, and press Enter.

27. Insert the media into the backup device, and press Enter.

Step 3: Review

This task covered the steps necessary for using SBACKUP. This procedure is complicated, so make sure that you know what you are doing. Make sure that the backup device you purchase is NetWare-compatible; that way you will have the proper device drivers. Read all available Novell and other vendor material you can before starting a backup. Good luck!

Restoring Files

Before restoring data to the target file server, make sure that the server has enough free disk space. The file server must have approximately 20 percent free disk space more than the amount needed for the restore. This space is needed to store temporary files and additional name space information called for in the restore process.

Task 22.2: Restoring data to your file server.

Step 1: Description

If you successfully backed up data in the preceding task, you can restore it using this task.

Step 2: Action

1. At the file server console prompt of the target server, type **LOAD WANGTEK** and press Enter. This command loads the device driver for your backup device.

2. At the file server console prompt of the target server, type **LOAD TSA** and press Enter. This command loads the TSA modules on the target file server.

> **Note:** The host server also can be the target server, but you still must load TSA on the server.

3. At the file server console prompt of the host server, type **LOAD SBACKUP** and press Enter. This command loads the SBACKUP NLM modules on the host file server. You should see a window similar to the one in Figure 22.4.

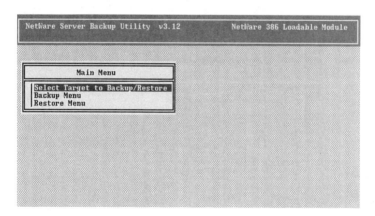

Figure 22.4. *SBACKUP Main Menu.*

4. Enter the username and password for the server. Generally, you can use the Supervisor account and its associated password.

5. Select the device driver corresponding to the backup hardware you will use to back up your server.

6. From the Main Menu, highlight Select Target to Backup/Restore, and press Enter.

7. Enter the username and password for the NetWare server you selected.

8. Press Esc.

9. From the Main Menu, highlight Restore Menu and press Enter.

10. From the Restore Menu, highlight Select Working Directory, and press Enter.

11. Enter the full path of the working directory, including the volume name and the directory path. If you don't know the full path, press Ins and build the path one level at a time.

12. Press Esc.

13. From the Restore Menu, highlight Restore Sessions or Restore Without Session Files, and press Enter. You should see a screen similar to the one in Figure 22.5. The Restore Sessions option enables you to use the session files created by SBACKUP during the backup process to restore data on your server. If you use this option, you can select the session you want to restore from the Restore Session list. Restore Without Session Files ignores the session files and scans the backup media to locate sessions to restore.

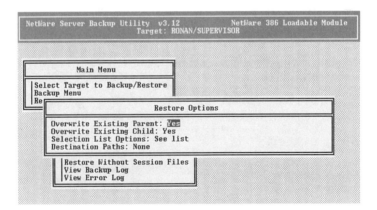

Figure 22.5. *The Restore Options screen.*

14. On the Restore Options screen, enter Yes for Overwrite Existing Parent:, and press Tab. If you select Yes, all the trustees and attributes of the parent are restored to the volume exactly as they were when they were backed up. This action could pose a problem if you modified the parents since the preceding backup.

15. Enter Yes for Overwrite Existing Child:, and press Tab. The Clear Modify Bit enables you to specify whether the backup process should clear the Modified since last archived bit field for the backed-up data.

16. With See List for Selection List Options highlighted, press Enter. A form is displayed on which you can specify the files and directories you want to include or exclude during the restore. This form is for fine-tuning what you selected in What to Back Up: during backup. The default is None, meaning that no changes are made to what you selected earlier.

17. Press Tab.

18. With None for Destination Paths highlighted, press Enter. Specify the Source Path and the Destination Path for the data.

22

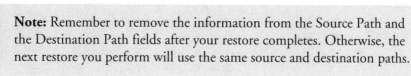

Note: Remember to remove the information from the Source Path and the Destination Path fields after your restore completes. Otherwise, the next restore you perform will use the same source and destination paths.

19. Press Esc twice.

20. Confirm your intent to proceed by answering the Proceed with Restore? prompt.

21. When prompted, insert the media into the backup device, and press Enter.

Step 3: Review

This task covered restoring data to your file server. As previously pointed out, backing up and restoring your system is one of the most important tasks of the system administrator. Do not hesitate to consult manuals, engineers, and NetWire for help.

SBACKUP Disadvantages

Earlier, you learned about the NMENU program, and you read that it was not as good as products from third-party suppliers of menu software. The same is true for the SBACKUP supplied with NetWare. SBACKUP has the following limitations:

☐ It does not itself support unattended backups. This means you must come in late, purchase a scheduling program, or kick your users off during the day. None of these alternatives is acceptable.

☐ It does not provide periodic verification.

☐ It provides limited hardware support. You have to use devices that support DIBI-II. The tape device you already have in your office might not work with SBACKUP. Therefore, it might be less costly to purchase backup software than backup hardware.

That concludes the material on NetWare disaster recovery, fault tolerance, and backup. Keep in mind that ensuring the availability of your network is an extremely important part of your job. If you do your homework properly, you should have no problem conquering this task.

Summary

The purpose of this chapter was to introduce one of the most important jobs an administrator has—keeping up the network. It is amazing how fast you'll lose users—and maybe your job—when the system is unreliable and unavailable.

To help you improve network availability, you learned

☐ About disaster recovery planning

☐ About some of NetWare's fault tolerance features

☐ About backup planning and operation

☐ How to use SBACKUP to back up and restore data on your network

Workshop

Terminology Review

backup—(n) A copy of a disk or of a file on a disk. (v) To make a spare copy of a disk or of a file on a disk.

backup procedures—The provisions made for the recovery of data files and program libraries, and for restart or replacement of equipment after the occurrence of a system failure or disaster.

exposure—A quantitative rating (in dollars per year) expressing the organization's vulnerability to a given risk.

fail safe—The automatic termination and protection of programs or other processing operations when a hardware or software failure is detected in a system.

fail soft—The selective termination of affected nonessential processing when a hardware or software failure is detected in a system.

risk—The potential that a given threat has of occurring within a specific period. The potential for realization of unwanted, negative consequences of an event.

risk analysis—An analysis of system assets and vulnerabilities to establish an expected loss from certain events based on estimated probabilities of the occurrence of those events.

System Fault Tolerance (SFT)—The capability of a Novell system to avoid and correct errors. Novell's SFT is tri-level.

threat—One or more events that might lead to either intentional or unintentional modification, destruction, or disclosure of data. An event which, should it occur, would lead to an undesirable effect on the environment.

vulnerability—The cost that an organization would incur if an event happened.

Task List

The emphasis of this chapter has been to introduce you to disaster recovery planning and backup. As a system administrator or supervisor, you must learn how to back up and restore data for your network. There were two very complicated tasks from this chapter:

☐ Using SBACKUP to back up data

☐ Using SBACKUP to restore data

Q&A

Q Should I send backup media off-site?

A Yes. You should find a secure off-site storage facility. This facility might be another of your offices with a safe, or it might be a site provided by a third party. You should ensure that tapes are stored off-site only when they are no longer required for day-to-day operations.

Q How many generations should I maintain?

A The answer to this question is really an operational decision. Most organizations maintain at least the Grandfather-Father-Son versions of backup media, such as tapes. Usually, the Grandfather is stored off-site and is replaced by the Father when a new Son is created. The Grandfather tape is then returned to the scratch pool.

Q How often should I back up?

A You normally back up data according to how often it is changed. Accordingly, you do not back up application software as frequently as the data created by the program.

Q Should users perform backups?

A Yes, however, studies show that users are unlikely to back up. You should encourage your users to store their group or departmental information to the server. If users store information they need for their work locally, you should encourage them to back up their information to the server or perform a backup. Again, you should use policies or accounting charges to move data to the server, where you can provide backup.

Q Should the NetWare LAN be included in the business resumption plan?

A Most assuredly, if the local area network stores, transmits, processes, or in any other way handles mission-critical data. You should perform a business impact analysis to quantify the criticality of the network for its inclusion in the business resumption plan. Business resumption planning is not a technical issue. It ensures that the necessary resources—be they human, computing, real estate, and so on—are available in the event of a disruption, catastrophic or not.

23

Setting Up Printing

Ask any system administrator—printing is a very difficult resource to share on a network. Network printing is both an extremely useful function of your network and a thorn in your side. Everybody wants to print reports, memos, letters, and such. These wants quickly turn into demands, and they can take over all your time. It is therefore extremely important that you understand printing concepts. This is why three chapters in this book deal exclusively with printing. To fully understand printing, you must fully understand printing components.

NetWare printing, as mentioned earlier in Chapter 20, revolves around three components:

- ☐ Print queues
- ☐ Print servers
- ☐ Printers

This chapter looks at these components in depth, including their use and function. You also will learn how to create and control print queues and servers.

Understanding Printing Basics

In Chapter 20, you learned about the differences between local and network printing. You also saw that a print queue is a shared area on a file server for storing print jobs in the order in which they are received. The print queue lines up the print jobs and sends them to the printer in an orderly and efficient manner. In turn, the print server directs the print jobs from the queue to the printer. The printer, which is the actual physical device, receives the job and typically outputs it to paper. You might want to refer to Chapter 20 to refresh your memory about printing terminology.

Using LAN-transparent applications, the users think they are printing directly to the printer down the hall. This illusion, however, is often quite difficult for the system administrator to achieve. Let's start our discussion by looking at printers.

Printers

Printers are the devices your users are most familiar with, after, of course, their workstations. Network printers are shared devices. You can attach them to a file server, print server, or local workstation acting as a remote printer. Printers attached to the file server or print server use PSERVER's printing functions. Printers locally attached to a workstation use the RPRINTER.EXE terminate-and-stay-resident (TSR)

program. RPRINTER talks directly to the print server and makes the printer available through the workstation's shell.

Today, you also will find intelligent printers—with print service and network interface cards built-in—that can attach directly to the network and act like workstations with remote printers attached. Apple's printers have worked this way since about 1986.

Printers get print jobs from print queues via print servers. You can mix and match printer, print server, and print queue configurations. For instance, you can have one queue per printer, multiple queues per printer, and multiple printers per queue. Your job as system administrator is to determine the mix that is correct for your environment. Before you can make this determination, you need a little more information. At this time, it is appropriate to refine the definition of a print server.

Print Servers

In Chapter 20, you saw that a print server is software that takes jobs from the print queue and sends them to the printer. Because it is software, you should think of the server more as a process than as a device. The print server can be a dedicated device or a process running on a NetWare file server. As a dedicated service, the print server process uses PSERVER.EXE, whereas as a nondedicated service, the print server process uses PSERVER.NLM.

Dedicated or nondedicated, that is the question. Each has its advantages. Running PSERVER.NLM on a file server costs less because it does not require additional hardware. However, a dedicated print server need not cost a fortune. You can retrieve your old PC from its current use as a boat anchor or doorstop, because the minimum configuration is an 8088 with a 20M hard drive and 1M RAM. On the other hand, using the file server as a print server really taxes I/O and memory—two resources used extensively by file service.

Figure 23.1 illustrates the various print services offered by NetWare.

Regardless of where the service runs, the print server has responsibility for controlling and redirecting print jobs from file server print queues to printers. They monitor the print queues and printers with vigilance. A job inserted into the print queue makes its way to the top of the queue, at which time the print server redirects it to the appropriate network printer. When a printer is out of paper, off-line, or jammed, the print server can notify the Supervisor, print server operator, or any other designated user.

23

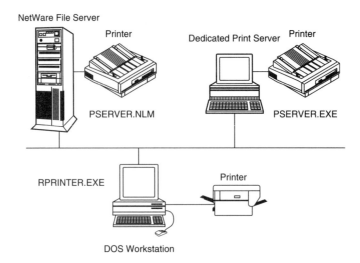

Figure 23.1. *NetWare print services.*

These are some of the pluses of print servers. Let's look at some limitations of NetWare printing as well. Because of DOS, a print server can have only 5 printers physically attached: LPT1, LPT2, LPT3, COM1, and COM2. As mentioned, DOS is a culprit in many a workstation's printing problems. To overcome this DOS limitation, NetWare provides remote printing. Remote printing allows workstations with locally attached printers to offer them as network printers. Using remote printing, NetWare supports another 11 printers: that is, 16 printers in total. In addition, a print server can service print jobs from print queues for up to eight file servers.

Starting Printing

When you run the print server process on a file server, you use the PSERVER NetWare Loadable Module. The Supervisor activates the NLM print server by typing **LOAD PSERVER** *print server* at the file server console. First, however, you must create and configure the print server using the PCONSOLE utility.

Similarly, you activate the print server process on a dedicated workstation by typing **PSERVER** *print server* at the DOS prompt. The only difference really is that you must open up enough connections so that the print server can communicate with multiple users, print servers, and file servers. To do this, you must include the following lines in the SHELL.CFG or NET.CFG file:

```
SPX CONNECTION = 60
SPX ABORT TIMEOUT = 2000
SPX LISTEN TIMEOUT = 300
SPX VERIFY TIMEOUT = 200
```

In addition, the workstation needs the following programs to run the print process:

- ☐ IBM$RUN.OVL
- ☐ PSERVER.EXE
- ☐ SYS$ERR.DAT
- ☐ SYS$HELP.DAT
- ☐ SYS$MSG.DAT

You also might want to modify the AUTOEXEC.BAT to boot the server as shown in this simple example:

```
@ECHO OFF
LSL
NE2000
IPXODI
NETX
PSERVER BALLIOL_PS
```

Refer to Chapter 19 for a refresher on configuring DOS clients. Back to the topic at hand, that is, setting up printing. Basically, you set up printing by taking the following actions:

- ☐ Creating print queues
- ☐ Creating print servers
- ☐ Defining printers
- ☐ Adding queues to printers

23

Creating a Print Queue

To create a print queue, the Supervisor creates print queues on the system and assigns print queue operators and users. Print queues are key to NetWare printing because they provide the link between the workstation and the shared printers. You must create a print queue before you assign it to a printer.

Task 23.1: Creating print queues.

Step 1: Description

You create a print queue using PCONSOLE. The PCONSOLE menu utility is found in your PUBLIC directory. This task works you through the creation of a print queue.

Step 2: Action

1. Type **PCONSOLE** and press Enter. You should have started the printer console utility, and you should see the screen shown in Figure 23.2.

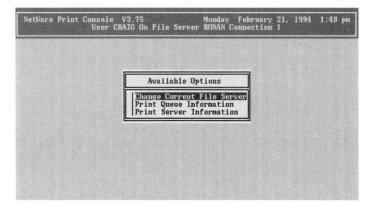

Figure 23.2. *The PCONSOLE screen.*

2. Use the down-arrow key to move the cursor to Print Queue Information and press Enter.

3. Press Ins and you should see the New Print Queue Name: window shown in Figure 23.3.

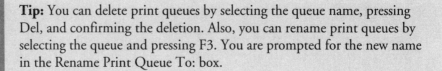

Tip: You can delete print queues by selecting the queue name, pressing Del, and confirming the deletion. Also, you can rename print queues by selecting the queue and pressing F3. You are prompted for the new name in the Rename Print Queue To: box.

4. Type **BALLIOL_Q1** and press Enter. You can use any queue name as long as it contains fewer than 47 characters.

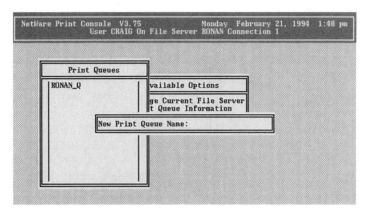

```
NetWare Print Console  V3.75              Monday  February 21, 1994  1:48 pm
                     User CRAIG On File Server RONAN Connection 1
```

```
        Print Queues
    ┌──────────────────┐
    │ RONAN_Q          │ vailable Options
    │                  ├──────────────────────
    │                  │ ge Current File Server
    │                  │ t Queue Information
    │        ┌─────────┴──────────────────────┐
    │        │ New Print Queue Name:          │
    │        └────────────────────────────────┘
    │                  │
    │                  │
    │                  │
    └──────────────────┘
```

Figure 23.3. *The New Print Queue Name screen.*

Note: The system assigns the print queue an eight-digit hexadecimal number and subdirectory in the SYSTEM directory. You can see this number using PCONSOLE|Print Queue Information|Print Queue ID.

5. From the Print Queues window, select BALLIOL_Q1 and press Enter.

6. Highlight Queue Operators and press Enter.

Note: Queue operators can manage print queues and assign queues to printers.

7. Press Ins and you see a Queue Operator Candidates list like the one in Figure 23.4.

Note: By default, the Supervisor is the only queue operator.

8. Using the down-arrow key, move the cursor to JANET and press Enter. This user is added as a queue operator, as shown in Figure 23.5.

9. Press Esc once.

23

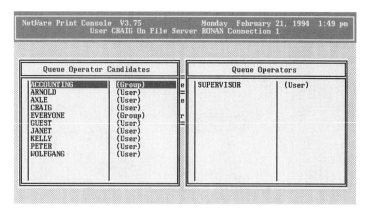

Figure 23.4. *Queue operator candidates.*

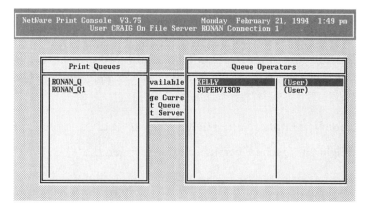

Figure 23.5. *New queue operators.*

10. Highlight Queue Users and press Enter. You can add users to the queue where the group EVERYONE does not belong to the queue.

11. Press Ins and you see a Queue User Candidates list like the one in Figure 23.6.

Note: By default, the group EVERYONE is assigned as a queue user. Queue users can add jobs to the queue.

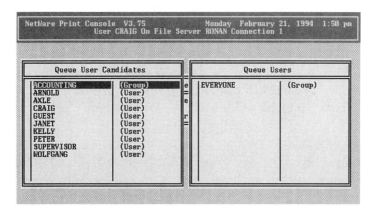

Figure 23.6. *Queue user candidates.*

12. Using the down-arrow key, move the cursor to JANET and press Enter. This user is added as a queue user, as shown in Figure 23.7.

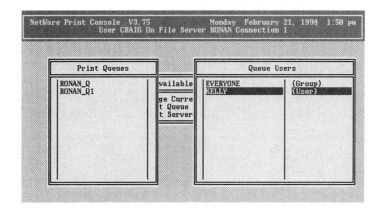

Figure 23.7. *New queue users.*

23

Note: Remember to use F5 to add more than one operator or user.

13. Press Esc repeatedly until you are asked to confirm your exit from PCONSOLE.

Step 3: Review

You can use PCONSOLE to create queues. Network printing revolves around queues. The system sends every print job first to a queue, stored on the file server's hard disk. Using queues, multiple users sending print jobs to the same printer do not have to wait for the printer to become free. Queues also provide a mechanism for assigning priorities to print jobs, which is FIFO—First-In, First-Out.

> **Tip:** You can see queue operators using PCONSOLE|Print Queue Information|print queue|Queue Operators. Similarly, you can see queue users using PCONSOLE|Print Queue Information|print queue|Queue Users.

Task 23.2: Deleting print queue operators and users.

Step 1: Description

You might want to delete operators and users from print queues you created. Use the PCONSOLE menu utility found in your PUBLIC directory.

Step 2: Action

1. Type **PCONSOLE** and press Enter.

2. Use the down-arrow key to move the cursor to Print Queue Information and press Enter.

3. Select BALLIOL_Q1 from the Print Queues list.

4. In the Print Queue Information window, highlight Queue Operators and press Enter.

5. Select JANET and press Delete.

6. Confirm your intention to delete the user JANET.

7. Press Esc once.

8. Highlight Queue Users and press Enter.

9. Highlight JANET and press Delete.

10. Confirm your intention to delete the user JANET.

11. Press Esc repeatedly until you are asked to confirm your exit from PCONSOLE.

Step 3: Review

PCONSOLE is a menu utility that you will use time and time again to set up print queues and queue operators and users. After you have defined queues and their operators and users, you are ready to create print servers.

Creating a Print Server

To create a print server, the Supervisor creates the print server and gives the print server a unique name and password. This process involves two steps: setup and installation. Setup involves creating a print server using PCONSOLE. Installation involves choosing a print server type and activating the right print server files—that is, PSERVER.NLM for a printer on a file server, PSERVER.EXE for a printer on a dedicated workstation, and RPRINTER.EXE for a printer attached to a client's workstation.

Task 23.3: Creating print servers.

Step 1: Description

Even though you can load print servers on different platforms, you configure them all in the same manner. You set up a print server using the PCONSOLE menu utility from the PUBLIC directory.

Step 2: Action

1. Type **PCONSOLE** and press Enter.

2. Use the down-arrow key to move the cursor to Print Server Information and press Enter.

3. Press Ins and you see the New Print Server Name: window shown in Figure 23.8.

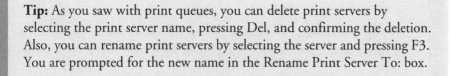

Tip: As you saw with print queues, you can delete print servers by selecting the print server name, pressing Del, and confirming the deletion. Also, you can rename print servers by selecting the server and pressing F3. You are prompted for the new name in the Rename Print Server To: box.

4. Type **BALLIOL_PS** and press Enter. You can use any server name as long as it contains fewer than 47 characters.

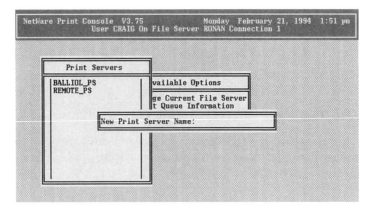

Figure 23.8. *The New Print Server Name window.*

> **Tip:** You might want to use the name of your file server and append _PS or _PS1 to create a print server name. This way, you won't be confused about the relationship between file servers and print servers. Don't name your print server the same name as your file server or you'll really confuse everybody.

5. From the Print Servers window, select BALLIOL_PS and press Enter.

6. Select Change Password and press Enter.

7. Type **NEWPASSWORD** after Enter New Password: and press Enter.

8. Retype **NEWPASSWORD** after Retype New Password: and press Enter. This password is now required to activate the printer.

9. Select Full Name from the Print Server Information window and press Enter.

10. Type **BALLIOL** *Print Server* after Full Name: and press Enter. You should see a screen like the one in Figure 23.9.

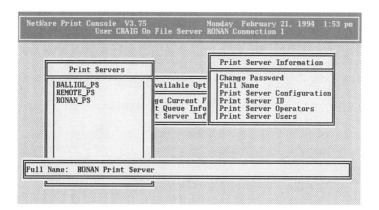

Figure 23.9. *The Full Name window.*

11. Highlight Print Server Operators and press Enter.

 Note: Print server operators can create notify lists for printers, change forms, change queue priorities, and down the print server.

12. Press Ins and you see a Print Server Operator Candidates list like the one in Figure 23.10.

23

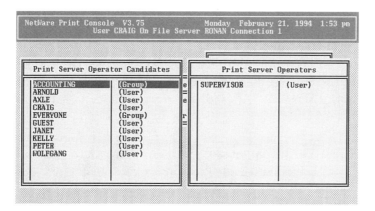

Figure 23.10. *The Print Server Operator Candidates name window.*

Note: By default, the Supervisor is the only print server operator.

13. Using the down-arrow key, move the cursor to JANET and press Enter. This user is added as a print server operator.

14. Press Esc once.

15. Highlight Print Server Users and press Enter.

16. Press Ins and you see a Print Server User Candidates list.

Note: By default, the group EVERYONE is assigned as a print server user. Print server users can send jobs to printers defined to this print server.

17. Using the down-arrow key, move the cursor to JANET and press Enter.

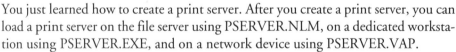

Note: Remember to use F5 to add more than one user.

18. Press Esc repeatedly until you are asked to confirm your exit from PCONSOLE.

Step 3: Review

You just learned how to create a print server. After you create a print server, you can load a print server on the file server using PSERVER.NLM, on a dedicated workstation using PSERVER.EXE, and on a network device using PSERVER.VAP.

Note: To load a print server on a router, the router loads the VAP automatically on initialization from the system directory. Refer to NetWare's manuals for the correct procedure for loading a print server on a router.

> **Tip:** You can see print server operators using PCONSOLE|Print Server Information|print server|Print Server Operators. Similarly, you can see print server users using PCONSOLE|Print Server Information|print server|Print Server Users.

Task 23.4: Deleting print server operators and users.

Step 1: Description

You might want to delete operators and users from print servers you created. Use the PCONSOLE menu utility found in your PUBLIC directory.

Step 2: Action

1. Type **PCONSOLE** and press Enter.

2. Use the down-arrow key to move the cursor to Print Server Information and press Enter.

3. Select BALLIOL_PS from the Print Servers list.

4. In the Print Server Information window, highlight Print Server Operators and press Enter.

5. Select JANET and press Delete.

6. Confirm your intention to delete the user JANET.

7. Press Esc once.

8. Highlight Print Server Users and press Enter.

9. Highlight JANET and press Delete.

10. Confirm your intention to delete the user JANET.

11. Press Esc repeatedly until you are asked to confirm your exit from PCONSOLE.

Step 3: Review

You might find yourself creating many print server operators. When you find that they cannot perform the function, you might want to remove their privileges. In addition, you might want to move users to another print server to improve their response. To delete print server operators and users, use the PCONSOLE menu utility.

After you define a print server, you need to configure printers and other resources.

Defining a Printer

To define printers, the Supervisor defines the printers, assigns names to them, and configures them. Configuring includes specifying port type, interrupt, and serial information.

Task 23.5: Defining printers using PCONSOLE.

Step 1: Description

You define printers using the PCONSOLE menu utility from the PUBLIC directory.

Step 2: Action

1. Type **PCONSOLE** and press Enter.

2. Use the down-arrow key to move the cursor to Print Server Information and press Enter.

3. Select BALLIOL_PS from the Print Servers list.

4. Use the down-arrow key to move the cursor to Print Server Configuration and press Enter.

5. From the Print Server Configuration Menu, select Printer Configuration and press Enter. You can define up to 16 printers for this print server.

6. Select the printer number from the top of the list that is not installed (Not Installed|0) and press Enter. In a new print server, all printers are labeled as Not Installed, and from 0 to 15.

7. Change the Name: if you want, to say HP LaserJet 4, and press Enter.

8. Press Enter at Type:.

9. Select Parallel, LPT1 from the 16 choices and press Enter. The first 7 choices are for printers attached to the print server. They are LPT1, LPT2, LPT3, COM1, COM2, COM3, and COM4. The next 7 are used for workstations acting as print servers. They use the same names but can be either parallel (LPT1, LPT2, or LPT3) or serial (COM1, COM2, COM3, or COM4). The last 2 are Remote Other/Unknown (for intelligent printers) and Defined Elsewhere (for printers serviced by print servers on other file servers).

10. Enter **No** for Use interrupts and press Enter.

11. If for some reason you entered Yes for Use interrupts, enter the interrupt for IRQ: and press Enter. Your screen should now look something like the one in Figure 23.11.

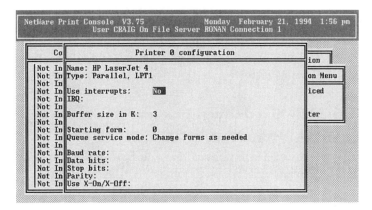

Figure 23.11. *HP LaserJet 4 configuration.*

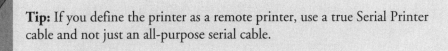

Tip: If you define a remote parallel port, you must choose the correct interrupt (IRQ) for that port. Ordinarily, LPT1 or LPT3 uses IRQ 7, and LPT2 uses IRQ 5. With standard IRQ assignments, COM1 or COM3 uses IRQ 4, and COM2 or COM4 uses IRQ 3. If you define the printer as local to the file server or as a dedicated workstation, you should define the port as No interrupt. Should you experience printing problems, you can always change No interrupt to the correct interrupt.

23

Note: Fill in the baud rate, data bit, stop bits, parity, and handshake (XON/XOFF) for serial printing. These parameters are printer dependent.

Tip: If you define the printer as a remote printer, use a true Serial Printer cable and not just an all-purpose serial cable.

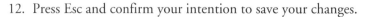

12. Press Esc and confirm your intention to save your changes.

13. Press Esc repeatedly until you are asked to confirm your exit from PCONSOLE.

Step 3: Review

Configuring printers is a complex task. Use PCONSOLE and take your time. You must map users to queues, printers to servers, and queues to printers. You can assign a queue to multiple printers.

Task 23.6: Deleting defined printers.

Step 1: Description

You might want to delete printers that you have defined to print servers. Use the PCONSOLE menu utility found in your PUBLIC directory.

Step 2: Action

1. Type **PCONSOLE** and press Enter.

2. Use the down-arrow key to move the cursor to Print Server Information and press Enter.

3. Select BALLIOL_PS from the Print Servers list.

4. In the Print Server Information window, highlight Print Server Configuration and press Enter.

5. From the Print Server Configuration Menu, select Printer Configuration and press Enter.

6. Select the printer HP LaserJet 4 from the list of Configured Printers and press Delete.

7. Confirm your intention to delete the printer HP LaserJet 4. You should see that the name changed back to Not Installed.

8. Press Esc repeatedly until you are asked to confirm your exit from PCONSOLE.

Step 3: Review

You can use PCONSOLE to delete printers you previously defined to print servers. Next you must assign queues you created earlier to the printer you just configured.

Assigning a Print Queue to a Print Server

To add a print queue to a print server, the Supervisor assigns queues to printers so that print jobs can find their way from specific queues to the correct printers.

Assigning queues to printers is important because it provides a path from the NetWare file server queue to the right printer. Can you guess what happens if you forget to carry out this step? Your users will send print jobs to print queues, and they will wait there forever for service.

Task 23.7: Adding queues to servers.

Step 1: Description

You assign print queues to print servers using the PCONSOLE menu utility from the PUBLIC directory.

Step 2: Action

1. Type **PCONSOLE** and press Enter.

2. Use the down-arrow key to move the cursor to Print Server Information and press Enter.

3. Select BALLIOL_PS from the Print Servers list.

4. Use the down-arrow key to move the cursor to Print Server Configuration and press Enter.

5. From the Print Server Configuration Menu, select Queues Serviced by Printer and press Enter.

6. Select the printer you want to delete from the Defined Printers list and press Enter.

7. Press Ins, select BALLIOL_Q1 from the Available Queues list, and press Enter.

8. Enter **1** for Priority: and press Enter. The priority is 1 to 10, with 1 given the highest priority.

9. Press Esc repeatedly until you are asked to confirm your exit from PCONSOLE.

23

Step 3: Review

After you have assigned a print queue to a printer and a print queue to a server and rebooted the print server, your users can print directly to the queue, and their jobs will end up at the right printer.

Task 23.8: Deleting queues from servers.

Step 1: Description

You remove print queues from print servers using the PCONSOLE menu utility from the PUBLIC directory.

Step 2: Action

1. Type **PCONSOLE** and press Enter.

2. Use the down-arrow key to move the cursor to Print Server Information and press Enter.

3. Select BALLIOL_PS from the Print Servers list.

4. Use the down-arrow key to move the cursor to Print Server Configuration and press Enter.

5. From the Print Server Configuration Menu, select Queues Serviced by Printer and press Enter.

6. Select HP LaserJet 4 from the Defined Printers list and press Enter.

7. Select BALLIOL_Q1 from the Available Queues list and press Delete.

8. Confirm your intention to delete the queue and press Enter.

9. Press Esc repeatedly until you are asked to confirm your exit from PCONSOLE.

Step 3: Review

Again, you used PCONSOLE. This time you used it to delete queues from print servers. After you have assigned a print queue to a printer and configured a print queue for a server, your users can print directly to the queue, and their jobs will end up at the right printer. You can use the PCONSOLE|Change Current File Server option to attach to other file servers to set up print queues and servers on any file server on the network. It is now time to activate the print server. You will activate the print server by typing

LOAD PSERVER BALLIOL_PS at the file server console prompt and then pressing Enter.

PSERVER BALLIOL/BALLIOL_PS at the dedicated workstation's DOS prompt and then pressing Enter.

RPRINTER BALLIOL_PS 18000001 (in which 18000001 is the printer number defined in the print server configuration for this remote printer) at the workstation's DOS prompt and then pressing Enter. Execute the RPRINTER command after you bring up a print server to service this printer.

Note: If you set up a password for the printer, the system prompts you for it.

Tip: You can get the print server number using PCONSOLE|Print Server Information|print server|Print Server ID.

Warning: If you make any changes to the print server, you must reload the PSERVER program to use the print server. You can use PCONSOLE to shut down the print server if you are currently running the print server program.

23

If you followed the directions in this chapter, your users should be merrily printing right now.

Print Server Security

As you already saw, you can assign a password to a print server. Figure 23.12 shows how you assign a password to a print server using PCONSOLE.

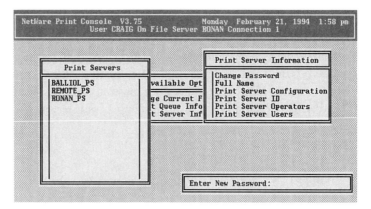

Figure 23.12. *Assigning a print server a password.*

When you start the print server, the system prompts you for the password necessary to establish the connection with the file server. Figure 23.13 shows PSERVER prompting you for a password.

```
                  Novell NetWare Print Server V3.76
                     Server RONAN_PS Initializing

0: Not installed                        4: Not installed



1: Not installed                        5: Not installed
              Password for file server RONAN:

2: Not installed                        6: Not installed



3: Not installed                        7: Not installed
```

Figure 23.13. *PSERVER prompting for a password.*

You assign passwords to print servers to prevent someone from starting a print server masquerading as a legitimate print server. If you don't use a password, any workstation with the PSERVER software can boot itself as another printer. For example, you have a printer in the Human Resources area that prints employee appraisals named HR_PS. Anyone can run PSERVER HR_PS and service print jobs destined for the other printer.

Physical Security for Confidentiality

The simplest control over printers and print servers is to ensure that they are provided the amount of protection warranted by the type of printing they are doing. For instance, in the Human Resources example, you would want to ensure that you adequately protected the printer and print server. You should physically protect access to a printer with confidential information being printed.

Unattended printers and print output represent a large exposure for most organizations. Any person can wait by any printer and get access to sensitive information. Also, many printers are strategically placed next to the office photocopier, increasing the risk of an unauthorized person photocopying confidential information. In fact, such a person might not take a risk by photocopying the document but might instead just walk off with the original because most users would decide that there was a printing problem and would try again. You must educate your users about confidentiality! Given that to think about, that's it for today.

Summary

The purpose of this chapter was to introduce you to printing. Printing is a very important part of your network. Most users will use network printing, and they will be quick to tell you when it doesn't work. It is amazing how fast you'll lose friends when printing doesn't work.

In this chapter, you learned

- ☐ How to create print queues and print servers
- ☐ How to define printers and add queues to printers
- ☐ About printer passwords and physical security

Workshop
Terminology Review

interface—The cables, connectors, and electrical circuits allowing communication between computers and printers.

parallel interface—A printer interface that handles data in parallel fashion, eight bits (a byte) at a time.

parity bit—A way of marking the eighth bit in a data byte, so that 7-bit ASCII characters between 0 and 127 are sent and received correctly. There are three kinds of parity: odd, even, and none.

print queue—A shared storage area on the file server where the system sends every print job before sending it to the print server.

print server—A print server is software that takes jobs from the print queue and sends them to the printer.

serial interface—A printer interface that handles data in serial fashion, one bit at a time.

transmission-on/transmission-off (XON/XOFF)—A type of software handshaking.

Task List

The emphasis of this chapter has been to set up network printing. As a system administrator or Supervisor, you need to learn how to set up print queues and servers, define printers, and assign operators and users for your network. There were many complicated tasks in this chapter:

- ☐ Creating, deleting, and renaming print queues
- ☐ Deleting print queue operators and users
- ☐ Creating, deleting, and renaming print servers
- ☐ Deleting print server operators and users
- ☐ Defining printers
- ☐ Deleting defined printers
- ☐ Adding queues to servers
- ☐ Deleting queues from servers

Q&A

Q I'm still confused. What printing programs do I run where?

A You run the following:

Printer attached to a file server: PSERVER.NLM at the file server console

Printer attached to a print server: PSERVER.EXE at the DOS prompt of the print server

Printer attached to a workstation: RPRINTER.EXE at the DOS prompt of the workstation

Q How many printers can be associated with a file server?

A You can have 5 printers directly attached to the file server and another 11 printers attached to print servers and workstations.

Q I have users fighting over paper trays, what should I do?

A You can buy a printer with multiple trays and software that allows users to select trays. Alternatively, you can set up printers for specific purposes; for example, one printer has letterhead, another has legal-size paper, another has plain bond, and yet another has envelopes.

Q Is the order important when creating queues and print servers?

A Yes, to save yourself trouble, you should create queues and printer servers in the following order:

1. Create a print queue

2. Create a print server

3. Define printers

4. Add queues to printers

24

Maintaining
NetWare
Print Services

In Chapter 23, you learned how to set up print queues and print servers so that your NetWare users could use network printers. For the system to work, you must have everything configured correctly on the user workstation, the file server, the print server, and the printer itself. Getting all the hardware and software on different network nodes to work together is an accomplishment—so congratulations are in order.

Of course, the job doesn't stop there. As users send output to the printers, as queues fill up and empty out, and as printers churn out more paper, things start to happen. Users lose track of their print files; print servers dutifully service queues and then seemingly abandon them; printers jam, run out of paper, and run out of ribbon or toner. Output stops appearing, and users (as we've noted many times) can be a vocal bunch when things don't work right. So they look to you to keep the output coming.

By now, you've learned that maintaining a NetWare LAN is no small amount of work—a fact that is especially true with print services. Printing never seems as though it should take up much time, given the simplicity of the task (after all, it is just printing). But in a high volume printing environment, you might be surprised at how much of your day you spend attending to various printing problems. Fortunately, as you learned in the preceding chapter, you can deputize your users as print queue operators and printer server operators. You then can let them handle the more routine tasks, while you focus on the tougher problems.

To help maintain print services, you and your deputies need tools. You need them to monitor and control the print queues your users send output to. You also need them to manage print servers and their attached printers. NetWare provides you with two main programs to maintain these services: the versatile PCONSOLE menu utility and the PSC command-line utility. In the following sections, you focus on using PCONSOLE to perform the important steps to administer your print services.

Controlling Print Queues

In previous chapters, you learned that users send their output to print queues, depositing print jobs at the end of a queue and then letting NetWare print services worry about getting the jobs to a printer. Users make their deposits in different ways, sometimes through network-aware applications that know about the queues, sometimes by intercepting output from applications that don't know about the network.

Whatever the method, NetWare's print services are responsible for getting the output from the queue to an actual printer. During the first stage of that process, the output moves through a print queue while waiting to be picked up by a print server. You can

control what happens to the output while it waits in the queue, as well as which servers may whisk it away for eventual printing.

NetWare enables you to establish, maintain, and view print queues set up on a file server. As you learned in Chapter 23, the PCONSOLE menu utility is the key facility you use to perform these tasks. PCONSOLE updates NetWare's bindery files with the definitions of your print queues.

Examining Queue Status

If you want to check on what's happening with the print queues established on your file server, the first task you probably want to do is see what their status is. The easiest way to examine status is by using PCONSOLE.

Task 24.1: Examining print queue status.

Step 1: Description
Using PCONSOLE, you can determine the status of any of the print queues established on your file server.

Step 2: Action
1. Type **PCONSOLE** and press Enter. You should see the main menu of the printer console utility.

2. Use the down-arrow key to move the cursor to Print Queue Information and press Enter. You then see a listing of Print Queues defined on the server, similar to that shown in Figure 24.1.

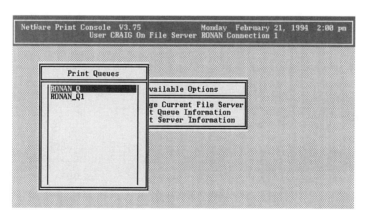

Figure 24.1. *Defined print queues.*

3. Use the cursor keys to select a print queue to examine and then press Enter. The Print Queue Information screen appears, as shown in Figure 24.2.

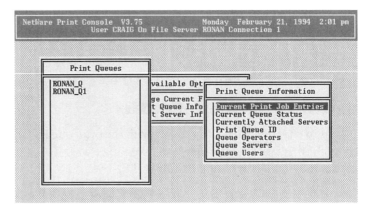

Figure 24.2. *Print Queue Information screen.*

4. Move the cursor down to Current Queue Status and press Enter. The status screen appears, similar to the one shown in Figure 24.3.

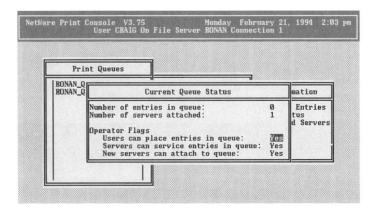

Figure 24.3. *Current Queue Status screen.*

The screen provides a concise summary of what is happening with the queue. Number of entries in queue refers to the number of print jobs that users have placed in the queue and that are now waiting for printing. Number of servers attached informs you how many print servers have attached to the queue and are trying to process print jobs.

5. Any Queue Operator defined for this queue can set the Operator Flags. You can update each of the fields by moving the highlight to the field using the cursor keys and then typing Yes or No to indicate your choice.

To prevent users from adding any new jobs to the queue (for example, if you are going to change or delete the queue), move the cursor to the field Users can place entries in queue and change the contents there to No. Similarly, even though you've defined some print servers as being able to service this queue, you can prevent them from processing any more queue entries. Move the highlight to the field beside Servers can service entries in queue and change it to No. Finally, if you want to prevent any new print servers from attaching to the queue, move the highlight beside New servers can attach to queue and change this field to No.

In later tasks, you will be submitting print queue entries. So if you did try setting these flags to No, set them back to Yes now.

6. Press Esc to return to the Print Queue Information menu.

> **Tip:** If the queue status screen indicates that there are one or more attached servers, you can determine their names by highlighting Currently Attached Servers from the Print Queue Information menu and pressing Enter. Also, if you are interested in the actual object number the print queue is known by on your server, highlight Print Queue ID and press Enter.

24

Step 3: Review

In this task, you learned that you can get an overview of print queue status, control whether entries can be placed at the end of the queue by users, and control whether print servers can service the queue, all within the Current Queue Status screen in PCONSOLE.

Examining and Changing Queue Entries

You also can view details on each print job that resides in the print queue. This capability enables you to see information such as who queued the job and when, how many copies will be printed, whether the job is on hold, and so on. You can also modify fields that affect how and when the job is printed.

Task 24.2: Maintaining print queue entries.

Step 1: Description

Using PCONSOLE facilities, in this task you first submit a file to the print queue and then view its details while it resides in the queue. Finally, you delete the queue entry prior to it being printed.

Step 2: Action

1. From Task 24.1, you should be looking at the Print Queue Information menu for a print queue on your server. If not, return to that screen now. Move the cursor to Current Print Job Entries and press Enter. Assuming that no jobs are to be printed, you should see an empty screen similar to the one shown in Figure 24.4. If you are using an active file server, however, you may see some print queue entries.

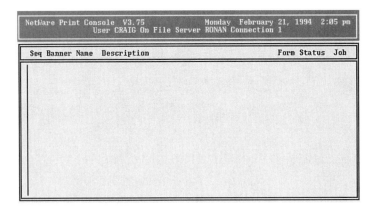

Figure 24.4. *Entries in print queue.*

2. So that you have something to work with, you should first create a print queue entry. As you saw in the preceding chapter, you can submit a file for printing from this menu by pressing Ins. In response, PCONSOLE offers the Select Directory to Print From box. In this box, you can build or enter a directory path in the same fashion as when you used the SESSION and FILER menu utilities. Use these techniques to select a directory containing a simple text file. After you enter or construct a directory path, press Enter and you are offered a menu of available files you can print. See Figure 24.5 for an example.

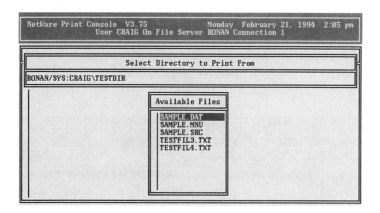

Figure 24.5. *Selecting a file to print.*

3. Highlight a file to print and press Enter. PCONSOLE then asks you to select Print Job Configurations. Choose (PConsole Defaults) and press Enter. You then see the New Print Job to be Submitted screen, which contains many details about the print job (see Figure 24.6).

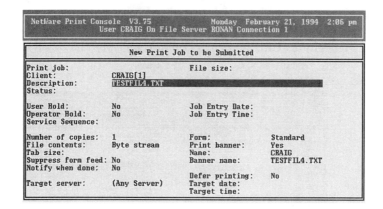

24

Figure 24.6. *Submitting a new print job.*

4. Because you want to examine this job while it is in the queue, you don't actually want this job to print. You can put the print job on hold by moving the cursor to the field beside User Hold, typing **Y**, and then pressing Enter. This step prevents the job from actually being picked up by a print server.

5. To submit the print job, press Esc. Confirm that you want to save changes by pressing Enter. You then see an updated screen indicating that your job has been entered into the print queue with a Status of Held. The Seq field shows in what order jobs are printed. Your screen should look like the one shown in Figure 24.7.

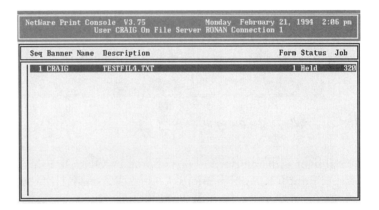

Figure 24.7. *Updated listing of queue entries.*

6. To view the details of an individual queue entry, use the cursor keys to highlight the entry and press Enter. The Print Queue Entry Information screen appears, as shown in Figure 24.8.

```
NetWare Print Console  V3.75            Monday  February 21, 1994  2:07 pm
               User CRAIG On File Server RONAN Connection 1

                      Print Queue Entry Information

Print job:          320             File size:       42
Client:             CRAIG[1]
Description:        TESTFIL4.TXT
Status:             User Hold On Job

User Hold:          Yes             Job Entry Date:  February 21, 1994
Operator Hold:      No              Job Entry Time:  2:06:30 pm
Service Sequence:   1

Number of copies:   1               Form:            Standard
File contents:      Byte stream     Print banner:    Yes
Tab size:                           Name:            CRAIG
Suppress form feed: No              Banner name:     TESTFIL4.TXT
Notify when done:   No
                                    Defer printing:  No
Target server:      (Any Server)    Target date:
                                    Target time:
```

Figure 24.8. *Print Queue Entry Information screen.*

Review the information on the screen. Most entries are self-explanatory, but some are noteworthy:

☐ The Status field shows whether the entry is simply waiting for service or is being held. If the entry is being serviced, the name of the print server doing the work is shown.

☐ Holds may be placed on the job by either the user or a Queue Operator. Operator holds cannot be removed by the user.

☐ Number of copies can be changed if additional copies are required.

☐ The server can send the user a message when the job is actually printed if you set Notify when done to Yes.

☐ Because the queue may be serviced by more than one print server, you might want to select which Target Server actually prints the entry. For example, you might want to select the server with a printer that is physically closest to you. Selecting this field gives you a menu of possible servers.

☐ Banners can be printed before the actual output, to help distinguish one user's output from another. If the Print banner field is set to Yes, you also can set banner text in the adjacent fields.

☐ If you expect your output to take a great deal of time to print, you can set Defer printing to print at a later time, say, the middle of the night. Setting this field to Yes enables you to enter a date and time, after which the entry is eligible for printing.

7. To accept the changes you made, press Esc. You return to the listing of print queue entries.

8. To delete a queue entry, use the cursor keys to highlight the entry and then press Delete. PCONSOLE asks you to confirm that you want to delete the queue entry. Confirm that you do by highlighting Yes and pressing Enter. You return to the listing of print queue entries, which no longer includes the entry you just deleted.

9. Return to the main PCONSOLE menu by pressing Esc three times.

Step 3: Review

The PCONSOLE utility gives you complete control over print queue entries, enabling you to set many parameters that affect how a particular entry is printed.

24

Controlling Print Servers

While users fill up your file server's print queues, print servers are busy trying to empty them out again. Using print queue configuration screens with PCONSOLE, you specify which print servers are allowed to service a queue. Then, using print server configuration screens, you attach print servers to the queues, and away your printing goes (assuming, of course, that you configured everything correctly for the print server).

But print servers want attention too—so PCONSOLE provides menu options that enable you to manage how print servers interact with print queues, as well as control what printers on the print server are up to. You see details on how to monitor and control print servers in the following sections.

Print Server Startup Configuration

Chapter 23 gave you details on setting up the initial configuration for a print server. Using the Print Server Configuration menu from within the Print Server Information section of PCONSOLE, you created a new print server name, defined a printer for the server, and assigned the printer to a print queue.

This process created a print server definition, which had a specific name and which you protected with a password. Then you started up an actual print server, either by loading the PSERVER NLM on your file server or by running print server software on a workstation. When you started the print server, you told it what name it should be known by, which corresponded to the name of the print server definition you created. You also had to supply a password, which allowed the print server to read the definition file and configure itself accordingly. And then the printing began.

Now that everything is up and running nicely, it's time to stir the pot a bit, with some further considerations about setting up print servers.

Servicing Print Queues on Other File Servers

You may remember that a NetWare print server can service print queues from up to eight different file servers. That's true, but getting everything to work properly can be tricky. It involves defining a regular print server, as usual, as well as defining a surrogate print server. The best way to learn how to do it is by way of example.

Assume that you have two file servers: BALLIOL and RONAN. BALLIOL runs the PSERVER NLM to service its print queues using a printer attached to BALLIOL. The

print server defined on BALLIOL to service the queues is called BALLIOL_PS. (See why we suggested adding "_PS" to differentiate the print server name from the file server name?) You want the printer attached to BALLIOL to output files that were sent to a print queue on RONAN. How do you do it?

The first thing to remember is that RONAN and BALLIOL have their own binderies and, therefore, their own set of print server definitions. So you must create two separate print server definitions, one on each file server. But they need to have the same name on both file servers.

You first log on to BALLIOL as Supervisor and use PCONSOLE to define BALLIOL_PS on the BALLIOL file server, as you learned in Chapter 23. Your definition should include printer hardware definition details for the attached printer. This is what we've referred to as the *real* print server.

On RONAN, you also log on as Supervisor and also use PCONSOLE to define a print server, which must be named BALLIOL_PS. This server is the surrogate print server. You can configure it just as if it were a local print server, including assigning which of the print queues on RONAN you can service. You can also give it a password, which may be the same as the one for the real BALLIOL_PS or a different one if you want. There is one difference, however: when you're configuring a printer for the file server, you select Defined Elsewhere for the Type field. This selection tells NetWare that the definition for the printer is on a different file server. You've now done everything you need to do on RONAN.

Back on BALLIOL, you have to do one more step. After you select BALLIOL_PS, under the Print Server Configuration menu, you select File Servers To Be Serviced. You then see a menu with your current file server (BALLIOL) listed. Press the Ins key to get a list of other available file servers, which includes RONAN. You select RONAN to include it in the list of file servers to be serviced by BALLIOL_PS. The real print server on BALLIOL now knows about the surrogate print server on RONAN.

When you start the PSERVER NLM on BALLIOL, it asks you for the BALLIOL_PS password as usual. The password you enter is the one you defined for the real BALLIOL_PS, that is, the one on BALLIOL. This permits it to read the print server definition contained in BALLIOL's bindery files. It then finds out that another BALLIOL_PS is on the RONAN file server—the surrogate print server. If you set the BALLIOL_PS print server password the same on both RONAN and BALLIOL, the print server starts servicing queues. If the password is different, you are asked to enter the other password.

24

That's all there is to it. While this process may seem complicated, if you follow these steps for your own environment, everything should work fine. The process even makes sense (but only after it all starts working).

Setting a Notify List

NetWare's print services include a handy notification feature. When a printer experiences an error, the print server sends a message to everyone on the notification list, stating which printer needs attention. If that person is logged on, he or she quickly becomes aware of the problem (and hopefully even goes to fix it).

Setting up a notify list is fairly straightforward, as you see in Task 24.3.

Task 24.3: Establishing a notify list.

Step 1: Description

In this task, you use PCONSOLE to set up a notify list for each printer on a print server. Each person on the notify list receives a message if the printer needs attention.

Step 2: Action

1. From PCONSOLE's Available Options menu, select Print Server Information and then the name of the print server. The Print Server Information menu appears.

2. Highlight and select Print Server Configuration. Then select Notify List for Printer. You then are given a choice of Defined Printers, as shown in Figure 24.9.

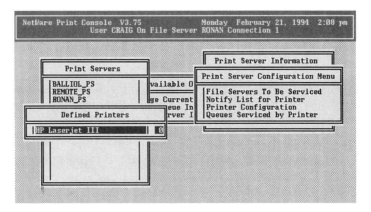

Figure 24.9. *Selecting a printer for notification.*

3. Use the cursor keys to highlight the printer for which you want notification and press Enter. You then see an empty list of notifications.

4. To add a notification name, press the Ins key. You then see a Notify Candidates list, as shown in Figure 24.10.

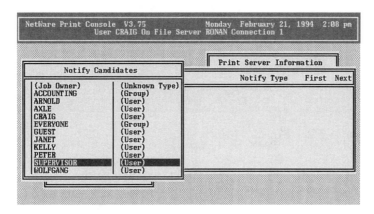

Figure 24.10. *Candidates for notification.*

A few items are worth noting in this list:

☐ The list of candidates includes both users and groups. So you can notify one person or an entire group of people with only one selection.

☐ The list also contains a special entry: (Job Owner). This person queued the job in the first place. The job owners are ideal candidates for notification, given their vested interest in seeing that the print function actually happens.

☐ The list of candidates are for the local file server only, not those on other file servers that also are serviced by this print server. To notify users on that file server, you must update the notification list for the surrogate print server.

5. Select the candidates you want to notify, either by highlighting individual entries or by using the F5 key to select a number of entries, and press Enter. The Notify Intervals menu appears, as shown in Figure 24.11.

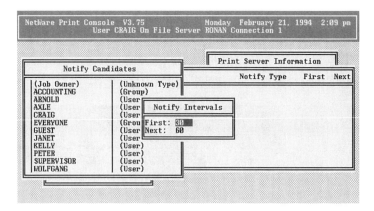

Figure 24.11. *Notify Intervals menu.*

6. By default, notification is sent 30 seconds after the problem is detected and every 60 seconds thereafter until it is corrected. You can change these settings if you want. To accept the intervals, press Esc and then confirm that you want to Save Changes. The updated notification list then appears.

7. Press Esc repeatedly until you return to the Print Server Information menu.

Step 3: Review

To notify a list of people when a printer problem is detected, use the PCONSOLE facility to create a notification list for each printer, as you learned in this task.

Print Server Status and Control

The process you've gone through so far has mainly used the Print Server Configuration menu to create a definition for a print server. This definition is read when a print server is started, either using PSERVER NLM on the file server or using PSERVER on a workstation. As such, the definition you created is really a startup configuration.

But you also can change how the print server operates after it has started. This alternative uses PCONSOLE's Print Server Status/Control option, which appears for any print server that is actually running. The Status/Control options can be confusing because they are similar to the Configuration menu, and both menus can be found on the Print Server Information box. The difference is that one (Configuration) creates a definition used when the print server starts, whereas the other (Status/Control) monitors and changes the way the server operates while it is running.

Let's look at some of the things you can do to manage a print server that's already running. First, you should get to the appropriate menu. From PCONSOLE's main

menu, select Print Server Information; then highlight and select the name of a print server. The Print Server Information menu then appears. Move the cursor down to Print Server Status/Control and select this option by pressing Enter. The following sections assume you have made these selections.

Getting Print Server Information

The Server Info menu selection provides a brief summary of print server status. Highlighting and selecting this option produces the Print Server Info/Status screen similar to the one shown in Figure 24.12.

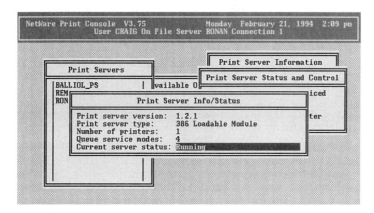

Figure 24.12. *Server information.*

In addition to the version number and server type, you see how many printers are attached to the server. You also see what the current Queue service mode is, which describes how the print server reacts to requests for form changes.

Finally, the Current server status shows whether the print server is running, down, or about to go down after completing the current jobs. Pressing Enter enables you to select from these three options. Choosing Down causes the print server program to end, wherever it is running.

File Servers Being Serviced

Choosing the File Servers Being Serviced menu option initiates a dialogue that is similar to the one you saw when configuring the server. The difference is that the selections show what is actually running, not what is configured to run when the print server starts. After you select this menu item, you see a screen similar to the one shown in Figure 24.13.

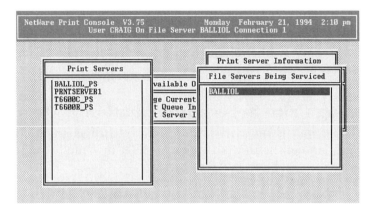

Figure 24.13. *File Servers Being Serviced screen.*

The file server on which you are running always appears. In addition, if you configured the print server to service other file servers, their names also should be listed.

You can delete a file server by pressing Delete. Pressing Delete stops the print server from servicing the file server and its print queues. You confirm deletion by highlighting Yes and pressing Enter in the normal fashion.

You use this same function to establish a connection between an active print server and a file server to be serviced. Pressing Ins opens a list of available file servers. If a print server of the same name is defined on the target file server, then highlighting a file server name and pressing Enter brings up a request for a password, as shown in Figure 24.14. The password you enter is for the print server definition on the target file server (that is, the surrogate file server you learned about earlier).

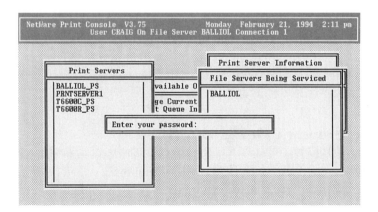

Figure 24.14. *Establishing a print server connection with another file server.*

Current Notify List

Selecting Notify List for Printer opens a menu that enables you to select from the currently defined printers. Choosing one printer produces the current notify list, just as it did under the configuration options. See Figure 24.15 for a sample.

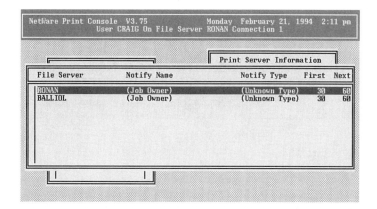

Figure 24.15. *Current notify list.*

The current list is based on the local print server definition, as well as notify lists set up on other file servers being serviced. That's why the list contains a File Server column in addition to the Notify Name and interval details. Using the same key sequences as you used for Task 24.3, you can add candidates for notification. However, you can select only from users and groups defined on the local file server. Notification for other file servers being serviced must be done on the surrogate print server's menu options.

You also can delete notification entries by highlighting the entry and pressing Delete. PCONSOLE asks you to confirm deletion by selecting Yes. You can delete any notification entries, even those for other file servers.

Queues Being Serviced

The Queues Being Serviced by Printer option provides details on the queues actually being serviced by the print server. After you select this option, you first are asked to pick which printer you want to review. You then get a list of queues being serviced for both the local file server, plus for any other file servers being serviced. Figure 24.16 provides a sample of what the screen looks like.

As for the notification lists described earlier, the list of queues is based on the local print server definition, as well as configurations set up on other file servers being serviced.

Note once again that the list contains a File Server column, in addition to the Queue and priority details. Using the same key sequences as you learned in Task 23.7, you can add new queues to be serviced. However, you can select only from print queues that are defined on the local file server. To link to print queues on other file servers being serviced, you must use the surrogate print server's menu options.

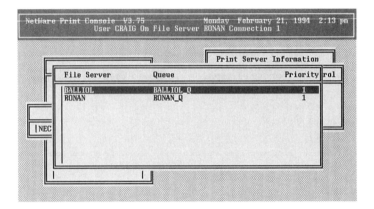

Figure 24.16. *Queues being served.*

You also can delete links to print queues simply by highlighting the entry and pressing Delete. PCONSOLE asks you to confirm deletion by selecting Yes. You can delete links to any print queues, even those on other file servers.

Printer Status and Control

The Printer Status menu option enables you to select a printer, then view its status, and control its operations. Because you haven't used these functions yet, let's do a task to help discover what's available.

Task 24.4: Controlling printers.

Step 1: Description
In this task, you use PCONSOLE facilities to control the operations of individual printers on the print servers.

Step 2: Action
1. You should be at the Print Server Status and Control menu. Select Printer Status to receive a list of printers configured for the print server.

2. Select one printer. A Status screen similar to the one shown in Figure 24.17 appears. If the printer actually is producing output, the details provided include the file server and queue where the job originated, job details, and percentage complete. If no printing is occurring, the Status field indicates `Waiting for Job`.

```
NetWare Print Console  V3.75          Monday  February 21, 1994  2:13 pm
                User CRAIG On File Server RONAN Connection 1

                        Status of NEC P2200

Status:              Waiting for job                    Printer Control

Service mode:        Change forms as needed
Mounted form:        1

File server:
Queue:
Job number:
Description:
Form:

Copies requested:                      Finished:
Size of 1 copy:                        Finished:
Percent completed:
```

Figure 24.17. *Printer Status screen.*

3. The highlight is on the Printer Control option. Press Enter to see a list of options like the ones shown in Figure 24.18.

```
NetWare Print Console  V3.75          Monday  February 21, 1994  2:13 pm
                User CRAIG On File Server RONAN Connection 1

                        Status of NEC P2200

Status:              Waiting for job                    Printer Control

Service mode:        Change forms as needed
Mounted form:        1                              Abort print job
                                                   Form Feed
File server:                                       Mark top of form
Queue:                                             Pause printer
Job number:                                        Rewind printer
Description:                                        Start printer
Form:                                              Stop printer

Copies requested:                      Finished:
Size of 1 copy:                        Finished:
Percent completed:
```

Figure 24.18. *Printer control selections.*

The available options include

☐ *Abort print job.* Ends the current print job and deletes it from the queue.

☐ *Form Feed.* Causes the printer to eject one page.

☐ *Mark top of form.* Places a row of asterisks across the page (used to align pages).

☐ *Pause printer.* Places the current job on hold until a start command is received.

☐ *Rewind printer.* Restarts printing in the middle of a job after a paper jam.

☐ *Start printer.* Starts printing after a Stop or Pause.

☐ *Stop printer.* Stops printing and returns the current job to the print queue.

4. Press Esc to leave the Printer Control selections. Then move the cursor down beside Service mode and press Enter. You then see the four service modes offered to deal with form changes.

5. Press Esc repeatedly until you are offered the chance to leave PCONSOLE. Confirm leaving by selecting Yes.

Step 3: Review

In this task, you learned that you can use PCONSOLE to remotely control printers that are attached to your print servers.

The PSC Command

During the previous two chapters, you focused on using the PCONSOLE menu utility to configure and maintain print services. PCONSOLE is the main tool to use for almost everything to do with setting up printing. You even can submit print jobs with it.

You also can use the command-line utility PSC to perform some of these tasks, however. Although not as user friendly as PCONSOLE, PSC is more direct and so can be faster to use.

The syntax of the PSC command is as follows:

```
PSC PS=print_server P=printer_number Flags
```

Most of the flags you can use are recognizable from the Printer Control options within PCONSOLE. They include `CancelDown`, `FormFeed`, `PAUse`, `STARt`, `ABort`, and `STOp`, as well as others. In addition, you can specify that a remote printer becomes `PRIvate` so it can't be used by others, or returned to duty with the `SHared` flag.

To determine the status of printers on a print server, type the following command at the DOS prompt:

```
PSC PS=[your print server name] STAT
```

Printing Configurations

The way you set up your printers, print servers, and print queues depends on your business printing needs and the number and types of printers. Many issues come into play, such as your users' needs for print quality, volume, and speed, as well as how far they are willing to walk.

Your budget, of course, is the biggest factor in the number and kind of printers you get. But given a fixed selection of printers, the flexibility of NetWare's print services can help you set up the best configuration to get the type of printers you have near the users who want them.

One Printer/One Queue

The most common way to set up printing is to create a print queue for each network printer. This one-to-one correspondence is usually the easiest configuration for users to understand. That way, they can direct output to a queue and know it will appear on a certain printer. Knowing exactly which printer is which enables them to select the one they need, based on quality (for example, laser versus dot-matrix) or location (for example, the printer that is the shortest walk or the one that enables the users to visit with their friends down the hall).

One Printer Serving Multiple Queues

With NetWare, setting up one printer on a print server and having it empty out multiple queues is easy. There are different reasons for setting up printing this way. For example,

☐ One specialized (and expensive) device may be connected to a print server that is servicing queues on many file servers. A large office might purchase a color printer and make it available to people using file servers on different floors.

☐ Multiple queues with one printer can implement a priority system. The printer is configured to print jobs coming from one queue prior to another so that output sent to that queue prints first. Individual users may be asked to use the high-priority queue only when necessary or might be restricted from accessing it at all.

☐ A printer may simply be assigned to fill in for another while maintenance or repairs are being performed. Rather than having users change their print configurations, having another printer doing its regular work temporarily and filling in for its ailing colleague is easier. (Of course, you should probably post a note around the old printer, telling the users where their output has gone.)

Whenever the printer starts to get overloaded, it may be time to get another one. Then creating new printer definitions and print servers and reassigning queues to the new printer are easy tasks. Your users don't even have to change their print configurations.

Multiple Printers Serving One Queue

You can assign a number of printers, either on one print server or on many, to empty out one single print queue. A typical application for this setup is high-volume printing environments like those found in a typing pool. In these environments, users probably don't care which printer actually produces the output, as long as they don't have to wait too long. So three or four printers may all be located right beside each other, all processing requests that were sent to one queue. The users simply look in the output trays for each printer to find their output.

If volumes continue to increase, you can add more printers to service the queue. At some point, however, you might consider separating users into different queues, simply to cut down on the number of printers they have to look at for their output.

Note: If you're a fan of symmetrical relations, you might consider having multiple printers serve multiple queues. It's possible, but it's not the greatest idea. Finding your output can start to become difficult. Unless you watch your job's progress each step of the way, you might not know where your output was actually printed.

Troubleshooting Printing Problems

As you can probably imagine, many things can go wrong with printing. Because printing is made up of so many separate components—the users' application software and workstation operating system, print queues definitions and files, print server definitions, print servers themselves, and their printers—it's almost a wonder that any of this process works. But it does, and usually works fairly well, once you are over the hump of getting things going in the first place.

The best approach to solving printing problems is being well informed and systematic. First, reread the chapters on printing and consult any other documentation you can get to make sure that you have a clear idea of how printing is supposed to work. Network printing can be an enigma, especially for a new administrator. Your queues and servers may be set up the way you think they should be, but maybe that's not the way NetWare needs them to be. Check and double-check.

Then approach the problems one step at a time. Follow the printing process from the beginning, that is, the creation of a print job on a user's workstation. Use PCONSOLE facilities to follow the job, first onto a queue, then to a print server, and finally to a printer. Pinpoint where the difficulty is and concentrate your efforts there.

If your problem appears to be hardware-related, it might be something as simple as cables that aren't hooked up properly. Or it might be in the more mysterious area of conflicting interrupts and input/output addresses. Make sure you can get a file server or workstation talking to a printer all on its own before you even try to configure NetWare print options. One way to get them talking, even on a NetWare file server, is by trying to use the Print Screen facility under DOS. If you can't get a printer to work this way, you need to fix this problem before trying to print with NetWare.

24

You also should refer to the Troubleshooting section of NetWare's Print Server manual. It describes a number of common network printing problems and gives suggestions to resolve them.

Summary

In this chapter, you focused on using the PCONSOLE menu utility for tasks required to

- ☐ Monitor your NetWare printing services

- ☐ Manage entries in print queues

- ☐ Reconfigure print servers and printers

You also received some suggestions on how to configure your printers to help improve throughput and work flows.

Workshop
Task List

The tasks you completed in this chapter involved managing print queues entries, and controlling print queues and servers on-the-fly. You practiced the following:

- ☐ Examining print queue status

- ☐ Managing print queue entries

- ☐ Setting who is notified when a printer needs attention

- ☐ Controlling the operation of individual printers

Q&A

Q If I change the configuration of a print server, does it take effect immediately?

A If you change items on the Print Server Configuration menu, they won't take effect until the server is restarted. Or, if you only make Status/Control changes, they will be lost when you restart the server. So to make a permanent change to the print server that takes effect immediately, you must update both the configuration and the current status.

Q What happens if I send printed output to a queue that doesn't have any print servers servicing to it?

A Your output is not lost. The print job remains in the queue, either until a print server picks it up and prints it, or until you (or a print queue operator) delete it.

Q Do I have to use any special types of printers with NetWare?

A You can use any of the commonly available printers that attach to today's personal computers. The main consideration is that you have the right kind of interface between the printer and the computer that is running as a print server. The most common type of interface is a parallel output cable, but serial output can also be used.

After you connect the printer and establish the right configuration, your users can start sending print output to the printers via NetWare. It is normally up to the workstation software to create a file that is recognized by the printer. The file created may include special characters that serve as instructions to a particular type of printer. NetWare then takes care of getting the file to the printer, without regard to its content. You can even use Postscript printers with NetWare.

24

25

Security Monitoring and Audit Trails

You might feel your organization is immune to security threats. At first blush, many organizations think their networks don't call for a great deal of protection. They respond that they don't process anything confidential or that they trust their employees. The network has only electronic mail and word processing. What happens if you look at the electronic mail or word processing documents. First, look at the mail and you see mail from the president of your company to the vice-president of research and development about the latest product, or to the vice-president of sales about the planned marketing campaign for the launch of your new product. These issues are sensitive. You can be assured that the president and the vice-presidents believe that using electronic mail is at least as secure as using the telephone.

Of course, you trust your employees. You know everybody on your network. Your organization does pre-employment reference checks on all employees. But does your organization do reference checks on maintenance staff or cleaning staff? It is not likely that they do. Besides, the number one threat to your organization is not from dishonest employees but from accidents caused by poorly trained or careless users. These users might erase files, rename files, overwrite files, trip on cabling, and spill coffee on their keyboards. They may install software on their machines without checking for viruses or reading the manual. Even though these acts are not intentional, they can cause you grief and money.

Regardless of the effectiveness of your pre-employment screening, you may end up with disgruntled or malicious employees who try to get you. Banks are careful in their hiring, yet they still get burned by employee theft. The temptation is just too great for some people to resist. These employees intentionally erase files, change or falsify data, or send messages on behalf of other employees. If you terminate these employees, make sure to escort them immediately off the premises and change all the access codes to which they were privy. You should work with Human Resources to ensure that you are informed about all terminations, transfers, and long-term leaves of absence.

The best protection against accidental errors or intentional acts is to segregate the areas on the file server where users have write or erase privileges. Backup also is an important control, which was covered in Chapter 22.

NetWare, like many operating systems, is a generalized product providing great flexibility to its purchasers. This flexibility is, however, what provides the system administrator with the greatest challenge. This chapter deals with some of the steps you can take to ensure that your system is both secure and available to legitimate users.

Scanning for Security Problems

A step you can take to ensure that your system is secure is to scan for problems periodically. In Chapter 21, you learned about scanning for viruses. You also can scan for security problems. Scanning involves reading the bindery and reporting on any potential security exposures. The SECURITY command-line utility is a scanning program provided with NetWare.

SECURITY

SECURITY is a DOS utility run from SYS:SYSTEM at a workstation by the Supervisor. You should leave SECURITY in this directory to prevent your users from running it to determine security holes you did not find. For instance, they might find out a particular account does not require a password. Upon using the account, they might find that the account has write access to the payroll file.

Note: Because SECURITY uses the bindery, you must be the Supervisor or Supervisor-equivalent to use it.

The SECURITY utility takes a single option, /C, which stands for continuous. Using continuous enables you to output the results of the security scan without pause. On a normal system, doing so means that a lot of data flies by on your screen. So you may choose not to use the continuous prompt.

Tip: You can stop scrolling by pressing Ctrl-S.

More likely, you may not want to view the results of the scan on your workstation's screen. Instead, you might want to direct the output of the scan to a file so that you can analyze or print it. You can send the scan to the file simply by typing the following:

```
SECURITY > SECURITY.DAT
```

Then press Enter.

SECURITY.DAT is any name that you choose for the output file. Remember that the file will be, and should be, found in the SYS:SYSTEM directory.

As you have already learned, you can print a copy of the security report by typing the following and then pressing Enter:

```
NPRINT SECURITY.DAT
```

Note: As well, you might have to specify a print queue.

The SECURITY command-line utility checks the bindery for possible security exposures. The utility is strictly a *detective* control. It is not a *corrective* control; that is, it does not correct any security exposures it finds. Correcting these exposures is up to you after you weigh the pros and cons of any corrective action.

SECURITY reports on security problems in the following categories:

- ☐ No password assigned
- ☐ Insecure passwords
- ☐ Accounts without FULL NAME specified
- ☐ Supervisor-equivalence
- ☐ Root directory privileges
- ☐ Login scripts
- ☐ Excessive rights

Sample output from the SECURITY utility is shown in Figure 25.1.

```
User JANET
    Groups managed: 2
    No Full Name specified


User PETER
    Is security equivalent to user SUPERVISOR
    No Full Name specified


User ARNOLD
    Is security equivalent to user SUPERVISOR
    Account has not been used for more than 3 weeks
        Last Login: Tuesday  January 25, 1994  11:20 pm
    No Full Name specified


Print Server RONAN_PS (Full Name: RONAN Print Server)
    Does not require a password


-- More --
```

Figure 25.1. *SECURITY output.*

In the following sections, you examine the possible network security deficiencies for which SECURITY scans.

Objects with No Password Assigned

If you find objects without a password assigned, you have just found a major risk to your network. Anyone can log in and impersonate this object. Depending on the privileges of the object, not having a password may or may not be a problem. The object might be a user account or printer. When NetWare installs, Guest is created without a password. Using Guest and SYSCON, anyone can obtain a list of all users on the file server (invaluable information to a potential uninvited guest). Using FILER, someone can peruse the entire directory structure. Even without File Scan rights, you can see the directory and subdirectory names (unless they are hidden). An intruder can deduce a great deal about your organization just by looking at these things.

In Chapter 9, you learned how to force users to enter a password.

Objects with Insecure Passwords

Insecure passwords are ones that the SECURITY utility thinks are easy for someone to guess, such as a password equal to the username. SECURITY also checks account restrictions and reports on the following:

- ☐ Users with passwords fewer than five characters

- ☐ Users not required to change their passwords at least every 60 days

- ☐ Users with an unlimited number of logins after password expiration

- ☐ Users not required to use unique passwords when they change their passwords

Review Chapter 9 if you forget how to set password restrictions.

Objects with Security-Equivalence to Supervisor

Supervisor-equivalence is a double-edged sword. It is necessary to have someone able to perform Supervisor functions, but having too many people with Supervisor-equivalence is a serious exposure. As previously mentioned, it is not even recommended that you use the Supervisor account for routine work. The Supervisor or

system administrator should have an account for daily work. Novell recommends that the Supervisor account should be used only for performing supervisory tasks.

The problem with having Supervisor-equivalents is as follows. Somehow a cracker finds out the name of a Supervisor-equivalent. Then this person inserts a *Trojan Horse* onto the Supervisor-equivalent's workstation—that is, replaces a legitimate executable with a modified one. When the user executes the Trojan Horse, everything appears normal to the user with Supervisor-equivalence, but the program actually is doing something like changing a user's password. This capability is difficult to detect. A similar exposure arises when you have an unattended workstation logged in by the Supervisor-equivalent. The moral is to be uncommonly wary of creating Supervisor-equivalent accounts.

Tip: One last word on Trojan Horses: Preventing the insertion of Trojan Horses in your workstation is difficult. You can write several easy ones using the ANSI.SYS program, the LOGOUT program, or login scripts. You should use Read Only, Delete Inhibit, and Rename Inhibit attributes to prevent the substitution of programs and files by unauthorized persons, or you should use a third-party product to protect the workstation.

In Chapter 8, you learned how to remove Supervisor-equivalence from a user.

Objects with Rights at the Volume Level

SECURITY reports any objects with trustee rights at the NetWare volume (root) level. In Chapter 15, you learned that rights flow down to the entire volume if rights are granted at the root level, unless they are revoked at a lower level (Chapter 16). Review the concept of rights in these chapters.

You should not grant the Access Control right at the root level because the person given this right can grant himself or herself all rights in any subdirectory on the volume.

Objects Without a Login Script

SECURITY reports on every user without a login script. Not having a login script might not seem like an exposure to you until you work through the logic.

The system stores user login scripts in the user's mail subdirectories in SYS:MAIL. The group EVERYONE has Write and Create rights to SYS:MAIL to deliver mail, which enables EVERYONE (all users) to create a file in another user's mail subdirectory. If a user does not have a login script, an intruder or cracker can create a login script file and dump it in that user's mail subdirectory. The next time the user logs in, the intruder's login script executes. For that reason, each user should have a login script.

In Chapter 11, you learned how to create and use login scripts.

Objects with Excessive Rights in Certain Directories

SECURITY checks system directories to ensure that they do not have more rights than they should. Users should have the following rights in these directories:

```
SYS:SYSTEM      [         ]
SYS:PUBLIC      [ R     F ]
SYS:LOGIN       [ R     F ]
SYS:MAIL        [   WC    ]
```

SECURITY also reports on users who have rights greater than Create and Write in SYS:MAIL subdirectories other than their own. Again, you learned about rights in Chapters 15 and 16.

You should run the SECURITY utility weekly on each server where you have responsibility. Take seriously each suggestion that the utility makes. Remember that the security of any system, like chains, is only as strong as its weakest link.

Other Automated Reviews

As you learned in Chapter 7, the bindery is key to the operation of NetWare. However, Novell provides only SYSCON and PCONSOLE for editing the bindery. It does not provide programs for looking at the bindery. You might want to get a product such as BindView Plus to look at bindery objects.

Collecting Data

You may want to use some command-line utilities frequently to collect security data. You can automate their use. Table 25.1 shows some reports you can run.

For the best results, you should run these reports from the ROOT directory as Supervisor or Supervisor-equivalent.

Table 25.1. Sample security reports.

Command	Description
FLAG *.DOC SUB > SECURE1.TXT	Lists the attributes of all files with the .DOC extension in the current directory and its subdirectories. The output is directed to a file for review.
FLAG *.EXE SUB > SECURE2.TXT	Lists the attributes of all files with the .EXE extension in the current directory and its subdirectories. The output is directed to a file for review.
FLAGDIR > SECURE3.TXT	Lists the attributes of the current directory. The output is directed to a file for review.
FLAGDIR * > SECURE4.TXT	Lists the attributes of all subdirectories for the current directory. The output is directed to a file for review.
TLIST . USERS > SECURE5.TXT	Lists the user trustees of the current directory. The output is directed to a file for review.
TLIST F: > SECURE6.TXT	Lists all trustees of the directory where F: points. The output is directed to a file for review.
LISTDIR /S > SECURE7.TXT	Lists the subdirectory structure for the current directory. The output is directed to a file for review.
LISTDIR /E > SECURE8.TXT	Lists effective rights in subdirectories in the current directory. The output is directed to a file for review.
LISTDIR /R > SECURE9.TXT	Lists the maximum rights mask in subdirectories in the current directory. The output is directed to a file for review.
NDIR /RIGHTS > SECURE10.TXT	Lists rights and attributes for all directories and files. The output is directed to a file for review.

Now that you have looked at the security for various files and directories, here are some recommendations in the following sections.

Directories

You should protect the system directories SYSTEM, MAIL, LOGIN, and PUBLIC. These directories should have Delete Inhibit and Rename Inhibit attributes.

Executable Files

You know that executable DOS files end in either .COM or .EXE extensions. Because these programs are likely candidates for viruses or Trojan Horses, you should protect them first. You should mark executables as Shareable to avoid conflicts when two users try to run the program at the same time.

Also, you should mark most executables to Read Only to prevent the files from being changed or deleted. Some programs are self-modifying and cannot be marked Read Only; however, none of NetWare's programs are self-modifying.

Where you can, set executables to Execute Only. You cannot use Execute Only if the program contains overlays or uses configuration information from its file.

Program-Related Files

Many files on your system are not programs but are necessary for a program to run. Some examples are DOS overlay (OVL) and Windows initialization (INI) files. Overlay files need not have an extension of .OVL. However, you should set the overlay files that you can find to Read Only and Shareable so that they cannot be modified or deleted, but they can be shared.

NetWare's own program-related files usually end in .DAT; you should mark these files as Shareable. Many users use these files concurrently. You also should mark them as Read Only to prevent them from being deleted or modified.

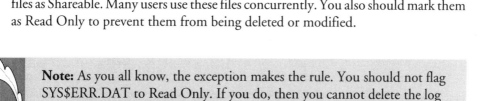

Note: As you all know, the exception makes the rule. You should not flag SYS$ERR.DAT to Read Only. If you do, then you cannot delete the log using SYSCON.

Data Files

Because user or application files are as varied as the users and applications themselves, no hard and fast rules exist for protecting data files. For applications with multiple users, however, you should set the attribute to Shareable. If you have applications that are not NetWare-aware, set the attribute to Nonshareable.

> **Note:** Before you set the Shareable attribute, check the product documentation. Some database products, such as Btrieve, do not like data files flagged as Shareable.

Database files on local area networks primarily are used for inquiry purposes and not updated. In these cases, you can set the attribute to Read Only, but do so only if the files will not be modified.

Temporary Files

You might want to set the Purge attribute for temporary files. Sometimes setting this attribute is not easy because the program that creates the temporary files must set the attribute. Most applications, including NetWare's, don't work this way. You can trick the program by telling the program to put its temporary files in a directory with Purge set. When a file is deleted from the directory, it is purged.

Now you're ready to turn your attention to NetWare's audit trails.

Audit Trails

In control methodology, there are three types of controls: *preventive*, *detective*, and *corrective*. Login security is a good example of a preventive control. The system prevents your access, for example, when you do not supply a valid username and password combination.

A corrective control detects a problem and makes a correction. Your house's thermostat is an excellent example of a corrective control. The thermostat constantly monitors the room temperature to make sure it doesn't go below 70 degrees Fahrenheit (21 degrees Celsius). When the temperature goes below the setting on the thermostat, the furnace is fired up. And when the temperature goes above 70 degrees, the furnace is shut down.

Detective controls provide a facility for determining after the fact that the process is out of control. The best example of a detective control is an *audit trail.* An audit trail provides a chronological record of system activities sufficient to track user and resource activity. Normally, the audit trail provides a reporting facility. An adequate audit trail for NetWare reports on the following:

- ☐ Program initiation
- ☐ File reads
- ☐ File writes
- ☐ Creation of files or directories
- ☐ Deletion of files or directories
- ☐ Renaming of files or directories
- ☐ Logins
- ☐ Logouts

Detective controls do not protect you against intruders but rather report on them. Likewise, an audit trial does not prevent unauthorized activity but provides clues that it happened.

Collecting, Filtering, and Reporting Data

An effective audit trail collects the information at the point closest to the service being offered. The file server therefore should do the data collection for the audit trail. Unfortunately, NetWare doesn't provide very good audit tools. You already know about the following tools for viewing audit information:

- ☐ ATOTAL
- ☐ PAUDIT
- ☐ SECURITY
- ☐ SYSCON | Supervisor Options | View File Server Error Log

You can use these tools to collect, filter, and report on the activity you want. More likely, you might want to purchase a third-party auditing package, such as Blue Lance's LT Auditor. LT Auditor can audit

- ☐ Drive
- ☐ Directory or directory tree

☐ FILESPEC

☐ FILESPEC to exclude

☐ File and directory operations

Whenever you like, you can look at the contents of the audit trail and print reports. You can be selective in the reporting you do. For example, you can produce a LAN Access Report that tells you who was connected to the server and for how long. Regardless of the product you use, you need to set an auditing mechanism to review access to key files and user activity.

An important part of any audit and control program is adequate documentation.

Network Documentation

Novell provides a variety of different worksheets with the installation manual for use by the system manager in detailing hardware and software configurations. You should complete these worksheets because they provide excellent documentation for the auditors. These worksheets also form the basis for your network documentation. The worksheets document information about the following:

☐ The file server

☐ The workstation Configuration

☐ Directories

☐ Groups

☐ Users

☐ User Defaults

☐ Trustee directory security

☐ Trustee file security

☐ Login scripts

Novell suggests that you complete these worksheets before you start building your network and that you have them handy during network setup. Let's look quickly at each worksheet.

File Server

The File Server Worksheet requires information about the server's name, make and model of the device, and the installer's name. The installer's name is particularly helpful if problems occur in the future, and you want to talk to the original installer.

The rest of the information on the File Server Worksheet is hardware-oriented. Some information the worksheet calls for includes

- ☐ Base and extended memory
- ☐ Network boards
- ☐ Nonnetwork boards
- ☐ Floppy drive format
- ☐ Hard drive
- ☐ Disk subsystems

You use the worksheet to document the LAN driver and network interface card configurations.

Workstation Configuration

The Workstation Worksheet documents hardware and software information. You complete a Workstation Worksheet for each workstation. Some nontechnical information that you want to capture includes the following:

- ☐ Owner of the workstation
- ☐ Serial number
- ☐ Type of workstation
- ☐ Installer's name

Much of the rest of the information on the Workstation Worksheet is hardware-oriented. The worksheet calls for the following:

- ☐ Board network address
- ☐ Base and extended memory
- ☐ Network boards

25

☐ Nonnetwork boards

☐ Floppy drive format

☐ Hard drive

☐ Disk subsystems

You also use the worksheet to document boot, remote reset, and redirector or shell information.

Directories

The Directories Worksheet is a matrix of directory structure and attributes and rights. The worksheet starts you out with the system installed directories of SYS:LOGIN, SYS:MAIL, SYS:SYSTEM, SYS:PUBLIC, and the users' home directories.

The worksheet suggests file attributes and inherited rights masks for these directories.

Group

The Group Worksheet provides the group name and full name, group's manager, and access to directories. The access information includes trustee directory assignments, access to files, and trustee file assignments. The worksheet also captures the usernames of group members.

The Group Worksheet and the following Users Worksheet form the basis of your security policy. You grant or deny access based on the information on these worksheets. When you complete these worksheets, you should review them with your users and management to get their approval and agreement.

Users

The Users Worksheet lists the full name, username, groups belonged to, and group manager for every user. In addition, you capture information about the applications used, access to directories, and any restrictions.

Using these worksheets, you also should track any special privileges that users have.

User Defaults

The User Defaults worksheet documents the user global restrictions set by the Supervisor. Information is gathered about account expiration, credit, concurrent

connections, intruder detection/lockout, password existence, forced passwords, grace logins, unique passwords, accounting, and time restrictions.

Again, this information affects every user, and you should get agreement and approval from your users and management. You should not set these authorities unilaterally unless you have the authority to do so. If you don't have the authority to set these defaults and you do, you will get nothing but grief. So find out who has the authority to make these decisions and get his or her approval after you have agreement from your users and their management.

Trustee Directory Security

The Trustee Directory Security and Trustee File Security worksheets provide useful information for system administration. This worksheet documents all trustees of all directories and their corresponding rights for directories.

Trustee File Security

The Trustee File Security Worksheet documents the path, all trustees of all directories, and their corresponding rights for files.

Login Scripts

The Login Scripts Worksheet is useful for working you through the coding of a system and user login scripts. The worksheet suggests the following login scripts:

- ☐ Preliminary commands
- ☐ Greetings
- ☐ Display login messages
- ☐ Attach to other file servers
- ☐ NetWare utilities mapping
- ☐ DOS directory mapping
- ☐ Application directory mappings
- ☐ Miscellaneous search drives
- ☐ Supervisor mappings

☐ Preliminary commands

☐ Home or username directory mappings

☐ Work directory mappings

☐ Default printer mappings

☐ Display directory path at prompt

☐ Display all current drive settings

☐ Run miscellaneous programs

☐ Set environmental variables for users

☐ Individual drive mappings

The login scripts and other worksheets provide an invaluable tool to the system administration during setup and installation, plus they provide valuable network documentation. If you are just setting up a network, you should fill out these worksheets first. Also, network documentation provides excellent help to a new administrator. To ensure that the new administrator gets worthwhile documentation, remember to keep it current. Outdated documentation is only marginally better than no documentation.

Summary

Establishing some security is an essential task of the system administrator, and NetWare provides several security tools. In this chapter, you learned

☐ To use the SECURITY command-line utility to evaluate security

☐ How to evaluate the various messages from the SECURITY command-line utility

☐ About the audit facilities in NetWare, including ATOTAL, PAUDIT, SECURITY, and SYSCON

☐ About the various worksheets—File Server, Workstation Configuration, Directories, Users, User Defaults, Groups, Trustee Directory Security, Trustee File Security, and Login Scripts—provided with NetWare

☐ That a good system is well documented

Workshop
Terminology Review

access guidelines—Used here in the sense of guidelines for the modification of specific access rights or attributes. It should be a general framework drawn up by you and your data owners or custodians to instruct you on the required protection for their data and programs.

accidental—Outcome from the lack of care or any situation where the result is negatively different from that intended. For example, poor program design and poor planning.

audit trail—A chronological record of system activities sufficient to enable you to reconstruct, review, and examine what happened on your system.

auditability—The physical or mental power to perform an examination or verification of your financial records or accounts.

breach—A break in your system security that results in admittance of unauthorized persons.

deliberate—Intended to harm you. The results of such deliberate actions might be different from those expected by perpetrators or victims. For example, arson and vandalism.

monitoring—The use of automated procedures to ensure that the controls implemented within your system are not circumvented.

security—Protection of all those resources that your users use to complete their mission.

security policy—The set of laws, rules, and practices that regulate how your organization manages, protects, and distributes its information.

sensitivity—The characteristic of your resources implying its value or importance and may include its vulnerability.

Task List

The emphasis of this chapter has been to introduce you to security and auditing. As a system administrator or Supervisor, you must learn how to protect your network. There was only one task in this chapter:

- ☐ Using SECURITY to scan for security exposures

Q&A

Q Does NetWare version 3.11 or 3.12 allow passwords equal to the username?

A No, these versions do not. Remember though that you may have NetWare 2.15 servers on your network. So you may want to check other servers, because if they are attached to you, they ultimately effect your security. A chain is only as strong as its weakest link.

Q Can I get a list of usernames from SECURITY?

A No, SECURITY provides only those usernames that have security exposures associated. If you want some other security reports, then again you should look at products from other vendors. In addition, you can find some utilities on NetWire to help.

Q NetWare's logging does not satisfy our auditor's requirements. What can I do?

A As mentioned, NetWare's logging could be improved. In some environments, it is probably sufficient. But if you are using it for mission-critical systems or rely on the log to prove accountability, you will need to acquire a product from a third-party software supplier.

26

Using the NetWare Accounting System

NetWare 3.11 and 3.12 provide a complete and flexible system of accounting and resource charging. In this chapter, you learn the purpose of resource accounting and the different tools for setting up monitoring.

First, you should not confuse NetWare's accounting system with an accounting application for recording debits and credits. Novell's accounting system serves a different purpose. Accounting on your server is the first step in implementing a comprehensive system for charging and billing users for resources they use.

Overview of the Accounting System

By setting up a well-planned accounting strategy, you can monitor the use of key system resources and assign rates for charging users. A good accounting system enables you to track network utilization, identify areas where resources are limited, and create a realistic upgrade strategy. By providing you with actual numbers about system usage, the NetWare accounting system helps you to justify proposed equipment purchases to management, and to better estimate the resources required to meet future demand. It also helps you to implement network services on a pay-per-use basis.

Not all networks need the accounting feature activated. Accounting makes sense when several departments use the same expensive resource, such as a file server for disk storage. It also makes sense when you plan to implement a charge back system, as often happens during the development of a product. When you track a group's use of resources for a length of time, you get a good idea of the real costs of product development.

In other instances, resource accounting is patently obvious. Universities, for example, need to control the use of resources. The system charges the student's use against a balance assigned to the student at the beginning of the semester. If the balance runs out, the student negotiates extra time.

Even if you are not in a university setting, you still may use this accounting system, so it helps to understand what the system is.

Understanding Resource Accounting

First, the accounting system is optional, and system administrators are free to set the appropriate level of accounting for their network. Your job is to determine when and how to implement resource accounting on your file server.

When the accounting system is activated, it records every user login to and logout from the server. The system also provides the means for system administrators to monitor and charge for the use of resources, such as the number of blocks read on the server, the number of disk blocks written to the server, the amount of disk storage used, and the number of services requested from the server by the user.

The Supervisor or Supervisor-equivalent must decide the resources that incur a charge and then set the charge for the use of those resources. You can assign a charge to any of the previously mentioned resources, indicating their cost to users.

Tip: Because accounting records every login and logout, you can use them as an additional security tool. The accounting system can provide a valuable audit trail of system access.

When accounting is activated, NetWare records events to the NET$ACCT.DAT file residing in the SYS:SYSTEM directory and charges users for resources. You see how you can use utilities provided with NetWare to create reports.

When accounting is deactivated, NetWare stops recording events. At any later time, you can reactivate accounting.

26

To use accounting effectively on your server, follow these steps:

☐ Activate accounting services.

☐ Set the charge rates for the resources to be tracked.

☐ Set account balances for users on the server.

The first step is required; the other two are optional. In Chapter 10, you touched on how to set account balances for users. You might want to refresh your memory and return there when you finish this chapter.

Starting Accounting

NetWare enables you to activate the accounting option for a server. You can activate the accounting features by using the SYSCON utility at a workstation. The Supervisor (or equivalent) must be logged in to activate the accounting features.

Task 26.1: Activating accounting.

Step 1: Description

This task shows you how to install accounting services on the network.

Step 2: Action

1. To change to the \PUBLIC subdirectory, type **CD\PUBLIC** and press Enter.

2. Type **SYSCON** and press Enter. The Available Topics menu appears.

3. Highlight Accounting and press Enter. An Install Accounting menu should appear, as shown in Figure 26.1.

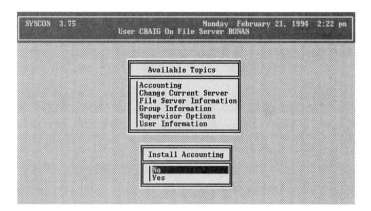

Figure 26.1. *Install Accounting menu.*

4. Choose Yes and press Enter.

5. Press Esc repeatedly until you are asked to confirm your exit from SYSCON.

Step 3: Review

When you activate accounting using SYSCON as you did in this task, the system tracks user logins and logouts and enables you to charge users for NetWare services. To charge users for system resources, however, you must specify a charge rate for every

resource to be monitored. By default, the system assigns no charge to NetWare resources when you first activate accounting. Therefore, no service incurs a charge unless you set a charge rate for the service.

You can use SYSCON to activate accounting on any server where you have the authority. Servers are not limited to file servers; you can specify other types of servers, including print servers and communication servers.

Managing Accounting Servers

After you turn on accounting, you can authorize other file servers and types of servers to charge your file server users for their specialized services. The first step is to list other accounting servers.

Task 26.2: Listing accounting servers.

Step 1: Description

In this task, you learn how to view the list of servers set up to charge for services on the network.

Step 2: Action

1. Type **SYSCON** and press Enter. The Available Topics menu appears.

2. Highlight Accounting and press Enter.

3. Move the cursor down to Accounting Servers and press Enter. You should see a list of servers similar to the one shown in Figure 26.2.

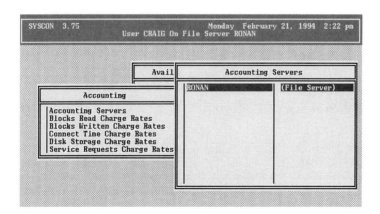

Figure 26.2. *Accounting servers.*

4. Press Esc repeatedly until you are asked to confirm your exit from SYSCON.

Step 3: Review

In this task, you learned how to view the list of servers set up to charge for services on the network. If the server you want is not listed, you can add it to the list.

Task 26.3: Adding accounting servers.

Step 1: Description

This task shows you the procedure for adding new accounting servers to charge for network services.

Step 2: Action

1. Type **SYSCON** and press Enter. The Available Topics menu appears.

2. Highlight Accounting and press Enter.

3. Move the cursor down to Accounting Servers and press Enter.

4. Press Ins to access the Select Server Type list. Your list should be similar to the one shown in Figure 26.3.

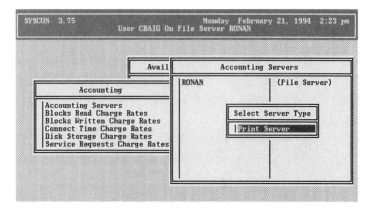

Figure 26.3. *Select Server Type list.*

5. Choose the server type and press Enter.

6. Press Ins to access the Other Servers list.

7. Choose the server or use F5 to choose more than one, and press Enter.

8. Press Esc repeatedly until you are asked to confirm your exit from SYSCON.

Step 3: Review

This task showed you the procedure for adding new accounting servers to charge for network services. If you add a file server by error, you can remove it.

Task 26.4: Deleting accounting servers.

Step 1: Description

Using this task, you can stop a server from charging for its services.

Step 2: Action

1. Type **SYSCON** and press Enter. The Available Topics menu appears.

2. Highlight Accounting and press Enter.

3. Move the cursor down to Accounting Servers and press Enter.

4. Highlight the server or use F5 to highlight more than one accounting server.

5. Press Delete.

6. Confirm your intent to delete the accounting server(s).

7. Press Esc repeatedly until you are asked to confirm your exit from SYSCON.

Step 3: Review

With this task, you learned how you can stop a server from charging for its services. Deleting a server may not be sufficient; you might want to remove accounting altogether.

Stopping Accounting

You easily can remove a server from the accounting list. If you want to deactivate accounting from a server, you must first remove all accounting servers from the list.

Task 26.5: Deactivating accounting.

Step 1: Description

This task shows you how to remove accounting services from the network.

Step 2: Action

1. To change to the \PUBLIC subdirectory, type **CD\PUBLIC** and press Enter.

2. Type **SYSCON** and press Enter. The Available Topics menu appears.

3. Highlight Accounting and press Enter.

4. Move the cursor down to Accounting Servers and press Enter. You should see a list of servers similar to the one shown in Figure 26.4.

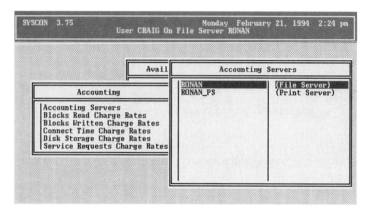

Figure 26.4. *Accounting Servers list.*

5. Use F5 to highlight all accounting servers.

6. Press Delete.

7. Confirm your intent to delete the accounting servers.

8. Press Esc to access the Remove Accounting menu.

9. Choose Yes and press Enter.

10. Press Esc repeatedly until you are asked to confirm your exit from SYSCON.

Step 3: Review

Although accounting performs a useful service to you, it adds overhead to the server's operation. When you deactivate accounting as you did in this task, the system stops recording events to the NET$ACCT.DAT file and stops charging users for resources. The file used for accounting remains, and you still can produce reports and audit trails.

Processing and Reporting Accounting Charges

After you activate the accounting system, you must determine the resources incurring a charge and the rate you want to charge for the use of those resources. NetWare

accepts as many as 20 different charge rates for each monitored resource, but you require only a few different charges for most resources.

As mentioned already, you can monitor and charge for the following resources:

- ☐ Connect time
- ☐ Disk blocks read on the server
- ☐ Disk blocks written on the server
- ☐ Disk storage used
- ☐ Services requested from the server by the user

The charge rate is set in half-hour increments and can vary based on the time of day or day of the week. By default, the accounting system uses Charge Rate 1 (no charge) for all services. For each resource, the entire accounting week is divided into half-hour periods, and you can set separate charge rates for each half-hour period.

Before you set rates, you should understand the services and resources that you can charge to users.

Connect Time

Connect time is the amount of time in minutes that the user connects to (or logs in to without logging out from) the NetWare server. This resource is commonly charged for on many computer systems, large or small. If you use a third-party supplier of computing resources—for example, a service bureau—you most likely pay for connect time.

You might want to charge for connect time when you have many users on a particular server competing for resources. By charging for connect time, you discourage users from logging in and staying logged in even when they have nothing to do. If you charge users for connect time, they probably will log in, do their work, and quickly log out.

26

Blocks Read

Blocks read is the number of blocks read from NetWare volumes. As you already know, you can configure NetWare blocks as either 4K, 8K, 16K, 32K, or 64K. But for the purposes of accounting, blocks are 4K.

You can charge for blocks read from a server when users access information services. Charging for blocks read is extremely useful when your file server provides an information service, such as a commercial database. When your department produces

technical reports that users of the server can access, for example, you may want to set a charge for blocks read on the server. By doing so, you can charge your users based on the amount of information they consume.

Remember, however, that charging per block read may not be a good idea on a file server shared by a workgroup in an office because you penalize users for loading and running large programs from the file server. Users certainly change their work habits to reduce the charges.

Blocks Written

Blocks written is the number of blocks written to NetWare volumes. Remember that you can configure NetWare blocks, but NetWare uses 4K for the purposes of accounting. What does this fact mean? Blocks written refers to the number of 4K blocks of data written to the file server, as opposed to the number of blocks stored (disk storage) at the end of the day when accounting checks.

You should be aware that charging for blocks written may prevent users from regularly saving important work. It also penalizes users of applications that make extensive use of temporary files.

Charging for blocks is, however, appropriate for an application such as word processing, where the user processes the data at the workstation and saves to the disk less frequently.

Disk Storage

Disk storage is the number of blocks of disk space used on NetWare volumes at the end of the day. As with other chargeable resources, the accounting system uses 4K blocks, regardless of the real block size.

Disk storage is quite a different measure from the number of blocks written to the server. Disk storage is a measure of the number of blocks used per day. Daily, the system tallies the disk space used by the system's users. Because this calculation is a disk-intensive operation, you should perform this operation when the server load is lightest, such as after midnight.

On most servers, disk storage is one of the most desired resources. Use the disk storage charge to reflect the value of this resource to your users. Be aware that disk space is an interesting commodity—your users tend to use as much as they can have. But resist the urge to use resource accounting to limit each user's disk space. You should use SYSCON to limit disk space.

> **Warning:** If you use DOS XCOPY or NetWare NCOPY to copy files for a user, then you assume ownership for those files and are charged for them. Use FILER to change the ownership back to the real owner to ensure proper disk storage charges.

Charging users for disk space might encourage users to keep their personal directories clean and to stop them from dropping jetsam on the server. But at what cost? They might not back up their critical files to the file server anymore. So carefully consider what your users are doing with the disk space on your file server before charging them.

Service Requests

Service requests are requests made of a NetWare server, such as when a user requests a list of a directory's contents. Almost any action performed on the file server is considered a service request, including logins, logouts, and even reading and writing blocks of data. So you should not charge for requests when you are using the other charge categories.

Setting Accounting Rates

By now, you should have a good idea of the services you want to charge users. So you need to figure out how much to charge.

The first step is to define the unit of charge. NetWare deals in charge units. It is not a measure in any currency. You must set up a system that relates the number of charge units to the amount of money actually charged. Many administrators suggest you use one cent as the basic charge unit, but you can use any appropriate equivalent where you don't have cents—for example, pesos or marks. Whatever value you choose, you must use that unit for all resources.

The next step is to decide how much you want to recover. You need to decide how much money you want to recover from the users for each charged service. Suppose, for example, you want to recover $36,000 over the next three years to fund upgrading the network. This means, you must recover $1,000 a month from your users. You can then decide how to recover the $1,000—for example, half from disk storage and half from connect time.

The next step is to monitor actual file server use for a short period.

26

After you have all your background information, you can calculate charge rate ratios. NetWare accounting uses a multiplier-divisor ratio to assign charge rates to system resources. The following equation comes right from the Novell manual and shows how the charge rate is computed:

$$\frac{\text{Total Charge for a Service}}{\text{Estimated Total Usage}} = \frac{\text{Charge Rate Multiplier}}{\text{Charge Rate Divisor}}$$

All you need to know is that when you divide the total money you want to recoup for a given service in a week by the average total use of the service in the week (from your monitoring), you get a *ratio* (fraction). This ratio represents how much you should charge (in charge units) for each unit of service (each block read or written).

Setting Up Charge Rates

As you learned in the preceding section, you must determine the rates to charge for each resource. To do so, you can use any method you want as long as it is equitable. The suggested method is to monitor resource use on the server over a period of time and then use this information to calculate the appropriate charge rates.

Let's look at how to set up accounting to charge at the rate of one charge unit for one minute of connect time.

Task 26.6: Setting connect time charge rates.

Step 1: Description
This task shows you how to set charge rates for the length of time a user connects to the server.

Step 2: Action
1. To change to the \PUBLIC subdirectory, type **CD\PUBLIC** and press Enter.

2. Type **SYSCON** and press Enter. The Available Topics menu appears.

3. Highlight Accounting and press Enter.

4. Move the cursor down to Connect Time Charge Rates and press Enter. A window like the one shown in Figure 26.5 appears, showing the days in half-hour segments. Notice that all the time periods are set to 1 (no charge).

```
SYSCON  3.75                           Monday  February 21, 1994  2:24 pm
                         User CRAIG On File Server RONAN

                                        Sun  Mon  Tue  Wed  Thu  Fri  Sat
         Connect Time Charge Rates  8:00am   1    1    1    1    1    1    1
                                    8:30am   1    1    1    1    1    1    1
                                    9:00am   1    1    1    1    1    1    1
Sunday                              9:30am   1    1    1    1    1    1    1
8:00 am To 8:29 am                 10:00am   1    1    1    1    1    1    1
                                   10:30am   1    1    1    1    1    1    1
Rate  Charge      Rate  Charge     11:00am   1    1    1    1    1    1    1
  1   No Charge    11              11:30am   1    1    1    1    1    1    1
  2                12              12:00pm   1    1    1    1    1    1    1
  3                13              12:30pm   1    1    1    1    1    1    1
  4                14               1:00pm   1    1    1    1    1    1    1
  5                15               1:30pm   1    1    1    1    1    1    1
  6                16               2:00pm   1    1    1    1    1    1    1
  7                17               2:30pm   1    1    1    1    1    1    1
  8                18               3:00pm   1    1    1    1    1    1    1
  9                19               3:30pm   1    1    1    1    1    1    1
 10                20               4:00pm   1    1    1    1    1    1    1
      (Charge is per minute)        4:30pm   1    1    1    1    1    1    1
```

Figure 26.5. *Charge Rate screen for connect time.*

Tip: You can assign different charge rates for different time periods—for example, off-peak time.

Tip: The first time you set charge rates, assign an arbitrary value, such as 1, and monitor use for a period of a week or more. Divide the weekly total you want to charge for connect time by the total weekly use. The result becomes your new charge rate.

5. Highlight the block of time you want. Use F5 and the arrow keys to highlight multiple blocks of time. Then press Enter. In Figure 26.6, Monday through Saturday, 9:30 a.m. through 6 p.m., is selected. If you scroll up, you can see that the block extends to 7 a.m.

6. From the Select Charge Rate menu, choose Other Charge Rate and then press Enter.

7. In the Other Charge Rate menu, specify a multiplier of 1 and a divisor of 1 (1:1) and press Enter.

26

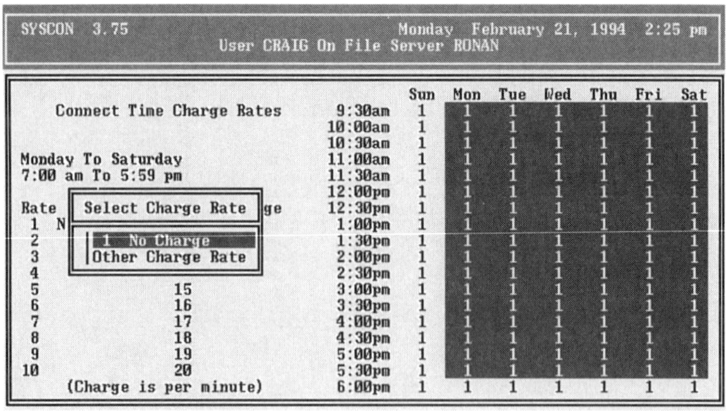

Figure 26.6. *Setting a block of time.*

8. Press Esc to return to the Connect Time Charge Rates screen. Your screen should look something like Figure 26.7. Notice that the block you previously highlighted has a 2 under each time slice. Rate 2, the rate per one-minute segment, now applies Monday through Saturday from 7 a.m. to 6 p.m. The rate is shown as 1/1 in the rate table on the left.

You can enter different charge rates for different blocks of time by repeating steps 5 through 8 for each block of time and charge rate you need.

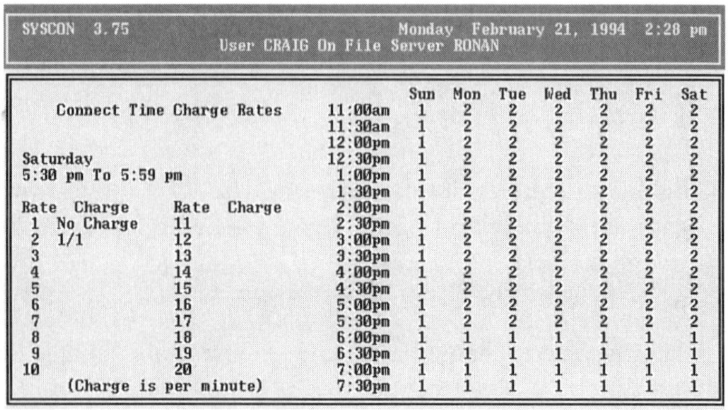

Figure 26.7. *New charge rate created.*

9. Press Esc repeatedly until you are asked to confirm your exit from SYSCON.

Step 3: Review

If you decide to set charges for connect time, then you use the procedure in this task to set charge rates for the length of time a user connects to the server. However, you might pick another resource for which to charge users.

Task 26.7: Setting blocks read charge rates.

Step 1: Description

This task shows you how to set charge rates for the number of data blocks read from the file server's disk drives.

Step 2: Action

1. To change to the \PUBLIC subdirectory, type **CD\PUBLIC** and press Enter.

2. Type **SYSCON** and press Enter. The Available Topics menu appears.

3. Highlight Accounting and press Enter.

4. Move the cursor down to Blocks Read Charge Rates and press Enter. A window similar to the one in Figure 26.5 appears.

5. Highlight the block of time you want. Use F5 and the arrow keys to highlight multiple blocks of time. Then press Enter.

6. From the Select Charge Rate menu, choose Other Charge Rate and press Enter.

7. In the New Charge Rate menu, specify a multiplier of 1 and a divisor of 1 (1:1) and press Enter.

8. Press Esc to return to the Blocks Read Charge Rates screen.

9. Press Esc repeatedly until you are asked to confirm your exit from SYSCON.

Step 3: Review

This task showed you how to set charge rates for the number of data blocks read from the file server's disk drives.

Task 26.8: Setting blocks written charge rates.

Step 1: Description

This task shows you how to set charge rates for the number of data blocks written to the file server's disk drives.

Step 2: Action

1. To change to the \PUBLIC subdirectory, type **CD\PUBLIC** and press Enter.

2. Type **SYSCON** and press Enter. The Available Topics menu appears.

3. Highlight Accounting and press Enter.

4. Move the cursor down to Blocks Written Charge Rates and press Enter. A window similar to the one in Figure 26.5 appears.

5. Highlight the block of time you want. Use F5 and the arrow keys to highlight multiple blocks of time. Then press Enter.

6. From the Select Charge Rate menu, choose Other Charge Rate and press Enter.

7. In the New Charge Rate menu, specify a multiplier of 1 and a divisor of 1 (1:1) and press Enter.

8. Press Esc to return to the Blocks Written Charge Rates screen.

9. Press Esc repeatedly until you are asked to confirm your exit from SYSCON.

Step 3: Review

This task showed you how to set charge rates for the number of data blocks written to the file server's disk drives. As you saw, you use SYSCON | Accounting | Blocks Written Charge Rates | Select Charge Rate.

Task 26.9: Setting disk storage charge rates.

Step 1: Description

This task shows you how to set charge rates for the amount of disk storage in blocks a user requires for file storage.

Step 2: Action

1. To change to the \PUBLIC subdirectory, type **CD\PUBLIC** and press Enter.

2. Type **SYSCON** and press Enter. The Available Topics menu appears.

3. Highlight Accounting and press Enter.

4. Move the cursor down to Disk Storage Charge Rates and press Enter. A window similar to the one in Figure 26.5 appears.

5. Highlight the block of time you want. Use F5 and the arrow keys to highlight multiple blocks of time. Then press Enter.

6. From the Select Charge Rate menu, choose Other Charge Rate and press Enter.

7. In the New Charge Rate menu, specify a multiplier of 1 and a divisor of 1 (1:1) and press Enter.

8. Press Esc to return to the Disk Storage Charge Rates screen.

9. Press Esc repeatedly until you are asked to confirm your exit from SYSCON.

Step 3: Review
To set up disk storage charge rates, you use SYSCON | Accounting | Disk Storage Charge Rates | Select Charge Rate, as you learned in this task.

Task 26.10: Setting service requests charge rates.

Step 1: Description
This task shows you how to set charge rates for the number of service requests a user makes of the server.

Step 2: Action

1. To change to the \PUBLIC subdirectory, type **CD\PUBLIC** and press Enter.

2. Type **SYSCON** and press Enter. The Available Topics menu appears.

3. Highlight Accounting and press Enter.

4. Move the cursor down to Service Requests Charge Rates and press Enter. A window similar to the one in Figure 26.5 appears.

5. Highlight the block of time you want. Use F5 and the arrow keys to highlight multiple blocks of time. Then press Enter.

6. From the Select Charge Rate menu, choose Other Charge Rate and press Enter.

7. In the New Charge Rate menu, specify a multiplier of 1 and a divisor of 1 (1:1) and press Enter.

8. Press Esc to return to the Service Requests Charge Rates screen.

9. Press Esc repeatedly until you are asked to confirm your exit from SYSCON.

Step 3: Review
To set up service requests charge rates, you use SYSCON | Accounting | Service Requests Charge Rates | Select Charge Rate, as you learned in this task.

Factors to consider in determining charge rates include the cost of providing the service and the load placed on the resources. If network traffic is heavy during peak periods, you can increase the rate at those times to discourage unnecessary use and to ensure that the network can provide the necessary throughput and response. Most of you already are familiar with this concept.

Consider your telephone, for example. Your regional operating company most likely charges more for calls during the day than for calls made after 6 p.m. Similarly, if hard disk space is at a premium, for example, then you can use the disk storage charge to influence the behavior of your users.

You should thoroughly discuss and communicate to your users any changes to charge rates. And you should value their input because they might have thoughts about your proposed change that you didn't have. For example, they might know that your change could adversely affect processing patterns. You also have other points to consider when making a charge change. When you change a charge rate for any resource, for instance, the user accounts are affected immediately. Any use of the resource after the charge rate has been changed is charged at the new rate. The actual charge to the account balance is made when the user logs out from the server.

Accounting Reporting

As you learned earlier in this chapter, accounting information resides in the NET$ACCT.DAT file, in the SYS:SYSTEM directory. Included in the file is information about the users' logins and logouts for the server, the users' total charges, users' connect time in minutes, number of service requests, the number of bytes read and written, and disk storage on the server. Simply, this file contains all accounting records for the server in chronological order in binary format. You therefore should use one of NetWare's utilities to access the information. Using either the ATOTAL or PAUDIT command-line utility, you can examine your network's accounting information.

To use ATOTAL, type the following at the DOS prompt:

`ATOTAL [>filename]`

ATOTAL records the daily and weekly totals of blocks read and written, connect time, disk storage, and service requests. It goes through the NET$ACCT.DAT file and totals every posted transaction. The resulting output shows daily and weekly totals for each service being charged on the server. Using the `filename` option, you can save the information to a file for further review or analysis. Figure 26.8 illustrates the output from ATOTAL.

```
F>atotal

Accouting Services Total Utility

02/21/1994:
      Connect time:        53      Server requests:     4499
      Blocks read:        430      Blocks written:       224
      Blocks/day:


Totals for week:
      Connect time:        53      Server requests:     4499
      Blocks read:        430      Blocks written:       224
      Blocks/day:



F>
```

Figure 26.8. *ATOTAL output.*

The PAUDIT command is similar to ATOTAL in syntax. To use PAUDIT, type the following at the DOS prompt:

PAUDIT [>*filename*]

As you can see in Figure 26.9, PAUDIT enables you to see records in the order they were created for each instance of an accounting service, including logins, logouts, and intruder detection.

```
2/21/94 13:59:25  File Server RONAN
     NOTE: about Print Server RONAN_PS during File Server services.
     Login from address 00000000:000000000000.
2/21/94 13:59:46  File Server RONAN
     NOTE: about Print Server RONAN_PS during File Server services.
     Logout from address 00000000:000000000000.
2/21/94 14:03:21  File Server RONAN
     NOTE: about Print Server BALLIOL_PS during File Server services.
     Login from address 123456AF:000000000001.
2/21/94 14:10:31  File Server RONAN
     NOTE: about Print Server BALLIOL_PS during File Server services.
     Logout from address 123456AF:000000000001.
2/21/94 14:11:19  File Server RONAN
     NOTE: about Print Server BALLIOL_PS during File Server services.
     Login from address 123456AF:000000000001.
2/21/94 14:29:32  File Server RONAN
     CHARGE: 53 to User CRAIG for File Server services.
     Connected 53 min.; 4499 requests; 1761105 bytes read; 919098 bytes written.
2/21/94 14:29:32  File Server RONAN
     NOTE: about User CRAIG during File Server services.
     Logout from address 00000001:0080C77A547A.
2/21/94 14:29:45  File Server RONAN
     NOTE: about User CRAIG during File Server services.
     Login from address 00000001:0080C77A547A.
F>
```

Figure 26.9. *PAUDIT output.*

26

Because ATOTAL and PAUDIT can display vast amounts of data, it generally is a good idea to capture the output to a file and view the contents of the file using

NPRINT. To print out the file or files you created to store ATOTAL or PAUDIT records, you type the following at the DOS prompt:

NPRINT *filename*

You learned how to print DOS files in Chapter 20 if you need a refresher.

Archiving Accounting Data

Keeping a printed audit trail of activity on your file server is a good practice. The audit trail becomes a series of records documenting individual transactions in the sequence that they occurred.

You can develop your audit trail by running ATOTAL and PAUDIT to get a detailed summary record of server usage. Monthly, you should archive contents of NET$ACCT.DAT to a DOS test file on another storage medium. After the data is archived safely, you can delete NET$ACCT.DAT. The system then creates a new NET$ACCT.DAT file to store the new accounting information.

Warning: The accounting system also creates the NET$REC.DAT file. PAUDIT uses this file to translate the raw data into nice reports. Under no circumstances should you delete NET$REC.DAT. If you delete it, the system does not automatically create it; you must restore it from a backup.

Even though the system compresses the data in NET$ACCT.DAT, you might notice that the file is too large. When you notice that the NET$ACCT.DAT file is too large, you can reclaim the disk space by deleting the file. If you delete the file, however, then all the accounting information collected so far is destroyed.

If you want to retain the current accounting records, then back up the file before deleting. You also might want to capture the output of the ATOTAL and PAUDIT utilities to a DOS file before deletion.

That's it for today; tomorrow you look at maintaining your file server.

Summary

You can use accounting for whatever means serves your purpose. Your organization can use it to charge for resources. Most organizations, however, do not use the accounting system actually to charge for resources but to track resource usage. As the system administrator, you can discover when, during the week, users use the file server the most. With this information, you can project what resources are needed and when.

In this chapter, you learned

- ☐ To activate and deactivate the accounting features of NetWare.

- ☐ How to calculate charge rates and to set up charge rates for connect time, blocks read and written, disk storage, and service requests.

- ☐ How to create audit reports and to archive the audit data in case it is called for later.

Workshop
Terminology Review

audit trail—A chronological record of system activities sufficient to enable the reconstruction, review, and examination of the sequence of environments and activities surrounding or leading to each event in the path of a transaction from its inception to output of results.

blocks read—Number of data blocks read from the server.

blocks written—Number of data blocks written to the server's disk.

connect time—Amount of time a user connects to the file server.

disk storage—Amount of disk storage, in blocks, used by the user on the server.

monitoring—Using automated procedures to ensure that the controls implemented within a system are not circumvented.

resource—In this instance, a data block read, a data block written, disk storage used, connect time, or any service request that may be requested or used by users and their programs.

service requests—Number of requests a user makes for any resource.

Task List

The emphasis of this chapter has been to introduce you to NetWare's resource accounting system. As a system administrator or Supervisor, you must understand how to use these tasks to use accounting effectively on your system. The tasks you should understand from this chapter are as follows:

☐ Activating accounting

☐ Listing accounting servers

☐ Adding and deleting accounting servers

☐ Setting charge rates for connect time, blocks read, blocks written, disk storage, and service requests

☐ Using ATOTAL and PAUDIT to print accounting reports

☐ Archiving accounting data

Q&A

Q Why would I use accounting?

A There are a number of reasons, but let's look at the three primary ones. First, accounting logs all logins and logouts. Second, your users may engage in activity that you want to discourage. For instance, they may store all information on the server. If you don't want them to store all information there, then you can use accounting to influence this behavior. Third, accounting can be used to charge back users for services. You can charge them to cover operating and upgrade costs.

Q Should I back up accounting information?

A You should back up every file of importance. The NET$ACCT.DAT file residing in the SYS:SYSTEM directory should be backed up. If you set accounting on, this file provides a valuable audit trail of logins and logouts.

Q Should I account for other services if I account for service requests?

A No, accounting for other services duplicates the accounting for service requests because service requests accounts for every request.

Day

14

27

Maintaining Your NetWare File Server

Despite what some mainframe zealots might have you believe, NetWare is not a toy. NetWare is a sophisticated network operating system, which facilitates the use of powerful and complex microcomputer hardware. It is definitely not a toy—that's evidenced by the fact that NetWare is used by more and more large companies to support business-critical applications and their users.

Although you've seen that NetWare can be easy to use, by now you've probably gained an appreciation of just how complex NetWare is. You've learned how to use many of its facilities, but you also might have sensed that a great deal is going on behind the scenes. For the most part, you don't need to worry about what's happening within the file server or on the network cable. Even in the role of administrator, you don't have to know all the intimate technical details about NetWare in order to use it—and even to help others to use it.

In some ways, NetWare is like your car. Most cars are easy to use and drive around when everything is working fine. Things continue to work well if you keep your eye on some basic indicators: the temperature, the oil pressure, the condition of the tires. You may even get adventurous and change your own oil. But when the indicators show trouble or when something major goes wrong, you depend on a mechanic to diagnose and fix the problem.

In the NetWare world, the role of the mechanic is played by a Certified NetWare Engineer (CNE) or Enterprise Certified NetWare Engineer (ECNE). These people have in-depth technical training on what makes your NetWare LAN tick, and they can help resolve the grittiest technical problems. They are the ones you should turn to when faced with tough network challenges and advanced uses.

But you can do many things as well. NetWare provides a great deal of information to help identify where problems may be occurring. Monitoring these details can help prevent network downtime and maintain good performance. And like the people who do some of their own automotive work, you may even take on certain repair and maintenance tasks yourself. (Or, you break down on the side of the information highway with no mechanics to be found, so you have to take on your own repairs.)

In this chapter, you examine two of the more common changes you can perform on your NetWare server and how you tell NetWare about them. You also learn about NetWare's MONITOR menu utility, the key diagnostic tool you can use to examine the health of your network.

In the next chapter, you discover how to change NetWare configuration options to affect the performance of your network (hopefully for the better).

Changing File Server Hardware

If you're used to taking care of your own PC, you might find that maintaining the hardware on your file server is just as easy—or as difficult. Changing and upgrading PC hardware can be one of the simplest and most satisfying tasks you ever undertake. When everything works, and you immediately start to experience faster performance or new functions, it can be a real thrill. But when things don't work, that's when you start to think your hardware could look much better as it sails through your open window and plummets to the sidewalk below. (Note that we don't recommend this approach to hardware changes. Although eminently satisfying, it tends to limit subsequent functionality.)

You'll find that dealing with file server hardware offers the same satisfactions and frustrations. NetWare offers its own unique tools to help you successfully install and configure new hardware. It also offers its own unique challenges. You learn about the NetWare commands you use to deal with some of the most common file server upgrades in the next section.

Note: The following sections assume that you are reasonably comfortable with digging in to your personal computer hardware—taking off the cover, pulling and installing add-on boards, pulling and replacing computer chips in sockets. If not, you might want to skip on to the "Looking for File Server Problems" section. Or, if you're feeling bold, go ahead and give these tasks a try. What have you got to lose, besides a major dollar investment in computer components? If you do decide to make your own changes, please be careful, as you should be with any electrical equipment. Make sure your computer is disconnected from its power source before doing any work inside.

Installing More Memory

27

As with most computer operating systems, one of the best ways to increase performance is by adding memory. More memory typically reduces the number of transfers of information to and from the hard disk, resulting in faster operations. NetWare is no exception because more memory enables you to have more file-cache buffers. (Recall from Chapter 3 that file caching is one of the keys to NetWare's performance.)

Adding memory to a file server is fairly straightforward. Your computer's motherboard normally contains sockets that accommodate a certain number of memory chips. The chips themselves might contain different amounts of memory. Some memory chip sets contain one megabyte of Random-Access Memory (RAM), whereas others contain four megabytes. If the motherboard provides sockets for eight sets of chips, you can add up to eight megabytes with one megabyte chips. If you want to go higher, you must pull the original chips and replace them with four megabyte chips. The exact number and combination depend on your motherboard, so it's best to consult the manual that came with the board.

After you add the memory, NetWare is clever about recognizing and using everything available. When you first start up NetWare, it tells you how much memory it finds in the file server. Or you can type **MEMORY** at the file server's console prompt and then press Enter.

NetWare responds with the amount of memory it finds.

If, after you add memory, you have up to a total of 16 megabytes (16M), you normally don't have to do another thing. Just start NetWare at the file server console the way you normally do. If you go over 16M, however, you have to register the amount with NetWare. How you register with NetWare depends on what type of bus your computer has.

When you use a computer with the *Industry Standard Architecture* (ISA) bus—the most common type of bus, particularly among less expensive computers—you use the following NetWare command and then press Enter:

```
REGISTER MEMORY starting_address memory_length
```

You may be pleased to know that specifying the starting address and memory length gives you a chance to practice your base-16 arithmetic, because these parameters must be specified in hexadecimal format. The *starting_address* actually refers to the starting point above 16M, which equals 1000000 in base-16 (often written as 0x1000000, or 1000000h, to indicate a hexadecimal number), so you can replace the starting address with 1000000. The *memory_length* is replaced by the amount of memory you have installed above 16M. Some common values appear in Table 27.1.

Table 27.1. Memory length parameters for REGISTER MEMORY command.

Amount of Memory above 16M	Memory Length Parameter in Hexadecimal
4M	400000
8M	800000
12M	C00000
16M	1000000
20M	1400000
24M	1800000

If your server has a total of 24M of memory (that is, 8M more than the key number of 16M), for example, you advise NetWare by typing the following command at the file server console prompt and then pressing Enter.

`REGISTER MEMORY 1000000 800000`

For convenience, you can add this command to the AUTOEXEC.NCF file for your file server. You learn about updating this file in Appendix A, which covers installing NetWare on the file server.

If you use a computer with the *Extended Industry Standard Architecture* (EISA) bus, things are a bit easier. All you have to do is use the following NetWare command and then press Enter.

`SET AUTO REGISTER MEMORY ABOVE 16 MEGABYTES = ON`

Note that you cannot simply execute this command at the file server command prompt. Instead, you must add it to the STARTUP.NCF file and restart the file server. You also learn about updating this file in Appendix A.

Adding Disk Drives

Installing new disk drives is not a task for the faint of heart. It can be incredibly simple—a matter of plugging in two cables and then using NetWare tools to configure the new disk space. Or you might end up losing all the data on the disks you already have. So the first task to perform before adding a new disk drive is to back up your file

27

server! Then ask yourself one more time, "Do I really want to try adding a disk drive on my own?" This job might be better left for your friendly neighborhood CNE or ECNE.

> **Note:** If you are setting up a NetWare file server for the first time, consult Appendix A for details on performing the installation. The following text makes more sense if you've already been through an installation.

The specific steps for installing a hard drive on your file server are highly dependent on the type of hard drive and controller card you use. This information determines the drive interface and, therefore, the disk driver that NetWare uses to talk with the hard disk. For example, two popular types of drive interfaces are the *Integrated Drive Electronics* (IDE) interface, and the *Small Computer System Interface* (SCSI). Don't buy a hard disk unless you know for certain that it will work with your chosen controller card. Two different controller cards might be able to coexist in your file server, but this arrangement can be tricky. To deal with all these issues, consult the manual that came with the hard drives and controllers. They should describe in great detail how to perform the physical and electrical installations.

Depending on whether you've installed a new controller card or simply added another disk to an existing controller card, you might have to load a new NetWare disk driver. Disk drivers are simply another type of NetWare Loadable Module (NLM). If you add only a drive but not a new controller, you probably do not have to add any new drivers. For a new type of card or a second card, however, you use the LOAD command at the file server command prompt. To load the disk driver for an IDE disk controller, for example, you type the LOAD IDE command and then press Enter.

NetWare then prompts you for additional technical information it needs. It asks which interrupt the disk controller uses and which input/output port to use. If you aren't familiar with these concepts, you may have to consult with someone who is. Fortunately, because NetWare is such a popular operating system, many controller card vendors include instructions on which NetWare disk drivers to use and how to configure and specify interrupts and I/O ports. If the specific instructions aren't available, you might do well to bow out and get help.

The real test of how well the installation went is to see whether NetWare recognizes the new disk drive. The first indication is whether the disk driver loaded, as described

earlier. If so, you can use NetWare's INSTALL file server menu utility to try configuring the new disk. At the file server prompt, type the following and then press Enter.

LOAD INSTALL

You should see a screen like the one shown in Figure 27.1.

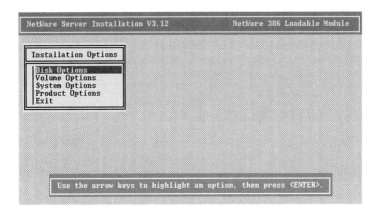

Figure 27.1. *INSTALL main menu.*

Select Disk Options and then Partition Tables. INSTALL tells you about the Available Disk Drives, that is, the drives that it knows about. Your new disk should appear on the menu. If it does, you are past a major hurdle. You can select the disk and define a NetWare partition, following the prompts on-screen. If the disk doesn't appear, you need to fall back to the installation and driver load procedures to try to find out what went wrong.

Assuming you've made it this far, you can return to INSTALL's main menu, select Volume Options and then define one or more NetWare volumes that make use of the free space on the new disk drive. Congratulations! Now you sit back and enjoy all the extra space.

If you didn't have success, take heart. You've probably run up against a technical problem that can be easily solved by someone with the technical expertise. Installing a new disk is a fairly advanced task, so don't be afraid to ask for help.

Looking for File Server Problems

By this point in the book, you should have a working NetWare file server. Your users can log in, store files, print documents, and send messages. You can run regular backups, and you can add and delete users and workgroups. Everything is working just fine. Why look for problems?

As you learned in your first lesson in Chapter 1, in your role as NetWare administrator, your users depend on you to deal with network problems. They want you to not only solve the ones that occur but ideally head them off before they happen. So you have to look for problems using whatever tools and procedures are available to you.

What You Can Do

One of the best diagnostic tools is using the system yourself. If you make regular use of your NetWare server, you can probably become aware of problems that might crop up, such as a crashed file server. Less dramatic situations, such as slow response time, also are apparent with regular use and can tip you off to the need for action.

Users, of course, are generally a pretty vocal group. So you can count on them to tell you when things don't work right. And tell you. And tell you. It is up to you to make sense of the symptoms they describe. Their descriptions may not always make sense, so it's best if you walk through the problems with them, observing everything they do. Then, assuming they haven't simply unplugged their network cable, you can make a determination of what the problem is, or at least isolate the circumstances that cause it.

One thing you can do to eliminate one source of user complaints is to test system changes yourself before you let users access the system. If you add new file server hardware or update software, for example, do some of your own testing—the more, the better. Too often, administrators make changes to the file server that they think are innocent enough but then hear a flood of complaints from their users. So do both yourself and your users a favor and test the changes out extensively, and under a number of different typical user configurations.

Another suggestion when you run into problems is to document the symptoms you find and the steps you take to remedy the situation. This approach can provide valuable reference information for you because you might run into similar problems later. Or a new problem that relates to the one you just solved might crop up; documenting the steps you took may help lead you to what went wrong. Your experience may also be invaluable to other administrators in your company.

Fortunately, NetWare gives you a few tools you can use to monitor how your network is running. You can use them to help prevent and detect file server and network problems. And because finding the problem can be half the battle, you are in a better position to remedy the situation, or call in the experts to fix it for you.

NetWare Console Commands

NetWare provides simple file server console commands that you can use to see what's happening on your file server. Each one provides you with useful information to tell you what's normal for your server and, in some cases, what's not.

A summary of the syntax and purpose of each of these commands appears in Table 27.2. Try each of them; you'll get to know your server better and be able to notice when things aren't quite right.

Table 27.2. Console commands.

Syntax	Purpose
SPEED	Provides an indication of your processor's speed rating, along with some comparative figures for different types of computers
CONFIG	Provides key file server and LAN details
DISPLAY NETWORKS	Shows which networks the file server is aware of
DISPLAY SERVERS	Shows a list of file servers that the built-in router is aware of
MODULES	Displays which NetWare Loadable Modules are currently loaded on the file server
PROTOCOL	Shows which communication protocols are in use on the server
VOLUMES	Displays a list of mounted volumes, as well as which name spaces are available on each

27

NetWare Troubleshooting Information

Despite NetWare's reputation for reliability and performance, problems invariably occur with such a sophisticated and complex collection of hardware and software. Troubleshooting problems is both a science and an art, requiring patience and experience. That's why you should always look to a CNE or ECNE when the going gets tough.

You also can look to the NetWare documentation, either in hard copy form or in Novell's ElectroText facility. In addition to the many manuals such as Concepts and those covering the setup of various facilities, a useful reference is the Troubleshooting Guide found in the System Administration Manual. These discussions might be technical in places, but may give you just the hint you need to get things up and running.

Using the MONITOR Utility

The file server console commands covered in the previous section give some useful details about your file server. But the main tool you use to follow what is happening within NetWare and its many modules is the MONITOR menu utility. MONITOR is like a viewer into the operating system, letting you see many statistics and indicators about activity and performance.

Starting MONITOR

Starting the MONITOR utility involves loading the MONITOR NetWare Loadable Module (NLM) from the file server command prompt. The format of the command is as follows:

```
LOAD MONITOR [option] <Enter>
```

The options you can use include the following:

- ☐ nh, which indicates that you do not want MONITOR's help screens loaded (used to save memory).

- ☐ ns, which loads MONITOR without its screen saver worm. The worm replaces the MONITOR screen at the file server console after the keyboard has not been used for ten minutes. The worm is an indicator of file server utilization—as utilization increases, the size of its tail and its speed increases.

- ☐ p, which loads MONITOR with an extra menu choice, the Processor Utilization option.

To start MONITOR, type the following at the file server console prompt and then press Enter.

`LOAD MONITOR p`

You'll see a screen like the one shown in Figure 27.2.

```
NetWare v3.12 (5 user) - 8/12/93              NetWare 386 Loadable Module

                        Information For Server RONAN

    File Server Up Time:    0 Days  0 Hours 59 Minutes 17 Seconds
    Utilization:                    1     Packet Receive Buffers:   100
    Original Cache Buffers:     1,691     Directory Cache Buffers:   26
    Total Cache Buffers:       1,095      Service Processes:          2
    Dirty Cache Buffers:           0      Connections In Use:         3
    Current Disk Requests:         0      Open Files:                11


                          Available Options
                       Connection Information
                       Disk Information
                       LAN Information
                       System Module Information
                       Lock File Server Console
                       File Open / Lock Activity
                       Resource Utilization
                     ▼ Processor Utilization
```

Figure 27.2. *MONITOR main menu.*

Information Provided for the Server

Once MONITOR is started, the main screen provides statistics in the top half and the option to select additional information on the bottom half. You see what the selections offer later in the chapter. First, let's review the Information for Server details. The following sections provide summaries of each of these key indicators.

File Server Up Time. This File Server Up Time field shows the amount of time since the file server was started.

Utilization Percentage. A Utilization Percentage field shows a value of 0 to 100, showing what percentage of time the file server's CPU is being used to do useful work such as filling requests for files. A low number shows that the system is not very busy, whereas a consistently high number shows that the system is being utilized heavily.

Original Cache Buffers. Recall from Chapter 3 that NetWare allocates as much memory as possible to the file-cache buffer pool but then surrenders it to other memory pools. The Original Cache Buffers value shows how many cache buffers were originally allocated when the server first started and before it started giving up memory.

27

Total Cache Buffers. The Total Cache Buffers parameter shows the number of file-cache buffers left at this point in time. Note that more buffer space may be given up as other pools require more memory. Remember also that file cache buffers are a key element of NetWare's performance. If this value starts to fall, performance suffers. You can control the minimum number of buffers that the server retains by setting a NetWare parameter. (See Chapter 28 for use of the SET command.) You might need to add more memory to allow more file-cache buffers. Or you might have loaded other modules, which take up permanent, semi-permanent, and short-term alloc memory but don't give it back for file caching. Downing and restarting the file server may be the easiest cure (as long as you don't reload the offending modules).

Dirty Cache Buffers. The Dirty Cache Buffers parameter shows file cache buffers that contain information destined for the disk but which are not yet written out. (Recall that this performance feature allows a program to carry on processing instead of waiting for the completion of a disk write.) Although a few are tolerable, too many cache buffers hanging around to be written out can be a concern. Dirty Cache Buffers may indicate that your hard disk is too slow (allowing many requests to build up). You also can control the time NetWare allows before it forces a write.

Current Disk Requests. The Current Disk Requests parameter shows the total number of disk requests for all disks on the server.

Packet Receive Buffers. Packet Receive Buffers are set up to hold requests received from workstations while they wait to be processed by the file server. The system automatically allocates additional buffers when needed, within minimum and maximum values you can set.

Directory Cache Buffers. The Directory Cache Buffers parameter shows the number of buffers used for directory entry caching. More are allocated when needed. Here again, you can control the minimum and maximum numbers within which the server automatically allocates cache buffers.

Service Processes. Service Processes handle requests from workstations. NetWare creates more service processes as the load increases, up to a maximum number you can specify.

Connections in Use. The Connections in Use parameter shows the number of workstations attached to the server. This number includes workstations that are attached but not necessarily logged in.

Open Files. The Open Files parameter shows the total number of opened files on the server. This number includes the bindery files and any transaction tracking files in use.

Other Available Options on the MONITOR Main Menu

The Available Options menu enables you to select other useful statistics and details. You find out more about the available selections in the following sections. (The menu options are discussed in order of importance rather than appearance on the menu.)

Resource Utilization

Selecting the Resource Utilization menu option changes the top part of the MONITOR screen. If you move the cursor down and select this option, you should see a screen like the one shown in Figure 27.3. Note the new set of statistics on the top half of the screen and the additional menu options on the bottom half.

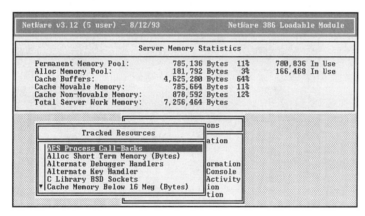

Figure 27.3. *Resource Utilization screen.*

This information is significant in that it provides a good picture of how memory on the file server is being used. The total number of bytes and relative percentages quickly show you whether, for example, too much memory is being taken from the file-cache buffer pool, which decrease the server's performance. In general, the higher the percentage of memory given to cache buffers, the better. And if the number of file-cache buffers falls below 25%, there is a good chance the server is about to crash.

Note that, for the permanent memory pool and alloc memory pool, both the total allocated and total in use are provided. This screen can give an indicator of situations where memory is being taken temporarily but not used on an ongoing basis.

The Total Server Work Memory value is less than the total memory installed on your server because the operating system itself and some DOS-related services also take up memory. The REMOVE DOS command frees up some additional memory for NetWare.

The Tracked Resources menu shows operating system resources, such as memory pools, which are tracked by NetWare. Each NLM that uses one of the tracked resources has a resource tag. Using the menu, you can select a tracked resource and press Enter. MONITOR then shows a list of the NLMs with resource tags. You can highlight and select one of the tags to receive additional resource information, such as a brief description of the resource. If the resource is a type of memory, the In Use value shows how much memory is tied up. A sample Resource Information screen is shown in Figure 27.4.

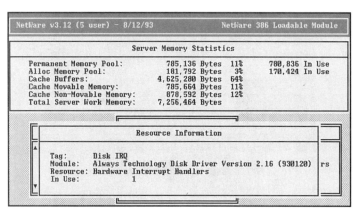

Figure 27.4. *Resource information sample.*

Processor Utilization

The Processor Utilization screen provides a measure of how much of the CPU load is used by processes and interrupt service routines running on the file server. You select which processes you want to track from those offered on the Available Processes & Interrupts menu. For the processes selected (either by moving the cursor to the process name or by highlighting a number of processes with the F5 key and then pressing Enter), NetWare generates and updates a histogram. A sample of the information provided is shown in Figure 27.5.

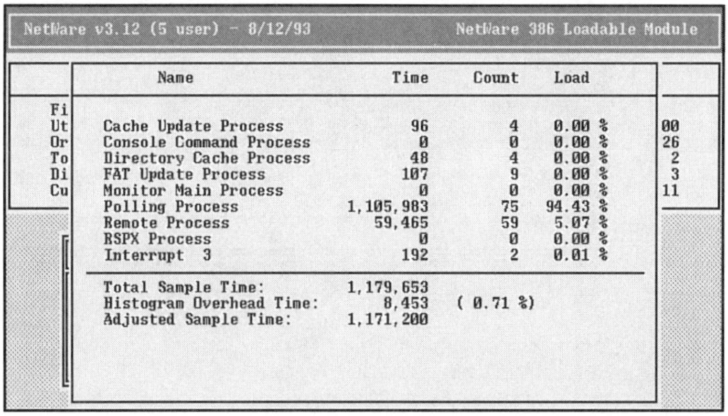

```
┌────────────────────────────────────────────────────────────────────┐
│ NetWare v3.12 (5 user) - 8/12/93         NetWare 386 Loadable Module │
├────────────────────────────────────────────────────────────────────┤
│       ┌──────────────────────────────────────────────────┐          │
│       │    Name              Time    Count    Load        │          │
│    Fi │                                                   │          │
│    Ut │ Cache Update Process     96       4   0.00 %      │ 00       │
│    Or │ Console Command Process   0       0   0.00 %      │ 26       │
│    To │ Directory Cache Process  48       4   0.00 %      │  2       │
│    Di │ FAT Update Process      107       9   0.00 %      │  3       │
│    Cu │ Monitor Main Process      0       0   0.00 %      │ 11       │
│       │ Polling Process   1,105,983      75  94.43 %      │          │
│       │ Remote Process       59,465      59   5.07 %      │          │
│       │ RSPX Process              0       0   0.00 %      │          │
│    ┌  │ Interrupt  3            192       2   0.01 %      │          │
│    │  │ ──────────────────────────────────────────       │          │
│    │  │ Total Sample Time:      1,179,653                 │          │
│    │  │ Histogram Overhead Time:    8,453   ( 0.71 %)     │          │
│    │  │ Adjusted Sample Time:   1,171,200                 │          │
│       └──────────────────────────────────────────────────┘          │
└────────────────────────────────────────────────────────────────────┘
```

Figure 27.5. *Performance utilization histogram.*

For each process or interrupt, the histogram shows the results of samples taken once per second, including the following:

☐ The name of the process or interrupt

☐ The amount of time spent executing the process or interrupt

☐ The number of times the process ran during the sample period

☐ The percentage of CPU time spent on the process

At the bottom of the histogram, NetWare displays adjustments for the overhead associated with collecting and processing the statistics themselves. The screen continues to update once per second.

Using this information, you can see where NetWare is spending most of its time. The majority of processor load is likely spent waiting for work, as indicated by the Polling Process statistic. Other processes with high load percentages may indicate resource hogs that require adjustment or correction.

Connection Information

The Connection Information selection displays details for each workstation attached to the file server. These details can be useful in monitoring how users make use of the file server and in helping diagnose any problems they are experiencing.

You can highlight any of the connections by moving the cursor to the username and pressing Enter to obtain additional details. A screen similar to the one shown in Figure 27.6 appears.

27

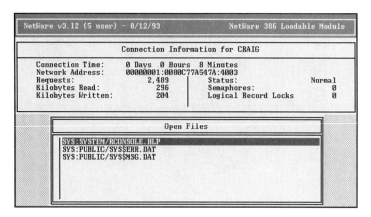

Figure 27.6. *Connection information.*

The top half of the screen shows how long the connection has been in place, as well as the network address, which is composed of the network number, the node address of the workstation, and the socket number in use. This screen also gives details on the number of requests issued by the workstation and the number of kilobytes of data read and written.

The Status field indicates one of the following:

☐ `Normal`, which means that the user is logged in and using the server normally.

☐ `Waiting On a Lock` or `Waiting on a Semaphore`, which mean that no more functions are performed until the lock is cleared or the semaphore seen.

☐ `Not Logged In`, which means that the workstation is attached, but no user is logged in.

The count of any semaphores or file locks in use by the connection is shown in separate field. Finally, the server files opened by the connection are shown in the lower half of the screen.

Disk Information

The Disk Information screen enables you to view details about disk drives and controller cards attached to the file server. When you select the Disk Information option, a menu appears showing what disks NetWare knows about. Selecting one of the disks produces a screen similar to the one shown in Figure 27.7.

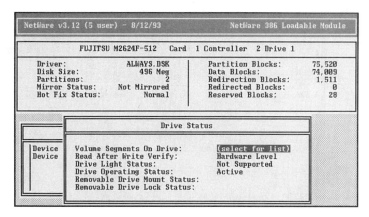

```
NetWare v3.12 (5 user) - 8/12/93          NetWare 386 Loadable Module

           FUJITSU M2624F-512    Card  1 Controller  2 Drive 1

    Driver:              ALWAYS.DSK    Partition Blocks:    75,520
    Disk Size:              496 Meg    Data Blocks:         74,009
    Partitions:                  2     Redirection Blocks:   1,511
    Mirror Status:     Not Mirrored    Redirected Blocks:        0
    Hot Fix Status:          Normal    Reserved Blocks:         28


                                    Drive Status

   Device    Volume Segments On Drive:       (select for list)
   Device    Read After Write Verify:        Hardware Level
             Drive Light Status:             Not Supported
             Drive Operating Status:         Active
             Removable Drive Mount Status:
             Removable Drive Lock Status:
```

Figure 27.7. *Disk information.*

The status information provided includes the name of the disk driver loaded which supports this disk, the disk size, the number of partitions that have been set up, and the current status for disk mirroring and use of the hot fix feature.

The number of blocks on the disk are displayed, divided into Data Blocks and Redirection Blocks. Recall that the hot fix feature notes when repeated disk write failures have occurred and moves data to the redirection blocks. A high number of Redirected Blocks indicates disk problems. You may need to reformat the disk or even replace it entirely.

Note also that a Drive Status menu appears, which enables you to get further details about which volumes are on the disk, the type of Read After Write Verify performed (if at all), and whether the drive has been activated. The status of features on removable drives is shown, if applicable.

LAN Information

Selecting LAN Information provides a menu showing the LAN Driver Information for each card installed on the server. Selecting one card provides details on the card's address and protocols in use, as well as a variety of generic and card-specific custom statistics. A sample of the information provided is shown in Figure 27.8.

You can use this information to provide basic information about the cards and protocols in use on the server. The screen also can provide clues about problems occurring on the network. A high number in Send Packet Retry Count, for example, might indicate a network problem such as too much traffic or a bad cable.

27

651

```
NetWare v3.12 (5 user) - 8/12/93                NetWare 386 Loadable Module

                         Information For Server RONAN

     File Server Up Time:      0 Days  1 Hour   3 Minutes 19 Seconds
     Utilization:                   2           Packet Receive Buffers:    100
     Original Cache Buffers:    1,691           Directory Cache Buffers:    26
     Total Cache Buffers:       1,091           Service Processes:           2
     Dirty Cache Buffers:           0           Connections In Use:          3
     Current Disk Requests:         0           Open Files:                 11

        ┌─────────────────────────────────────────────────────────────┐
        │         NE2000 [port=300 int=3 frame=ETHERNET_802.3]          │
        ├┬────────────────────────────────────────────────────────────┤
      ┌─┤│  Version 3.25                                                │
      │NE20│ Node Address: 00006E22837A                                 │
      └─┤│  Protocols:                                                  │
        ││    IPX                                                       │
        ││      Network Address: 00000001                              │
        ││                                                             │
        ││  Generic Statistics:                                        │
        │▼   Total Packets Sent:                             13,361     │
        └──────────────────────────────────────────────────────────────┘
```

Figure 27.8. *LAN card information.*

System Module Information

Selecting the System Module Information option provides a list of System Modules currently running on the server. Selecting one of the modules displays the module's name and the number of bytes it uses. It also displays a list of resource tags associated with the module. Highlighting a tag and pressing Enter yields the same kind of details available from the Resource Utilization screen and can be used for troubleshooting in the same manner. Figure 27.9 provides a sample.

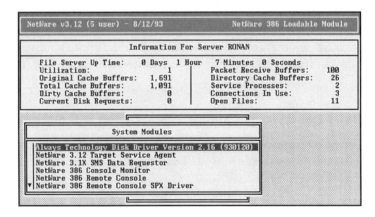

Figure 27.9. *System module information.*

File Open/Lock Activity Information

At some point, a user may approach you with the problem that he or she can't get to a file because it is locked. You can use the File Open/Lock Activity Information menu selection from the MONITOR utility to select a file and determine whether any locks are in place. If they are, you can quickly determine who is using the file from the connection number. Figure 27.10 shows a sample display for a file in use.

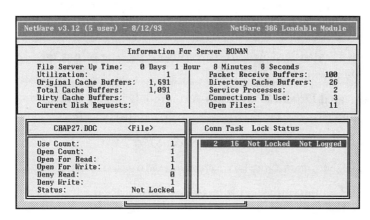

Figure 27.10. *File lock information.*

As you can see, using the MONITOR utility is key to gaining insight into how your NetWare file server is running and where problems can occur.

Summary

In this chapter, you covered a number of areas related to maintaining your NetWare file server. You saw details on the following:

☐ Performing certain kinds of upgrades to your server and what NetWare commands to use after performing the upgrades.

☐ Some of the tasks you can perform to help prevent and detect problems from occurring.

☐ Useful NetWare commands you can use to see what is running on a file server.

☐ How to use the MONITOR file server console menu utility to get an in-depth look at how NetWare and its related modules are making use of the file server.

27

Workshop

Terminology Review

EISA Bus—See *Extended Industry Standard Architecture Bus.*

Extended Industry Standard Architecture Bus—A type of bus, less commonly found than the ISA Bus, but capable of better performance.

IDE—See *Integrated Drive Electronics.*

Industry Standard Architecture Bus—The type of bus used in most of today's personal computers.

Integrated Drive Electronics—A commonly used disk drive interface for personal computers.

ISA Bus—See *Industry Standard Architecture Bus.*

SCSI—See *Small Computer System Interface.*

Small Computer System Interface—A disk drive interface used for many personal computers that offers higher performance than IDE.

Q&A

Q Can I use the MONITOR command to watch NetWare from a workstation?

A The MONITOR NLM only runs from the file server console prompt. However, you can use NetWare's RCONSOLE facility to remotely run MONITOR and view its results on your workstation.

Q Do I have to format a disk drive from DOS before NetWare can use it?

A You don't need to use DOS to format a disk before allowing NetWare to access it. NetWare takes an unformatted disk partition and prepares it for its own use—it doesn't need DOS. The INSTALL program provides the required functions to prepare the disk. See Appendix A for more details on creating a NetWare volume.

28

Fine-Tuning
Your NetWare
File Server

A system administrator often is caught up in the quest for increased performance and greater reliability. User demands for more resources must be balanced against budgetary constraints. So you are forced to try to extract the most bang-for-the-buck from your investment in computer technology.

NetWare is a network operating system known for its performance. Functions that used to run on large mainframe computers can now be transferred to a NetWare LAN and perform just as well, or even better, at a fraction of the operating cost. NetWare is also flexible. It can be configured to deliver the best balance of speed and reliability in a variety of different operating environments—from a general-purpose file server to the foundation of a sophisticated client/server database management system.

In the preceding chapter, you learned how to use the MONITOR menu utility to view some of the elements that control how NetWare operates. Key factors such as the amount of memory available for file caching, the number of packet receive buffers, and the number of service processes affect NetWare's performance. Indicators such as the status of dirty cache buffers and redirected blocks can point out potential problem areas.

NetWare version 3.12 has more than 60 operating parameters that affect these elements and, therefore, affect how NetWare itself runs. Each has a default value, which has been set to meet the needs of typical installations. In most cases, you don't need to make any changes at all. If you need to, however, you can adjust these parameters to customize NetWare so that it performs the way you want it to.

In the following sections, you learn how to use the file server console SET command to adjust these parameters. But before you go any further, a word of caution: Tuning NetWare, or any advanced computer operating system, is a complex task. What may seem like a minor change can quickly leave your system unbelievably slow, or even unusable. It's just like working under the hood of your car—a quick turn of a screwdriver, and the car might not start any more. Approach this task with great care.

We suggest that you don't make too many changes at once. A better approach is to adjust one parameter at a time and then observe how that change affects system performance. Keep a record of every parameter you reset, including the details of what it was before you made the change, and what you changed it to. If you get into trouble, return everything to its default value and start again. And as always, don't be shy about consulting with a NetWare CNE or ECNE for help. They have more experience and training in this advanced area (and besides, they love this stuff).

Tuning NetWare Using the *SET* Command

You use the SET command at the file server console prompt to change key NetWare parameters. Its format is as follows:

```
SET parameter=value <Enter>
```

If you simply type the command SET and press Enter, NetWare provides you with a menu of different categories, as shown in Figure 28.1.

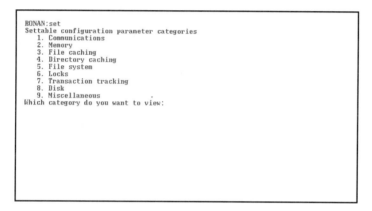

```
RONAN:set
Settable configuration parameter categories
    1. Communications
    2. Memory
    3. File caching
    4. Directory caching
    5. File system
    6. Locks
    7. Transaction tracking
    8. Disk
    9. Miscellaneous
Which category do you want to view:
```

Figure 28.1. *The SET menu.*

Entering the number of the category produces a listing of the parameters within that category. For each parameter, NetWare tells you its current value and gives a brief description of its purpose. The acceptable limits are given for numeric parameters, in terms of the discrete values or range of values you can set. NetWare also tells you whether the parameter *can be* set in the STARTUP.NCF file, or if it *must be* set there (as opposed to being available at the console prompt). Some parameters from the Communications category are shown in Figure 28.2. As you can see, this screen provides useful online documentation of the parameters you can set.

```
Console Display Watchdog Logouts: OFF
    Description: Display on the console watchdog connection failure logouts

Enable Packet Burst Statistics Screen: OFF
    Description: Display NCP packet burst statistics screen

New Packet Receive Buffer Wait Time: 0.1 seconds
    Limits: 0.1 seconds to 20 seconds
    Description: Minimum time to wait before allocating a new packet receive
                buffer

Maximum Physical Receive Packet Size: 4202  (only settable in STARTUP.NCF)
    Limits: 618 to 24682
    Description: Size of the largest packet that can be received by an MLID

Maximum Packet Receive Buffers: 400  (also settable in STARTUP.NCF)
    Limits: 50 to 2000
    Description: Maximum number of packet receive buffers that can be allocated
                by the server

Reply To Get Nearest Server: ON  (also settable in STARTUP.NCF)
    Description: Does this server respond to GET NEAREST SERVER requests from
                workstations that are attempting to locate a server

<Press ESC to terminate or any other key to continue>
```

Figure 28.2. *Sample* SET *online documentation.*

If you don't reset any parameters, you can use this method to review the default settings for each. Before you change anything, make sure that you try the defaults for a long enough period of time. They serve many NetWare users well, so don't be in a hurry to alter their values.

In the following sections, you review the parameters you can set. Some of the parameters affect system performance; others affect security and set warning indicators; still others are for administrative convenience. The focus of these sections is on the more commonly used parameters, but you also see a summary of others, including their default settings and possible values.

Setting Memory Parameters

At many points during your exploration of NetWare, you have heard about the importance of memory and its effect on file server performance. Our rule of thumb has been that the more memory is available for file caching, the better your server performs. Two key parameters have an influence over file-cache memory and are described in the following section.

Maximum Alloc Short-Term Memory

Recall from Chapter 3 that certain information used by the server (for example, connection information, drive mappings, and NLM tables) make use of the alloc memory pool. But this pool takes space away from file caching (through the permanent memory pool) and does not return it, even if its requirement for memory ends. As a result, you might want to limit exactly how large this pool can grow.

For version 3.12 of NetWare, this parameter has a default of 8M (that is, 8,388,608 bytes). It can range from 50,000 bytes to 32 megabytes (33,554,432 bytes). Novell suggests that this default is adequate for up to 1,000 users, each with 26 drive mappings. Decreasing the default maximum value—say, to two or three megabytes— helps retain memory for file caching. But it may also prevent you from loading NLMs or doing any other activity that requires alloc memory. In this case, NetWare advises you that operations cannot be completed due to lack of space in the alloc memory pool. If you run out of memory, you might have to decrease memory use by unloading NLMs, for example. Or you might have to add memory to your server and raise the maximum memory available to the alloc memory pool.

Cache Buffer Size

This Cache Buffer Size parameter simply specifies the size of buffers used for file caching. By default, it is set to 4K; this setting makes sense because the default file block size is also 4K, and file blocks are placed in file-cache buffers.

You can increase the cache buffer size to 8K or 16K. The value, however, should not be larger than the smallest file block size in use on your server. Cache buffers larger than this amount actually slow down your server and waste memory. Only increase the buffer size if all your disks are set up with blocks larger than 4K.

Note that you can set this parameter only in the STARTUP.NCF file. You cannot change it at the console prompt.

The only other memory parameter relates to registering memory above 16M for EISA machines. See Chapter 27 for details on how to use the Auto Register Memory Above 16 Megabytes parameter.

Setting File-Caching Parameters

Just like setting memory parameters in the last section, when you're setting file-caching parameters, the emphasis is on controlling how much memory is reserved for file-cache buffers. One parameter sets a minimum number of buffers, whereas another sets a warning limit advising you when you are close to the minimum. You also see one other parameter that balances performance between disk writes and reads.

Minimum File-Cache Buffers

Because file-cache buffers are so key to performance, the Minimum File-Cache Buffers parameter enables you to specify a minimum number of buffers that must be kept available. When this minimum is reached, NetWare no longer gives up memory from the file-cache buffer pool. Note that if this situation occurs, other processes such as NLMs may not be able to load because they can't get needed memory.

The default value for this parameter is 20, which is actually quite low. If you get down this low, you receive the message `Cache memory allocator exceeded minimum cache buffer left limit`. But chances are you will experience other problems first. You shouldn't change this value, however, unless you actually experience problems with running out of file-cache buffers. One approach to preventing problems is to use the next parameter, a warning threshold for running out of file-cache buffers.

You can specify anywhere from 20 to 1,000 for the minimum number of buffers.

Minimum File-Cache Report Threshold

Hitting the minimum number of file-cache buffers is something you want to avoid. For that reason, NetWare enables you to specify a threshold number of buffers. The threshold is relative to the minimum number of buffers you set with the last parameter. With the default threshold of 20 and the default minimum number of buffers, for example, you are warned when the number of buffers available falls below 40 (20 plus 20). The message `Number of cache buffers is getting too low` appears on the console.

You can set the threshold to any value from 20 to 1,000.

Maximum Concurrent Disk Cache Writes

The Maximum Concurrent Disk Cache Writes parameter specifies how many disk write requests are placed in NetWare's elevator algorithm before it begins its sweep across the disk surface. (The elevator seeking algorithm approach to disk access was touched on in Chapter 4.) A higher number permits the elevator to be loaded up, emptying out dirty file-cache buffers at a faster rate. If the number of dirty cache buffers starts to climb, you might find it necessary to increase this value.

Unfortunately, if NetWare pays more attention to writing out dirty cache buffers, it must pay less attention to disk read requests. Once again, it is necessary to find the right balance.

The default number for maximum concurrent disk cache writes is 50 but can be set to anything from 10 to 1,000.

Other File-Caching Parameters

NetWare maintains other useful file-caching parameters; they are listed in Table 28.1. You can consult your NetWare documentation or the SET command menu for more details on when and how you might change these values.

Table 28.1. Other file-caching parameters.

Parameter	Default Value	Range of Values
Dirty Disk Cache Delay Time	3.3 sec	0.1 sec to 10 sec
Read Ahead Enabled	ON	ON, OFF
Read Ahead LRU Sitting Time Threshold	10 sec	0 sec to 1 hour
Reserved Buffers Below 16M (can only be set in STARTUP.NCF)	16	8 to 300

Setting Directory-Caching Parameters

The approach to improving NetWare performance by directory caching is similar to that used for file caching. More memory allocated to directory-cache buffers normally means faster performance. Since directory caching takes memory away from file caching (directory caching uses the permanent memory pool), you are faced with yet another trade-off. The three key parameters discussed in the following sections play the biggest roles in this area.

Minimum Directory-Cache Buffers

The Minimum Directory-Cache Buffers parameter specifies the number of directory-cache buffers that are allocated immediately upon starting the server. The default number of buffers is 20 but can be set to any number from 10 to 2,000.

After the minimum number of buffers has been allocated, NetWare waits a set amount of time before it allocates another buffer (see the Directory Cache Allocation Wait Time parameter in Table 28.2). You use this approach to prevent many new directory-cache buffers being allocated in the face of a sudden but temporary surge of activity. However, this approach also slows down directory searches once the minimum number of directory-cache buffers has been reached. Increasing the

28

minimum number therefore postpones this slowdown and keeps directory searches running quickly. But don't forget, more directory-cache buffers mean less space for file-cache buffers.

If directory searches start to slow down shortly after you've started the server, you might want to increase this value.

Maximum Directory-Cache Buffers

Using the Maximum Directory-Cache Buffers parameter limits the amount of memory that can be allocated to directory-cache buffers. Of course, you would set this parameter to constrain the amount of memory taken from the file-cache buffer pool and given for directory-cache buffers in the permanent memory pool. The default value is 500 but can be set to any number from 20 to 4,000.

If the MONITOR Resource Utilization screen indicates that your server is losing too much file-cache buffer memory to the permanent pool, decreasing this parameter is a good alternative. Of course, the trade-off is that directory accesses can become too slow.

Directory-Cache Buffer NonReferenced Delay

The Directory-Cache Buffer NonReferenced Delay parameter sets how long a directory entry must remain in cache until it can be overwritten. Higher values cause more directory entries to stay in memory longer because the increased delay forces NetWare to allocate new buffers, rather than reuse old ones. With more directory entries in cache, the one you need is more likely to be found, and response time quickens. As usual, this result is at the cost of more memory in the permanent pool (and less available for file caching) because NetWare must take space for more buffers.

The default value for the delay is 5.5 seconds but can be set to any time from one second to five minutes.

Other Directory-Caching Parameters

NetWare maintains other directory-caching parameters, which are listed in Table 28.2. You can consult your NetWare documentation or the SET command menu for more details on when and how you might change these values.

Table 28.2. Other directory-caching parameters.

Parameter	Default Value	Range of Values
Maximum Concurrent Directory Cache Writes	10	5 to 50
Dirty Directory Cache Delay Time	0.5 sec	0 sec to 10 sec
Directory Cache Allocation Wait Time	2.2 sec	0.5 sec to 2 min

Setting Communication Parameters

The communication performance of your NetWare file server is influenced mainly by the number and size of packet buffers you can allocate. As usual, more space for packet buffers can speed communication but rob memory from file caching.

In addition, one set of communication parameters is designed to control network connections, dropping workstations that have disappeared from the network for whatever reason.

Key Packet Buffers Settings

The parameters used to control packet buffers are similar to those used for directory-cache buffers. There's a minimum number, a maximum number, and an amount of time to wait until a new buffer is allocated.

Minimum Packet Receive Buffers

The Minimum Packet Receive Buffers parameter specifies the number of packet receive buffers that are allocated immediately upon starting the server. The default number of buffers is 100 but can be set to any number from 100 to 1,000. Note that you can set this parameter only in the STARTUP.NCF file. You cannot change it at the console prompt.

After the minimum number of buffers has been allocated, NetWare waits a set amount of time before it allocates another buffer (see the New Packet Receive Buffer Wait Time parameter in Table 28.5). This approach prevents many packet buffers being allocated in the face of a sudden but temporary surge of activity. However, this approach also slows down the allocation of new packet buffers in response to more network activity once the minimum number of packet buffers has been reached.

28

Increasing the minimum number therefore postpones this slowdown and enables you to add new buffers more quickly. But there's the usual catch: having more packet cache buffers means less space available for file-cache buffers.

If network communications start to slow down after you've started the server, you might want to increase this value.

Maximum Packet Receive Buffers

Using the Maximum Packet Receive Buffers parameter limits the amount of memory that can be allocated to packet buffers. Of course, you set this parameter to constrain the amount of memory taken from the file-cache buffer pool and given for directory-cache buffers in the permanent memory pool. The default value is 400 but can be set to any number from 50 to 2,000. You can set the maximum packet receive buffers at the console prompt or from within the STARTUP.NCF file.

If the MONITOR Resource Utilization screen indicates that your server is losing too much file-cache buffer memory to the permanent pool, decreasing this parameter is a good alternative. Of course, the trade-off is that network communications with your server might slow down.

Other Packet Buffer Settings

Two other parameters—Maximum Physical Receive Packet Size and Allow LIP—have an affect on network throughput because they regulate the size of network packets the server can handle; see Table 28.3. As you might expect, larger packets mean more data can be sent in each, which speeds communication. Use of these parameters depends on other technical details concerning your network, such as the type of network, the type of NICs you use, the capabilities of devices such as routers. You therefore have to do some extra investigation before you use them.

Table 28.3. Packet buffer size parameters.

Parameter	Default Value	Range of Values
Maximum Physical Receive Packet Size (can only be set in STARTUP.NCF)	4202	618 to 24682
Allow LIP (Large Internet Packets)	ON	ON, OFF

Key Watchdog Settings

The watchdog feature is designed to drop unused connections with workstations. If a user simply shuts off his or her computer without logging off the network, for example, that user's NetWare session still is in place. Therefore, the memory allocated for his or her use still is tied up. This situation can also pose a tempting target to the network cracker, who might try to take over a session that is still active.

If the file server has not received a packet from the workstation in a given period of time (Delay Before First Watchdog Packet), it sends a watchdog packet. If the file server does not get a response within a set time (Delay Between Watchdog Packets), it sends another packet. The file server repeats this process a certain number of times (Number of Watchdog Packets), and if it still does not receive a reply, the connection is cleared. These parameters are summarized in Table 28.4.

Table 28.4. Watchdog parameters.

Parameter	Default Value	Range of Values
Delay Before First Watchdog Packet	4 min 56.6 sec	15.7 sec to 4 min 56.6 sec
Delay Between Watchdog Packet	59.3 sec	9.9 sec to 10 min 26.2 sec
Number of Watchdog Packets	10	5 to 100

A message appears on the file server console whenever a connection is dropped, as long as the Console Display Watchdog Logouts parameter is set to ON (which is the default value).

Other Communication Parameters

NetWare maintains other communication parameters, which are listed in Table 28.5. You can consult your NetWare documentation or the SET command menu for more details on when and how you might change these values.

Table 28.5. Other communication parameters.

Parameter	Default Value	Range of Values
New Packet Receive Buffer Wait Time	0.1 sec	0.1 sec to 20 sec
Enable Packet Burst Statistics Screen	OFF	OFF, ON
Reply To Get Nearest Server (can also be set in STARTUP.NCF)	ON	ON, OFF
Enable IPX Checksums	1	0, 1, 2
NCP Packet Signature Option (can also be set in STARTUP.NCF; after startup, can only be increased in value)	1	0, 1, 2, 3

Setting Other Types of Parameters

You've touched on many of the key parameters under the categories of memory, file caching, directory caching, and communications. But many more are available under the categories listed in the following sections. You see details on the most important ones, plus a summary of the other parameters available.

 Tip: Remember, you can always type the SET command at the console prompt to get a brief reminder of the meaning for each parameter and its possible values.

Key File System Parameters

One set of File System parameters is geared toward controlling warnings associated with running out of space on file server volumes.

Volume Low Warn All Users

Although the Volume Low Warn All Users parameter has its default value of ON, users are warned through a broadcast message from the server when the amount of free space on a volume goes below a certain threshold (set through the next parameter).

Volume Low Warning Threshold

When the number of disk blocks available on a volume falls below the number set by Volume Low Warning Threshold, a warning is broadcast to users. The default value is 256 blocks but can be set from 0 to 1,000,000. Note that the actual free space on the volume measured in bytes depends on the size of the file allocation block.

Volume Low Warning Reset Threshold

To prevent frequent broadcast warnings while a volume hovers around the warning threshold, the Volume Low Warning Reset Threshold parameter sets how many free blocks must be regained before any future broadcasts are issued. The default value of 256 blocks above the warning threshold must become free; then the original threshold must be crossed again before a broadcast message is sent by the file server. You can set this value from 0 to 100,000 blocks.

Another set of File System parameters regulates when deleted files are actually purged from the system.

Immediate Purge of Deleted Files

The Immediate Purge of Deleted Files parameter normally is set to OFF, meaning that deleted files are not immediately purged when deleted. You may still be able to use SALVAGE to recover the file, as long as other conditions have not caused it to be purged (for example, if the volume filled up beyond a certain point).

Minimum File Delete Wait Time

Deleted files are not eligible to be purged until the time specified by the Minimum File Delete Wait Time parameter has passed. These files are not purged automatically by the system, even if the volume is full. The default time is 1 minute 5.9 seconds but can be set from 0 seconds to 7 days.

File Delete Wait Time

Files that have been deleted for more than the amount of time set by File Delete Wait Time are marked as candidates for purging. As NetWare tries to maintain a minimum amount of space on a volume (at least 1/32 of the available space), it begins purging the oldest files meeting this criteria. The default time is 5 minutes 29.6 seconds but can be set from 0 seconds to 7 days.

Note that, if the file server runs out of space and needs to create a file for a user, it might delete any file older than the Minimum File Delete Wait Time, not just those files past the File Delete Wait Time. The latter parameter affects purging to maintain minimum space, not purging to obtain room for a new file when no other space is available.

You can find additional file system parameters in Table 28.6.

Key Disk Parameters

The most important disk parameter is Enable Disk Read After Write Verify, which normally is set to ON. This setting ensures that NetWare rereads all data written to the disk to verify it is correct. Read After Write Verify is the starting point for NetWare's hot fix redirection capability. If the parameter is set to OFF, hot fix can still work, but it relies on errors reported by the disk drive during read or write operations. Read After Write Verify is more reliable, however, and is the preferred method. You can set the parameter at the file console prompt and in the STARTUP.NCF file.

You can find a summary of the Concurrent Remirror Requests parameter in Table 28.6.

Key Lock Parameters

Lock parameters set the maximum number of record locks and file locks that can be in place. Four separate parameters specify the maximum number of record and file locks for each connection and for the system as a whole. See the Lock Parameters section in Table 28.6 for details on the default values and range of acceptable values.

Transaction Tracking Parameters

You learned about NetWare's Transaction Tracking facility in Chapter 22. Four parameters are important to its operation and are included in Table 28.6.

Key Miscellaneous Parameters

Other parameters worthy of special note are described in the following sections, and the remaining parameters are included in Table 28.6.

Maximum Service Processes

The Maximum Service Processes parameter, with a default value of 20, sets the maximum number of processes NetWare creates to serve workstation requests. After you first start the file server, NetWare creates service processes in response to increasing load, up to the maximum number. A higher number can provide better throughput, but at the expense of memory available for file caching. You can set this parameter to any number from 5 to 40.

New Service Process Wait Time

Before creating a new service process, NetWare waits the amount of time set by the New Service Process Wait Time parameter. As for directory-cache buffers and packet buffers, this approach prevents many service processes from being created in the face of a sudden but temporary surge of activity. The default value is 2.2 seconds but can be set from 0.3 second to 20 seconds.

Allow Unencrypted Passwords

The Allow Unencrypted Passwords parameter normally is set to OFF. The result is that user passwords traveling between workstations and the file server normally are encrypted. Having encrypted passwords helps prevent network crackers from intercepting passwords from the network cable and trying to log in to the system.

Table 28.6. Summary of other parameters.

Parameter	Default Value	Range of Values
File System Parameters		
Maximum Percent of Volume Space allowed for Extended Attributes	10	5 to 50
Maximum Extended Attributes per File or Path	8	4 to 512
Maximum Percent of Volume Used by Directory	13	5 to 50
Maximum Subdirectory Tree Depth (can only be set in STARTUP.NCF)	25	10 to 100
Turbo FAT Re-Use Wait Time	5 min 29.6 sec	0.3 sec to 1 hour 5 min 54.6 sec
NCP File Commit	ON	ON, OFF
Disk Parameters		
Concurrent Remirror Requests (can only be set in STARTUP.NCF)	4	2 to 30

continues

28

Table 28.6. continued

Parameter	Default Value	Range of Values
Lock Parameters		
Maximum Record Locks per Connection	500	10 to 10,000
Maximum File Locks per Connection	250	10 to 1,000
Maximum Record LocksTransaction Tracking Parameters	20,000	100 to 200,000
Maximum File Locks	10,00	100 to 100,000
Transaction Tracking Parameters		
Auto TTS Backout Flag (can only be set in STARTUP.NCF)	OFF	OFF, ON
TTS Abort Dump Flag	OFF	OFF, ON
Maximum Transactions	10,000	100 to 10,000
TTS UnWritten Cache Wait Time	1 min 5.9 sec	11 sec to 10 min 59.1 sec
TTS Backout File Truncation Wait Time	59 min 19.2 sec	1 min 5.9 sec to 1 day 2 hours 21 min 51.3 sec
Miscellaneous Parameters		
Maximum Outstanding NCP Searches	51	10 to 1,000
Pseudo Preemption Time	2,000	1,000 to 10,000
Display Spurious Interrupt Alerts (can also be set in STARTUP.NCF)	ON	ON, OFF
Display Lost Interrupt Alerts (can also be set in STARTUP.NCF)	ON	ON, OFF
Display Disk Drive Alerts (can also be set in STARTUP.NCF)	OFF	OFF, ON
Display Relinquish Control Alerts (can also be set in STARTUP.NCF)	OFF	OFF, ON

Parameter	Default Value	Range of Values
Replace Console Prompt with Server Name (can also be set in STARUP.NCF)	ON	ON, OFF
Display Incomplete IPX Packet Alerts (can also be set in STARTUP.NCF)	ON	ON, OFF
Display Old API Names (can also be set in STARUP.NCF)	OFF	OFF, ON
Allow Change to Client Rights (can also be set in STARUP.NCF)	ON	ON, OFF

Where to Use the *SET* Command

You can type most of the parameters covered in Table 28.6 at the file server console prompt or place them in the AUTOEXEC.NCF file. You can set some of the parameters in the STARTUP.NCF file, whereas you must set others there. You probably noted in the parameter descriptions where this is the case. If, at the console prompt, you try to enter a parameter that can be set only via the STARTUP.NCF file, NetWare advises you accordingly.

In summary, you can set the following parameters only in the STARTUP.NCF file:

☐ Auto Register Memory Above 16M

☐ Auto TTS Backout Flag

☐ Cache Buffer Size

☐ Maximum Physical Receive Packet Size

☐ Maximum Subdirectory Tree Depth

☐ Minimum Packet Receive Buffers

☐ Reserved Buffers Below 16M

☐ Concurrent Remirror Requests

You can set the next set of parameters either from within STARTUP.NCF, within AUTOEXEC.NCF, or at the file server console prompt:

28

☐ Display Spurious Interrupt Alerts

☐ Display Lost Interrupt Alerts

☐ Display Disk Device Alerts

☐ Display Relinquish Control Alerts

☐ Display Old API Names

☐ Maximum Packet Receive Buffers

☐ Reply to Get Nearest Server

☐ NCP Packet Signature Option

☐ Maximum Alloc Short Term Memory

☐ Enable Disk Read After Write Verify

☐ Display Incomplete IPX Packet Alerts

☐ Replace Console Prompt with Server Name

☐ Allow Change to Client Rights

All remaining parameters you can set within the AUTOEXEC.NCF file or at the file server console prompt.

Note that if you change the setting of a parameter in either the STARTUP.NCF or AUTOEXEC.NCF file, the change does not take effect until you restart the file server.

Summary

In this chapter, you focused on using the SET command to alter key NetWare parameters, including the following:

☐ Memory parameters

☐ File-Caching parameters

☐ Directory-Caching parameters

☐ Communication parameters

Choosing the appropriate values most often involved a trade-off between the amount of memory used, and the speed of the system.

Well, you've come to the end of a long journey. In the last 14 days, you've taught yourself many important details about using and administering a NetWare LAN—from how to log on and find your way around, to tuning the performance of your file server. You've covered a great deal of challenging material, and you deserve a pat on the back. Congratulations!

We hope you enjoyed your trip. Thank you for choosing this book to help in your discovery—we hope that it continues to serve you as a useful reference while you administer your LAN.

We also encourage you to keep learning and discovering. As Confucius said, "Acquire new knowledge whilst thinking over the old, and you may become a teacher of others." What better advice for a network administrator?

Good Luck!

Workshop
Q&A

Q Is it important to spend time tuning my NetWare file server?

A The default settings for the file provide good performance for most applications. You probably don't need to change a thing. If you do, it should be in response to an identified problem. Remember the old adage, "if it ain't broke, don't fix it."

If you can't resist the urge to "tinker", make your changes to a test system, that is, one which isn't used for an important business information system. In that way, if you mess up a test system, you won't cause any harm to a server your business depends on.

Q How do I edit parameters in the STARTUP.NCF or AUTOEXEC.NCF files?

A Use the INSTALL NLM on the file server. Its System Options menu includes choices for creating and editing each of these files. The editor works in the same manner as in other NetWare menu utilities (like entering login scripts), so you should be familiar with how to use it.

Q **Are there similar parameters that can be changed to make a workstation perform faster?**

A A DOS-based workstation doesn't have nearly as many parameters that affect its performance. However, there are some features, such as caching, that can be used to speed up the workstation. And as with the NetWare file server, more memory helps, especially when using programs like Windows. The best thing to do is consult a good DOS reference text for tips on how to configure your workstation for maximum performance.

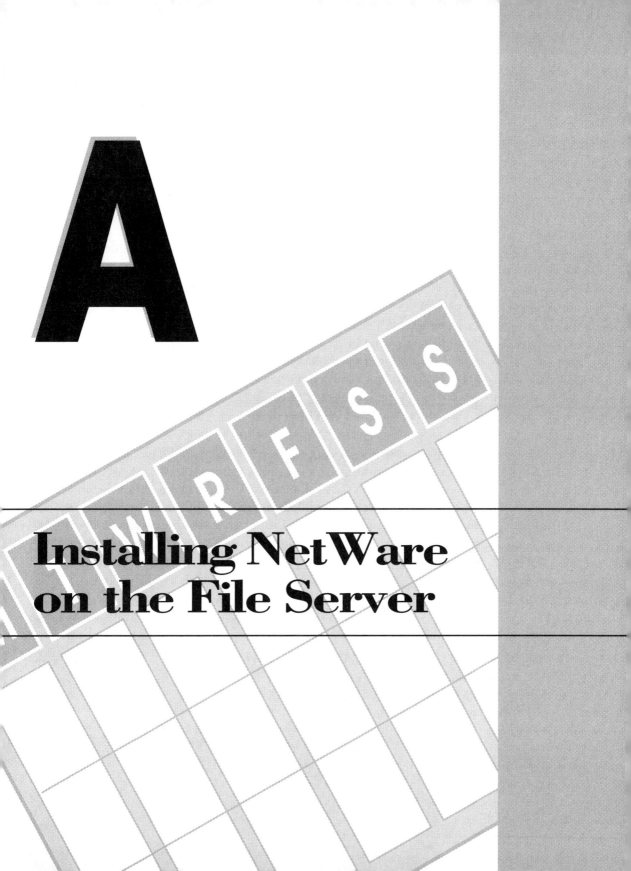

A

Installing NetWare on the File Server

Ah, ah—I know what you're thinking: "Should I try to install NetWare on the file server myself, or get help from a CNE or ECNE?" Well, seeing that this is NetWare, one of the most powerful network operating systems in the world, and it could make you want to blow your head *clean off*, you've got to ask yourself one question: "Do I feel lucky?"

Well administrator—do ya?

Trying to install NetWare isn't quite as threatening as an encounter with certain famous movie police inspectors, but it can pose some real challenges. It's one of those tasks that could go very smoothly and take an hour or so. Or it could be a battle every step of the way.

To a large extent, it all depends on the particular pieces of hardware you've pulled together to form your file server. It's the hardware, particularly disk controllers, and NICs that dictate which of the NetWare Loadable Modules (NLMs) you need. If the NLMs recognize your hardware and work properly, your installation will be easy. If they don't, you will have to determine what the problem is and fix it. It may mean reconfiguring your hardware, or possibly getting custom NLMs from the hardware vendor.

Solving these problems can require a great deal of technical knowledge and experience. That's why usually it's a good idea to get a Certified NetWare Engineer (CNE) or Enterprise Certified NetWare Engineer (ECNE) involved with your installation, especially if you aren't that familiar with the details of PC hardware. Someone who has gone through many installations can quickly recognize the cause of problems. And they probably have a nice collection of NLMs to interface with unusual types of hardware, which might be just what you need to get up and running.

But not everyone has the luxury of their own personal CNE. So you might be the one who *must* install the software on your server. In that case, read on—you'll get an overview of the installation process that will help you when you roll up your sleeves to start.

Installing NetWare involves many steps. The actual steps you follow depend on the hardware you use, so we won't be able to cover all the possibilities here. Consult NetWare's Installation and Upgrade manual for step-by-step instructions to follow for your particular configuration.

Rather than detailed steps, you'll see the big picture of a NetWare installation. This information should help you when you perform the detailed steps, as well as determine the cause of any problems which might arise.

The Installation Process

First, you look at some of the hardware issues for a NetWare file server. Then you walk through the installation process itself.

Required Hardware

Because your file server will be one of the most heavily-used computers in your office, you should try to get a machine with as much power and performance as possible. NetWare will run on a surprisingly small machine, but for serious business use, a larger machine is required. Following are some examples of systems you can use:

☐ You can use a PC with a 386SX processor, but a 486DX is preferable, and a DX2 (running at 66 megahertz) is even better.

☐ As we've mentioned throughout this book, the more memory you have, the better. You can get away with the minimum 4M (megabytes) of RAM required, but 8M is more realistic, and 16M or 32M is much better, particularly if you have many users.

☐ Your hard disk should be have at least 50M available for storage. This allows 5M for a DOS partition, and 45M for NetWare's SYS: volume. However, because 250M is becoming a common disk size for workstations, you might as well not even bother creating a server with less than 300 to 500M of disk storage. One or two gigabytes (Gs) is not uncommon.

You also will need a network interface card (NIC) compatible with the type of network you are installing, such as Ethernet or Token Ring. For a video card and monitor, you can get away with almost anything, since NetWare's file server console doesn't make use of very elaborate graphics. A tape drive attached to the server computer also is very useful if you plan on performing regular backups of files (and you should). At the very least, have a tape drive available on one of your workstations, which can also be used for backup.

The Need for a CD-ROM Drive

NetWare version 3.12 is available on diskette, as usual, but you also can get it on CD-ROM. If you've ever gone through the process of swapping floppy disks for large programs such as NetWare, the ease of installing from CD-ROM is very appealing. You simply insert the CD-ROM into the drive, issue a few commands, and then sit

back and watch. Waiting for the prompt to insert yet another floppy disk becomes a thing of the past. With the number of diskettes required for NetWare (and especially ElectroText) growing with every release, the CD-ROM option definitely is worth considering.

CD-ROM drives may be a new technology for you, however. If you haven't installed and used one in the past, this can seem like yet another hurdle you must overcome before your NetWare file server is up and running. And the last thing you want now is another hurdle.

Using a CD-ROM drive may not be as difficult as you think. If you didn't purchase a drive with your file server, the add-on installation may be as simple as plugging the drive into the connector on a SCSI disk controller. At the very worst, you will need to add another card to the file server that supports the CD-ROM drive. Note that the drive should be able to read a CD in standard format (which is known as ISO 9660).

After it is physically installed, just two files normally are required to make the CD-ROM drive functional. One, a driver in the CONFIG.SYS file, recognizes the drive and provides an interface to programs running on your computer. The other, a program executed from the AUTOEXEC.BAT makes the CD-ROM appear as just another DOS disk drive. From that point on, you use the CD-ROM like any other DOS disk. You can change to the CD-ROM drive letter (for example, the D: drive), move around its directories, and read its files. The only thing you can't do is write to it, because it's Read Only.

So if you *do* decide to use CD-ROM, just follow the manufacturer's instructions for installation, and make sure you can use it as a DOS drive before even attempting to install NetWare.

As a test, mount the NetWare 3.12 CD-ROM, and use DOS commands to look at some of the files. For example, change to the directory

`NETWARE.312\ENGLISH\README`

This directory contains updates to the NetWare manuals, and additional information on installing and using various products. Of particular interest is the following file:

HELP.CD

The file contains text on how to install NetWare from a CD-ROM drive. It includes information about a potential source of problems when using a CD-ROM drive that shares a SCSI disk controller with a hard disk used for NetWare. A work-around solution is described.

Creating a DOS Partition

Because you start NetWare from DOS, you must start the file server by first booting DOS. While it is possible to start the server from a floppy drive, this is not recommended. Starting from a hard disk drive is much easier, so your file server needs a bootable DOS partition on its hard disk.

If you've ever installed DOS from scratch, you may remember that you used the FDISK command to *partition* the hard drive. This allocates a section of the hard disk for use by DOS. Normally, you enable DOS to use the entire hard disk.

But now, you will allocate only a portion of the hard disk to DOS, as little as 5 M of space. The rest will be used by NetWare when it creates a NetWare partition. Your hard disk will end up having two different partitions, each one maintained by a separate operating system—DOS and NetWare.

To create the DOS partition, you can use your DOS distribution diskettes to run FDISK, create the DOS partition of at least 5M, and FORMAT the partition as a bootable disk ready to accept files. You can restart your computer, and see your C: drive as usual.

Warning: You probably realize this, but by using FDISK and FORMAT, you lose whatever files were on the hard disk. If you are pressing this computer into service from a previous life as a DOS machine, make sure you first back up the existing DOS files.

Note: If you create a larger DOS partition, you will have less available space for your NetWare partitions. NetWare will create and format its own partition later in the installation process.

If you are using a CD-ROM drive, you will need to add the two required driver programs mentioned earlier. Then reboot your computer so that the CD-ROM drive is recognized and available.

This is a good time to run your computer through a full suite of tests. You should make sure all the hardware functions correctly before trying to install NetWare.

> **Tip:** The NetWare install program also gives you the option of creating a DOS partition. But it's easier, and a bit less confusing, to do this before starting the installation process.

Starting the Installation

The first step of the installation process involves copying some key NetWare files onto the DOS partition. Remember, NetWare is a program (called SERVER.EXE) that is started from the DOS prompt; it takes over the computer once it has started. So you need to copy SERVER.EXE, plus some other key files, onto the DOS partition on the hard disk. You do this using the NetWare supplied INSTALL program. Later, you'll start NetWare and complete the installation process under its control.

If you are installing from floppy disks, insert the one labeled Install in the file server's floppy drive A:. At the A: drive prompt, type the following and then press Enter.

`INSTALL`

If you are installing from CD-ROM, remember, it's just another DOS drive. Running a program from the CD-ROM isn't any different than running one from the hard drive or floppy disk. For example, assume that you configured it as drive D:. Switch to the D: drive and change to the following directory:

`NETWARE.312\ENGLISH`

Then start the installation program by typing the following and then press Enter.

`INSTALL`

INSTALL leads you through the installation process, so simply follow the prompts. For example, when it asks you to name the file server, you can enter any name up to 298 characters long, as long as there are no periods or spaces. INSTALL will also offer to assign automatically an IPX internal network number. It's easiest to simply accept the number it proposes.

Even if you're installing from CD-ROM, you'll be prompted to insert the disk labeled SYSTEM_1 into the floppy drive. INSTALL gets SERVER.EXE, plus disk drivers and certain key NLM files from this diskette, and copies them to the C: drive in directory SERVER.312.

INSTALL then prompts you for some more choices, such as your country code, DOS filename format, if you want to enter startup commands, and if you want SERVER.EXE

added to your file server's AUTOEXEC.BAT (so that NetWare will start automatically when you boot the computer). Answer these however you like.

INSTALL then leads you into the next phase of installation by starting NetWare. To do this, it simply executes the program SERVER.EXE for you.

Loading a Disk Driver

At this point, you are actually running NetWare, except your file server doesn't have a NetWare disk it knows about, nor can it talk on the network. It does recognize your DOS partition, but won't offer those files to the network. That's not too impressive right now, but it gets much better.

NetWare needs to know how to access the disk drive where your NetWare partition is going to be created. You have to load a disk driver NLM so that NetWare can recognize the hard disk controller and drive. The INSTALL program you ran from a floppy disk or CD-ROM copied a few disk driver NLMs to your DOS partition. These are files with an extension of .DSK. Two common ones include the following:

- [ ] IDE.DSK, used for IDE-type controllers

- [ ] ISADSK.DSK, used for many built-in AT-class disk controllers, as well as older controllers

The increasingly popular SCSI disk controller cards usually come with their own .DSK file designed for use with NetWare. If you have one of these cards, you'll need to copy the correct .DSK file onto the DOS partition on the hard disk. Leave NetWare by typing the following two commands at the console prompt and press Enter after each command:

DOWN
EXIT

Doing this takes you back to the DOS prompt. You can then find and copy the .DSK driver from a diskette supplied by the disk controller vendor to the \SERVER.312 directory on the C: drive. After you've copied the disk driver, restart NetWare by typing the following command and then press Enter:

SERVER

After you select the disk driver, you load it with the LOAD command at the console prompt. Because NetWare still knows how to talk to your DOS partition, it looks back in the \SERVER.312 directory for the appropriate file. For example, to load the IDE.DSK disk driver, type the following command and press Enter.

LOAD IDE

Depending on the type of disk you use, the disk driver will prompt you for additional information. This probably will include the interrupt number and the address of the input/output port it should use. The driver will likely offer defaults that you can choose if you are unsure of the real values. The trial-and-error method can be a bit dangerous, however, so it's much better to have a good idea of the actual parameters. They should be available from the documentation supplied with the computer or controller card. You even may be able to get the details by using a diagnostic program such as MSD, but this must be done back at the DOS prompt (that is, after leaving NetWare and returning to DOS).

If everything has gone well, you will get a message indicating that the driver has loaded successfully, and you're ready for the next step.

Creating a NetWare Partition

NetWare now knows how to talk with your disk drive directly, without having to use DOS. You can create a NetWare partition from the space you left on the hard disk, and from that space, create the NetWare SYS: volume.

To do these functions, you use another installation program, this one a NetWare Loadable Module called INSTALL.NLM. To start INSTALL, type the following at the console prompt and press Enter:

LOAD INSTALL

You first must create a NetWare partition on the disk drive. Use the Disk Options selection followed by Partition Tables. NetWare then lists the Available Disk Drives.

If you don't see your drive listed, NetWare doesn't recognize it. You'll have to go back to the previous step and determine why. But if you do see your drive, you can select it and press Enter. In response, INSTALL displays a partition table. You should see the small DOS partition on the disk, and a lot of free space. That's where you're going to create the NetWare partition. From the Partition Options menu, select Create NetWare Partition, and follow the prompts, accepting the defaults as you go.

After creating the partition, press Esc to return to the Installation Options menu.

Creating a NetWare Volume

You now have a NetWare partition that is ready to accept a NetWare volume. Because every file server requires a SYS: volume, that's the one you'll create. If you want, you can create additional volumes as well.

To create a volume, select the Volume Options item. INSTALL displays a list of Volumes, which should be empty at this point. Press Ins, and NetWare will enter the name SYS: on the New Volume Information screen. By default, it will assign all available free space to SYS:. So if you want to create volumes other than SYS:, decrease the value in the Initial Segment Size field. This leaves space for you to follow this same procedure in order to create other volumes. Otherwise, just accept the defaults NetWare has proposed.

When you are ready to create the volume, press Esc, and confirm that you want to create the volume. After creating the volume, you must mount the volume so that NetWare can use it. To do this from within INSTALL, select Volume Options from the main menu, and then select the volume. You should see the Volume Information screen.

Select the Status field, press Enter, and select Mount Volume. The SYS: volume now is open for business.

Copying SYSTEM and PUBLIC Files

Now that you have a place to put them, you are ready to copy the many files NetWare needs to put in the SYSTEM and PUBLIC directories. NetWare gets these either from the installation diskettes or the CD-ROM.

> **Warning:** If you're using CD-ROM, you might be faced with a decision. Recall mention of the HELP.CD text file that described a potential problem with using a CD-ROM. This step is where the problem can arise. Try the following procedure. If it doesn't work, you'll have to try the steps listed in HELP.CD that involve mounting the CD-ROM drive as a NetWare volume.

To copy the required files, you use another option from the INSTALL.NLM. From its main menu, choose System Options, and then select Copy System and Public Files.

If you are installing from disks, simply insert the one labeled Install and press Enter. INSTALL prompts you for the other disks.

If you're installing from CD-ROM, press F6 which enables you to enter a new pathname as the source of the files. Remember that your CD-ROM is just a DOS drive? All you have to do is type the drive letter, followed by the correct path for the

files. If your CD-ROM is DOS drive D:, for example, you would type the following command and press Enter:

```
D:\NETWARE.312\ENGLISH
```

INSTALL then copies the files to the SYS: volume.

Loading the LAN Driver

Now all NetWare has to do is find out about the NIC installed at the file server—how to talk to the card, and what protocol it should use to speak to other stations on the network.

At this point, NetWare knows how to find files on the SYS: volume. In particular, the SYS:SYSTEM directory contains many NetWare Loadable Modules with an extension of .LAN. These are the LAN drivers NetWare uses to talk to the NIC installed on the file server. You load one of these drivers in the same way as other NLMs, by using the LOAD command. For example, to talk with an NE2000 NIC, type the following command and press Enter.

```
LOAD NE2000
```

> **Note:** NetWare comes with LAN drivers for many NICs. However, if a driver for your NIC isn't included, you will have to load one from a diskette supplied by the NIC vendor. To do this, if you place the diskette in drive A, you preface the driver name in the LOAD command with "A:". You should eventually copy this driver to the SYS:SYSTEM directory so that you don't need to insert the diskette each time you start NetWare.

Depending on the type of NIC you use, the LAN driver will prompt you for additional information. This probably will include the interrupt number and the address of the input/output port it should use. The driver will likely offer defaults that you can choose if you are unsure. (It's a little less dangerous here, as compared to playing with the file server's hard disk controller.) The details should be available from the NIC vendor's documentation.

Note: If you are using Ethernet NICs, by default, NetWare version 3.12 uses a frame type of 802.2. This frame will not be recognized by other servers running the older 802.3 frame type, and it won't be seen by workstations that have not been configured for 802.2. You may need to load support for frame type 802.3, as well.

If everything has gone well, you will get a message indicating that the driver has loaded successfully. The last step is to associate the IPX protocol with the LAN driver you just loaded. To do this, you use the BIND console command. If you loaded the NE2000 LAN driver, for example, type the following command and press Enter:

```
BIND IPX to NE2000
```

BIND prompts you to enter a network address, which can be any hexadecimal number up to eight characters long. Note that this isn't the same as the internal IPX number you were prompted for by INSTALL. Enter a number of your choosing.

You then should make selections from Install's System Options menu to Create the STARTUP.NCF and AUTOEXEC.NCF files. Commands in these files are executed when you start your NetWare server. The command to load your disk driver is normally placed in STARTUP.NCF, while loading the LAN driver and binding the protocol are in AUTOEXEC.NCF. After you create them, review each of these files to ensure that NetWare has gathered the correct information from your previous entries. It's a good idea to test the files by downing the file server and restarting NetWare from scratch. If the server isn't restarted with the same commands and option choices you typed earlier, you'll have to Edit the .NCF files to provide the correct information.

You should now have a NetWare server available for use by all your users. Congratulations!

What if It Doesn't Work?

If everything *hasn't* gone well, you should review the above material again. Also review NetWare's Installation and Upgrade manual. If you can, get help from a CNE or an ECNE. Then try it again, one step at a time.

B

Novell NetWare Certification Programs

Novell has established four different certification programs for NetWare, namely the Certified NetWare Administrator (CNA), the Certified NetWare Engineer (CNE), the Enterprise Certified NetWare Engineer (ECNE), and the Certified NetWare Instructor (CNI) programs.

Certified NetWare Administrator (CNA)

The Certified NetWare Administrator (CNA) program provides guidelines and certification testing for individuals performing day-to-day system administration functions. These functions include backing up servers, adding and deleting users, creating login scripts, and maintaining security.

CNA Courses

Anyone with a thorough understanding of DOS and a particular NetWare operating system can become a CNA. The Novell Education program offers the courses listed in Table B.1 for preparation.

Table B.1. Certified NetWare Administrator (CNA) Courses.

Version	Course
NetWare 2.2	501—NetWare 2.2 System Manager, 502—NetWare 2.2 Advanced System Manager
NetWare 3.1*x*	508—NetWare 3.1*x* Administration
NetWare 4.*x*	520—NetWare 4.*x* Administration

CNA Tests

By passing the appropriate Certified NetWare Administrator test shown in Table B.2, a candidate can become certified. Becoming a CNA may also help you if you decide to go on and work toward CNE certification. The current Certified NetWare 4.*x* Administrator and Certified 3.1*x* Administrator tests count toward CNE certification, though the NetWare 2.2 Administrator test does not.

Table B.2. Certified NetWare Administrator (CNA) Tests.

Test	Test Number
Certified NetWare 2.2 Administrator	50-115
Certified NetWare 3.1x Administrator	50-390
Certified NetWare 4.x Administrator	50-391

B

Certified NetWare Engineer (CNE)

The Certified NetWare Engineer (CNE) program is the next level of Novell certification for technical support personnel. The program prepares individuals to provide superior network maintenance and diagnostics. Individuals receive in-depth training in Novell hardware and software support. To certify as a CNE, applicants must earn 19 credits as shown in Table B.3.

Table B.3. Certified NetWare Engineer (CNE) Credit Requirements.

Prerequisite Requirement	2 credits
Operating System	5 credits
Core Requirements	8 credits
Electives	4 credits
Total credits required	19 credits

To receive these required credits, applicants must pass a series of tests as laid out in the following tables.

CNE Prerequisite Requirement

The CNE applicant can satisfy the prerequisite requirement by passing either UNIX OS Fundamentals for NetWare Users or DOS/Microcomputer Concepts (Table B.3).

Table B.3. CNE Prerequisite Requirements (2 credits).

Course Number	Course Name	Test Number	Credits
220	UNIX OS Fundamentals for NetWare Users	50-107	2
or			
1100-1	DOS/Microcomputer Concepts	50-15	2

CNE Operating System Requirements

The operating system requirements are currently in two tracks—the NetWare 3.1x Track and the NetWare 4.0 Track (Table B.4). Novell is phasing out a number of older courses and tests in the operating system category. CNE candidates wishing to complete their operating system requirements on the NetWare 2.2 track must complete their CNE certification before June 30, 1994, otherwise their 2.2 tests will count as elective credit only. NetWare 3.11 System Manager and NetWare 3.11 Advanced System Manager (tests 50-91 and 50-82 respectively) will no longer be available as of May 12, 1994.

Table B.4. CNE Operating System Requirements (5 credits).

Course Number	Course Name	Test Number	Credits
508	NetWare 3.1x Administration	50-130	3
518	NetWare 3.1x Advanced Administration	50-131	2
or			
520	NetWare 4.x Administration	50-122	3
525	NetWare 4.x Advanced Administration	50-123	2

CNE Core Requirements

The CNE core requirements are two tests—NetWare Service and Support and Networking Technologies (Table B.5).

Table B.5. CNE Core Requirements (8 credits).

Course Number	Course Name	Test Number	Credits
701	NetWare Service and Support	50-46	5
200	Networking Technologies	50-80	3

CNE Elective Requirements

Candidates can choose among several different courses and tests to satisfy the four elective credits (Table B.6). Generally, any operating system track test not used to complete the operating system requirement may be used toward elective credits. There are numerous restrictions and limitations, however, so contact Novell education or a local NAEC for details.

Table B.6. CNE Electives (4 credits).

Course Number	Course Name	Test Number	Credits
205	Fundamentals of Internetwork and Management Design	50-106	2
526	NetWare 3.11 to 4.x Update	50-124	2
535	Printing with NetWare	50-137	2
550	NetWare Navigator	50-138	2
605	NetWare TCP/IP Transport	50-86	2
610	NetWare NFS	50-87	2
615	NetWare for Macintosh Connectivity	50-93	2
625	NetWare NFS Gateway	50-119	1

continues

Table B.6. continued

Course Number	Course Name	Test Number	Credits
630	NetWare/IP	50-139	1
715	NetWare Dial-in/Dial-out Connectivity	50-112	2
720	NetWare for SAA Installation and Troubleshooting	50-85	3
740	NetWare Internetworking Products	50-117	2
750	NetWare Global MHS	50-108	2
804	NetWare 4.0 Installation and Configuration Workshop	50-126	2
904	Btrieve: An Overview	50-127	1
905	Programming with Btrieve	50-129	2
1125	LANalyzer for Windows	50-105	1

ECNE and CNI

The Enterprise Certified NetWare Engineer (ECNE) program is for individuals who wish to acquire a more in-depth knowledge of Novell products and who have successfully completed the CNE program. This program is suited for individuals who are involved in the management of enterprise networking environments.

The Certified NetWare Instructor (CNI) program is for those who want to teach Novell courses. CNI candidates are required to attend the courses they plan to teach, and then pass a special CNI version of the equivalent test. CNI candidates also must pass an instructor performance evaluation.

Certification Benefits

Certification brings benefits. These include

- ☐ Technical support: CNEs receive priority attention from Novell Technical Support, including two free support incidents, and a 50 percent discount on all additional support incidents.

- ☐ NSE: CNEs receive a free issue of the Network Support Encyclopedia (NSE) Professional volume, which is an electronic information base containing technical information needed for installing, maintaining, and troubleshooting a network.

- ☐ CNEPA membership: CNEs receive membership to CNEPA, a non-profit international organization, and can access their NetWire special forum.

Novell recognizes that many system engineers and network administrators have acquired a great deal of knowledge and experience about NetWare. Should you feel after reading this book that you are ready, you may take the Plato Challenge Test without attending classes. Classroom work supports your effort in attaining accreditation.

Novell has two different testing methods. In the first method—adaptive testing—candidates are challenged by questions drawn from a computer data base of thousands of questions. Each question has three associated levels of difficulty. The first question for each topic has a low level of difficulty. Answering the question correctly allows the candidate to progress to the next level of questions, through to the highest level. If a candidate fails to answer any question at any level, the system will fall back to the previous level. So, a candidate who knows the material well will complete the challenge within three questions, and move on to the next related topic in the test. Otherwise, the candidate will receive questions that attempt to assess the candidate's understanding of the topic. If no questions for a particular subject are answered correctly, the examination program will move on to the next topic.

The second method—non-adaptive testing—uses standard computerized testing methods. The tests contain between 60 and 75 questions and take from 60 to 90 minutes. The number of questions answered correctly provides the grade and percentage.

For more information about Novell's NetWare certification programs, in the United States and Canada, contact Novell Education at 1-800-233-EDUC. In other locations, call 1-801-429-5508.

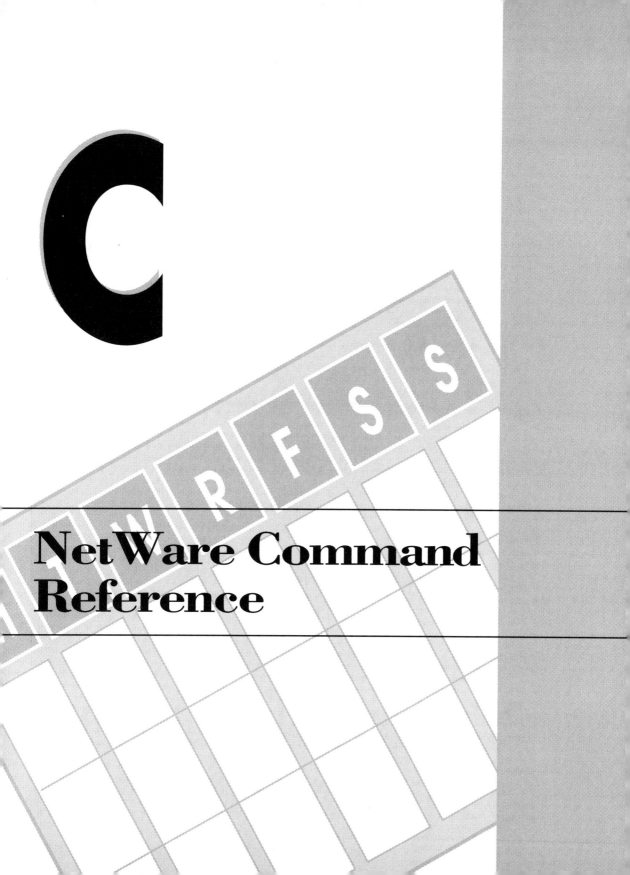

C

NetWare Command
Reference

This appendix serves as a useful reference of NetWare commands. The information for each command may include

☐ The name of the command

☐ A description of the command

☐ The command syntax

☐ Command parameters

☐ The procedure for using the command

☐ Notes about the usage of the command, if appropriate

ATOTAL

Enables a Supervisor to either see the accounting services records or create a file showing the records.

ATOTAL records the daily and weekly totals of blocks read and written, connect time, disk storage, and service requests.

Syntax

```
ATOTAL [ > filename ]
```

Procedure

Type the command at the DOS prompt.

Usage Notes

You can use the > *filename* option to redirect the information to a file, where you can then access it.

ATTACH

Enables you to log in your workstation to another file server while you remain logged in to your default server.

Syntax

```
ATTACH file server/username
```

Procedure

1. Type the command at the DOS prompt. Enter the name of the file server you want to attach to as *file server* and your username as *username.*

2. Type your password for the attached file server if required.

Usage Notes

You can attach your workstation to all file servers where you have login rights. You repeat the procedure for every file server to which you want to attach.

BIND

Enables the Supervisor to link a LAN driver to a communication protocol or to a network board in the file server.

Syntax

```
BIND protocol TO LAN driver [driver parameter]
BIND protocol TO board name [protocol parameter]
```

Parameter

The driver parameters you can use are:

DMA=n	DMA channel number
FRAME=*name*	Frame type
INT=n	Interrupt number
MEM=n	Memory address number
PORT=n	I/O port number
SLOT=n	Slot where the board is installed

The IPX protocol parameter you can use is

NET=n	Network number for cabling system

Procedure

1. Install the board and load its corresponding LAN driver.

2. Type the command at the file server console, with the name of the protocol, such as IPX for *protocol* and the name of the driver or the board for *LAN driver* or *board.*

BINDFIX

Enables the Supervisor to repair the bindery to fix problems such as the incapability to delete or modify user information and rights, error messages regarding the bindery on the file server console, or an "unknown server" message during printing on the default server.

Syntax

```
BINDFIX
```

Procedure

1. All users should log off the network.

2. Type the command at the DOS prompt.

3. Answer Yes or No to whether you want to delete mail subdirectories for users who no longer exist on the network.

4. Answer Yes or No to whether you want to delete trustee rights for users who no longer exist on the network.

5. When BINDFIX completes, check to see if old problems are reoccurring.

Usage Notes

If the old problems persist, restore the old bindery.

BINDREST

Enables the Supervisor to restore the old bindery files when an attempt to fix the bindery fails to work.

Syntax

BINDREST

Procedure

1. All users should log off the network.

2. Type the command at the DOS prompt.

Usage Notes

If the bindery files you restore are too old, passwords may be set to old passwords that the users no longer can remember. You will need to reset the passwords and have the users set new passwords.

BROADCAST

Enables the Supervisor or console operator to send a message from the file server to all users, or to selected users.

Syntax

BROADCAST "message" [username] [connection number]

Procedure

Type the command at the file server console. You should add either the username or the connection number option to restrict the message to certain users or workstations.

Usage Notes

When using BROADCAST, separate usernames or connection numbers with commas.

You always should send a broadcast message before taking down the file server.

CAPTURE

Enables you to print text files, files from applications, screen displays, and any other print output not designed for network printing. This command enables you to print from applications not supporting network printing.

Syntax

```
CAPTURE options
```

Parameters

Options	Description
AU[TOENDCAP]	Sends job automatically to printer or file upon exiting the application
B[ANNER]=*banner*	Prints a word on banner page
C[OPIES]=*n*	Prints specified number of copies
F[ORM]=*n*	Specifies the printer form defined by Supervisor
F[ORM]F[EED]	Enables form feed after your print job is through
J[OB]=*job*	Tells the printer the print job configuration
K[EEP]	Retains what data is in the queue if your workstation hangs
L[OCAL]=*n*	Specifies the LPT port number to capture
NAM[E]=*name*	Prints a name on the banner page
N[O]A[UTOENDCAP]	Prevents the job from automatically going to the file or printer upon exiting the application
N[O] B[ANNER]	Prevents a banner page from printing
N[O] F[ORM] F[EED]	Prevents form feed from functioning
N[O] T[ABS]	Keeps tabs exactly as in your application. Do not use if your application has a print formatter
Q[UEUE]=*queue*	Specifies the queue for the print job
S[ERVER]=*server*	Specifies file server, if not default server

Options	Description
SH[OW]	Shows the LPT ports that are captured
T[ABS]=*n*	Makes all tabs the uniform number of spaces specified. Do not use if your application has a print formatter
TI[MEOUT]=*n*	Sends job automatically to printer if nothing is added in specified number of seconds

Procedure

1. Type the command at the DOS prompt, with any option.

2. Enter the application and access the file you want to print.

3. Press Shift+PrntScrn.

4. Exit the application. If Autoendcap is set to Yes or Timeout is enabled, your job will print, otherwise type **ENDCAP** at the DOS prompt.

Usage Notes

You can include this command in your login script.

CASTOFF

Enables you to block other workstations and the file server from sending you messages.

Syntax

CASTOFF [ALL]

Procedure

Type the command at the DOS prompt. Include the ALL if you want to block file server messages.

Usage Notes

The most recent file server message sent to you while the block was in place appears when you unblock messages.

CASTON

Enables you to resume getting messages from other workstations and the file server after you have blocked them with CASTOFF.

Syntax

CASTON

Procedure

Type the command at the DOS prompt.

Usage Notes

The most recent file server message sent while the block was in effect will now appear. Clear it by pressing Ctrl+Enter.

CLEAR STATION

Enables the Supervisor to close files and delete internal tables for a workstation that has crashed.

Syntax

CLEAR STATION *n*

Procedure

Type the command at the file server console, using the connection number for *n*.

CLS

Enables the Supervisor to clear the file server console screen.

Syntax

CLS

Procedure

Type the command at the file server console.

COMCHECK

Enables you to test the cabling between the file server and a workstation.

Syntax

COMCHECK

Procedure

1. Make sure that DOS is booted on both the file server and the workstation and that IPX is loaded on the workstation.

2. Type the command at the DOS prompt.

3. Type any name in the Unique User Information Box.

4. Check to see that the screen displays the network number, node number, the unique name you typed in, the date, and the time. If it does not, first check the cabling and replace if necessary.

CONFIG

Enables the Supervisor to see the file server name, its network address, loaded LAN drivers, board settings, node addresses for boards, communication protocol bound to the board, cabling number for network boards, frame type assigned to boards, and board names.

Syntax

```
CONFIG
```

Procedure

Type the command at the file server console.

Usage Notes

You see slightly different information for boards with different versions of NetWare.

DISABLE LOGIN

Enables the Supervisor or console operator to block all users from logging in to the file server.

Syntax

```
DISABLE LOGIN
```

Procedure

Type the command at the file server console.

DISABLE TTS

Enables the Supervisor or console operator to shut off the Transaction Tracking System in the file server.

Syntax

```
DISABLE TTS
```

Procedure

Type the command at the file server console.

DISMOUNT

Enables the Supervisor to restrict access to a volume while repairing it or upgrading disk drivers.

Syntax

```
DISMOUNT volume name
```

Procedure

1. Send a broadcast message to all users to close all files on the volume.

2. Type the command at the file server console, with the name of the volume for *volume name.*

DOWN

Enables the Supervisor to ensure that all cache buffers are written to disk, that all files are closed, and that the Directory and File Allocation Tables are updated before turning off the power to the file server.

Syntax

```
DOWN
```

Procedure

1. Send a broadcast message to all users to log out.

2. Type the command at the file server console.

Usage Notes

If you issue this command and do not turn off the power, the file server still receives packets, and you can issue any command that deals with the packets.

ENABLE LOGIN

Enables the Supervisor or console operator to reverse a disable login command, or a change of status command, so that users can once again log in to the file server.

Syntax

```
ENABLE LOGIN
```

Procedure

Type the command at the file server console.

Usage Notes

You can use ENABLE LOGIN to reenable the SUPERVISOR account after it has been locked by the intruder detection program.

ENABLE TTS

Enables the Supervisor or console operator to restart the Transaction Tracking System in the file server when it has been disabled due to insufficient memory or to the SYS: volume becoming full, or when the Supervisor has manually disabled it.

Syntax

```
ENABLE TTS
```

Procedure

Type the command at the file server console.

ENDCAP

Enables you to end the capture of LPT ports.

Syntax

```
ENDCAP options
```

Parameter

Options	Description
ALL	Ends capture of all LPT ports
C[ANCEL]	Ends LPT port capture and discards data without printing
C[ANCEL] L=n	Cancels a particular port and discards data without printing
C[ANCEL] ALL	Cancels all ports and discards data without printing
L[OCAL]=n	Specifies the LPT port number to end capture

Procedure

Type at the DOS prompt the command with the option.

Usage Notes

You cannot ENDCAP without first using CAPTURE.

EXIT

Enables the Supervisor to access DOS after downing the file server, if the power is not turned off. It also enables the Supervisor to warm boot the file server after removing DOS with the REMOVE DOS command and then downing the file server with DOWN.

Syntax

```
EXIT
```

Procedure

Type the command at the file server console.

FLAG

Enables the Supervisor or users with the modify access right to view or change the file attributes of a given file..

Syntax

FLAG *file name [attributes]*

Parameter

file name   Lists or sets the attributes for a file.

Attributes	Description
A	Archive needed
CI	Copy Inhibit
DI	Delete Inhibit
H	Hidden
HELP	Provides all available attributes in the version of NetWare
I	Indexed
N	Reset a file's attributes to the default setting
P	Purge
R	Rename inhibit
RO	Read Only
RW	Read Write
S	Shareable
SY	System
T	Transactional
X	Execute only

Procedure

Type the command at the DOS prompt.

FLAGDIR

Enables you to set a directory's security attributes.

Syntax

```
FLAGDIR directory name [attributes]
```

Parameter

Attributes	Description
DI	Delete inhibit
H	Hidden
N	Normal
P	Purge
R	Rename
SY	System

Procedure

Type at the DOS prompt the command with the letters of the *attributes*.

Usage Notes

You must have rights in a directory to modify its attributes.

GRANT

Enables you to add trustee rights in a directory you control to a user or group.

Syntax

GRANT *attribute* TO *user*

Procedure

Type the command at the DOS prompt.

Usage Notes

For GRANT, substitute a group name for a username if you want to add group trustee rights instead.

LISTDIR

Enables you to sort and view the entire contents of a directory.

Syntax

LISTDIR */option*

Parameter

Option	Descripton
D	Creation date of each directory
E	Effective rights in each directory
R	Rights: Inherited Rights Mask of NetWare version 3.*x* directories
S	Subdirectory structure
T	Creation date of each directory
A	All of the above

Procedure

Type the command at the DOS prompt.

Usage Notes

LISTDIR shows subdirectories and subsequent subdirectories, not files. Use NDIR to view subdirectories and files.

You can get help with LISTDIR syntax by typing **LISTDIR** **/HELP** at the DOS prompt.

LOGIN

Enables you to change your default file server by logging in to another file server.

Syntax

```
LOGIN file server / username
```

Procedure

1. Type the command at the DOS prompt with the file server name for *file server*, and your name for *username*. You do not need to log out of the current file server, since this command automatically logs you out of that file server.

2. Type your password, if required.

LOGOUT

Enables you to log out of your workstation from any or all file servers.

Syntax

```
LOGOUT file server
```

Procedure

Type the command with the name of the file server you want to log out from as *file server* at the DOS prompt. If you type LOGOUT without *file server*, then you logout from all file servers.

Usage Notes

Using LOGOUT, you can log out of more than one attached file server by adding file server names to the command.

MAP

Enables you to view, create, or modify drive mappings to make getting around in your directory easier.

Syntax

```
MAP [parameter] letter:=path
```

Parameter

Options	Descriptions
DEL	Deletes an existing drive mapping
INSERT	Inserts a new drive mapping into the search list
NEXT	Assigns the next available drive letter as a regular drive pointer
ROOT	Establishes a regular drive mapping as a false root

Procedure

Type the command at the DOS prompt.

MEMORY

Enables the Supervisor to see how much memory is installed in the file server.

Syntax

```
MEMORY
```

Procedure

Type the command at the file server console.

MENU

Enables you to run a menu you created.

Syntax

```
MENU [filename]
```

Procedure

Type at the DOS prompt the command with the name of file. If the file name has an extension of *.mnu*, then you need only type the high level qualifier for the file name.

Usage Notes

You can create a menu tailored to your needs.

MODULES

Enables the Supervisor to list the NetWare Loadable Modules currently running on the file server.

Syntax

```
MODULES
```

Procedure

Type the command at the file server console.

MOUNT

Enables the Supervisor to make a volume available for network use after repairing it, upgrading it, or returning it for some other reason.

Syntax

```
MOUNT volume name
```

Procedure

Type the command at the file server console, with the name of the volume for *volume name*, or with the option *all* if all volumes need to be mounted.

NAME

Enables the Supervisor to see the name of the file server.

Syntax

```
NAME
```

Procedure

Type the command at the file server console.

NCOPY

Enables you to copy a directory and its contents or files from one location to another.

Syntax

```
NCOPY path1 [TO]  [path2] [/option]
```

Parameter

Options	Description
A	Copies modified files without resetting the archive bit
C	Copies without preserving file attributes or name space information
E	Copies empty subdirectories
F	Forces sparse files
I	Warns if destination does not support file's attributes or file space information
M	Copies modified files while resetting the archive bit
P	Preserves the hidden and system file attributes
S	Copies subdirectories
V	Copies and verifies the copy

Procedure

Type at the DOS prompt the command with the name of the directory or file you want to copy for *name*, the source for *path1*, and the destination for *path2*.

Usage Notes

You can copy a directory to another file server only if you are attached to that file server.

NDIR

Enables you to sort and list directories and files.

Syntax

NDIR /*option*

Parameter

Options	Description
Sort by directory structure	
DO	Directories only
FO	Files only
SUB	Subdirectory files in addition to files in the default directory
Sort by platform	
MAC	Macintosh files and subdirectories
LONG	Long names, such as Macintosh, OS/2, and NFS
Sort by owner	
[REV] SORT OW	Directory and file owners in alphabetical order, or reverse
OW [NOT] EQ *name*	Directories and files owned by one user, or excluding one user
Sort files by attribute	
[NOT] A	Archive needed
[NOT] CI	Copy inhibit (Macintosh only)
[NOT] DI	Delete inhibit
[NOT] EO	Execute only
[NOT] H	Hidden
[NOT] I	Indexed
[NOT] P	Purge
[NOT] RI	Rename inhibit
[NOT] RO	Read only
[NOT] S	Shareable

Options	Description
[NOT] SY	System
[NOT] T	Transactional

Sort files by date

Options	Description
AC [NOT] BEF ¦ EQ ¦ AFT *mm-dd-yy*	Accessed before, on, or after the date
AR [NOT] BEF ¦ EQ ¦ AFT *mm-dd-yy*	Archived before, on, or after the date
CR [NOT] BEF ¦ EQ ¦ AFT *mm-dd-yy*	Created before, on, or after the date
UP [NOT] BEF ¦ EQ ¦ AFT *mm-dd-yy*	Updated before, on, or after the date
[REV] SORT AC	Accessed in order from earliest to latest, or reverse
[REV] SORT AR	Archived in order from earliest to latest, or reverse
[REV] SORT CR	Created in order from earliest to latest, or reverse
[REV] SORT UP	Updated in order from earliest to latest, or reverse

Sort files by size

Options	Description
[REV] SORT SI	Smallest to largest, or reverse
SI [NOT] GR ¦ EQ ¦ LE *n*	Bytes greater than, equal to, or less than the number

Other options

Options	Description
DATES	Creation, last modified, last accessed, last archived dates
RIGHTS	All rights and attributes

Procedure

Type at the DOS prompt the command with options for additional information.

Usage Notes

The use of NOT excludes that attribute, date, and owner.

NETX

Enables you to see, load, or unload the shell file for a file server in your workstation.

Syntax

```
NETX option
```

Parameter

Options	Description
I	Information about the current NetWare shell
PS=*file server*	Loads the file server shell into the workstation
U	Unloads the NetWare shell from the workstation

Procedure

Type the command at the DOS prompt, with the option.

Usage Notes

The use of *x* denotes the version of DOS you have; for example, if you have NetWare 3.*x* you will use shell NETX.

If you use NETX to log in to another shell, type your username and password at the prompts.

NPRINT

Enables you to print text files from the command line.

Syntax

NPRINT *file name [option]*

Parameter

Options	Description
B[ANNER]=*banner*	Prints a word on banner page
C[OPIES]=*n*	Prints specified number of copies
D[ELETE]	Automatically erases file after printing
F[ORM]=*n*	Specifies the printer form defined by Supervisor
F[ORM] F[EED]	Enables form feed after print job is through
J[OB]=*job*	Tells the printer the print job configuration
NAM[E]=*name*	Prints a name on the banner page
N[O]A[UTOENDCAP]	Prevents the job from automatically going to the file or printer upon exiting the application
N[O] B[ANNER]	Prevents a banner page from printing
N[O] F[ORM] F[EED]	Prevents form feed from functioning
N[O] NOTI[FY]	Prevents notification that print job is done
N[O] T[ABS]	Keeps tabs exactly as in your application. Do not use if your application has a print formatter
NOTI[FY]	Notifies you when your print job is done
Q[UEUE]=*queue*	Specifies the queue for the print job
S[ERVER]=*server*	Specifies file server, if not default server
T[ABS]=*n*	Makes all tabs the uniform number of spaces specified. Do not use if your application has a print formatter.

Procedure

Type the command at the DOS prompt, including the directory path if the file is not in your default directory and with desired options.

NVER

Enables you to see what version of NetWare your file server is running, including the versions of NetBIOS, IPX, SPX, LAN driver, Shell, DOS, and the file server name.

Syntax

NVER

Procedure

Type the command at the DOS prompt.

OFF

Enables the Supervisor to clear the file server console screen.

Syntax

OFF

Procedure

Type the command at the file server console.

PAUDIT

Enables the Supervisor to see the records of accounting services used on the screen or to create a file showing the records. This command chronologically records each instance of an accounting service, including logins, logouts, and intruder detection activity. The Supervisor can use this information to monitor whether intruders have tried to access the network.

Syntax

```
PAUDIT [> filename]
```

Procedure

Type the command at the DOS prompt.

Usage Notes

The > *filename* option enables you to redirect the information to a file.

For information displayed to the screen, scroll through the dates until you find the one you want.

PROTOCOL REGISTER

Enables the Supervisor to register a new protocol on the file server, along with the protocol's frame type and protocol identification number.

Syntax

```
PROTOCOL REGISTER name frame id#
```

Procedure

Type the command at the file server console, with the name of protocol for *name*, the name of the frame type for *frame*, and the protocol id number (or Ethernet type, or SAP) for *id#*.

PROTOCOLS

Enables the Supervisor to see what protocols are registered on the file server, along with their frame types.

Syntax

```
PROTOCOLS
```

Procedure

Type the command at the file server console.

PURGE

Enables you to purge files you have deleted from the directory you are in, freeing up disk space.

Syntax

PURGE

Procedure

Type the command at the DOS prompt.

Usage Notes

Once you purge files, you cannot salvage them.

REMOVE DOS

Enables the Supervisor to return memory used for DOS to file caching; it also keeps NLMs residing on DOS partitions or local drives from being loaded at the file server console.

Syntax

REMOVE DOS

Procedure

Type the command at the file server console.

Usage Notes

To reverse the REMOVE DOS command, you must reboot the file server.

RENDIR

Enables you to rename a directory.

Syntax

```
RENDIR path1 [TO] path2
```

Procedure

Type the command at the DOS prompt with the old directory path and name for *path1* and the new directory path and name for *path2*.

Usage Notes

You can use the following in the directory path

period (.):	If it is your default directory
drive letter (F:):	If it is mapped to the directory you want to rename
colon and slash (:/):	If the directory you want to rename is a root directory on the volume

RESET ROUTER

Enables the Supervisor to fix the router table if it has become corrupted from a router or file server going down.

Syntax

```
RESET ROUTER
```

Procedure

Type the command at the file server console.

Usage Notes

Resetting the router causes it to update its routing table by sending messages to each file server or bridge nearby. Normally, this table updates every two minutes anyway.

REVOKE

Enables you to restrict a user's or group's rights in a directory you control.

Syntax

```
REVOKE attribute FROM user
```

Procedure

Type the command at the DOS prompt.

RIGHTS

Enables you to see what your rights are in a file or directory.

Syntax

```
RIGHTS path
```

Procedure

Type the command at the DOS prompt, with the filename (and directory path if it is not your default) for *path*.

Usage Notes

The use of RIGHTS only enables you to see your rights in the default directory.

SALVAGE

Enables you to recover files accidentally deleted.

Syntax

```
SALVAGE path
```

Procedure

Type at the DOS prompt the command with the full directory path (including the volume) for *path*.

Usage Notes

You can recover multiple files using a wildcard character if you used a wildcard character to delete them as a group.

SECURE CONSOLE

Enables the Supervisor to disable DOS without removing it from file server memory, keep unauthorized users from loading NLMs from floppies, local drives, or different directories, prevent entry into the OS debugger, and prevent changes to the file server date and time.

Syntax

```
SECURE CONSOLE
```

Procedure

Type the command at the file server console.

Usage Notes

To reverse the SECURE CONSOLE command, you have to reboot the file server.

SECURITY

Enables the Supervisor to check system security for possible problems, by either viewing the security summary on the screen or redirecting the information to a file.

Syntax

```
SECURITY [> filename]
```

Procedure

Type the command at the DOS prompt, adding the option if you want to redirect the information to a file.

SEND

Enables anyone to send a brief message to all users, multiple users, one user, workstation, or another file server.

Syntax

```
SEND "message" [TO] destination [option]
```

Procedure

Type the command at the DOS prompt, with message enclosed in quotes. You can add the following destination options to restrict the message to certain users or workstations, alone or in any combination separated by commas:

☐ Username

☐ Group name

☐ Connection number

☐ Console

Usage Notes

Maximum message is 45 characters, minus the number of characters in your username.

Use the `fileserver/` option only if the user is not on your file server.

Only IBM-compatible workstations support the SEND command.

SERVER

Enables the Supervisor to boot the file server using a DOS executable file on the file server console.

Syntax

```
SERVER -option
```

Parameter

Options	Description
-C *number*	Boots with different cache buffer size
-NA	Boots without AUTOEXEC.NCF file
-NS	Boots without STARTUP.NCF file
-S *[path] filename*	Boots with alternate STARTUP.NCF file

Procedure

Type the command at the DOS prompt at the file server console, with option if needed.

SET

Enables the Supervisor to see or set how the operating system parameters are configured for communications, memory, file caching, directory caching, file system, locks, transaction tracking, disk, password encryption, and other miscellaneous settings.

Syntax

```
SET
```

Procedure

1. Type the command at the file server console to access the parameter category list.

2. Type the number of the parameter category you want to view and press Enter.

3. For version 3.11, press Enter to view normal parameters. To view normal and advanced parameters, type **Y** by itself.

Usage Notes

To change parameters to enhance your file server's performance, type the **SET** command at the file server console followed by the revised parameter. Then make the same change in the AUTOEXEC.NCF file. You can only change some parameters noted in the screen display by editing the STARTUP.NCF file.

SETPASS

Enables you either to change your password or to set one on any file server. Enables the Supervisor to set or change any user's password.

Syntax

```
SETPASS file server name
```

Procedure

1. Attach to all file servers where you have the same username.

2. Type at the DOS prompt the command with your default file server for *file server name*.

3. Type your old password at the prompt.

4. Type your new password at the prompt.

5. Retype your new password at the prompt.

6. Confirm that you want to synchronize passwords.

SET TIME

Enables the Supervisor to set the date and time kept by the file server.

Syntax

```
SET TIME month/day/year hour:minute:second
```

Procedure

Type the command at the file server console.

Usage Notes

You can set either the time or the date without setting the other by typing in just the one you want. The other remains as it was.

By typing **SET TIME** by itself, the Supervisor can see the date and time set on the file server.

SETTTS

Enables you to set TTS manually.

Syntax

```
SETTTS [logical level [physical level]]
```

Parameter

☐ Logical level: Record locks that TTS ignores before beginning to track a transaction.

☐ Physical level: Physical locks that TTS ignores before beginning to track a transaction.

Procedure

Type the command at the DOS prompt, with options set to a number set between 1 and 254.

Usage Notes

Logical locks do not require using physical locks too. However, physical locks require using logical locks.

SLIST

Enables you to view a list of available file servers where you currently are physically attached.

Syntax

```
SLIST file server
```

Procedure

Type the command at the DOS prompt, with the name of the file server for *file server.*

SMODE

Enables you to set the search mode for an executable file to use when it must access a data file. This tells the executable file how to search the default directory and the search drives for the file it needs.

Syntax

```
SMODE [path] file name mode [/SUB]
```

Parameter

The search modes are

0	Looks for search mode instruction in SHELL.CFG
1	Searches if a path is not specified
2	Never searches
3	Searches if a path is not specified and the request is to read (not modify or write to) a file
4	Reserved
5	Always searches
6	Reserved
7	Always searches if the request is to read (not modify or write to) a file

Procedure

Type the command at the DOS prompt, with the directory path for *path* (if it is not the default), the executable file name for filename, and the number of the search mode for *mode*.

Usage Notes

Include the /SUB option if you want the mode to apply to executable files in all the subdirectories below the directory you specified in *path*.

SYSTIME

Enables you to see the date and time set on a file server you are attached to (not the default).

Syntax

```
SYSTIME file server
```

Procedure

Type the command at the DOS prompt, with the name of the file server for *file server*.

TIME

Enables the Supervisor to see the date and time set on the file server.

Syntax

```
TIME
```

Procedure

Type the command at the file server console.

TLIST

Enables you to list the users and groups who are trustees of any directory where you have trustee rights.

Syntax

```
TLIST
```

Procedure

Type the command at the DOS prompt.

TRACK OFF

Enables the Supervisor to free up file server memory by turning off the Router Tracking Screen and its display of network advertising packets.

Syntax

```
TRACK OFF
```

Procedure

Type the command at the file server console.

TRACK ON

Enables the Supervisor to start the Router Tracking Screen displaying three types of packets: server, network, and connection, formatted according to whether they are incoming, outgoing, or connection requests.

Syntax

```
TRACK ON
```

Procedure

Type the command at the file server console.

Usage Notes

If you do not need to have the tracking feature on, you should turn it off to free up file server memory.

UNBIND

Enables the Supervisor to remove the link between the LAN driver and the communication protocol.

Syntax

```
UNBIND protocol [FROM] LAN driver [driver parameter]
```

Parameter

Driver parameters	Description
DMA=n	DMA channel number
FRAME=name	Frame type
INT=n	Interrupt number
MEM=n	Memory address number
PORT=n	I/O port number
SLOT=n	Slot the board is installed in

Procedure

Type the command at the file server console, with the name of the protocol, such as IPX, for *protocol*, with the name of the LAN driver for *LAN driver*, and with a driver parameter only if the file server has more than one network board of the same type.

Usage Notes

The driver parameters must be typed within square brackets.

UPS STATUS

Enables the Supervisor to check the following information for the file server's uninterruptable power supply:

- ☐ Type of power being used
- ☐ Discharge time requested
- ☐ Discharge time remaining
- ☐ Battery status, such as charged or being recharged
- ☐ Recharge time requested
- ☐ Recharge time remaining
- ☐ Current network power status

Syntax

```
UPS STATUS
```

Procedure

Type the command at the file server console.

USERLIST

Enables you to view information about users.

Syntax

```
USERLIST [file server/] [username] /option
```

Parameter

Options	Description
A	Addresses of all users
C	Continuous scrolling through the list
O	Object type of all users

Procedure

Type the command at the DOS prompt, using options after the slash to see different information.

Usage Notes

Your username appears with an asterisk next to it in the list USERLIST provides.

View information on attached file servers by typing the name of the file server in the command.

VOLUMES

Enables the Supervisor or console operator to view all the volumes mounted on a NetWare version 3.x file server.

Syntax

VOLUMES

Procedure

Type the command at the file server console.

WHOAMI

Enables you to view information about yourself on all file servers where you are attached.

Syntax

```
WHOAMI /option
```

Parameters

Options	Descriptions
G	Groups belonged to
O	Object Supervisor
R	Effective rights
S	Security equivalencies
SY	System (network) information
W	Workgroup manager
A	All of the above

Procedure

Type the command at the DOS prompt, with options after the slash.

WSUPDATE

Enables you to update your workstation shell file with the latest version in the SYS:PUBLIC directory.

Syntax

```
WSUPDATE SYS:PUBLIC/NETX.EXE ALL_LOCAL:NETX.EXE
```

Procedure

Type the command at the DOS prompt.

Usage Notes

Make sure the latest shell files are in the SYS:PUBLIC directory.

Add /L=*path:filename* if you want to create a log file of this command.

The Supervisor can update all workstation shell files automatically by entering the command in the system login script, using the pound sign (#) before the command.

D

Glossary

access—The capability and the means necessary to approach, to store, or to retrieve data, to communicate with, and to make use of any resource of a computer system.

access guidelines—Used here in the sense of guidelines for the modification of specific access rights. A general framework drawn up by the owner or custodian to instruct the data set security administrator on the degree latitude that exists for the modification of rights of access to a file without the specific authority of the owner or custodian.

access period—A segment of time, generally expressed on a daily or weekly basis, when access rights prevail.

access type—An access right to a particular device, program, or file, such as read, write, execute, append, allocate, modify, delete, or create.

accidental—Outcome from the lack of care or any situation where the result is negatively different from that intended, such as poor program design, or poor planning.

accountability—The quality or state that enables violations or attempted violations of a system security to be traced to individuals who may then be held responsible.

administrator—The person responsible for managing a NetWare file server, and supporting NetWare users.

alloc memory pool—The portion of memory used by NetWare for short-term memory needs. Alloc memory space is borrowed from the permanent memory pool, but is not returned.

annotating—The practice of including comment lines within a program such as a login script in order to explain the purpose of instructions.

ARCnet (*Attached Resource Computer Network*)—A local area network scheme developed by Datapoint.

attach—To log in a workstation to another file server while the workstation remains logged in to the first.

audit trail—A chronological record of system activities sufficient to enable the reconstruction, review, and examination of the sequence of environments and activities surrounding or leading to each event in the path of a transaction from its inception to output of results.

auditability—The physical or mental power to perform an examination or verification of financial records or accounts.

authentication—The act of identifying or verifying the eligibility of a station, originator, or individual to access specific categories of information.

authorization—The process that grants the necessary and sufficient permissions for the intended purpose.

backup—The process of copying data files, usually from a hard disk to another media such as magnetic tape. Used to enable the restoration of data in the event of disk failure or file corruption.

backup procedures—The provisions made for the recovery of data files and program libraries, and for restart or replacement of equipment after the occurrence of a system failure or a disaster.

bandwidth—The range of frequencies available for signaling; the difference expressed in Hertz between the lowest and highest frequencies of a band.

bindery—NetWare database for identifying objects, such as users, groups, file servers, and other network objects.

block—The basic unit of file storage for NetWare. A block can be any size from 4 kilobytes to 64 kilobytes (in integral powers of two).

blocks read—Number of data blocks read from the server.

blocks written—Number of data blocks written to the server's disk.

breach—A break in the system security that results in unauthorized admittance of a person or program to an object.

bridge—A device used to connect LANs by forwarding packets addressed to other similar networks across connections at the Media Access Control data link level. Routers, which operate at the protocol level, are also called bridges.

broadcast—A LAN data transmission scheme in which data packets are heard by all stations on the network.

brute-force attack—A computerized trial-and-error attempt to decode a cipher or password by trying every possible combination. Also known as *exhaustive attack*.

buffer—An area of memory used as a temporary window that data is moved into and out of.

bus—A common connection. Networks that broadcast signals to all stations, such as Ethernet and ARCnet, are considered bus networks.

cabling system—The type of cable used to network computers together. Also refers to the protocol used to govern use of the cable by each computer.

cache movable pool—A sub-pool within the file-cache buffer pool used for system tables.

cache nonmovable pool—A sub-pool within the file-cache buffer pool used for loading NLMs.

clear text—Information that is in its readable state (before encryption and after decryption).

client—In a client/server system, the computer (usually a workstation) that makes service requests.

client/server—A network system design where a processor or computer designated as a server (file server, database server, and so on) provides services to other client processors or computers.

collision—A garbled transmission resulting from simultaneous transmissions by two or more workstations on the same network cable.

command line—The DOS (>) or NOS (:) prompt.

communication protocol—The agreed-on set of rules that are followed by every computer on a network to allow exchanging data over the common cable.

connect time—Amount of time a user connects to the file server.

control codes—Nonprinting computer instructions such as carriage return and line feed.

current directory—A pointer to the current location in the file hierarchy. Commands usually operate on files in the current directory, unless a full pathname is provided.

data-dependent protection—Protection of data at a level commensurate with the sensitivity level of the individual data elements, instead of with the sensitivity of the entire file that includes the data elements.

default login script—The login script built in to the functioning of the LOGIN.EXE command.

define user/group—The process of creating an entry in NetWare's bindery database so that it knows the identity of each user or group using the file server. Access control mechanisms are based on this identity.

deliberate—Intended to harm. The results of such deliberate actions might be different from those expected by perpetrators or victims. For example, arson and vandalism.

directory—A special file that contains information about files and subdirectories within the directory. The directory provides details such as a file's name and its size.

Directory Entry Table—A NetWare data structure containing details about NetWare files, such as filename and size.

disk storage—Amount of disk storage, in blocks, used by the user on the server.

distributed password system—For security systems, one where passwords are created by the users. The passwords may be accounted for centrally.

DOS command interpreter—The DOS program that accepts user instructions to DOS, and performs the appropriate action. The normal command interpreter is known as COMMAND.COM.

dynamic object—An object removed from the bindery when you reboot the server.

effective rights—The actual rights a user has to a file or a directory based on trustee assignments, inheritance, and masks.

EISA bus—See *Extended Industry Standard Architecture bus.*

encryption—Incorrectly used as a synonym for cryptography; the transformation of plain text into coded form (encryption) or from coded form into plain text (decryption).

enterprise-network—A network bringing all sites together through a communication medium.

error log—An audit trail of system warning messages displayed for the file server.

Ethernet—A local area network protocol developed by Xerox.

exposure—A quantitative rating (in dollars per year) expressing the organization's vulnerability to a given risk.

Extended Industry Standard Architecture (EISA) bus—A type of bus, less commonly found than the ISA bus but capable of better performance.

extended memory—That portion of memory on an Intel 80x86 computer above one megabyte.

fail safe—The automatic termination and protection of programs or other processing operations when a hardware or software failure is detected in a system.

fail soft—The selective termination of affected non-essential processing when a hardware or software failure is detected in a system.

file—A single, named collection of related information stored on a medium.

File Allocation Table (FAT)—A NetWare data structure containing information about every block on a NetWare volume.

file caching—A process that uses memory as a temporary storage area for portions of disk files. Programs that need data from the file, or that want to write new data into the file, actually access the cache in memory (and therefore move the information more quickly). Portions of the file are moved between the file cache and disk as a separate operation.

file server—A computer attached to a LAN which allows other computers to access its data in the form of individual files. In a NetWare LAN, the file server is normally a personal computer running the NetWare Network Operating System.

file-cache buffer pool—The portion of memory used by NetWare for file caching.

frame type—Format used for the contents of a network packet. NetWare uses two main frame types for Ethernet packets. Ethernet_802.3 is the default type for version 3.11, while Ethernet_802.2 is the default for version 3.12.

full pathname—The complete list of the path to a file, including file server name, volume name, and all directories on the path to the file.

gateway—A device that provides routing and protocol conversion among physically dissimilar networks and computers, for example, LAN to Host, LAN to LAN, X.25 and SNA gateways.

grace login—A login to the system after the password interval has expired.

grant—To authorize.

hacker—A computer enthusiast; also, one who seeks to gain unauthorized access to computer systems.

handshaking—Used in this context to refer to the controlled movement of bits between a computer and a printer.

hub—(1) A device used on certain network topologies that modifies transmission signals, allowing the network to be lengthened or expanded with additional workstations. The hub is the central device in a star topology. (2) A computer that receives messages from other computers, stores them, and routes them to other computer destinations.

IDE—See *Integrated Drive Electronics.*

identification—The process that enables, generally using unique machine-readable names, recognition of users or resources as identical with those previously described to a system.

identifier variable—The name of a value tracked by NetWare. An example is the identifier variable DAY, which is set to the number of the current day.

Industry Standard Architecture (ISA) bus—The type of bus used in most of today's personal computers.

Inherited Rights Mask—A mechanism that blocks some rights for a file or subdirectory, which you can inherit from a directory.

Integrated Drive Electronics (IDE)—A commonly used disk drive interface for personal computers.

interface—The cables, connectors, and electrical circuits allowing communication between computers and printers.

intruder—A user or other agent attempting to gain unauthorized access to the file server.

IPX/SPX—The Internet Packet Exchange/Sequenced Packet Exchange network communication protocol; NetWare's native communication protocol.

ISA bus—See *Industry Standard Architecture bus.*

item—A single value in a property.

kernel—A group of programs that perform most of NetWare's basic tasks; the core of a NetWare file server. The kernel is started from the DOS command prompt using the command SERVER. Thereafter, it takes over operation of the file server computer.

key—In cryptography, a sequence of symbols that controls the operations of encryption and decryption.

LAN—See *local area network.*

Least Recently Used algorithm—The methodology used by NetWare to decide which buffers can be reused.

Link Support Layer (LSL)—A set of programmed routines that examines packets coming in from the network, and routes them to the appropriate handlers, according to the type of protocol found. For example, the LSL sends IPX packets to software responsible for IPX/SPX, while IP packets are sent to the TCP/IP protocol handlers. The LSL can be found on NetWare file servers and clients using the ODI architecture (see Chapter 18 for more details on client software).

local area network (LAN)—A communications system used to allow connected computers shared access to resources on the network.

login—The process of accessing a file server or computer after logical connection has been established.

login script—A text file containing commands that are executed when a user logs in to NetWare.

logout—The process of disconnecting from a file server or computer.

low memory—The first 640 kilobytes of memory on an Intel 80x86 computer.

LSL—See *Link Support Layer.*

mainframe—A large computer system that supports hundreds or thousands of users with one machine.

MAKEDISK—A program included with the NetWare CD-ROM. It creates diskettes that are used to install workstation software.

map—To assign a workstation drive letter to a server directory.

menu—A list of options from which users select.

menu options—An option that may perform some action, prompt the user for additional information, or lead to another menu.

monitoring—Using automated procedures to ensure that the controls implemented within a system are not circumvented.

multitasking—More than one program active (running) on the computer at a time.

multithreaded—More than one thread active (running) on the computer at a time. A thread is a unit of execution that can be an entire program, or only a portion of a program.

NetWare Loadable Module (NLM)—A program module that is loaded on a file server, and which interacts with the kernel.

network—A collection of interconnected, individually controlled computers, printers, and hard disks, with the hardware and software used to connect them.

network drive—An online storage device available to network users.

Network Interface Card (NIC)—A device installed in a computer which serves as the gateway between the computer's internal components and the network cable.

network operating system—Normally refers to an operating system running on a computer which is designed to provide network services such as file sharing. May also refer collectively to all network programs running on both client and server computers.

NIC—See *Network Interface Card.*

NLM—See *NetWare Loadable Module.*

node—A point of interconnection to a network. Normally, a point at which a number of terminals are located.

object—A passive entity that contains or receives data. Access to an object potentially implies access to the information it contains.

off line—Indicates that the printer is not ready to receive data.

OSI model—The Open Systems Interconnect model, formulated by the International Standards Organization to illustrate functional layers needed for data communication.

packet—A group of bits transmitted as a whole on a network.

parallel interface—A printer interface that handles data in parallel fashion, eight bits (byte) at a time.

parity bit—A way of marking the eighth bit in a data byte, so that 7-bit ASCII characters between 0 and 127 are sent received correctly. There are three kinds of parity—odd, even, and none.

password—Given to or created by the user, privileged information that is entered into a system for authentication purposes. A password is a protected word or secret character string used to authenticate the claimed identity of an individual, a resource, or access type.

pathname—The path to a directory or file, usually with respect to the current directory.

peer-to-peer network—A network where each node may act as a server, a client, or both at the same time.

permanent memory pool—The portion of memory used by NetWare for long-term memory needs. Permanent memory space is borrowed from the file-cache buffer pool, but is not returned.

permission—A particular form of allowed access, such as permission to Read as contrasted with permission to Write.

preemptive scheduling—Programs/threads are allowed a certain amount of CPU time. If they are not completed, they are stopped temporarily, and another is allowed its turn.

print queue—A shared storage area on the file server where the system sends every print job before sending to the print server.

print server—Software that takes jobs from the print queue and sends them to the printer.

property—Field name in the bindery database for information related to a bindery object.

protocol—A set of characters at the beginning and end of a message that enables two computers to communicate with each other.

read—A fundamental operation that results only in the flow of information from an object to a subject.

read access—Permission to read data.

remote procedure call—A request for some type of processing activity, issued by one computer and sent across the network to another computer.

resource—In this instance, a data block read, a data block written, disk storage used, connect time, or any service request that may be requested or used by users and their programs.

rights—User capabilities given for accessing files and directories on a file server.

ring architecture—A hardware feature offered on Intel 80386 and 80486 microprocessors. It prevents programs running in lower number rings from being interfered with by those in higher number rings.

risk—The potential that a given threat has of occurring within a specific period. The potential for realization of unwanted, negative consequences of an event.

risk analysis—An analysis of system assets and vulnerabilities to establish an expected loss from certain events based on estimated probabilities of the occurrence of those events.

run-to-completion—Programs/threads running on the CPU are not interrupted after a certain time allocation. Instead, they are allowed as much time as they need to finish.

SCSI—See *Small Computer System Interface.*

security—Protection of all those resources that the client uses to complete its mission.

security policy—The set of laws, rules, and practices that regulate how an organization manages, protects, and distributes sensitive information.

segment—An area of a physical disk that has been prepared for use by NetWare.

sensitivity—The characteristic of a resource that implies its value or importance and may include its vulnerability.

serial interface—A printer interface that handles data in serial fashion, one bit at a time.

server—A network device that provides services to client stations. Servers include file servers, communication servers, and print servers.

service requests—Number of requests a user makes for any resource.

set—Multiple values for a property.

shell—A terminate-and-stay-resident (TSR) program acting as a redirector on the DOS workstation.

Small Computer System Interface (SCSI)—A disk drive interface used for many personal computers which offers higher performance than IDE.

software bus—The facility that allows NLMs to be loaded, interact with the NetWare kernel, and be unloaded.

static object—An object that remains in the bindery even when you take down and bring back up the file server.

subdirectory—A directory within another directory. (Other than the root directory, which resides at the top of a file system, all directories are also subdirectories.)

submenu—A menu below the main menu.

Supervisor—The Network Supervisor is the person responsible for the operation of the network. The Network Supervisor maintains the network, reconfiguring and updating it as the need arises.

System Fault Tolerance (SFT)—The capability of a Novell system to avoid and correct errors. Novell's SFT is tri-level.

system login script—The login script executed for all users logging in to NetWare.

TCP/IP—The Transmission Control Protocol/Internet Protocol, a widely used network communication protocol which is also supported by NetWare.

threat—One or more events that may lead to either intentional or unintentional modification, destruction, or disclosure of data. An eventuality which, should it occur, would lead to an undesirable effect on the environment.

topology—The physical layout of the network cabling.

transmission-on/transmission-off (X-ON/X-OFF)—A type of software handshaking.

tree—A representation of NetWare's hierarchical file structure. The hierarchy starts at the root directory and expands out, through many directories, subdirectories, and files. The structure, therefore, appears as an upside-down tree.

troubleshooting—Diagnosing and solving problems that invariably occur when using computers.

trustee—A user assigned rights to a file or directory.

trustee rights—Rights to a directory or file directly or indirectly assigned to a user or group. They are a combination of a user's rights, the group's rights, and security equivalence rights.

uninterruptible power supply (UPS)—A device that provides continuous and regulated electrical power even when the main power lines fail or experience power fluctuations. It is normally used with an important computer, such as a NetWare file server, to protect against loss or corruption of data in the event of a problem with normal electrical power.

UPS—See *uninterruptible power supply.*

user login script—The login script executed for an individual user when he or she logs in.

user—An individual who accesses and makes use of a NetWare file server.

username—A name used to identify a user account.

utilities—Useful programs provided with a system. Some examples include tools that enable you to view, rename, copy, format, delete, and otherwise manage accounts, files, and volumes.

verification—Confirmation that the object is what it purports to be. Also, confirmation of the identity of a person (or other agent external to the protection system) making a request.

virus—A self-replicating program that attaches itself to either a program or data so that it can hide and travel throughout your network. Viruses are either benign or malignant.

volume—A logical data structure analogous to a physical disk. However, a NetWare volume can be spread across many physical disk segments.

vulnerability—The cost that an organization would incur if an event happened.

wiretapping—Monitoring or recording data as it moves across a communications link; also known as *traffic analysis*.

workstation—A desktop computer that performs local processing and accesses LAN services.

workstation operating system—Software that controls the internal operations (housekeeping chores) of the workstation. Operating systems are specific to the type of computer used.

worms—Similar to viruses, except their aim is simply to replicate themselves repeatedly until they use all the memory in your network so that nothing can be done.

write—A fundamental operation that results only in the flow of data from a subject to an object.

write access—Permission to write to an object.

Index

L

tasks

X

Add to Your Sams Library Today with the Best Books for Programming, Operating Systems, and New Technologies

The easiest way to order is to pick up the phone and call

1-800-428-5331

between 9:00 a.m. and 5:00 p.m. EST.
For faster service please have your credit card available.

ISBN	Quantity	Description of Item	Unit Cost	Total Cost
0-672-30206-3		Networking Windows, NetWare Edition	$24.95	
0-672-30097-4		Windows Programmer's Guide to Resources	$34.95	
0-672-30298-5		Windows NT: The Next Generation	$22.95	
0-672-30295-0		Moving into Windows NT Programming	$39.95	
0-672-30364-7		Win32 API Desktop Reference	$49.95	
0-672-30382-5		Understanding Local Area Networks	$26.95	
0-672-30209-8		NetWare Unleashed	$45.00	
0-672-30026-5		Do-It-Yourself Networking with LANtastic	$24.95	
0-672-30173-3		Enterprise-Wide Networking	$39.95	
0-672-30170-9		NetWare LAN Management Toolkit	$34.95	
0-672-30243-8		LAN Desktop Guide to E-mail with cc:Mail	$27.95	
0-672-30005-2		Understanding Data Communications	$24.95	
0-672-30119-9		International Telecommunications	$39.95	
0-672-30485-6		Navigating the Internet, Deluxe Edition	$29.95	
0-672-30326-4		Absolute Beginner's Guide to Networking	$19.95	
❏ 3 ½" Disk		Shipping and Handling: See information below.		
❏ 5 ¼" Disk		TOTAL		

Shipping and Handling: $4.00 for the first book, and $1.75 for each additional book. Floppy disk: add $1.75 for shipping and handling. If you need to have it NOW, we can ship product to you in 24 hours for an additional charge of approximately $18.00, and you will receive your item overnight or in two days. Overseas shipping and handling adds $2.00 per book and $8.00 for up to three disks. Prices subject to change. Call for availability and pricing information on latest editions.

201 W. 103rd Street, Indianapolis, Indiana 46290

1-800-428-5331 — Orders   1-800-835-3202 — FAX   1-800-858-7674 — Customer Service

Book ISBN 0-672-30481-3